This book provides a survey of the development of scientific disciplines and technical projects under National Socialism in Germany. Each contribution addresses a different, new aspect which is important for judging the interaction between science, technology and National Socialism. In particular, the personal conduct of individual scientists and engineers as well as the functionality of certain theories and projects are examined.

All essays share a common theme: continuity and discontinuity. All authors cover a period that reaches back to the Weimar Republic and forward beyond the end of National Socialism to the post-war period. This unanimity of approach provides answers to major questions about the nature of Hitler's regime and about possible lines of continuity in science and technology which may transcend political upheaval. The book is also the most comprehensive to date on this subject, and includes essays on engineering, geography, biology, psychology, physics, mathematics and science policy. It thus offers something of interest for the specialist, scientist, engineer and historian as well as an unprecedented overview of science and technology before, during and after the Third Reich.

Science, Technology and National Socialism

Science, Technology
and National Socialism

Edited by

Monika Renneberg
Assistant Professor in the Institute for the History of Science,
Technology and Mathematics, University of Hamburg

and

Mark Walker
Assistant Professor of the Department of History,
Union College, Schenectady

CAMBRIDGE
UNIVERSITY PRESS

Published by the Press Syndicate of the University of Cambridge
The Pitt building, Trumpington Street, Cambridge CB2 1RP
40 West 20th Street, New York, NY 10011–4211, USA
10 Stamford Road, Oakleigh, Victoria 3166, Australia

First published 1994

Printed in Great Britain at the University Press, Cambridge

A catalogue record for this book is available from the British Library

Library of Congress cataloguing in publication data

Scientists, engineers, and National Socialism / edited by Monika Renneberg and Mark Walker.
     p.   cm.
Includes index.
ISBN 0 521 40374 X
1. Science – Germany – History.   2. Engineering – Germany – History.
3. National Socialism and science – History.   4. Fascism – Germany – History.
I. Renneburg, Monika.   II. Walker, Mark, 1959–   .
Q127.G3S36 1993
509.43'09'04–dc20   92–41633   CIP

ISBN 0 521 40374 X hardback

CE

This book is dedicated to all those critical voices who have tried to illuminate this ambivalent chapter of history, but were unappreciated, ignored and discouraged.

Contents

Illustrations

Contributors

Ulrich Albrecht is Professor of Peace and Conflict Studies at the Department of Political Science of the Free University of Berlin. He also holds a degree in aeronautical engineering. His recent books are *The History of the Soviet Armaments Industry* (1992) and *Die Abwicklung der DDR* (The Liquidation of the GDR: 1992).

Ute Deichmann teaches biology and chemistry at the Georg-Büchner-Gymnasium in Cologne. She has published *Biologen unter Hitler – Vertreibung, Karrieren, Forschung* (1992).

Ulfried Geuter is a freelance journalist and scientific author and psychotherapist in Berlin. He is the author of *The Professionalization of Psychology in Nazi Germany* (1984; English edition 1992) and the editor of *Data on the History of German Psychology* (2 vols., 1986 and 1987) and (with Mitchell G. Ash) of *History of German Psychology in 20th Century* (1985).

Andreas Heinemann-Grüder is Lecturer at the Humboldt University in Berlin. His publications include a book on Soviet policy in the Middle East and a book on the history of the first Soviet atomic bomb (1992). Most recently he has written (as co-author) *The Specialists. German Natural Scientists and Technicians in the Soviet Union after 1945* (1992).

Kristie Macrakis is Assistant Professor of the History of Science at Michigan State University. She is the author of *Surviving the Swastika: Scientific Research in Nazi Germany* (New York: Oxford University Press, 1993).

Herbert Mehrtens is professor of history at Technische Universität Braunschweig, Germany. He has edited *Naturwissenschaft, Technik und NS-Ideologie* (1980). His latest book is *Moderne – Sprache – Mathematik* (1990).

Benno Müller-Hill is Professor of Genetics at the University of Cologne. He has written articles in Molecular Biology and *Murderous Science. Elimination by Scientific Selection of Jews, Gypsies, and Others. Germany 1933–1945* (1988).

Michael J. Neufeld is a curator in the National Air and Space Museum, Smithsonian Institute. He is the author of *The Skilled Metalworkers of Nuremberg* (1989), *The Rocket and the Reich* (1994), as well as articles in German social history and history of technology.

Maria Osietzki, Ruhr-University Bochum, Germany, has published on the history of big science in nuclear research. She is coauthor of the book *Wissenschaft für Macht und Markt.* Her publications include articles about gender in the history of science and technology. She is preparing a book about the history of energy and entropy.

Monika Renneberg teaches at the Institute for the History of Science, Mathematics and Technology at the University of Hamburg. She is author of *Gründung und Aufbau des GKSS-Forschungscentrums Geesthacht. Ein Beitrag zur Geschichte der Großforschungseinrichtungen in der BRD* (Ph.D., 1989).

Mechtild Rössler is a programme specialist in the World Heritage Centre at UNESCO in Paris. She has written a number of articles on the history of geography and spatial planning in Germany, 1918–1945 and has published *Wissenschaft und Lebensraum. Geographische Ostforschung im Nationalsozialismus* (Berlin, Hamburg: Dietrich Reimer, Verlag, 1990).

Reinhard Siegmund-Schultze is currently Fellow of the Alexander von Humboldt Foundation and visiting scholar at Harvard University. His publications include papers on the history of mathematical ideas and on the social history of mathematics in Nazi Germany in particular, *Mathematische Berichterstattung in Hitlerdeutschland* (1993).

Helmuth Trischler is Director of Research at the Deutsches Museum, Munich, and Senior Lecturer at the University of Munich. His books include *Luft- und Raumfahrtforschung in Deutschland 1900–1970. Politische Geschichte einer Wissenschaft* (1992).

Mark Walker teaches history at Union College in Schenectady, has written *German National Socialism and the Quest for Nuclear Power 1939–1949* and edited (with Teresa Meade) *Science, Medicine, and Cultural Imperialism.*

Burghard Weiss is Assistant Professor in the History of Science at the Technische Universität Berlin and the author of publications on the evolution of Physics and Technology in the 18th and 20th centuries, including *Zwischen Physikotheologie und Positivismus* (1988).

Sheila Faith Weiss is Associate Professor of History at Clarkson University. She is the author of *Race Hygiene and National Efficiency* (California, 1987). At present she is working on a history of social biology education during the Third Reich.

M. Norton Wise is Professor of History at Princeton University where he specializes in nineteenth- and twentieth-century physics. He is co-author with Crosbie Smith of *Energy and Empire: A Biographical Study of Lord Kelvin* (1989).

Acknowledgments

We are grateful to the University of Texas Press, Campus Verlag, and Springer Verlag respectively for permission to republish the following articles: Herbert Mehrtens, 'The Social System of Mathematics and National Socialism: A Survey'; Herbert Mehrtens, 'Irresponsible Purity: The Political and Moral Structure of Mathematical Sciences in the National Socialist State'; Ulfried Geuter, 'The Whole and the Community: Scientific and Political Thought in the Holistic Psychology of Felix Krueger'. We are also grateful to Philips Company and the Archives of the Max Planck Society for permission to reproduce illustrations.

Abbreviations

AAW	(former) Archives of the Academy of Sciences of the German Democratic Republic
AEG	German General Electric Company
AQ	*Die anschauliche Quantentheorie*
ARGB	*Archiv für Rassen- und Gesellschafts-Biologie*
AVA	Aerodynamic Experimental Centre
BAK	Federal German Archives, Koblenz
BA/MA	Federal German Military Archives, Freiburg
BDC	Berlin Document Centre
BSC	Bohr Scientific Correspondence, Archives for the History of Quantum Physics (American Institute of Physics)
CIOS	Combined Intelligence Operations Service
DBV	German Union of Biologists
DFG	German Research Foundation
DFL	German Research Centre for Aviation
DFR	German Research Council
DFW	German Aircraft Works
DIB	German Industrial Bank
DMV	German Union of Mathematicians
DNDS	*Die neue deutsche Schule*
DNVP	German National People's Party
DVL	German Experimental Centre for Aviation
FHJ	Flying Hitler Youth
GAMM	Society for Applied Mathematics and Mechanics
GDR	German Democratic Republic

HA/DLR	Historical Archives of the German Research Centre for Aeronautics
HJ	Hitler Youth
HN	Heisenberg Papers, Max Planck Institute for Physics, Munich
HU	University Archives of the Humboldt University, Berlin
HWA	Army Ordnance
ICBM	Intercontinental Ballistic Missile
IFZ	Institute for Contemporary History
IG.	I. Physical Institute, University of Göttingen
KPD	Communist Party of Germany
KWG	Kaiser Wilhelm Society
KWI	Kaiser Wilhelm Institute
LAB	State Archives of Berlin
MPG	Max Planck Society
MPGA	Archives of the Max Planck Society
MPI	Max Planck Institute for Chemistry, Mainz
MPIA	Archives of the Max Planck Institute for *Strömungsforschung*
MR	Reich Union of Mathematicians
NASM	National Air and Space Museum
NKVD	Soviet Secret Police
NS	National Socialist
NSBO	National Socialist Factory Organization
NSDAP	National Socialist German Workers Party
NSFK	National Socialist Teachers Union
NSV	National Socialist People's Welfare
NWM	*Naturwissenschaftliche Monatshefte für den biologischen, chemischen, geographischen und geologischen Unterricht*
OHI	Oral history interview
OKW	Armed Forces High Command
OMGBS	Office of Military Government, Berlin Sector
OSB	Higher School Authorities
PD	*Physikalisches Denken in der neuen Zeit*
PMS	Philips Medizin-Systeme (formerly C. H. F. Müller), Hamburg
PZ	Pedagogical Center
RAF	Royal Air Force
RBE	Radium-Beryllium-Equivalent
R&D	Research and Development
REM	Reich Ministry for Education
RFR	Reich Research Council

RLM	Reich Aviation Ministry
RM	Reich Marks
SA	Storm Troopers
SAM	Siemens Archives, Munich
SB	Prussian State Library, Berlin
SBZ	Soviet Occupation Zone
SCI	Science Citation Index
SED	Socialist Unity Party of East Germany
SO	Suicide (as in SO mission: suicide mission)
SPSL	Society for the Protection of Science and Learning
SRW	Siemens Reiniger Werke
SS	Defense Squadron
STA-HH	Hamburg State Archives
TH	Technical University
UA	Archives of German and Austrian Universities
UAM	University Archives, Mainz
V-1	Revenge Weapon 1
V-2	Revenge Weapon 2
VfR	Society for Space Travel
VTOL	Vertical takeoff and landing (plane)
WGL	Scientific Society for Aviation
ZstA	(former) Central State Archives, Potsdam

1 | Scientists, engineers and National Socialism

MONIKA RENNEBERG and MARK WALKER[1]

The three related yet separate parts of this essay move from the general to the specific: (1) science and technology are placed in the context of National Socialist Germany by means of a model based on Franz Neumann's *Behemoth*; (2) the main unifying theme of this book, 'continuity and discontinuity', is analysed; and (3) the contents of this volume are surveyed, including a brief description of each essay.

1 Behemoth revisited

1.1 Behemoth

How did scientists and engineers fare under National Socialism? Did Hitler's regime accelerate or obstruct the push towards technocracy in Germany which was both already prominent during the Weimar Republic and inherent in modern science and technology? How did technocracy affect science and engineering? These questions are interconnected: an investigation of science and technology under Hitler facilitates an understanding of technocracy; an examination of technocracy in turn illuminates the structure of the Third Reich; and finally the structure of the National Socialist state provides insight into science and technology. This essay suggests a model for National Socialism which hopefully will give both answers to these questions and stimulate further inquiry.

In 1942 the émigré social scientist Franz Neumann proposed a suggestive and insightful model of National Socialism as a cartel of power blocs, including the Army, Big Business, the Civil Service and the National Socialist German Workers party (*Nationalsozialistische Deutsche Arbeiterpartei*, henceforth NSDAP): the *Behemoth*, or un-state.[2] These blocs sometimes cooperated, sometimes conflicted, always competed with each other, and

1

combined to form National Socialism. The tensions between them produced much of the dynamic energy that ran the regime.[3] This model of a cartel of power blocs also tacitly argues that other groups were powerless: the working class, the churches, women, and so on.

In a recent study of Adolf Hitler's power, Ian Kershaw has demonstrated[4] that these power blocs – like most individuals or organizations during the Third Reich – accessed power only through the fulcrum of the *Führer*. Thus one could argue that the cartel of power blocs operated through and around Hitler like spokes around the hub of a wheel. This image of the power cartel allows a marriage of the intentionalist and the functionalist approaches to the structure of the Third Reich.[5] The fact that power and authority originated with Hitler or had to go through him – as a prominent National Socialist explained in 1934, it was 'the duty of everybody to try to work towards the Führer along the lines he would wish'[6] – does not necessarily mean that he was in control. If Hitler's power was the hub of National Socialism, he still could behave either as master in his Reich or as a weak dictator, depending on the context and the power blocs involved.[7]

The contrasting fates of rockets and nuclear weapons research during the Third Reich provide an example of the limits of Hitler's power.[8] For any major research and development project to be successful, it had to be approved by Hitler. However, the fact that Hitler's approval was necessary does not mean that his ability to make definitive decisions was sufficient. The rocket project's enthusiastic supporters managed to force their pet project onto Hitler's agenda, including a personal audience. Hitler was sceptical at first, but eventually became convinced, so that the project was supported. The nuclear weapons project was effectively frozen at the laboratory level of research, far down the ladder of command from Hitler, so that Hitler was merely informed of its existence. In the former case, Hitler found himself in a position to make a decision, and he did; in the latter case, Hitler was never presented with an opportunity to say yes or no.

It is not enough to recognize the central role played by Hitler's power in the Third Reich. The members of this cartel also should be revised, for several reasons. Neumann could not have foreseen how the SS (*Schutzstaffeln*, loosely translated as 'defense squadron') would expand into its own empire, that a plethora of special agencies devoted to specific (and often overlapping) tasks would grow within the German state like a cancer, or how the war economy would affect Germany and the occupied or annexed territories. The revised power cartel includes the different branches of the Armed Forces (Army, Navy and Air Force); Big Business; the Civil Service; the NSDAP (both the central organization and the regional satrapies of the Party *Gauleiter,*); the SS; and the various spheres of '*Führer* power': Hermann Göring's Four Year Plan; the Todt Organization and its successor, Albert Speer's Ministry of Armaments and later War Production; the

Hitler Youth organization; the occupation governments in occupied Europe.[9] The effectiveness of a bloc depended on two main factors: relative strength and relative autonomy, or, in other words, the ability to cooperate as well as to compete.

The relative position of the blocs changed with the evolution of the Third Reich. The Armed Forces were strong throughout, were quite independent until 1938, but lost almost all independence after the winter of 1941–2.[10] Big Business was strong throughout, but beginning in 1936 and especially from 1939 onwards it became more and more entangled in the political, military and ideological goals and policies of National Socialism; strength did not necessarily imply independence, for although Big Business in Germany regained some autonomy (parallel to science and technology) during the war and certainly prospered, it was often in a way not wholly of the businessmen's own choosing.[11] The Civil Service steadily lost independence and power;[12] the NSDAP was strong and independent up until the very end;[13] the power and independence of the SS grew steadily.[14]

Neumann had probably conceived the blocs as discrete and autonomous, but in fact, as Michael Geyer has pointed out, the opposite was true.[15] Some blocs were relatively clearly defined and bounded, like the Armed Forces. Membership of the NSDAP was suspended when an individual began active military service. But even the autonomy of this bloc was compromised by the introduction of *Waffen*-SS units and 'political' officers during the war. In fact, the second adaptation to be made to Neumann's theory is to recognize that most blocs overlapped with each other to a considerable degree. Thus the image of a spoked wheel is not completely satisfactory because the spokes were not distinct and separate.

Exactly how the power blocs overlapped can best be seen by examining individuals. For example, Rudolf Mentzel and Erich Schumann,[16] important science policy-makers in the Third Reich, were connected to several blocs. Mentzel, an Old Fighter of the Party and honorary member of the SS, carved out a mini-empire within the Reich Ministry of Education which included control over the Reich Research Council and the German Research Foundation, conduits for most of the funds given to scientific research. Schumann, a professor at the University of Berlin and one of the many opportunists who rushed to join the Party in the spring of 1933, held influential positions in the Ministry of Education and headed the research branch of Army Ordnance. Similarly one could take Carl Krauch, an I. G. Farben executive hired by Göring to run the Four Year Plan, who at times worked closely with the SS and Speer's ministry.[17] It is striking that these 'middle managers', who often wielded considerable power in the National Socialist state precisely because of their divided loyalties, have been relatively neglected by historians.

But even if the power blocs were not distinct, the cartel model is nevertheless useful because the National Socialist state was to a considerable degree divided up into relatively autonomous groups. The great majority of individuals making up these blocs did have a dominant or overriding loyalty or responsibility. Thus despite Mentzel's ties to the party and the SS, his power base lay in the Education Ministry and he generally worked to further the interests of this ministry; Schumann's real influence and loyalty lay with the Army, not the Civil Service; despite Krauch's longstanding connection to the I. G. Farben colossus and his consequential dealings with the SS, his overriding responsibility and loyalty remained with the economic pseudo-ministry headed by Göring.

Focus on the individual within the power blocs also allows recognition of the fact that ideological groupings existed within this cartel that cut across bloc lines, such as anti-Semitism, anti-Socialism and anti-Communism, nationalism and, most importantly for our purpose, technocracy.[18] These groupings of individuals definitely cut across all the blocs, often overlapped with each other, but usually did not completely cover any bloc. Thus not even the membership of the NSDAP was completely anti-Semitic.

The introduction of ideological groupings in effect multiplies the levels of the power cartel model. Instead of asking how particular blocs cooperated or came into conflict, particular ideological groupings can be studied which owe allegiance both to their power bloc and to common ideology. For example, the debate over the mobilization of German women for the war effort can be interpreted as a conflict between technocrats in various blocs, who wanted to exploit the labour of German women, and another ideological grouping, spread over several blocs as well, which insisted that German women remained limited and foreign forced labor made up the difference.[19]

1.2   Technocracy

Although this revised model of the National Socialist *Behemoth* may be useful for the Third Reich in general, its main function here is to facilitate understanding of the fate of scientists and engineers under Hitler by means of the concept of *technocracy*, usually defined as the 'management of society by technical experts'.[20] Here the engineers and scientists are the actors, not merely the tools.

The technocratic movement first became influential in the United States of America[21] and subsequently spread to other countries. Technocracy was often considered incompatible with capitalist democracy; a centralized government run by technocrats would be better, with Fascist Italy and National Socialist Germany as possible candidates. But the German technocratic movement[22] encountered a fundamental dilemma at the start of the Third Reich: how to reconcile the international and rational elements of technocracy with the demands of the extremely nationalistic and often irrational Third Reich.

This conflict is perhaps best illustrated by the brief life of the journal *Technokraties* organ of the German Technocratic Society. *Technokratie* first appeared shortly after Adolf Hitler's appointment as German Chancellor in 1933. The first editorial admitted that technocracy had to be accommodated to National Socialism and distinguished from its American counterpart: technocracy was an example of 'German intellectual goods'.[23] The following article, entitled 'German Technocracy', paid lip service to National Socialist 'Blood and Soil' ideology, but also warned that if this ideology was taken too far, then Germany would revert to 'primitive circumstances'.[24]

These two cautiously critical essays were followed in turn by Hans Triebel's analysis of 'National Socialism and Technocracy'. The author and NSDAP member begins with ritual praise for Hitler, who had 'solved' practically all of Germany's economic problems. In other words, Hitler too was a technocrat. However, Triebel also refers to the National Socialist technocrat Gottfried Feder, who probably would have supported the technocratic society, but had already begun his precipitous fall from power within the National Socialist movement. The technocratic society either chose, or was forced to choose the wrong patrons in the Third Reich.

Triebel made great efforts to accommodate technocracy to the requirements of the 'new state'. For example, technocracy was now portrayed as compatible with autarchy – a policy usually pursued for political, not economic or technical reasons. German technocracy's fundamental similarity to technocratic movements in other countries was admitted, but Triebel asserted that this similarity in no way contradicted the staunch nationalism of German technocracy. Most important was Triebel's unconditional abdication of political influence: 'technocracy does not have political ambitions ... and does not want technicians to dominate politics ...'[25]

But despite these concentrated efforts to make technocracy more palatable to National Socialism, a survey of the three years *Technokratie* appeared reveals that the German society was in fact dependent on its American counterpart. Very many articles were translations of American articles, not to mention a British article that imprudently praised the physicist Albert Einstein, a special target of National Socialist attacks.[26] The journal section devoted to 'Technocracy around the world' perhaps unwittingly underlined the fundamental conflict between the international technocratic movement and the racist (*völkisch*) nationalism of National Socialist Germany. The journal *Technokratie* and with it the German Technocratic Society came to a sudden end in 1935, ironically just when opportunities for technocrats within the National Socialist state began to improve. The Third Reich had room for individual technocrats, but not for a technocratic movement.

The historian Walter McDougall has proposed a different definition of technocracy: the 'institutionalization of technological change for state purposes'.[27] Here engineers and scientists are the tools, not the actors, and this technocracy does not necessarily aim at or serve a rational state.[28] McDougall has demonstrated that this concept of technocracy is a valuable way to investigate radically different political and ideological systems by comparing the space race in the post-World War II Soviet Union and United States.[29] Unfortunately, neither of these two definitions for technocracy fits the Third Reich well.

A generation of scholarship has demonstrated the often contradictory, self-destructive and chaotic nature of the Third Reich. National Socialism did not allow technical experts to manage society rationally. Such specialists often had considerable influence, but only as the tools of various power blocs. The Third Reich was also unable to institutionalize technological change for its own purposes: the polycratic cartel of overlapping, competing and contradictory power blocs effectively hindered and sometimes prevented the systematic and thorough development and implementation of specific technologies and policies, let alone technological change in general; for similar reasons coherent and consistent 'state purposes' are hard to find except in a very general sense, such as territorial and economic expansion, a racially 'pure' population, and totalitarian control over every aspect of society. Yet despite the Second World War, the SS police state and genocide, not even these goals were realized.

Perhaps the most striking and novel aspect of technocracy under Hitler was the use of rational means and technocratic principles to achieve both rational and irrational ends. In other words, technocratic methods were decoupled from technocratic goals. State purposes were similarly replaced by the purposes of power blocs or ideological groupings. Thus the main differences between technocracy under National Socialism and elsewhere were: (1) German technocrats were able and willing to help further irrational and thereby un-technocratic goals and policies; (2) clear, coherent and consequent state purposes scarcely existed.

The above discussion has taken for granted that both technically- and scientifically-trained experts could be technocrats. But this assumption ignores a fundamental historiographic conflict: how to judge the relationship between science and technology, between engineers and scientists? Historians and sociologists of science often argue – explicitly or implicitly – that scientists and engineers are comparable, if not equivalent. The transformation of some technologies from trouble-shooting by more or less well-trained inventors to a science-based enterprise was arguably one of the fundamental trends of the first half of the twentieth century and made technology more attractive for some engineers, scientists and state officials. The sociologist Bruno Latour has argued that this transformation has had a profound effect on science as well, leading to what he calls 'technoscience', including both the 'scientification' of technology and the 'technologization' of science.[30]

Historians of technology often argue – sometimes implicitly, without even mentioning science or scientists – that engineers and scientists are fundamentally different and must be treated as such. Since engineers and scientists generally had positions and functions which differed from those of scientists, they may also have a different attitude towards National Socialism and the economic, political and social problems of their time.[31]

The distinction between engineers and scientists clearly breaks down in exceptional circumstances like the second world war, when science was mobilized and applied for the war effort, and science-based military technologies were researched, developed, manufactured and used. Indeed much of the available literature on technology under National Socialism, including the papers in this volume, has been devoted to science-based or military technologies. There are very many aspects of technology and engineering during the Third Reich that have scarcely been examined, but could fruitfully be. The relationship between scientists and engineers remains one of the most important still open questions about science and technology under Hitler.

If we apply the revised *Behemoth* model to technocracy during the Third Reich and interpret the latter as an ideological grouping within several power blocs, then this model facilitates an investigation of the thorny question of the relationship between modernization and National Socialism: did National Socialism deliberately or unintentionally contribute to the modernization of German society?[32] Ian Kershaw, who argues that the concept of modernization is unhelpful for evaluating National Socialism, defines this concept as follows:

> As conventionally deployed in sociological and historical writing, 'modernization' implies long-term change spanning centuries and transforming 'traditional' society based on agricultural and artisanal production, personal relations of dependence, local loyalties, rural cultures, rigid social hierarchies, and religious world-views, into industrial class society with highly developed industrial technologies, secularized cultures, 'rational' bureaucratic impersonal socio-political orders, and political systems of mass participation.[33]

Indeed, perhaps the concept of technocracy can be used instead of modernization; the historian need only interpret what looks like modernization as either the relative success of one ideological grouping, the technocratic, in competition with the others, or the cooperation of more than one grouping towards a common goal. For example, as Hans Mommsen has argued, it took both technocrats and anti-Semites to realize the Holocaust: 'if one wants to speak of modernization in the Third Reich, then its specific forms were the perverse applications of medical theories as well as mass extermination engineered with technical means.[34]

In Germany, as elsewhere, there was a growing tendency towards technocracy both before and after 1933, and especially during the Weimar Republic.[35] Opposition to technocracy and to rationalization also existed, even in the sciences themselves.[36] There was no inherent contradiction between technocracy and conservative, romantic ideologies, as Jeffrey Herf's study of reactionary modernism demonstrates,[37] and technocrats were scattered throughout German society between the wars, including from the beginning in the National Socialist movement. How else can one explain the sophisticated use of modern technology for propaganda by the NSDAP? Many more technocratic enthusiasts flooded into the Party or ancillary organizations after 1933, and it was these technocratic National Socialists who facilitated the opportunistic marriage of 'Blood and Soil' ideology with the power of the most modern science and technology, thereby making possible the nightmare of the Third Reich: repression, persecution, war and genocide.

The application of the concept of technocracy to the National Socialist period thus merely recognizes that technocrats existed before, during and after Hitler's rule, that they always faced strong practical and ideological opposition, and that this particular conflict played an important role in the history of the Third Reich. How else can we explain the transition from mass shootings to gas chambers,[38] the sterilization[39] and euthanasia campaigns, the propaganda network and the secret police system?[40] In fact the contrast between SS and SA (*Sturmabteilung*, storm troopers) provides a paradigmatic example of conflict between a pro-technocratic (if contradictory) and an anti-technocratic part of the National Socialist movement. Just as the 'Night of the Long Knives' decided this rivalry in favor of the SS,[41] so the technocrats won most of the battles they fought within the polycratic structure of the Third Reich.

The influence of the technocracy grouping grew sharply after the concerted efforts at rearmament accelerated in 1936 and especially after the Lightning War (*Blitzkrieg*) failed in the winter of 1941–2. As we shall see, scientists and engineers benefited as the technocratic grouping within the cartel grew more powerful. Here is one of the insights offered by the Behemoth model: conflict and cooperation between blocs were two sides of the same coin.

If a Party technocrat, an SS technocrat, technocrats from a special agency like the Four Year Plan, the General Government, or Speer's Ministry, and a technocrat from the Armed Forces were to meet together – as, for example, such technocrats did at the Wannsee Conference – they would all see each other as rivals, they would all be jealous representatives of their bloc, but they would all agree that scientific, technological and bureaucratic rationality and efficiency was the way to solve their and Germany's problems, in this case the 'Final Solution of the Jewish Question'. Thus bloc representatives may in certain situations have divided loyalties because of an ideological commitment, with the result that their reaction becomes unpredictable or at least more complex. In any case, by the end of the war and the 'Thousand Year Reich', technocracy – and with it science and engineering – was emerging as one of the most powerful and last pillars of the National Socialist state.

1.3   Scientists and engineers under Hitler

The historians and scientists who have studied science and technology during the Third Reich usually focus first of all on two aspects of that experience; (1) the 'synchronization' or 'coordination' (Gleichschaltung) of science and engineering carried out during the first years of the new regime,[42] symbolized by Albert Einstein's emigration to the United States;[43] and (2) the so-called 'Aryan' science and technology movements (literally translated as 'German'), which in fact were political movements within individual disciplines that agitated for a more 'German' and 'Aryan' chemistry,[44] mathematics,[45] physics[46] and psychology.[47]

But the common assumption that the National Socialist movement deliberately set out to purge science or engineering in particular is questionable. Most scientists and engineers who were thus affected were purged automatically as a small part of the general National Socialist 'cleansing' of the Civil Service. Moreover, after 1933, since many positions in science and engineering were connected directly or indirectly to the Civil Service, many prospective researchers were also liable to this automatic synchronization.

Einstein is the exception that proves the rule. He drew the attention and ire of the new German rulers precisely because his influence transcended the limits of his profession and affected the political sphere. Parts of Hitler's movement undoubtedly held some parts of science in contempt, but this scorn was not universally applied and was never held for technology.

There were two separate categories for science and engineering from the perspective of National Socialism: (1) those disciplines obviously useful to the Third Reich in an ideological or practical sense, including biology,[48] chemistry, geography and engineering, which hardly need to be synchronized; and (2) other disciplines, such as mathematics, physics and psychology, which now had to demonstrate convincingly their utility for the 'new' Germany. It is no coincidence that the latter disciplines all experienced an 'Aryan' science movement or the equivalent which challenged the existing professional hierarchy, but the former did not. Chemistry did experience an 'Aryan' chemistry movement, but it was supported only by a few theoretical chemists and could not compete with the obvious economic and military value of modern chemistry, which had been demonstrated so clearly in World War I. The 'useful' disciplines needed only to be purged of politically unreliable and racially objectionable individuals. The apparently useless disciplines would be purged in any case, but also had to struggle for recognition and support from the state and thereby were vulnerable to political attack. This distinction can also be seen in terms of more practical versus more theoretical disciplines: the latter apparently lacked both utility and immediate applicability.[49]

All the 'Aryan' science movements fit into a similar pattern which in turn mirrors the face of the SA during the early years of the Third Reich: an uncoordinated and often – from the perspective of the National Socialist leadership – unwanted 'revolution from below' pushed for change that went beyond the official synchronization; the state's responding calls for 'evolution, not revolution', a thinly-veiled threat to the National Socialist movement's own rank and file not to overstep its bounds; the obtuse reaction of continued agitation for a 'second revolution' which would achieve what the first had not; and finally a purge of the would-be revolutionaries by the state itself, a 'Night of the Long Knives'.[50]

In other words, because certain disciplines were not obviously useful to the National Socialists, they were vulnerable to political attacks emanating from within their own ranks by scientists or engineers who called for change under the banner of creating a more 'German' or 'Aryan' science. But these attacks or intrigues were not planned by or controlled from the top of the National Socialist hierarchy; instead they often were unwanted and were considered counterproductive. The responsible state authorities usually responded to the 'Aryan' science agitation by insisting that any and all change occur through official channels, but since the 'Aryan' science rebels were rarely satisfied with such prospects, they continued their 'revolution from below'.[51]

Eventually the National Socialist state effectively terminated all the rogue 'Aryan' science or technology movements, although the dates and severity of these measures varied, because in the meantime these disciplines had, sometimes after great effort, demonstrated their willingness and ability to help further the goals of National Socialism. The adherents of 'Aryan' science did not suffer the fate of Ernst Röhm and the SA leadership, but the professional and especially political influence of these researchers was either effectively eliminated or severely diminished.

This pattern for science and engineering under Hitler fits well into the revised Behemoth model. As mentioned above, scientists and engineers were purged as part of the cleansing of the Civil Service bloc. Most of the relatively few 'Aryan' scientists were either attached to or sought support from the Civil Service or relatively weak individuals in the NSDAP. The classic example is Johannes Stark, Nobel Prize-winner and co-founder of 'Aryan Physics', who sought to exploit bureaucratic power within the Reich Education Ministry and the support of National Socialist idealogue Alfred Rosenberg, but whose precipitous fall from political influence was arranged by the SS and the powerful *Gauleiter* (Regional leader of the NSDAP) Adolf Wagner.[52]

In contrast, the scientists and engineers who eventually quashed the rebellion within their own ranks did so by allying themselves with the technocrats within the National Socialist state, whether in industry, the Armed Forces, or in a special agency of 'Führer Power' like Hermann Göring's Office for the Four Year Plan or Albert Speer's Armaments Ministry. Such alliances allowed these researchers to escape the relative decline in power of the Civil Service and hitch a ride on the precipitous rise of technocrats within the National Socialist power cartel, beginning in 1936 with massive rearmament, picking up speed with the start of war in 1939, and accelerating after the winter of 1941–42.[53] This alliance of scientists and engineers on the one hand and National Socialist technocrats on the other also had an unforeseen consequence: it hastened the transition towards 'Big Science' in Germany and thereby facilitated the ability of the two post-war Germanies to compete with rivals such as the United States and the Soviet Union.

Thus the newly-found (or new heights of) appreciation of science and engineering by National Socialists was really only a consequence of the ability and desire of technocrats to fill niches within and help to further the goals of National Socialism. Technocracy, like technology, is fundamentally ambivalent and proved compatible with the most extreme aspects of German Fascism. Without technocracy the most barbaric, irrational and backward-looking policies of the Third Reich, including 'euthanasia', involuntary sterilization, the brutal repression of the Socialist movement, ruthless imperialism, ideological warfare on the eastern front, genocide and efforts to create a 'master race', would have been impossible. Scientists and engineers eventually managed to carve out a place for themselves in Hitler's Germany with the help of technocracy, usually not as the perpetrators of crimes against humanity nor as the wagers of aggressive war, but instead often as the technocratic experts or assistants who actively or passively made it all possible.

2   Continuity and discontinuity

The contributions to this volume not only cover a broad spectrum of scientific disciplines and technological projects under National Socialism; they also offer individually and collectively a starting point for investigating the question of *continuity* or *discontinuity* in scientific or technological developments before, during and after the Third Reich. All articles share first of all a common span of time, reaching from the Weimar Republic over the twelve years of National Socialist rule into the post-war years, although different authors emphasize different parts of this period. All authors go significantly beyond at least one of the political breaches in 1933 or 1945, whether they investigate a theoretical concept, an institution, a project or a discipline. The choice of this common time period should facilitate the search both for a particularly National Socialist science or technology and for lines of continuity over the political breaches in the areas of science and technology.

The question of continuity or discontinuity conceals abysses in German history which are closely connected to the difficult digestion since 1945 of the German past.[54] Both concepts are laden with values that in turn have molded the patterns of argumentation and how they have been used, and have normalized the historical judgment of science and technology under National Socialism. The problems bound up with these value-laden concepts will be discussed below.

When the Allies won the Second World War in 1945, they had defeated a criminal National Socialist regime which had murdered, enslaved and oppressed other peoples in the name of German racial superiority. The incomprehensible horror remains. A moral judgment is still required for the historical examination of National Socialism.[55] The Third Reich remains unlike any other historical episode.[56] The historiography of National Socialism, including the study of science and technology during the Third Reich, persistently questions the personal guilt or responsibility of the people involved, as well as their excuses or justifications. The answers to these questions vary greatly.

The National Socialist domination also came to an end for the Germans in 1945. They too distanced themselves from the worldwide horror provoked by German actions during the preceding twelve years, if for no other reason in order to secure their future under the occupying Allied powers. But psychological repression followed such distancing.[57] The interpretation of National Socialism as an 'accident' in the historical development of Germany dominated the German historiography of the post-war period.[58] This characterization also fulfilled an apologetic (in the sense of apologia) function by offering a theoretical justification of the simple distancing from these 'foreign bodies' in German history. Moreover, it allowed Germans involved with the post-war reorganization thereby to connect themselves uncritically to unburdened traditions from the Weimar period.[59] The reorganization of the West German research organizations is one example of this uncritical connection with Weimar.[60] This background endows the concepts of continuity and discontinuity with a specific meaning. Continuity is *positive* and means a connection between the post-war science and technology and developments in the Weimar period – but excluding the Third Reich. National Socialism makes up the *negative* discontinuity in German history. This unpleasant epoch has usually been omitted from the literature on the history of science and technology.[61]

It is precisely this omission which touched off the critical examination of science under National Socialism that was renewed in the Federal German Republic during the sixties. The student movement mounted a political protest against the silence over the 'brown past' (a reference to the brown-shirted SA) of the universities and demanded a critical examination. The considerable continuity in personnel from the Third Reich into post-war West Germany at the universities, in the legal system and among physicians as well as among scientific and technical experts was tolerated if not actively supported by the western Allies as part of the Cold War and contributed to this generational conflict.

The need to demand the right to speak despite considerable resistance made the question of political and moral guilt a central part of the debate – here the guilt of having remained silent for so long about victims and perpetrators. In contrast, for a long time the mere discussion of the National Socialist past of the universities was a political issue. This experience also molded subsequent historical work on science and technology under National Socialism.

The wave of publications on *Vergangenheitsbewältigung* (dealing ambivalently with an unpleasant past) which began in the sixties fits the previous pattern.[62] On the one hand, the silence over the victims of National Socialism was broken. A large part of the literature was concerned with the persecution, expulsion and murder of the Jews. On the other hand, attempts – whether successful or not – were made to justify past conduct, especially in the few lecture series held by universities on their history during the Third Reich. The few statements by scientists and engineers in these lectures exhibited a common pattern of justification: a blatant distancing which presupposed a complete separation between the practice of science and its political abuse.

Thorough historical investigations of science and technology under National Socialism were first carried out in the seventies. Their number increased enormously in the eighties, especially in connection with the 1983 and 1985 anniversaries of milestones in the Third Reich.[63] These investigations have collectively contributed to the fact that the study of science and technology under National Socialism is today an established component of historical research in Germany. Yet this research remains connected to a moral judgment of the conduct of scientists and engineers during the Third Reich, and this connection is jealously guarded in particular by the representatives of the respective scientific or technical disciplines.[64]

New assessments of continuity and discontinuity can be found in these studies, which in turn are again closely connected with efforts to construct a particular type of past for a scientific discipline. The first historical investigations concentrated on conspicuous aberrations. The National Socialist period was still considered to represent discontinuity in the history of science and technology, but it was now at least recognized, not omitted. The expulsion of Jewish colleagues, the political attacks on scientific autonomy and the claims of the *völkisch* (literary translated as 'people's', but also including a distinctive racist component) ideologies were characterized as specific to National Socialism. The different *völkisch* variants of scientific disciplines, from the so-called 'Aryan Physics' to race biology, were now of interest as aberrations in the development of science.[65]

The scholarly value of this work should in no way be denigrated through reference to the moralizing function it has had in the hands of some historians and scientists. A simple identification has often been made between 'the National Socialists' in the scientific disciplines and the *völkisch* variants,[66] which were then portrayed as pseudo-scientific or unscientific. This characterization facilitated an equally simplistic argument: all non-*völkisch* parts of the scientific work carried out during the National Socialist period – and that was by far the greater part – should thereby be excluded from questions of responsibility or guilt.[67]

The discontinuity of National Socialism in the history of scientific development was thereby specified and restricted. Its condemnation in turn strengthened the positive assessment of continuity in scientific conduct from the Weimar Republic through the period of National Socialism into the post-war years. Of course the historical examination of these clearly aberrant developments in science and technology need not be reduced or limited to these apologetic function. They continue to form an important part of research into National Socialism.[68] Ulrich Albrecht's contribution in this volume offers a good example of the potential of such work.

Historical research has recently been extended to the 'normal' sciences and technologies themselves, which are no longer simply contrasted with the *völkisch* variants. Herbert Mehrtens[69] has transcended the reduction of specific National Socialist influences on science and technology to the *völkisch* variants with the thesis that the ideology of 'service to the Volk' (*Dienst am Volk*) could suffice for binding scientists and engineers to the National Socialist system. His own studies, along with many others from different fields, have shown that a place could be sought and found in National Socialist ideology, in addition to the legitimation of scientific research through its economic and military significance for the goals of the Third Reich. In turn, the material and political support for the sciences increased significantly with the intensification of rearmament in 1937 and then grew even stronger during the war. These studies demonstrate the functionality and productivity of individual disciplines and their representatives for the technocratic side of National Socialism.[70] The contributions by Trischler, Neufeld and Rössler in this volume also offer such examples.

However, the technocratic side of National Socialism cannot be so easily separated from the ideological, for they could have common goals.[71] Mechtild Rössler has demonstrated for the field of geographic *Ostforschung* (literally 'Eastern Research') just how close the connection could be between the ideology of 'living space' (*Lebensraum*), racist population policy and scientific planning.[72] Her contribution to this volume handles a similar theme. The contribution from Ute Deichmann and Benno Müller-

Hill shows that in the field of biology a sharp separation between ideology and science is also impossible.[73]

This extension of the historical research can neither be summarized completely nor differentiated for the difficult disciplines, but it has had consequences for our understanding of continuity and discontinuity. It is clear that the negative assessment of discontinuity can no longer be reduced to a narrow, restricted region of National Socialist 'pseudo'-science, nor can the positive continuity in scientific activity be separated from National Socialist goals.

An extended approach to science and technology under National Socialism also allows historians to include developments before 1933 in their work. It is already well known that the racist foundation of National Socialist ideology was built upon a tradition of biologistic and social darwinistic concepts begun during the German Empire. The most prominent examples of precursors to National Socialist developments come from the area of race hygiene and eugenics.[74] The contributions by Ulfried Geuter, Sheila Weiss, Norton Wise and others in the collection offers examples for such continuities of theoretical concepts in scientific disciplines.[75] They all demonstrate that even if theoretical concepts in science are close to National Socialist ideology and policy, they may not necessarily be equated with the ideology of the Third Reich. Instead, concepts and programmes developed in the Weimar Republic were much more often accommodated to the requirements of the National Socialists and in turn functionalized by them. Omissions, changes in accent and reinterpretation were all part of this process, and need to be recognized.

Along with the work which 'moves backwards' from National Socialism, other significant studies examine the long-term development of a discipline or a project in which the Third Reich makes up only one part. Of course no disciplinary history that wants to trace cognitive development can exclude the results achieved in Germany between 1933 and 1945. But some historical work examines social and political structures that extend far beyond the two temporal boundries of the Third Reich.[76] Examples of such work in this volume include in particular the contributions from Trischler, Neufeld, Rössler, Sheila Weiss and Osietzki.[77] Since concepts or projects could be redesigned or made functional for different National Socialist goals, the desire for professional security and the realization during the Third Reich of previously conceived projects represent elements of continuity.

The institutional histories that do more than merely handle developments in the Third Reich also deserve mention.[78] Examples from the history of the Kaiser Wilhelm society (*Kaiser-Wilhelm-Gesellschaft*, henceforth KWG) can be found in the contributions from Deichmann and Müller-Hill, Macrakis and Burghard Weiss. The recent university histories,[79] which emphasize the inclusion of National Socialism, have once again made clear how many university scholars fit unconditionally and smoothly into the Third Reich. The political disposition of university teachers, often expressed as a continuity from 'no to the Weimar Republic' to 'yes to National Socialism,' also included anti-Semitism. Moreover, it has become clear that the ethos of science did not oppose National Socialism.[80] A corresponding investigation of the political disposition of engineers has been available since the seventies.[81] Heinemann-Grüder's article on armaments engineers in this volume is another contribution to this field of research.

Historical investigations of science and technology under National Socialism that take into account preceding developments in turn affect continuity and discontinuity. The multifaceted lines of continuity that stretch from clearly identifiable National Socialist developments back into the Weimar Republic, as well as the lines of continuity that illustrate the functionality of scientific and ideological concepts, technological projects and scientific disciplines for National Socialist goals, force a revision of the positive assessment of continuity. These lines of continuity release 'fears of condemnation'[82] from those individuals in particular who are used to a positive connection between the post-war period and the traditions of the Weimar Republic for their discipline. The simple strategies of distancing no longer work, since the 'normal' professional-interest politics obviously sufficed for an ordering in and functionalizing for the goals of the National Socialist system.[83]

Finally, developments in German science and technology that reach beyond the end of National Socialism need to be considered. The fact that there was neither a great reckoning nor a completely new beginning in 1945 has now become a truism. Diverse studies have shown that the functionary elite of the Third Reich were integrated into the post-war society of the Federal German Republic.[84] Countless examples of institutional and personal continuity in the area of science and technology can be found in the works already cited.[85] Examples in this volume are offered by Trischler, Burghard Weiss and Rössler. The policy of the victorious powers to recruit or carry off scientists, engineers and their equipment as reparations was especially significant.[86] Although personal careers and 'German' projects were thereby interrupted, this policy offered the possibility of continuing the work somewhere else.[87] The contributions from Neufeld and Heinemann-Grüder in this volume illustrate such examples. The victorious powers were particularly interested in the professional skills of technical specialists, not their political conduct. In turn scientists and engineers in these fields could make the transition to another political system with hardly any friction.[88]

Few investigations have been undertaken of the question of continuity in scientific or technical concepts, or in projects that transcend personal and institutional continuity,[89] perhaps because of the clearly controversial and sensitive nature of serious breaches in science policy. Nevertheless, the fact that the victorious powers halted projects in Germany did not necessarily mean their end. Neufeld's example of rocket technology makes it much more evident that it was possible to transfer to the United States an entire project structure that had been developed in Germany. The constraints that were placed in particular upon different scientific and technical fields of German research until 1955 represent a break with the past. Yet even these areas of research, which were taken up again in the mid 1950s, contain elements that connect to developments under National Socialism.[90]

The fact that a transfer of people, institutions and concepts from National Socialism into democratic structures was possible without political reflection is based upon, and in turn strengthened, the 'apolitical' self-understanding of scientists and engineers. Reinhard Siegmund-Schultze handles historical aspects of this self-understanding in this volume. In the final article, Herbert Mehrtens gives a sociological interpretation for the relative independence of the discipline of mathematics from concrete political conditions, an interpretation that can be generalized to cover all the sciences.

When scientific disciplines are viewed as social systems, they are provided with a self-definition, alongside that of the 'pure' science, which is subordinated to the legitimation and accommodation necessary in every political system. In exchange for the general loyalty and functionality of the individual disciplines, political systems guarantee in turn non-interference in scientific decisions. The restrictive self-definition in turn allows a construction of the history of the discipline that can boast of a continuity of 'pure' science. In the concrete, political-revolutionary situations of 1933 and 1945, however, first of all accommodation was necessary; researchers also made omissions and reinterpretations in 1945. The articles from Neufeld, Rössler and Heinemann-Grüder offer such examples. Scientists and engineers obviously tried to distance themselves from racist theory and practice, whereby the technocratic and military elements of their work were unquestionably continued; indeed, precisely these elements were attractive for the new political systems.

The lines of continuity that reach out of the Third Reich into the Federal German Republic or into one of the victorious powers are rarely seen as threatening.[91] The continuation under democratic conditions of projects supported under National Socialism is what has simultaneously consecrated them. This process is exactly as apologetic as its converse would be. In fact a comparison is necessary, for the functionality of science and technology for National Socialism obviously did not exclude functionality for other industrial nations with different political structures. Such a comparison would enrich and extend an analysis of the modernity or – as suggested above – the technocratic dimensions of the National Socialist system in a way that would illuminate the functions of science and technology in a modern society.

3   Outline of this book

The individual contributions to this volume include: (1) four articles that deal with different aspects of technology under National Socialism; (2) nine essays that handle individual scientific disciplines; (3) and two concluding articles which transcend individual scientific or technical disciplines. Extracts from original German sources are given in English; unless otherwise stated, all translations are by the author(s) of the chapter concerned.

3.1   Technology

Andreas Heinemann-Grüder concentrates on the personal motives of the German armaments engineers who worked in military research and development during both National Socialism and the post-war period. Leading National Socialist ideologues re-evaluated technology before and during the Third Reich. An ideological connection was made between German technology and racial superiority, material rewards were promised to the engineers and the occupation of engineer received enhanced prestige. Armaments research in particular was strongly supported and encouraged at the technical universities after 1933. The integration of armaments research into the engineering curriculum made the path from engineering studies into military research and development an option that was taken for granted. Many engineers were prepared to carry out armaments research under National Socialism, and this willingness was founded on the privileges connected with this work. The high prestige enjoyed by engineering in National Socialist ideology contributed as well. This prestige was enhanced once more during the last two years of the war when the search for 'wonder weapons' began and the engineers were upgraded to 'ideological soldiers.' Heinemann-Grüder concludes that the wishes of the engineers in no way contradicted the demands of the National Socialist system.

A survey of the technological reparations policies of the victorious powers, which recruited the German armaments engineers in great numbers for their respective skills, illustrates that the main reason for the willing collaboration of these engineers was once again the offer of professional and material security. Heinemann-Grüder's argument goes further: it was precisely the possibility of continuing projects from the National Socialist period in the service of one of the victorious powers that allowed the engineers to avoid self-critical reflection. Since their new employers did not ask about the researchers' National Socialist past, the Germans could interpret their invitations to go and work for the victorious powers as both an appreciation of their technical abilities and a justification of their previous work.

Michael Neufeld employs Thomas Hughes' concept of a 'technological system' in his examination of a concrete project: rocket technology, argu-ably the greatest technological achievement of the Third Reich. The begin-nings of rocket technology during the Weimar Republic were more show-manship than scientific enterprise. The actual expansion of the technological system began only when the Army took over the project. The concentration of development and production in a military research centre, first of all in Kummersdorf, became the centrepiece of the rocket project. After the Air Force had been brought into the project in 1935, it continued on a significantly larger scale in 1937 at the newly-built experimental grounds in Peenemünde. The transition to Big Science entailed in this project facilitated the technological successes which were necessary for the production of the V-2.

Financial resources were increased further at the beginning of the war, but at the same time new problems arose which needed to be solved. First of all, the project was pulled into the polycratic power struggles of the Third Reich. Underestimation of the technological problems caused still greater difficulties. The British air attack on Peenemünde in August of 1943 forced organizational changes, including a shift of production to the infa-mous underground *Mittelwerk* (literally translated as 'Middle Works') in the Harz mountains, where the lives of concentration-camp prisoners were murderously exploited as slave labour. Nevertheless, in September of 1944 the first V-2 rockets were fired against Paris and London.

Neufeld does not find specific National Socialist influence on the rocket project, except for the use of concentration-camp prisoners. However, he concludes that the leap from a small rocket research project to a massive technological system in so little time would have been inconceivable without National Socialism, in particular without the megalomania which the strained research and industrial capacities of the German Reich simply could not satisfy.

The technological system built around Peenemünde fell apart with the victory of the Allies, yet a group of 120 researchers around Wernher von Braun did continue their work as rocket engineers in the USA. The preser-vation of the decisive documents, materials and key personnel, as well as the transfer of the project from the German Army to its American counter-part, all facilitated the reconstruction of the entire technological system in the USA. The obvious and specifically National Socialist feature of the project, the exploitation of concentration-camp inmates, was not con-tinued.

Helmuth Trischler's article investigates German aeronautic research from the Weimar Republic to the Federal German Republic. His differen-tiated investigation of these scientists and the pattern of their conduct during National Socialism demonstrates once again the impossibility of a simplistic black and white judgment.

The development of aeronautic research since the turn of the century into an institutionalized science is used as background for the investigation of personal conduct. A stormy phase of expansion during the First World War was followed by constraints in the twenties, from the prohibitions of the Versailles Treaty to the poor material conditions of the Great Depression. The National Socialists' promises to support aeronautic research generously, which were in fact realized immediately after the National Socialists took power, thereby enhanced the prestige of aeronautic research and were one reason why the leading scientists 'quickly became friends' with the new political system. The fact that there were hardly any political attacks on the autonomy of these scientists made agreement with National Socialism still easier.

Trischler examines closely the conduct towards the political rulers of Ludwig Prandtl, conduct which the author classifies under the concept of *Resistenz*,[92] individual acts of opposition coupled with a fundamental loyalty to authority. This *Resistenz* in no way excluded participation in 'self-mobilization': the efforts during the war years to make research, as well as research planning more effective. German aeronautic research was rebuilt after the destruction of National Socialism by essentially the same scientists who had dominated science policy during National Socialism. Finally, instead of critical reflections by these scientists on their participation in National Socialist war research, Trischler finds only the usual retreat into supposedly apolitical science.

Ulrich Albrecht examines another area of aeronautic research which he characterizes as specifically National Socialist: three projects for fighter planes which were proposed and produced by various aircraft firms near the end of the war. The projects were begun at a time when a military defeat already loomed over Germany. German armaments production clearly could not match the quantitative Allied superiority in war materials. In this context the National Socialists propagated the hope that the clear quantitative superiority of the enemy could be matched and even overcome by a qualitative, technical superiority. Albrecht places the development of three fighter planes in this context.

The first project, the 'People's Fighter' (*Volksjäger*), went from the invitation for bids to its first flight in the breathtaking time of only three months. Because of the shortage of raw materials, the 'People's Fighter' was partially constructed from wood. Moreover, the planes were built by concentration-camp prisoners. The second project was a so-called 'Suicide Plane' (*Selbstopferflugzeug*) without landing gear. The last desperate project was the production of motorless fighters designed as gliders because of the shortage of fuel. All three projects featured a prone position for the pilot – in order to increase the centrifugal force a pilot could endure – and the use of half-grown boys as pilots. Certainly the most cynical 'special feature' lay in the construction and implementation of fighter planes as suicide weapons, thereby condemning the pilot to death.

These projects were not continued in the post-war period, yet Albrecht describes most impressively how post-war technical historiography has changed these inhuman projects to a celebration of the 'greatest technical performances'. The post-war descriptions of these projects speak of 'sacrificial weapons' (Verlustwaffen) or 'manned attrition devices (bemannten Verschleissgeräten), and thereby completely deny the fate of the people involved. Albrecht thus calls for a revision of this type of historiography.

3.2   Scientific disciplines

The first group of the following articles, which are concerned with individual scientific disciplines, investigate important aspects of National Socialist ideology, especially the aggressive demand for an extension of German 'living space'.

Mechtild Rössler analyses the origin and goals of the new discipline of 'area research and spatial planning' from the Weimar period into the post-war years. The first efforts at spatial planning in the Weimer Republic were a reflex reaction to the urbanization of industrial society. Individual scientific careers begun in this period often led seamlessly through to the Federal German Republic. The legal foundation for a comprehensive central spatial planning was first laid and corresponding national institutions were first created under National Socialism. Rössler singles out the Reich Office for Spatial Planning and its research organization, which in particular were engaged in economic, settlement and transportation planning in the *Altreich* (Germany's pre-war boundaries), from the profusion of planning institutions, responsible ministries and competing sections in the Third Reich. In contrast to the work in the *Altreich*, the racist model of the 'People's Community' (*Volksgemeinschaft*) provided the basis for planning in the conquered eastern regions. The Reich Office was involved with the 'General Plan for the East', which was overseen by the SS Planning Staff under Heinrich Himmler. This plan embodied the aggressive realization of National Socialist war aims as well as a ruthless and racist occupation policy, foreseeing the expulsion and murder of the Polish, Jewish, Russian and Ukrainian populations as well as the racist selection and control of the new Aryan settler population. The area research concepts which were developed for the east on the basis of this policy followed the same technocratic and disciplinary principles as did the concepts developed for the *Altreich*.

The plans for the east were neither realized not continued in the post-war period. In contrast, the concepts for the *Altreich* formed the basis for the reconstruction of western Germany. This work was carried out during the Federal Republic in the same institutional sphere as under National Socialism. Rössler argues that the distinction made by the victorious powers between planning as a means 'to solve problems of a modern, highly industrialized and urbanized society' and planning as a means of National Socialist population policy allowed the seamless continuation of the area research and spatial planning created under National Socialism.

Kristie Macrakis investigates an interesting aspect of the Kaiser Wilhelm Society, the most influential German scientific research organization outside the universities. National Socialist ideology played a role in the foundation of agricultural and biological KWG institutes during the war years in eastern and southeastern Europe. These institutes were the result of a connection between: (1) an ideological matrix which intertwined the concepts of 'living space', 'blood and soil' (*Blut und Boden*) and 'people's soil' (*Volksboden*); (2) the economic potential of the rich agricultural regions in the east and southeast of Europe; and (3) the ambitions of individuals. For example, the director of the 'Institute for the Science of Agricultural Work in the KWG', founded at the end of 1940 in Breslau, argued that this institute was intended to help integrate the conquered regions in the east. The other institutes were in theory joint partnerships between two nations. The German–Bulgarian Institute for Agricultural Research in Sofia was set up as an equal partnership, perhaps because of a cultural imperialist intent on the German side. Sofia was to become the leading agricultural institute for all of southeast Europe. A joint Greek–German biology institute was to be set up in the Piraeus as well, but Greek interest in the project was dampened after the German occupation of their country.

The foundation of these three institutes was bound up in the 'ideological matrix' of 'living space', cultural policy and National Socialist agricultural policy; they were first founded in this context, for there had been no such demand during the Weimar Republic. Thus Macrakis sees this ideological influence on institute foundation as a discontinuity in KWG policy. The two institutes in Bulgaria and Greece were not continued in the post-war period, but the Breslau institute continued to operate (first at Imbhausen, then at Bad Kreuznach), under the same director, as a Max Planck Institute, until 1976.

Ute Deichmann and *Benno Müller-Hill* give a survey of biologists at universities and KWG institutes during the Third Reich, investigating for the first time the losses to biology through the National Socialist dismissal policy and comparing them with developments in other disciplines. In a second section, they examine the support of biology through the German Research Foundation at universities and KWG institutes. Membership of the NSDAP was not a necessary criterion for such support. The number of biologists working at KWG institutes continually rose under National Socialism when compared to academic researchers. Why were the KWG institutes supported so generously? The willingness of the KWG to accommodate itself to the goals of National Socialism, as well as economic and military opportunities in the conquered regions in the east, made such support possible. Thus Deichmann and Müller-Hill are able to place research at various KWG institutes into the context of the 'General Plan for the East'. Further examples of war-related research in the field of biology within the KWG are also relevant in this regard. The collaboration between biologists and National Socialists in no way stopped at the cooperation with the SS and the concentration camp at Auschwitz. There were ideological reasons for the willingness of geneticists in particular to identify themselves with the race-hygiene policy of the National Socialists. Finally, Deichmann and Müller-Hill throw light on the further development of research organizations after the war: the scientists in the KWG advocated a centralized variant of research organization since they had had the best experience with precisely such an organization under National Socialism.

Sheila Weiss handles a prominent aspect of National Socialist ideology, race biology, in her contribution. Weiss investigates in particular school plans from the Weimar Republic through to the post-war period. She demonstrates that the Weimar Republic opened up a broad field for school reform and in particular for biology instruction. The new reformers attributed extensive tasks to biology: instilling love of the Fatherland, providing citizenship training, cultivating a sense of community and teaching health and hygiene. While a few of the suggested tasks did find entry into teaching, the persistent demands from the pedagogues for a broader consideration of biology in the teaching plan fell on deaf ears. Exactly this demand was fulfilled by the National Socialists both rhetorically and practically, thereby finding the enthusiastic agreement of many biology teachers. An unbroken continuity existed between these concepts in the Weimar period and under National Socialism. What was new was the extreme emphasis on racism in all areas, which was supposed to demonstrate the superiority of the Nordic race. The new school plan, which actually was not officially adopted until 1938, reinterpreted old concepts from the Weimar Republic in a particular way. For example, demands for biology as a life science were reduced to biology as the 'laws of life', that is, as 'selection and elimination'.

According to Weiss, biology lost significance for governmental and Party officials with the outbreak of war, since the hard sciences and their potential contributions to military research and development obviously were now more highly regarded than the predominantly ideological function of biology. The racist textbooks were pulped after 1945. However, Weiss argues that the politicization of biology remained. For example, the Soviet occupation demanded that biology now prove that members of all races had the same rights and responsibilities.

Ulfried Geuter's article examines the holistic psychology of Felix Krueger in order to determine whether Krueger's theory contained elements of political thought related to National Socialist ideas. His differentiated investigation clearly illustrates the pattern and limits of a simple ordering of Krueger as a predecessor or pioneer of National Socialism.

Geuter shows how Krueger developed his psychological theory during the twenties in close connection with right-wing conservative political discourse. The concept of holism was widespread in the scientific and political thought of the Weimar Republic as an answer to the problems of industrialization. Krueger's holistic psychology promised order and consistency and his conception of the dominance of the whole over the parts was a particularly right-wing conservative idea that recognized no interrelation between the whole and its parts. Important in this regard is the determination of the community as ahistorical and timeless, which, however, in Krueger's concrete, general determination embodied features of contemporary German Nationalist and young Conservative thought. Krueger applied his theory to political relations, limited the community to the German 'People's Community', and correspondingly called for Germans to be obedient followers of an authoritarian leader. If he thereby also saw community and holism as biological units, he did not conceive of them as units of blood and race. To this extent Krueger's community psychology was not National Socialist. Krueger greeted the National Socialist succession to power even though he was critical of how racist Jewish policy and political persecution were implemented in practice. He did not build the race policy into his theory and he suffered from National Socialist university policy due to his pro-Semitic remarks: he was first removed from his position as rector at Leipzig and finally forced into early retirement.

Krueger was a representative of the type of professor who rejected the democracy of the Weimar Republic and instead wished for an internal right-wing conservative renewal of Germany and an external expansion, and who saw his science as making a contribution towards these goals. Thus Krueger's theory could 'feed National Socialist policy', even if he himself was too independent to accommodate his theory completely to National Socialist ideology. Instead he used his strong institutional position to try and make the Leipzig holistic psychology into the obligatory research programme under National Socialism – but failed. Geuter comes to the conclusion that even if Krueger developed no National Socialist psychology and personally suffered, he did create an intellectual contribution for National Socialist ideology and policy.

Norton Wise also investigates an individual scientist's theory and its political implications: the system of the physicist Pascual Jordan, which connected aspects of quantum physics, philosophy, psychology and sociology.

Jordan's consistent worldview rejected determinism and took as its starting point the anti-causality that the historian Paul Forman has described for the quantum physics of the Weimar Republic.[93] In contrast, Jordan designed a new causality, statistical and psychological, which reached far beyond the field of quantum mechanics. Jordan proposed a quantum-mechanical holism as a positive 'holism of the organism', which at once contained all possibilities for behaviour, which could not be broken down into individual parts, and which could be determined only at the moment of measurement. According to the physicist, this holism decomposes during the transfer from the microscopic to the macroscopic level; in the latter, objects are then once again causally determined, but in the microscopic region they have a freedom of decision.

Jordan's amplifier theory allowed the transfer of the 'acausality' of certain atomic reactions, with the help of the 'leader principle' (*Führerprinzip*), to the macroscopic level. The physicist saw analogous structures in the field of biology, in which the 'decisions' of a central molecule was supposed to deliver the directives for an entire organism, and in the area of mass psychology, in which leading personalities could use the subconscious mind to produce conscious actions. Jordan thereby assumed an hierarchical organization structure of the natural as well as the social order. His worldview was based on mutual legitimation of quantum mechanics and National Socialist culture.

Jordan borrowed many elements of his theory from other contexts, for example from the school of the physicist Niels Bohr, from the Vienna Circle and from Freudian psychology. Wise shows how Jordan reinterpreted the representatives of these schools as supporters of his dictatorial model, thereby simultaneously and emphatically warning against a global assignment of all holistic concepts to National Socialist ideology.

The next two articles also examine aspects of physics in National Socialism. They both handle the technology of particle accelerators, but from completely different perspectives. *Burghard Weiss* investigates the 'Minerva Project', a linear accelerator at the KWG Institute for Chemistry, from the beginning of the project during the thirties until the sixties.

The KWG chemistry institute had an early, relatively small-dimensioned model of a linear accelerator which was used for the production of neutrons. Only in 1938 did Otto Hahn see the need for a larger linear accelerator, after Josef Mattauch had succeeded Lise Meitner and in any case had insisted on physical changes in the institute for his research. Moreover, Weiss sees the new accelerator project in the context of the discovery of nuclear fission at the end of 1938, which made a stronger source of radiation very desirable. In addition, the project promised increased prestige for the institute. Otto Hahn was unsuccessful in his efforts to gain financial support from military and industrial sponsors until scientific research began to be organized centrally after the end of the Lightning War in 1941: the remaining funds came in particular from Göring's Ministry of Aviation. In the middle of 1942 the first production contracts were distributed to industrial firms. However, the continuation of the project was severely constrained by the ever-worsening effect of the war in Germany. In 1944 the entire institute was evacuated to southern Germany; at the end of the war eighty per cent of the equipment for the linear accelerator was stored there.

The post-war French occupation government guaranteed the continuation of research and a new reconstruction of the institute at the University of Mainz. However, first of all a joint decision on the further fate of the entire Kaiser Wilhelm Society had to be made by the victorious western powers. Moreover, the financing of research in the Federal Republic had to be regulated. In 1949 the future of the institute as a Max Planck Institute was decided and the financing sorted out. The linear accelerator was finally finished by the beginning of the sixties. Weiss argues that the continuation of the project in the post-war period was possible because there was a continuity of personnel and an availability of apparatus, and because the project was actively supported by the allies. Moreover, the relative backwardness of the project when compared to international developments secured its existence: it was no threat to or competition for the western powers.

Maria Osietzki investigates the ideology embodied in the technology of the particle accelerator, a highly technical instrument of modern physics. This 'accelerator ideology' facilitates a special connection between science and power.

The origin of this ideology lies in the transition from classical to quantum and nuclear physics. In particular the accelerator was integrated into the conceptual field surrounding nuclear physics, which in turn was molded by fantasies of inexhaustible amounts of energy lying dormant in atomic nuclei as well as of the transmutability of matter. In addition accelerators symbolized the fact that new scientific results often depended on the availability of highly technical apparatus. The maxim 'the bigger the accelerator, the higher the research performance' molded the dynamic in the development of accelerators and research practice. Moreover, the author places the higher estimation of the apparatus and simultaneous devaluation of the individual researcher bound up in this maxim in the context of the institutional transition to Big Science. The development of accelerators in Germany, which began in the thirties, was already based on technological and ideological developments in the USA. In particular, it was already clear that an accelerator would lend great prestige to such a research institute. The legitimation of the requests for accelerators which scientists made under National Socialism were correspondingly tailored to this principal desire for prestige.

Osietzki describes in detail the activities of the Siemens Company, which wanted for economic reasons to achieve a monopoly over the construction of synchrotron accelerators. Rolf Wideröes' betatron is a good example of an accelerator project embedded in the military context of National Socialism. Yet the author concludes that even in the Third Reich accelerators were predominantly important as symbols for scientific superiority and economic power. Osietzki interprets the multiplication of accelerators after 1945 as an act of liberation by the nuclear physicists from the stigma of 'extermination science', since elementary particle physics counted as basic research.

Herbert Mehrtens chooses a sociological approach for his survey of mathematics under National Socialism. First of all, he develops his concept of mathematics as a 'social system'. Such a system includes the internal structure of the discipline, processes of identity formation, setting up boundaries against other social systems, and making connections to the system's surroundings all the way up to the more important political connections. Beginning with the formation of the 'social system' of mathematics, which reaches back into the nineteenth century, Mehrtens can show how the necessary dynamic balance between disciplinary autonomy and national society took concrete form under National Socialism.

Mehrtens places the well-known phenomenon of 'Aryan Mathematics' into the conflict between mathematical modernity, which had dominated the discipline since the end of the twenties, and counter-modernity. Ludwig Bieberbach, as the leading representative of 'Aryan Mathematics', with the help of National Socialism attempted to push through his counter-modern criticism and his own mathematical research programme. Mehrtens uses his concept of mathematics as a 'social system' in order to illustrate the reasons for Bieberbach's failure. Bieberbach's connection between mathematics and National Socialist worldview did serve an ideological function for his discipline, but Bieberbach could not satisfy the far greater interest in the instrumental character of mathematics. It is clear why Bieberbach failed within the social system: (1) by assaulting 'modern' mathematics he thereby attacked the nucleus of a well-established social system; (2) his projection of general desires and values onto a mathematical program contradicted the purely professional structure of the system.

Mehrtens analyses the integration of mathematics into National Socialist society by means of the German mathematical societies. The example of the German Mathematicians' Association illustrates that the politically powerful were prepared to respect professional autonomy so long as sufficient loyalty was guaranteed towards the state. Moreover, the hasty accommodation of the Reich Union of Mathematical Societies to National Socialism, which in particular was concerned with mathematics in schools, reduced the political pressure on the German Mathematicians' Association by means of a sort of division of labour. In addition, other requirements of National Socialist society were fulfilled by the Society for Applied Mathematics and Mechanics.

Mehrtens comes to the conclusion that the cognitive and social universality of the social system of mathematics, together with its social differentiation, formed the basis for the survival of the discipline under the extreme changes brought about by National Socialism, that is, for the integration of mathematics into the political and social system of National Socialist Germany.

3.3   General aspects

Reinhard Siegmund-Schultze investigates patterns in the political conduct of scientists, which are molded by a fundamental contradiction. First of all, scientists are integral parts of modern industrial society and thereby represent a significant political factor. Yet scientists are hardly politically active in the broader sense; instead they constrain their political activities in general to professional matters. Moreover, scientific productivity is coupled to the apolitical conduct of the representatives of individual disciplines.

The ethos of science, the social position of scientists, the special interests of particular scientific disciplines and their historical roots are all important for an understanding of the political conduct of scientists. In conflicts between 'pure scientific interests' on the one hand and national-cultural, national-political and national-scientific traditions on the other, the latter always prevail, especially in the five political systems found in Germany during the last century. The author thereby demonstrates the importance of considering the political behaviour of scientists over a long period of time. Building on this point, Siegmund-Schultze offers the thesis that it is precisely the radical political changes in the past hundred years that have contributed to the fact that scientists have developed 'apolitical conduct' as their most promising and certain strategy.[94]

Siegmund-Schultze provides a survey of the pattern of political conduct by scientists under National Socialism, from the lack of solidarity with Jewish colleagues to efforts to preserve and expand capacities for education and research. He closes with the thesis that the restoration of the ideal of apolitical science in the Federal German Republic after the war hindered a critical examination of this ideal until the sixties. Such a discussion also did not take place in the German Democratic Republic.

The strategy of demarcation from the Third Reich and the 'anti-Fascist' attitude in the German Democratic Republic produced many similarities with National Socialism, so that coping with the Nazi legacy was intimately connected with political coordination and indoctrination. Thus a deeper understanding of the historical after-effects of National Socialism can be gained by studying the political history of science in East Germany. While the author calls for studies comparing the situation in the former German Democratic Republic and under National Socialism, arguably it is also important for this theme to compare the respective treatments of National Socialism in the Federal German Republic.

In his second essay in this collection, *Herbert Mehrtens* formulates theses for the political and moral structure of mathematical sciences, which once again can be carried over to other scientific disciplines. He analyses National Socialism as a concrete political system which makes especially clear those structures which mold the sciences in the twentieth century.

Mehrtens begins with a criticism of the contemporary self-understanding of scientists which is based on the 'purity' of their results. He criticizes as politically inconsequential in particular an ethics of science which refers to the image of 'pure' science and understates connections to technology, politics and economics. The basis and function of this image are illustrated in the context of the author's thesis of mathematics as a social system. The fundamental self-definition of the system 'orientates itself on the product and process of pure research work as an exclusively cognitive entity'. It is functional for drawing boundaries and for the productivity of the system.

Interest politics is of course a recognized part of the system, yet the restrictive self-definition allows it to disregard political or moral considerations as long as they are not relevant for the professional politics of the discipline. Self-definition and acceptable interest politics facilitate a far-reaching independence of the disciplines from the concrete changes taking place in the political surroundings. But the market for science is publicly financed and organized, and thus power lies on the side of the state. The disciplines gain public legitimation and participation in social power through accommodation. Yet scientists and mathematicians produce only potential means to power – the basis of their existence is that they produce the means to power; that it potentially remains in the hands of scientists is connected with the self-definition, which indeed constitutes a non-interference declaration in matters of politics, economics and morals. Mehrtens closes with a call to reconsider as well parts of the social system of science which, as a prerequisite for responsible political conduct (and not just of scientists), transcend the effective self-definition of 'purity'.

2 | 'Keinerlei Untergang':[1] German armaments engineers during the Second World War and in the service of the victorious powers

ANDREAS HEINEMANN-GRÜDER

The growing relevance and public discussion of the responsibility of science and technology enhances the significance of historical research into the political, socio-psychological, ethical and institutional context of technology. However, the behaviour of armaments engineers during the Nazi period and the military intentions and implications of their work have not yet been taken up by historians. With the exception of several studies on the socio-political conduct of engineers, armaments engineers have been excluded from socio-historical analysis and criticism.[2] This fact is all the more surprising because the conduct of the German military and scientists during the Nazi period has been studied in detail. The few studies of engineers mostly deal with specific projects or individuals.[3] In contrast, historical analyses of armaments have usually been devoted to economic and structural aspects.[4]

Studies from an ethical point of view of the history of science during the Nazi period deal primarily with those branches of knowledge that have been proclaimed 'pure', or with the disciplines that clearly were compromised.[5] Engineers have never had the sort of pretenses of self-righteous purity that historians usually contrast with actual conduct. This difference might be the essential explanation for the lack of research on the morality of armaments engineers.

This paper will be devoted primarily to the personal motivations of German armaments engineers conducting military research and development (R&D) during World War II and immediately thereafter. The attitude of these engineers towards the military goals of their research will be studied. The inherent internal connection between technology and armaments will be examined. The institutional aspects of Nazi technology have already been analysed by Karl-Heinz Ludwig.[6]

The empirical basis is naturally limited by the existing sources, so that only an incomplete mosaic can be reconstructed out of quite different auto-biographical accounts. Besides some contemporary publications on the philosophy of technology, the memoirs of armaments engineers and information collected through personal interviews will serve as the primary basis for this work.[7]

The term 'armaments engineer' should be clarified. There is neither a definite boundary between science and technology nor one between scientists and engineers, but engineers' work might be understood as the practical application of scientific principles.[8] I will therefore include under the term 'armaments engineers' all engineers responsible for the calculations, design and development of weapons as well as the running of weapons-producing industrial plants. Admittedly, this term thus has a broad meaning, and therefore makes it difficult to distinguish it from the term 'armaments scientist'.

Technology as battle[9]

Historically the terms 'armaments' and 'engineering' have been very closely connected.

> '*Ingenere*' was at one time nothing more than the title of a person in charge of constructing military installations and digging trenches for defense against the newly-invented artillery. This title was then applied to the next generation of professionals whose functions were similar in substance, but totally different in spirit.

Ludwig Brinkmann wrote this in 1908 in his Engineers' Manifesto.[10] By 'different in spirit' he did not mean that the modern engineer rejected military goals. On the contrary, engineers immersed themselves in supra-sensual abstract ideas. In other words, they became more like scientists.[11]

When philosophers like Brinkmann at the beginning of the twentieth century compared the engineers' profession with the taming of the shrew, they meant that the engineer's work is necessarily violent. Brinkmann makes a comparison with the art of torture.

> It is one thing to observe objectively as a researcher and notice things with a cool and clear head; it is another to perform purposefully and highly subjectively a preconceived idea. When sometimes Nature persistently resists, it allows the veils concealing it to be torn. But the engineer, whose task it is to enslave it, struggles to tame the eternal shrew, who is scratching and biting fiercely in defense. And this is an everlasting battle. This guerilla war, which becomes practice, or is identified with it, provides engineers with their trademark and distinguishes them from their fellows, pure scientists.[12]

Authors like Brian Easlea have concluded from similar opinions expressed by engineers and scientists that the essence of the natural sciences is the rape of Nature.[13] By extending statements on nature-destroying technology, weapons-producing technology would only be a radical consequence of an intrinsic disregard for nature.

Even if we disagree with this radical statement of the relationship between technology, the destruction of nature, and armaments, we cannot assume any fundamental contradictions between technology and military purposes. Moreover, the professional ideology of pure science is basically alien to the philosophy of technology. The basic conflict that exists in the pure sciences between the cognition process and the ideals of enlightenment on the one hand and the social system on the other, cannot be applied to technology.

Such major programmatic works as Brinkmann's laid the groundwork for the psychological and social elevation of engineers as a social group. Engineers in turn promoted an aggressive cult of feasibility. But the ideologues of National Socialism went much further. They promoted the idea, at least theoretically, that engineers or simply 'technology' should be 'constructively' involved in politics. As opposed to the romantic 'back to nature' movements and the anti-modernism criticisms of technology, the spiritual pioneers of National Socialism made a myth of technology. They effectively used the latest technological innovations for propagandistic purposes. They elevated the social prestige of engineers, who at that time felt unappreciated.[14]

Before the Nazi era, widespread social insecurity among engineers caused by the Great Depression was coupled with previously existing professional insecurity. As engineers and technicians of various qualifications and rank, they lacked solidarity and group identity and had no specific social image.[15] They had neither political conscience as a social group – if you take for example the publications of their professional organization, the Union of German Engineers (Verein deutscher Ingenieure) – nor a relatively high proportional representation in the Nazi party before 1933.[16] But Nazi propaganda adroitly manoeuvred the subconscious wishes of a caste that felt discredited, which might be one of the major reasons why, as early as the beginning of the summer of 1933, all the larger professional engineering organizations joined the Nazi-controlled Reich Society for Technological and Scientific Work (Reichsgemeinschaft technisch-wissenschaftlicher Arbeit). From then on they showed nothing but goodwill towards the Nazi system.[17]

The spiritual ideologue of the Nazi movement, Alfred Rosenberg, embraced the underprivileged engineers in his famous 'Myth of the Twentieth Century':

> whoever blindly condemns 'technology' nowadays, and piles up curse
> upon curse against it, forgets that it is based on an everlasting German
> drive which would disappear together with the downfall of technology.
> That would deliver us to the barbarians, and leave us in the condition to
> which the Mediterranean civilizations once declined. It is not the tech-

nology that kills everything vital, rather it is human beings who have degenerated.[18]

'Aryan Technology' (*Deutsche Technik*), which was also the programmatic title of the professional engineering journal during the Nazi era, was expected to prove the racial superiority of Germans and solve the universal crisis of bourgeois society. Rudolf Heiss saw technicians as a

> crucial force, upon whose unbending will, reliability in difficult situations, and inner power shall depend the victory of emotional mobilization ... They will decide whether the main demands of National Socialism will find their practical application, or otherwise merely become a meaningless catchword.[19]

The new appreciation of 'Aryan Technology' had an anti-Semitic connotation and was hostile to the natural sciences. Modern physics, for example, was considered excessively theoretical, senseless, and as having Jewish overtones.[20]

According to the very foundation of Nazi ideology, technology proper carried an immediately political and explicitly ideological function. Some famous Nazi ideologues even promoted technocratic concepts of technology as a leading political force in society. However, engineers were only marginally involved in the decision-making process for economic policy as a whole, and in armaments technology (*Wehrtechnik*), in particular, until the beginning of the forties.[21]

'Ultimately, by declaring technology a creative political force, national law contributed to the determination of the ideological purposes of the technical intelligentsia.'[22] '*Völkisch*' (literally translated as folk, including nationalist and racist overtones) ideology was not perceived as something superficial or as a by-product of technology. In the Nazi ideology of technology – as opposed to that of science – the 'service to the *Volk*' and the *völkisch* disposition were organically integrated. The 'pure German' should find his expression in technology, which was the achievement of the 'racial society' (*Rassegemeinschaft*).[23] Naturally not all engineers perceived their professional activity from that point of view. But their psychological elevation, combined with the Nazis' promise to answer their material deprivation, made them match the performance expected of them at the very beginning of the Nazi era.[24] In early 1943, the journal *Deutsche Technik* claimed that the success of the Nazi efforts was already clear:

> the technicians who were looked down upon by humanists, and who were criticized by moralists for their aspiration towards practical application, and were insulted by economists as the world's Cinderella for being an innocent source of social faults ... are now recognized as full-fledged members of the 'People's Community' (*Volksgemeinschaft*). In fact they have become a force called upon to answer the extraordinary quest for leadership.[25]

Armaments technology as part of education

The political and organizational efforts in Germany to train engineers specializing in military technology and, moreover, to give military personnel technological skills, go back as far as the turn of the twentieth century. The education of engineers and the research and development of armaments was to be combined according to the example of the French *École Supérieure Politechnique* and the *École de l'Application de l'Artillerie et du Génie*. But the Military and Technical Academy (*Militärtechnische Akademie*) founded in Potsdam in 1903 was only able to train a small number of engineering officers in the few years of its existence. Because of the provisions of the Versailles Peace Treaty, the recently established military and technological academy had to be closed down. Thus the technical education of military personnel and armaments engineers had to be transferred directly to technical universities.[26] However, this transfer was not completed during the Weimar Republic.

Only after Hitler came to power did the individuals who had already begun the appropriate preparations during the Weimar Republic bring together the Armed Forces, the universities and the bureaucracy. Special mention should be made of Major Karl Becker, who in the twenties was the representative of the Army Commission on Weapons and Equipment (*Inspektion Waffen und Geräte*, subsequently called Army Ordnance, *Heereswaffenamt*). In 1932 the Ministry of Culture appointed him honorary professor of military sciences at the University of Berlin. As head of a department in Army Ordnance, and after 1938 as its chief, he championed the introduction of military sciences at the Technical University of Berlin.[27] Also foremost among the promoters of military research in universities was Erich Schumann, physicist and private lecturer (*Privatdozent*) at the University of Berlin. Schumann worked in the Ministry of War (*Reichswehrministerium*) from 1923 on, and in 1932 became chief of both the research department of Army Ordnance and of military political institute (*Wehrpolitisches Amt*) in the Nazi party (another name for the *Nationalsozialistische Deutsche Arbeiterpartei*, henceforth NSDAP). It was Schumann who, while serving, first from 1934 in the Reich Ministry of Education (*Reichsministerium für Wissenschaft, Erziehung und Volksbildung*), and then from 1938 to 1945 as a deputy minister in the Ministry of War, promoted the interests of the Army in the scientific research being conducted at universities.[28]

The interest of the Army in cooperation in the field of armaments technology with technical universities and in educating a corps of qualified engineers is hardly surprising. What is noteworthy, however, is that technical universities were themselves interested in attracting armaments research.

University professors became actively engaged in armaments research. It was much easier to attract funding when they could prove that the results of their research could be used for military purposes. During the planning stage of the pompous 'Faculty of Armaments Technology' (*Wehrtechnische Fakultät*) in Berlin-Grunewald, numerous professors tried to secure posts and funding in advance. Hans Ebert and Hermann-Josef Rupieper have summarized the whole affair.

> The arguments in favor of establishing these institutes are of considerable importance for the connection between scientific interests and National Socialist armaments policy, because professors thereby demonstrated their professional contribution and their interest in military-technological research and instruction. The exaggeration in their scientific arguments should not mislead us into doubting that they actually expressed their convictions, even if the latter were not decisive for the development of research. However, it is clear that in their minds they made a distinction between military research and National Socialism, and that their main purpose was 'to serve their people' by enhancing the military power of the Army. Although they did not always explicitly express their own scientific position, these testimonials indicate the scientists' willingness to put their efforts and research in the service of National Socialism.[29]

Thus it is significant that the National Socialist state planned to send military professionals to the Faculty of Armaments Technology for their education in armaments engineering, rather than to retrain 'civilian' professors for this task. The Ministry of War, the Aviation Ministry (*Reichsluftfahrtministerium*), the High Command of the Navy and Army Ordnance were to provide a large share of university professors in this faculty.

Armaments research was not only found in the specially established Faculty of Armaments Technology. It was quite common in all technical universities.[30] University students naturally became involved in the armaments sector through the integration of armaments research into the technical universities, where work on military contracts was encouraged.[31]

According to Karl-Heinz Ludwig, the trend towards armaments research at technical universities gained ground, especially after 1942, because participation in armaments research often protected students from conscription. It also provided them with a privileged distribution of materials and equipment. But institutional cooperation between scientific research institutes and high-ranking armaments research staffs (*Wehrforschungsstäbe*) was only successful in the field of chemistry.[32] It proved impossible to establish a long-term inter-institutional exchange between technical education, technological R&D and the military during the twelve years of Nazism.[33] Plans for such an explicit military research organization under the domain of the party and the SS remained wishful thinking.[34] Nevertheless, Minister of Armaments and Munitions Fritz Todt, who as of 1939 also headed the Union of German Engineers, managed from early 1940 to his death in 1942 to strengthen significantly the influence of engineers in the armaments economy. This goal was realized on 23 February 1940 by the appointment of the chief of the main department of technology in the NSDAP to the post of 'General Inspector of the Four Year Plan'. Ludwig has interpreted this event as the 'engineers' gradual power takeover in the war economy', caused by the obvious lack of armaments in the early stages of the war.[35] But engineers saw it differently.

Motives of armaments engineers

The personal history of an Austrian engine designer named Ferdinand Brandner was typical of the attitude young engineers held towards military aims and Nazism. He started as a locomotive engine designer, and in time worked at Humboldt-Deutz-Motoren A.G. in the Rhineland. By 1936 Brandner was designing aircraft engines at Junkers-Motorenbau in Dessau.[36] Brandner came from a petty bourgeois family. His father was a low-ranking official. After his engineering studies, he started building a successful professional career. Yet by the end of the twenties he started feeling anxious about his position, after seeing so many engineers lose their jobs.[37] In 1930 Brandner joined the National Socialist Factory Organization (*Nationalsozialistische Betriebszellenorganisation*) and even the Technical Engineers Division (*Ingenieurtechnische Abteilung*) of the NSDAP, at that time illegal in Austria. It is easy to understand his motivations: he was seeking a responsible and challenging position, a good income and family security.

Disappointed by the chauvinistic *Anschluss* ('connection', in this case absorption) of Austria by Germany, he resigned all his party functions in 1938. Thereafter he devoted himself entirely to his work, namely to the development of a 2,000 horsepower aircraft engine at the Junkers industrial works in Dessau. According to his own account, he 'was yearning for creative work'.[38] It is impossible to establish whether the possible military application of his work was either a stimulus or a barrier for him. As far as we can judge from his memoirs, he was only interested in seeking technical solutions to problems.

According to the now rank-and-file NSDAP member Brandner, the outbreak of war 'took us all by surprise. None felt inspired by it. We all felt that we had set out upon the path of no return'.[39] No thoughts other than 'straight ahead' – this concise motto was the theme of Brandner's memoirs.[40] The power engines built by Brandner's team were to make the Ju 288 aircraft 'the fighting machine that would decide the war'.[41] The Ju 288 project was designated top priority by the Aviation Ministry and was to go into serial production in April of 1941. Brandner brought the spirit of war to his design table.

> The fate of the Air Force depended upon whether the Ju 288, the fastest fighter, could replace the Ju 88 as soon as possible. Every specialist knew

that bringing the series to fruition, the most important phase of the development, was very important for serial production.[42]

Under pressure from the military for results, the Junkers engineers astonishingly beat all records. Following the 24 December 1941 directive from the Ministry of Aviation, they 'worked even more doggedly' on the further development of a Jumo 222 engine with a power output of 3,000 horsepower.[43] Similar time pressure was exerted on other aircraft engineers, for example on the subsequently famous Ludwig Bölkow from Messerschmitt. From the end of 1942 until the autumn of 1943, Bölkow developed the Me 109 fighter, an airplane that provided strong competition for the American Mustang fighter. For a young engineer of thirty-one it was a stressful but prestigious job, or, as he put it, 'it was a fabulous education'.[44]

Many corporate research departments were frequently burdened with military directives by higher ranking offices. The reorientation of corporate research programmes to armaments projects was not always carried out on the basis of free will.[45] But among ambitious engineers striving for more independence, financial support was as a rule a primary motivation for turning to military projects. Thus the Peenemünde rocket development programme, initially promoted by technical director Wernher von Braun of the Army Testing Grounds (*Heeresversuchsanstalt*) and by their military chief Colonel Walter Dornberger, was only comprehensively funded after the potential military benefits were proven, and after the War Ministry took over rocket development.[46]

Another example is the famous Baron Manfred von Ardenne, an engineer with his own private research laboratory. Beginning in 1936, he tried to develop 'with all vigor' a 'panorama radar system'.[47] However, Aviation Minister Hermann Göring did not pursue the idea proposed by von Ardenne in October of 1940. Later, von Ardenne legitimized his motives to contribute to air defense long before the outbreak of war with his 'honest wish to help defend German lives'. Disingenuously he admits in his autobiography that his aspirations 'in view of this aggressive [German] policy might at least appear suspiciously like an illusion'.[48] The words 'at least' and 'appear' are remarkable. Von Ardenne made his proposals long before the Allies started bombing Germany, long before even the possibility of air war was publicly discussed in Germany. Von Ardenne's proposal to design defence radars against incoming bombers and his offer to Postal Minister Wilhelm Ohnesorge to use nuclear power for military purposes 'appear' to be more of an eagerness to procure funding by accepting military aims and to win political and administrative influence in the Nazi system through participation in weapons projects.

Armaments researchers do not mention in their memoirs whether they had any scruples about the fact that this 'detour' towards weapons projects meant that they would also have to bear the responsibility for their application and implementation.[49] Secret zones, barbed wire, strict security, constant Gestapo surveillance and the presence of forced labour during the war – all this was taken for granted by the engineers involved with Peenemünde. The opportunity to participate was honour enough. For example, Hermann Oberth, the 'father' of rocket technology and the mentor of von Braun, was unhappy that he had to work in Vienna, far away from Peenemünde. He also wanted to be there.[50]

Working in armaments R&D was considered prestigious because armaments corporations and their research laboratories never lacked governmental contracts. They could provide career-oriented engineers with opportunities to prove themselves, bestowing on them good wages, job security and, during the war, exemption from a 'hero's death at the Russian front'.[51] Elevated by Nazi ideology to the level of members of the 'master race' (*Herrenmenschen*), these armaments engineers sought to prove the legitimacy of this title, especially in the last two years of the war.

The reliance on 'salvation' through technology grew with the approach of the end of the war. Armaments technology turned into a battlefield. The journal *Deutsche Technik* stated frankly in January of 1943 that 'very strict criteria should be applied – war criteria'.[52] In the same issue Minister of Armaments Albert Speer called upon 'the men of German technology':

> through fabulous victories the German soldier has greatly extended the frontiers. He has provided an incomparable example for the workers of the fatherland. I call upon the men of German technology to ensure that in the coming year the front has the weapons, ammunition, and equipment needed. The task falls upon you to enhance the military might of our people. Your work in the coming year should be guided by the necessity to conserve manpower, material, energy, and transport.[53]

The working atmosphere of armaments engineers became that of military comradeship. The presence of forced labour, of the SA, and often that of concentration-camp prisoners at the corporate facilities became the status quo for the working routine in the last years of the war.[54] With growing military problems came a stubborn will to pull through. Corresponding descriptions can be found during the last stages of the war. Thus Brandner wrote from the recently relocated Jumo production facilities in Oberursel to his wife, who had also been evacuated to the countryside because of the Allied bombardments in June of 1944:

> it was a crazy trooper's life, in spite of work and so on it was a stubborn struggle for survival and this welded the team together ... SA patrolled the facilities ... Meanwhile I have to push for the priority of constructing my engine, and of course the program cannot be interrupted.[55]

Brandner continues in his memoirs: 'I welcomed complete devotion to my work because in view of approaching fate it seemed to be the only way to save me from despair'. Brandner was ordered by his corporate chiefs during

Easter of 1945 to 'prepare and transport the strategic engine 004 under the thunder of cannons'.[56]

From the engineers' point of view, the requirements for productivity set by the Ministries of Aviation or Armaments frequently seemed absurd, ignorant and careless, especially towards the end of the war. For example, the seventh regulation imposed by the Armaments Ministry's 'Concentration Decree' of February 1945 stated that from then on only such 'projects would be allowed, whose estimated time requirements did not exceed twenty-three days for design and 500 workshop hours, and whose implementation would be expected within a period of two months after the beginning of work'.[57] However, we have no evidence of noncompliance. As Brandner noticed, he and his colleagues worked with 'self-abandon'. This 'self-abandon', of course, resulted in a lowering of production quality.

The pressure on engineers to produce 'revenge weapons' or 'wonder weapons' towards the end of the Second World War opened the way to projects which under normal conditions would have been considered technological charlatanism and brushed off as simply irresponsible. Kamikaze weapons and other ill-conceived and hastily completed projects represented the desperate and irrational approach to technological solutions of a sinking National Socialism.[58] The language of the 'final struggle' (*Endkampf*) could not conceal the fact that armaments engineers were exempted from military service. They did not have to face the contradictions between the Nazi pathos of the 'final struggle' and the realities of the war.

The open-mindedness of engineers towards military aims, if we do not include convinced Nazis, was the result of privileges: work security, good wages, available product financing, exemption from military service, and the opportunity to prove themselves intellectually and physically far from the danger, on the 'home front'.

We should make one last general observation in order to understand the motives of armaments engineers. Once begun, projects reveal their own inner dynamics and engineers find themselves under pressure to carry the ideas through to a successful end. The pressure to see projects through to a successful conclusion later became an effective stimulus for German armaments engineers. After the war Soviet officials quickly learned to exploit this professional ethic. For example, Brandner reports that Stalin tried to stimulate the team of Germans working on the further development of engine 004 in the Soviet Union by making condescending remarks about the German work. Nothing could more effectively urge an engineer towards a better performance than such criticism.

Dealing with the Nazi past

The attitude of armaments engineers toward the military defeat of the Third Reich is very characteristic of their own self-image. The defeat was blamed on the lack of technocratic rationality, haste, a lack of planning, and the political recklessness of the Nazi system. In regard to the disorder in which the decision was made to launch the serial production of 'his' Jumo 222 engine, Brandner asserts with a disingenuous air of innocence that: 'Nazi Germany lost the war only because of such disorganized decision making'.[59] This statement has the hidden meaning that German engineers remained unbeaten in the field of technology. The anarchy of competences, the reckless political intervention into scheduling and the distribution of materials and equipment, changes in priorities – all these criticisms of inefficiency are present in the memoirs of, for example, aircraft designer Kurt Tank, Gerhard Fieseler, the designer of the V-1 rocket and the 'Fieseler Stork' airplane, and Walter Dornberger, the military commander of the Army Testing Grounds at Peenemünde.[60]

One of the leading causes of anxiety for Germany's top development engineers was that military research planning by the Nazis was completely paralyzed by the chaos among competing personalities and organizations. Development engineers constantly pushed for greater efficiency. Aircraft designer Willy Messerschmitt, who was the first person in the world to develop a jet-powered aircraft, the Me 262, first received a rejection when he recommended it to Field Marshal Milch before the attack on the Soviet Union. When the Me 262 was built two years later in a desperate hurry, it came too late to be an effective 'wonder weapon'.[61] From this constant criticism we can determine the implicit demand for a more efficient and leading role by engineers in armaments production, in other words a technocratic mentality.

Along with an obvious assumption of responsibility, the isolation due to the secrecy of military technology and the pressure caused by the work itself served as self-legitimation for carrying out military research.[62] Brandner writes that:

> due to the work pressure and the top priority level neither I nor my colleagues nor my chiefs came into contact with the death camps for Jews. We did not believe the rumors spread about such camps. We all believed that inhuman and simply impossible in civilized nations.[63]

In any case, Brandner witnessed forced labour, and he does not mention it. In an interview a Siemens engineer admits at least to knowing about forced labour, but he immediately and tellingly adds that: 'I did not know anything about Jews'.[64] Having known about the fate of the Jews was one of the strongest taboos of the immediate post-war period. In contrast, forced labour, especially concerning Slavs, was tacitly justified by continuing anti-Bolshevism. This Siemens engineer used financial security, *esprit de corps* and intense work pressure to explain the lack of concern over the work with weapons. 'It did occur to me that we contributed to the war, but how could we help it? It was war, and we had to work for the war, without too much reflection.'[65]

There was a prevalent fear among German armaments engineers during the last months of World War II. They were concerned by the approach of the Allied forces, the intense aerial bombardment and the possibility of being imprisoned. Fanatical '*Wehrwolf*' and SA troops also caused great consternation. Engineers were occupied with thoughts of fleeing, concern for their families and the rescue of their possessions. They could think of little else except their own survival. The engineers allowed themselves little time for reflection on their situation: the most common pattern of behaviour for this period was a willingness to flee to the countryside until the fighting was over and then, as quickly as possible, to return in order to begin collaborating with the victorious powers.[66]

The retreat into purely technical work and the obscuring or functional legitimization of the military nature of their work as a rule are present in the attitudes of armaments engineers towards their Nazi past. This has a clear parallel in the nuclear scientists.[67] Walter Dornberger characterizes the development of the V-2 rocket as an achievement for civilization. 'From the very beginning we wanted to reach space, the limitless void. For that we needed an inconceivable speed ... The A4 [V-2] was only an intermediate step.'[68] The journal of the former Peenemünde rocket designers contains this note: 'we developed this machine [V-2] as a transport vehicle of the future'.[69] They take advantage of the widespread acceptance of space research in their self-serving interpretation of the V-2 development as an achievement for mankind. According to this account, the military purpose of the V-2 was merely a necessary evil. 'It was absolutely clear to us that development would be impossible without providing some kind of military use.'[70]

Klee and Merk write in reference to the interpretation preferred by Peenemünde rocket designers: 'if any development of great rockets was possible at all ... it was only through weapons research. This was merely a deviation for a project that would one day serve peaceful purposes.'[71] The 'peaceful purposes' argument is supposedly given weight by the temporary arrest of the rocket designers von Braun, Klaus Riedel and Helmut Gröttrup on 13 March 1944. These three leading designers had debated the possibility of space travel instead of 'vengeance weapons' during a visit to a restaurant. A fanatical Nazi informer took this to be sabotage.[72] For some uncritical historians, this arrest is proof of the alleged opposition of these three Peenemünde rocket designers to National Socialism. But even if these engineers did regard the development of the V-2 weapon as a necessary evil, neither the quoted study by Klee and Merk nor the completely sympathetic biography of von Braun by Bernd Ruland contains any hint of a justification for this 'deviation'.[73]

When the attitudes of armaments engineers during the Nazi period are examined, it is difficult to employ differentiated categories. One would not find a group of 'pure scientists' among the technicians. Moreover, the degree of Nazi conviction apparently was unimportant for professional self-perception. The usual categories for describing political behaviour during the Nazi period, such as 'Nazi convictions', 'opportunism' and 'inner opposition' do not fit. There is no stigma with regard to armaments research, either instilled during education, in the scientific community, or in the work environment.[74] Instead, armaments research was justified as a noble service to the people. There were very few outspoken opponents of Nazism. Among the prominent German inventors or technicians, the air pioneer Hugo Eckener stands alone, of whom Rolf Italiaander has written a comprehensive biography.[75] It becomes clear that it is irrelevant, not to say absurd, to juxtapose the spiritual idea of science serving truth with its military applications when examining armaments research.[76] The requirements of researcher and developer did not contradict the demands of the Nazi system; on the contrary, they were asking for a more efficient Nazi research policy.

Common reasons for the successful use of engineers for the war machine follow from a socio-psychological point of view, which can also be generally applied to the Nazi system as a whole.[77] The impersonality of technical sciences and narrow fields of specialization can prevent an engineer's conscience from perceiving the social consequences. A new study of the risk perception by engineers of their work concludes that engineers who reject the cult of technical feasibility must pay for their doubts with their jobs. According to the engineers interviewed by Eva Senghaas-Knobloch and Birgit Volmerg, job security was more important than social responsibility.[78]

But it would be insufficient to explain attitudes of armaments engineers in the Nazi era merely in terms of technology and career opportunity. National Socialism integrated engineers into its political and military goals and policies by elevating them explicitly to the rank of ideological soldiers. Performance expectations for engineers involved with military projects were based on an obligatory 'service to the people' and subsequently were seen as a technical contribution to the 'final struggle'. From the engineers' perspective, most difficulties came from their adoption of the Nazi ideology of technology. That is why it was difficult for them afterwards to hide behind allegedly purely innocent technical positions. On the one hand – similar to Nazi logic – they complained about the inefficiency of Nazi technology, but on the other they claimed to be occupied only with technical duties.

German specialists as reparation servants

At the end of the war German armaments engineers did not have to face an existential crisis. The formerly feared victorious powers did interrupt their careers, but at the same time they offered new employment opportunities for adapting to the post-war era. To understand the new circumstances in which German armaments 'specialists' (as they were generally called by the Soviets) found themselves, we should outline how these specialists were used by the Allied forces.[79] The key concerns of the Allied powers' policy were dismantling the war industry and military research, obtaining reparations and, finally, competing for the German scientists' brains.

The guidelines and contradictions of the Allied occupation policy had already become obvious during the Yalta conference (4–11 February 1945). The common agenda at this conference included war reparations and the economic disarmament and suppression of Germany. The use of German labour was discussed in Yalta. Due to the Allies' disagreement on this issue, Molotov tried in a memorandum to have this critical point postponed until later negotiations.[80] The Yalta conference protocol mentioned three forms of German reparations, among them the very concisely phrased 'use of German labor'.[81] The use of German labour by the Allies in Germany as well as abroad received a far-reaching stamp of approval in Allied control council proclamation N. 2 of 5 June 1945. The characteristic absence of any clear explanation is understandable, because the Allies implicitly accepted the mutual possibilities of using German specialists, among them armaments engineers, without desiring to define dubious legal terms for reparation services.

The remainder of this chapter will concentrate on the Soviet use of German armaments engineers because by comparison the use of such German labour by the Americans, British and French has already been studied in detail.[82] I will also discuss the fate of scientists, particularly nuclear physicists, since their practical work did not differ greatly from the work of engineers.

If one tries to follow the stages of Soviet reparation policy, it is possible to discern a period of a few weeks directly after the end of the war when Soviet troops took war trophies at random.[83] Immediately after the end of the war the Soviets made one significant exception to their policy of dismantling. Those branches of arms research and weapon production that could not play an important role in providing food or in reconstruction in the Soviet Union, or whose transfer to the Soviet Union would be very time-consuming, remained initially in the Soviet Occupation Zone. The reconstruction and production of weapons was much easier and faster in the occupation zone with the help of German workers. At the same time, Soviet scientists and engineers could gain very valuable experience in the occupation zone through their cooperation with German specialists.

The first wave of relocation of German specialists to the Soviet Union was related to nuclear research. In April of 1945 Zavenyagin, Deputy Chief to Beriya, the infamous head of the Soviet secret police (henceforth NKVD), asked leading Soviet scientists participating in the Soviet uranium project to help find and choose their German counterparts. The Soviet military administration and NKVD had to act promptly on this matter because they had already agreed with the other Allies to the partitioning of Berlin. Whoever and whatever had not been removed before the arrival of the Americans, British and French could no longer be taken. NKVD began the task of finding German physicists and chemists for the Soviet uranium project. Some individuals who had worked in nuclear research or uranium technology were known to the Soviets through the technical literature, others were found through espionage, and finally some volunteered their services to the approaching Red Army.[84]

For example, the private researcher Manfred von Ardenne, Peter Adolf Thiessen, head of the Institute for Physical Chemistry in the *Kaiser-Wilhelm-Gesellschaft*, and professors Max Volmer and Gustav Hertz took it upon themselves to form a 'defense ring' in the face of the approaching Red Army. Whoever first contacted the Soviet military would speak for the rest of them.[85] They hoped that through their mutual recommendation of each other's scientific reputation it would be possible to prevent the plunder of their institutes, to continue their work without interruption under the protection of the Soviets and, above all, to protect themselves and their families from prosecution. The decision to remain in Berlin, in spite of the approaching Red Army and calls for the evacuation of scientific institutes to western Germany, were made for various reasons. Cooperation with the Soviets would enable them to continue with their work, keep their co-workers together and protect them from the insecurities and hardships of the refugee life. They hoped that the Red Army would treat highly qualified specialists with due respect. Some of the Nazi party members among the nuclear scientists obviously presumed that the Soviets would value their scientific cooperation more than their political past. Here they judged correctly. Whether a Nazi or a communist – the Soviets were not interested in this aspect. Peter Adolf Thiessen, for example, a member of the Nazi party since the twenties and a leading figure in Nazi armaments research, never had to face 'denazification' procedures. But a pro-Soviet attitude was also unwelcome. Heinz Barwich, who openly expressed his communist inclinations in 1945 and afterwards in the Soviet Union, met with the Soviets' cold shoulder. Later statements, for example by von Ardenne, that the decision to cooperate with the Soviets had political grounds, are unconvincing. But risk still remained. The Soviets could consider them enemies, in spite of all loyalty.

Soviet contractors also attracted some German specialists through financially lucrative offers, including researchers located in the western zones. Nobel Prize laureate Otto Warburg was approached in this way, but he turned down the offer. Werner Heisenberg also received an invitation to the Soviet Union in the summer of 1946. His former Leipzig colleague Heinz Pose wrote enthusiastically to Heisenberg about the good working conditions, the resources placed at their disposal and the confidence they enjoyed, as well as about the Soviets' great interest in Heisenberg's

research. If he was interested in their offers he was to signal his agreement
to the Soviet courier. Heisenberg politely refused – obviously he wanted
first to explore the possibility of cooperation with the British.[86] NKVD
Deputy Chief Zavenyagin formally invited Nobel Prize laureate Gustav
Hertz to work in the Soviet Union. He was expected to continue his work
on isotope separation. Hertz, who had suffered during the Nazi period
because of his Jewish background, gratefully accepted.

There was a special rivalry between the Americans, British and Soviets
for possession of the German rocket designers. When the American troops,
who had occupied Thuringia at the end of April 1945, relinquished this
territory as promised to the Soviets at the end of June, they took about
1,300 German missile workers and related specialists with them.[87] When
the Americans visited the Harz underground facilities where the V-1 and
V-2 had been produced, they took all the blueprints that had not been
destroyed. After combing the Harz, the Soviets found the underground V-1
and V-2 production facilities.[88] The Soviets seized the remaining raw
materials, spare parts, and unfinished V-1 flying bombs and V-2 missiles.[89]
Part of the find was sent to the Soviet Union, but a Soviet 'Special Committee' considered it wiser to use German engineers to reconstruct the missing
blueprints.[90]

The Americans set up an internment camp for former armaments specialists on their side of the zone border, in particular for the missile designers
they had taken with them during their withdrawal from Thuringia. Soviet
recruiters in plain clothes turned up in the American zone in order to lure
the specialists to work on the reconstruction of the V-2 in the Harz by
offering them superior food, lucrative pay, apartments and clothes. At that
time such Soviet recruiting in the western zones was common practice.[91] An
unspecified number of German rocket designers returned to Thuringia after
their forced evacuation by the Americans, which provoked special
measures by the American Military Administration in order to prevent any
further returns. Within a year the team at the rocket facility the Soviets
called 'Zentralwerke' included as many as 600 qualified specialists who
were above all involved in reconstruction and assembly of the V-2 missile
for the Soviets.[92]

Stalin asked Truman personally by letter to return those specialists who
had been taken by the Americans. This request was again repeated by
General Sokolovskij to Lucius D. Clay. But it fell again upon the deaf ears
of the Americans who were already suspicious of Soviet claims.[93] For its
part, the British secret service found it necessary to make comparable offers
to Germans attracted by the Soviets, including similar pay and family
support, either in the British zone or in Great Britain itself.[94] Private British
companies were allowed to employ German specialists because not only
the Soviet government, but also the governments of Canada, Australia,
some Latin American countries and India all showed interest in German

armaments engineers.[95] To the annoyance of British Intelligence, the Americans claimed German specialists for themselves under the pretext that they would otherwise fall into the hands of the Soviets.[96]

Dismayed that the Americans had outwitted them, British agents made barely disguised offers to German specialists in the Soviet Occupation Zone.[97] Sometimes the Allied competition to win German armaments specialists over to their side had remarkable consequences. The Allied powers involved not only raised their bids offering material wealth; some German engineers exercised pressure by way of threatening to take their services to the Soviets in order to raise their salaries and improve their families' living conditions.[98]

With the exception of the initial recruiting, arrests or simple deportations of nuclear scientists who seemed to be useful for the Soviet uranium project, there was no programme for the employment of German specialists in the Soviet Union during the first year of occupation. A new practice of dismantling started in October of 1946. It involved primarily the armaments production that went on after the war and was accompanied by a forced transfer of qualified Germans to the Soviet Union.[99] About 3,000 specialists were deported in the course of such transfers in October of 1946. The work on the V-1 and V-2, to name only the most prominent projects, was to be continued in the Soviet Union with all the necessary specialists. They were told that they would stay for five years in the Soviet Union and would receive good pay. In the early morning of 22 October 1946 military patrols turned up at the apartments of armaments specialists in the Soviet zone, forced the specialists and their families to pack up their belongings, and escorted them to the nearest railway stations where the trains were already waiting.

The main reason for the collaboration with the Allied authorities of the German armaments engineers or scientists who had participated in weapons R&D during the war was the professional and material insecurity they felt towards the end of the war. Indifferent whether they continued Nazi armaments projects under Soviet guidance in the Soviet Occupation Zone, or whether the work involved moving to countries that had won the war, they took every opportunity to continue their vocation and achieve material security. Nuclear physicist Heinz Barwich, who later became known for his escape from the German Democratic Republic to the West, described his decision to work in the Soviet Union in simple words: 'I decided to go to the Soviet Union on 10 June 1945. I was thirty-three years old, married with three children, was expecting a fourth. I was also jobless. So the decision was not difficult.' And he added: 'of course work in Russia was attractive with regard to money'.[100] Political convictions very rarely played a decisive role in the choice of a particular victorious power. German 'specialists' expected better working conditions from the Americans and the British because of a common underlying anti-Bolshevism, supposedly better treatment and pay, and fewer language barriers. The previous Nazi propaganda undoubtedly played a role here. Engineers and scientists who suffered under the Nazis quite often chose to collaborate with the Soviets.[101] But engineers and scientists who occupied prominent positions in Nazi armaments R&D also favoured the Soviet Union. At least the Soviets did not confront them with denazification.

It was the ability to continue former armaments projects in the service of the victorious powers that allowed these engineers to avoid any self-critical analysis of their work during the Third Reich. Military aims were hardly immoral, once disassociated from Nazi contractors. Moreover, even the deeds of the armaments engineers were legitimized in retrospect by the separation of military aims from Nazism and their political insignificance so shortly after the downfall of the Nazi regime.

As far as armaments engineers deported to the Soviet Union are concerned, we can witness a subjective transformation of a suppressed awareness of being a perpetrator to that of being a victim. The forced move to the Soviet Union was perceived as brutal despotism, a crying injustice. This fitted very nicely into the widespread image held by Germans in particular of Russians as Asiatic barbarians. The specialists forcefully moved to the Soviet Union perceived themselves to a certain extent as representatives of a civilized nation, as messengers from a technically and scientifically developed society, who had survived Nazism intact.

Comparison of the use of German specialists by the Allied powers

In the now defeated Germany, British and American secret services organized departments that dealt with the procurement of information, documents, equipment, and scientific and other personnel. Most of all, their goal was to prevent the Soviets from seizing these first.[102] Joint British and American intelligence teams (henceforth CIOS teams) initially had three tasks before them: first, to find out what the Germans knew about weapons, radar, synthetic rubber, synthetic propellants, torpedos, missiles, jet engines, and infrared and telecommunication systems; second, to collect information that would help defeat the Japanese; and third, to locate and seize German scientists and engineers who could provide information about the above-mentioned items. In July of 1945 the US Joint Chiefs of Staff decided to transfer 350 German rocket designers, among them von Braun, to the United States as part of the top secret 'Project Overcast'.[103] The German nuclear research project was explored and its results immediately confiscated by the Mission, codenamed 'ALSOS', especially founded for this purpose. The centrally commanded CIOS missions enjoyed top priority and they could rely upon the complete support of the occupation forces. CIOS, ALSOS and other ventures to transfer German scientists and technicians to the United States, bearing such code names as 'Overcast' or

'Paperclip', had highly qualified employees and potent communication and command structures at their disposal.[104] The lack of a corresponding literature on the similar activities of the British and the French allows only a comparison between the exploitation and transfer of German specialists by the Americans and Soviets. There are remarkable similarities between their policies towards German armaments specialists.

First, these two countries pursued their own economic interests, aided by the confused legal definitions of war trophies and permissible reparations. It is impossible to estimate even approximately the scope of economic reparations, either for the Soviets or for the West.

Second, the evacuation of German scientists and engineers from Thuringia by the Americans had already been carried out more or less under the threat of force – those who did not want to cooperate voluntarily with the Americans would have been arrested, exactly as happened with the Soviets.

Third, secret services were guided only by general national military and economic interests in technology, know-how and qualifications, no matter what the political consequences might be for the relations with the other Allied powers or how this might affect the economic situation in Germany in the long run, and without regard to ethical implications.

Fourth, there was another parallel between the American operations 'Overcast' and 'Paperclip' on the one hand and the similar Soviet projects on the other: the Nazi past of the German scientists was of no importance when the qualifications of the person in question could be exploited and, therefore, should be kept out of the hands of the competing Allies. Sometimes Soviet officers were even impressed when some of the Germans admitted having a Nazi past instead of regarding themselves as unfortunate victims or opportunists.[105]

Fifth, not only the Soviets but also the US military administration in no way bound themselves to the terms of the Potsdam Treaty in the transfer of scientific know-how, equipment and highly qualified personnel. This treaty was adhered to only with regard to war materials and personnel. When American companies considered German technology economically interesting, it was declared part of the reparations. Whether it was in the form of patents or not was of secondary concern.[106]

Sixth, the German scientists and technicians who were transferred, both to the Soviet Union and elsewhere, were not always strictly tested for their qualifications. Many specialists were included on the transport lists only to prevent a rival power from seizing them. The evacuation from Germany had in those cases only the function of forced quarantine. According to John Gimbel, Truman's final approval of 'Project Paperclip' was definitely a product of the Cold War with the Soviets.[107]

Finally, American–Soviet parallels exist in the circumstances of the later repatriation of specialists to Germany. Before they were allowed to return, they had to go through a 'cooling-off' period.[108]

Consequences

The use of Nazi scientists has recently been criticized with great vigor in the USA. The American reputation has allegedly been damaged by their luring of Nazi scientists.[109] And indeed the practical usefulness of these researchers was given priority, whether they were innocent or not. In addition, the reference to the Soviets seemed to justify the pragmatism of the Western Allies.[110]

It is only at first glance surprising that a similar moral rigour is lacking in the Soviet case with regard to their use of German armaments know-how. The Soviet Military Administration abandoned the practice of denazification from the very beginning during the reinstatement of armaments companies in the Soviet Occupation Zone.

> Whether one was a high-ranking SS leader or a war criminal or whatever, as long as he was an expert, a 'specialist,' everything was forgotten, forgiven, became null and void ... They valued 'specialists' so much, especially in the field of armaments engineering, that all other considerations were neglected.[111]

The quick and unconditional readiness of famed German nationalists or even Nazis to cooperate might have astonished the Soviets. Work for the Soviets was only very rarely the result of a political conversion to Soviet ideology. Their collaboration often helped suppress personal feelings about the fallen Germany. The experience of working conditions during wartime and the adjustment to military aims may have played a beneficial role for the easy integration of German specialists in the Soviet Union. Used and honoured by the Soviets as 'technocrats', the specialists could bury their personal and collective past in a double manner. They plunged into their work and perceived themselves as victims of Soviet despotism.

Repatriates have reported many times that the transfer to the Soviet Union offered them new working and living conditions which the prohibitions on further military R&D in post-war Germany would have forbidden. They did not mention any political scruples. Instead a type of allegedly apolitical researcher and engineer dominated, who drew satisfaction from the solution of intellectual and technological problems. In the face of the insecurities faced in the aftermath of war, the threat of denazification, the lack of research opportunities in Germany and often the spectre of unemployment, many of them found a new sense of purpose in serving the victorious powers, at least temporarily. They perceived service for the victorious powers as an appreciation of their abilities. There were no reflections on the military aims of the work already carried out during the Nazi era and merely continued under the Allies' guidance. Employment by the Allies meant more a continuity rather than a break with the past. Content, work organization, work group and technocratic self-perception stayed practically the same. Continuity through employment by the victorious powers also allowed these researchers to avoid critical questions about their joint responsibility for National Socialist Germany's war.

The easy integration of German specialists into the Allies' armaments programmes leads to the question of similarity between the armaments research organization in Nazi Germany and that of its victorious opponents. A systematic comparison of Nazi and Stalinist research organization is needed and would be very fruitful. This comparison cannot be made here, particularly in view of the lack of systematic analysis in the existing literature on the Soviet Union.

The fundamental thesis of this essay is that the momentous activities of German armaments engineers under National Socialism were a continuation of a previously existing professional self-perception, of a technocratic way of working and opportunistic political accommodation. This continuity explains the applicability of these behaviour patterns to the work for the victorious powers after 1945. In other words, the exaggeration of the specific Nazi convictions in the conduct of German armaments engineers would be a mistake. The Nazis did achieve one thing: the social self-awareness of engineers grew enormously. The appreciation of German know-how through employment by the Allies continued this tradition. A feeling of surrender or of having been involved in a shameful deed could be avoided or denied. The contributions of German engineers to armaments research and technological development both under the Nazis and after the Second World War in the service of the victorious powers are impressive precisely because neither the National Socialist system nor the victorious powers demanded a break in their traditions.

3 | *The guided missile and the Third Reich: Peenemünde and the forging of a technological revolution**

MICHAEL J. NEUFELD

Within a decade, from late 1932 to late 1942, the technology of rocketry was transformed by a German Army team based first at Kummersdorf and then at Peenemünde. Starting with small, unreliable amateur rocket experiments in the late Weimar Republic this group created a technological revolution: the first large guided missile, the A4 or V-2. Although this missile was ultimately a poor weapon and was responsible for a massive diversion of scientific, engineering and production resources from more sensible armaments projects, at the same time it embodied spectacular advances in liquid-fuel rocket propulsion, supersonic aerodynamics and inertial guidance. Indeed, it must be considered the greatest technological achievement of the Third Reich.[1] Yet the scholarly literature on this topic is extremely meagre; the subject has been too long the captive of popular historians who gave myth-making a higher priority than analysis or accuracy. The only major exception is Heinz Dieter Hölsken's *Die V-Waffen*, which illuminates the internecine German struggles over the 'vengeance weapons'. Hölsken, however, shows little interest in the history of science and technology in the Third Reich.[2]

In fact the German Army rocket programme was one of the first examples of state mobilization of massive engineering and scientific resources for the forced invention of a radical, new military technology. It preceded by a decade and was not dramatically smaller in scale than the even more revolutionary Manhattan Project in the United States. It is thus part of the intertwined stories of the rise of 'big science' and the growth of the military-industrial complex, which might be better called the military-industrial-university complex.[3]

But a more useful lens for viewing the creation and growth of Peenemünde is the 'technological systems' approach of Thomas P. Hughes. Hughes has shown, in his studies of the electrical pioneers, how successful 'system builders' had to overcome social and political obstacles just as much as technical, scientific and economic ones. John Law has called this 'heterogeneous engineering' – the social must be engineered as much as the technical if new inventions are to be converted into functioning technological systems. In the growth of systems, their builders encounter 'reverse salients' – Hughes' military metaphor for difficulties that impede the smooth advance of the system. By converting reverse salients into better-understood 'critical problems', system builders can concentrate financial and human resources to solve those problems. Successful systems acquire 'momentum': the mass of their capital investment and human organizations acquire a direction and velocity, and through 'conservative' inventions perpetuate and extend the control of the system. But as Law has pointed out, system growth is far from inexorable. Systems can fail or be dismantled if they are confronted by 'radical' inventions that supersede the technology on which the system is based, or if political, technical or economic problems run out of control.[4]

The construction and growth of the Germany Army guided missile programme differs significantly, however, from the corporate model on which Hughes concentrates, because it was a technological system growing out of a military bureaucracy in which economic considerations were largely irrelevant. The revolutionary possibilities of a long-range missile based on liquid-fuel rocketry alone motivated the engineering officers who launched the programme. They built, over time, a viable research, development and production system for the missile that, because of the need for secrecy and the inadequate technology base in industry, centred on a large government laboratory. The growth of the Peenemünde technological system was also furthered by the 'polycratic' character of the Nazi system, divided as it was into warring bureaucratic empires. The Army, as one of the most powerful actors in the regime, at least until the early years of the war, was able to promote its rocket project in the absence of a coherent system for setting priorities.[5] But in order to understand why the Army succeeded where the original inventors failed, it is necessary to look first at the origins of the missile in the spaceflight movement of the Weimar Republic.

1 The Weimar origins of the rocket programme

The liquid-fuel rocket was, in Hughes' terms, a 'radical' invention – that is, one which potentially could initiate a whole new technological system, and thus one subject to a great deal of initial scepticism. The idea of using liquid fuel to produce a quantum leap in performance over the black-powder rocket was originated primarily by the three main pioneers of the spaceflight movement: Konstantin Tsiolkovsky, Robert Goddard and Hermann Oberth. Of the three, Oberth, a German-speaking Transylvanian, had the most impact in Europe. While Tsiolkovsky was the first, his publications were buried in obscure Russian journals and he was virtually unknown until after Oberth's seminal 1923 work, *Die Rakete zu den Planetenräumen* (The Rocket into Interplanetary Space). Goddard, a physicist at Clark University in Massachusetts, attempted to avoid public controversy. His famous *A Method of Reaching Extreme Altitudes* (1919/20) made only opaque references to advanced rocketry. Nonetheless, Goddard's discussion of a staged powder rocket capable of hitting the moon unleashed a wave of sensationalism and ridicule in the newspapers that only furthered his reclusiveness. He waited a decade before publicly acknowledging his launch of the world's first liquid-fuel rocket in 1926, although wild rumours of his activities did circulate in the press. Goddard was anything but a system builder. Supported by funds from the Guggenheim Foundation, Goddard eventually withdrew to the New Mexico desert and worked out of the public eye. He had neither the personality to convert the technology into a viable system, nor the historical context to do so – that is, energetic military support. As a result, his technological influence on later missile development was practically nil.[6]

Thus it was Oberth's 1923 book that had the most enduring impact. His open discussion of how the obstacles to spaceflight might be overcome included detailed discussions of possible alcohol/liquid-oxygen and liquid-hydrogen/liquid-oxygen multi-stage vehicles. Although *Die Rakete* initially did not provoke a large reaction, Oberth's cause was soon taken up by Max Valier, a freelance writer of dubious books on cosmology and the occult, but also a tireless propagandist. Valier's campaign eventually led to a brief alliance with Fritz von Opel, heir to the car-manufacturing fortune, and to a spectacular set of rocket-car stunts in the spring of 1928 using black-powder rockets. This unleashed a popular fad for rocketry and spaceflight in the Weimar Republic. Rocket stunts with cars, rail cars, gliders and even ice sleds followed, and famed director Fritz Lang released a serious moonflight movie, *Frau im Mond* (The Woman in the Moon), in October 1929. While some ridicule accompanied this activity, it appears that Germany had the most positive public reaction to the idea of spaceflight in the world at this time. Weimar culture in the 'stabilization period' (1924–30) seems to have been particularly open to radical technological change, and there was a nationalist pride in any German accomplishments that signalled recovery from the humiliations of the war and Versailles.[7]

The fad naturally boosted the fortunes of the small spaceflight movement in Germany, which had already formed an organization, the *Verein für Raumschiffahrt* (The Society for Space Travel or VfR), in 1927. One of the consequences of this fad was the beginning of serious liquid-fuel experiments – in contrast to the stunts with commercial black-powder rockets which served no useful purpose except publicity. Johannes Winkler, the first president of the VfR, carried out private experiments and worked at the Junkers aircraft company in Dessau from 1929 to 1931 and from 1933 to 1938 on the application of rocketry to aircraft. Meanwhile, Max Valier made an alliance with the Berlin liquid-oxygen equipment manufacturer Paul Heylandt in late 1929, and began to build a new rocket-car engine using paraffin fuel. Valier was killed in a laboratory explosion in May 1930, but his work was carried on in the factory by his Heylandt assistants, Walter Riedel and Arthur Rudolph – both to play very important roles at Peenemünde. The rocket car that was finished in 1931 was a public-relations flop, however. As the Depression deepened the rocket fad slowly died.[8]

But the group of experimenters that sustained rocketry more than any other in the years of economic collapse was the VfR's own *Raketenflug-platz* (Rocketport) in Berlin. It had its origins in Oberth's attempt to build a liquid-fuel rocket in 1929, as a publicity stunt for Lang's *Frau im Mond*. The technologically naive Oberth had hired a self-proclaimed engineer and shameless con-man, Rudolf Nebel, to help him. (It is ironically appropriate that 'Nebel' means 'fog'.) After the whole thing ended as a fiasco, Nebel went on an endless search for money and resources for further experiments. In the fall of 1930 his efforts led to the setting up of a rocket experiment group on an abandoned munitions dump in northern Berlin. The group attracted a number of unemployed craftsmen and engineers, and included a student, Wernher Freiherr von Braun, who was 18 in 1930 and was enrolled at the *Technische Hochschule* Berlin in mechanical engineering. The *Rake-tenflugplatz* built a number of engines and staged many launches from 1931 to 1933. The group's engine technology was based on trial-and-error experimentation, with liquid oxygen and gasoline as propellants (Figure 3.1). Alcohol was later substituted as the fuel, in line with Oberth's original suggestions – it was less explosive than gasoline and had the useful property that water could be added to reduce its concentration, thereby lowering burning temperature. Burn-throughs of engines nonetheless continued, along with frozen valves, leaky lines and innumerable other failures. The problem of rocket stability in flight was solved only poorly by giving the vehicles rather baroque configurations. The whole enterprise was a lot more showmanship than science.[9]

Compared to what would be needed to convert liquid-fuel rocketry into a viable technological system, the resources of the rocket groups and inventors were, of course, completely inadequate. The rocket pioneers, from Oberth to Nebel, had all pinned their hopes largely on some corporation or millionaire financing development or on forming their own corporation. They seem to have been influenced by the heroic independent inventor of the late nineteenth and early twentieth centuries, such as Edison and Diesel, and they marketed as possible commercial applications intercontinental transport by rocket plane, or in the nearer future, rocket mail. Nobody could imagine how expensive this technology would be, or what kind of military-industrial-university complex would be necessary to create it.

Fig. 3.1 Rudolf Nebel, at left, is shown at the *Rakentenflugplatz* in April 1931, along with space popularizer Willy Ley and engineer Klaus Riedel. The engine test stand in the background was made out of the launch rail for the ill-fated Oberth *Frau im Mond* rocket of 1929.

2   The Army takes command – and builds a technological system

When officers in the Army Ordnance Office (*Heereswaffenamt*) first took an interest in rocketry they were no clearer on what would be required. The key figure at the beginning was Lt. Col. Dr Ing. Karl Becker, head of the ballistics and munitions section of the Weapons Testing Division. Undoubtedly as a result of the rocket fad, in 1929 Becker obtained the permission of the Reichswehr Ministry to investigate the rocket as a weapon. Because that technology had been militarily insignificant since the mid nineteenth century, there was no specific prohibition of it in the Versailles Treaty. But the lack of a clause banning rocketry has often been overrated as a cause of the programme. In fact, Becker's section was interested in using solid-fuel rockets as artillery for chemical warfare. Versailles forbade Germany the possession of poison gas, but that and other prohibitions had been continually violated by the Reichswehr in its secret rearmament programme. It is thus doubtful that the Treaty would have made much of a difference even if it had banned the rocket.[10]

Becker and his subordinates – of whom Capt. Walter Dornberger would later be the most important – also became interested in the long-term possibilities of liquid fuels for something much more ambitious. The ballistics and munitions section played a hidden hand in letting Nebel lease the *Raketenflugplatz* and, in 1931, as a result of Heylandt's rocket car, secretly began to give contracts to that company for engine development. Various rocketry inventors were investigated, and many turned out to be frauds. The *Raketenflugplatz* was paid to give a rocket launch demonstration in mid 1932, but the result was unimpressive, reinforcing the officers' disgust with the circus-like atmosphere surrounding Nebel. By this time it became clear that the inventors were achieving little while creating unwanted publicity, and that an in-house research-and-development group might make better progress. It took some years, however, before this became the central organizational concept of the new technological system.[11]

In late 1932 Wernher von Braun was hired as the first employee of the new group. He was of old Prussian Junker stock and his father was Minister of Agriculture in the reactionary Papen and Schleicher cabinets of 1932–3. This background helped the twenty-year-old von Braun overcome the officers' skepticism about his youth, but it was his technical brilliance that had most impressed Becker and Dornberger. He was put into a doctoral programme in applied physics at the University of Berlin after only two years of engineering school. His secret dissertation, defended with high honours in June 1934, amounted to a summary of the rocket development carried out under his direction at the artillery range at Kummersdorf, southwest of Berlin.[12] A number of assistants were brought to Kummersdorf as well – most notably Riedel, and later Rudolph, both originally from Heylandt.

Between 1932 and 1936, two factors pushed the Army Ordnance rocket group toward concentrating development in a large in-house laboratory: secrecy, and the frustrating inadequacy of the technology base in industry. Utter secrecy was an obsession with the engineering officers who supervised the rocket programme. Although the exact form of a large guided missile was unclear, the aim was to maintain Germany's 'sizable development lead' over foreign countries 'above all because of the element of surprise', Capt. Leo Zanssen stated in 1935.[13] The Nazi seizure of power provided the police state needed to suppress other rocket work and establish an Army near-monopoly over the technology, as well as the armaments build-up necessary to fund it. Army Ordnance worked hand in glove with counter-intelligence and the Gestapo to drive the rocket experimenters out of business in 1934; discussion of the subject was virtually banned from the press; unwanted people like Nebel were excluded from Kummersdorf while useful people like Rudolph were brought on board; and non-Germans, including the Romanian citizen Oberth, were kept at arm's length.[14]

The obsession with secrecy encouraged the construction of a large government laboratory. It also added to the difficulties of contracting out rocket-engine and vehicle parts to companies – something that was problematic in any case because of the lack of an adequate technology base in industry. While various firms working with aluminium did build engines, tanks and parts in the first few years, the problems involved drove the rocket group to concentrate more and more hardware fabrication in-house at Kummersdorf and to plan the new facility at Peenemünde on the Baltic coast with a complete manufacturing capability for test vehicles. Thus the heart of the nascent Army guided-missile system was the concentration of development and fabrication in one military facility, with corporate contractors playing only secondary roles. Contracting to private industry only became important when there were technological reverse salients that could not be easily attacked with in-house expertise. That was particularly the case in guidance and control; von Braun and his assistants had come out of an amateur tradition that, out of necessity, had emphasized propulsion to the neglect of all else. The crude stopgap measure of using a large rotating mass on the two A2s – the first Army liquid-fuel rockets launched in December 1934 – had to be replaced with a true three-axis guidance system based on gyroscopic principles. Kreiselgeräte GmbH (Gyro Devices Ltd), a research-and-development company secretly owned by the Navy, was given that task.[15]

The decisive breakthrough in the growth of the Army rocket programme came in 1935 through an alliance with the *Luftwaffe* (Air Force), which possessed enormous political capital in Göring's leadership. The new service's technical staff and the Army Ordnance group at Kummersdorf made an agreement to cooperate in exotic propulsion technologies. Five years of joint experiments with rocket planes and a rocket-assisted take-off system

Fig. 3.2   Test stand I at Peenemünde, which could accommodate engines of up to 100 metric tons of thrust, was completed in spring 1939. Its massive size shows the huge investment made by the Army in rocketry since the *Raketenflugplatz* era.

for aircraft followed. Even more important was the decision to establish a joint research centre for the testing of missiles and other secret weapons. The Peenemünde site was purchased in early 1936, and it is clear that the *Luftwaffe's* influence and free-flowing money had much to do with the sudden acceleration in the scale of the Army rocket programme – not least because Becker, now a general and head of the Testing Division, was determined not to let the *Luftwaffe* outdo the Army in spending. Further support was received in 1936 from the Commander-in-Chief of the Army in return for the promise of a viable weapon. Out of this sprang Dornberger's idea for the A4 – a missile to deliver a one-ton warhead at twice the range of the Paris Gun of World War I – the prestige weapon of the heavy artillery, the area of specialization out of which Dornberger and Becker had come.[16] The *Luftwaffe* undertook construction of both halves of the Peenemünde facility and, beginning in April 1937, most of the Kummersdorf team moved to the Baltic coast. In September 1937 the Army side of Peenemünde had 349 employees. By mid 1942 it would have almost 6,000 in development alone (Figure 3.2).

3   The system expands – and incorporates the universities

With the growth of the new facility and with money no object, Dornberger's role as the key system builder became steadily more apparent. By 1936 he was head of an independent rocketry section and he possessed the full backing of Becker, who became head of Army Ordnance in 1938. Dornberger's ambitious concept for Peenemünde as a large in-house facility is shown by his desire to build a production line for the A4 there, rather than giving the vehicle to a corporation for quantity production. According to Arthur Rudolph, Dornberger sprang the idea of an in-house production facility on von Braun and himself during the December 1937 launches of the unsuccessful A3, a test vehicle. Rudolph and von Braun protested that they knew nothing about production, but within a year the plan had been approved by the new Army Commander-in-Chief, von Brauchitsch, and Rudolph had been named chief engineer in Peenemünde for the project.[17]

The second critical system builder was von Braun. His role was, first and foremost, to motivate and manage the engineers at Peenemünde – and indeed the key personnel in the project were overwhelmingly engineers or engineering professors, not scientists. Through his charismatic leadership and matchless command of difficult technical issues in all areas, von Braun kept morale high and development on track. He also played a crucial role in the integration of the universities into the research process. Contrary to many assertions in the English-language literature, the incorporation of many academic institutes into the Peenemünde system did not begin after secrecy was loosened in September 1939 to accelerate A4 development. Since 1935–6 Dr Rudolf Hermann, an assistant at the *Technische Hochschule* (Technical University) Aachen, had been involved in testing subscale rocket models in the supersonic windtunnel there. Von Braun and Dornberger attracted him to the Peenemünde team in 1937 with the promise of a new, much larger, world-class supersonic windtunnel to be built in the Army facility. Until it was completed in November 1939, however, von Braun and his development people still depended on Aachen, *Luftwaffe* facilities and the Zeppelin company for aerodynamic research. Measuring systems and other apparatus were also designed by Prof. Dr Hase at the TH Hannover. It is true, however, that the involvement of university institutes became much larger during the war; particularly important were the *Technische Hochschulen*, especially Dresden and Darmstadt.[18]

The reasons why institute directors were willing to accept many of Peenemünde's research problems included scientific interest, nationalist or National Socialist ideological commitment, and funding and draft exemptions for key people. More interesting is how the von Braun team incorporated the universities into the research process. Von Braun seems to have cultivated his contacts with academic scientists and engineers in part to find key personnel for the massive build-up of on-site development capability.

During the war he also assiduously promoted an academic atmosphere, including the exchange of ideas and research results among the Peenemünde laboratories and between the Baltic-coast facility and the universities. It is noteworthy that von Braun and Dornberger incorporated the university institutes by evading all centralized mechanisms like the weak Reich Research Council which, ironically, Becker headed from its founding in 1938 until his suicide in April 1940. But even Becker seems to have had little interest in the Council, and in the polycratic ruling system of the Third Reich no one was able to organize research centrally or produce a coherent scientific war effort. In this context Peenemünde was able to divert a significant percentage of German research resources into the militarily questionable guided-missile programme. It also fended off attempts later in the war to strengthen Research Council control.[19]

With the relentless expansion of its resources between 1935 and 1942, Peenemünde had finally entered the realm of 'big science', or better, *Grossforschung* ('big research'). This transformation both fostered dramatic breakthroughs in the three key technologies necessary for the A4 and was a result of them, since success helped ensure continued growth. In liquid-fuel rocket propulsion, Dr Walter Thiel, formerly of the Research Section of Ordnance Testing Division, produced a quantum leap in performance between 1936 and 1941. He scaled up the alcohol/liquid oxygen engine from the A3's 1.5 metric ton thrust to the 25 ton thrust needed for the A4, while drastically reducing engine size, overcoming perplexing injection and burn-through problems and increasing efficiency to near the theoretical maximum. This effort was almost entirely in-house, except for the contracts for the steam generator/turbopump combination needed to move large volumes of propellants. In aerodynamics, Hermann's group, through laborious subsonic and supersonic wind-tunnel work, drop tests and launches, was able to refine the fin and fuselage shape to produce the first fin-stabilized supersonic projectile – something some artillery specialists said was impossible.[20]

But it was the third key technology, guidance and control, that was the biggest technological reverse salient. Simply contracting the problem to Kreiselgeräte for the A3 proved illusory as the difficulties were far larger than the company or the Army anticipated. In the aftermath of the failure of the A3 guidance platforms, a new test vehicle (the A5) was designed, other firms, primarily from the aviation instruments sector, were given parallel contracts to those of Kreiselgeräte, and the formerly weak guidance-and-control section of Peenemünde was greatly expanded in personnel under the direction of Dr Ernst Steinhoff. This change greatly expanded the large in-house laboratory concept at the heart of the system. After the war started, university research also made significant contributions. Prof. Dr Wolman of the TH Dresden was the key figure in the design and refinement of the radio cut-off and tracking systems for the A4, and many institutes at Darmstadt were involved in the calculation and simulation of trajectories, the design of accelerometers and the perfection of the control system.[21]

4   The battle for priority

The attack on Poland brought an acceleration of A4/V-2 development, making possible the appropriation of greatly expanded research resources. But the war also plunged the programme into the Third Reich's internal struggles for power and priority. Although Dornberger was only a lieutenant colonel in the Army Ordnance at the start of the war, he proved to be a talented in-fighter and system-builder who cultivated contacts at the highest levels of the Army and the regime. His close alliances with Becker, and above all with von Brauchitsch, who had been his regimental commander in the Weimar Republic, were particularly important.[22] In the very first days of the war Dornberger secured top priority for the rocket programme from the Army Commander-in-Chief by promising field deployment of the missile in two years: a risky gamble. Another key ally was cultivated at this time – Albert Speer, Hitler's chief architect and, after 1942, Armaments Minister. Speer's organization began supervising the construction of the Army installation in 1939. He explained in his memoirs the peculiar fascination exercised by the von Braun team ('these mathematical romantics'), and with the technology ('the planning of a miracle').[23] The romantic appeal of the technology was not a trivial factor in the support rocketry received from leading personalities in the Third Reich – above all because of the anticipated morale effect on target populations of this exotic new weapon. The guided-missile technological system of the Army also acquired a great deal of 'momentum' through its first-rate installations and research staff. These factors made it difficult to question the logic of an enormously expensive weapon that could, as it turned out, only drop conventional explosives randomly over large urban areas.

Nonetheless, the Army rocket programme went through a number of vicissitudes between 1939 and 1943 as a result of the incoherent leadership of the war economy and because of episodes of scepticism on the part of both Hitler and Fritz Todt, who became the first Armaments Minister in 1940. Von Brauchitsch's assignment of top priority without regard to other authorities – like his approval of the production plant in 1938 – symbolized an arrogant independence on the part of the Army which could not be sustained. Hitler cut back the steel quota for Peenemünde in November 1939, and showed himself unenthusiastic for the project at times. A mythology has been constructed around this fact, however, based on the memoirs of Dornberger and von Braun. Far from Hitler withholding top priority until mid 1943, missile development was reduced to second priority only for six months in 1940–1. This temporary reduction plus other transitory priority problems did not delay the A4 for more than a few months; the missile lagged behind because the technical difficulties were so challenging. It was production that was delayed – in the shape of the separate Peenemünde plant that was being built. But that project was mired in a morass of problems of its own making, and even if it had been built faster it would have been ready too soon – before the A4 itself. In fact in August 1941 the Army leadership succeeded in making an end run around the increasingly sceptical Todt by securing the support of Hitler, who in a meeting with Dornberger and von Braun declared the A4 'revolutionary for the conduct of warfare in the whole world'. He made an absurd demand for hundreds of thousands of missiles! The production plant was upgraded to top priority immediately afterward.[24]

This incident reveals clearly the 'polycratic' character of the war economy and priority system and the lack of perceptive strategic leadership in the Reich. By one estimate it cost 550 million Reichmarks to build the Army facilities at Peenemünde, and the cost of production was considerably more.[25] The Army was able to push the programme forward because of its substantial, though declining, influence, and because skilfull manoeuvring by Dornberger and his superiors allowed them to reach the Führer and exploit his desire to punish Britain.

But even a Führer order did not end the priority battles over the Army project. During the early years of the war, relations with the Luftwaffe deteriorated and the rocket plane experiments were ended. After the failure of the air arm in the Battle of Britain, the Army's long-range weapon project began to look too much like competition: 'the Army is beginning to fly', grumbled some Air Force officers. Eventually the Luftwaffe launched its own long-range weapons project in 1942, the later V-1, in part to get back at the Army, but this never proved a decisive threat to the A4/V-2. The interservice rivalry has, however, been exaggerated. In 1942 a new cooperative Army/Luftwaffe project was launched, an anti-aircraft missile name Wasserfall. That project has hampered not so much by interservice rivalry as by disarray in the Aviation Ministry itself, and by an underestimation on all side of its technical difficulty.[26]

5   Production, concentration-camp labour and the collapse

The Wasserfall project brought new manpower and resources to the Army side of Peenemünde, but also complicated further the immense difficulties in putting the A4 into production and deploying it in the field. Aided by the Führer's support in August 1941, Dornberger accelerated planning for production, and extended his system-building to include new production sites, liquid-oxygen plants, and the fabrication of vehicles and equipment for mobile and fixed launches. But there is every sign that the technology of the A4 was rushed prematurely into production by Dornberger

Fig. 3.3   The first successful A4 (V-2) is prepared for launch on 3
October, 1942.

Fig. 3.4 After the first successful launch, General Fellgiebel, head of the radar programme, congratulates Peenemünde-East Commander Col. Leo Zanssen, standing at centre. Third from left is Col. Walter Dornberger, followed by Dr Wernher von Braun, Dr Ernst Steinhoff (in *Luftwaffe* uniform), Dr Rudolf Hermann, and Dipl.-Ing. Gerhard Reisig, head of the measurement group.

because he had 'bet the company': promising early deployment was the only way for the missile programme to grow rather than to shrink or to be cancelled. As a result, the engine was too complicated for cost-effective mass production, the guidance system too immature to deliver the accuracy promised. Von Braun's development team struggled with innumerable failures, but did achieve a successful launch on the third attempt in October 1942. However, due to the ever-changing configuration of the vehicle as it was refined, the production drawings remained in a terrible mess[27] (Figures 3.3 and 3.4).

The morass into which the production plans had sunk was only overcome when Speer, who had become Armaments Minister after the February 1942 death of Todt, obtained approval from Hitler for mass production in December of that year. Speer ruthlessly pushed through a speed-up and reorganization, just as he had done with the war economy. Inevitably, many of his top people collided with Dornberger, who like most officers resented the intrusion of the civilian armaments bureaucracy into his bailiwick. Dornberger even had to fend off attempts to hand over the production plant to the electrical engineering giant AEG and then to convert the whole facility into a company.[28] But all plans to build A4s at Peenemünde and elsewhere became irrelevant after the harmful but not decisive RAF air raid on the secret weapons centre on 17–18 August 1943. Himmler, arguing that spies must have betrayed the location, convinced Hitler to move production underground. The result was the murderous Mittelwerk factory built with concentration-camp labour by SS-General Hans Kammler and run by an Armaments Ministry corporation. It began producing A4s at the end of 1943 – at the cost of thousands of prisoner lives[29] (Figure 3.5).

After the war the SS provided a convenient scapegoat for all crimes connected with the rocket programme. Actually Dornberger, Rudolph and the Armaments Ministry had already arranged to have SS prisoners brought to Peenemünde and planned the same for other factories.[30] The desperate shortage of manpower and the relentless drive to expand the guided-missile technological system necessarily implicated the programme more and more in the Third Reich's growing system of forced and slave labour. Nonetheless, Himmler and the SS presented an even more formidable challenge to the Army's control over the system than had the Armaments Ministry. Himmler made his next move in February–March 1944 by attempting first to entice von Braun, who held honorary SS rank, to take his team into the SS, then, when he refused, by arresting him and two others as punishment. Von Braun and the others were rescued by the efforts of Speer and Dornberger.[31]

Only after the assassination attempt against Hitler on 20 July 1944 was Himmler able to make further strides toward his goal of absorbing the rocket programme. As new head of Army armaments, he named Kammler

Fig. 3.5 An American soldier guards a captured and nearly completed A4 missile in the underground *Mittelwerk* facility, 1945.

'special commissioner for A4 matters'. In what may have been a counter-move, on 1 August the Army establishment at Peenemünde completed its transformation into a civilian government corporation, the Elektrome-chanische Werke GmbH, with a director from Siemens as its chief. It was a further sign of the collapse of the Army's position in the Third Reich.[32] In the last months of the war Kammler became the ultimate authority in a technological system run by a coalition of the SS, the Speer Ministry and the Army. While Dornberger retained an important position in the system directing the training and outfitting of the guided-missile troops, he was more and more reduced to carrying out the orders of Kammler and Speer.

On 8 September 1944 the first operational missiles – now called V-2s – were successfully fired against Paris and London. Their effect has often been greatly overrated; the total explosive load of all the V-2s fired was less than a large RAF bomber raid.[33] But impelled by desperation, von Braun's team at Peenemünde, Dornberger, Speer and Kammler all worked to produce as many missiles as possible without regard to the cost to the prisoners. Work also continued on Wasserfall; many test launches were made in 1944–5, but the guidance system was very incomplete. The Baltic-coast installation was finally evacuated in February–March 1945, and the team was concentrated around the Mittelwerk in central Germany. Nothing much could be done there. In April Dornberger and some of the team members moved to Bavaria, where they successfully contacted the US forces on 2 May.

6 Transfer to the United States

Within weeks the United States had seized most of the documents and key people from the German Army missile programme, plus parts and equipment for about 100 V-2s. Much of this material was quickly evacuated from areas that were to be in the Russian and British zones of occupation. 'Project Overcast', to exploit German scientists and engineers for the war against Japan, soon became 'Project Paperclip', aimed at a broader use of German personnel in the United States. As is well known, a group of about one hundred and twenty researchers led by von Braun was assembled at Fort Bliss, near El Paso, Texas, and was involved in the Army Ordnance/ General Electric Hermes programme for guided-missile research (Figure 3.6). V-2 launches were carried out at White Sands, New Mexico, for scientific and military purposes. But the von Braun group was underutilized and frustrated at Fort Bliss, and only in 1950 when they were moved to Redstone Arsenal in Huntsville, Alabama, did they return to accelerated missile development. They designed the Redstone missile, really an upgraded A4, and later the Jupiter and Pershing (Figure 3.7). In 1960 the Huntsville group was transferred to NASA as the Marshall Space Flight Center, along with their giant booster programme, Saturn.[34]

The details of these developments need not distract us here. For our purposes what is interesting is the manner in which the German Army guided-missile programme was transferred to the United States. The end of the war meant the collapse of the technological system centred at Peenemünde. But the preservation of its documents and its core personnel relatively intact, plus the transfer from German to US Army Ordnance allowed the reconstruction of the system in another country – something that may be unique. The 'arsenal system' of development and production of weapons in Army installations was an old tradition in the United States, despite the general hostility to state ownership in American ideology. At Redstone Arsenal the von Braun group was able to reconstruct the model of in-house development and manufacture of test and prototype missiles, with contracting limited to subsystems and mass production. The only functional elements missing were close university contacts – and concentration camps.

This system was in marked contrast to the Air Force, which contracted development to aerospace corporations with limited supervision/ programme management by officers. In the interservice battles over missiles and space in the Sputnik era, the arsenal system was often attacked as

Fig. 3.6 Peenemünde engineers brought to the United States under 'Project Paperclip' are assembled at White Sands Proving Ground, New Mexico, in 1946. Von Braun is standing seventh from the right in the first row, with his hand in his pocket. Fourth from left is the front row, in the short white jacket, is Arthur Rudolph.

Fig. 3.7 Counterclockwise from left, at the US Army Redstone Arsenal in Huntsville, Alabama, c. 1955, are Gen. Holger Toftoy, Dr Ernst Stuhlinger, Hermann Oberth, Dr Wernher von Braun and Dr Robert Lusser.

expensive, old-fashioned and incompatible with American capitalism. Under NASA, the Marshal Space Flight Center was forced more and more to depart from the old system, due to the agency's preference for the Air Force system and the massive scale of the Saturn V project – the launch vehicle for the Apollo lunar landings. Even so, the von Braun group retained more intense supervision, more in-house work and a more conservative technological style, which contributed to the astonishing standards of reliability of the Saturn vehicles. Only with the post-Apollo cutbacks of the early 1970s was the Huntsville system finally gutted and most of the Germans pushed into retirement.[35]

7   Conclusions

The transfer of Peenemünde's system to the United States obviously raises the question as to what, if anything, about the German guided-missile programme was specifically Nazi in character, other than slave labour. As part of the story of the rise of the military-industrial-university complex, Peenemünde had some of the features seen elsewhere, such as at Los Alamos: ultra-secrecy, massive state investment, the need to scale up exotic technologies to an industrial level, and the harnessing of university research for weapons development. For enterprises like Peenemünde and the Manhattan Project to be successful, they needed system builders who had a vision of how military, corporate and academic resources might be reorganized for the purpose of creating radical new weapons technologies almost regardless of cost. Even the feature that appears to be unique to the German missile programme – the dominance of the central military laboratory, with production as well as research-and-development capability – turns out to be fairly similar to the US arsenal system. It is possible that older German Army Ordnance traditions resembled those of the United States, since armories and arsenals had a long history in all Western armies. But such influences are not readily visible in the Peenemünde documents.

What clearly was influential for the in-house development system at Peenemünde was secrecy, plus the lack of any industrial base for rocket technology. Becker, Dornberger and other leading officers were obsessed with secrecy because they thought the revolutionary possibilities of the guided missile justified launching Germany first into a new arms race. (They were in fact convinced that they were in a race with other powers, especially the United States, until late in the war – an ironic mirror image of the assumptions behind the Manhattan programme.) Secrecy plus the Nazi police state allowed the Army to put the amateurs out of business, but also hampered the contracting out of development to corporations, which had proven frustrating in any case because of the inadequacy of the technology in industry. As a result, Peenemünde was planned with the capability to fabricate entire test rockets and Dornberger, as chief system-builder, pushed this philosophy further in 1938 with his idea for a production plant. The unanticipated need to build a large guidance-and-control laboratory only added to the trend toward extensive in-house capability as the core of the system.

Corporate contractors thus played a secondary role as extensions of the system, as did a number of university institutes which were increasingly integrated after the beginning of the war. Only with the shift to mass production and the forceful intrusion of the Speer ministry in 1942–3 was the corporate role expanded. National Socialist anti-capitalism – as fraudulent as it often was – therefore cannot be shown to have played any role in the shaping of the German guided-missile programme, and Nazi ideology in general had little effect. The desire for an aggressive military buildup and the search for decisive new weapons technologies already flourished in the old Reichswehr officer corps. Versailles, by stripping the Army of most of its men and armaments, had fuelled both revanchist attitudes and an openness to radical inventions with military potential.

We are thus left with the question: what was specifically Nazi about the German guided-missile programme? Other than the use of concentration-camp labour, the answer is, not very much. But posing the question in this way misses what is really important: the Third Reich as historical context. The leap at such an early date from small-scale rocket research to a massive technological system is difficult to imagine without National Socialism. Becker, Dornberger and von Braun's system-building flourished as a result of the rearmament drive and the Army's autonomous position in a polycratic regime of competing power blocs. The division and incoherence in the leadership of the military and war economy also contributed to the lack of a coherent weapons development policy or perceptive strategic leadership – something that was a problem in any case with dilettantes like Hitler and Göring as supreme commanders. In the end, despite episodes of disinterest on the part of the *Führer*, almost no one fundamentally questioned the wisdom of an extremely expensive weapons system that was supposed to destroy enemy morale by scattering relatively small amounts of conventional explosives over large urban areas. As a result, the rocket programme built an institution and a weapon which made little sense given the Reich's limited research resources and industrial capacity – a prefect symbol of the Nazi regime's pursuit of irrational goals with rational, technocratic means. Because of the in-fighting in the Third Reich, the guided missile came not 'too late' but, as Hölsken has suggested, too early – before electronics, computers and nuclear weapons could make it effective.[36] Only in other places and at other times could the technology of Peenemünde reach its logical conclusion: the ICBM.

4 | *Self-mobilization or resistance? Aeronautical research and National Socialism*

HELMUTH TRISCHLER

1   Definition of concepts

During the past decades, historical research has invested considerable time and energy in the analysis of the relationship of varying classes and groups within German society to the National Socialist regime. Although denazification, which was largely ineffective in its aim, had clearly revealed the diversity of conduct during the Nazi period, the interest of most historians has been focused on the protagonists and leading personalities of the regime on the one hand, and on those of the resistance movements on the other. This very understandable concentration on the extreme polarities of the collective and individual responses to National Socialism has long dominated the manner in which research has approached the subject.

However, this historical reality is generally much too complex to be relegated to categories of black and white. The deeper the historical analysis delves into societal structures, the more confusing the definition and interplay of acceptance and rejection, of support and disobedience, appear. Words such as 'opposition' or 'resistance' lose more and more of their actual meaning.

When the *Institut für Zeitgeschichte* (Institute for Contemporary History) in Munich began an extensive project on *Bayern in der NS-Zeit*[1] (Bavaria under National Socialism) in the 1970s, one of the greatest problems turned out to be an insufficient and inadequate conceptualization. It is not surprising that in this context a new concept was formed to express better the behaviour of a large part of the population in their confrontation with the regime: the concept of '*Resistenz*'.

The term resistance includes aspects that clearly refer to the rejection of and, more accurately, the active combatting of a political system. Resist-

72

ance, in reference to National Socialism, must be seen as a type of response that rejects the Nazi regime as a whole and which, as far as the individual or societal groups are able, attempts to overthrow the system.

The concept of 'Resistenz' does not include systematic efforts for overcoming the system. It is characterized instead by the rejection of and refusal to support the system, the limitation and the containment of Nazi power and its claims, irrespective of the reigning powers or dominant interests involved. The term itself is a controversial one and, admittedly, has its weaknesses, particularly with regard to an adequate translation. If an attempt is made to translate Resistenz into English or French, the results are precisely those words this writer has sought to avoid: 'resistance' and 'résistance'. Nevertheless, the fact that the term includes forms of the effective limitation of the powers of National Socialism which were hardly or not at all a politically motivated, conscious anti-Nazi stance, has made it decidedly useful, if not integral, for the purposes of social historical analysis.[2]

The title of this essay includes a second term which may be thought of as being the opposite of Resistenz, namely 'self-mobilization' (Selbstmobilisierung). This term should also not be considered principally in the light of politically motivated actions. Self-mobilization, in reference to National Socialism, can be defined as voluntary involvement, the free devotion of an individual's ability, above and beyond the professional call of duty, to advance the objectives of the regime.[3]

The range of potential responses exhibited by scientists in their confrontation with the Nazi state is extremely varied. The counterpole to resistance may be seen as being unconditional activism, a complete identification with Nazi ideology. This position was indeed evident among scientists, but it was fairly rare, even in the field of aeronautical research. National Socialist ideology was largely anti-scientific and thus unavoidably came into conflict with the modern sciences.[4] Movements such as 'Deutsche Physik' were dominated by the mentality of typical anti-modernists who were not able to fathom the concepts of pure physics (quantum mechanics, theory of relativity) as these concepts were developed in the decades after the turn of the century.[5] The few scientists who actively spouted Nazi propaganda were usually either second-rate or insignificant graduates who hoped through the party to embark on a brilliant career. In the field of aeronautical research, the best-known exception is the aerodynamicist Wilhelm Müller, who was appointed by the Education Ministry, under strong pressure from the Party, to the chair for theoretical physics previously held by the renowned Arnold Sommerfeld at the University of Munich in 1941. However, many scientists of the younger generation rebelled against the hierarchical and patriarchal structure of the institutes and departments at universities and research centres. National Socialism may thus be viewed as the manifest expression of the structural generation gap.

Self-mobilization was well represented in aeronautical research. A whole range of varying gray areas existed between the milky white of *Resistenz* and the anthracite of self-mobilization. Historical realities are difficult to classify as black or white. Most scientists during the Third Reich cannot be relegated to either category, but were somewhere in the twilight zone. Self-mobilization and *Resistenz* may be seen as opposite sides of a coin which portrays the historical German mentality as one that understands the natural sciences as part of society far removed from any political influence.

2   The development of aeronautical research during the Third Reich

The rise of aeronautical research as an institutionalized science began in the years between the turn of the century and World War I. Three important organizations must be mentioned in this connection:[6]
(1) the establishment of the *Modellversuchsanstalt der Motorluftschiffstudiengesellschaft* (Experimental Model Institute of the Society for the Study of Motor Airships) in 1907 in Göttingen which, during World War I, served as the birthplace of the world-famous *Aerodynamische Versuchsanstalt* (Aerodynamic Experimental Centre, henceforth AVA)
(2) the foundation of the *Deutsche Versuchsanstalt für Luftfahrt* (German Experimental Centre for Aviation, henceforth DVL) in Berlin-Adlershof in the year 1912; and
(3) the combining of state, research and industry in the *Wissenschaftliche Gesellschaft für Luftfahrt* (Scientific Society for Aviation, henceforth WGL), also established in 1912.

Until 1933, further developments in the field were largely influenced by the political situation in Europe. The stormy expansionism during the First World War was followed by a deep depression resulting from the Treaty of Versailles. Military aviation was generally forbidden in Germany, and civil aviation was severely limited in its possibilities until the mid 1920s. This resulted in industry's backing out of research programmes and left the sciences to fight for survival during the inflationary period between 1918 and 1923. From the mid 1920s onwards, the sciences, supported financially by the state, revived and were thus able to make plans for the future. These few years of apparent normalcy were followed by another major setback: world depression.

During this phase, in the years between 1928/29 and 1933, it became clear, as far as aeronautical research was concerned, that the parliamentary democratic state was generally not in a position to support the interests of science. The departmental bureaucracy was only convinced with difficulty of the necessity of supporting an increase in working capacity for aeronautical research. In contrast, however, the parliamentary decision-making bodies seemed to have virtually no understanding of the supposed vital interests of research. They simply cut all funding for research centres. This attitude of the state toward the sciences shows once again to what extent the Weimar Republic was truly caught in a crisis during the late 1920s and early 1930s. Large sections of society, among them the scientists, had ceased to accept the Republic as a valid form of government and were looking for alternatives.

Thus, the removal of the democratic parliamentary bodies by the National Socialists was largely well received by those in aeronautical research. The scientists noted with undisguised satisfaction that aeronautics was granted autonomy under the Reich. With the appointments of the director of the *Lufthansa*, Erhard Milch, to undersecretary and of one of the most avid promoters of aeronautical research in the face of the departmental bureaucracy of the Weimar Republic, Adolf Baeumker, as head of the research department of the newly formed *Reichsluftfahrtministerium* (Reich Aviation Ministry, henceforth RLM), hopes increased that, after years of 'unjustified penny-pinching', the importance of research for the good of the state would finally be recognized, as Ludwig Prandtl, one of the leading members of the scientific community, stated.[7]

Prandtl and his colleagues were not to be disappointed. Initial contact with the RLM resulted in permission being granted to the AVA to construct a new windtunnel, a request they had petitioned for in vain for over five years. It is not surprising that at the celebration of the 25th anniversary of the AVA on 30 May 1933, under the auspices of Undersecretary Milch, the future seemed to be bathed in a golden light.

The general policies at the DVL were also changed with surprising swiftness. The increase of the budget for aviation by more than 40 million Reichsmark from the job creation programme made it possible for the DVL to put plans for expansion into effect which had been gathering dust since the late 1920s.

The effect on morale of the immediate measures taken by the Nazi regime simply cannot be overestimated. The call which had supposedly gone unheard for years, '*Forschung tut not*' (research must be supported), was suddenly of the utmost importance. Aeronautic scientists soon discovered that their demands could not be outrageous enough as far as those in power were concerned. Infinite possibilities seemed to present themselves. Research installations, previously unthinkable due to the high costs involved, were suddenly approved without question. The financing problem, which had always been the limiting factor of research, seemed no longer relevant. The expansion of the DVL alone consumed over 28 million Reichsmark by the start of the Second World War, a huge amount, inconceivable by the standards of the Weimar era. The staff of the centre increased threefold within a two-year period. At the outbreak of World War II, the research institute had a workforce of some 2,000 employees. The AVA grew just as rapidly. It was staffed by 80 employees in the year Hitler seized power, and grew to over 450 by the year 1936 and to approximately 700 in the last year of peace.

In addition to these centres, completely new research institutions were established. In 1935 plans were made for the foundation of the *Deutsche Forschungsanstalt für Luftfahrt* (German Research Centre for Aviation, henceforth DFL), the most important installation of the pre-war period. Within just a few short years, the centre seemed to shoot up on the green fields outside Braunschweig. With research installations of this magnitude, the Germans hoped to resume at an international level the leading position they had held in the 1920s. Göring dictated the goals to be attained: the foreign advantage must be curbed by 1938/39 so that Germany might assume the lead.[8]

The field of aeronautical research benefited enormously from these policies of expansion. Scientists generally tend to judge themselves by their colleagues at home and abroad. Scientists in aeronautical research in Germany looked to America, which since the 1920s had been a shining example of well-equipped research and organization. The German scientists were forced to sit in silence as, in Great Britain, France and, particularly, the USA, the groundwork for excellent research opportunities was laid, while in Germany, working with obsolete equipment, it was not even possible to conduct model tests on new aircraft types. What a difference it made, after the apparent lack of interest by the parliamentary democracy in the necessity for research, to be confronted with the generosity of the new ruling powers. An additional aspect was the increase in the prestige of aeronautics and aviation. Research centres were suddenly openly visited by the leaders of the Reich. Aeronautics, as part of the directed psychological preparation for war, was also allotted a prominent position in the school curriculum.

In view of these conceptually favourable general policies, it seemed reasonable that the traditional professional organizations of aeronautics scientists and engineers had to be sacrificed. The traditional WGL tried in vain to retain its membership. The *Vereinigung für Luftfahrtforschung* (Union for Aeronautical Research), founded by the National Socialists in 1933 as an opposing party (i.e. competitor) to the WGL, succeeded in undermining their authority. Since the National Socialists had cut off all funding and membership had dropped dramatically, the board of the WGL finally conceded defeat in 1936 and agreed to a formal disbanding of the organization. At the same time, the *Vereinigung für Luftfahrtforschung* was reorganized and renamed *Lilienthal-Gesellschaft für Luftfahrtforschung* (Lilienthal Society for Aeronautical Research). Göring personally assumed the sponsorship of the organization. The presiding committee consisted of three chairmen, Prandtl, Baeumker and Carl Bosch, one of Germany's leading industrialists who went on to become president of the *Kaiser-Wilhelm-Gesellschaft*.[9] The general meeting of the *Lilienthal-Gesellschaft*, conducted with great pomp and ceremony, was without a doubt among the highlights of the German scientific community's existence. The *crème de la crème* of international aviation were in attendance: Bruno Mussolini, Jerome Hunsacker, Charles Lindbergh, Curtis Douglas and Melville Jones.

The crowning event of the organizational reshuffling of the year 1936 was the founding of the *Deutsche Akademie der Luftfahrtforschung* (German Academy of Aeronautical Research). Adopting the constitution of the time-honoured Prussian and Bavarian academies, an academy of technical sciences was created, a novelty in the German scientific structure. Nothing can better exemplify the spectacular increase in the power and importance of aeronautical research than the foundation of this academy despite violent opposition from the established sciences.

All in all, within just a few years the political policies surrounding research and development had undergone a revolutionary change. Shortages of money were replaced by generous funding. As far as the sciences were concerned, 'parliamentary tightfistedness' had been replaced by 'unlimited generosity'. It is thus not surprising that the scientists did not regret the passing of democracy, or that they quickly aligned themselves with the new dictatorship, particularly when, with regard to their actual work, virtually no limits were set on their traditional autonomy.

3   **Courses of action during the armament phase: between *Resistenz* and self-mobilization**

The political stance of university professors in Germany with regard to the Weimar Republic had generally not been one of support, but, at most, one of toleration of and loyalty to authority.[10] Hitler's purging of the '*Schandfrieden*' (dishonourable peace) of Versailles, which had directly hindered aviation's advancement, guaranteed the Führer the political sympathies of those who otherwise would have had much to criticize in the measures taken by the new rulers. This ambivalence between criticism of individual actions of the regime, on the one hand, and absolute loyalty to and approval of the person of Hitler on the other, as described by Ian Kershaw so impressively in his studies on the actual mood of the population of Bavaria, is also true of the sciences.[11] Albert Betz, for example, the head of the AVA, incurred the Party's indignation when he saw fit to criticize policies of the regime at an institute party to commemorate the fifth anniversary of Hitler's rise to power. His Catholic background contributed to his ability to look critically at the social consequences of the regime's policies. Nazi loyalists within his staff were outraged and reported him to the authorities. As a result of this incident, Betz was on the Party's 'undesirables' list for some time. However, it was finally possible for the departmental bureaucracy of the RLM, together with the *Kaiser-Wilhelm-Gesellschaft* (Kaiser Wilhelm Society, henceforth KWG), to moderate the complaints submitted against Betz by the *Kreisleitung* (Regional Director) of the NSDAP and by the *Deutsche Arbeitsfront* (German Labour Front).[12] In the end, the interests of rearmament were to prove mightier than the influence of the *Arbeitsfront*. One and a half years later, a few weeks after Hitler's invasion of Poland, this same Betz, in a symbolic gesture of his unfailing belief in the Führer's dedication to peace, sent colleagues abroad copies of Hitler's speech before the *Deutsche Reichstag* (German parliament). Strangely enough, although Betz retained his critical eye with regard to the reduction of workers' rights, he was apparently blinded by Hitler's supposed foreign policy successes. He rigorously defended Hitler against attacks by the foreign press in correspondence with a Swiss friend and colleague, Jakob Ackeret.[13] Finally, during the war Betz devoted his entire energy to the goals of the regime. His zeal went above and beyond the normal degree of loyalty to authority. The following account will show that Betz was certainly no exception within the scientific community, but rather the rule.

Another example is the undisputed '*primus inter pares*' of German aeronautical research, Ludwig Prandtl. He is typical of the mentality and behaviour of German scientists during the Third Reich and is thus best suited to our analysis. Prandtl is typical of the scholar who considers himself to be absolutely apolitical. His work meant everything to him. Organizational and representational tasks resulting from his prominent position at home and abroad as the 'Father of Aerodynamics' were grudgingly endured, rather than gladly fulfilled.[14]

Prandtl can certainly not be termed a supporter of the parliamentary democracy of Weimar during the 1920s. Rather, like so many professors, he was closer politically to the *Deutschnationale Volkspartei* (DNVP – German National People's Party). Nevertheless, he was always willing to answer and fulfill any requests the state approached him with. When in 1928 questions arose in the *Reichsverkehrsministerium* (Reich Ministry of Transport) as to how the efficiency of German aeronautical research could be improved, it was Prandtl who, together with his protégé and colleague Theodore von Kármán and the departmental bureaucracy, created the *Deutscher Forschungsrat für Luftfahrt* (German Research Council for Aviation) as a coordinating body and advisory commission.[15]

Basic loyalty to state authority regardless of its form, and thus loyalty to the National Socialist regime, did not stop Prandtl from voicing his criticism wherever he felt the regime's actions interfered with his interests as a scientist. Two spectacular instances of his unyielding personal and civil courage follow:

(1) In the years between 1928 and 1933, large and active groups of the *Nationalsozialistische Betriebszellen-Organisation* (National Socialist Factory Organization, henceforth NSBO) were formed within the AVA and the associated Kaiser Wilhelm Institute for Hydrodynamics. After Hitler's rise to power, this organization had attained a certain legitimacy and

members presented their demands to Prandtl as their '*Führer des Betriebes*' (Factory Leader) and to the head of the *Kaiser-Wilhelm-Gesellschaft*. In addition to the typical goals of the National Socialist radicals, such as the dismissal of moonlighters, an equalization of wage differences between blue- and white-collar workers and a guarantee of fair wages defined by new pay-scale regulations, a call went out for the removal of 'politically unreliable elements'.[16]

The NSBO's attacks were directed specifically at Johann Nikuradse, a Georgian, who had succeeded in putting himself in Prandtl's favour and had thus advanced to the position of departmental head. The NSBO suspected Nikuradse of spying for the Soviet Union and of stealing books from the institute. The case against Nikuradse became a political issue when written accusations by the NSBO cell fell into the hands of the *SS-Standartenführer* and director of police of the city of Göttingen. He in turn passed the information on to Bernhard Rust, the *Reichsminister für Erziehung, Wissenschaft und Volksbildung* (Minister of Education and Science), a good friend of his, and to Johannes Weniger, the head of the Information Service of the SS.

The shot the instigators of the written accusations sought to fire at Nikuradse backfired. Nikuradse had joined the Nazi Party in 1923 and had excellent contacts with the SS. In an attempt to clear his name, he launched a counter-attack and presented the matter to the judicator at the University of Göttingen. Suddenly it was not just a single scientist who stood accused, but a group of seven employees of AVA.

Prandtl initially defended Nikuradse. As Nikuradse's aims became clear, Prandtl abandoned him. He saw the absolute threat to the expansion of his newly founded institute that would be posed by the dismissal of an entire group of experienced scientists. Moreover, he felt it was his duty to support his employees in combatting what – in his opinion – was unjustified dismissal. The board of the KWG had its hands full trying to calm the stormy 'political' waters. In the end, the KWG was successful in that only three of the key figures involved in the revolt were dismissed.

Prandtl, however, continued his own investigation in secret. For months thereafter, he stubbornly refused to cooperate with the dismissal resolution issued him by the NSDAP and the KWG. On the other hand, Nikuradse was soon to realize just whose anger he had provoked. Despite protection by the party hierarchy, Prandtl dismissed him a few months later.

With this dismissal, Prandtl alienated Weniger completely. A member of the SS Secret Service, Weniger was appointed head of personnel at the *Deutsche Forschungsgemeinschaft* (German Research Foundation, henceforth DFG) in July of 1933, thanks to his connections with Rust. From this prominent position, he did all he could to damage Prandtl. He not only accused him of being anti-Nazi, but also suggested that he had outrageously exaggerated his requests for funding from the research association.

Prandtl's position was significantly strong, due to the immense importance of aeronautical research to the war effort, for him to be able to ignore
the threat of incarceration in a concentration camp. Moreover, Prandtl
tried to compensate for the tarnish on his reputation – his and Betz's failure
to join the NSDAP – by deliberately hiring party members for administrative positions within the institute. The 'political evaluation' drawn up by
the local Kreisleiter in Göttingen in May of 1937 was more a reflection of
the differing thought processes between the Nazi elite and the scientific
community than it was an accurate description of Prandtl's person:[17]

> Prof. Prandtl is a typical scientist in an ivory tower.
>   He is only interested in his scientific research which has made him
> world famous. Politically, he poses no threat whatsoever. I would go so
> far as to say that he is ignorant of even the most basic political matters,
> since they in no way affect his research work ...
>   In conclusion, Prandtl may be considered one of those honourable, con-
> scientious scholars of a bygone era, conscious of his integrity and respect-
> ability, whom we certainly cannot afford to do without, nor should we
> wish to, in light of his immensely valuable contributions to the develop-
> ment of the air force.

The ambivalence of Prandtl's behaviour is typical: on the one hand, he
was never afraid of arguing with influential, power-wielding party
members, if it was to serve his interests or those of his staff; but on the
other hand, he conformed to the current situation by making concessions
with regard to personnel.

(2) Physics in Göttingen was to suffer greatly due to the expulsion of
Jewish scientists from their positions and professorships.[18] The prelude to
these dismissals was the Gesetz zur Wiederherstellung des Berufsbeamten-
tums (Restoration of Permanent Civil Service Act) of April 1933. Prandtl
did not hesitate to complain at the highest level of the irreparable damage
his field would sustain if 'politically and racially undesirable scientists'
were removed from their positions. As early as the end of April 1933, he
began badgering the Reich's Minister of the Interior, Frick, with petitions.
Prandtl could often be quite naive regarding political matters, but he was
sufficiently astute and enough of a tactician to word his message skilfully.
He protested to Frick that the rigid system devised by the race theorists
should be flexible enough to allow scholars who were half or a quarter
Jewish, who were then logically half or three-quarters German, to be per-
suaded to join the people's cause. In correspondence with his colleagues, he
clearly articulated his fundamental aim. The National Socialist activists
had demanded that the internationally recognized Gesellschaft für angewandte Mathematik and Mechanik (Society for Applied Mathematics and
Mechanics) should exclude its Jewish members. Prandtl, the president of
this society, advocated opposing this demand. Not, as might be assumed,
because this would have been an expression of respect and honour for the

'Father of Mathematics', Richard von Mises, who was principally affected by the decree, but, more accurately, because Prandtl felt the discipline would suffer. The point had finally been reached where he was no longer willing to comply with the changing political situation. He was in any case willing bravely to contend that politics should be excluded from scientific activity.[19]

Prandtl retained this courage even when the regime had firmly established itself and despite the notable increase of National Socialist influence on research. Two of his actions are particularly noteworthy in that they clearly placed him at the head of his field.

His first act was in conjunction with the filling of the post of Arnold Sommerfeld's former chair. The University of Munich and the Bavarian Ministry of Cultural Affairs and Education had selected the rising star in the sky of theoretical physics, Werner Heisenberg, a student of Sommerfeld's, to be his successor. Heisenberg's appointment came to nothing, however, due to violent attacks launched in the *Völkische Beobachter* and in the *Schwarze Korps*, a newspaper belonging to the SS, accusing him of being a '*Jude im Geiste*', (Jewish in spirit). Prandtl took the opportunity at a meeting of the Academy for Aeronautical Research to point out to the head of the SS, Heinrich Himmler, the damage the SS was inflicting with their attacks on Heisenberg. Later, in reference to their conversation, he forwarded a petition to Himmler in which he again vehemently defended Heisenberg.[20]

In the end, there was nothing Prandtl could do to prevent the appointment of Wilhelm Müller, the aerodynamicist and representative of *Deutsche Physik*, in place of Heisenberg. The fact that the most important centre for theoretical physics in Germany was to be led by a second-rate proponent of experimental physics was more than the '*sture bayerische Dickschädel*' (literally 'stubborn, thick-skulled Bavarian' – Prandtl came from Freising, near Munich) could bear. He had attempted as early as 1933/34 to question the authority of the Ministry of Aviation by calling Undersecretary Milch's attention to the detrimental effects on the war effort in aviation which were sure to result from the expulsion of Jewish scientists of merit.

Milch actually responded immediately and protested to the Minister of Education, Rust, against the decision. During the war Prandtl again tried to call attention to the situation and directed his petition to the Minister for Aviation and Hitler's acting representative. In an appeal directed to Göring, Prandtl termed Müller's appointment an explicit attempt to sabotage the German war effort. Further petitions were submitted during the course of 1941 and the spring of 1942 which contained contributions from his confederates within the scientific community and which were exceedingly clear in their demands.[21] The petition, submitted to Göring on 28 April 1941, is a clear example of Prandtl's grasp of language and rhetoric:

> Recent developments have created a situation within the discipline of physics at German universities which could prove threatening to the education of future leaders within the field and which, if the situation is not

remedied, shall undoubtedly result in German inferiority in this important area for the war and the economy.

Unchanged, it will definitely put us at a major disadvantage with regard to American competition ... To state the matter simply, I refer to a group of physicists, who unfortunately have good connections to the Führer, who rage against theoretical physics and denounce the most creditable of the theoretical physicists, who have succeeded in placing unqualified persons on the chairs of vital institutes, etc., and, indeed, have done so with the explanation that modern theoretical physics is some sort of a Jewish hoax, which cannot be gotten rid of fast enough and which should be replaced by a *'Deutsche Physik'* ...

Theoretical Physics is indisputably recognized as essential for the education of future leaders within the physics discipline. Its goal, after all, is to give a logical order to physical processes and phenomena as a whole and develop their physical laws in order to provide a tool for the technical physicist and engineer with which he will be able systematically to design new constructions as well as calculate their effectiveness. A study of physics, excluding theoretical physics, will do nothing more than produce good, but inept, workmen, rather than leaders able to grasp and command the field in its entirety.

It may be that one would tend to consider Prandtl's ten-year efforts to protect his Jewish colleagues as well as those suspected of being *'Juden im Geist'* to be a manifestation of resistance. Somewhat less spectacular, but nevertheless still active opposition was exhibited by numerous circles in aeronautical research to the political situation during the Third Reich. Examples include Jonathan Zenneck and Hermann Blenk, who vehemently criticized the grossly exaggerated secrecy regulations, which only succeeded in cutting off all interdisciplinary communication, a factor absolutely necessary within the field; Georg Madelung, who complained about the omnipotence of bureaucrats and military men, who with their superior arrogance, dismissed scientists as 'aesthetical eccentrics'[22] with no idea of the importance of the war efforts. These examples show – even more than Prandtl's initiatives – the specific character of the scientists' actions. In general these were not feats of resistance aimed at conquering the system. On the contrary, they sought to strengthen the powerful position of the Reich and thus to keep National Socialism in power by removing barriers to efficiency – whether ideologically motivated attacks on the sciences by Nazi activists or political clashes of competence by competing powers within the polycratic chaos of the Nazi regime.

It should be clear from these examples that *Resistenz* and self-mobilization are not merely opposites, but may be seen as complementary. The acts Prandtl and his colleagues undertook to express their opposition were actually motivated by fears that all of their energies and efforts, expended in the cause of mobilization and for the *'Vaterland'*, were to be thwarted by individual political decisions. An understanding of this ambivalence is necessary to comprehend the merits of the term *Resistenz*. Its meaning is varied enough to be able to include manifestations of opposition to the established power structures and conformity and loyalty to the system.

4   The self-mobilization of research during World War II

After the head of the powerful 'Technical Office' in the Ministry of Aviation, Ernst Udet, committed suicide in November 1941, the inherent weaknesses of the German war effort in aviation could no longer be denied. Aircraft production with fewer than 1000 planes per month had fallen well below the planned output target. At the same time, it became clear that the bureaucratic, political attempts to channel research which had been attempted since the outbreak of the war had failed. The state was neither able to present concrete production goals to the scientists, nor were the scientists as successful in combining research and development as their American counterparts. Duplication and overlap of tasks and a lack of coordination between research and industry were everyday occurences. Complementary to the transfer of decision-making powers back into the hands of industry in 1942, the Ministry of Aviation was now also willing to return the direction of further research to the scientists themselves.[23]

This meant, however, that senior staff like Prandtl, who already had more than enough to do, were saddled with even more work. This initiative would have been an utter failure without their inner preparedness to dedicate themselves fully and completely to a more efficient use of research for the war effort. Despite some doubts that they were neglecting their actual responsibilities as research scientists, in the end none of them rejected any of the unreasonable requests put to them by the Ministry of Aviation. Thus the *Forschungsführung des Reichsluftfahrtministeriums* (Research Direction in the Ministry of Aviation) could be established in June of 1942. This four-man commission under Prandtl's chairmanship, working under the worst possible conditions, met with remarkable successes during the last few years of the war, if these are gauged by the immanent logic of the war industry. The regime was well rewarded for having resorted to the scientific community's ability to direct its own activities, a policy which largely contradicted the Party's and state's claim to leadership. The members of the Research Direction repaid the trust they were afforded by mobilizing all their efforts for the objectives of the Nazi regime. 'That research during this crucial time of war should successfully complete all tasks put to it, is surely what all of us want.' Walter Georgii, managing member of the Research Direction, thus articulated the new credo of a science which now had political responsibility.[24]

Attempts to limit and control the freedom of individual scientists had been decidedly rejected during the Weimar Republic; now, however, under different circumstances, scientists were suggesting and enforcing this policy of their own accord. The Research Direction went so far as to cancel current research projects in favour of a concentration on tasks supposedly essential to the war efforts, a virtual sacrilege for the scientific community. During the total war, the otherwise sacrosanct freedom of research was sacrificed to the optative of the fastest possible military translation of their results.

The complex diversity of thousands of scientists makes generalization impossible. There was individual resistance to the programming of working goals according to the necessities of war. Particularly those involved in fundamental research work, like Hermann Schlichting, were incensed by the limits placed on their autonomy. With the growing disillusionment regarding their chances of ending the war with a victory, an increasing sense of vexation prevailed. Nevertheless, this vexation did not develop into a challenge directed at the primacy of the Research Direction's policies. At most, it led to a renewed absorption with their work, as the scientists buried themselves in their projects. True examples of active resistance in aeronautical research are nonexistent. Critical remarks from individuals are not so much an expression of a stance in opposition to the system, as, rather, a result of the frustration resulting from the lack of recognition of their willingness to mobilize all of their abilities for the cause. Particularly scientists like Georg Madelung, who were active in areas of practical application, complained about the lack of contact with the front lines. World War I proved the point. Madelung surmised that the reason aeronautical research between 1914 and 1918 was so successful was that scientists were able to work realistically and in a practice-oriented way. The current situation left their requests for contact with industry and the military unanswered.[25]

5   Interpretations of the scientists' actions

The ambivalence of scientists to the Nazi regime requires interpretation. The following cases can be made in an incomplete attempt at an explanation:

(1) Even though a steady stream of complaints about the state's interference in the autonomy of scientific study and research was to be heard, aeronautical research had largely remained amenable to cooperation with the state since its inception around 1910. Having come to the realization that only the state was in a position to finance large-scale research facilities, Prandtl and his colleagues had placed their expert knowledge at the government's disposal during the First World War and, again, from the mid 1920s onwards. Thus, the state had employed the services of scientists in an 'age-old tradition', going back long before the Third Reich.

(2) A sense of loyalty to every form of state authority was deeply rooted

in the scientists of the period. It resulted from the authoritarian sociali-
zation of the educated middle class which rose during the German Empire.
Prandtl often referred to this 'willingness to serve' the state.[26]

(3) Coupled with this willingness to serve was the expectation that the
state and society should place the best possible facilities at the disposal of
the sciences they expected to serve them. As far as research was concerned,
the government of Weimar had violated this 'contract of natural law'
during the world economic crisis by implementing emergency budgeting.[27]
The Nazi regime responded differently: the services of the scientists were
secured thanks to a generous research budget.

(4) Aeronautical research and the Third Reich were to form a mutually
dependent coalition. The regime needed scientists and was willing to offer
the best working conditions available to get them. The head of the Institute
of Engine Research in Stuttgart, Wunibald Kamm, recognized that research
had succeeded during the Second World War in manoeuvring itself into a
position from which there was only one escape, namely complete identification with the objectives of the regime. The National Socialists had provided leading scientists with the research institutes they had long desired. In
the interests of protecting their life's work, they were then forced to give the
Nazi state their full support. As Kamm saw it, World War II was for them a
question of 'life and death'.[28]

(5) This chapter has examined the objective behaviour of scientists based
on their experiences in the twenties and thirties. This approach was intentional since the misconception is all too prevalent that, given the criminal
nature of the Nazi regime, resistance to the Third Reich must inevitably
arise. On the contrary, resistance must be considered in the context of the
circumstances and experiences of groups within society and the actual
manifestations and unreasonable demands of the regime which provoke
acts of resistance. Seen from this perspective, the factors conducive to
resistance were absent from the field of aeronautical research. Scientists
profited from the regime's policies perhaps more than any other single
group within society. Thus it is not surprising that opposition was limited
to protests against individual policies without challenging the overall
loyalty afforded state authority.

(6) An apolitical ideology of science is closely related to a willingness to
serve. Those involved in the natural sciences saw themselves and research
as something value-free, objective and thereby also politically neutral.
According to the conventions of the scientific community, the active
support of a ruling class, regardless of its political shade, was not political,
but opposition of any form was profoundly political.[29]

6   After National Socialism: reconstruction – Arguments for and
        against aeronautical research at and outside universities

Even after the events of the years between 1933 and 1945, it never
occurred to a great majority of those active in aeronautical research that
their sacrificing dedication to the Nazi regime and war machine was in and
of itself a political statement. In his manuscript '*Gedanken eines unpoliti-
schen Deutschen*' (Reflections of a unpolitical German), written in 1947,
Prandtl makes the claim that he had 'never played a role in politics', but
had always only served 'State and Science'.[30]

Aeronautical research in Germany was reorganized during the period in
which research was banned by the Allies (1945–1951/55) by virtually the
same scientists who had defined the policies of the scientific community
prior to 1945: Prandtl, Betz, Kamm, Madelung, Georgii, Schlichting,
Friedrich Seewald, Hermann Blenk and many others. The younger generation was actively mobile and increasingly began to accept attractive positions abroad. The older generation saw their life's work as being in
Germany and attempted to rebuild what had been destroyed as quickly as
possible.

Second thoughts about the resumption of research projects relevant to
the military were the exception rather than the rule. In an atmosphere of
tense East–West relations which climaxed during the Korean War in
1951/52, the possibility to re-establish applied aeronautical research by way
of military contracts presented itself. The department headed by Hermann
Blenk, which supervised the reorganization of the German armed forces
before the foundation of the Ministry of Defense, approached the leading
figures in aeronautical research almost immediately. Proponents of the
applied sciences were ecstatic at this ray of hope in the otherwise cloudy
sky of German aeronautics. It is not surprising that the DVL intended –
even before its official reopening in May of 1954 – to pursue projects on
guided missiles and thus become genuinely involved in military research.[31]
It is also not astonishing that, in the early 1950s, the scientists had already
established a centre in Stuttgart euphemistically entitled, *Forschungsinstitut
für Physik der Strahlantriebe* (Jet Propulsion Physics Research Institute).
This institute facilitated international contact with the latest technology
abroad in the field of rocket research. Head of the institute was Eugen
Sänger. During the Third Reich, Sänger had worked on '*Antipodenbom-
ber*', initially in Trauen, near Braunschweig, and later in Ainring, in
Bavaria.[32]

Penetrating reflections on the political dimensions of scientific activity,
which were typical of the American scientists at the time, were not conducted in Germany. The scientific community in the USA, with its typically
American understanding of democracy, argued its differences in public as
to whether or not it was legitimate to continue military research after the

Second World War. In contrast, only rudimentary discussions were held in West Germany on this highly controversial topic in an atmosphere of 'self-appeasement', and then only in a select circle by those directly affected.

These discussions were hardly justified on ethical or moral grounds, but were rather a result of diverging professional interests. The community of aeronautical researchers was split into two factions in the early 1950s over the question of whether the newly created research organizations should be made part of the universities or be reorganized in centres outside the universities. Scientists from the *Kommission für Luftfahrtforschung* (Commission for Aeronautical Research) from the DFG were united on the one hand. They advocated the expansion and improvement of research capacity at the universities and clearly rejected efforts to expand centralized testing facilities. They were opposed by scientists from the WGL, refounded in 1952, who insisted on the renewed establishment of research and testing centres outside the universities. The debates of the competing groups were of a fierceness 'beneath the dignity' of scientific associations and, in the opinion of one shocked participant, made the 'conflict of interests in the business world' appear mild in comparison.[33]

Far be it from me to deny the moral energy of the scientists from the DFG in their committed argument against the re-establishment of research centres outside the universities. They have, at any rate, never tired of pointing out the role that research outside the universities played in the organization of the Nazi air offensive, thus contributing to the infamous bombing raids. In their opinion, similar situations could be avoided in the future, if research were returned to the universities.[34] They have been able to recognize partially that research and politics are structurally bound to one another. By the same token, their subsequent willingness to accept military research contracts reveals that the ethical and moral arguments tendered in the bitter disputes in the early fifties were principally used to support their particular interests. To put it bluntly, they were primarily interested in the research funds offered by the federal government. Both factions realized that this phase would set the course for the future structure of aeronautical research in West Germany. The differences between scientists at universities, with fewer staff and less equipment, and their privileged colleagues at large-scale research installations, still exists today. In contrast, the demand for a new ethic of science and thus for a departure from traditional, apolitical ideas of science has been made only recently, and that with a 'time lag' of several decades.[35]

5 | Military technology and National Socialist ideology[1]

ULRICH ALBRECHT

According to a widespread assumption, modern weapon systems and their principles of construction follow universal rules that are independent of the type of society in which this technology is created and immune to ideological disputes. The example of National Socialism shows, however, that this assumption is invalid. Nazi ideology had a specific impact upon the development of armaments technology in the Third Reich, especially during its downfall.

The German engineers and scientists involved in the efforts to keep the Nazi war machine running were presumably not only National Socialists because of individual membership in the Party or one of its organizations, or belief in the ideology. Certain groupings of scientists and engineers responded to the dramatic challenge presented by the threatened downfall of the Third Reich with enormous activity and technological contributions which remain uncommon in the world of armaments, and which distinguish this technology from developments elsewhere. The project proposals for military technology submitted by some branches of the German war economy thus represent artifacts that mirror National Socialist policy, especially its inhumane features. In other words, the technical projects discussed below were not only unique because they were prosecuted with phenomenal effort, under grossly inadequate working conditions, using slave labour and in underground facilities to avoid Allied bombing. Some of the high-tech items created in this period show distinct features of National Socialist approaches to military technology, and to modern technology in general.

Hitler repeatedly stressed the ideological role of technology. For example, in his recorded table conversations he said: 'decisive for the winning of any war remains, however, that one is always in possession of the "technically superior weapons"'.[2] However, this ideological position would not have had such dramatic implications if it had not been paired with the rational capitalism and industrialism of the arms manufacturers, their tremendous will to persist and to prevail. Both motives escalate in the final phase of the Third Reich *in furioso*. Thus this study focuses upon the final months of the Nazi empire in 1944–5.

The twelve years of National Socialism do not constitute an isolated stage either in the course of German history or in the progress of technology. Did the perversions of technology found in this period have predecessors during the Wilhelmine empire or the Weimar Republic? Can traces of National Socialism be found in technological developments in post-war Germany? Are these perversions unique for the Third Reich? Certain lines of technology may be found extreme, sometimes even perverted, but they will not necessarily be National Socialist. In order to determine whether or not a certain technology was exclusively National Socialist, it is useful to ask whether there was a continuity or discontinuity in technological developments before, during and after the Third Reich.

The question is thus not a simple one; lines of continuity may exist everywhere. It is also complicated by a view of history in which National Socialism and World War II are embedded as a specific stage in German history. After the 'power grab for global hegemony' (*Griff nach der Weltmacht*) by the new German Empire was frustrated in World War I, the army commenced preparations for a war of revanche without much attention by the politicians of the Weimar Republic and long before Hitler took over. The Research Agency for Military History (*Militärgeschichtliches Forschungsamt*) has researched this bleak chapter of German history in impressive detail.[3]

Military historians, however, naturally tend to focus upon military developments. Progress in armament technology is generally neglected in this literature. However, the fact that some military technologies from the Third Reich can be traced back into the Weimar Republic makes it necessary to determine the specific influence of National Socialism on technology. In contrast, until very recently German historians of technology have often portrayed these technological developments as if they were divorced from the policies of the National Socialist dictatorship.

In the thirties the German elites, who were not necessarily National Socialists, worked to get rid of the 'shame of Versailles', the denial to Germany of an appropriate position in world affairs. After this second attempt for world hegemony was thwarted in World War II at a much bloodier cost than the first effort, both Germany's neighbours and the Germans themselves wondered whether a third outburst might emanate from German soil in an effort to correct history. The general consensus is that there is a great discontinuity indeed; since 1945 the new Germany has not turned out giant aircraft, suicide weapons, poisonous chemicals or long-range missiles. Because of the enormous significance of this great historical divide, the specific aspects of Nazi military technology and its role in German history, as well as the relationship between discontinuity and continuity, all merit special study.

1 Aeronautical technology before 1933

A review of developments in German military technology before 1933 reveals that there were indeed special activities generally unknown to the contemporary public, and that these projects subsequently played an important role in the Third Reich. Because the air force was commonly considered to be *the* National Socialist element among the German armed forces, examples in this study will be mainly drawn from aeronautical technology. The army and especially the navy were generally considered by the Nazis and others to be too conservative to be open-minded towards Hitler's 'revolution' and new military technologies. There certainly were specifically National Socialist approaches to other types of military technology as well, above all to chemical munitions. Chemical weapons, after all, had been invented in Germany: mustard gas in 1916, chlorides like Clark I and Clark II in 1917. The three decisive inventions in nerve gases were made during the Third Reich: Tabun in 1936, Sarin in 1941 and Soman in 1944. The massacre of huge numbers of human beings by poison gas demonstrates a particular tendency of the National Socialists to use chemicals as means of mass destruction, a goal that is reflected in the invention of most toxic agents for military purposes. But this line of technological development merits separate studies.[4] Gigantomania, another candidate for the manifestation of National Socialist technocracy, can also be studied in other sectors of German technological development for both civilian and military purposes, for example in Albert Speer's architecture or the plans for a 'wide gauge' railway with tracks four meters wide and wagons two stories high.[5]

1.1 Aeronautic R&D

Any study concerned with continuities or discontinuities in national technological developments would find Germany to be a special case; political factors remain overriding for any evaluation. The German record is fundamentally different from circumstances in Western democracies, where societies only took up arms as the requirement of the day, and afterward returned to business as usual. Advanced military technologies such as aircraft played a crucial role in the two brief expansionist phases during the Wilhelmian era and under National Socialism. The national R&D effort within the science establishments and industry gave priority to novel types of technology and, within those, to supposed superior technologies, such as super-heavy machines.

The expansionist phases of German history were followed by phases in which Allied prohibitions hindered technological progress. The development of militarily relevant technologies, aircraft prominent among them, was denied to Germany during the Weimar Republic after World War I, the period of occupation after World War II, and in the early years of the Federal German Republic. Efforts recorded during the 'prohibition' phases to continue with former high-tech ambitions under clandestine conditions are especially relevant for the continuity/discontinuity problematic. The will to prevail with such technologies and under the most adverse conditions is worthy of attention.

The conditions for the subsequent rise of aeronautical R&D in Nazi Germany will be scrutinized in this section using Trischler's contribution to this volume, especially the most useful notion of 'self-mobilization' of scientists. Aeronautical research in Germany followed two, apparently unrelated, tracks during the Weimar Republic. They both reflect directly the political conditions.

First of all there were the grand accomplishments of basic aeronautical research, highlighted by the name of Ludwig Prandtl,[6] and the Göttingen airfoils which remain a basic tool for any aeronautical engineer designing the lift surfaces of a flying machine. The work of these aerodynamicists did not concern the powerful Allied control commission because this high-quality academic work was considered far removed from any military application – at least by the Allied supervisors, who greatly misunderstood the motivations of the German scientists and engineers who conducted those numerous measurements. But these latter researchers developed a double-blind negative view, which made these groups susceptible to the appeal of National Socialism: on the one hand, that the democratic Weimar Republic had failed to recognize their academic accomplishments and proved unable to render the financial support that this internationally very successful area of research deserved; on the other hand, the leading aerodynamicists also clearly perceived that the Western powers were against them, that their academic successes raised concerns in Western capitals because they were German.

Secondly, there was the will of German industrialists, notably in the small aeronautical firms, to survive until better times, in this case the National Socialist period. These industrialists demonstrated an ability to manoeuvre in extraordinary ways: they went abroad in order to work in technologically less well developed countries like Sweden or Spain so as to avoid Allied controls. In contrast, there is no record of a British or French firm, to name only the leading nations in the field, which ever took comparable steps. The German industrialists were also looking for extraordinary technological solutions to their problems, like giant planes, quite in contrast to what commercial wisdom would have demanded from them. This emphasis on exceptional technology did not immediately pay off. But the very fast Heinkel transport planes with their aerodynamically clean surfaces, the flying boats by Dornier, or the reliability of diesel-engined Junkers[7] passenger aircraft, which all appeared during the Weimar years, contributed greatly to raising world aviation standards. The lack of state support for the aircraft makers, despite the noted successes of German designs in the export business and in international contests, also contributed to the susceptibility of these groups to the appeal of the flight-minded National Socialists. The army and a few state agencies during the Weimar Republic were interested in such technological developments, but had little to offer in terms of financial or other support.

1.2   Giant aircraft

A concept of excess size, which might be interpreted as National Socialist gigantomania, became apparent in the development of German aeronautical technology. But giant constructions may be found elsewhere as expressions of extreme or misguided approaches to technology which are not necessarily Teutonic in nature.

The technological programmes of the German military before, during and after the Third Reich will be examined first of all with regard to gigantism. For example, there is indeed a tendency in aircraft construction towards gigantic designs. Ironically, it was not these German giants, but instead the step-by-step approach subsequently taken in America and the United Kingdom which produced the 'flying fortresses' that proved decisive for strategic bombing in the war. The development of large rockets was similar. These examples will serve as a useful comparison to those technologies that were exclusively National Socialist in nature.

'Without doubt the most remarkable aircraft built by the Germans during the First World War were the "R" (*Riesenflugzeug*) type giant machines with four, five or six engines', write two British air historians.[8] The main contractor for giant planes was the Zeppelin Werke Staaken GmbH, in one of the Berlin suburbs, earlier active in the production of the famed Zeppelin airships. The history cited emphasizes that:

> There was no previous experience in the design of aircraft of such gargantuan proportions. As an example of just one of the many difficulties which had to be faced, that of engine failure may be instanced ... Undercarriage problems too were a constant headache, again due to there being no previous material of this size to draw upon and the fact that stressing problems were not fully understood ... Construction of these monster machines, which spanned almost 149 ft, was a complicated and lengthy process, and the total number of man-hours must have been prodigious.[9]

Zeppelin was not the only company which strove to set the pace by means of exotic technologies. A number of German firms hoped to win World War I by turning out giant planes, among them some of Germany's best-known companies: General Electric (Allgemeine Elektrizitätsgesell-schaft, henceforth AEG), the German Aircraft Works (Deutsche Flug-zeugwerke GmbH, henceforth DFW), and the railcar producers Linke-Hofmann S.S.W. and Gothaer Waggonfabrik. The scope and timing of this broad involvement are important.

AEG only entered the competition for a giant bomber aircraft, a new field of activity for the firm, during the final stage of the war, with the 'R I' type. The prototype broke into pieces during the maiden flight on 3 Sept-ember 1918. The DFW submitted two designs to the Reich bomber com-petition, 'R I' and 'R II'. This firm's concept represented a most unortho-dox approach in bomber design. The power plants were placed inside the hull of the aircraft, thereby denying the advantages of air-cooling engines by exposing them to the airflow. The DFW 'R I' experienced teething prob-lems with the transmission of power to the air screws of the four Mercedes engines buried in the fuselage. However, the prototype bomber was reportedly deployed successfully against the Russians on the Eastern Front beginning in April of 1917. The supreme army command ordered six additional giant aircraft of the improved 'R II' type. These were also plagued by problems in power transmission. Only the German capitulation brought an end to the time-consuming efforts to iron out the snags in this approach.

A third competitor, Linke-Hofmann, transferred its experience in making large railway engines to aircraft construction. The two entries sub-mitted by this company to the giant bomber competition, also labeled R I and R II, reflect this approach. The designers placed four engines inside the hull of the bomber as did DFW, a common design for locomotives, and geared the power plants to a single oversized propeller. This entailed enor-mous technological difficulties in cooling the engines and mastering vib-ration. The increased size was based on completely untried technologies which were immediately applied to operational equipment – an approach which re-emerged in military technological developments in the Third Reich.[10]

A fourth competitor, the young engineer Claudius Dornier, designed his concept of a giant plane as a flying boat. In contrast to his rivals, Dornier continued with his giant flying boats during the Weimar years. Count Zep-pelin had, during the war, entrusted Dornier with the task of designing the first all-metal amphibious aircraft in Friedrichshafen at Lake Constance. The result was the biggest aircraft in the world at that time, a remarkable achievement for the first construction by a young engineer.[11] The wingspan of this monster, which Dornier christened 'Rs I' in reference to the wartime giant planes, amounted to 142 feet. A sultry wind brought this large con-struction to a premature end. Despite Dornier's precautions – pulling the flying boat out to open waters so that it faced the storm with engines running under full power and anchoring it firmly to a buoy – the craft was smashed on the shore and destroyed. The design was apparently unfit for the rugged conditions of military service.

Dornier and his team immediately began work on a successor, 'Rs II'. This plane actually flew, but showed many features of a too-ambitious leap in technology. The entire tail assembly was not nearly rigid enough and whipped about during the landing after the maiden flight. Furthermore, at this time aeronautical engineers were insufficiently familiar with the hydro-dynamic requirements for the design of flying boats. For example, since water exerts suction on boats and seaplane hulls, the hull must have a break or 'step' cut sharply into it in order that the plane be able to break loose and take off. Rs II did not have this 'step', soon common for any seaplane. The Imperial German navy was willing to acquire Dornier's giant seaplane despite such shortcomings. However, RS II was destroyed in mid-air during the ferry flight.

Dornier turned without pause to 'Rs III', an even more gargantuan design, which included no less than three 'steps' in the hull. The engine compartment was located above the airframe, and above this engine was the huge 121-foot wingspan and fuselage running back to the tail. An external ladder enabled the crew to move between the three levels of the plane. The maximum speed of this construction and its engine, capable of producing 1000 HP, barely reached eighty kilometers per hour. The military commissioned Rs III a fortnight before the armistice.

In 1921 the Allies demanded that the giant flying boat be scrapped. The German government protested, valuing the ship at exactly one million marks. Dornier went on after the war to design a fourth giant plane, 'Rs IV', again with three fuselages in vertical arrangement. The positioning of the four engines resembles the designs of subsequent long-range bombers. This huge aircraft was also scrapped on Allied demand. The technical literature stresses the accumulation of valuable experience that Dornier was able to extract from these experimental designs.[12]

Dornier never gave up his dream of designing the largest flying boats in the world, even under the adverse conditions of the Great Depression and the political constraints of the Weimar Republic. The new project received the unusual designation 'Do-X'. 'X' meant 'unknown quantity' – Dornier was convinced that the most powerful flying boat in the world would beat any competitor. In Germany the Do-X was and still is considered to be one of the great accomplishments in aviation technology, despite the fact that only three planes were actually built. From the technological perspective the design approach was rather conservative. The fuselage was subdivided into three decks. Empty weight was thirty-three tons, sixty-one loaded, sur-passing anything then flying. The giant was propelled by twelve engines. The first flight took place in 1929.

It was soon clear that sheer size was the sole significant feature of the new giant. Despite propulsion by 6,000 HP engines, when fully loaded the ship was unable to fly higher than 1,400 feet. Even after the plane was re-engined with more powerful British motors, its ceiling remained under 2,000 feet. Hostile warships could easily have fought the low-flying plane. A trans-Atlantic flight portrayed to the German public as a resounding success in fact experienced a series of problems. The rear engines in the tandem arrangement ran permanently over-heated and tended to erupt into flames. Landings in rough waters incurred damage and repairs caused enormous delays. The Do-X crossed the open waters of the Atlantic mostly by exploiting the so-called ground effect which provided extra lift when flying only twenty feet above the sea. The Do-X was supposedly designed as a passenger plane, but operating costs were prohibitive. Only Fascist Italy showed interest as a customer. Mussolini acquired two aircraft which the Italian air force deployed for experimental flights. However, it soon became clear that these slow- and low-flying giants were of little military use, and both aircraft were scrapped.

Gigantomania still exists in Germany. James Gilbert, whose verdict on Dornier's giant flying boat has been cited above, even found visions of combining nuclear power plants, the ultimate in propulsion technology, with the German giants:

> Claudius Dornier still has dreams of building a giant flying boat freighter, a flying container ship with a gross weight of a thousand tons, a length and span of about 100 meters, and a range of over 4,000 miles. The engines would be ten huge turbofans, though later versions, said Dornier, *could even be nuclear powered.*[13]

2   National Socialist technology

The approach of National Socialism to technology in general was complex and contradictory. First of all, the Nazis combined one of the most important technical ideas of the early twentieth century, mass production, with their recognition of the significance of masses of humans and material. Secondly, they developed further the concept of the serial destruction of life by means of modern technology. Progress in military technology up until the turn of the century had been characterized by the involvement of machines for destruction: guns, warships, infantry weapons. Techniques of serial destruction by automatons accompanied the introduction of mass-production equipment. The mechanical serialization of killing by machines on a large scale available at the end of World War I, culminating in the machine gun and chemical weapons, thus appears to offer particular insight into the Nazi understanding of technology. Certainly machine-type weapons were not peculiarly German, let alone National Socialist. These military technologies represent a considerable degree of continuity from the Wilhelmine Reich to the Weimar Republic, through the Nazi era and beyond to the post-war world. But the army in the Weimar Republic and later the National Socialists used the various options differently.

An investigation of armament technology during the Third Reich has to compare and contrast various technologies in order to try and filter out what was and was not specifically National Socialist. Single-mission or suicide weapons comparable to better-known equipment introduced by Imperial Japan represent one pole in a spectrum of uniquely National Socialist technology. Other types of technology, such as large numbers of technologically advanced jet fighters to be operated by under-age, juvenile pilots, and in particular equipment where ideological commitment was to compensate for deficiencies of technology (for example, unpowered combat aircraft) come close to this pole.

This chapter will pinpoint specifics of National Socialist approaches to military technology by referring to exceptional characteristics such as demanding Herculean pilot performance, the lowering of recruitment age, suicide weapons and hypertrophic vengeance weapons. Of course these examples are not the whole story, rather they need to be seen in a more general framework. A deeper understanding of the interaction between technology and National Socialism would be provided by placing the developments scrutinized in the following sections in the context of the social and economic history of the Third Reich, especially during the final hypertrophic phase of its dissolution.

Both the causes of the thriving dynamism of technological advance under National Socialist rule, as well as the interaction of engineers with other institutions like the army, SS and industry, deserve more penetrating analysis than can be offered here. In particular, the role of the SS in high-tech R&D at the end of the war remains a neglected yet very important area of research.[14] It may be true that the SS followed a long-term strategy in the acquisition of advanced technology, and that the gargantuan projects considered below reflect more the short-lived irrational efforts of Party ideologues to escape the dictate of events. The respective relationships of German industrialists, here the arms makers, with the various National Socialist groupings and institutions remain an especially difficult research topic. This study and its more modest scope can only shed some light on this taboo period of German history.

National Socialist technology must be judged not only by the artifacts that emerge, but also by *how* these were accomplished. The massive use of slave labour in high-tech priority projects is an important example of this second aspect. National Socialist authorities originally opposed the use of foreigners in military production, because they were afraid of sabotage and espionage. However, the employment of concentration-camp prisoners in National Socialist high-tech projects, eventually in underground facilities, became a common feature during the second half of the war. In particular, the huge so-called Mittelwerke in the Harz mountains used slave labour for

the mass production of V-1 and V-2 missiles and 'people's fighter' aircraft
(*Volksjäger*), recruiting labour from the Buchenwald concentration camp.[15]
Other major production sites for advanced weapons became 'external
camps', which obtained their manpower from the bigger and better-known
concentration camps.

One purpose of this chapter is to provoke a more critical historiographic
approach to the history of technology in Germany and especially its reference to National Socialism.[16] A thorough discussion of the economic
history of the Third Reich or the necessary differentiation of groups within
the NSDAP or military lies beyond the scope of this essay. The relationship
between National Socialism and technology remains a matter in its own
right, and the creation in practice of institutional structures as part of this
relationship is considered here only as a secondary matter.

2.1   Aeronautic research and technology, 1933–41

Distinctions must be made between phases in the brief history of
the Third Reich in order to separate out the core of National Socialist
understanding of military technology. From the appointment of Adolf
Hitler as German chancellor in 1933 until the war with the USSR and the
end of the 'lightning war' (*Blitzkrieg*) in the winter of 1941–2, it is difficult
to delineate specifically National Socialist features in the development of
German technology. Mark Walker has demonstrated the importance of the
periodization of the war and the role of technologies in the war effort for
the nuclear programme: the war economy and armament technologies followed a conventional, perhaps even conservative course as long as the
lightning war was successful.[17] Michael Neufeld points out in this volume
how guided-missile development was boosted from 1942 onwards. By comparison, even though the speed of the National Socialist military build-up
during this first phase, 1933 to 1941, was still remarkable, the new technologies that were launched in these years were not unique: the development
of jet engines for high-performance aircraft was paralleled in Britain, and
the work of the rocket pioneers around Wernher von Braun is comparable
to Marshal Tukhachevski's promotion of missile technology in the USSR
during the thirties.[18] The true Nazi contribution to armaments, suicide
technology, was developed mainly during the last three years of the war,
after the lightning war had ground to a halt in the Soviet Union. Once it
had become clear that the war had now turned into a war of attrition
which Germany was ill-equipped to fight, the National Socialists responded
with a frantic and unprecedented effort to develop high-tech weapons. It
was in this second phase of the Third Reich and the war, 1941–5, that the
quest for 'wonder weapons' began in earnest, and that both the National
Socialist leadership and also the rank and file in the workshops and design
rooms dropped any concern for the 'humanization' of warfare, opting

instead for a 'total war', which also meant 'total technology'. The development of suicide weapons after the failure of the 'wonder weapons' to change Germany's fate thus appears as the purest manifestation of the National Socialist approach to technology.

The peculiar features of National Socialist weapon technology will be examined using three examples of aeronautical technology from the final phase of the Third Reich: (1) the 'people's fighter' programme in the autumn of 1944; (2) the subsequent suicide fighters for a point-by-point defence by National Socialist elite formations; and (3) the final effort, unpowered combat gliders as fighter aircraft. These were not even the very last projects. On 12 March 1945 Göring proclaimed even more ambitious technological programmes as part of the 'new defence programme of the *Führer*', for example a new tailless jet fighter designed by the Horten brothers, and ordered production of the six-engined tailless bomber Horten H XVIII.[19] The peculiarity of National Socialist technology could also be investigated in other contemporary technologies. Parallels to giant planes can be seen in the army's development of super-heavy tanks and guns. For example, Ferdinand Porsche's combat tank of 1944 weighed 185 tons and the Adler company's tank design E 100 had tracks measuring one meter in width. Both tanks were outfitted with guns of the then sensational fifteen centimeter caliber. The final National Socialist demand was for a 1000 ton tank.[20] Excessive vengeance weapons were developed for heavy artillery like the supergun (*England-Geschütze*) and other wonder weapons.[21]

The 'wonder' aeronautical technologies addressed here in detail represent only part of the broad spectrum of efforts made during Nazi Germany to gain a winning edge in the military confrontation with the anti-Hitler coalition by resorting to extreme, forced technological development. As Neufeld shows in this volume, after 1941 the missile projects were also pushed to the extreme. Comparable weapons were subsequently developed for the arsenals of all major military powers. The sole distinctly National Socialist feature in the missile programme was the widespread use of concentration-camp slave labour.

There are a number of concepts which also appear overly ambitious and gigantic, but which are not exclusively National Socialist. The VTOL (vertical takeoff and landing) plane concepts proposed by Heinkel in 1945, the 'wasp' and 'lark' programmes, anticipate post-war experimental developments like the French SNECMA *Coléoptère* which appeared in 1958 (Figure 5.1).

The 'superfast bomber projects' (*Schnellstbomberprojekte*) from Daimler-Benz during the final days of the war may reflect a certain technological mania. Beginning in March 1944, Daimler-Benz filed a number of patents for the exotic bomber. The person in charge was none other than the engineer Fritz Nallinger, subsequently a highly respected technical director of the company during the Federal Republic. On 19 January 1945

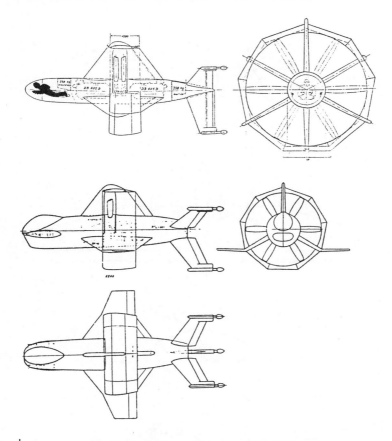

Fig. 5.1   German high-tech projects at the end of the war: Heinkel
projects 'Wespe' (wasp) and 'Lerche' (lark). (The drawings reprinted in
this chapter originated, if not otherwise indicated, at the respective
companies, and were confiscated by the victorious Allies in 1945.
Reproductions are taken from the former German originals.)

Nallinger presented the detailed project proposal as 'Reflections on the
development of a superfast bomber carrier' to the Reich Aviation Ministry
(*Reichsluftfahrtministerium*, henceforth RLM) (Figure 5.2).

The description of the mission profile for the bomber seems excessive
even by today's standards:

> The carrier plane takes off with the bomber fitted beneath it and flies to
> the limit of its range, there reaching maximum altitude. At this point the
> bomber starts its engines and separates. The carrier plane then returns to
> base, while the bomber uses its untouched fuel reserves to fly to its distant

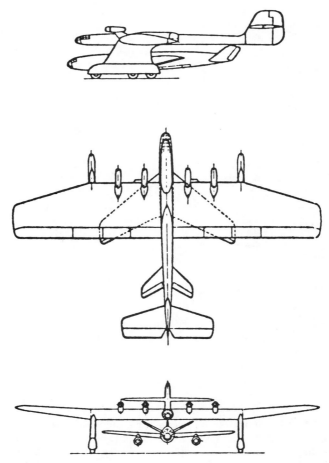

| **Fig. 5.2**   Intercontinental bomber project by Daimler-Benz (late 1944).

target. After fulfilling the long-distance mission, the crew lands the bomber at a pre-determined point of enemy coast territory in order to be picked up by a submarine. For this purpose the bomber has been designed purely as disposable equipment, and does not have an undercarriage or expensive equipment. There also is no protective equipment or guns.[22]

The Mercedes bomber project, which was submitted in four variants, may appear dubious in a number of ways, including with respect to the language in which it is portrayed, by today's standards. But the project was neither exclusively National Socialist, nor as extreme as the 'suicide technology' discussed below.

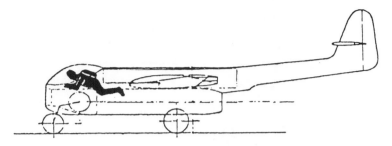

Fig. 5.3 Jet fighter project by BMW, with pilot in prone position (November 1944).

The important techno-political background of the final days of the Third Reich is not well known. Hitler's decree of 25 September 1944 for the creation of the 'people's storm' (*Volkssturm*), a final mobilization of all males able to fight, was accompanied by some last-ditch efforts to develop and adjust technologies. The 'emergency fighter programme' (*Jäger-Notprogramm*) called for simplified jet fighters that could be produced from surrogate materials (*Sparstoffe*), mainly plywood, and piloted by Nazi youth (*Hitlerjungs*) against the armadas of Allied bombers. The jet power plants and aerodynamics of these emergency fighters made these aircraft high-tech programmes indeed. When the difficulties in the implementation of this emergency programme became apparent at the end of 1944, the emergency fighter programme turned to even more radical and simplified kinds of fighting equipment. Now the call came for suicide fighters propelled by rocket motors which would be launched within sight of Allied bombers and which, according to a subsequent proposal, should down enemy aircraft by ramming them. Here parallels to the Japanese *kamikaze* approach become clear. Finally, when fuel supplies were drying up, in a last desperate campaign German expertise in gliding was applied to conceptualize unpowered combat gliders outfitted with machine guns.

The main German competitor in the manufacture of aircraft engines, BMW, also discovered long-range bombers at the end of the war, submitted a number of proposals, and even suggested their deployment from 1950 onwards. Yet a number of jet fighter proposals by this firm are more interesting. Variant 2 (figure 5.3) contains one aspect which should be evaluated as a first implementation of purely Nazi approaches to technology: the pilot is placed in a prone position in order to increase the performance limits of fighting men. Combat jet pilots can endure up to nine g in dogfights in a seated position without 'blacking out', but the human capacity to withstand g forces may be increased to fourteen g if the pilot is in a prone position. Such an arrangement hampers the general ability to pilot an air-

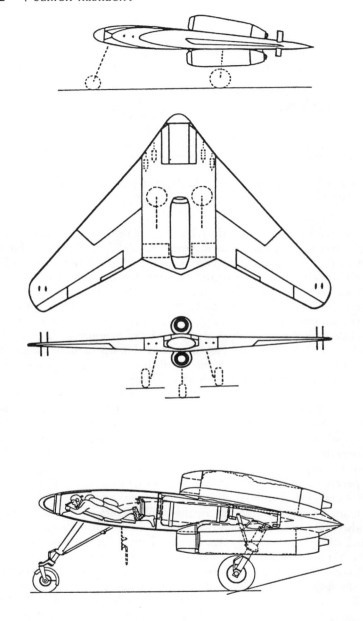

Fig. 5.4 High-tech at the end of the Third Reich: flying wing jet fighter Gotha P60. Top: three-view drawing: bottom: arrangement of pilot in prone position.

craft, but it might provide a decisive advantage in a dogfight. Only the Nazis ever opted for the prone position of pilots in combat aircraft.

A number of German firms hoped to gain a specific advantage for their combat designs by suggesting a prone position. This motive also sheds a different light on the Heinkel VTOL planes mentioned above, for they also envisaged a prone pilot. Other German companies besides BMW and Heinkel proposed designs at the end of the war based on the National Socialist concept of gaining a tactical advantage by placing excessive stress on the man in the cockpit. For example, the Gothaer Waggonfabrik sought to make a name for itself in corporate circles (figure 5.4), and the Arado company designed a mini-fighter (*Kleinstjäger*). Even the Zeppelin research centre proposed a prone pilot in their 'flying bazooka' (*Fliegende Panzer- faust*). The Henschel works in Berlin-Schönefeld, up until this time not a very successful competitor for aeronautical contracts, suggested a ground- support jet aircraft with wooden wings and a prone pilot (figure 5.5) 'who in this position was able to withstand significantly higher g-forces when intercepting or making tight turns'.[23] In March 1945 four prototypes were under construction. The rival mini-fighter from the Arado works, project AR E 381 of December 1944 (figure 5.6), was based on a more specific design philosophy. The craft had an extremely small cross section (0.45 square meters, which Arado proudly compared to the 1.8 square meters of the standard air force fighter, the Me 109) and was designed to fly as close as possible to Allied bomber formations, because 'it is a generally accepted fact that the possibility of a kill increases the more the fighter is able to close in on the enemy'.[24] 'The pilot should open fire in frontal attack at the closest possible range with the one MK 108 [machine gun].' Because the rocket fighter would carry fuel sufficient for only two attacks, the plane carried austere munitions, limited to only forty-five rounds. The survival kit for the pilot consisted of a small landing skid and brake parachute. Superb piloting abilities would have been required to land such an aircraft without power ('dead stick') and with such minimal shock absorbers. The rocket motor was also dangerous: 'they apparently were not fully aware of the dangers posed by T-fuel for AR, which blew pilots of the Me 163 into small pieces in unsuccessful landings'.

The selection of a prone arrangement for the pilot in order to push fighting men to the limits of their potential performance, a unique feature not found in aircraft designs in other countries, indicates a first specific aspect of National Socialist approaches to military technology. A second step in this direction was the extreme lowering of the age limit for fighting personnel and the recruitment of teenagers. Parallel to the draft of Nazi youth to the people's storm, the air force accepted people's fighter concepts which envisaged adolescent pilots (see section 2.2 below). The place of youth in National Socialist ideology played an important role in these developments. A third specific National Socialist aspect is seen in the

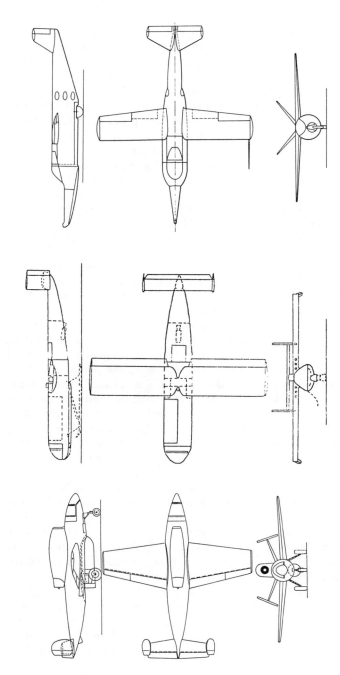

Fig. 5.5 German combat aircraft projects with pilot in prone position. Left: ground attack aircraft Henschel HS 132 (March 1945); centre: project Arado E 381; right: 'Flying bazooka' by Zeppelin.

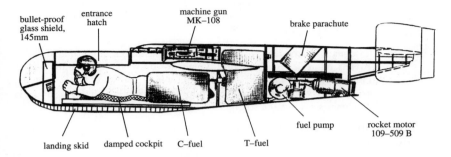

Fig. 5.6 General arrangement drawing. Arado AR E 381 mini-fighter (December 1944) (Archiv Kurz).

decision to break with established military traditions and to opt for suicide missions (see section 2.3 below). Not even this stage was the last of the desperate approaches to armaments technology and usage. Unpowered fighter aircraft or combat gliders were designed in the final days of the Third Reich which made no attempt to provide fighting men with equal armaments and whose utility as a weapon rested solely with the Herculean efforts of the heroes in the cockpits (see section 2.4 below). Thus the double nature of National Socialist weapons technology emerges: (1) the glorification of death, the foreseeable fall, accompanied by an enormous concentration of force, and (2) the Herculean performance.

The three examples scrutinized in the following sections highlight pure National Socialist approaches to armaments technology. First of all, excessive demands are made on the abilities of fighting men, in this instance pilots, mirroring elitist conceptions of the role of German soldiers. Secondly, the programmes indicate the excessive use of manpower resources, calling for boys to combat Allied troops. Finally, there is a culmination in suicide weapons, the final step in the same direction, to total war.

2.2   The people's fighter

The people's fighter programme embodies far-reaching National Socialist ambitions to impose their own concepts on the industry programmes for combat aircraft. 'The control of air force supplies was transferred to the Minister for Armaments and War Production, [Albert] Speer during the winter of 1941/1942, when it had become obvious that the RLM was unable to ensure sufficient support and corresponding technological developments', notes a post-war publication in a remarkably partisan manner.[25]

Karl-Otto Saur, a high-ranking National Socialist official (*NS-Hauptdienstleiter*) and engineer subordinate to Speer,[26] was made responsible for the fighter programme,

> whose main objective was among others the fastest creation of a so-called 'people's fighter', a construction which not only was to be built with a minimum effort of material and time, but which also should be easy to fly. Nazi youth were supposed to pilot this people's fighter in mass deployments against the stream of Allied bombers.

Adolf Galland, a combat ace and General of Fighter Pilots, gives a more precise hint:

> The Flying Hitler Youth [*Flieger-Hitlerjugend*, henceforth FHJ], boys aged sixteen, seventeen, and eighteen, were to be deployed as the last levy for the defence of the Reich without training in motorized flying or interception as pilots of the new 'people's fighter', a single-engined jet fighter. Thank God, this 'people's storm in the air' did not come into being ... Mass deployment was prepared with juvenile pilots after cursory training in gliding while production and missions was to have been supported and controlled by the *Gauleiter* [regional Party leaders]. The people's fighter was supposed to provide some sort of '*levée en masse*' in the air.[27]

The exploitation of adolescents by the air force had been prepared. The members of the FHJ, numbering 78,000 in 1938, usually started their career in aviation by building model planes. Later they progressed to gliding, where three different qualifications could be earned (the so-called A-, B- and C-certificates). 'Often air force bases were visited, where Hitler Youth [*Hitlerjugend*, henceforth HJ] were permitted to join flights in bombers and two-seater combat aircraft – yet only in training flights and not in combat missions.'[28] There was no other air force in the world where youngsters were allowed to fly in military aircraft. Apparently, the National Socialist Flying Corps (*Nationalsozialistisches Fliegerkorps*, henceforth NSFK), the parent organization for the FHJ, was 'the true promoter and initiator of the idea' of a people's fighter: 'if the people's storm deployed in ground-fighting was to use a "people's rifle" and a "people's pistol", then it was only reasonable to let the NSFK pilots fly a "people's fighter"'.[29]

The National Socialist leadership had high hopes with regard to the juvenile HJ pilots. Colonel General Alfred Keller, the head of the NSFK, 'complained about the "lack of guts" of air force pilots. He would demand more combat devotedness from his HJ pilots. One kill per mission must be the rule.'[30]

The preparations for the required training programme again reflect Nazi ideology.

> Training aircraft shall mainly be built by the NSFK itself and an unpowered version should serve for the quick training of a full age-cohort of the HJ. If possible, they should proceed directly from glider training to

mission 162 flights without intermediate piston engine aircraft. Details of both the shooting training, which should be carried out in a suitable manner on the ground, and of the full training program, shall soon be determined with the prominent participation of holders of the Iron Cross who had been members of the HJ or NSFK.[31]

In late autumn 1944, numerous HJ members were commanded to take training exercises in gliding.

The shortage of fuel halted the training of voluntary HJ pilots in people's fighter jets on 4 February 1945. The larger part of the HJ trainees were then transferred after meagre training to the infantry for use in the final battle for Berlin. The NSFK, however, continued working with unpowered gliders until Soviet tanks arrived.

The invitation for tenders for the people's fighter was sent to Arado, Blohm & Voss, Focke-Wulf, Heinkel and Junkers on 8 September 1944. Focke-Wulf excelled in addressing the ideological aspects of the tender with two submissions, named 'people's aircraft' (*Volksflugzeug*) and 'people's racer' (*Volksflitzer*). Others like the Horten brothers also competed without invitation for the contract, submitting project H X, with a juvenile pilot in a prone position.[32] The required tempo for prototype development remained unbelievably rapid, exceeding any standard in the aviation industry: on 20 September 1944, twelve days after the formal invitation, the companies had to furnish full sets of drawings of the people's fighter to the RLM. On 23 September 1944 'a decisive "people's fighter review" took place at the headquarters of the Reich Marshal' and was chaired by Göring himself (the main tenders are illustrated in figure 5.7).[33] The location of the meeting was the Wolfschanze near Rastenburg, Hitler's final command post in the East. 'Göring and Saur reportedly enthused over [the idea of] thousands of people's fighters taking off from highways against the streams of Allied bombers.'[34] The beginning of mass production was set at the meeting for 1 January 1945.

The then head of aircraft development at the Arado company remembers the conditions under which the people's fighter was made:

> ... one day, in mid September 1944, an official of the Technical Agency showed up without prior warning at the development section which had been moved to Landshut in Silesia. He wanted to create a light fighter project with a BMW 003 power plant within a couple of days. He apparently knew very well what should be made. He did not leave the design room for two full days and tried to steer the project into the direction he desired ... A few days later the industry projects were presented to the [government] Fighter Staff. To the best of my memory, there must have been nearly a dozen, because most of the firms, especially those whose planes had been eliminated in the big type reduction programme of 1 July, tried to get an order in the fighter sector by submitting more than one project. Some of these projects had been redesigned in terms of weight and performance at the last minute after the discussion of other drafts.[35]

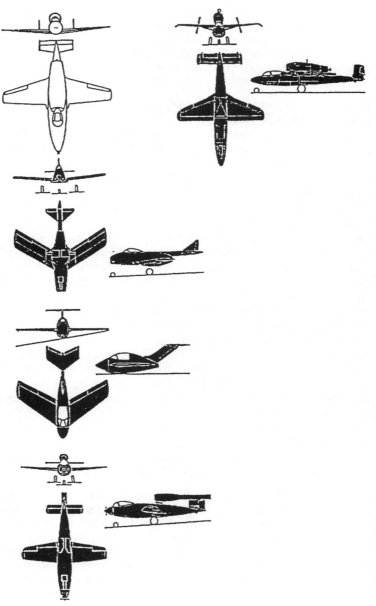

Fig. 5.7 Bids by German industry for the Emergency Fighter Programme (*Jägernotprogramm*), 1944. Left, from top: Arado Flugzeugwerke Project E 580; Blohm & Voss Schiffswerft BV P211; Junkers Flugzeug- und Motorenwerke, EF126. Right: the winning Heinkel He 162.

The Heinkel company, which sought to re-enter high-tech programmes and which laboured with problems of capacity utilization,[36] was especially able to keep pace. The firm received the order for mass production of their project one week after submission of the tender on 15 September 1944. Blohm & Voss, the main competitor with Project P 211 (see figure 5.7), was finally beaten. The maiden flight of the first prototype He 162 salamander took place on 6 December 1944, sixty-nine days after receipt of the contract. This document stated that the Heinkel works should commence production of 1000 people's fighters on 1 January 1945, the Junkers company should launch another batch of 1000 planes, and the Mittelwerke GmbH, the underground facility exploiting prisoners from concentration camps mentioned above, should build another 2000 aircraft. Later, in a significant increase in effort, the output of Heinkel's people's fighters was planned at 1000 planes per month (Figure 5.8).[37] The Junkers works were going to mass-produce the people's fighter in another underground facility, the Tartun salt mine near Stassfurt. Alongside production, full-scale engineering and preparatory work was undertaken underground: in the cellars of the famed Schwechat brewery near Vienna, in a department store in Mariahilfer Street in Vienna, and especially in a cave near Mödling in the Austrian Alps (code-named Languste).

Besides the inhumane intent to use adolescents as pilots, the people's fighter programme incorporated further dimensions of National Socialist military technology: the accelerated timetables and the speed of innovation, where one novelty was to be followed by an even more innovative piece of armament at ever shorter intervals. In sum, when examining National Socialist technology, it is not only a matter of looking at the finished project. Other dimensions are *how* it was made, and at *what cost*. These notions remain multifaceted: they include the immeasurable human costs in slave labour, just to mention the extreme pole. The people's fighter programme was explicitly designated a 'forced action' (*Gewaltaktion*), as Saur noted:

> The one-seater single-jet mini-fighter designed by Heinkel, which after thorough examination has been selected by the main development committee for production, is released for the immediate launch of serial production ... at a monthly output of 1000 units for the time being. Final development, full-scale engineering, testing, and production will be carried out in strictest concentration as a forced action in a joint undertaking of the administrative offices and plants concerned ... The *Führer* agreed that leadership of the forced action is entrusted to director general Kessler.[38]

Common practices of testing and proving new equipment were abandoned for the overriding goal: technical progress, as fast as possible. The awards used to motivate the design team for this forced action seem meagre: 10,000 cigarettes and 500 bottles of vermouth.[39]

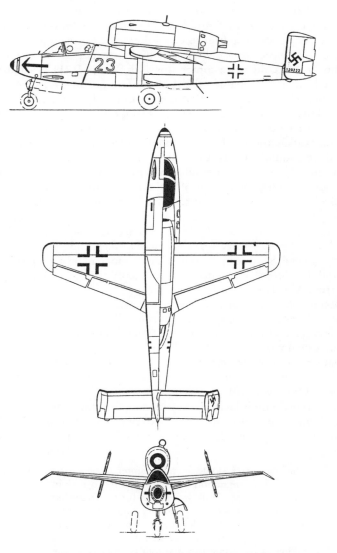

Fig. 5.8 Heinkel He 162 'Volksjäger' (People's Fighter), the winner of the *Jägernotprogramm*.

The [amount] of time worked per week remained a secondary [consideration]: ninety hours were worked in the first week alone. Later we fell back to the seventy-hour week, because the shorter work time was compensated for by a higher speed of work. The designers rarely slept on their mattresses at their work stations.[40]

The final assembly of the people's fighter was supposed to take place at air force bases.

The final weeks of the people's fighter design team in spring 1945 again indicate the absurdity of the whole project. Construction efforts continued until the last possible moment:

> Otto Butter [deputy chief designer] was ordered to evacuate the more important engineers of the design and project section by rail ... to the Gandersheim Heinkel plant in the Harz mountains. The remaining staff was to be deployed with the people's storm. Because the Allies were in the vicinity of Gandersheim, the train had to be re-routed after a one-week bewildering trip to Jenbach in Tyrol. There they got instructions from the Tyrolean *Gauleiter* Hofer to proceed into Germany's pre-war boundaries [the *Altreich*]. Heinkel and Frydag then agreed that senior engineer Butter should escape with the very best technicians to Bavaria, some thirty-five people, in order to continue work on the people's fighter on a reduced scale. Using part of the He 162 drawings moved to Jenbach, a small team of technicians worked on technical improvements of the mini-fighter in a Landsberg youth hostel until the Americans occupied the location.[41]

The clauses of the contract for the 'one-seater single-jet power plant mini-fighter' of 29 September 1944 warned that

> given the harshness of conditions an uncompromising fulfillment of the task is possible only if any additional equipment or changes are dispensed with. Furthermore, there is agreement that serial production will be based on the first drawings and that the risk of a potential failure escaping notice has to be accepted.[42]

In technological terms Heinkel's people's fighter represented an emergency product. The plane was built partly of metal, partly of wood. The centre fuselage carrying the power plant at the back was made of metal. Wings and ailerons were made of plywood. In the summer of 1942 an instruction was sent out to spare light metal in German aircraft manufacturing:

> According to the instruction by State Secretary General Milch of 17 August 1942, a conversion committee was established in the Industrial Council with the task of ensuring far-reaching savings of light metal by conversion to steel, wood, or other materials in air force equipment.[43]

Wooden aircraft or wooden parts for planes are also found in other countries. Yet jet fighters made from plain wood remain a German speciality.[44] The western high-performance aircraft that used wood resorted to choices of exotic timbers unavailable to German industry. Two production chains centred in Erfurt and Stuttgart were formed to make the wooden parts of the people's fighter, including a great number of small craft firms. Ernst Heinkel, who as the owner of his company was the nominal head of the programme, gives a vivid description of the production conditions in the winter of 1944–5:

Production was farmed out to numerous plants and shops above and beneath the ground. Instead of rail transportation, which was increasingly destroyed by air attacks, columns of trucks ferried the parts to the assembly points. Smaller parts were carried by messengers with backpacks.[45]

The famous designer apparently found it difficult to recollect the specific Nazi aspects of this project: the 'messengers' were not ordinary civilians; the backpack campaign for people's fighter production was 'a HJ action'.[46] The official organization of these efforts is worth noting:

The manufacturing of the wooden parts (wings, ailerons, etc.) was planned in the form of a collective action by the SS, the NSFK, timber shops, and industry, under the leadership of SS-official Dr Kurt May.[47]

Allegedly because of faulty cement, the wooden planking on the leading edge of the wing dismembered on 10 December 1944 during a flight demonstration of the people's fighter before Party and army officials, causing a crash, killing the pilot and dampening the enthusiasm of the guests.

The people's fighter showed other serious shortcomings in addition to inadequate materials. Its weapon, a single Rheinmetall MK 108 machine gun, was adjusted to a firing distance of only 450 meters – well within the range of the multi-barreled defensive armour of the Allied 'flying fortresses'. According to official calculations, a people's fighter needed to score at least three direct hits to fell a bomber, thus a suicide attack probably would be necessary in order to be successful. With the less powerful MG 151 built into the Heinkel-produced people's fighter, twenty to twenty-five hits would be needed. Adolf Galland, someone who would not be suspected of being critical towards the National Socialists, repeatedly submitted his criticism of the whole concept, at Hitler's request also in a special memorandum for the *Führer*. Galland writes in his memoirs that two leading aircraft designers joined him in his scepticism:

Messerschmitt and Tank shared the opinion with me that these specifications and conditions must produce an aircraft which would hardly be interesting in technical and tactical performance, and which would presumably end in a complete failure. Even the calculations indicated a minimum in every area ... I had opposed the people's fighter project from the beginning in the sharpest manner. In contrast to the founding fathers of the idea, I had only professional objections, such as too limited performance, endurance, and firepower, poor visibility from the cockpit and insufficient flight safety. Furthermore, I was convinced that the plane could not be successfully deployed until the end of the war.[48]

Messerschmitt submitted his criticism in a letter dated 23 October 1944:

(1) the technical requirement is wrong because the tasks of this people's fighter can be fulfilled better with existing and proven aircraft ... (2) the assumption is mistaken that the single-engine jet fighter will enable us to

throw enormous numbers of aircraft into combat in spring and summer of 1945.[49]

Messerschmitt continued with his opposition until May of 1945![50]

Actual experience showed that the people's fighter was far from being a truly operational fighting vehicle. When the machine gun was fired, muzzle pressure tore away parts of the aluminium covering. The landing gear showed weaknesses. The ribs of the leading wing edge were under-dimensioned. Lateral stability was poor. Stalling characteristics needed to be improved. Since adequate solutions such as the lengthening of the air-frame were impossible because of the tight production schedule, unrealistic emergency measures such as the addition of extra ballast weights in the nose of the aircraft were introduced, which in turn reduced the flight per-formance of the design. Pilot routines added to the shortcomings of the vehicle. In order to reduce high landing speeds, air force pilots preferred to 'slip' fighters, but manoeuvring the people's fighter into a small oblique angle to the landing path in order to slow down the high landing speed of 200 kilometers per hour regularly produced a deadly effect: one rudder was caught by the jet exhaust like a ping-pong ball by a fountain, and collap-sed, ending in a fatal crash.

General Galland notes wryly that people's fighter technology was not continued after the war, which confirms him in his scepticism: 'in contrast to many other German projects, add-on engineering did not take place on this basis [the He 162], neither in the West nor in the East'.[51]

2.3   Suicide aircraft

The peak of National Socialist influence on armament technology dismissed, among other things, the idea of the soldier fighting for his survi-val, and knowingly built the death of the warrior into the concept of some military equipment. Such an approach denies all standards of defensive combat and reflects the pure desire for destruction which dominated the latter days of the Third Reich.

Contemplating the threat of an Allied invasion on the Continent, the air force officer and devoted National Socialist Heinrich Lange founded

> a small group of air force members who supported suicide [Selbstop-ferungs-, henceforth SO] missions. Following a precisely defined plan, one landing craft of the invasion fleet would be sunk by one SO plane. The SO pilot had to steer the SO aircraft, which was designed as disposable, into the target until impact, thereby causing his death.[52]

The prominent German flyer Hanna Reitsch, who flight-tested both tech-nological prototypes of the SO concept, the manned V-1 as well as the Messerschmitt Me 328, defended the idea even after the war:

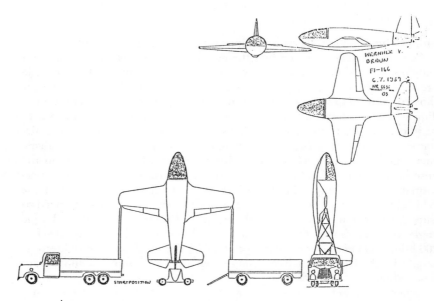

| Fig. 5.9   Wernher von Braun's rocket plane of 1939 (Kunz Archive).

> The suicide mission called for people who were prepared to sacrifice themselves with the clear conviction that nothing else would rescue them. This position had nothing to do with misguided idealism, because it was not only a question of inner preparedness, but also of extremely sober calculation.[53]

In the winter of 1943–4, the (Nazi-founded) German Academy of Aeronautical Research convened for the SO project

> experts of all war technology-related areas, including explosives, torpedoes, navigation and radio, shipbuilding, naval officers and experienced aircraft designers. Generals in charge of combat fighter planes delegated representatives. There were also aeronautical physicians.[54]

Remarkably enough, the National Socialist leadership was unenthusiastic. The RLM rejected the whole idea. Hanna Reitsch submitted the project to Hitler on 28 February 1944, 'who also refused it, but who allowed further work in this direction'.[55] 'In the meantime', the same source continues, 'thousands of voluntary applications came in. First a group of only seventy men was selected, while the others were to be called up after the flying equipment had been finished.'[56] Applicants for the mission signed the following declaration: 'I hereby report myself to the SO mission as pilot of the manned gliding bomb. I am aware of the fact that

Fig. 5.10   'Vengeance weapon 1', the V-1.

this mission will end with death [signature].'[57] This technological concept had been under consideration for a number of years in Nazi Germany. An early submission stems from the hero of German rocket technology, Wernher von Braun. For undisclosed reasons, he sketched a vertical take-off rocket plane in 1939 (figure 5.9), which clearly resembles the features of later point-by-point defence fighters on suicide missions.

After other vehicles were rejected, SO experiments started in earnest with a manned version of 'vengeance weapon 1', the buzz-bomb V-1 (figure 5.10). The programme received the code name 'Reichenberg', a reference to the capital of the formerly Czechoslovakian territory 'Reichsgau Sudetenland'. The manned flying bombs were called 'Reichenberg apparatus' (*Reichenberg-Geräte*). Perhaps the most distinctive feature of the SO planes was the lack of landing gear; the aircraft were not supposed to return back to base. In the words of Reitsch: the 'mission equipment [was] a single-seater, powered, without the possibility of landing, i.e. without landing skid or landing flaps'.[58]

The SS became responsible for the programme in due course. Hanna Reitsch describes how the engineer and SS official Dr Otto Skorzeny came in to save the project. Skorzeny was one of the troubleshooters in the National Socialist system, the man who in a bold mission had freed Mussolini from jail in Gran Sasso in July of 1943, and who arrested Admiral Horthy in Hungary in October of 1944. 'Skorzeny was sent by Himmler, who had informed him about our plan ... Independent from us, he also came up with the idea of using the V-1.'[59]

There were even efforts to build a manned version of the V-2, the intermediate-range missile designed by von Braun. Given the context of the war, subsequent claims that the piloted version of Aggregate 9 (A 9) 'did not have any military significance'[60] are hard to believe. A cockpit and wings were added. A technical description gives details:

> Computations showed that under optimal conditions we could reach a shooting distance of 550 kilometers with this design. This was twice the range of the A-4. Our missile grew into a fully automated supersonic aircraft. Its flight path led it through the layer of air around the globe and through nearly airless space ... Since spring 1940 our windtunnel was operating successfully to develop suitable wings and to provide the design data required by the engineers and flight path specialists.[61]

A report co-authored by von Braun illustrates the hubris of the manned rocket plane: 'if it were put on top of a booster with 200 tons thrust, the pilot would be able to cross the Atlantic with the A-9, and with an even heavier booster the A-9 ought to be able to reach orbit'.[62]

In the autumn of 1944 the RLM issued another invitation for tenders in the emergency fighter programme, calling for a simple point-by-point defence aircraft which could be produced cheaply and easily. Because at the time Allied bombers needed only short flights to reach their targets, the fighters had to be able to take off in sight of the attackers and to intercept them before they arrived over their destinations.[63] This demand could only be satisfied with rocket propulsion, a troublesome, if not dangerous, and rarely tested technology. In any event, the fighter planes conceived in this tender turned into suicide weapons, even though saving the life of the pilot was one of the original design goals.

The three biggest German aviation concerns participated in this tender: Messerschmitt submitted the wooden P 1104, Junkers model EF 127 'Walli', and Heinkel type P 1077 'Julia'. But the contract was given to an outsider who originally had not been invited to the tender, engineer Erich Bachem, a former director of the Fieseler works, the designers of the V-1. During the last phases of the war, Bachem established his own enterprise, the Bachem-Werke GmbH in Waldsee in Württemberg. His main asset was the design drawings of the winning BP-20 (figure 5.11). It may have helped the new firm that – according to the SS Main Office – it 'worked on a special task by order of the head of the SS and Commander of the reserve army and all offices and agencies will have to support it'.[64] Other aircraft companies also entered into a closer relationship with the SS, for example by taking more and more labour from concentration camps.

The leading companies did not capitulate. They tried to use improved submissions to eliminate the newcomer Bachem from the race for the

Fig. 5.11   Bachem 'Natter' point defence fighter (Deutsches Museum München).

expected mass-production order. Junkers assumed that the RLM had found the concept of their EF 126, with the wooden components and the Schmidt-Argus buzz pipe at the back, to be too close to the Reichenberg apparatus. Thus Junkers submitted a heavily redesigned version, the EF 127 (see figure 5.12), propelled by a liquid rocket motor from the Walter company. Heinkel also repeatedly offered improvements of model Julia, 'an intermediate solution between a manned flak rocket and an inexpensive fast mini-fighter'.[65] On VE day prototypes of the Heinkel machines were nearly completed. One specimen of the Junkers design was completed under Soviet supervision and tested. Junkers test pilot Mathies was killed during the trials.[66]

The winning Bachem design (figure 5.12) was of all the bids the most thorough proposal and openly incorporated features of a National Socialist technological ideology during the final phase of the Third Reich. The whole bow of the 'adder' (*Natter*), as the vehicle was called, was designed to house a battery of unguided rockets. Rescuing the pilot presented problems: 'after firing the rockets the centre of gravity of the machine was shifted to such an extent that it could no longer fly'.[67] In aerodynamic terms this judgment was the death verdict for any attempt to build it as a flyable aircraft. Yet the report already cited continued:

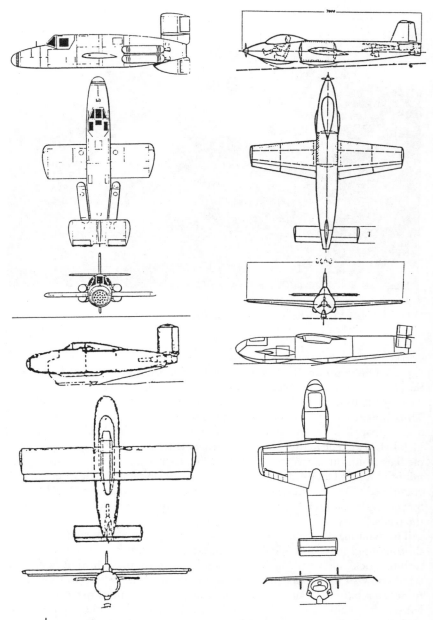

Fig. 5.12 Submissions by German industry for the Emergency Fighter Programme (*Jägernotprogramm*), 1944. Clockwise from left: Bachem, Junkers, Messerschmitt, Heinkel.

The rescue of the pilot at high speed caused special problems. In order to find a feasible solution, a separation of the front section was considered. After separation the main parachute would pull the pilot's seat backwards, saving at the same time the most expensive instruments in the cockpit. Because in the context of total war even the adder could not be deployed as purely disposable equipment, the rear section of the fuselage with the power plant and flight controls was also designed to separate. These precious parts would also be saved by parachute.[68]

The first flight of the Bachem construction took place on 25 February 1945, using a dummy pilot for the test. Afterwards 'the RLM immediately demanded a launch with a manned vehicle'.[69] According to a better-informed source, in the meantime the SS had taken over responsibility for the adder and tried to accelerate the programme.[70] A first lieutenant, Lothar Siebert, volunteered to pilot the maiden flight. He was killed during the first start at the end of February, 1945:

> The head of the pilot must have been jerked backwards, which made him lose consciousness or immediately suffer a broken neck ... The craft turned into an inverted flight position and disappeared in fast horizontal flight. About a minute later it exploded.[71]

Experimental testing with the adder was continued until April 1945. There were twenty-two launches, four of them manned. Otto Pabst judges that 'development work for the Ba 349 adder can only be understood in the emergency situation of the war ... Taking into account the expected stresses [on the plane], the [wooden] construction was a more or less war-related risk.'[72]

2.4   Unpowered combat gliders

When fuel supplies dried up during the last months of the war, the very last series of desperate projects to fight Allied bombers were heavily armoured combat gliders without power plants. Plans to use unpowered combat planes to ram Allied bombers or to fire upon them at close range did not proceed beyond windtunnel and prototype testing. But the concept fitted directly into the people's fighter idea. A historical account of the people's fighter project states that in particular a 'combat glider', which was to be 'towed by a fighter to an appropriate height', was considered for training.[73] The Hamburg company Blohm & Voss in particular proposed a number of combinations of combat gliders and suicide aircraft. The description of project P 214 is revealing:

> Officially designated 'a manned anti-aircraft bomb', this was an aircraft which, directed by a pilot, would bring a heavy explosive charge close to an enemy bomber formation. At a sufficient distance from the formation the pilot would bail out and detonate the by now unmanned aircraft with

its charge. Because parachuting during the approach was theoretically possible, [but] presumably was practically excluded, one could label this a 'suicide bomb'.[74]

After a series of trials with glider aircraft, Blohm & Voss decided on a final project, designated 'combat glider BV 40', a year before the official proclamation of the people's storm (figure 5.13).

> The Technical Director and Chief Contractor of the Blohm & Voss company, Dr Richard Vogt, designed such a gliding fighter without propulsion in the spring of 1943. Four prototypes were made under the designation BV 40. The greatest emphasis was placed upon simple construction and the use of surrogate materials. Dr Vogt dealt intensively with the people's fighter concept and became the most dangerous rival of Heinkel in the subsequent competition.[75]

The craft BV 40 'was conceived as a relatively small fighter without propulsion, which would be built at minimum production cost and labour input in mass series and be pitted against Allied bomber units'. The *Book of German Aviation History* describes the mission concept as follows: 'after disengaging, the prone pilot in the BV 40 should attack the bomber formation in a dive of about twenty degrees at a speed of 400 to 500 kilometers per hour with one single burst of fire, break through, and land somewhere'.[76]

Another early submission for this technology, once again long before the official proclamation of the concept, came from the Messerschmitt company, famed for its fighter aircraft. In cooperation with the German Research Agency for Gliding (*Deutsche Forschungsanstalt für Segelflug*), the firm designed type Me 328 (figure 5.14), a 'one-seater fighter which would be carried to the enemy bomber formation and then carry out its attacks gliding down'. Flight trials by Hanna Reitsch and others showed meagre results: 'flight characteristics were not excellent, but sufficed for the intended SO mission'. The composite airframe of the combat glider, made from wood and pressed layers of other materials,[77] did not stand the stresses of flight manoeuvres, 'so that testing was discontinued after the first fatal crash'.[78]

A parallel project of Messerschmitt's arch rival Heinkel was conceived right from the start as 'manned disposable equipment'. The Heinkel designers began with the assumption 'that apparently the pilot was unable to bear the high g-forces during the launch'.[79]

There also were mixes between unpowered gliders and rocket-propelled suicide weapons. For instance, the Zeppelin research centre suggested a manned 'flying bazooka', which included a 'propulsion on demand' set of solid-fuel rockets. This construction would be towed 'by an aircraft starting to intercept bombers and ... be separated at an appropriate moment. Protected by an armour plate the pilot could release his rockets close to the

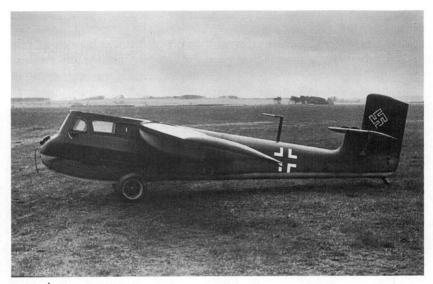

Fig. 5.13   Unpowered combat glider, Blohm and Voss BV 40 (Deutsches Museum München).

Fig. 5.14   Messerschmitt's unpowered fighter Me 328 (Deutsches Museum München).

target.'[80] The pilot of the craft did not have much to release; the small vehicle carried two unguided rockets. The firm submitted additional designs, for example the concept of a ramming fighter. Like other last-minute submissions, these designs did not proceed beyond the stage of experimental development.

3   A new historians' dispute?

The debate surrounding these irrational projects entails to some extent a critique of the historiography of technology in Germany. This literature does not deny the artifacts under scrutiny, but rather often defends them as extraordinary technological accomplishments achieved under extremely adverse conditions; the ingenuity of German engineers in their selection of exotic technological solutions is praised, accompanied by bitter attacks against those critical voices which dare to trespass into this arcanum of technological history.[81] What is required is a specific 'historians' dispute' (*Historikerstreit*[82]) over the historical verdict on Nazi technology: did German industry and German engineers only carry out unrealistic projects because they were forced to do so, or did they make their own contribution to the fanaticism of the last days of the Third Reich?

For instance, the people's fighter project demonstrates that industry correctly foresaw the forthcoming call for inhumane, low-tech fighter aircraft. After the war, Ernst Heinkel, the head of the firm that made this aircraft, understandably put it another way:

> Saur's ambition that this aircraft so to speak must become a 'people's fighter', with which after very brief training Nazi youth could have taken off for the 'defence of Germany' of course far exceeded reality and fits the misguided fanaticism of those days.[83]

However, in 1944 Heinkel did not say that the people's fighter programme 'of course far exceeded reality'; he built the aircraft instead. The programme was also not 'so to speak ... a people's fighter'; this was the official designation of the project.

Thus the usual assumption that German arms makers merely satisfied the demands of state or Party organs needs to be challenged. The NSFK allegedly started to recruit juvenile pilots for missions in such aircraft in the spring of 1944, long before the official programme for a people's fighter was launched the following autumn, demanding that the registering volunteers forego the otherwise mandatory air force officer training. When National Socialist officials proclaimed the cynical concept of 'people's defence', they did not ask for something previously unknown; instead they gave political credit to preconceived technocratic concepts within the ranks of industry and the Party.

The jargon used in the historiography of the people's fighter reveals a great deal about the persistence of idiosyncratic Nazi attitudes towards technology. One study states that the Heinkel design 'additionally had one small blemish: it required an experienced pilot or at least specially trained flying personnel',[84] thereby mirroring the people's storm ideology. Another account of the Heinkel jet states: 'using a modern term: "disposable equipment" [*Verschleissgerät*] was required', but why should such a term be 'modern'? Moreover, the 'time constraints set by the RLM ... indeed were almost unreal'. Why 'almost'? Such statements strongly suggest that fascination with the Nazi approach to military technology is not limited to the year 1945.

The literature often prefers to describe the failure of the demonstration flight of the people's fighter in 1944 as an annoying trifle – without the slightest appreciation of the fact that, taken together, poor cement, insufficient gluing techniques and wooden jet fighters symbolically mirror the hypertrophy of technological development in the decaying Third Reich.

This bias is certainly not limited to studies of the people's fighter. An aviation history states without comment with regard to suicide aircraft that: 'in the final days of the war trials took place with manned V-1s with the mission of ramming Allied bomber formations'.[85] A recent account of the adder project, reflecting well the language of the National Socialists, also says without emotion that: 'during work on the project a decision was made for a combination between aircraft and missile as disposable equipment'.[86] The continuity of the jargon is once again impressive. The author of the report seems to share the regret that the adder could not be deployed as 'pure disposable equipment'. The rescue of the human pilot was not as important as saving the 'precious parts' of the aircraft: 'because the rear section with the power plant and controls could be completely incorporated into a new machine, the loss of the remaining parts was tolerable'.

In the meantime, some participants in this strange arms race have shown reservations about the concept. The former head of the design department of the Arado works speaks of 'unclear thoughts' and reports that: 'the testing of the Ba 349 incurred many disagreeable interruptions because of the lack of preparatory work and the haste in which it was carried out'.[87] The author was also astonished by the organizational mess at the end of the war: 'that work was continued until the arrival of enemy troops, despite the fact that the Ba 349 had already been cancelled by the Armaments Staff on 5 January 1945, can only be understood in the psychosis linked with the approaching end of the war'.[88]

The evaluation of the armament projects briefly portrayed here remains very controversial. There is a mainstream of writers, mostly retired industry men and, rarely, professional historians, who, accompanied by a few conservative historians, care for military history and the history of technology with a benevolent attitude. This group is confronting a small group of authors who dare to write in a critical tone about National Socialist technology. For example, the historian Karl-Heinz Ludwig, an authority on technology during the Third Reich, quotes with reference to the people's fighter a bitterly polemical letter by Fritz Hahn (an author of a book on German secret weapons) which sought to dismiss the significance of this technological project: 'for the critical expert the "plywood bird He 162" as a weapon for fighting was nothing more "than a joke", and "even experienced pilots did not master this machine"'.[89]

One should expect a stiff controversy about the appropriate assessment of the technological remnants of the Third Reich. But given the horrific legacy of National Socialism, those authors who still find technological excellence and nothing else in all those people's fighters, suicide weapons and combat gliders must be confronted with the full picture: slave labour used to make the weapons, unrealistic performance and production requirements, and the personal record of the individuals involved in directing these frantic efforts. There now are a few historians critical about National Socialist technology whose writings should challenge the authors cited above: Andreas Heinemann-Grüder, Karl-Heinz Ludwig, Herbert Mehrtens, Michael Neufeld, Hartmut Petzold, Helmuth Trischler and others.

Future studies in this vein should not investigate only the political attitudes of engineers and plant managers. This has been researched sufficiently by Heinemann-Grüder, Hortleder and Kogon,[90] who have found that if need be German engineers explain their political roles in abstract terms, and that despite their self-perception as innovative men, when pressed they tend to take more conservative positions.

These findings point to a more general context in which an analytically more profound investigation can be made of the engagement of technical elites in the downfall of the Third Reich. Anglo-Saxon authors in particular remain impressed by the turn German technologists made towards National Socialist concepts during the last days of the war – when the average citizen, the notorious 'man in the street', was convinced that the war had been lost and that survival was the order of the day. Jeffrey Herf[91] has suggested identifying the high-tech orientation of the National Socialists as 'reactionary modernism'. He is referring to a more general debate about 'progressive reaction' and is not specifically talking about armaments. This debate has already been stirred up in the fine arts.[92] It might well be the case that the formula of technological progress that serves reactionary purposes may help provide a deeper understanding of the interrelationships between engineers, industry and National Socialism. This formula would fit both the self-esteem of the engineers and the objective role that the system offered to them.

Karl-Heinz Ludwig has contributed the useful notion of 'self-mobilization', which Trischler highlights in this volume. The concept seems to be perfectly suited to understand the extraordinary commitment of the Nazi technologists during the final years of the German war effort. The voluntary will of those individuals to transcend accepted standards in the fulfillment of professional duties proved very helpful during the last spasm of the National Socialist will to prevail, even resorting to technologies which obviously were of limited military value. Trischler correctly emphasizes that certainly not every engineer was fiercely motivated to work frantically in the apocalyptic scenario of the collapse of the Third Reich, and that there were grey areas of motivation. Yet the combination of the National Socialist leadership principle (*Führerprinzip*) with the psychological forces of group behaviour under stress nevertheless produced a high rate of 'mobilization'.

6 | 'Area research' and 'spatial planning' from the Weimar Republic to the German Federal Republic: creating a society with a spatial order under National Socialism

MECHTILD RÖSSLER

1 Introduction

> Like all great cities, it was made of irregularity, change, falling behind, collision of things and affairs, indescribable points of silence in between, the beat and eternal disonance and dislocation of all rhythms with each other, and in general it resembled a boiling bubble, which moves around in a vessel made of the durable material of houses, laws, regulations and historical traditions.[1]

Musil, who rendered the masterly description of the city of Vienna at the turn of the century given above, simultaneously directs our attention to the densely developed environment, this permanent material, into which other conditions of society are inscribed. History that has taken on the forms of stone, tar and concrete can be fundamentally changed only with difficulty and in long cycles, if one disregards individual phenomena and destruction through war.

This structure surrounds us and in a way influences our everyday life and behaviour. The petty bourgeois nuclear family has imprinted its structure upon the living-room–bedroom–children's-room–apartment. Highways have become the cutting and separating symbol of the modern mobile transportation society.

Organized planning is not a phenomenon of the twentieth century. The regular layouts found in ancient cities, as well as blueprints from the absolutist era, demonstrate city planning. At the turn of the century a complex process began, and not only in Germany, which brought up the question of a more coherent and complex type of planning: increasing industrialization in regions such as the Rhine–Ruhr valleys, Silesia and the metropolitan areas of Berlin and Hamburg, massive migration and economic restructuring all resulted in a process of rapid urbanization. Industrialization and

126

urbanization are part of a general process of the production of Modernism, an overall social, economic, spatial and scientific-technological change.[2]

A new utopia of rational planning of social development, which can still be found today in the contributions of town and regional planners, emerged with this development. This essay will examine the formation of a new, autonomous research discipline (*Raumforschung*), and the development of its planning side, spatial planning (*Raumordnung*), within the many-layered modernization process of the German Reich, with special attention to the construction of society in the theories, models and plans in the twenties, thirties and forties.

2   The first approaches to regional planning in the Weimar Republic: institutions and careers in the urbanization process

The first measures for regional planning were taken in heavily developed areas with a high density of population and industry. This planning went beyond the kind of urban and municipal planning that had been employed by local governments. In order to organize the legal framework for planning on this scale, new institutional forms were required. In Berlin a *Zweckverband Berlin* was founded as early as 1910, whereas in the Ruhr valley a regional development corporation was founded in 1920. The backgrounds of these two endeavours were thoroughly different: the latter was created to 'secure the natural resources'[3] such as water as pure resources for industrial production, whereas in the Berlin area the main aim was to coordinate town and traffic planning. In both regions, however, it was also a matter of creating space and green zones in order to improve living conditions in these agglomerations.

The first group of planners of the twenties was very much influenced by the reform ideas of the youth movement or by Ebenezer Howard, who affected urban design and blueprints with his book *Garden Cities of Tomorrow*.[4] Reulecke describes how the first collection of material and plans in 1912, which were based on middle-class reform ideas, provided a starting-point for planners in the twenties.[5]

Another organization of regional planning was founded in a metropolitan area in 1928: the 'Hamburg–Prussian Regional Planning Committee', which coordinated the plans of the city of Hamburg and the interests of the surrounding Prussian regions. During the Weimar Republic this committee made important contributions towards laying the foundations for comprehensive planning. In 1929, towards the end of the Weimar Republic, a working association of the regional planning organizations was established.[6]

Another process was connected with this institutionalization: the professionalization of scholars and technicians who had taken their degrees at engineering and architecture schools or in the local government sciences

(*Kommunalwissenschaften*). A kind of civil engineering (*Städtetechnik*) had already been established by the middle of the nineteenth century. As part of the local authorities, it was responsible for gas, water and (industrial) effluents. In the early industrialization period, therefore, a new group of specialists grew up which occasionally influenced the wider field of city planning.

The first phase of the institutionalization process was linked with professional careers, specialized journals such as *Der Städtebau* (City Planning, founded in 1904) and their influence on universities and disciplines. The Chicago School of Social Ecology,[7] which was reviewed and emulated in Europe, emerged during this period. However, such new and interdisciplinary approaches of socio-spatial research as a basis for area and city planning were not adopted in Germany. The more traditional disciplinary boundaries between architecture, geography and sociology were retained.

At the end of the 1920s, however, new discussions began on the function of cities and areas. In the field of geography, Walter Christaller developed the central place theory, which in 1932 became his PhD thesis in Erlangen.[8] During the 1933 International Congress of Architects in Athens the so-called 'Charter of Athens' was formulated, a discussion of the interrelations between the urban functions of traffic, housing, work and recreation, a model which had a fundamental influence on the city planning of the post-World War I period.

The first planning careers in the German Reich were 'home-made': for example, those of the local government administrator Robert Schmidt in Essen, who became the Director of the *Ruhrsiedlungsverband* (Ruhr Housing Association); the urban development administrator, Kurt Schumacher, from Hamburg; or Josef Umlauf, whose career is characteristic of the development of the early period.[9]

After studies in architecture and urban planning at the universities in Vienna and Berlin, Umlauf worked for professional journals like *Baugilde* and *Form*. He took part in the urban development planning of Berlin and in 1933 made a proposal for the reorganization of the open spaces around Berlin Castle (*Berliner Schloss*) in connection with the construction of the *Reichsbank*. His actual career is inseparably linked with the institutionalization of planning studies in the Third Reich, which will be examined in the next section.

Umlauf became head of the planning office at the *Reichsheimstätten-amtes der Deutschen Arbeitsfront* from 1934 to 1937, moved to the *Bezirks-planungsstelle Arnsberg* in the *Landesplanungsgemeinschaft Westfalen* in 1937 and worked at the *Siedlungsverband Ruhrkohlenbezirk* in 1938. In 1940 Konrad Meyer asked him, as well as other first-generation planners, to join Heinrich Himmler's 'Office for the Strengthening of Germandom' (*Reichskommissariat für die Festigung des deutschen Volkstums*) in the planning division, the *Stabshauptamt für Planung und Boden*.

Even Umlauf's third career after 1945 was typical of the professionalization of the planning disciplines: he became director of the *Ruhrsiedlungsverband* and subsequently received a new chair for spatial and area planning at the Technical University of Stuttgart. He was also a member of professional organizations like the *Akademie für Städtebau und Landesplanung* and the *Akademie für Raumforschung und Landesplanung.* This exemplary biography of research and planning in three very different social and political systems (from the Weimar Republic to the German Federal Republic) only marginally distinguished itself from others. What was extraordinary was his theoretical-methodological approach displayed in his 1958 dissertation 'Structure and Organization of Regional Planning' as well as his historical reflections on his work.[10]

Planning in the Weimar Republic was, in general as well as individually, an urban phenomenon; regional planning was only developed in metropolitan areas. 'The city is the instrument of impersonal life, the mold in which people, interests and tastes in their complexity and multiplicity flow together and can be socially experienced.'[11] The complex process of urbanization and modernization in science, technology, architecture and literature would be unthinkable without the discourse on the cities. New literary forms like reporting reflected the process of urban life in a special form.[12] Lindner has portrayed in a masterly way the reporters' milieu in the metropolis of the 1920s.[13]

But the modern produced the 'anti-modern'.[14] An even broader discourse among different political and cultural movements on the inhabitable city, the hostility of the metropolis and anti-urbanism, a critique of civilization and flight from the city received attention. The big city as a symbol of civilization and modernity, the metropolis of noise and dust, the deserts of stone and anonymous masses were juxtaposed against the countryside as a more healthy environment and living space.

This criticism of the metropolis, developed 'in the cities themselves',[15] was a many-layered and complex discourse which can be found in very different discussion circles. 'This two-front position of the avant-garde against tradition as well as against the criticism inherent in modernization was also expressed in the discussion surrounding *Neues Bauen* [Build Something New] and *Neues Wohnen* [Live in a New Way].[16]

Urban critique and utopias, traditional and modern concepts, the avant-garde of new design and living and anti-urban ideologies were also reflected in contradictory ways in the city planning utopias and the planning literature and are necessary for understanding developments after 1933. In particular Peukert has warned against hasty interpretations and pointed out that the vocabulary of this critique of modernization made use of metaphors from the traditionalist critique of modernization, so that the two discourses have been mixed up in a special way and have to be separated and analyzed.[17]

3   New institutions of area research and spatial planning after 1933:
spatial order as National Socialist social planning

     After the National Socialists took power, they created a centra-
lized state step by step, which for the first time in German history introduced the kind of far-reaching legislation required for comprhensive planning. There were several laws in Prussia, like the Prussian city reform law
of 1808, which were more an administration reform than a step towards
organized planning.[18] Several such laws were enacted: a housing estate law
in 1933 (*Wohnsiedlungsgesetz*), the settlement organization law (*Siedlungs-
ordnung*) in 1934, the Reich's environmental protection law (1935) and the
'Public land regulation law' (*Regelung des Landbedarfs der öffentlichen
Hand*) in 1935. The latter was the basis for the creation of the first centralized planning agency of the Reich: the Reich Office for Spatial Planning
(*Reichsstelle für Raumordnung*). It was led by Hanns Kerrl (1887–1941),[19]
a figure of little significance, but like all other planning and architecture
institutions the office was placed directly under Hitler.[20] In contrast to his
interest in architecture and urban planning and his involvement in the town
planning of Berlin, Munich and Linz, however, Hitler exerted no influence
on the general planning of the Reich office.

     In the self-definition and historiography of the Third Reich, planning
stood in the first row:

> In the 19th century, as a result of the general lack of restraint under
> liberalism, the idea of planned cities was gradually lost. The dis-
> advantages of this licentious development have been demonstrated in an
> especially blatant manner by the extremely rapid urbanization caused by
> recent technical-industrial development ... Only in the Third Reich has
> purposeful and systematic planning been demanded, both in the area of
> legal regulation as well as through support of community work. Since the
> restructuring of local communities is part of restructuring the entire
> German living space, community planning can only take place in the
> closest connection with state and Reich planning, which formulate more
> general ideas and plans.[21]

     The Reich office had its own research organization, the 'Reich Associ-
ation for Area Research', with branches at every university. This concept
was developed by Konrad Meyer, the first head of the Reich Association.
Surveys of the entire German Reich were carried out by regional research
units based at the universities and bound together in the Association. In
this respect Meyer realized his model of interdisciplinary work for the
entire Volk.[22] He recognized that scientific production was higher in units
with voluntary scholars. In the first phase statistical information and
economic evaluations were collected and were brought together to form
charts and maps. The material was immediately used for economic, settlement and traffic planning by the *Reichsstelle*. The main aim of this office

was the construction of a spatial order for the German *Volk* in the *Altreich* (Germany in its borders of 1937). As we shall see, other institutions were planned for the occupied eastern territories.

Pahl-Weber has pointed out that the Reich Office was not at all influential in the East. It developed planning instruments which were the basis for general spatial planning inside Germany until 1961, when the *Bundesbaugesetz* (Federal Constitution Law) was enacted. Moreover, this office was less concerned with racial categories, and invented a more technocratic and functional approach towards planning.[23]

The National Socialist model of society

The so-called '*Volksgemeinschaft*' (People's Community) became the model for the National Socialist society. This construction of a new social entity bridging all classes, all walks of life and social strata, was not defined by status or profession, but rather by 'blood'. This model therefore functioned on a racial basis and excluded non-Aryans and Jews. The interests of the *Volksgemeinschaft* were dictated by National Socialist policy. This almost mythical construction of a *Volksgemeinschaft* was intended to conceal social and internal conflicts in society. This aim also becomes clear in an article on 'community' in a contemporary dictionary:

> In contrast, the National Socialist worldview, through its practical concept and organization of the community, has helped the original essence of the community to reemerge victorious. The idea and form of the community at the front, born out of the world war as the archetype of the true, closed community ... in which the essence of human existence is revealed as community life. The community experience extends itself from the foundation to a complete *Volksgemeinschaft*. There the separation into nation-less, international classes find its end, especially through the cultivation of the common *Erbmasse* [hereditary matter] as the constant factor of a community.[24]

In general, an all-embracing concept of *Volk* and society in the Third Reich did not exist. On the contrary, several institutions and offices fought against each other with different concepts in the typical competence chaos and power struggles.[25]

In particular, each planning institution had a different conception of society or tried to realize what it understood by *Volksgemeinschaft* in different ways. A letter to the Reich Ministry of the Interior criticized that regional planning was organized too loosely and demanded that all planning efforts be coordinated and centralized under the leadership of one ministry. At the time, the different planning institutions were: *Reichsstelle für Raumordnung, Reichskommissar für die Festigung deutschen Volkstums, Reichslandwirtschaftsminister für die West-Ost-Siedlung, Reichs-*

minister Dr. Todt für die Autobahnen, Reichswirtschaftsminister für industrielle Umsiedlung, Reichsamt für Wirtschaftsausbau, Reichsarbeitsminister, Prüsfstelle für Gemeinschaftsiedlungen, Reichskommissar für den sozialen Wohnungsbau, and *Reichsverkehrsminister für die Eisenbahn.*[26]

These conflicts became exacerbated during the Second World War and the National Socialist expansion towards the East. In the new 'unpopulated' areas of the East, several planners saw the potential for realizing their ideas on a grander scale than in the densely developed areas of the *Altreich.*

The concept of a 'comprehensively designed German living space' and its significance in the war programme of the Reich Association for Area Research

As early as September 1939 a new research programme entitled 'The German East' was developed by the Reich Association and transmitted to its university branches, including general surveys as well as the 'strengthening of Germandom', the creation of new German soil, and so on. The scholars had to analyse the East in order to find out how many German settlers could live there as well as where to construct new industrial sites and agrarian regions. Upper Silesia was to be developed as a new economic region and 'living organism'. One research unit would also make a survey of the existing 'central places' and would make proposals for the best possible central-place hierarchy in strategic, economic and population terms.[27]

A letter written by the head of the 'Central Places' committee, Prof. Geisler, addressed to the director of the Reich Office, Jarmer, illustrates the nature of their work and the state of their progress. He discussed the problem of the *Gau*-towns (regional towns), district and provincial capitals, and displayed their borders on a secret map. The members of the committee also developed a preliminary layout for the central places in the East of the German Reich near the border of the General Government.[28]

Furthermore, they published a volume for the Reich Association for Area Research, 'Structure and form of the Central Places of the German East',[29] with contributions from the members of the central places committee: the geographer Christaller, the economist Isenberg, the sociologist Hilberath and the regional planners Ziegler and Reiser. Their aim was the transformation of the East into 'German land' and a German landscape which was also demonstrated by a map made by Christaller. Here he presented a new hierarchy of central places (in parentheses are the planned population numbers):

> main village (600);
> major main village (1200);
> administrative centre (3000);
> major administrative centre (9000);
> district centre (30000);

major district centre (100,000);
Gau-capital (450,000).

He traced the borders between the hierarchical districts and proposed new ones, as well as a development or reduction to typical size. Christaller built the idea of the 'strengthening of Germandom' into his theory.[30] However, he was also accused of being too theoretical and of constructing a purely theoretical spatial model without any links to the 'Volk'. He was asked to think more 'organically'. Yet the dispute between him and the economist Bülow in a newly founded journal[31] had no consequences, because most planning agencies and National Socialist offices used Christaller's concepts. Even more important, one of the most influential men in the Third Reich, SS leader Heinrich Himmler, used Christaller's concepts as a model for the planned transformation of the East into a new Nazi society.

Spatial and social order in the 'General Plan of the East': a model for National Socialist social planning

When Heinrich Himmler (1900–45) took over the 'Reich Commission for the Strengthening of Germandom' in 1939, he created a new office of 'Planning and Soil', *Stabshauptamt Planung und Boden*. He asked Konrad Meyer to head this office after a private meeting in the newly occupied Poland.[32] Himmler, a former member of the Artamanen movement,[33] saw his agency as an instrument to realize his far-reaching plans of selection and breeding, of agrarian culture and Aryan race. He drew up a programme aimed at the Germanization (*Eindeutschung*) of the people in the occupied areas and at the settlement of German peasants there.

In order to achieve the scientific realization of Himmler's ideas, Konrad Meyer brought together a team of specialists to plan for a new National Socialist society and its spatial form. This team included the regional planner Josef Umlauf (already mentioned above), the sociologist Herbert Morgen, the geographer Walter Christaller and even a landscape planner.

Research and planning by this office were based on the studies of the Reich Association for Area Research, not only because of the personal continuity, but also because they worked in the same building in Berlin-Dahlem. One of the first results of their work was the 'General Plan for the East. Legal, Economic and Spatial Bases for the Development of the Eastern Territories' in 1940. The document was modified by several other offices[34] and existed in different forms for 1940, 1941 and 1942, when Himmler received a 'final version'. Historians today consider this plan the 'official programme of National Socialist occupation policy'.[35] The plan shows three interrelated levels: settlement theory and spatial planning; population policy and social planning; and the policy of conquest and occupation.

To summarize the first aspect,[36] Christaller's theory of central places was already well known among planning experts. It had been published in 1933 and discussed in the Reich Association in 1937. Now the team in the Planning and Soil office tried to modify and apply it. Meyer, who was in charge of Himmler's planning office, wrote in 1970 that he had asked Christaller to come to work in Berlin because of his new approach:

> Until this authority was dissolved Christaller worked there as a scientific colleague on formulating the concept of the projected new post-war structure of the German Reich. He was able then to verify ... the theoretical results of his dissertation on the basis of the reality of culturally and geographically different settlements.[37]

During the Third Reich Christaller had already modified his theory, which included the principles of traffic, consumption and administration. The latter was now linked to the new structure of National Socialist administration. On the lower level of the hierarchy of central places he included a National Socialist celebration hall, buildings for the Hitler Youth or a central parade square, in other words the visible buildings of the model for National Socialist society.

The organic growth of society, as demanded by Bülow in the theoretical debate, would not be possible because of the National Socialist destruction of the East and because of the intended speed of the transformation of the Eastern territories. The best way, therefore, seemed to lie in a *rational* creation of a National Socialist society based on plans for an optimal distribution of people and goods, industry and traffic lines. Christaller's urban theory was therefore modified to fit the huge agrarian country in the East of Germany. For example, the planners developed the new '*Hauptdorf*', main village, which was to fulfill important functions for Nazi administration and to act as a unifying core for the area surrounding the village. The General Plan of the East planned thirty-six settlements with 20,000 people each as a new level in the hierarchy of central places. There were no cities in the plan and no equal distribution of central places because of the linear development (along the railroads and highways!) of these huge areas. In this manner, the Nazi administration and the military assumed that Poland and the USSR could be filled by German settlers easily, and controlled in a rational and simple way.

The second aspect of population policy was connected with the first, settlement theory, and the third, occupation policy. The General Plan was a 'long-range regional development programme' as well as a programme of selection, Germanization and genocide. Therefore, occupation policy was a two-stage process: first, expulsion and extermination of the Polish, Jewish and Russian populations; second, racial selection and control of the settlement of German peasants; and finally the creation of the 'East wall' by means of military villages.

This plan is an example of the transformation and realization of an ideal National Socialist society. Himmler secured all powers of decision for this project for himself. The Reich Office for Spatial Planning had no influence at all. But there must have been some conflicts over jurisdiction, as is indicated by a remark made by Meyer's boss about the Reich Office after the war:

> The Reichsführer SS explained that he did not make any arrangements with Speer's ministry. The creation of a big ministry for building and construction is planned for the post-war period. It is necessary to separate the fields of designing the environment (*Gestaltung des Lebensraumes*) and of technical construction.[38]

A separation is made here between individual aspects such as technical development, infrastructure, railroads, highways and communication lines, and a total 'environmental design' as the creative part, i.e. the design of the buildings, the landscape and even the people in terms of Himmler's racial categories. This division would facilitate both Himmler's creation idea and the more technical rational approach of the planner in the Reich Office, or Todt's or Speer's organizations.

In the recent literature on Himmler, his part in the creation and construction of the *Volksgemeinschaft* in the East is played down, often, because these plans were never realized because of the war. But the racial selection of people and the extermination by the SS was nevertheless translated into action, as well as the parallel formation and design (*Gestaltung*) of the new landscape through resettlement, family relocation and settlement of Aryan peasants. Moreover, the General Plan of the East was in fact realized in one district in occupied Poland, Zamos.[39]

Here the ideas of healthy, 'popular' design and construction, agrarian romanticism and anti-urbanism already developed in the Weimar Republic found their expression. Design did not by any means exclude technocratic approaches, as shown by the example of Christaller's concept. the main point is the model of racial planning in the East on the one hand, and the approach applied by the planners of the *Altreich*, which was based on economic and technical categories, on the other. This division between the total design of the expanded environment (*Lebensraum*) in the East and the purposeful, rational planning by the Reich Office enabled the silent transition to the planning of the post-war period.

4   The silent transformation: institutions of area research and regional planning in post-war reconstruction

> That there was no totally new beginning, rather multifarious lines of political and economic continuity became effective again very quickly ... today is almost a truism.[40]

The first preparations for the post-war period were made by architects and planners as early as 1944 and 1945. Speer created a *Wiederaufbaustab* (Rebuilding Staff), a group of well-known architects and town planners who influenced the town planning and the planning concepts (Leitbilder) of the post-war era.[41]

Facing the lost war and the victory of the allies, the Reich Association for Area Research destroyed vast quantities of records and files.[42] The rest of the material and the staff were brought to Hannover. There was no disruption in their work. A report stated that they resumed their research on 20 May 1945, twelve days after the collapse of the Third Reich and the end of war![43] They were assisted by the geographer Kurt Brüning, the last head of the Reich Association. He was involved in the foundation of the 'Academy for Area Research and Regional Planning' in Hannover, which took over the inheritance of the Reich Association. Brüning became the first president. The material of the Reich Office remained in Berlin and the old staff moved to Bonn and founded a new 'Institute for Spatial Planning', which later took over that material and some assistants.

In 1949 a conflict broke out between these two institutions in Hannover and Bonn on the division of research themes and the forms of organization. The debate was linked to financial problems and the question of who should pay for two institutions with the same research profile. Should the German Federal Republic pay for both or should the State of Lower Saxony (*Land Niedersachsen*) pay for the one in Hannover?[44]

In the end the two institutions of the Third Reich became two institutions of the German Federal Republic. They became the immediate legal successors, retaining all academic staff and material. The institute in Bonn later became the well-known *Bundesanstalt für Landeskunde und Raumordnung*.

The developments in Bonn and Hannover were not influenced by the Allies or by occupation policy at all. The Control Commission for Germany only criticized the term 'Reich'. In fact, they had to do little more than changing their names.[45] The same happened at the Nuremberg trials, where Konrad Meyer was among the accused and the General Plan of the East was discussed. In the American understanding, the plan was never realized and therefore Konrad Meyer and his staff were innocent. No connection was made between National Socialist planning, population policy, social structure and extermination. Planning was not connected to politics, governmental or economic systems. In the Americans' opinion it had been used to solve problems of a modern, highly industrialized and urbanized society.

At the same time, the new institutions were confronted with huge tasks: reconstruction and rebuilding, the organization of the refugee problem[46] and the refugees' distribution, traffic planning and housing programmes. The necessity for these programmes was demonstrated by the terrible economic and social situation in a destroyed Germany. Nobody asked for a critical reflection on the theoretical approaches and planning concepts. The new task was to help the broken-down society (*Zusammenbruchsgesell-*

schaft)[47] to find a new order and to establish principles for reconstruction. These research questions had been familiar since the thirties and forties. They had been fully developed and worked out, so that the staff could use old material, maps and charts, or even programmes and plans made for the 'reconstruction' after victory', for example in the home-building programme.

As a consequence of the heavy destruction and great displacement of population, home construction was one of the main tasks and an urgent social-political aim,[48] as were evacuation, resettlement, reconstruction of the transportation and traffic system, energy and resource supply, and new construction of economic planning and administration.

5   Conclusion

In the twentieth century spatial and regional planning became important instruments applied by the highly industrialized countries of the West to organize settlement, traffic and economics. In the Third Reich, the ideas and structures of self-organized planning associations developed during the Weimar Republic were used to form the first centralized planning agency. This Reich Office for Spatial Planning existed between 1935 and 1945. Within this office, regional planning, once developed in response to the problems of urbanization and industrialization after the turn of the century, was transformed into comprehensive planning. In the highly developed *Altreich* it was pragmatically oriented, in the East after 1939 it was organized and directed towards the creation of a new agrarian community, the *Volksgemeinschaft*. One must therefore distinguish between different types of planning as instruments of modernization. Especially with the National Socialist expansion to the East, the planners wanted to construct a new society, including the environment, houses and people. In this field the competence of the Reich Office was reduced and cut by other agencies. Central ideas for the new community were formulated by the specialists of Himmler's planning office. Their tasks could be described as the general preparation of plans for occupied Poland and Russia as well as of individual plans for German villages. The General Plan of the East combined theoretical concepts with racial planning and a kind of 'total environmental design'.

Because of this division of labour, area research and spatial planning could be re-established after 1945 using the Third Reich institutions. Specialists, records and legal succession were taken over by organizations of the Federal Republic of Germany, and several laws were carried over from the Third Reich. The professionalization of the planning disciplines also continued with the new wave of modernization in the reconstruction period. Spatial and regional planning in the Federal Republic of Germany has its foundations in organizations, laws and instruments of the National

Socialist period. Between 1933 and 1945 several planning approaches existed, which can be traced back to two directions: on the one hand, the technocratic approach of the Reich Office and the regional planning agencies; and on the other hand, Himmler's plans for the East, aiming at the realization through planning of a National Socialist *Volksgemeinschaft.*

7 | The ideological origins of institutes at the Kaiser Wilhelm Gesellschaft *in National Socialist Germany**

KRISTIE MACRAKIS

When examining the relationship between science and ideology in National Socialist Germany, historians of science have hitherto been concerned primarily with the origin of race ideology and how it, in turn, affected the development of biology and physics and their transformation into race hygiene and *deutsche Physik* (Aryan Physics).[1] While this is clearly an important and interesting question, it is also necessary to examine other types of ideology and their relation to scientific development and organization. The role of agricultural science in National Socialist Germany combined with the notion of *Lebensraum* (living space) and cultural imperialism as a core ideological matrix is an area that has received scant attention.[2] This is unfortunate because these strands in the ideological matrix were central to National Socialist ideology.

This chapter will examine the influence of National Socialist ideology, broadly conceived, on the founding of Kaiser Wilhelm Institutes during World War II. The *Kaiser Wilhelm Gesellschaft* (the forerunner of the *Max Planck Gesellschaft*; literally in English Kaiser William Society; henceforth KWG) was Germany's premier scientific research organization during the first half of the twentieth century. Founded in 1911, by 1933 it maintained about thirty research institutes concentrating on basic scientific research. During the Third Reich it enjoyed more freedom of movement than many other scientific institutions or the universities. The degree of influence of National Socialist ideology on the Society and its institutes was differential, however, and changed during the course of the Third Reich. By the time of World War II the Society had aligned itself more closely with the government in a number of ways and became more influenced by some kinds of ideology.[3]

One way to test the influence of ideology on aspects of the scientific enterprise is to examine the founding of institutes. The discussions, plans

139

and programmatic statements accompanying foundation periods often illuminate the state of a science at the time as well as the influence of society on science. Most of this chapter will concentrate on the creation of several new agricultural and biological institutes by the Society during the war while simultaneously examining the way certain types of ideology shaped the agendas of the institutes. I will argue that there was discontinuity and change in the traditional ways in which new institutes were founded during the war as a result of ideological considerations and the political culture of National Socialism, yet simultaneously there were continuities, especially in the continuing general influence of the social, political and scientific context on institute creation since the Society's founding in Imperial Germany.

Traditions, patterns and philosophy of institute creation at the Kaiser Wilhelm Gesellschaft before 1933

Although there is no rule-book for the founding of new institutes at the Society, since its founding in 1911 traditions, patterns and procedures developed during the last years of the Empire, the first World War and the Weimar period which were peculiar to its special institutional character. These characteristics can be conveniently divided between the Society's notion of the appropriate elements that go into founding a new institute and the resulting procedures, on the one hand, and the influence of the social, political and scientific context on institute founding, which the actors are usually unaware of, on the other. Over the course of time, as the Society grew older, it did not rigidly adhere to one pattern. But in normal times (and National Socialism was not considered a normal time in the Society's eyes; nor was it in historian's eyes) the influence and role of politics was considerbly less than during the Third Reich.

The two key characteristics of Kaiser Wilhelm Institutes, according to the Society, were: (1) the field to be institutionalized should not be prominently represented at a university institute; and (2) one finds an outstanding scientist and builds an institute around him. In the final analysis, however, much of the desire for institute creation came from the strong interest of a scientist or group of scientists to found a new institute. During the founding years of the Society in Imperial Germany, there were, of course, other interests or interest groups as well. For example, a group of chemists played a major role in the initiative to found the Society because of the abortive attempt to found a Chemische Reichsanstalt (Imperial Chemical Institute).[4] As a result, the first two institutes of the Society were chemistry institutes: the chemistry institute, headed by Ernst Beckman, and the physical chemistry institute, created for Fritz Haber.

More interesting, perhaps, was the founding of the Kaiser Wilhelm Institute for Biology. Although members of the Society agreed there was a strong need to have a biology institute, most of the founding members were not biologists. Consequently, the Society solicited twenty-nine *Gutachten* (expert reports) from biologists all over Germany in which the scientists pleaded for the institutionalization of certain branches of biology. In the end, heredity was judged to be a science that was weakly institutionalized in Germany, yet important enough to merit a new research institute. After it established the type of biology to be housed at the institute, the Society searched for a distinguished senior scientist to serve as director. Although it lost its initial choice of Theodor Boveri due to illness and his fear of losing university ties, the Society appointed the distinguished botanist Carl Correns to lead the institute. In the case of the founding of this institute, the currents in biological research and what was seen to be 'hot' influenced the choice of field, while ideology and the political constellation of the times were not overt or overriding factors.[5]

During the Weimar period institutes proliferated in industry-related sciences during the early twenties, while basic science research institutes for anthropology and breeding research opened by the end of the decade. There is no doubt that industry played an increasingly influential role in founding research institutes during World War I and the immediate post-war period. In some cases it also determined or influenced the research activities of the institute. The industrialists' role in founding new institutes was not a surprising development, since university chemists and industrial chemists had already taken part in the founding of, and had contributed to the financing of, the Society from its earliest years. Under the pressures of the post-World War I economy, the Society welcomed the contributions of wealthy industrialists. As a result of the war, it recognized the importance of developing the manufacture of raw materials. Between 1914 and 1926 seven industry-related institutes opened for coal, iron, metal, leather, textile chemistry and silicate research. These new institutes departed from the classic basic research Berlin-Dahlem institutes built, or conceived of, before the war. The Society also expanded the location of its institutes to the *Ruhrgebiet* (Ruhr River Valley) – the major industrial area of Germany.[6] It is clear from these examples that the social and economic context of the early Weimar years influenced and shaped the founding of new institutes. One principle remained the same, however, the choice for director was always an outstanding scientist in the field.

The founding of the Kaiser Wilhelm Institute for Anthropology, Human Genetics and Eugenics in 1927 is a prime example of the way in which an institute was imbedded in the Weimar social structure. The social context played a role both in the institutional support found for the institute and in the way in which the science of eugenics was tied to the aims and goals of social welfare.[7] By the late twenties sources of financial support for institute creation at the KWG had shifted from an industrial base to federal and state support from the Prussian and Reich administrations. The institute had received almost a million marks from the latter in 1927, while only 23,300 marks came from private and industrial sources.[8] Another break with the institutional patterns in Imperial Germany was the new emphasis during the twenties on the importance of applied science (this is also reflected in the founding of industry-related institutes) for the nation, in contrast to the earlier value placed on pure science. This was manifested at the Institute for Anthropology in the emphasized relationship between the applied science of heredity and social problems. Geneticists and biologists at the institute also began to see a major role for biology in the social and economic reconstuction of the state after the destruction of World War I. Hermann Muckermann, a Roman Catholic interested in the importance of eugenics for family and social welfare, stimulated the founding of the institute. By 1927, Eugen Fischer was institute director and head of the Anthropology department, Muckerman led the eugenics department and Othmar von Verschuer headed the department for human heredity.[9]

From this quick overview, one can see that social, scientific and, to a lesser degree, political factors continually influenced the founding of new institutes. Particularly striking is the proliferation of industry-related institutes during and after World War I. In the case of the biology institute, developments in the field were of central importance, while the social context shaped the founding of the Institute for Anthropology. Despite these social and scientific influences no reigning ideology in society at large seems to have found its way into the founding discussions and justifications. During the Third Reich, however, a reigning ideology did play an important role in the creation of new institutes; in part because it was a major element of the social and political structure, and in part because of the magnified and pervasive influence of politics and ideology on many aspects of life in a totalitarian regime. In particular, during the war the Society aligned itself more closely with many governmental agencies and complied with some aspects of the state's policies. National Socialist leaders sometimes even sat on the boards of the Society. Yet, even the Society recognized the effect of ideology, and was often unwilling to accept whole-heartedly some of the new institutes into its band of Kaiser Wilhelm Institutes.

The ideological background

Living space and a National Socialist agriculture

The notion of *Lebensraum*, hardly a construct of Nazi Germany, can be traced back to Imperial Germany and was an outgrowth of migrationist colonialism and romantic agrarianism. It is an ideology that was created in quasi-scientific ways by geopoliticians and in turn was later applied as an ideological rationalization (or now a transformed political construct) to the areas of agriculture and biology. The geographer Frie-drich Ratzel and the geopolitician Karl Haushofer made key contributions to the development of the concept of *Lebensraum*. Ratzel originated the term *Lebensraum* and used it as a central concept in a biological theory. He was influenced by Darwinism and believed that species migration was the most important element of social adaptation. Haushofer also legitimated his imperialist notions with science, and his geopolitics strongly influenced the National Socialists. Haushofer's radical conservative ideology integra-ted *Weltpolitik* (economic imperialism) with *Lebensraum* to form his geo-politics. He thought of the *Volk* – represented socially as the nation and politically as the state – in cultural, economic and geographic, and not racial, terms. The 'science' of geopolitics focused on the identification of the environmental factors required for developing the *Volk*, investigated the relationship between space and politics, and reflected the way in which geographical knowledge could be transformed into intellectual equipment for politicians. The most important environmental factor for the *Volk* was an adequate amount of *Lebensraum*. In particular, a growing and vigorous people like the Germans needed more living space.[10] It was ideas like these which became policy in the Third Reich.

Associated with the notion of *Lebensraum* were the ideological under-pinnings of the culture of agriculture. Agriculture is a science that appeals to romantic yearnings – blood and soil (*Blut und Boden*), living space (*Lebensraum*) and people's soil (*Volksboden*) are all slogans closely tied to a National Socialist conception of the goals and function of agriculture in society. In the Third Reich agriculture was both reactionary and modern – reactionary in its romanticism, but modern in its technology.[11] By expanding into the rich agricultural territories of the east and southeast, the German *Volk* could achieve more economic independence. Another phrase commonly used during the Third Reich was *Nahrungsfreiheit* – nutritional freedom; the Third Reich aspired to meet its nutritional needs from its own resources and geared agricultural policies towards this goal.[12] It is therefore not surprising to find that over 650 agricultural institutes existed by 1939, and that over fifty new institutes related to agriculture, breeding research and nutrition were created in Nazi Germany by 1939.[13]

Cultural imperialism: a war without weapons

Within weeks after the outbreak of World War II in 1939, cultural and science policies for use in foreign countries were formulated by the leaders of ﹨National Socialist Germany. Just as *Lebensraum* had its roots in Imperial Germany, so too was foreign *Kulturpolitik* (cultural policy in the broadest sense) an old tradition in Germany. By the time of the Third Reich, however, the emphasis turned to cultural imperialism with the defined goal of national expansion of power and the use of power politics to achieve this; it had become a vehicle of foreign policy.[14] The *Reichsministerium für Wissenschaft, Erziehung und Volksbildung* (Reich Ministry of Science and Education, henceforth REM) perceived the cultural policies of the Reich as a 'war without weapons' and it was their goal to 'secure and influence' similar policies in Germany's occupied territories. These policies would be implemented and spread through the German scientific institutes abroad (*deutsche wissenschaftliche Institute im Ausland*) which were founded during the war by the Reich and the foreign office to spread German propaganda to occupied territories.[15] Institutes had already opened in Bucharest, Sofia and Belgrade, and twelve more were being built. The institutes planned and took the lead in implementing German *Kulturpolitik*.[16]

By the autumn of 1941, German troops had occupied almost all of continental Europe as part of Nazi Germany's expansionist policy. This territorial expansion led to a more conscious advance of cultural policies and, in particular, of science policy. Of central importance for science in this scheme were a series of secret meetings held at the REM in the winter of 1940/41 which dealt with the question of transferring international organizations from Brussels to Germany. It was also during this time that the Rosenberg Ministry, which was responsible for research in the East, approached the KWG asking for a collaborative effort.

Within weeks after the outbreak of war, the Reich Ministry of the Interior had already announced that 'scientific and cultural relations to neutral countries abroad must be cultivated even more during the war'.[17] By the autumn of 1940 a victorious outcome of the war seemed likely for Germany and plans were therefore made for the immediate post-war world under German leadership. There were many meetings among the appropriate ministries where the 'importance of scientific cooperation within the international organizations for future foreign cultural policies of the Greater German Reich' were discussed. The question of restructuring international organizations and the influence of Germany on these institutions was not considered to be an independent problem, but only part of the 'foreign relations of science and its extra-political [significance], that is, its importance for cultural policies'.[18]

As part of this new international politics for science, the Foreign Office began to consider the question of whether to bring international organizations, which originally had their home in Brussels or Paris, to Germany.[19] This question led to an important conference on 12 November 1940 with scientists and officials from the ministries. Among the scientists asked to participate in the meeting and advise the Ministry on the question of moving the headquarters of international organizations to Germany were six directors of Kaiser Wilhelm Institutes: Fritz von Wettstein (Kaiser Wilhelm Institute for Biology), Richard Kuhn (Kaiser Wilhelm Institute for Medical Research), Peter Thiessen (Kaiser Wilhelm Institute for Physical

Chemistry), Eugen Fischer (Kaiser Wilhelm Institute for Anthropology), Ernst Heymann (Kaiser Wilhelm Institute for Private Law) and Victor Bruns (Kaiser Wilhelm Institute for Law and International Law).

The responses of these Kaiser Wilhelm Institute scientists varied with regard to the role of international unions and societies, but many displayed nationalistic tendencies while conceiving of Germany as the leader of a united European science in competition with American science. Von Wettstein stands out as a representative of this type of thinking as shown by his statement:

> I believe the best way [to restructure international organizations] would be to organize Europe under German leadership as a European section. We can forget about America. The struggle with America will start after the war and ability will decide whether the right to lead will lie with America or with Europe.[20]

Other Kaiser Wilhelm Institute scientists had similar views. Richard Kuhn, who was vice-president of the Chemical Union, thought that German leadership was possible in Europe (in other words, Germany did not have the chance to be competitive with America), but he also believed that the headquarters should only be moved if the American president of the union agreed. If he did not, it would create bad feelings between Europe and America.[21] Thiessen, who was probably the most convinced National Socialist of the group, thought that the war-like position (*Kampfstellung*) between Germany and America that Kuhn foresaw already existed, and therefore steps should be taken to limit *Kulturpolitik* to European territory.[22]

Wettstein's and Brun's contributions to *Kulturpolitik*, or cultural imperialism and exploitation, did not end with this important meeting. By early 1942 two developments occurred almost simultaneously: von Wettstein and Bruns, with the support and complicity of Ernst Telschow (as the responsible representative of the Kaiser Wilhelm Gesellschaft), agreed to cooperate with both the Reich Nutrition Ministry and the Rosenberg Ministry on scientific research in the east.

Alfred Rosenberg's Office, a party agency, approached Bruns in February 1942 with detailed plans for a future cooperative venture between the Office and the KWG. The agenda for this cooperation was detailed and telling:

1 Appointment of teaching and research personnel in all areas of science for deployment in the east.
2 Arranging the military exemptions (*UK-Stellung*) through the Reich Ministry of the East for KWG scientists participating in tasks important for the war effort.
3 Scheduled deployment of scientific personnel in the east.

4 Introduction of scientists to the practical problems and tasks of the east. Research contracts for the institutes and exchange of results.

5 Financial support for the contract research in the east through the Ministry.

6 Creation of an East Office within the KWG, for the purpose of regulating business with the Ministry.

7 The support of future generations of scientists (*Nachwuchs*).

8 Cooperation with the *Hauptamt Wissenschaft* (Science section of the REM) in cultural areas.

9 Deployment of teaching and research personnel at the KWG for the '*Hohe Schule*' (Literally 'Higher Schools', run by the Nazi Party).

10 Deployment of scientists in the camps of the Reich Teacher's Association (*Reichsdozentenbundes*).

11 Cooperation between the *Hauptamt Wissenschaft* and the KWG for the deployment of scientists in the scientific work of the Party and its affiliates.

12 Publication of scientific articles, especially those related to cultural areas, in the journals of the Party.[23]

This plan soon led to a meeting at the *Hauptamt Wissenschaft* with Bruns, Telschow and two representatives of that office, where they discussed 'problems arising from research in the east, especially the maintenance and safeguarding of the Russian Institutes there'. Telschow 'promised the support of the KWG as long as the personnel existed and as long as' the Society's 'advice was needed'.[24] These plans, however, seemed to have remained in the preliminary stages since no full-scale deployment of Kaiser Wilhelm Institute scientists in the east occurred.

Negotiations for institutes in Russia had begun with the Reich Nutrition Ministry about the same time as the overture was made to Bruns. Von Wettstein suggested a plan for Vavilov's breeding research stations which lay in European Russia. These were partly in German-occupied territory and partly in Russian territory. Von Wettstein 'recommended taking the stations and caring for them through the Kaiser Wilhelm Gesellschaft in order to save the valuable material and to make further work there possible'.[25] By 9 March von Wettstein had drafted a list of the most important places in Russia for the biological institutes in the east which would make up part of the 'biological network' of the KWG.[26]

The *Kaiser Wilhelm Gesellschaft* recognized the effect of the 'New Order' ideology on its international scientific relations and reported in 1941 that 'the recent events of the war and the concomitant new order of European territory is increasingly affecting the international scientific relations of the KWG'.[27] The various cultural agreements had led to visits by foreign guests to Germany and the Kaiser Wilhelm Institutes. In part independently, and in part in collaboration with the Foreign Office's new *Kulturpolitik* for the occupied eastern territories, the Kaiser Wilhelm Gesellschaft created several new institutes in territories either occupied by the Reich or under its indirect control, and scientists travelled to eastern countries to deliver lectures as goodwill ambassadors.[28]

Ideology and the founding of new institutes for agriculture and biology at the Kaiser Wilhelm Gesellschaft during the war

Three new institutes for agriculture and biology were founded by the KWG after the war broke out: one in Breslau (for agriculture), another in Sofia, Bulgaria (for agriculture), and a third in Athens/Piraeus, Greece (for biology).[29] On closer inspection, it seems that the Sofia and Athens institutes were conceived of before the outbreak of war, but the new political circumstances were more favourable to the enterprises outlined, therefore it was also possible to gain government support through the Reich Nutrition Ministry, the REM and the Foreign Office. With agriculture and *Lebensraum* as parts of a core National Socialist ideology, projects relating to agriculture and to the ideals of *Lebensraum* flourished.

One of the first institutes for agriculture to be founded after the war broke out in the autumn of 1939 was the 'Institute for the science of agricultural work in the *Kaiser Wilhelm Gesellschaft*' in Breslau. It had its founding meeting on 6 December 1940. Although Breslau was not a city in one of the occupied territories, it was located on Germany's most easterly border near Poland. Even before the war broke out it began to conceive of itself as the 'cultural centre of the Ostmark (Eastern Borderland)'.[30] It was also an agricultural centre. After the German victories in Poland in 1939, the east began to assume even greater importance. For these reasons it became a good location from which to organize agricultural activity for the east and a place from which to look towards the southeast.

Otto Fitzner, president of the Chamber of Industry and Commerce in Breslau, a Party Member since 1931 and a KWG senator since 1937, approached Telschow in April 1940 suggesting the establishment of an institute for research on the physiology of work in agriculture. Funding would come from Fitzner, from the City of Breslau and from agriculture. Initially, Telschow was sceptical about the project. Konrad Meyer, the doyen of agricultural research, also thought other problems were more important and Rudolf Mentzel, head of the *Hauptamt Wissenschaft* at the REM, agreed.[31]

The institute was motivated by the need to find ways to master effectively the work necessary for agriculture. With the rise of technical methods available since the middle of the nineteenth century, machines and the labour of guest workers from abroad were used for this purpose, but no systematic methods were developed. More recently Germany had been beset with a decrease in numbers of workers interested in agricultural work because of the flight to the cities. In order to remedy the situation in an efficient way it was proposed that the new institute would have the task of researching all methods available for use in agricultural business. The second task of the institute would be to advise agronomists about questions arising from the economics of work. Finally, the institute would work closely with the agricultural machine industry in order to find new technical solutions. Breslau was considered to be a favourable location for the institute because it lay in the 'big agricultural area of the east and the institute could help considerably with the expansion of the new territory there'.[32]

By the autumn of 1940 both the Nutrition Ministry and the REM still did not support the founding of this new institute. The Nutrition Ministry saw it as a rival institute to a state agricultural institute; it is not clear why the REM initially did not support the institute. Fitzner, however, sought out Telschow yet again, pledging 100,000 RM for the institute. He planned to interest Mentzel and Lammers (the head of the Reich Chancellery) in the project as well. Because of the tasks for the institute in the east, Fitzner thought the institute should be called the 'Adolf-Hitler-Institut'. Telschow wanted to delay the KWG decision until the final verdict of the Reich Nutrition Ministry and of the REM, because the KWG could 'in no way provide funding for this goal'.[33]

By the end of September, however, Mentzel, Meyer and the Nutrition Ministry supported the creation of such an institute.[34] Fitzner and Gerhardt Preuschen, the future director of the institute, also gained the personal support of Herbert Backe, who wanted to sit on the board of trustees.[35] Backe, who with his position as Secretary of State in the Reich Agriculture and Nutrition Ministry (by 1943 he was appointed Reich Minister and Reich Farmer's Leader by Adolf Hitler) was one of the leaders of the National Socialist regime, had also been a member of the KWG senate since 1937. The REM sent its official support by the middle of October with 'an order' for the KWG to begin the preparations necessary to found the institute.[36]

The organizational stages of the institute progressed quickly, and by the founding celebration on 6 December 1940, Telschow was able to draw attention to the 'exceptional quickness' with which the institute had been set up. A number of leaders from the Party, the state and business showed interest in the project by joining the board of trustees and the Society was 'satisfied' that the new institute could contribute to 'questions of the German east'.[37]

The new director of the institute was Dr Gerhardt Preuschen. Before taking up the position of director of the agricultural institute, Preuschen had been the founder and director of an institute for agricultural technology and workers' physiology in Eberswalde from 1932 to 1940. Because he had not yet written his *Habilitation* (a second dissertation needed to qualify for a professorship in Germany) Mentzel and Meyer did not believe it was a good idea to create an institute under his leadership, but perhaps his background in mechanical engineering, practical training in agriculture and experience in the technology of agriculture compensated for this.[38] Although his political affiliation was not openly discussed in the negotiations, he had been a member of the NSDAP since 1 May 1937.[39] The appointment of a director who was not 'habilitated' marks a change in the general policies of the KWG, and in general German academic policy.[40]

Preuschen gave the opening lecture and thereby outlined the tasks and methods for the new institute. 'Safeguarding the new living space [*Lebensraum*] of the victorious campaign in 1939', began Preuschen, was the task that awaited the German people in the future. He made his National Socialist views clear, and brought to light the motivation behind the founding of this institute: 'The territory in the east must be integrated into German living space over the next few years'.[41] In his talk, Mentzel also emphasized the new tasks in the east as a result of the successful military campaign in 1939. He drew attention to the important contribution of science for these political goals. The creation of a new institute in the middle of the war 'proved Germany's strength', he said, and was done through German diplomacy and using the importance of science for the new Europe.[42] Backe began his talk with the oft-repeated National Socialist slogan about the 'danger' of the 'flight from the land'. The reason for this flight, he claimed, was the 'devaluation of agricultural work'. Because the east was assuming great importance, this flight from agricultural work, which was primarily occurring in the eastern parts of Germany, posed a threat. By creating new technical methods for agricultural work, Backe hoped the institute could help eradicate the causes of 'flight from the land'.[43] Common to all three speeches was the emphasis on the Breslau connection to the Balkans or southeast Europe. Backe identified the new institute as a 'bridge to southeastern Europe'. Mentzel thought the institute would not only have an impact on Germany, but also on southeastern Europe, which had a longstanding relationship with Breslau. Therefore foreigners from the southeast, like Iwan Bagrianoff, the Minister for Agriculture in Bulgaria, would be appointed to the Board of Trustees. Preuschen also discussed Breslau's close relations to southeastern countries and the interaction of Balkan agriculture with the German economy.[44]

Since the KWG had no president from the time of Carl Bosch's death in April of 1940 until June 1941, as managing director Telschow assumed the role in absentia and participated in the founding of the new institute. As a member of the NSDAP since May 1933 it is no surprise that Telschow would support National Socialist goals in agriculture. But if a strong president had been present at the time, then perhaps the Society might have been able to resist the intrusion of National Socialist politics into the founding of a new institute. The KWG viewed the institute with reservation, as is indicated by its name: 'Institut für landwirtschaftliche Arbeitswissenschaft in der Kaiser Wilhelm Gesellschaft' (Institute for the Science of Agricultural Work in the *Kaiser Wilhelm Gesellschaft*). This institute, in fact, inaugurated a 'new type' of institute for the Society, one under the general framework (*'Im Rahmen'*) of the KWG.[45] Administratively it was loosely connected to the KWG but the inspiration and running of the institute came from other individuals and institutions.

Soon after the opening celebration of the agricultural institute in Breslau, another agricultural institute was projected for Bulgaria, occupied by Germany but under indirect control. Bulgaria, according to Norman Rich, a leading authority on the German occupation, 'retained a greater degree of control over its domestic and foreign affairs during the war than any other country in southeastern Europe'.[46] Yet, simultaneously it was Hitler's 'self-willed ally'.[47]

Just as the Breslau agricultural institute had political origins, so too did the German–Bulgarian Institute for Agricultural Research. The institute seems to be the outcome of an agreement for cooperation in agriculture made on 25 June 1940 between Konrad Meyer, the head of the Research Service and Director of the section for agriculture and biology in the Reich Research Council, and Dontscho Kostoff, director of the central agricultural experimental and research institute in Sofia. In this agreement, Meyer and Kostoff resolved to deepen scientific cooperation through personal contacts between scientists. These contacts would be cultivated through mutual invitations for research trips and lectures. According to the KWG, it was the Bulgarian Agricultural Minister Iwan Bagrianoff's idea to create a joint German–Bulgarian Institute for agricultural research.[48] Bagrianoff had visited the Kaiser Wilhelm Institute for Breeding Research in 1940 and during that time had made overtures to the ministries and to the KWG about creating a similar institute in Sofia. Therefore, by April of 1941 the KWG began preparations for an institute based on 'strict parity' whereby there would be both a German and a Bulgarian president and director. Both countries would also share the costs; the Bulgarian government would build the institute and contribute the land, while the KWG would supply the instruments and other necessities for running an institute.[49] Such joint efforts were not unprecedented in the history of the Society. For example, even before the Third Reich a German–Italian institute for Marine biology had been founded in 1931. This in turn was built on a long tradition of German involvement in the Naples station and a desire for a Mediterranean centre. But the context of Greater Germany and the war cannot be overlooked in evaluating the founding of a new institute in the forties. Although it seems as though a Bulgarian stimulated the project, the KWG was taking advantage of, and contributing to, the state's *Lebensraum* policy. *Lebensraum* had found its way into the world of science as the Society expanded its foreign relations to the southeast. The cooperative nature of the project probably mirrored the general attitude of the occupied countries (or those countries under direct control) who saw the Germans as providers of needed equipment and instrumentation while the poorer rural countries would provide the rich agricultural resources, or whatever resources were available.

The political goals of the Bulgarian institute fit the notion of a 'new Europe' under German rule:

> ... without a doubt, the results won here in the continental climate of southeast Europe will also have fundamental importance for the *new Europe*. Indeed, in the future the main emphasis of Europe's total agricultural production will lie in the territories of the European East and Southeast.[50]

The KWG planned to uphold the 'basic research' tradition of its institutes in this project even though, by its nature, agriculture is primarily applied research. The memorandum on the tasks of the German–Bulgarian Institute for Agriculture paid lip-service to basic research and argued that one must conceive of research in the long term. Basic research, so the argument goes, eventually leads to practical fall-out. Accordingly, the institute would focus on problems of plant production not only for the 'new Europe' but also for Bulgaria.

Unlike the Breslau institute, plans for the institute in Bulgaria did not develop quickly and it was not until late 1942 that the institute celebrated its founding. Unlike the Breslau institute, however, the KWG, the REM and the Foreign Office supported the project unequivocally. The role and importance of the Foreign Office in the affairs of the Society at this juncture are also significant. Not only did it support the creation of the institute financially and scientifically, but its general influence in the affairs of the Society is reflected also by the presence of Ernst von Weizsäcker as a member of the president's advisory board (as of 24 April 1942). It was at the 24 April 1942 senate meeting that Weizsäcker suggested naming King Boris of Bulgaria an honorary member of the KWG. The head of the cultural department of the Foreign Office, Fritz von Twardowski, was a member of the board of trustees of the institute and participated in its founding.

The political and scientific importance of the project is reflected by the three-day programme prepared by Bulgarians for the president and his entourage from the KWG. On the first day the German guests visited the Bulgarian Minister President and the Agricultural Minister. The evening ended with a dinner headed by the German consulate.[51] The next day, 12 September 1942, the institute in Bulgaria opened officially in the presence of Albert Vögler, von Twardowski, the director of the cultural policy department of the Foreign Office, Mentzel, Beckerle, the German consulate in

Sofia, the Bulgarian Minister President and the Bulgarian Agricultural Minister.[52] Speeches extolled the new cooperative venture and after the 'auspicious intensification and deepening of mutual political, economic and cultural ties' between Germany and Bulgaria it was clear that activity would develop in agriculture, said a spokesman for the Bulgarians.[53] After the celebration, there was time for some sightseeing. The next day the KWG entourage visited agricultural schools near Sofia and ended the visit on 14 September with more dinners with German and Bulgarian dignitaries.

The founding of a new institute in Bulgaria raised suspicion, and a few days before the official celebrations the English radio announced:

> The German government is now establishing an institute for agriculture with the help of the *Kaiser Wilhelm Gesellschaft* which has the singular goal of exploiting Bulgarian agriculture for the interests of the Reich.[54]

This statement was in part true. In fact, when Telschow outlined the origins of the project to Mentzel, he stated:

> The stimulus for the founding of the institute came when the former Bulgarian Agriculture Minister, his excellency Bagrianoff, and his Secretary of State Kostoff, visited Germany. The Kaiser Wilhelm Gesellschaft, *as a representative of the German Reich* [emphasis added] brought the negotiations to a successful conclusion.[55]

This retrospective explanation would seem to substantiate the claim that the German government was building the institute with 'the help' of the KWG. Although the KWG was not a Reich institution but an autonomous organization, it became, perhaps, 'a representative of the German Reich' when its administrators or scientists went abroad. The KWG was certainly exploiting Bulgarian agriculture, but in a reciprocal way. Another unanswered question involves the motivations of the Bulgarians. It seems that, in addition to Iwan Bagrianoff, Slaw Antonoff, a Bulgarian scientist who had studied in Germany and was a Germanophile, campaigned for the founding of the institute. As a result of his efforts Telschow nominated him for a 'German order'. Antonoff's friendly attitude also earned him the name 'betrayer' from the English radio. In addition to making the best of a bad situation there were probably a number of fellow travellers from the political right in Bulgaria, as there were in other countries.

The German director of the institute was Professor Arnold Scheibe who came from an institute for agriculture at the technical college in Munich. Scheibe had been a member of the NSDAP since 1 May 1937 and of the SS since 1 October 1933. After becoming institute director in Bulgaria on 1 April 1942 he was given a leave of absence from the university in Munich. As early as September 1940, he was exempt from military service (*UK-Stellung*) because his work on plant breeding was considered important for the war effort. He had been working on a project for the Research Service since 1935 on oil and food plants. This work was, in turn, based on his participation in the German Hindukusch Expedition in Afghanistan (supported by the Reich Research Council, RFR) where he collected materials for research on plant breeding.[56] Scheibe's research received ample support from the Reich Research Council, and by 1944 he had at least two contracts for research designated important for the war and the state: one for the breeding and preparation of fibrous plants and the other for fruit and vegetable preservation especially for the army.[57] In addition, German agriculture could profit from his research on fat and protein, which had become an important topic during the war.

The Bulgarian director was to be Professor Dontscho Kostoff. But because of difficulties in gaining approval for Kostoff as a result of his activities in Russia, no Bulgarian director existed by 1943. The plans for equity in the board of trustees were realized, and twelve representatives from both the German and Bulgarian authorities sat on the board. On the German side there were two representatives from the KWG, one from the Foreign Office, one from the REM and one from the Reich Nutrition Ministry. The Bulgarian board of trustees consisted of the Agricultural Minister, Bagrianoff, Antonoff, the director of the natural history museum, a biologist and the director of the Bulgarian Sugar Trust.[58]

The KWG thought the institute would become the 'leading agricultural institute for the whole southeast'[59] and therefore it was advantageous for the Society's network of institutes abroad in agriculture and biology. Another institute to be added to the KWG network abroad was one for biology in Piraeus, Greece, a country occupied by Germany in April 1941.

The German–Greek biology institute also seemed to have received its initial stimulus from the foreign country participating in the joint arrangement. According to the record, it was Dr Tzonis, the director of a chemical-biological and cancer research institute in Athens, who proposed the idea of founding a joint German–Greek research institute for biology.[60] Even before the war, in January of 1938, Max Hartmann, a department head at the Kaiser Wilhelm Institute for Biology, evaluated and approved very highly of Tzonis' plan. Hartmann called attention to the existence of biological institutes in the Mediterranean – in Spain, France, Italy, Yugoslavia and Egypt; yet no similar institute existed in Greece. 'With its strong geographic structure, its great climatic differences, its rich coastal formations and rich island world ... Greece is very favourable for modern experimental-biological researches', wrote Hartmann in his assessment. Therefore, German biologists had a strong interest in founding the institute. By exploring the land and sea thoroughly it would also be of great use for Greek agriculture and fishing. Finally, young Greek biologists would benefit and be educated through their contact with German personnel.[61]

The institute was designed to create a 'firm connection between Greek and German culture'.[62] The 'cultural goals' of the institute were also stressed in the statutes, where the first sentence read: The KWG is building an institute, with the approval of the German Reich government and the Greek government, 'in an attempt to intensify and cultivate the cultural and scientific relations' between the two countries.[63] Some scientists involved in the founding discussions also saw it in this 'cultural propagandistic way' – a significant departure from the traditional pure science institutes created by the Society. Fritz von Wettstein even went so far as to say that the institute abroad would 'never only have the character of a pure research institute' like the ones at home, but rather he thought it was an 'important task' for the institute to be used as a 'German cultural propaganda institute'.[64]

Dr Tzonis visited the cultural department of the Foreign Office in Berlin on 24 August 1940 to discuss the founding of the institute again. Hartmann reported to Telschow that Tzonis was in Berlin to realize his plan 'under the present more favourable political conditions'. Hartmann advised Tzonis to found the institute as a KWG Institute and not as a direct state institute.[65] The KWG wrote to the Foreign Office expressing 'great interest' in the project should funding from the Reich be forthcoming.[66]

Although Tzonis sponsored the project, as preparations continued for the institute in Athens Hartmann began to sense a dampening of interest by the Greeks towards the end of 1941. The war context had begun to penetrate more deeply into Greece as German troops had occupied much of Europe; Greece was invaded in April 1941. The German military had apparently taken over many scientific institutes for their own use. Hartmann reported in December 1941 that he had the impression that the 'attitude of Greek academic circles – also those who had been very friendly towards Germans before – had become much more reserved since the summer'. One Greek scientist apparently declined to join the board of directors of the institute because the political context in Greece made it 'psychologically impossible' (*seelisch unmöglich*).[67] As a result of these reservations it was not until 1942 that a contract between the KWG and the Greek government was signed.[68]

Failed plans for founding joint institutes in southeast Europe

In addition to the agricultural institutes in Breslau and Bulgaria, another joint institute for agriculture was planned for Hungary, an agricultural country in southeast Europe. Discussions began in the autumn of 1941 at a time when the Bulgarian institute was well on its way towards completion; it was therefore often referred to as a model for the prospective Hungarian institute. The initial written stimulus for a joint German–Hungarian institute for agriculture came from Baron Tilo von Wilmowsky, an Austrian and president of the Central European Economic Association, on 2 September 1941. As a result of discussions with Vögler, the president of the KWG, German and Hungarian colleagues from the economic association, Reichsminister for Finance Lutz Count Schwerin von Krosigk, and Herbert Backe, the idea to create such an institute found great interest and warm support, especially from the latter two individuals. Wilmowsky thought that German scientific results could be used on the special climatic and soil conditions in Hungary and the Danube basin. The Hungarians were interested in such a project because they had a longstanding interest in exporting agricultural products and importing industrial ones.[69]

The KWG was interested in the project and financial support was available, but there did not seem to be a leading scientist on hand; after all, it had been the tradition of the Society to find a scientist and build an institute around him. Telschow, the general director of the Society, approached the foreign office. They also supported the project as an analogue to the Bulgarian institute, although they did not want it to become 'the central agricultural station in the southeast' because of rivalries among countries.[70]

Yet, even before detailed plans could develop for the institute, interference came from the REM. Mentzel claimed that the Society had not told him of the plans for an agricultural institute in Hungary. In a power-play that reflects the changing relation of the KWG to the state, Mentzel wrote to the Society on 21 October 1941 claiming that in accordance with his decree of 30 July 1941 'all future negotiations about foreign questions at the *Kaiser Wilhelm Gesellschaft*' could only be undertaken with his prior permission. Therefore he required a report about the founding of this institute in Hungary. Annoyed at this interference in its internal administration, Vögler wrote to the Ministry reminding them that they had reported the discussions to the Ministry in a letter predating Mentzel's and clearly the Society would contact the appropriate ministries on such questions, but the senate of the Society was finally responsible for founding such institutes. Furthermore, wrote Völger, according to its statutes, the president led the whole Society and was not bound to the directives of a ministry. Three months after Vögler's letter of 6 November, Mentzel replied and repeated his assertion that the Society's plans abroad had to be undertaken in agreement with him and his directives. He wrote to Vögler that he did not subscribe to the basic attitude in his letter and referred to the first paragraph of the Society's statutes (as of 1937) where it was stated that the KWG is 'under the ministries' control' ('*untersteht .. meiner Aufsicht*'). He then referred to paragraph fourteen where the statutes stated that the creation of research institutes could be undertaken after a hearing by the senate and scientific council in agreement with the minister. By the end of the letter Mentzel was asking the Society to defer the plan because no scientist was available for the task.[71] In the end, the plan failed because no suitable scientist was found to head the proposed institute, a problem that had plagued the negotiations from the start and did not seem to be a result of Mentzel's interference.

It is significant that two institutes were created, and that one was planned, in southeastern Europe. The Balkans were seen by the National Socialists as an important element of the New Order of Europe under German rule. These countries would provide agrarian products in exchange for industrial growth and would thereby benefit the German economy. In fact, by 1939 Germany led France and England with the lion's share of exports from southeastern countries; and by June 1941 Germany's influence in the Balkans was growing.[72] But, in particular, Germany saw the southeastern European countries as providers of agricultural raw materials. During the war the most important task of German agriculture was the provision of protein and especially fat. Sunflower seeds from Roumania, Bulgaria and Hungary, for example, were considered to be an important raw material for oil. Walter Darré proclaimed at an exhibition that southeastern Europe could supply Greater Germany's needs for plant oil.[73]

No institutional commitments in Poland

Interestingly enough, the KWG had no institutional commitments in Poland, the country targeted for living space, the first country occupied by Germany during the war, and a country where other scholars and scientists set up ideologically inspired or influenced institutes. A few examples of institutions set up by other scholars and scientists show how much less the KWG was influenced by, and contributed to, *Lebensraum* ideology in the east. And it should be emphasized here that *Lebensraum* is generally applied to areas in the east, especially Poland and European Russia. The two most important and notorious institutes founded in Poland during the Third Reich were the 'Institute for German Work in the East' (*Institute für Deutsche Ostarbeit*) in Krakow and the *Reichsuniversität* Posen.

The Institute for German Work in the East was supposed to become the intellectual bulwark of German culture in the East and a centre for research and teaching.[74] Located in the *Generalgouvernement* of occupied Poland, the institute was headed and conceived by Hans Frank, who was also the Governor of the *Generalgouvernement*. It consisted of eleven departments ranging from Race and *Volk* Research, law, history and philology to agriculture; it also organized conferences and published its own journal. The *Reichsuniversität* Posen, on the other hand, was one of three Reich universities founded in the occupied countries of the newly won *Lebensraum* (the other two were in Strassburg and Prague). The Reich universities were model National Socialist universities and were created to serve cultural, economic and political rule in the occupied areas and to build up *Lebensraum* policies.[75] The KWG and its scientists were not involved in these institutions nor were comparable institutions created by the Society. This comparison it reflects the different and subtle nature of the relationship between National Socialist ideology and the *Kaiser Wilhelm Gesellschaft*.

Epilogue

During the last two years of World War II, the Society had begun to evacuate many institutes out of Berlin to southwest Germany because of heavy Allied bombing.[76] The newly founded institutes discussed above were not affected by this measure because of their locations. The war context, however, made it increasingly difficult to work under the deteriorating conditions. The work at the German–Greek Institute for Biology never really got off the ground and once the work at the German–Bulgarian Institute for Agriculture was ready to begin, the rapidly changing military and political events in Bulgaria and Germany in August 1944 made it necessary for Arnold Scheibe to evacuate the equipment, materials and books from the institute to Germany. Bulgaria basically capitulated and the Soviet Army entered the country. This marked the end of the joint project. In his 1956 retrospective history of the institute, Scheibe relates that further German–Bulgarian cooperation was discontinued because the 'iron curtain' cut off contact between the two countries.[77] But, in fact, it was discontinued because of its World War II origins, as was the German–Greek Institute for Biology. Both these institutes represented discontinuities in the policies and politics of institute foundation at the Society.

The institute for agricultural work in the KWG survived the war, although its work was also limited during the last few years when the director and staff members were drafted. By January 1945 it had to move from Kleinau, near Breslau, where it had been working in rooms in the university, because of the advancing Russian troops. By the autumn of 1945 the institute had leased an agricultural plant in Imbshausen, its members having fled through Leipzig where they left much equipment. Although the director initially wanted to re-found the institute in Darmstadt in Hessen, the American zone of occupation, he ended up in the British zone where he would not be arrested, because of his party membership.[78] The institute was kept on during the early post-war years with a change of emphasis in its tasks. Because of the miserable state of agriculture and nutrition, the ministries of the state were very interested in the work of the institute and its task was to increase production in the agricultural sector.[79] The newly founded *Max-Planck-Gesellschaft*, however, did not believe that the research undertaken at the institute belonged to the tasks of the Society and by 1948–9 did not want to keep it.[80] Nevertheless, by 1950, after the leasing arrangement ran out in Imbshausen, the institute had moved to Bad Kreuznach and in 1956 was renamed 'Max Planck Institute for Agricultural Work and Agricultural Technology', thus being formally integrated into the band of Max Planck Institutes. After Preuschen retired in 1976, the institute closed.[81] In some respects there was interest in maintaining the institute in the early post-war years for the same reason it was founded during the Third Reich – in order to help Germany become self-sufficient in agricultural production and to improve the desperate state of nutrition, during the early post-war period as much as during the war; this represented a continuity in goals. Both during the war and in the post-war period the Society was reluctant to maintain it as a *Kaiser-Wilhelm/Max-Planck-Gesellschaft* institute.

Conclusion

The concepts of *Lebensraum* and *Kulturpolitik,* and the increased importance of agriculture to the National Socialists all played important roles in the creation of new institutes at the Society and in the participation of some KWG scientists in National Socialist *Kulturpolitik.* There was hesitation on the part of the KWG to integrate the three new eastern/ southeastern institutes into its band of Kaiser Wilhelm Institutes. This was reflected in the names of these institutes: Institute for Agricultural Science *in* the KWG, 'German–Bulgarian Institute for Agriculture' and 'German–Greek Institute for Biology'. These institutes inaugurated a new type of institute which was administered by the Society but not fully incorporated into it or credited with the name 'Kaiser Wilhelm Institute'. The joint institutes were conceived of in a cooperative way and, in the two cases above, the initial stimulus had come from the partner countries abroad. It was not simply a matter of the Society implementing new National Socialist cultural policies for southeast Europe. After World War II, the Society considered the two institutes abroad to be 'war foundings' and they were therefore not continued. In the case of the two institutes abroad, the political and ideological context played major roles in the founding, which usually did not occur at the Society prior to the Third Reich.

The ideological origins of the institute for agriculture in Breslau were seemingly forgotten after the war, and that institute was re-founded as a Max-Planck-Institute for Agricultural Work and Agricultural Technology in Bad Kreuznach in 1956, thus becoming fully integrated into the refounded *Max Planck Gesellschaft.* The director, Gerhard Preuschen, also stayed on.[82] In itself, the study of agriculture was not ideological, but during the Third Reich its justification in the context of a growing Greater Germany made it so. During the Weimar period there had been little interest in creating an institute for agriculture at the Society; this type of work was seen as too applied and could be carried out in conjunction with existing institutes. With new masters who greatly valued agriculture both for its contribution to *Nahrungsfreiheit* and for the ideological importance of *Blut und Boden,* agricultural institutes flourished at the Society and in general.

The ideological matrix of *Lebensraum*, *Kulturpolitik* and National Socialist agriculture flavoured programmatic statements, which in turn served to legitimate the various projects to National Socialist governmental agencies. Furthermore, the notions dovetailed with the underlying aims of the scientific projects before these ideas were realized in the political realm. In fact, the Sofia and Athens institutes were conceived of before the war, but could only be created under more favourable political circumstances. The Society exploited the political situation in order to gain financial support from the REM, the Reich Nutrition Ministry and the Foriegn Office. The war years were also a period in the Society's history when it established closer ties to these offices. This is reflected in the election of Ernst von Weizsäcker, the Secretary of State in the Foreign Office, to the Advisory Board and Senate of the Society in 1942. Herbert Backe, minister of the Reich Nutrition Ministry, was named vice-president of the Society in 1941, and there had been an immense increase in financial support from the Nutrition Ministry during the war.[83] Backe had referred to this increased financial support when he vied to become vice-president. Finally, a senator of the Society and industrialist – Otto Fitzner – had stimulated the creation of the Breslau institute. All these developments reflect the way in which members of the new National Socialist society infiltrated the decision-making bodies of the *Kaiser Wilhelm Gesellschaft*.

While the social and scientific context of the times often entered into and influenced the creation of scientific institutes at the Society, by the beginning of the war years the social structure of National Socialist Germany was totalitarian and it had strong ideological programmes. Although pure scientific elements also played a role in institute founding, the scientists used the political context to legitimate and find support for their creation, yet the institutes also had strong ideological origins, which represented a discontinuity for the Society.

8 Biological research at universities and Kaiser Wilhelm Institutes in Nazi Germany

UTE DEICHMANN and BENNO MÜLLER-HILL

1 Introduction

When the American physicist Samuel Goudsmit analysed the development of nuclear physics in Germany during World War II, he came to the rather devastating conclusion that:[1] 'Scientific work did not advance under the administration of men like SS-Brigadier *General Ministerial Direktor Professor Doktor* Rudolf Mentzel, and *Ministerial* Manager *Professor Doktor* Erich Schumann[2] ...'

Many scientists and historians agree with Goudsmit that poor administration and funding of scientific research, as well as the general hostility of the National Socialist leaders towards the sciences, severely crippled science in Germany. The exodus of Jewish scientists is also widely considered to be an important reason for the poor performance of German science during and after the Third Reich.[3] On the other hand, recent publications on the history of sciences during National Socialism question the general truth of the claim that all science radically deteriorated during the Nazi era.[4] To the best of our knowledge no one has explored the question of continuity or discontinuity of scientific research in biology during these years.

How did the National Socialist regime influence the development of biological research at universities and the Kaiser Wilhelm Institutes? Here we will demonstrate that the impact of the forced emigration on biology was smaller than in other fields. Scientific research at universities during the Third Reich, like science today, was difficult without funding from outside sources. Thus we analyse the funding of biological research at universities and Kaiser Wilhelm Institutes by the *Deutsche Forschungsgemeinschaft* (literally translated as 'German Research Foundation'), the main state funding agency. Neither ideologically oriented nor senseless

160

research projects were funded in biology. The total volume of funding for fundamental research grew until 1944. Moreover the relative amount of money appropriated to the Kaiser Wilhelm Institutes (KWIs) increased from about ten percent before 1933 to about fifty percent in 1944. The decline in German biology after World War II was not caused by lack of money during the Third Reich.

2   The expulsion and forced emigration of 'non-Aryan' and politically incriminated biologists, 1933–9

The National Socialist policy of *Gleichschaltung* of the universities has been analysed in many publications.[5] It can be summed up as the application of the *'Führerprinzip'* (Leadership Principle) to the university administration and the expulsion of all Jewish and the few outspoken liberal or left wing university teachers. Detailed information about the process of *'Selbstgleichschaltung'* at KWIs can be found in for example, Vierhaus and Brocke.[6]

At the Austrian universities the National Socialist laws aimed at *Gleichschaltung* were implemented immediately after the *'Anschluss'* on 13 March 1938. Here, followers of the former Dollfuss-Schuschnigg-Regime and persons who belonged to Catholic political unions were among those dismissed for political reasons. The expulsion of university teachers according to these laws took place at the German University in Prague immediately after the German occupation of Czechoslovakia in March 1939. In Strassburg and Posen, new German universities were established in 1941 and 1940, respectively, with German staff. All members of the previously existing French and Polish universities were dismissed.

In spite of the fact that the *Kaiser Wilhelm-Gesellschaft* (literally translated as Kaiser Wilhelm Society, henceforth KWG) was a private institution, according to the Civil Service Law in 1933 'non-Aryan' assistants, fellows and employees had to be dismissed in 1933 in those institutes that relied upon public money for more than fifty percent of their finances.[7] However, most of the directors could stay in their positions until 1935 and some until 1938.

2.1   *Biologists who were dismissed either as 'non-Aryans' or for political reasons, and who emigrated*

In 1933 there were 249 'habilitated' biologists at universities in Germany and 25 'non-habilitated' biologists at KWIs; in 1938 there were 61 'habilitated' biologists at Austrian universities and at the German university in Prague.[8] At least thirty of these 337 biologists (8.9%) lost their positions in Germany during or after 1938, either as 'non-Aryans' or because they were married to a 'non-Aryan'; almost all of them emigrated, see

Table 8.1. *The dismissal and forced emigration of biologists of Jewish origin or married to a Jewish wife*

Name	First name	Position	Institution	Subject	Year of dism.	Successor	Year of emig.	Countries of emigration	First permanent position	Year of return	Institution
Bodenstein	Dietrich	res. fell.	KWI Biology	Zoology	1933		1933	Italy, USA	Stanford Univ.	0	
Brauner	Leo	ao Prof	Univ. of Jena	Botany	1933		1933	Turkey	Univ. Istanbul	1955	Univ. of Munich
Bresslau	Ernst	o. Prof.	Univ. of Cologne	Zoology	1933	O. Kuhn	1934	Brazil	Univ. Sao Paolo	0	
Brieger	Friedrich	Pdoz.	Univ. of Berlin	Bot/Gen	1934		1934	England, Brazil	Univ. Sao Paolo	0	
Fraenkel	Gottfried	Pdoz.	Univ. of Frankfurt	Zoology	1933		1933	England	Imp. Coll. London	0	
Freund	Ludwig	ao. Prof.	Germ. Univ. Prague	Zoology	1938		—a			1949	Univ. of Halle
Gams	Helmut	ao. Prof	Univ. of Innsbruck	Botany	1938		—			(1945)	Univ. of Innsbruck
Goldschmidt	Richard B.	Dir.	KWI Biology	Zool/Gen	1935	A. Kühn	1935	USA	Univ. Calif. Berk.	0	
Gross	Fabius	Ass.	KWI Biology	Zool/Gen	1933		1933	England	Marine Biol. Ass.	0	
Hamburger	Victor	Pdoz.	Univ. of Freiburg	Zoology	1933		1934	USA	Washington Univ.	0	
Heilbronn	Alfred	ao. Prof.	Univ. of Münster	Botany	1933		1933	Turkey	Univ. Istanbul	1956	Univ. of Münster
Heitz	Emil	ao. Prof.	Univ. of Hamburg	Bot/Gen	1937		1937	Switzerland	Univ. of Basel	0	
Hermann	Siegwart	Pdoz.	Germ. Univ. Prague	Botany	1938		1939	France, USA		0	
Hertz	Mathilde	Pdoz.	KWI Biology	Zoology	1935		1935	England		0	
Hirmer	Max	ao. Prof.	Univ. of Munich	Botany	1936					0	
Japha	Arnold	ao. Prof.	Univ. of Halle	Zoology	1936					0	
Jollos	Victor	ao. Prof.	KWI Biology	Zool/Gen	1933		1934	USA	–	0	
Kalmus	Hans	Pdoz.	Germ. Univ. Prague	Zool/Gen	1938		1938	Yugosl., England	Univ. of London	0	
Marcus	Ernst-G.	ao Prof.	Univ. of Berlin	Zoology	1935		1936	Brazil	Univ. Sao Paolo	0	
Merton	Hugo	ao. Prof.	Univ. of Heidelberg	Zoology	1935		1936	Scotland		0	
Peterfi	Tibor	guest res.	KWI Biology	Cytology	1935		1935	Engl., Denmark	Copenhagen Univ.	0	
Philip	Ursula	res. fell.	KWI Biology	Zool/Gen	1933		1933	England		0	
Pringsheim	Ernst G.	o. Prof.	Germ. Univ. Prague	Botany	1938	V. Czurda	1939	England	Cambridge Univ.	0	
Przibram	Hans	ao. Prof.	Univ. of Vienna	Zoology	1938		—c			0	
Schwarz[d]	Walter	Pdoz.	TH Darmstadt	Botany	1933		1933	Palestine	Hebr. Univ. Jerusalem	0	
Steinitz	Walter	Pdoz.	Univ. of Breslau	Zoology	1935		1935	Palestine		0	
Stern	Curt	Pdoz.	KWI Biology	Zool/Gen	1933		1933	USA	Univ. Rochester	0	
v. Ubisch	Gerta	ao. Prof.	Univ. of Heidelberg	Bot/Gen	1933		1934	Brazil	Seruminstit. S.Paolo	0	
v. Ubisch	Leopold	o. Prof.	Univ. of Münster	Zoology	1935	H. Weber	1935	Norway		0	
Wolf	Ernst	Pdoz.	Univ. of Heidelberg	Zoology	1933		1933	USA		0	

Note: ao. Prof.: associate professor; Ass: assistant; Dir: director; guest res.: researcher not employed by the KWG; o. Prof.: full professor; Pdoz.: assistant professor; Bot: Botany; Gen: Genetics; Zool: Zoology; Disrn: Dismissal; Emig: Emigration; Return: Return to a position at a German or Austrian university. The names of successors are given only for dismissed full professors.

a Ludwig Freund was deported to KZ Theresienstadt in 1943.   b Arnold Japha committed suicide in 1943.   c Hans Przibram died from starvation in the KZ Theresienstadt in May 1944.

d [partially obscured] ...ered his name into Michael Evenari after his emigration.

Table 8.1.[9] Nine biologists were dismissed on political grounds and two for unknown reasons. Four of these eleven biologists emigrated, four biologists emigrated for unknown reasons; see Table 8.2. The total number of biologists who emigrated during or after 1933 is 33 out of 337 (9.7%);[10] two others most probably also emigrated. Four of the emigrants accepted a position at a German or Austrian university after World War II, among them two of the émigré Jewish biologists.

The comments of the president of the KWG, Max Planck, on the expulsions illustrate the readiness of these scientists to subordinate themselves to the regime almost without protest, and to veil the active participation of the KWG. In the 1934 annual report of the KWG, Max Planck described the dismissal of Curt Stern, Victor Jollos and Fabius Gross as follows:

> Dr Stern accepted a call from the university in Rochester. Professor Jollos followed a call from the Institute of Genetics of the University of Wisconsin in Madison. Dr Gross went as an assistant to Huxley and Fisher in London.[11]

In fact, Victor Jollos never managed to obtain a permanent position in the USA. When, after the Nuremberg laws were passed, the 'Second Director' of the KWI for Biology, Richard Goldschmidt, was dismissed in December 1935, Max Planck commented in the report of 1937 that: 'Prof. Dr R. Goldschmidt accepted a position at the University of California, Berkeley'.[12] Unlike the KWI for Biology, no Jewish scientists worked at the KWI for Breeding Research. A gardener, Fanny du Bois-Reymond,[13] was, however, dismissed from this KWI.[14]

2.2   Biologists who were dismissed for political reasons but continued biological research in Germany

Elisabeth Schiemann lost her *venia legendi* (the right to teach) at the university in Berlin in 1940, because she openly contradicted anti-Semitic views. She continued her research, however, obtaining a research stipend from the DFG with the help of Fritz von Wettstein. In 1943 she was appointed head of a department in the newly founded KWI for *Kulturpflanzenforschung* (Cultivated Plants Research).

Three assistants at the KWI for Breeding Research, Hermann Kuckuck, Rudolf Schick and Hans Stubbe, were dismissed in 1937 after having been accused of disturbing the peaceful working conditions. The political background for these dismissals was the strong pressure of members of the NSDAP and the SS at this institute, who wanted to get rid of these three non-National Socialists. Stubbe could continue his research at the KWI for Biology under von Wettstein. He was appointed Director of the KWI for *Kulturplanzenforschung* in 1943. Kuckuck and Schick somehow managed to continue plant breeding research, the former with a private firm, and

Table 8.2. The dismissal and emigration of non-Jewish biologists

Name	First name	Position	Institution	Subject	Year of dism.	Reason for dism. or emig.	Successor	Year of emig.	Countries of emigration	First permanent position	Year of return	Institution
Arens	Robert	Pdoz.	Univ. of Cologne	Botany	–	unknown		1936	Brazil	Univ. Rio de Jan.	0	
Daumann	Erich	Pdoz.	Germ. Univ. Prague	Botany	–[a]	political		?	Tasmania?		0	
Eckert	Friedrich	Pdoz.	Germ. Univ. Prague	Zoology	1938	unknown[a]					0	
Gaffron	Hans	guest res.	KWI Biology	Biochem		unknown		1937	USA	Univ. Chicago	0	
Gassner	Gustav	o. Prof.	TH Braunschweig	Botany	1933	political	Jaretzky	1934	Turkey	Univ. Istanbul	1945	TH Braunschweig
Holtfreter	Johannes	Pdoz.	Univ. of Munich	Zoology	1938	unknown		1939	Engl. Canada, USA	Univ. Rochester	0	
Kisser	Josef	Pdoz.	Univ. of Vienna	Botany	1938	political		–			1945	Univ. of Vienna
Kosswig	Curt	ao. Prof.	TH Braunschweig	Zool/Gen	1937	political		1937	Turkey	Univ. Istanbul	1955	Univ. of Hamburg
Mainx	Felix	ao. Prof.	Germ. Univ. Prague	Botany	1938	political		–			1947	Univ. of Vienna
Matthes	Ernst	o. Prof.	Univ. of Greifswald	Zoology	–	unknown	Heidermanns	1937	Portugal	Univ. Coimbra	0	
Penners	Andreas	ao. Prof.	Univ. of Vienna	Zoology	1938	political		–			0	
Schaxel	Julius	ao. Prof.	Univ. of Jena	Zoology	1933	political[b]		1933	USSR		0	
Seiler	Jakob	ao. Prof.	Univ. of Munich	Zoology	–	unknown		1933	Switzerland	Univ. of Zurich	0	
Storch	Otto	o. Prof.	Univ. of Graz	Zoology	1938	political	J. Meixner	–			1945	Univ. of Vienna
Strouhal	Hans	Pdoz.	Univ. of Vienna	Zoology	1938	political		–			1945	Univ. of Vienna

Note: Abbreviations: see Table 8.1.

[a] His fate after 1939 is unknown to us.

[b] Julius Schaxel was arrested under the Stalin purges in 1937 and died under obscure circumstances in 1943 in Moscow.

the latter on his own farm. Both became university teachers only after the war.

Three full professors were retired (*emeritiert*) against their will: Hans Driesch (philosopher and biologist in Leipzig) and Richard Hesse (zoologist in Berlin) for political reasons, and Carl Zimmer (zoologist in Berlin) for reasons unknown.

2.3   A brief summary of the impact of the expulsion of biologists

It is not possible in this chapter to describe in detail the suffering that was caused by anti-Semitism, political persecution and the expulsions. The period of hardship often lasted for many years, and some emigrants were never able to cope with the new situation. Many of the Jewish emigrants shared a deep attachment to Germany. The expulsion thus caused a particular humiliation, which transcended the hardship of losing a position and finding a new one in another country.[15] The outstanding scientific achievements of the emigrants also cannot be discussed in detail here. Instead, we will try briefly to assess the impact of the dismissal and forced emigration on biological research in Germany, first of all by comparing it with the losses in other disciplines. The results show that, with 9.7%, the loss in biology was lower than that in physics or mathematics. Here, however, older figures of 26% and 20% respectively, for emigrants[16] could not be confirmed in a more recent study, according to which 15.5% of the university teachers of physics emigrated.[17] No university lost both all of its botanists and all of its zoologists, whereas at the University of Göttingen virtually all of the mathematics lecturers had to emigrate, and in physics the majority of them.[18] Finally, zoologists constituted a larger percentage of the emigrants than did botanists.

An often neglected sinister aspect of the expulsion should also be mentioned. In biology as elsewhere, most of the vacancies were refilled within a short time. Assistant professors became full professors, postdoctoral workers moved up and became assistant professors. This ability to advance rapidly in their career was an important factor in ensuring the loyalty for the National Socialist regime of a large group of young academics.

3   Funding of biological research by the *Deutsche Forschungsgemeinschaft* (DFG) and the *Reichsforschungsrat* (RFR)

3.1   The founding and the aims of the DFG and RFR

The *Notgemeinschaft der Deutschen Wissenschaft* (Emergency Association of German Scientists) was founded in 1920 by representatives of universities and other research institutes. This self-administrated association became the most important German organization for the funding of scientific research. In 1937 its name was changed to the *Deutsche Forschungsgemeinschaft* (German Research Association, DFG). The *Notgemeinschaft* was *gleichgeschaltet* in June 1934 when Johannes Stark, Nobel prize-winner and one of the anti-Semitic founders of 'Aryan Physics', was appointed president by the Minister of Education, Bernhard Rust. Stark imposed the *'Führerprinzip'* on the institution (that is, he abolished democratic decision-making in the organization) and denied grants to Jews. Because of Stark's conflicts with the Ministry of Education, he was replaced in late 1936 by Dr Rudolf Mentzel, a member of the SS and official in the Ministry of Education. In 1937 Rust founded the *Reichsforschungsrat* (Reich Research Council, RFR) in order to coordinate scientific research with the Four Year Plan for economic autarky established in 1936. The RFR did not have its own administration, but instead remained part of the DFG and was responsible for research grants in the natural sciences. Grant applications for biological research were handled by the heads of three departments of the RFR: Professor Konrad Meyer of the department of Agricultural Sciences and General Biology; Professor Ferdinand Sauerbruch of the department of Medicine; and Professor Kurt Blome of the department of Genetics, Population Policy and Racial Care. Meyer had a very influential position in the RFR. He was professor of agricultural sciences in Berlin, held a high SS rank and was also head of the *'Forschungsdienst'*, the association of agricultural scientists (see also under 5.2). His department had the most money at its disposal.[19]

The *Notgemeinschaft* decided whether to approve grant applications after consulting two anonymous referees (*Gutachter*). After the foundation of the RFR in 1937, the system of anonymous referees was abolished. According to the available documentation, grant applications made by biologists after May 1937 were decided by a single appointed expert.

3.2   The volume of funding for biology, 1933–45

How did the funding of biologists by the *Notgemeinschaft*/DFG develop after 1930, and what was the impact of the RFR? This question can be answered by determining the amount of money from the DFG/RFR given to the biologists who applied for grants from 1931 to 1945. (Research at the universities relied heavily on funding from outside but most KWIs had their own research money.)

Only a few individual grants by the *Notgemeinschaft* are documented for the years prior to 1933. Records of the *Notgemeinschaft* concerning preliminary decisions on grants, however, give information on grants before 1933.[20] According to this list, in 1930 74,000 RM were granted to the biologists analysed in this study. The documentation for grants since 1933 is also incomplete but is available for most grants particularly from 1937,

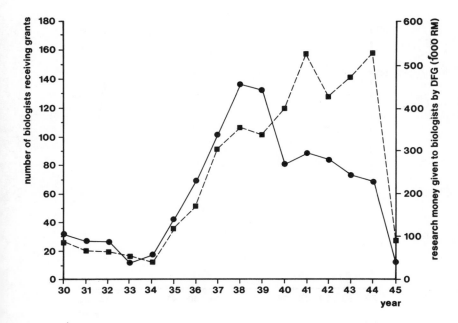

Fig. 8.1 Funding of biologists by the DFG/RFR from 1930 to 1945. The grants from January to May 1934, before the DFG was *'gleichgeschaltet'*, are listed under 1933. The data for the years 1930 through 1932 were derived from records of the *Notgemeinschaft* about preliminary decisions on grants (see note 20).
● — ● number of biologists receiving grants.
■ -- ■ money (RM) given to biologists.

when the RFR was founded, to 1945. Figure 8.1 shows that funding of biologists increased from 300,000 RM in 1937 to 520,000 RM in 1944. The number of biologists funded per year increased from 101 in 1937 to 135 in 1938, then decreased to 80 in 1940 and 67 in 1944. After 1940, all research had to be designated 'war-relevant' in order to receive financial support. The buying power of the RM did not change between 1937 and 1944.

3.3   *Was membership of the NSDAP among biologists a prerequisite for being well funded?*

Like other German professionals, many biologists became NSDAP ('party') members in 1933. When the moratorium on applications introduced in April 1933 was ended, a second wave of biologists joined in 1937. The membership increased further in 1938 when Austrians could become

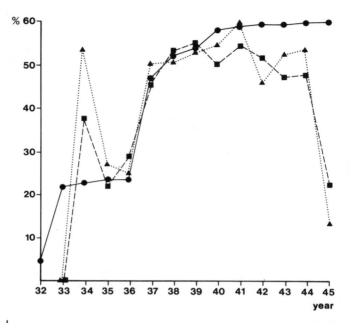

Fig. 8.2 Relationship between membership in the NSDAP and funding by the DFG/RFR. As in figure 8.1, grants until May 1934 are listed under 1933.

● — ● percentage of NSDAP members among the biologists who applied for grants between 1933 and 1945.

■ -- ■ percentage of NSDAP members among grant recipients.

▲ ... ▲ percentage of money given to NSDAP members of money given to biologists.

legal party members, and again in 1940, presumably due to German successes in the war (Figure 8.2).

Figure 8.2 shows the percentage of NSDAP members among biologists applying for DFG support during the years 1933–45. In order to find out whether the grants were preferentially given to party members, we compared the amounts per year given to members and to non-members (Figure 8.2).

A preference for party members is evident in 1934. Later, however, the percentage of party members among grant recipients corresponds to the percentage of membership among biologists. After 1941, it is even lower. Party membership was thus not a prerequisite for financial support. Though it can be assumed that in some cases money was given because of a scientist's influential political position, the research topic and the scientific respectability of the researcher seem to have been more important.

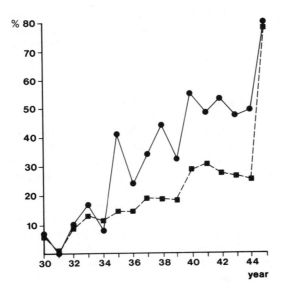

Fig. 8.3 Funding by DFG/RFR of biological research at KWIs in comparison to universities. As in figures 8.1 and 8.2, grants until May 1934 are listed under 1933. As in figure 8.1, the data for the years 1930 through 1932 was derived from records of the *Notgemeinschaft* about preliminary decisions on grants.
■ -- ■ percentage of biologists at KWIs among biologists receiving DFG/RFR grants.
● — ● percentage of total research money of DFG/RFR given to biologists at KWIs.

3.4 *Comparison between the funding of biologists working at KWIs and at universities*

Did universities and KWIs profit equally by the increase in funding?

According to the records of the preliminary grants of the *Notgemeinschaft* (see above), the percentage of money given to biologists at KWIs from 1929 to 1932 never exceeded 11% of the money given to biologists at universities (Figure 8.3). Biologists working at KWIs received 10% in 1932, 48% in 1941, and 49% in 1944, of the DFG/RFR financial support given to biologists (Figure 8.3). In 1945, they received 80% of the DFG/RFR support, but due to the low number of grants (9) in this year, a statistical evaluation is hardly possible. We note, however, as a curiosity that biologists at the KWIs had more trust in the continuation of the funding of their science when faced with the end of Nazi Germany than had their university colleagues. The KWIs not only obtained sufficient funding from the DFG/RFR, they also enjoyed a huge increase in financial support from the state. Due to this support, which was disproportionately provided by a few Ministries, the total budget of the KWG increased from 5.7 million RM in 1932 to 7.4 million RM in 1937, 10.9 million RM in 1940 and 14.4 million RM in 1944.[21]

After 1935, the average grant given to a biologist at a KWI was more than twice as large as a grant given to a biologist at a university. In 1944 the size of grants differed by a factor of 2.9. The data on grant rejections – though incomplete – show clearly that grant applications by biologists at KWIs were rejected less often than those of biologists at universities. Twenty-seven (8.2%) of 326 applications from universities, and three (4.2%) of seventy-one from KWIs were rejected from 1937 to 1939. From 1940 to 1941 there were fifteen rejections of 133 grant applications (11.2%) from universities, and 2 of 52 (3.8%) from KWIs. According to the information in the DFG files, there were no more rejections after 1941. On the whole, the KWIs profited from the increase in funding for biologists during the National Socialist period, whereas the percentage of financial support given to biologists at universities decreased drastically from 1932 to 1944.

4   DFG funding and the quality of research

4.1   General considerations

The content and results of biological research funded by the DFG/RFR will be described and analysed in a forthcoming publication by Ute Deichmann. Here the quality and the influence of the research of a selected group of biologists working at universities or at KWIs will be estimated by counting the number of citations and of cited articles of these biologists in the Science Citation Index from 1945 to 1954 (SCI) (see note, 'Methods and sources').

Unless stated otherwise, biologists who received DFG grants between 1933 and 1945 are analysed. They were either full professors at universities between 1937 and 1945 (fifty-six persons), or they were directors or heads of departments at five KWIs[22] (seventeen persons). Emigrants are thus not included. The money given by the DFG/RFR to each person is counted uniformly between 1937 and 1945, independent of the year of appointment as director or full professor. The year 1937 was chosen as the starting-point, because at that time the Jewish directors of KWIs had been replaced by successors from universities.

4.2   The comparison between universities and KWIs

The average number of citations per person, 96.5 (universities) and 109.8 (KWIs), is almost equal in universities and KWIs (Table 8.3).

Table 8.3. *DFG-funding between 1937 and 1945 and number of citations for all cited papers in the SCI 1945–1954 of biologists, who received DFG-grants between 1933 and 1945.*

	Univ.	KWG	Univ./KWG
Researchers funded by DFG			
Total	56	17	3.3
Members of NSDAP	27	9	
Non-members	29	8	
DFG 1937–1945 (RM)			
Total	818 139	899 191	0.9
Members of NSDAP	463 149	263 146	
Non-members	354 980	636 045	
Citations			
Total	5 402	1 866	2.8
Members of NSDAP	1 730	628	2.6
Non-members	3 672	1 258	2.9
Articles			
Total	2 642	836	3.2
Members of NSDAP	871	290	3.0
Non-members	1 771	546	3.2
Citations × 1000/RM			
Total	6.6	2.0	3.3
Members of NSDAP	3.7	2.3	1.6
Non-members	10.0	1.9	5.3
Citations/article			
Total	2.0	2.2	0.9
Members of NSDAP	2.0	2.2	0.9
Non-members	2.1	2.3	0.9
Citations/researcher			
Total	96.5	109.8	0.9
Members of NSDAP	64.1	69.8	0.9
Non-members	126.6	157.2	0.8

Note: Univ.: 56 full professors, who between 1937 and 1945 held chairs at botanical, zoological and genetic institutes of universities; 27 members of the NSDAP, 29 non-members. KWI: 17 directors and heads of departments at 5 KWIs (see 22) between 1937 and 1945; 9 members of the NSDAP, 8 non-members.

Table 8.4 *The 15 full professors at universities respectively directors and heads of departments of KWIs who collected the highest number of citations in the SCI 1945–1954*

Name	Subject	Institution	Citations	Articles	Citations/article
Schmidt, Wilhelm J.	Zoology	Univ of Giessen	480	241	2.0
Frisch, v., Karl	Zoology	Univ of Munich	379	143	2.7
Timoféeff-R., N.W.	Genetics	KWI Brain Research	318	123	2.6
Schramm, Gerhard	Virology	KWI Biochemistry	287	68	4.2
Bünning, Erwin	Botany	Univ of Strassburg	278	106	2.6
Lorenz, Konrad	Zoology	Univ of Königsberg	264	56	4.7
Höfler, Karl	Botany	Univ of Vienna	256	111	2.3
Bauer, Hans	Zoology	KWI Biology	252	56	4.5
Küster, Ernst	Botany	Univ of Giessen	238	155	1.5
Harder, Richard	Botany	Univ of Göttingen	237	93	2.5
Kühn, Alfred	Zool/Gen	KWI Biology	234	127	1.8
Oehlkers, Friedrich	Bot/Gen	Univ of Freiburg	233	70	3.3
Weber, Friedrich	Botany	Univ of Graz	226	95	2.4
Hartmann, Max	Zool/Gen	KWI Biology	212	78	2.7
Tischler, Georg	Bot/Gen	Univ of Kiel	178	80	2.2

Note: Bot: Botany; Gen: Genetics; Zool: Zoology; Cit/art: Average number of citations per article.

If the fifteen most cited persons are compared and the ratio of citations per article is taken as a measure of excellence, three researchers are clearly superior (Table 8.4): Konrad Lorenz, Hans Bauer and Gerhard Schramm. Lorenz received the Nobel prize in 1973 together with Niko Tinbergen and Karl von Frisch (the latter being number five on this scale). Schramm came very close to winning the Prize for his work on the Tobacco Mosaic Virus. The placement of the later Nobel prize winners suggests that this table is not altogether misleading. The influence and quality of research did not differ substantially between KWIs and universities. But, as stated above, we are dealing here only with biologists who received DFG grants.

We do not know the total cost of the research described in the articles cited in the SCI. Thus the ratio of citations to DFG money has to be used with care. This value differs by a factor of 3.3 between universities and KWIs (Table 8.3). If we generalize this value, biologists at KWIs spent 3.3 times more DFG research money than university professors in order to receive the same number of citations. As stated above, we are only dealing with money from the DFG and do not consider the research money provided by the KWG or the universities themselves.

At universities, non-party members received 2.7 times more citations (10 versus 3.7) for a given amount of DFG research money than members of the NSDAP. Party members collected only about half of the citations per person of non-members, both at universities and at KWIs. There is, however, no difference between party members and non-members in the number of citations per article. Non-party members apparently just worked much harder and published more. Yet three party members belong to the group of the fifteen most cited biologists in this study.

4.3   DFG money and the quality of research at universities

When funded full professors are compared with non-funded ones, DFG grants exerted a positive influence on the number of citations. The control group consists of the twenty-two biologists who were full professors between 1937 and 1945 and who did not apply for a DFG grant during the period from 1933 to 1945. In fact, more than two-thirds of all full professors at universities applied for grants from the DFG at least once during this period. Professors who received DFG grants collected 3.8 times more citations per person than the non-funded professors from articles published between 1933 and 1945. Funded professors received 45.1 citations, non-funded ones 11.8. An increase in productivity and, to a much lower degree, in the apparent quality of research, existed when the funding was higher than 2,000 RM; that is, with persons who applied for grants more than once (Table 8.5).

These data suggest that sufficient funding is one of the prerequisites for good research, i.e. research resulting in a large number of citations.

Table 8.5. *The influence of DFG funding on the quality of research at universities*

Funding 1937 to 1945 (RM)	Number of Professors	Citations/ Professors	Articles/ Professors	Citations/ articles
0	22	28.5	18.4	1.5
1–2000	7	41.4	23.0	1.8
2001–4000	10	137.2	65.0	2.0
4001–6000	6	97.6	52.5	1.9
6001–10000	7	110.8	62.0	1.8
10000–20000	11	93.0	37.6	2.5
20001–30000	7	68.1	37.8	1.8
>30000	6	95.1	43.5	2.2

Note: The average number of citations for all cited papers in the SCI 1945–1954 per person is listed for eight groups of full professors at universities, which differed by the amount of funding per person. All full professors who held chairs at German and Austrian universities between 1937 and 1945 are included.
RM: DFG-money, which was given between 1937 and 1945;
Citations: Average number of citations per person;
Articles: Average number of cited articles per person.

However, this conclusion does not mean that generous funding necessarily resulted in a large number of citations. According to the data in table 8.5, beyond 4000 RM an increasing amount of funding did not produce an increasing number of citations. The number of persons in each of the groups in Table 8.5 is too small for a statistical evaluation. In spite of this, and in spite of the fact that we do not have information about the total costs of the research involved, we may conclude that full professors at universities were not funded according to their scientific influence as estimated by the number of citations.

5   Why were biologists at KWIs funded so well?

Though the content of German biological research between 1933 and 1945 cannot be discussed here in detail, most of it, both at universities and at KWIs, was basic research.[23] What caused this large increase in the funding of basic research at KWIs during the Third Reich?

5.1   Politics

Some general remarks on the position of the KWG in National Socialist Germany may help to explain the impressive support for biological institutes. It was the policy of the KWG after 1933 'to contribute to the rise of the new Germany'.[24] In 1935 Secretary General Friedrich Glum wrote on the occasion of the 25th anniversary of the KWG: 'The KWG does not need a special justification for being joyfully at the disposal of the new *Reich* of Adolf Hitler and thus to contribute to the work of reconstruction of our German *Vaterland*'.[25] The KWG placed itself voluntarily at the disposal of the new regime and was rewarded. To quote Glum:

> the Reichgovernment, particularly the Reich Education Minister, has amply rewarded the readiness of the Society to serve the great tasks of the Third Reich. It has given increasing support to the Society, which has greatly suffered under the economic crisis, and it has acknowledged the Society's outstanding position in German science.[26]

As mentioned above, the total budget of the KWG increased from 5.7 million RM in 1932 to 14.4 million RM in 1944 due to the growing financial support from the state.[27] The establishment of two KWIs for basic or applied biology in occupied countries may be mentioned as symbols of the willingness of the KWG to participate in the nationalistic aims of the Reich government: the Bulgarian–German Institute for Agriculture, founded in Sofia in 1941, and the German–Greek Institute for Biology in Athens–Piraeus.

In spite of the fact that part of the National Socialist movement was hostile towards science, other members of the regime and the state funding organizations shared an interest with the KWG in having outstanding, internationally recognized scientists as directors of KWIs. The *Reichserziehungsminister* (Minister of Education) Bernhard Rust, for example, urged Fritz von Wettstein, a non-party member who ranked as the best plant geneticist in Germany, to accept the position of first Director of the KWI for Biology in Berlin. Von Wettstein refused the offer twice. In 1934, he wrote to the Bavarian Minister of Culture: '[Shortly after my refusal] ... [Rust] informed me in a personal conversation ... that he considered my move to Berlin to be absolutely necessary'.[28] He had two further meetings with Rust, with the result that: 'I can no longer refrain from the opinions of the *Reichsstellen* (Reich officials) that my presence in Berlin is my duty to the Reich'.[29]

In their grant applications submitted to the DFG between 1937 and 1942, von Wettstein and Alfred Kühn, the other Director of the KWI for Biology, emphasized repeatedly the danger of losing priority in all fields to researchers in the USA. They received the support they had requested. In spite of the fact that Nikolaj V. Timoféeff-Ressovsky was a citizen of the USSR, the Education Ministry increased the budget for his research institute after he received an offer of employment from the Carnegie Institution at Cold Spring Harbor in 1936.[30] Timoféeff, an internationally renowned geneticist, was Director of the Department of Genetics at the KWI for Brain Research. He turned down the offer to go to the USA.

During the war the KWG agreed to play an important role in reorganizing biological research in the occupied parts of the USSR. Many Soviet plant-breeding institutes, including those belonging to the Vavilov organisation, with their outstanding collections of primitive strains of crops, in 1941 and 1942 fell into German hands. Von Wettstein wrote a detailed memorandum outlining the future importance of these institutes for German science. He recommended to Ernst Telschow (Secretary General of the KWG), Herbert Backe (Secretary of State in the Ministry of Agriculture) and Konrad Meyer that these institutes become part of the 'biological institutional network' of the KWG.[31] According to von Wettstein, they should be associated with the KWI for *Kulturpflanzenforschung*. In fact, the director of the Erwin-Baur-KWI for Breeding Research, Wilhelm Rudorf, wanted them as part of his KWI, and he contacted Alfred Rosenberg, Minister of the Occupied Eastern Territories, in this regard.[32]

One might argue that Rudorf and von Wettstein had humanitarian motives for their intervention on behalf of the Soviet institutes. They might for example have intended to prevent them be taken over by unqualified biologists or the SS, and to preserve the lives of their colleagues. In any case, von Wettstein believed in a total German victory over the Soviet Union. In his letter to Telschow of 9 March 1942, he mentioned five Soviet biological institutes which 'for the time being were held in reserve (*vorläufig als Ergänzung*)', because 'we have not yet taken possession of them (*denn sie sind ja vorläufig noch nicht in unserem Besitz*)'.[33]

5.2   Economics and the military

Botanists at KWIs emphasized the importance of their mutation research, particularly of research in polyploidy, for the fast breeding of new crop strains. The support given to botanical research during the forties should also be regarded as part of the political concept of 'expansion of German living space (*Erweiterung des deutschen Lebensraums*)'. This policy, the '*Germanisierung*' (Germanization) of the already annexed Polish territories and land not yet under German control, was begun under the authority of SS leader Heinrich Himmler in October 1939. The fundamental importance of the concept of '*Lebensraum*' for the future was expressed by Prof. Konrad Meyer in a lecture on 'planning and reconstruction in the occupied eastern territories' delivered to the representatives of the KWG in the *Harnack Haus* of the KWG on 28 January 1942.[34]

> You have to have faith, imagination, and courage in order to contribute to the tasks of reorganization in the East. We thus also have to try to retreat from the half-solutions of former times and instead of treating symptoms to have the courage for a surgical operation. That is, from the viewpoint of our politics and economy, to dare a reorganization of the whole structure of the people. The *Ostaufgabe* [task in the East] is the

unique opportunity to realize the National Socialist will, and unconditionally to let it become action.[35]

Meyer, who held a high rank in the SS and was also head of the *Planungs-
abteilung* (Planning Department) of the *Reichssicherheitshauptamtes*, that
is, the headquarters of the NS police and security forces, was also the
author of the '*Generalplan Ost*' (General Plan for the East).[36] This plan
contained a comprehensive scheme for the legal, economic and spatial
reconstruction of the annexed or to be conquered territories between the
Oder river and the Ural Mountains. New settlement areas for German
farmers were to be placed under the control of Himmler during the period
of reconstruction, and the new settlers were to be racially selected according to the conception of the SS.[37] The concept of the *Generalplan Ost* was
part of the '*Germanisierungspolitik*' of the SS in the East. It assumed a
successful 'final solution of the Jewish question' and outlined the expropri-
ation and expulsion of millions of citizens of the USSR, Poland and other
East-European countries from these territories.[38] Alternatives like deprivation of rights with the obligation to do slave labour (see below, *nicht
eindeutschungsfähige Slowenen*), deportation to Siberia and 'scrapping
(*Verschrottung*) by labour' of those people who were 'racially undesirable'
were discussed by various committees, to which at least one member of the
KWG, Eugen Fischer, belonged.[39]

The botanical expeditions of the RFR after 1941, research at the KWI for
Kulturpflanzenforschung and, above all, at the KWI for Breeding Research,
were all funded as part of this political agenda of '*Erweiterung des Lebens-
raumes*'. For example, in his 1942 grant application, Hans Stubbe from the
KWI for Biology stated that,

> The systematic collection and maintenance of such plants [primitive
> strains of crops – UD and BMH] is the priority of the German breeding
> research, because the extraordinary diversity of these plants in the
> hitherto still unexplored mountains of the Balkans and their adaptation to
> extreme living conditions guarantee the finding of cold-, drought-, and
> parasite-resistant strains among them. These plants, with their precious
> qualities, play a decisive role in the breeding of generally resistant strains
> for the German East.[40]

The above-mentioned Backe, who was also a member of the KWG Senate,
and from 1941 to 1945 vice-president, emphasized in a meeting with von
Wettstein, Rudorf and Telschow that a central institute ('*Zentralstelle*') for
primitive plant strains was urgently necessary.[41] Backe was responsible for
the coordination of agricultural production for the Four Year Plan and for
army logistics and supply in the war against the USSR. In 1942 he succeeded Darré as head of the Ministry of Agriculture, and in 1944 he became
Minister of Agriculture.[42]

An official KWG statement declared that Rudorf and several of his

Fig. 8.4   Reichsmarshal Göring in the Kaiser Wilhelm Institute for Breeding Research. The photograph was published by the KWG in the *Jahrbuch 1940 der Kaiser Wilhelm-Gesellschaft*, p. 49.

collaborators in the KWI for Breeding Research were carrying out 'important tasks in the agricultural reconstruction of the occupied eastern territories'[43] (Figure 8.4).

Plant breeders from the KWI carried out research on fat- and oil-yielding crops adapted for agriculture in the East. After Joachim Hackbarth had become head of the division '*Ölpflanzen und Körnerleguminosen*' (oil-yielding plants and grain-yielding plants that are self-sufficient concerning nitrogen) in the branch in East Prussia of the KWI for Breeding Research in 1941, all of his wartime research projects served the agriculture in the East (*Anbau im Osten*).[44] This branch of the KWI was enlarged during the war with the help of '*Ostarbeiter*' ('Eastern Workers', forced labour).[45]

The contribution of scientists from this KWI and also of biologists from other institutions (see below) to the German war economy even included cooperation with Himmler and with officials from the concentration camp in Auschwitz. After Himmler received an order from Hitler to facilitate the growing and breeding of the rubber (caoutchouc) plant 'kok-saghyz' by all possible means in Germany, the KWI for Breeding Research agreed to work under the leadership of Himmler.[46] An SS-*Obersturmbannführer* was ordered to search for the kok-saghyz plant under the codename 'the plant

4711' in Russia, and the first plants were found in 1941.[47] The KWI for Breeding Research then took over the scientific breeding.[48] Rudorf took advantage of the fact that he was provided with 50 '*nichteindeutschungsfähigen Slowenen* ('Slovenes not capable of becoming Germans'), that is slave workers from a nearby 'resettlement camp' (*Umsiedlungslager*), to work in the plantations.[49] On 25 June 1943 there was a work-meeting on 'kok-saghyz-caoutchouc' in the *SS-Wirtschaft- und Verwaltungshauptamt*. The participants from the breeding and basic research sections included the following: Prof. Christiansen-Weniger and Prof. Ries from Pulawy/Lublin, (*Landesforschungsanstalt*) Prof. Walter (working for the army), Prof. Rudorf and Dr R. W. Böhme (KWI for Breeding Research), Prof. Kappert (Institute of Genetics, University of Berlin), Dr Amlong (represented by Mr March and K. Lausche from Posen, *Gauforschungsanstalt*), Dr Zimmermann (*Forstliche Hochschule, Eberswalde*), Prof. Tobler (*Technische Hochschule, Dresden*), Prof. Krause (Botanical Garden, Berlin). Four participants came from the *Kommandatur* (Command) of the concentration camp in *Auschwitz*: the *Diplom* (Masters degree) chemist Weinmann, SS-*Hauptsturmführer* Kudriawtzow, SS-*Obersturmführer* Dr Schattenberg, and the SS-*Sturmbannführer* Dr Joachim Caesar.[50]

Caesar presided at the meeting as representative of the SS-*Hauptamt*. The working programme was delivered by Rudorf.[51] Caesar was head of the agriculture department in the Auschwitz concentration camp. Beginning in 1942 the work in the newly founded plant-breeding station in Auschwitz concentrated on the kok-saghyz plant.[52] According to the planned division of labour, the KWI was assigned to send samples of all seedgrains to the Auschwitz concentration camp where their properties, such as the amount of caoutchouc, would be tested and the breeding selection would take place.[53] After the war Rudorf never mentioned his close contact with Auschwitz.[54]

From December 1939 all KWIs in Berlin and Brandenburg were declared *kriegswichtig*, that is, important enough to receive support during wartime. They were thus able to acquire the raw materials needed for their research.[55] In all of the KWIs mentioned, some of the research was classified at different levels of priority; such classifications increasingly became a prerequisite for DFG funding and for receiving supplies of the necessary raw materials and equipment during the war. This kind of research, however, did not necessarily have anything to do with the war. At the KWIs, very few projects with priority could really be considered relevant to the war. Thus the purely basic research at the Division of Virology at the KWIs for Biology and Biochemistry, 'investigations in the field of virology', was granted a high priority. The war-related research at the KWI for Brain Research and the KWI for Biophysics, with their well-equipped radiobiological laboratories, was, above all, research in radiation biology and radiation protection. One special war-related project was the testing of gas masks by radioactive isotopes.

From 1943 to 1945, part of the research was also funded by the '*Bevoll-mächtigter des Reichsmarschalls für Kernphysik*' (Plenipotentiary for Nuclear Physics) in the RFR (Professor Abraham Esau and, from late 1943, Professor Walter Gerlach)'. This administrator was responsible for the entire uranium project, including radiobiological effects and radiation protection. Since researchers had discovered that the effect of neutrons and strong gamma rays on human beings was much greater than had been assumed, Gerlach considered neutron dosimetry to be of particular importance from the viewpoint of nuclear physics.[56]

The Genetic Department in Berlin-Buch conducted research into the biological and genetic effects of fast neutrons on small mammals (mainly rats), and into neutron dosimetry.[57] Due to the emergency programme 'energy production from nuclear processes', which was introduced in January 1945 by a decree from Hitler, the '*Bevollmächtigter* for nuclear physics' concentrated this research in six working groups. These groups were provided with energy, materials and personnel. The group 'radiation protection and dosimetry' included the Genetic Department in Berlin-Buch, and the *Physikalische Technische Reichsanstalt*.[58]

The research at the KWI for Biophysics was funded by the '*Bevollmächtigter* for nuclear physics' until 1944. In his grant application of 1944, Boris Rajewsky, Director of this institute, claimed that his research served to clarify the 'biological effects of corpuscular radiation incl. neutrons *in consideration of the possibility of their use as a weapon* (*Kampfmittel*), but above all the biological basis of radiation protection'[59] (emphasis in original). Despite the emphasis on possible military applications of radiation research, this request was not funded. Gerlach was simply not interested in Rajewsky's research.[60] But Gerlach also envisaged the possibility of nuclear explosives. In a meeting between Mentzel (RFR), Erich Schumann (*Bevollmächtigter für Sprengstoffphysik*) and Gerlach in October 1944, it was decided that the three million volt apparatus, which had been ordered and designed by Rajewsky but was not yet set up, should be taken away from him so that it could be used for the production of neutrons and for '*sprengstoffphysikalische Versuche*'.[61]

5.3   Ideology

There was also an ideological rationale behind support for genetic research, work which made up a large proportion of the biological research at KWIs. Renowned geneticists like Timoféeff and Stubbe emphasized the importance of their basic research in modern genetics for race hygiene, possibly in order to obtain financial support. Writing in *Der Erbarzt*, the principal journal for race hygiene, Stubbe suggested that genetic diseases in botany and zoology were models for the 'genetic doctor' ('*Erbarzt*'):

> When the breeder realizes the nature of genetic diseases, he has many
> more possibilities to make a positive racial selection than the doctor and
> human geneticist, who, in most cases, have to extinguish without being
> able to create the healthy and resistant combination.[62]

In the same journal, Timoféeff also called for measures against the genetic
burden found in human populations, which he claimed was increasing due
to reduced natural selection.[63]

Timoféeff was invited to give a lecture on 'experimental mutation
research' at a training course in '*Rassenkunde*' and genetics organized by
the Office of Race Policy (*Rassenpolitisches Amt*) in October 1938.[64] The
participants in this course visited Timoféeff's institute in Berlin-Buch.
There were other cases of cooperation between geneticists and race hygienists: in 1938 Timoféeff reported on his cooperation in the field of population genetics with Prof. Hermann Boehm's Institute for Genetics at Alt-
Rehse.[65] This institute belonged to the SS-Leadership School for German
Doctors, which was established by the Nazi physicians league in 1935. The
Institute for Genetics was established in order to familiarize participants in
the training courses for physicians with the principles of genetics and racial
policy. Timoféeff and Stubbe supported Boehm by designing the construction of, and the equipment for, the institute.[66] They also provided mutant
strains of maize, *Antirrhinum* and *Drosophila* for the courses. Timoféeff
was helped in turn by Boehm, who was a longstanding party member,
when in 1938 the former refused, in spite of pressure, to become a German
citizen.[67]

Fundamental research in genetics was considered important for National
Socialist race ideology by most leading[68] and many lower party and SS
members. Thus when the *Kreispersonalamt* (local personnel office) of the
NSDAP made inquiries about Kühn, referring to rumours that he had been
a member of the German Communist Party (KPD), the *Gauleitung*
(regional office) *Süd-Hannover-Braunschweig* of the party responded that
Kühn had never been a member of the KPD.

> His attitude towards the [NSDAP] party has always been, if not dismiss-
> ive, at least neutral. Without any doubts his work as a scientist is out-
> standing. I had the opportunity to attend a lecture by him about genetics
> last autumn, which I enjoyed. From this point of view, I would like to say
> that he is working in accordance with our aims, without feeling connected
> to the NSDAP.[69]

6   The German Research Council and Research Association after 1945

The Max Planck Society (*Max-Planck-Gesellschaft*, MPG) for the
Advancement of Science was founded on 26 February 1948, as the West

German successor to the KWG. The allies demanded that the name be changed. In 1949 two competing research organizations were established. An initiative by the rectors of universities and the Ministers of Culture of the individual Federal states revived the *Notgemeinschaft* in January 1949 with almost the same statutes as in 1920. The *Notgemeinschaft* was a self-governing body and the influence of the state governments on the *Notgemeinschaft* was very small, though they provided most of the money. Two months later, the MPG and the academies of science in Göttingen, Heidelberg and Munich founded the German Research Council (*Deutscher Forschungsrat* DFR) as the official representative organization of German science.

The decisive initiative for the DFR came from the physicist Werner Heisenberg who became president of the organization. The DFR, which was oriented towards the central Federal government and away from the states, was supported by Konrad Adenauer, the first chancellor of West Germany. One of the aims of the DFR was to promote not only small-scale research, which already existed in many places in Germany, but also large-scale research projects.[70] The DFR proposed that financial support for the MPG should be provided by the central Federal government (an office connected to the Chancellor's department was to be established, '*Dienststelle für Forschung beim Bundeskanzleramt*'), whereas research at universities should remain the responsibility of the states. The DFR made substantial financial requests of the Federal government, but never received much money. The universities and the state governments were opposed to the DFR, primarily because it would allow the Federal government to dominate scientific research, traditionally a prerogative of the states. They favoured the *Notgemeinschaft*. The physicist Walter Gerlach, vice-president of the *Notgemeinschaft*, also reproached Heisenberg: 'Particularly you, who has always stood up for the autonomy of research, should understand that we cannot give up a well conceived plan towards self-organization of research when not even the government compels us to do so'.[71] The DFR did not succeed in its efforts to control funding for scientific research. On 2 August, 1951, the *Notgemeinschaft* and the DFR merged to form the new DFG on the terms of the *Notgemeinschaft*. The idea of the DFR was abandoned.

What were the reasons for outstanding scientists like Heisenberg to found a new Research Council shortly after the National Socialist Research Council disappeared? The founder and first president of the KWG, Adolf Harnack, had said in 1910: 'Army and science are the two pillars of Germany's greatness; their cultivation must never cease or stand still'.[72] After World War II Germany was not only beaten militarily. In reality what the biologists had warned against in their grant applications also happened: Germany had been overtaken by the Americans in science.[73]

The founders of the DFR believed that Germany's greatness should be restored through its scientific achievements. Heisenberg, for example, spoke of 'attempts to regain the position that German science held in the international world of scholars up to 1939'.[74] In the financing programme proposed by the DFR, the physicist Max von Laue is cited to the effect that 'today scientific research is almost the only way that Germany can conduct foreign policy. If we give up the struggle in this field, after ten years we shall become as uninteresting for the rest of the world as any Bantu tribe'.[75] The DFR complained that 'two World Wars, emigration, dismantling of industry, an often absurd denazification hitting everybody (*sinnlos wütende Entnazifizierung*) ...' had harmed Germany severely.[76] Because of the lack of sufficient funding for research, the most talented young men might take advantage of the good career opportunities in the USA or in England. (On the other hand, the report written in 1951 on behalf of the MPG, *40 Jahre Kaiser Wilhelm-Gesellschaft*, did not mention the forced emigrations after 1933).[77] A central policy of science, which would above all support outstanding German scientists in research institutes, would enable the Germans to overcome foreign supremacy in scientific research.

In contrast to the universities, the MPG supported the idea of the DFR. The support of big science projects was one of the major aims of the DFR. In order to explain the necessity for large-scale funding of German scientific research, Heisenberg wrote in 1949:

> During the Third Reich Germany barely participated in this development [of scientific research – UD and BMH] ... There was a general restriction on applying the results of science available in 1933 to armaments, and to promote any kind of armament industry, whereas support of basic scientific research, on the whole, was severely neglected.[78]

This assertion was not true, at least for biological research at KWIs. On the contrary, the good relationship that the KWG had had with the National Socialist Research Council suggests plausibly that the MPG and its scientists favoured the new Research Council so strongly because they expected to be well funded, particularly in 'big science' projects. The universities, on the other hand, were obviously not interested in having another Research Council in Germany.

However, the question, what was the reason for the decline in German biology after World War II, in particular why was the start in molecular genetics delayed in Germany, has not yet been answered. German traditionalism, international isolation due to the legacy of National Socialism and perhaps to still-existing anti-Semitism, may all have played a role in this delay, but these factors have yet to be analysed.[79]

9 | Pedagogy, professionalism and politics: biology instruction during the Third Reich

SHEILA FAITH WEISS

> ... In the new state and the new school, it is a self-evident duty of biology instruction to aid in the political education of our youth ... Biology, more than any other science, establishes a foundation for political understanding.[1]

Given the centrality of biological discourse for National Socialist ideology and policy, comments such as these by biology educator and secondary-school principal Otto Rabes seem neither particularly surprising nor revealing – until one learns when they were written. Rabes' remarks were not printed in one of Germany's many 'coordinated' pedagogical journals sometime after the Nazi seizure of power. His 'new state' was not a reference to the 'völkisch'[2] state. Indeed, Rabes articulated this relationship between biology education and politics during the early months of the Weimar Republic. Yet it is precisely the Weimar origins of Rabes' comments that render them so important for understanding biology education under National Socialism. His remarks point out that the politicization of biology education was not an invention of Nazi pedagogues and was not merely imposed from above after 1933.

In fact, an examination of Weimar and Nazi biology education reveals significant avenues of continuity in terms of pedagogical style, intellectual content and, to a certain extent, even broader philosophical goals. After the Nazi seizure of power, activist school biology teachers were able to emphasize those pedagogical and intellectual components of Weimar biology education that could be of ideological or instrumental use to the Party and State – couching them, of course, in the appropriate National Socialist discourse. While there were significant differences in the training, status and motivations of primary- and secondary-school biology teachers, the driving motive of both groups of biology instructors was professional self-interest. There was a community of interest between biology teachers and Nazi Party officials. Biology teachers were desperate for the status and prestige that the new regime was willing to bestow upon them; Party officials were dependent upon the commitment of biology instructors in order to carry out their plans for the racial education of all German children. Moreover, it is fair to say that this community of interest was mutually beneficial: biology teachers achieved many of their longstanding goals and biology instruction appears to have been successful in supporting Nazi relations of domination and, to a far lesser extent, serve broader Nazi economic and military aims.

Biology instruction and the professional interests of biology teachers during the Weimar Republic

The enthusiasm with which many school biology teachers greeted the Nazi seizure of power is explicable only after examining their pedagogical and professional interests during the Weimar Republic. The momentous events of 1917 and 1918 sent a clear signal to reform-minded pedagogues that long-awaited curriculum changes in the German schools were imminent and urgent. In a 1919 treatise Walter Schoenichen, Director of the Pedagogical Department of the Prussian Institute for Education and Classroom Instruction and Weimar Germany's leading biology didactician, spelled out the new goals awaiting all school instruction. The impact of the war and revolution, he contended, required that German education focus on love of the homeland, citizenship training and the cultivation of a sense of community, as well as health and hygiene. These instructional tasks should not, however, be delegated solely to German or civics but must become the guiding principle of all school subjects including, of course, biology.[3]

Schoenichen emphasized the unique contribution that biology could make to the first of these tasks, love of homeland. Even prior to the introduction of formal instruction in biology, primary school teachers could ensure that *Heimatkunde* – an interdisciplinary subject taught in the early primary-school grades – foster love of country by linking its biological and German components. Teachers might stress, for example, the role of plants and animals in German myths and sagas.[4] More significantly, however, since a child's love of the fatherland was predicated on its emotional bond to its immediate natural environment, Schoenichen insisted that only local fauna and flora form the core of natural history instruction and that children become acquainted with their natural surroundings directly through frequent class outings to nearby woods, streams or lakes.[5]

Schoenichen's stress upon biology instruction as a means of cultivating love of homeland was echoed in the writings of other German biology didacticians, especially those preoccupied with primary-school education. Like Schoenichen, they recognized that love of homeland could not be cultivated through the use of dry biology textbooks but rather by embracing the tenets of the *Arbeitsschulgedanke* – a pedagogical reform emphasizing active, experiential learning.[6] For biology instruction that meant not only taking schoolchildren on nature walks but also involving them in the care of animals and plants – the latter to be accomplished through the use of school gardens.[7] Indeed the school garden not only promoted love of homeland by enabling schoolchildren to gain hands-on experience growing things in their native soil but also by giving them the sense that they were contributing, however nominally, to the food production of their war-ravished country.

Not only was school biology instruction particularly well suited to promote love of the homeland, it was also invaluable for citizenship training. Biology education served a civic function by making children aware of important German agricultural products and their role in the economic life of the country.[8] Even more significantly, it could also cultivate a 'sense of *völkisch* community'.[9] Schoenichen demanded that biology teachers instruct children in the proper understanding of the concept of 'organism'. Critical here was the idea that the state, like all higher organisms, was more than the sum of its parts and that its efficiency depended on the 'strong harmonic working together' of its members.[10] For Paul Brohmer, another highly-regarded biology pedagogue, biology demonstrated 'that the individual is a link in a higher level of organization, and that it cannot free itself without giving up its existence'. The practical political lesson was clear: 'the school child must feel that he is a part of his *Volk*; he must bow to the laws of the community and offer his energies to strengthen it and protect it from harm'.[11]

Inseparable from citizenship training – especially in the aftermath of a war that took a heavy toll on Germany's stock of human resources – was what Schoenichen termed 'health education'. Central to its goals was the idea that individual health was not merely a private but also a political affair: children must be taught that it was their duty to remain healthy and efficient in the interest of the state and combat anything detrimental to Germany's '*Volkskraft*'.[12] While it was clear that biology would shoulder the lion's share of the burden of health education, it could do so only by adopting important curriculum changes – changes advocated not only by Schoenichen but also by numerous other biology schoolteachers and didacticians. First, the study of human beings must become an important, if not the most important, focus in biology instruction. In addition, biology classes must deal adequately with such issues as alcoholism and infectious diseases. And finally, heredity and eugenics should occupy a prominent place in the biology school curriculum, at least in the secondary schools.[13]

Many of the practical and political aims of Weimar biology didacticians found their way into primary- and secondary-school curricula. The Prussian secondary-school curriculum of 1925, for example, mandated that biology foster love of homeland, the health of the nation and a sense of community.[14] The Hessian secondary-school biology curriculum focused on the 'homeland' in all classes.[15] And the 1928 Hamburg secondary-school curriculum legislated that biology instruction 'awaken the interest in the economic and technical importance' of plants and animals by examining the role of Germany's former colonies as well as familiarizing students with the political and ethically relevant subjects of genetics and eugenics.[16]

Yet at odds with both the goals of biology pedagogues and the programmatic statements in the curriculum guidelines was the actual amount of time allotted to biology in all German schools. This was not a new problem.[17] German biology teachers had long since complained that their subject was grossly undervalued by those formulating school curricula, especially in Germany's largest state, Prussia. Generally viewed by non-biology educators as being little more than a descriptive science possessing no particular educational value, biology was unable to compete with the so-called 'cultural disciplines' of religion, German and history in the constant battle for school hours. Indeed in 1879, largely owing to a fear of the ideological costs of permitting Darwin's theory to be taught in the biology classroom, biology was eliminated from the upper level of Prussian secondary schools entirely.[18] Although the situation was remedied somewhat in the first decade of the twentieth century, even the educational reforms of the Weimar Republic left Prussian school biology teachers far from their stated goal of two hours of classroom instruction per week in all secondary school grades.[19] The 1925 Prussian secondary-school curriculum found no place for biology in the fourth and fifth classes of all secondary schools, and in the more traditional, classics-oriented secondary schools, the *Gymnasien*, it was absent from the sixth class as well. Only in the scientifically-oriented secondary schools, the *Oberrealschulen*, was biology taught in the thirteenth class, the *Prima*.[20] What this meant in practice was that there was a two- or three-year gap in the schoolchild's biology education – a situation teachers found pedagogically frustrating as well as intellectually inexcusable,[21] especially considering the lip-service paid to the importance of biology in the Prussian curriculum. Even in Hamburg, where biology was better represented than anywhere else in Germany, it took a back seat to all the 'cultural subjects'.[22]

Secondary-school biology schoolteachers publicly lamented the sad state of affairs of their subject in Germany's numerous pedagogical journals. In addition to the complaints regarding the shortage of hours, instructors bemoaned attempts to eliminate biology as an independent subject, at least in the middle schools, and were outraged over the teaching of biology by non-biologists – indeed by non-scientists. Though perhaps an extreme example, a man who allegedly could not tell the difference between a spider and a beetle had a position as a secondary-school biology teacher.[23] The situation in the primary schools was even worse. There biology was only taught as a small part of *Naturkunde* or natural science – a subject which itself was the stepchild of the primary-school curriculum.[24] Moreover, in the primary schools, biology instruction was devoid of any philosophical perspective. With its scientifically old-fashioned and pedagogically unsound emphasis on morphology, school biology, and primary-school biology in particular, did not reflect current trends in biological research.[25] It was not presented as the 'science of life' and did not study animate nature in its interrelatedness.[26]

During the financially and politically troubled final years of the Weimar Republic, biology didacticians and secondary-school biology instructors sought to promote their interests by joining hands with university biologists in the establishment, in 1931, of a new professional organization, the German Association of Biologists (*Deutscher Biologen-Verband*) (DBV). Although certainly some activist biology teachers joined the DBV owing to a shared political commitment with its chairman, the Tübingen botanist and Nazi sympathizer Ernst Lehmann, most were probably simply fed up with the lack of attention which the older German Association for the Promotion of Mathematical and Scientific Instruction (*Deutscher Verein zur Förderung des mathematischen und naturwissenschaftlichen Unterrichts*) devoted to biology.[27] In any event, the pedagogical, philosophical and professional goals of secondary-school biology teachers were clearly articulated in the organization's journal, *Der Biologe*. In a March 1932 article entitled 'Guidelines for Secondary School Biology Education', one finds virtually all the longstanding demands for 'relevant' and experiential biology instruction, for the introduction of heredity and eugenics, and for the broader political goals of biology education. The last of the ten guidelines ended with the sentence: 'biology is to be accorded a place among the central subjects (*Kernfächer*) in all schools'.[28]

The mandatory introduction of racial science into the school biology curricula

At the time, most biology teachers did not expect a quick realization of their goals. Yet in just a few short months the Nazi seizure of power altered the fortunes of biology education dramatically. Comments by important Party and State functionaries such as Hans Schemm and Wilhelm Frick suggested to even the most sceptical biology pedagogues that Germany finally had leaders who took their subject's civic function seriously.[29] Moreover, words were quickly backed up by deeds. In September 1933 the then Prussian Minister of Culture, Bernhard Rust, issued a decree mandating the introduction of a new constellation of subjects into the final grades of the Prussian secondary and primary schools with the aim of safeguarding the racial and genetic substrate of the *Volk*. These pillars of racial improvement – genetics, race hygiene, population policy, genealogy and ethnology – comprised what might best be termed a new Nazi metafield, 'racial science'. Although Rust emphasized that 'racial science' was to have a place in all subjects, the 1933 statute decreed that the lion's share of the new material would naturally fall to biology; more concretely, in the struggle over additional time in the school curriculum, biology would be accorded two to three hours per week to assure the success of its mission.[30]

Even before Rust extended the Prussian statute to the entire Reich two years later,[31] the reaction of German biology teachers to the decree was unabashedly enthusiastic. One Hamburg secondary-school teacher spoke for many of his colleagues when he proclaimed, '[we] biologists are unbelievably happy that a place has been created for these important [biological] questions in the new Reich and that our Führer Adolf Hitler and his helpers have such an interest in them'. This will ensure, he continued 'that our youth will begin to think biologically early and view the future of the state as being dependent upon noble biological laws'.[32] In the pages of Lehmann's *Der Biologe* – a journal that hardly required any 'coordination' after 1933 – biology instructors also spoke of better times to come for their discipline.[33] Undoubtedly they felt gratified by the new official name of their subject, '*Lebenskunde*' or 'science of life' – a name that seemed to support the broader philosophical outlook long since held by most biology teachers. School biologists repaid the new leadership and simultaneously promoted their professional interests by publishing a flood of pamphlets, handbooks and textbooks devoted to the teaching of racial science in the schools, by willingly staffing special courses and organizing training camps (*Schulungslager*) designed to instruct teachers in the new material, and by serving the National Socialist Teachers League (NSLB) as biology and 'race' experts. And although there was a healthy dose of self-aggrandizement in their proclamations of support for racial science in the schools, most secondary-school biology teachers had either taught portions of it during the final years of the Weimar Republic or had longed to do so. Genetics had been part of the biology curriculum of most German states before the Nazi seizure of power; race hygiene, at least in its non-racist, meritocratic form, had already been taught in Baden, Hessen, Hamburg, Thuringia and possibly Württemberg.[34] Moreover, since genetics and race hygiene were considered the most modern, most advanced subdisciplines of academic biological research, the new opportunity to teach them could only have been viewed as a professional boon, at least to secondary-school teachers, who both identified with their university colleagues and tended to measure the worth of biology education by the degree to which it reflected current research trends. Indeed prominent university geneticists and race hygienists such as Günther Just, Eugen Fischer and Walter Scheidt were more than willing to lend a helping hand in the promotion of their disciplines in the schools – a task directly or indirectly benefitting them.[35]

The situation was more complicated with that subfield of racial science stressing the superiority of the so-called Nordic race, *Rassenkunde* or ethnology. Here there was no real continuity, at least in terms of subject matter, with biology education prior to 1933. Not only was there no mention of ethnology in any Weimar biology curriculum,[36] but even a future Nazi biology school-textbook author such as Jakob Graf, a Party member since 1931, omitted all discussion of the race question from his 1930 handbook on heredity and eugenics.[37] Yet despite the lack of continuity of intellectual content, biology teachers had been accustomed to their field serving distinctly political ends. Certainly there were many biology teachers who were convinced that ethnology, in its attempt to preserve Nordic blood, was every bit as important as race hygiene in protecting the health and efficiency of the *Volk*. While some secondary-school instructors might have had reservations regarding the objectivity of Hans Günther's description of Europe's six so-called European races, ethnology was clearly too central to the Nazi Party programme for it to be ignored by any biology teacher. The most a teacher could do, should he or she find the eugenic leg of 'racial science' more scientific than the anthropological, was to teach ethnology in a manner that stressed *Leistung*, or efficiency, rather than outward appearance, as the best evidence of good 'race'.[38] As might be expected, there was no way to circumvent the blatantly anti-Semitic approach to the 'Jewish question' in the classroom.

An analysis of the vast body of primary literature dealing with the teaching of 'racial science' in the primary and secondary schools suggests that it functioned to sustain Nazi relations of domination. In particular, it sanctioned support for the 'national community' (*Volksgemeinschaft*) and legitimized the dichotomy between the useful 'national comrade' and the social and racial outsider, 'the community alien'. Biology pedagogues, many of whom had also been writing prior to the Nazi seizure of power, could use pre-1933 trends in biology education emphasizing the 'superorganic' as the basis for such pat Nazi racial-science textbook statements as 'you are nothing; your *Volk* is everything' and 'the individual is nothing more than a simple link in a chain'.[39] Attacks against individualism were also commonplace in Weimar eugenics education. What changed in race hygiene instruction after 1933 was not the emphasis on the 'national community', but rather the development of a racial qualification for entry into it. Textbook authors and biology pedagogues, however, also launched a far more brutal attack against those who, for reasons of health or attitude, had been rhetorically excluded from the 'national community' by race hygienists even before the Third Reich. In what was certainly an attempt to offer biological support for the draconian 1933 sterilization law, textbook authors now labeled genetically unhealthy Germans 'devoid of value' or 'subhumans' – phrases and terms seldom, if ever, used before.[40] In the clear hierarchy of human values depicted in textbook graphs, students quickly learned which groups of people were 'very valuable from the standpoint of the efficient functioning of the national community' and which were deemed 'worthless'. In at least one primary-school class, for example, Nazi racial-science truths regarding the 'defective' were hammered home in a genetics experiment linking high-grade and low-grade peas with people.[41]

Yet a continuation of the elitist eugenic tradition notwithstanding, lip-service had to be paid to Nazi egalitarianism. Especially in texts designed for primary-school children and their teachers, longstanding prejudices in favour of the higher social classes were watered down with the strictly Nazi view that a person's worth was not determined by what occupation he held but by what level of commitment he worked at for the good of the whole.[42]

It goes without saying that racial science textbooks also examined the 'Judenfrage'. Although the degree of crudity and brutality with which text-books examined the 'Jewish question' varied according to author and time, all classroom books sanctioned the officially prescribed distinction between 'national comrade' and 'community-alien' by portraying the Jew as the negative counterpart of the German. The Jew, unlike the Aryan, was the product of two non-European races, the so-called Near Eastern and the Oriental. Whereas the Aryan, especially the Nordic stock among it, had lived as honest peasants, in constant struggle only with the harsh northern environment, the Jew was in essence a nomad – someone for whom a per-manent abode was foreign and hence someone who was only able to secure his existence by deceiving and exploiting others. This unflattering character portrait of the Jews, often with equally denigrating photographs accom-panying the text, was then used by authors to justify the 1935 Nuremberg Laws. Many of the textbooks went so far as to provide graphs and charts in an effort to explain to children what a 'full Jew,' 'half Jew' and 'quarter Jew' was, and who was now allowed to marry whom.[43]

Biology instruction and the Nazi curricula reforms

Although 'racial science' was by no means the sum total of Lebenskunde, it was the only facet of biology instruction specially legisla-ted during the early years of the regime. Prior to the introduction of the first new curriculum plan in 1937,[44] primary- and secondary-school biology teachers still technically operated under Weimar curricula guidelines, com-plaints by Nazi pedagogues notwithstanding. This, of course, should not suggest that school biology instruction was unaffected by Nazi philosophi-cal and pedagogical principles; what it does mean is that in the absence of clearly articulated statutes governing all aspects of biology education, acti-vist biology pedagogues themselves had the opportunity to help shape the contours of their discipline. Many biology instructors at all school levels published 'relevant' articles in a wide variety of pedagogical journals; several authored textbooks and handbooks. Others served their discipline and their own careers by becoming involved in the activities of the Biology Section (Reichssachschaft) of the National Socialist Teachers League.[45]

Years before Rust's curriculum guidelines for the secondary schools were put into place in 1938, the Biology Section of the NSLB was busy drafting plans of its own for Lebenskunde instruction.[46] An examination of the 1937

NSLB biology draft curriculum reveals important similarities to that of the 1925 Prussian biology curriculum in terms of methodological approaches and intellectual content. Both curricula (1) maintained a division between the plant and animal kingdoms for instructional purposes; (2) combined a systematic and ecological approach to the organic world; (3) emphasized plants and animals of the child's immediate environment and viewed 'love of homeland' as an important educational goal of biology; (4) included environmental protection, a study of useful animals and medicinal plants, and an emphasis on human physiology and health; and (5) stressed the importance of biological excursions and experiential learning based on principles of the *Arbeitsschulgedanke*.[47]

This continuity was no accident. The NSLB, like other Nazi professional organizations, had to represent not only the interests of the Party but also, at least to some degree, the professional aspirations of its members.[48] Neither Party nor State could expect teachers to adopt a completely new curriculum that would make their former training obsolete, and in the case of biology education it was certainly not necessary. Although there was clearly a wealth of new 'racial science' material in the NSLB draft curriculum, much of it designated for the higher secondary-school grades, what is surprising is how much 'usable past' existed. What Party and biology teachers appeared to have worked out together was a new, blatantly National Socialist discourse in which to couch the material. This language is evident in the programmatic statement accompanying the draft curriculum as well as in the justifications given for the way in which material was structured in it. The language could also be gleaned from sentences bearing the unmistakable mark of the school biologists' self-interest. The framers of the curriculum argued, for example, that whereas all subjects were expected to promote racial consciousness instinctively, only biology provided the scientific foundation for it.[49] They also naturally demanded far more curriculum hours for their subject than Prussian biology school-teachers enjoyed during the Weimar years.[50]

It seems likely that the NSLB draft curriculum for biology and the activities of the Biology Section strongly influenced the shape of the 1938 secondary-school biology curriculum. The twenty-four pages devoted specifically to biology instruction in the Reich Education Ministry's *Education and Instruction in the Secondary Schools*, nearly twice the space accorded to physics and chemistry combined, both reflected the ideological importance of the new *Kernfach* and attested to significant avenues of continuity with pre-Nazi traditions. In addition to the similarities between the Prussian biology curriculum and the NSLB draft curriculum already mentioned, Rust's biology curriculum emphasized the role of plants and animals in German fairy tales and sagas, the practical and ideological utility of the school garden, and the economic importance of organic nature – themes stressed in the writings of biology didacticians during the Republic.[51]

But just as in the case of the NSLB draft curriculum, Rust's biology curriculum placed this older material together with the Nazi-specific racial-science subjects in a blatantly Party-political instructional framework. The guiding principle of *Lebenskunde* instruction became 'the unity and interdependence of life'. While not new, this emphasis on *Ganzheit* and the superorganic was now designed to lead children to the National Socialist truth that 'the *Volk* as a community of blood and fate is the highest of all transindividual units'.[52] The Weimar biologists' demand that biology education be taught as the 'science of life' was also reinterpreted. It was one-sidedly reduced to a preoccupation with the 'laws of life' – with 'selection and elimination' and heredity – a knowledge of which demonstrated 'the biological nonsense of the theory of equality'.[53] Whereas biology education had been politicized in the past, *Lebenskunde* instruction in the secondary schools – at least in theory – was now the handmaiden of Party-political interest. An analysis of the 1939 and 1940 curriculum reforms for middle schools and the upper primary-school grades points in the same direction.

By the time the curriculum reforms were instituted, the community of interest between school biology teachers and Party and State was already well developed and mutually beneficial. Secondary-school biology teachers received what they had demanded since 1901: two hours a week of biology instruction in each school year. Indeed, in virtually all higher secondary-school forms, biology now enjoyed more hours than physics and chemistry combined.[54] Moreover, at least in Prussia, all secondary-school children were required to take an oral examination in biology, albeit only those portions of it falling under the rubric of racial science, in order to obtain their secondary school diploma, the *Abitur*.[55] Biology also appears to have won a more prominent place in the last four grades of the primary schools, although it continued to be taught in close association with physics and chemistry; during the first four primary-school years it was taught as part *Heimatkunde*.[56] Whereas the number of hours accorded to biology paled in comparison to the number earmarked for German and history, biology teachers could feel satisfied that their subject now occupied a central position in the educational curriculum. The long-proclaimed view by biology didacticians that their subject was unique among the sciences in its educational value appeared finally to have won official recognition. In an influential treatise examining the significance of various school subjects from the standpoint of 'racial education', Nazi pedagogues Rudolf Benze and Alfred Pudelko omitted all the natural sciences except biology. The other sciences, they argued, 'were not as ideologically important as *Lebenskunde* and the so-called German-related subjects'.[57]

The Party and State were also well served by school biologists. In numerous articles published in pedagogical journals both before and after the biology curriculum reforms, biology instructors went beyond the call of duty in demonstrating the compatibility of their subject matter with Nazi doctrine. They also authored the four sets of secondary-school biology textbooks designated for classroom use after 1938.[58] Whereas these texts functioned primarily as 'a vehicle of transport of ideology', to use a phrase coined by Herbert Mehrtens,[59] they also possessed an instrumental function. Much in the racial-science portion of the textbooks, as well as in other sections, served to induce social conformity and efficiency – behaviour necessary for the well-functioning of the Nazi regime.[60] In addition, biology education as a whole aided the regime, however marginally, though its involvement with Göring's Four-Year Plan[61] and the production of raw silk needed for the air force.[62] Although it is not clear how enthusiastically instructors greeted these new tasks, the economic and civil importance of applied biology education had certainly been a familiar theme for most teachers since the Weimar years.

Yet despite this community of interest between biology teachers and Nazi Party and State officials, neither side could have been completely satisfied with the actual *practice* of biology education under the swastika. Nazi Party pedagogues may have laid the theoretical foundations for a new racially relevant form of biology instruction, but the slow-moving wheels of the state educational bureaucracies, conflicts of interest between Party and State institutions, as well as the intellectual lethargy on the part of many biology teachers all mitigated against the quick and total realization of their plans. For example, although there were literally dozens of newly approved textbooks available for racial science instruction, virtually none of the Prussian secondary schools chose to adopt them. Older biology textbooks, some originally written under the Empire, continued to be employed for classroom use. Indeed, even after Rust's 1938 reforms, the four state-mandated sets of secondary-school biology textbooks written to reflect the new curriculum were not immediately used.[63] Moreover, an examination of the annual reports of Prussian secondary schools reveals that many biology teachers continued to stress more traditional areas of biology in the *Abitur* examination. Even when racial science topics were assigned, they very frequently focused on straight Mendelian genetics. What is clear is that ethnology and the 'Jewish question' were among the least popular subjects for either the oral or the written biology *Abitur* examinations – suggesting, perhaps, that these topics were viewed by the university-trained biology teachers as less 'scientific' than genetics, population policy and eugenics.[64] Whatever the real motives behind the biology teachers' trend to stress the 'scientific' portions of racial science, it ran counter to the intentions of Nazi diehards.

Biology instructors also had plenty to complain about. Although their subject had gained status – both real and rhetorical – during the early years of the Third Reich, evidence suggests that biology instruction waned in importance with the outbreak of war. While biology did not lose any hours in the primary- or secondary-school curriculum, *Abiturienten* were no longer permitted to take a written examination in biology after 1939.[65]. In the scientifically-oriented secondary schools, boys had to write examination in either physics or chemistry – subjects that were more immediately relevant to the war effort – in addition to mathematics and German.[66] Moreover, it appears that with the start of hostilities, the once compulsory oral examinations in biology/racial science became voluntary. At the very least, not all schoolchildren graduating from Prussian secondary schools were given an oral test in biology, although Rust never officially changed his 1935 policy mandating that all pupils be tested in racial science before leaving school.[67]

Postscript

Dissatisfaction over specifics on the part of both Nazi officials and biology teachers notwithstanding, avenues of common pedagogical, intellectual and philosophical interest combined with the latter's drive for more professional recognition made it relatively easy for most school biologists to serve the new order. While it is difficult to generalize about the attitude of all teachers, there is little evidence to suggest that many had strong reason to oppose the manner in which their subject was taught during the Third Reich. As we have seen, much of the content of biology education under the swastika was not specifically Nazi – it was largely traditional material that was effectively repackaged for consumption under new conditions. Even much of the 'racial science' material – genetics, race hygiene, population policy – was supported and taught during Weimar. Moreover, whereas school biology was certainly politicized far more radically than it had been in the past, Otto Rabes' statement mentioned at the beginning of this paper should remind us that the politicization of biology education did not begin in 1933.

Nor, one might add, did it end in 1945. In the Soviet Occupation Zone (SBZ) every attempt was made to eliminate all Nazi-tainted books and publications from both schools and public libraries. Included on the lengthy list of 'brown' publications were numerous treatises on genetics, race hygiene and racial science – texts that had been standard works for the training of biology teachers under the Nazis.[68] Officials either had them destroyed or ordered them placed in 'poison cabinets' (*Giftschränke*) where they remained largely inaccessible to the public until recently.[69] Yet the new authorities did not rest content in eliminating Nazi-tainted biology books. The 'misuse' of biology instruction during the Third Reich was corrected by assigning new political goals for the subject. According to a 1946 *Lehrplan* for the SBZ, biology education's task was to demonstrate that 'Darwin's theory of struggle for survival is not applicable to human social life and that one cannot use this principle to legitimize bloody conflicts between individuals, groups, or nations...' In addition, it was hoped that proper biology instruction would make it clear that 'science does not sanction the discrimination of members of one race by those of another ... and that all members of the human race have the same rights and duties'.[70] Whereas the *Lehrplan* did mandate genetics instruction in the final year of all secondary-school education, children learned both the teachings of Mendel as well as those of the Soviet agrobiologist, T. D. Lysenko.[71] By the time uniform biology texts were introduced in the early 1950s, Lysenkoism had totally eclipsed Mendelian genetics in biology classrooms of the new German Democratic Republic (GDR).[72]

The situation regarding biology education in the British, French and American Occupation Zones is less clear-cut. As was the case in the SBZ, Nazi biology textbooks and handbooks were removed from the classrooms. In the immediate post-war years, biology texts predating the Third Reich appear to have been used when available. Soon, however, biology textbook authors who had served the Nazi state were allowed to publish revised versions of their works.[73] Expunged of all doctrines of Nordic supremacy but not always of eugenics, biology education in the Western Zones and the future Federal Republic was similar in structure and content to school biology in the Weimar Republic – with the important exception that the post-war *Lehrpläne* set no political goals for the subject.[74] This trend has not been universally applauded. Interestingly enough, in more recent years the intentional depoliticization of biology education has become as much a source of frustration to certain critical West German biology pedagogues as has claims of residual forms of racism and biologism in school textbooks.[75] Whether, given the serious environmental problems now facing the Federal Republic, biology education will once again set a political agenda – this time, for the good – remains an open question.

10 | The Whole and the Community: scientific and political reasoning in the holistic psychology of Felix Krueger[1]

ULFRIED GEUTER

During the methodological conflict within German psychology at the end of the 1950s, it almost appeared as if the anti-intellect (*Ungeist*) of German psychology had dominated the holistic psychology of Felix Krueger more than other psychological schools during the National Socialist period. Although scrutiny of the development of psychology under National Socialism in general had been avoided after the war, now the political past of the Leipzig School in particular became the subject of insinuation and criticism. The reasons for this had less to do with the special role played by Felix Krueger and his school under National Socialism, than with the fact that throughout the 1950s holistic psychology continued to dominate academic psychology in the Federal Republic of Germany.[2] Representatives of the generation of psychologists who had been trained in the psychological institutes during this period now wanted to replace the irrational Weltanschauung and subjective methodology of holistic psychology with a measurable and mathematical psychology oriented towards developments in the United States.[3] The disagreement over these different paths for psychology was paralleled by differences concerning Krueger's political conduct and the fate of the Leipzig School under National Socialism. While Friedrich Merz, an opponent of holistic psychology, portrayed it as the school which profited most from National Socialism,[4] its main defender, Albert Wellek, declared that Krueger was a political opponent of the National Socialist system.[5] While Krueger was described by the psychologists Wyatt and Teubner, who had emigrated to the USA, as 'one of the early sympathizers of the NS movement',[6] his successor in the Leipzig professorship, Werner Fischel, wrote after the war that Krueger had come into conflict with National Socialism and for that reason had been forced into early retirement.[7]

When later in the 1970s a new generation of psychologists determined the image of their discipline, they proceeded to make fun of the old German psychology. In 1974 this ridicule was expressed clearly and cleverly in the festschrift for (the fictional psychologist) Ernst August Dölle, who – like Krueger – had tried to achieve a 'holistic way of thinking' (*Verganzheit-lichung der Denkweise*).[8] However, even in this phase of the post-war devel-opment of psychology, there was no systematic attempt to come to terms with the connection between psychological theory formation and political conviction in the work of Felix Krueger. Only in the past fifteen years, encouraged by the centennial anniversary of the Leipzig institute in 1979 and the debate over science under National Socialism reinvigorated by the fiftieth anniversary of the 'seizure of power' by the National Socialist German Workers Party (henceforth NSDAP) in 1983, have discussions begun into this connection between psychology and politics.[9]

A relevant question has already been asked for the history of philosophy and individual sciences in Germany: whether certain theories, developed before the National Socialist period, contributed to National Socialist ideology or at least to its acceptance by public opinion. According to Lukács, the development of the 'philosophy of life' (*Lebensphilosophie*) included a 'destruction of reason', which made the intelligentsia receptive to the philosophical arbitrariness of National Socialist ideology.[10] Gasman sees the origins of National Socialist ideology in the Social Darwinism of Ernst Haeckel.[11] Sontheimer has investigated the conceptions of society that allowed National Socialism to propagate its ideas.[12] Such studies were developed in the context of the experience that, at least when it came to theory, German intellectuals had been helpless when confronted by National Socialism. If even before 1933 their reasoning carried features of National Socialist ideology, then it is no wonder that they greeted the 'seizure of power' with conviction.

Felix Krueger was one of those established professors who celebrated the new political direction in 1933, but who subsequently turned away from this path. Thus the question is also valid for him: were there elements of political reasoning in his scientific theory which were related to National Socialist ideology or to the right-wing conservative thought congenial to National Socialism? Or to put it more generally, how did scientific and political reasoning interact within his psychological theory? This question stands at the centre of the following investigation, which will illuminate the position of Felix Krueger and his holistic psychology in and towards National Socialism. The first sections examine the development of Felix Krueger's theory before 1933; here I will concentrate on the aspects that are important for my argument. Subsequently I will attempt to place changes in his theory into the context of contemporary political developments, especially the situation around 1933. One problem lies in Krueger's work style. He rarely put down his thoughts in a systematic fashion, rather he published them in a sometimes only implied and vague way in a number of articles. He linked these statements relatively openly to political diagnoses

of the time, although unsystematically and associatively. In part, this connection is found in political speeches, which will be incorporated into this
analysis together with Felix Krueger's political conduct. Finally I will
examine more closely the circumstances surrounding Krueger's retirement
under National Socialism, since this fact has led to him being declared a
victim of the Nazi regime.[13] The political climate at the Leipzig psychology
institute will not be examined unless it concerns Krueger himself. The
tension in this institute caused by the psychology professor and active
NSDAP member Hans Volkelt has been examined elsewhere.[14]

Holism and feeling

Felix Krueger, who in 1917 took over the Leipzig professorship
made famous by his teacher Wilhelm Wundt, opposed even in his early
writings those who, in contrast to Wundt, wanted to restrict psychology
methodologically to experimentation and to concentrate on sensory psychology. In his article 'on developmental psychology', he pleaded that
psychological facts be investigated through their development and determination by social conditions,[15] and called for the introduction of developmental and social-genetic perspectives in psychology. If sensory psychology
had tackled the empirical study of human cognitive processes by studying
the effect of the sensory gates to the external world, Krueger began from a
different epistemological standpoint. In his opinion, and corresponding to
the philosophy of life, the cognitive process was based on experience. For
Krueger it is an epistemological principle that 'only experiential reality pos-
sesses an immediate, certain, and primary reality'.[16] The 'last' touchstone'
for statements about reality was not the practical evaluation of cognition
using reality, but rather the 'immediate fact of the real experience'.[17]
Because only experiential reality and not what had already entered the
consciousness can be seen as immediate reality, psychological phenomena
cannot be comprehended using the methods of experimental sensory
research.

When Krueger was developing the foundations of his theory, sensory
psychology faced the problem of explaining perceptions such as melodies
or movements, for which the whole perception no longer can be deduced
from the association of individual stimuli. Krueger developed the concept
of *complex quality* in his early work as a response. If Krueger thereby said
what was asserted by the Berlin school of gestalt psychology, that the
whole is more than the sum of its parts, in contrast to this school he also
claimed that experiential reality is always unstructured and holistically
diffuse, but on the contrary a gestalt is only a special case of a whole: an
organized whole. If the experience of a gestalt is that of a fully developed
form, then feelings could not possess gestalt qualities, since they would be
complex qualities of a given unstructured holism.

Experiential wholes entailed a threefold primacy for Krueger: (1). a 'phenomenal' primacy, that is, they appear first of all; (2) a 'functional' primacy, in other words they dominate psychological events; and (3) a 'genetic' primacy, meaning that they appear earlier during development. As essential proof for the thesis of the primacy of unstructured feelings, he argued that onto- and phylogenetical diffusiveness precedes structure:

> The behavior of children is distinguished in particular from that of adults by determination through instantaneous feelings and blunt, disorganized dull impulses. Here in turn children are similar to primitives, to a considerable extent also to animals, which of course are more rigidly bound by instinct than all human beings. This disorganization, just like the incoherence, the instability of behavior, and the simultaneous experience, are all based on an undeveloped, relatively formless state of the psychological fabric.[18]

The Sander method of 'actual emergence' was used in an attempt to prove the phenomenal primacy of experiential wholes. In this experiment a picture was presented in stages, at the beginning diffuse and unclear and subsequently becoming sharper and sharper. According to the results, at the beginning diffuse and emotionally determined 'proto-forms' were perceived, while a completely organized experience, according to gestalt psychology the basis of all perception, only appeared later. The experiment was based on the idea that, as the clarity of stimulation is vague, the determination by internal psychological structure increases, or, as Krueger once said, 'the structure' was brought through the diminution in clarity of external stimulation 'to intensified response'.[19]

Holism, structure and value

The paths of gestalt and holistic psychologies diverged not only at Krueger's theory of feelings, rather also at the theoretical explanation for the experimental results of perception research. The gestalt psychologist Wolfgang Köhler, from the perspective of Krueger an adherent of a physical-science approach, asserted a structural identity between the external world and the cognizant organism. In contrast, Krueger based his approach on a subjective theory of cognition when he argued that the holistic perception of feeling takes the character of an immediate experience. He assumed that the psyche had an inherent impulse towards wholeness and sense.[20] Wellek subsequently characterized this impulse towards wholeness as 'a general biological fundamental fact ... (the fact that makes life and its conservation possible) ...'[21] The sensible answer of an experimental subject in the actual emergence experiment thus spoke less for the experience that in the external world things stand in an objectively sensible, and indeed usually man-made connection, than for the manifestation of this internal impulse of the psyche.

Krueger was concerned with more than the formation of theoretical models for the explanation of empirical data. He wanted to penetrate through to concepts of the holistic psychological being and finally to a concept of the ideal holism.[22] The concept of *structure* was central in this regard. Beyond the experiential wholes, accessible on a phenomenal plane, there existed for Krueger an existential whole of a special type: the naturally predisposed whole of the psycho-physical structure. Structures were something that lay behind, that could only be inferred, something that appears in the colourings of experience, that in particular becomes clear in the depth of the feelings, yet exists as a disposition by nature. Structure was not only an explanatory concept, rather something he supposed to exist:

> In the end, considering very diverse phenomena with respect to life, structure is: the entire being, which bears the respective phenomena, has a structurally-bound unity ... According to the type of bodily organism, we have to consider the entire structure of every *psychological* being: as relatively persistent with regard to psychological phenomena, at the same time as a naturally disposed substance (*Seinsgrund*) for experience ... Structure means an organized and coherent wholeness of what exists (*Seiendes*). That is more than the holism and organization of experience, behavior, and the manifestation of self in general. A structured psychological being must be considered as a real precondition for everything that we encounter in psychological phenomena.[23]

Krueger's concept of structure transcends this philosophical imputation of an existent substance. Structure is — just like wholeness — something charged and required in a value-bound way:

> *Structure* is given by experience as the holistic (inherited from the fundamental arrangement) composition of organisms, as a coherent and organized essence capable of strong growth; and indeed the human being is charged with this essential form of life; it alone is capable of unbound growth. Structureness forms the kernel of life, it is the most certain type of what exists; and simultaneously it is what absolutely should be.[24]

In 1932 Krueger spoke of the 'Law of remaining whole through inner organization' as the 'fundamental law of our true existence' and as a 'bio-psychological necessity for evolution', which would be the 'vehicle of ethical necessity'.[25]

There were scientific reasons for the introduction into psychology of the concept of holism; new phenomena had created scientific problems that should be explained. However, Krueger went further, both in the foundation as well as in the expansion of the validity of his concepts. The concepts were not only introduced as theoretical assumptions, rather also as philosophical, value-laden demands; finally they took on the character of philosophical concepts of being, which were supposed to cover the entire 'bio-psychological' field of life. As Moritz Schlick has criticized,[26] the concept of holism was not supposed to describe the phenomena better, rather to express additional regularities inherent within the objects. According to Schlick, contradictions in the question of the better description were thus elevated to ontological problems and metaphysical controversies in psychology.

The search for holism, order, and sense in the Weimar period

Krueger himself made no attempt to deny the fact that the development of his concepts should not only solve scientific problems but also questions should be answered which 'life itself drives at this time, especially in Germany ... with a more than theoretical necessity'.[27] His theoretical efforts paralleled conservative criticism of civilization, the content of which molded the theory to the degree that the scientific and political discourses in Krueger's reasoning can scarcely be separated.

Krueger often warned of the apparent disintegration of the modern period. For example, in 1930 he complained:

> Well-bred civilization is also endangered if the 'mind' arbitrarily separates itself out of the supra-personal orders of human life, like when animal drives, the 'economy', or technology demoniacally absolve themselves. Then the kernel of human structures always loosens itself, that is the inner bond of values in the soul. Psychological *structure itself* decomposes, as the form of being given to people[28]

In his theoretical article on 'The Problem of Holism' from 1932, Krueger criticized that in all areas of life goal-oriented rationality was being emphasized 'to the detriment of the inner, durably bound values'.[29] In psychological research, psychoanalysis, a mechanical theory of the psyche, had reinterpreted the 'central structure of personality' as 'conventional illusions'.[30] Ludwig Klages and Oswald Spengler were also targets of Krueger's criticism, because they presented a one-sided view of the diffuse nature of the psyche, neglecting the consistently creative forces, and thereby expressing only cultural desperation. In a period in which people were no longer one with themselves and their environment,[31] scientific theory should help restore unity and wholeness.

The desire for holistic thought was widespread in both the scientific and political reasoning of the Weimar period. For example, in the natural sciences the descriptive scope of the concept of holism was extended, which originally was introduced as a scientific working-concept applying to the individual organism. Just as for Krueger the whole was what the soul should be, for the biologist and philosopher Hans Driesch it was the goal of the development of the organism. When arguing for the category of holism, which he considered a fundamental category for the study of life, even Driesch, at that time certainly the best-known representative of a vitalist position in biology, who consequently insisted on the autonomy of organic life compared with the inorganic, went beyond the experimental facts and declared that wholeness was an indefinable fundamental meaning, which could only be perceived.[32] According to Schlick,[33] the polarization in bound or unbound forms was spread throughout the natural and social sciences. Inorganic nature was contrasted with the organic, physical nature with the psychological, the individual with the whole. It was assumed that the latter member of each pair could never be completely put together from pieces of the former, as each was characterized by certain holistic properties from the beginning. Sontheimer[34] has shown that similar reasoning was widespread both in constitutional law and in the political thought of the Weimar period. A democracy conceived as a mechanical and artificial order, and a unity of the *Volk*, seen as natural, were widely regarded as being diametrically opposed to each other.

Since few investigations into the holistic theories of the time for the different sciences are available, we will have to be content with this brief outline discussion. However, there is a certain striking parallel between scientific and political reasoning. According to Sontheimer,[35] it was a sign of the times to want to overcome relativism through constructions of absoluteness. The period created both relativism as well as the need for order and sense. For example, Paul Forman[36] has described how for physics during the Weimar period, concepts of causality and determinism were abandoned as a reaction to the hostile cultural environment. This reaction created the climatic preconditions for the acceptance of quantum theory. Yet it also created, so to speak, as a conservative pendant to the disintegration of order, a yearning for order, but an order that would no longer be sought in the causal progress of history, rather in the cross-section, in the structure, in the morphology – on which, for example, Ludwig Klages wanted to found his psychology – in holism, in outlasting unity.[37]

Different authors have pointed out that the theoretical reasoning of the intelligentsia in the first decades of this century has to be seen as an answer to the new problems created by the industrial age. The thesis from Ringer[38] is widely accepted (see also the criticism by Jürgen Habermas[39]) in the historical literature that only a minority of the German professors were oriented towards modernity and wanted a progressive democracy; the majority, discredited in their previous function as intellectual interpreters of the nation and under more social pressure, in contrast held firm to the old political concepts of order. Perhaps it went far beyond this political dimension of a reaction to social change, namely to what Horkheimer called the revolt of subjective nature against objectification. The subjectivity that had been lost was reclaimed in the arts or in the youth movement; this was a response to civilization and its discontents, the theory of centring the person in feelings was a protest against a rationalization which focused entirely on the cognitive and instrumental.[40] But, for example, psychoanalysis – which reacted to the same historical situation – spoke of the costs of this rationalization, of the restriction of the satisfaction of human needs considered necessary due to denying reality; it thereby led to a criticism of culture, where Krueger released the individual from his social and individual history and referred him back both to a psychological structure understood as outlasting the individual but not defined any further, and to his values as the kernel of his personality.

In 1935 Ernst Bloch described the tendency in different fields to look at the whole and the gestalt – thereby excepting the Wertheimer-Köhler school of gestalt psychology – as a 'feudal dam in the river of history', since laws were replaced by invariant essence.[41] One can ask whether Krueger's theory, which was centred on such 'invariant essences', had something to do with the search for sense by the intelligentsia in a period which, according to Bloch, was so lacking in sense.

Krueger gave his psychology a pronounced ideological accent with regard to both religion and politics. Throughout his writings, comments can be found on religious consciousness and its certainty with regard to what psychological research can never completely comprehend.[42] In particular, his writings from the middle of the 1920s, a period of consolidation for the Weimar Republic, contain religious confessions. In contrast, previously, just as afterwards, Krueger's ideological references were of a more political nature. In June of 1919, when delivering the keynote address at a university ceremony honouring fallen soldiers and greeting the returning soldiers, he emphasized the spiritual tasks that were the result of defeat and class conflict. During the war Germany's spiritual powers had not sufficed to give Europe a 'morally justifiable form'.[43] Considering the 'bitter class conflict of the present', the task was to create 'spiritual unity of life for the nation'.[44] In his comments on Wundt, Krueger later emphasized that the rationalism of Descartes should be opposed and a German *Weltanschauung* (ideology) with a place for valid values be created.[45] In 1932 he connected the religious and nationalistic bases of his theory. According to his description of the philosophical history of holistic reasoning, the true metaphysic systems rooted in religion, which spoke to the reality of the soul as holistic and living, carried on the Germanic tradition.[46]

The holistic theory of Felix Krueger was also a theory directed against the disintegration of a firm. *Weltanschauung* in the Weimar period, a theory that propagated order and stability. This political dimension of his scientific reasoning and his wish to contribute in the area of theory to a renewal of the community of the *Volk* becomes even clearer in his psychology of the community, a topic to which Krueger turned, if only programmatically, with the increasing crisis of the Weimar period. When he transferred his concepts to social circumstances, the theory practically became a political programme.

The psychology of the community and political ideology

As early as 1915, Krueger had determined that psychological development was determined through community and culture. For him communities were transpersonal holisms; at that time he listed 'family, male companionship, club, art school and the like, church, state, language community, *Volk*'.[47] However, this idea became a central theme for Krueger only towards the end of the Weimar period. The most important elaborations appeared in 1935 by Krueger and his student Karlfried Graf von Dürckheim-Montmartin. In the way they transferred holistic psychological ideas to social facts and defined concrete communities, the connections between the scientific and political discourses became ever tighter. Even before the National Socialist period, the political discourse had dominated Krueger's scientific concepts of community which remained completely on the level of an eloquent programme carried over to everyday politics. During the National Socialist period, the psychology of community life received greater attention and new accentuations in holistic psychology. More than other parts of his theory, the psychology of community life facilitates study of how far Krueger helped prepare the ground theoretically for National Socialism.

At first the fundamental idea of Krueger's community psychology was to transfer the doctrine of the dominance of the whole to social structures. Since social units were interpreted as supra-individual *psychological* wholes, social-psychological, and not only historical or sociological research, was responsible for these units and thereby also Krueger's theory itself.[48] As Krueger himself said, the fundamental concepts of the Leipzig school made a psychology of community life possible.[49] However, even at the methodological starting-point arbitrariness was applied in the definition of what a community is. Krueger advocated connecting the fundamental knowledge of social psychology with the 'unobstructed view' and 'life knowledge' of natural communities, thus fastening science to a 'natural and proven' knowledge.[50] In the sole systematic realization of community-psychological ideas by the Leipzig school, the methodological arbitrariness becomes even clearer. Dürckheim-Montmartin[51] emphasized that a true community is to be recognized by seeing whether it realized the idea of community. The determination of this idea is attached to everyday experiences, when one truly experiences a community, but the type of experience itself is not understood as historical. So, for example, the whole of a community is defined such that it exists within each individual as a fabric of obligations (*Sollensgefüge*) and that it is visible in the responsibility of every member of the community towards the whole, especially in times of danger.

What is interesting for the ideological starting-point of the theory is how the relationship between 'member' and 'whole' is conceived. Krueger's theory does not recognize the interaction between part and whole, rather only the law of the dominance of the whole; in the area of society it appears as the superimposition of the community over the individual and the subordination of the individual to the community. A comparison of Krueger with William Stern for the transfer of holistic ideas to social facts shows concisely in what very different ways a political conviction can mold scientific interpretation.

Stern also supported the tendency in psychology towards a holistic approach. Holism was for him a central category of his personalism (as he called the science of the person), the wholeness of the person was an original wholeness and thus underivable. However, for Stern personal wholeness was not only fixed structure, rather at the same time vagueness, so not only structure, but rather also diffuseness.[52] In contrast to Krueger, Stern did not recognize a value-bound required superimposition of the whole over its parts. Stern also applied the concept of the whole to social facts, but he characterized the relationship between individual and community as a tension. This tension might be transcended through the 'introception' of the outer goals of the superimposed holisms like *Volk* and humanity (a category which Krueger did not use) in the inner goals of the individual, without, however, abandoning the autonomous individual as the reference point:

> No matter how much the person is codetermined by all transpersonal areas to which he belongs, he does not take his individual wholeness from them, rather he asserts his wholeness as something autonomous, and he enriches his wholeness through the incorporation of those influences in his own being.[53]

Even with the strongest connection to the human community, people retain 'their personal fundamental characteristic "self-determination", especially in the tensions with the outer determinations which throng around it'.[54] One can recognize a different political starting-point in this difference between Stern's and Krueger's determination of the relationship between individual and community. Stern based his psychology on a theory of the autonomous person; this corresponded to the liberal idea of democracy, which is founded on the concept of free individuals and their association. In contrast, the German nationalist Krueger did not recognize the ideas of autonomy or self-determination. He wanted to embed the individual organically in a superimposed social community that the individual would accept as natural. This corresponded to the criticism of democracy by the opponents of the Weimar Republic, who wanted to base the state on the so-called natural units, especially the unity of a biologically understood *Volk*, and did not want to recognize a contractual state of associated individuals.[55]

The polarization between the theory of a contractual state and an organic conception of the state, which shines through in the contrast between Stern and Krueger, was older than the political conflicts of the Weimar Republic. We find theories in the aftermath of the French Revolution and the Enlightenment in which the legal and political nature of the state is no longer, as had already been the case in the ancient world, conceived in an analogy to animate nature only in certain respects, rather systematically after the model of a living organism. In contrast to the theory of a contractual state, the state has conferred on it its own value independent of the individuals. In Johann Gottfried Herder's writings the idea emerges for the first time that the individual is only itself when it fulfills its part of the whole.[56] The holistic conception of the state after the model of an organism was widespread in the nineteenth century. But it would be too easy for the evaluation of Krueger simply to contrast the thesis of the predetermination of the individual through social relations as a monocratic thesis with the thesis of the self-determination of the individual in the sense of the Enlightenment as a democratic thesis.[57] Not only the general transfer of the holistic idea to social facts marked Krueger's conservatism, but rather also the specifics of his conceptualizations. This distinction becomes clear when we, for example, take as a striking contrast to Krueger's conceptions the social theory of Karl Marx, which Krueger consistently and vigorously opposed. Marx also explained many social processes through organic metaphors. His theory also asserts that a totality of social relationships prevails behind the back of individuals, however with the decisive difference to Krueger, that this totality is itself historical and thereby transient, and that the freedom of the individual consists in the determination of its development through the knowledge of the laws of the supra-individual units. In any case, the mere fact of the placement of the individual in transpersonal holisms did not constitute an affinity of the theory to conservative social criticism of the twenties or even to National Socialist ideology.

Under the pasty surface of his words, here and there a clear piece of social reality shines through in Krueger's writings. For example, he, who wanted to have Marxism banned as a soul-destroying theory, demanded 'that human work, and especially economics, become the subject of philosophy';[58] for 'what always signifies *reality* for the developed human being depends on human work'.[59] Krueger is close to the theme of alienation. However, he sees causes and cure only in the psychological attitude towards reality and not in social relations. The questions of the sociality of the individual and of the connection between social and psychological reality are not developed in his work. For one reason social reality is not analysed historically, rather it is shifted to the region of a supra-individual psychological reality; and for another, the individual is not seen as being determined by these relations and simultaneously constituting them through its actions, rather it lives from an emotional rooting in the given community. The essential idea of the determination of psychological events through society and culture is thereby sacrificed to mystification. A community which is understood as timeless, but which nevertheless fits well into the times, takes the place of the interaction of individual and society as the last fundamental root of psychological values.

Since the industrialization at the end of the nineteenth century at the latest, scientific theory had to find a response to the new social fact, that social interdependence was becoming ever greater and social relationships between people ever more opaque. A large number of scholars answered by means of a conservative criticism of civilization. Whereas Max Weber supported the democratic form of state, despite all his criticism of bureaucratization and of the depersonalization and mechanization of life, phenomena which Krueger also chose for the starting-point of his philosophizing, in the German-language sociology of the twenties a type of reasoning became more and more dominant, which wanted to reach back to natural forms of community beyond the concrete historical forms of state in order to frame a renewal of society. The negative phenomena of civilization were confronted by the positive fundamental facts of life; original communities, in which leading and being led existed, were considered such facts. The search for the future resulted in an often vaguely conceptualized past; past and future became dimensions uncomprehended by a 'mythical view'.[60] The polarity of society – civilization maintained through external order – and community – the natural, living and organic order – developed in 1887 by Ferdinand Tönnies, was made useful for the conservative criticism of society. Democracy appeared as the mechanical rape of life, which was contrasted with the more highly valued forms of community.[61]

For Krueger the crisis of society was a crisis of culture, a crisis of the disintegration of the living, the dissolution of parts out of 'holistic associations'.[62] He did not perceive its phenomena in historical categories. Thus for example in a 1930 speech before the National Socialist Students and Teachers League (*Nationalsozialistischer deutscher Studenten-und Lehrerbund*) in Leipzig he spoke out for the strengthening of the family without considering the social background of its dissolution, and as a way of obtaining salvation from the cultural emergency he recommended that women go back to the family and have more children.[63]

Krueger appropriated the usual slogans popular at the time from the German National or Young Conservative movements for his scientific theory of the community. At the end of the Weimar period and finally during National Socialism he thereby manufactured an ever tighter connection between his psychology and the dominant politics of the day. At the 1928 Conference of the German Philosophical Society (*Deutsche Philosophische Gesellschaft*) Krueger said that due to the contemporary hardship and the loosening of the bindings in society, a 'deeper will for community' was needed. 'We must responsibly make ourselves ready for new social forms and orders'.[64] Responsibility 'for the whole and its future' would be necessary; this assumed, among other things, 'leadership and faith of the followers, each at their place secured through instinct'.[65] Concepts like 'faith of the followers' or 'security through instinct' did not belong to the usual framework of Krueger's psychology, but they were built without hesitation into his statements when he applied his theory to the politics of his day. The diction corresponded at this point to the categories of all the right-wing revolutionary currents in the Weimar Republic. However, at that time the interpretation of existence still had a 'religious nature' for Krueger.[66] Two years later, at the 1930 Breslau Congress of the Philosophical Society, Krueger made a turn – even if only vaguely and unsystematically – in an explanation of the necessity of philosophy, towards the Nordic mysticism of blood:

> We Germans have to philosophize in order to live ... Our development as a *Volk* is repeatedly blocked or confused, and without a doubt the mixture of blood is at work. Until today in Germany the confessions, the political camps, and the economic interests are, if not enemies, certainly more irreconcilable than elsewhere; likewise the classes, the generations, even the schools. The down-to-earth Nordic nature has had the most difficult struggle in the history of the German mind with the genotype of classical antiquity.[67]

On the eve of the Third Reich in 1932 Krueger raised in his theoretical work 'The Problem of Holism'[68] the necessity for the Germans to become a community and ended his argument with a strongly German-expansionist and this time also racist chord. The starting-point is also here at first criticism of the ubiquity of machine technology and a 'factory organization' of social life:

> Human existence is now fundamentally threatened. And no one can withdraw himself from this situation. Least of all can the Germans within their boundaries, which have been sharply contested for ages and recently once again mutilated, reassure themselves with all that has happened, given the open wounds that every adult and their collective body has ... For them it has become a pressing problem, how the individual and the communities to which he belongs can remain whole or should win a new stability ...
>
> Since the war these same Germans, plagued by disaster, have been plundered and maltreated worse than cattle. That has finally reopened their eyes to see through the cloud of western phrases and the Eurasian haze. Their dammed-up powers are concentrating. From the inside they are beginning to line up, as has often been the case in great emergency ...
>
> Unless one opens the path for a reformation at the head and the limbs, like that now required for human existence, the West will revert to chaos and the less noble races will win the upper hand. It must be reformed from scratch, so that finally politics and the economy will be embraced. The *Volk* of Master Eckhart, Luther, and Johann Sebastian Bach will have to work for such a formation of the whole ...

> What now needs to be done cannot be brought about by science and philosophy alone ... But the greater the danger, the more necessary become the powers of order, symbol formation, and spiritual leadership. And all the more decisively ... these must. orientate themselves to that place, where the essence of all living being and at the same time all essential community is rooted, that is the holistic, which demands inner form.[69]

Krueger did not strictly separate scientific paper from political speech, rather he openly introduced his political standpoint into scientific papers and mixed his political speeches with his psychological theory. If he spoke on the decline of the family before the National Socialist Students and Teachers League, he attacked the Russian collective raising of children as biological nonsense (thereby he did not forget to refer to the brooding responsibilities of birds and the construction of nests) and legitimated the family as being a 'living, supra-personal whole'.[70] His theoretical belief that a community is characterized by the fact that the individual members feel obligated to what the whole demands, becomes a political demand, when as a strategy against the decay of naturally understood communities like the family, he calls for the cultivation of readiness to serve:

> ... stabile, transmitting creative formation is necessary ... For every individual this means in the end to surrender himself for communal tasks with his neighbors in inner solidarity, with faithfulness; that he be prepared to sacrifice, to suffer, and if it must be, to fight obligingly for a *suprapersonal* whole.
>
> Many now yearn to be part of a new, unquestionable following under true *leadership* ... Authority should grow again, living and naturally.[71]

In a speech at the National Meeting of the German Boy Scouts (*Bundesfeuer der Reichsfachschaft der deutschen Pfadfinder*) at New Year 1932, Krueger became even more concrete in the determination of timeless communities, from which he expected saving stability in an unstable time. The *Volk* was the 'psychological and spiritual bond encompassing everything', the '*Volksgemeinschaft* ('people's community') is ... more than the sum of individual beings';[72] to create it would require the duty of the 'labour service', journeys to the 'bleeding boundaries' of Germany, the revival of *Volk* songs or community dance. He wanted to reinstate the 'unities of blood and love': motherhood, marriage, family, tribe, and male companionship.[73] Pressure from the outside compelled a solidly structured state on the inside, which could 'demand anything from its men'; 'he who does not want to subordinate himself, should be legally forced to'.[74] With respect to the threatening destruction of *Volk* and Reich, one had to 'prepare youth for war'.[75] Krueger exhorted the boy scouts: 'if you now orientate yourselves with your leaders to the encompassing whole of the *Volk* and the state, insert yourself willingly into the orders which this whole has recently demanded'. However, he went on admonishingly: 'but that must be done like the limb of an organism by remaining true to yourselves, holding fast to your own well-developed nature'.[76]

Krueger's concrete determinations of trans-personal holisms were keyed to contemporary right-wing conservative politics. But can one say that he also helped to develop a National Socialist theory? A clear answer to this question is difficult because there was no unified theoretical edifice for a National Socialist ideology which could be used to measure the degree to which a scientific theory agreed with this ideology. Yet beyond all of the fluctuations in day-to-day politics and beyond all of the contradictions between different National Socialist leaders and institutions, there were a few universal fundamental Nazi convictions, such as the superiority of the Nordic race, the necessity of the struggle for more space for the German *Volk*, and the organization of society according to the leadership principle. The militant anti-Semitism and the explanation of history as the struggle between races were probably the essential unifying elements of National Socialist beliefs.

Krueger's early theoretical efforts had not necessarily led to the propaganda of leadership and *Volksgemeinschaft*. However, the de-historization of social formations, the explanation of holism as an ontological principle of the living, and the principle of the dominance of the whole over its parts and its transfer to social facts all created the preconditions for a way of thinking that could easily accommodate itself to National Socialist ideas. The psychology of community met with the National Socialist ideology of the *Volksgemeinschaft*, but it did not take its fundamental ideas from this ideology, which itself had only amalgamated them. The concept of a transpersonal social unity that exists before the individual, can already be found in the organic conception of the state in German idealism.

However, Fichte had constituted the nation as a spiritual unity, and for Schelling the state was denied every goal-means-relation, was conceived as an embodiment of the spirit and was derived from the absolute, thereby elevating the state to the status of an idea.[77] The 'organic theory of community' in the twenties, which can be found in Krueger's work, no longer explained the pre-personal unit as a spiritual unit – or as historical and thereby transitory – but rather as biological. For Krueger, the holism, as well as that of the individual and the community, was a 'fundamental bio-psychological state'.[78] But just such an idea was so widespread at that time that one cannot yet identify it with a National Socialist concept, even if it comes close to this. For example, Mommsen has showed that the intellectual polarity of 'organic community' and 'amorphous mass society' was common in the groups surrounding the attempt on Hitler's life on 20 May 1944.[79] The transition from this idea to National Socialist ideas appears to me to take place where the biologically-understood social units are founded in racist terms on the unit of blood or race. If this point of transition is not reached in a scientific theory, then we can diagnose in it a conservative ideological content – which could also prepare the ground for National Socialist ideas; however, we should then not speak of a fusion of theory with National Socialist ideology. This transition is suggested repeatedly in Kreuger's writings. However, racism, Nordic expansionism and anti-Semitism did not become systematic reference points of his theory; I will come back to this matter below. Thus Krueger's psychology of community was not National Socialist. Yet the thesis certainly does hold that the holistic psychology developed by him in the Weimar period helped contribute to the 'creation of a scientific climate in which the Fascist worldview' could flourish.[80]

Holistic psychology and National Socialist state power

Even if they were not necessarily close to the NSDAP as a party, at first most holistic psychologists nevertheless saw in the erection of the National Socialist state the solution of the spiritual and political crisis in Germany. At the thirteenth Congress of the German Society for Psychology (*Deutsche Gesellschaft für Psychologie*) in 1933, Krueger greeted Hitler in his opening speech as the 'farsighted, courageous, and soulful Chancellor';[81] in 1935 Hitler was for Krueger the 'inspired and beloved leader of our *Volk*', according to Friedrich Sander he was even 'a brilliant psychologist by the grace of God'.[82]

Holistic psychology saw itself confirmed as a theory by the change in political fortune. Albert Wellek, who after the war attested to a difficult fate for this school in the National Socialist period, in 1934 wrote on the theory of 'transpersonal wholes': 'our contemporary spiritual circumstances are favorable for the research now being forcefully implemented'.[83] The new political reality was interpreted according to holistic psychology; and the making of this reality was considered to confirm the psychological theorems. The National Socialists portrayed their 'seizure of power' as if the artificial social structure of democracy had been replaced by the timeless, true units of the community: the unprecedented thousand-year Reich could now begin. According to the categories of holistic psychology, the true community, in particular the community of the *Volk* described by Krueger as the most peculiar 'supra-personal power of the whole', had been created in opposition to destructive civilization, mechanization and loss of soul.[84] In political reality, however, the whole was only a fictitious whole, a myth that turned the real contrasts inside out. The political creation of the National Socialist *Volksgemeinschaft* also required terror: the elimination of those who might contradict, in order to ensure the required unity. Just as in theory the whole was supposed to possess primacy over the parts, in political reality it was prescribed to the individuals. The wholeness did not have to prove itself to them, but they had to prove themselves to it.[85]

The psychology of the community had only partially anticipated such a reality of a *Volksgemeinschaft* defined by the National Socialists in terms. of a friend–enemy dichotomy and enforced by terror. Krueger had indeed spoken of subordination and of the necessity to enforce this through coercion. But the political reality, especially in the anti-Jewish policy and political persecutions, went further. If holistic psychology also wanted to correspond to this reality, then it had to accommodate its theory still further.

As early as 1932, in a speech against the Treaty of Versailles, Krueger had demonstrated that he wanted to reinstate the unity of the German *Volk* in opposition to those whom he defined as not belonging:

> Let us not be weakened by merely negative voices or feelings of envy. In our conduct with each other, every emotion, every motion is evil which is limited to a rigid anti. Our country and life must be so completely filled with German nature capable of strong growth that the alien, that which is contrary to the *Volk*, can find no place. It must transform itself into the characteristic German or get out.[86]

In 1935 the word 'unholistic' appeared, if only once:

> The state's jurisdiction and ability to defend itself cannot dispense with harsh measures. Masterfully it demands the sacrifice of the individual will and even of life, for as in any whole that will endure, even its finest parts must yield to it. People have been given the ability to recognize what is *unholistic* in their existence, that is, what is contrary to life and hostile towards formation. They sacrifice their fallibility by consciously obeying their state and recognizing voluntarily the authority ordered above them.[87]

Sander went beyond this point; along with the law of the good gestalt he invented the law of the elimination of that which is alien to the gestalt and openly applied it to the persecution of Jews and the so-called hereditarily sick:

> ...he who wants to lead the German *Volk* back to its own gestalt after the distortion of its essence ... must eliminate everything that is alien to the gestalt, in particular he must neutralize all the demoralizing influences of alien race. The elimination of the parasitically proliferating Jewish race, as well as making infertile the carriers of inferior inheritance of one's own *Volk*, has its deeply ethical justification in this will to the pure gestalt of the German essence.[88]

National Socialism had realised the priority of the whole, the 'will to the *Volksgemeinschaft*', it had legally recognized the *Volk* as 'an organic whole ... of a racially-determined character'.[89] For Sander, holism and gestalt are at the same time 'inspirational ideas of the German movement' as well as 'fundamental concepts ... of German psychology'.[90]

Yet the question of the *Volksgemeinschaft* and the method of its realization by the National Socialist state was also a point of contradiction for Krueger. Although at first Krueger conceived of National Socialism as the realization of his theory, in contrast to Erich Rudolf Jaensch, for example, he was no apologist who wanted to accommodate his theory to the required political reality no matter what the cost. When Krueger had conceived his communities, he did not mean the marching in the street, the persecution of the Jews and the extension of the state to machinery that dominated everything. In 1934 he opposed a trivialization of the holistic concept – practised by Sander – and the concept of the 'total state'.

> ... the call for *holism*. Now the same call is propagated even in the newspapers, and mass meetings are excited by it ... The main emphasis is diverted into the '*Volksgemeinschaft*', and lately the 'total state' is accepted in outline along with it. The guild, family, and companionship withdraw behind these preferred topics of public opinion, even more the timeless products of the spirit, most of all the creative personality ... So it is high time that the science of experience turn its attention to the facts common to all.[91]

Science was now being evoked by Krueger as a guardian against National Socialist reality, whereas previously he had seen it as its interpreter. What was happening was not what had been intended by the German nationalist intellectual. Thus Krueger complained in the same lecture:

> Words like bonding, comradeship alternating with solidarity, front, common nature-like worldview, especially, however, *Volksgemeinschaft* are popular. Serious considerations of guild, guild honor, and guild organization, of clan association and tribal characteristics, of neighborhoods, self-administration, and not least of economic, psychological, and spiritual bonds would belong there and be generally less ambiguous ...
> Science has the duty always to examine as rigorously as possible which 'we' is seriously meant or actually available, how the solidarity of living persons is there truly achieved, to what degree it is dependable and productive; moreover, whether the purported unity is actually possible and could last, therefore could also create something lasting.[92]

In a lecture at the fifteenth Congress of the German Society for Psychology in 1936, Krueger once again contrasted clearly the 'communities of blood', clan, family, *Volk*, comradeship and work community, based 'on instinct and feeling', with the 'other purely masculine associations', which 'are determined more by the spiritually-led will, thus the army, the companies, first of all the state with its legally enforced dominance'.[93] But both 'main forms of community are real structures of human existence. They are bound by psycho-biological laws ... in particular, in both cases the *predominance of the whole* over its parts holds'.[94] Thereby the communities, which at first could have been seen as being created by people, were nevertheless once again biologized. The opposition to the National Socialist realization of the *Volksgemeinschaft* on the one hand, and its mystification through the naturalization of social facts on the other, were not far apart from each other. Thus Krueger, with regard to theory, could not come to an anti-National Socialist position. Just as the criticism of culture in the twenties was psychological as a criticism of the loss of soul and did not grasp the social and historical causes of change, so also now it could only be regretted, but not grasped that the embodiment of holistic psychological ideas in the reality of National Socialism took another form than intended. In contrast to the Leipzig psychologist Johannes Rudert, who attempted towards the end of the National Socialist period in his booklet 'Character and Fate' to digest the experiences of the National Socialist period by asking whether we live 'only on the surface or only through the accommodation to what everybody says and does' or through the 'actual center of our existence',[95] Krueger only became more restrained in his statements over the course of time. In his 'Developmental Psychology of Wholeness', published during the war, he once again summarized the theory of holistic psychology. He repeated that the fundamental laws of holistic psychology would also be valid for communal life, like the superiority of the whole or the determination of the community through feelings, the internal structuring, the hierarchical order, and the internal tension between the parts. However, he did not again refer to political reality as he had done during the thirties. As if he wanted to hold up the ideas of a conservative revolution from the right as a contrast to National Socialist reality, he wrote:

> At times every *Volk* has to renew itself fundamentally, in its entire structure, thus also in its legal order. The *Volk* is blessed if that happens through reforms, that is, if it is achieved steadily from the inside out, as a totalitarian unified new *formation*, not through continual revolutions, which destroy irrevocably the well-grown.[96]

Felix Krueger, National Socialist anti-Jewish and racist policies and racist typology

Although the holistic psychological theory had allowed itself to be combined with the Fascist ideology of the *Volksgemeinschaft*, it did not contribute to the central and unifying element within all that was propagated as National Socialist ideology, the race doctrine and anti-Semitism. Holistic psychology as a theory did not recognize the superiority and inferiority of races; it did not propagate war as a means to solve the supposed racial conflicts. In his political statements Krueger also generally kept his distance from racism. Because of a pro-Semitic remark he eventually even found himself in political difficulties, which I will discuss in the next section. Since Krueger's views on anti-Jewish and racist politics, like those he held on racist typology, are not made clear by his writings alone, but rather also from a few political acts, I will include the latter in what follows.

Krueger was not free from racist ideas. In 1932 he criticized the 'logicalizing' Arab and Jew and contrasted them with the 'Germanic type of thinking'.[97] He emphasized in his inauguration speech as rector that the 'efforts to achieve the pure truth have racial roots and *völkisch* preconditions'.[98] During the first years of the National Socialist regime he consented to the policy of persecution of Jews at the universities. In contrast to Wolfgang Köhler, he did not protest against the dismissal of Jewish university instructors. It was he who, after the departure in early 1933 of William Stern as chairman of the German Society for Psychology, completed the anti-Jewish 'coordination' (*Gleichschaltung*) of the Society. As the new chairman, he worked to fill the chairs in psychology made vacant by the dismissal policy, but not for the return of their Jewish former occupants.[99] Krueger arranged the transfer of the thirteenth Congress of the Society in 1933 to Leipzig and its programmatic political orientation.[100] He also prepared in cooperation with political authorities the concentration of the fourteenth Congress on the themes of race, psychology of the community and education for the community.[101]

But in contrast to his successor Erich Jaensch, who became chairman of the Society in 1936, or the typologist Gerhard Pfahler, Krueger did not try to connect his theory systematically with National Socialist racial doctrine. Krueger rejected the theory of Jaensch, who connected his types of perception with the classification of races by Hans F. K. Günther. This opposition had not only political, but also methodological reasons.[102] It becomes clear, however, in an internal faculty conflict over the *Habilitation* (approximately a second PhD) of Johannes Rudert at the University of Leipzig, who had submitted a criticism of Jaensch's typology as a *Habilitationsschrift*, that Krueger also wanted to repudiate the political arbitrariness of such a type of theory formation.[103] According to the referees' reports, in his unfortunately unpublished *Habilitationsschrift* Rudert asked how far typology allowed a consideration of the main forms of character. As the first referee of the thesis, Krueger gave a clearly positive characterization:

> After an appropriate outline of the major theories of Kretschmer and Jung, Jaensch's theory of types is confronted with both a precise representation of all its ambiguity and a thorough criticism. In my opinion, it is definitively made clear that this theory lacks clarity and consequences with respect to the emotionality of the holistic, and the structures of experience. In particular, the time-bound functionalism of Jaensch failed to appreciate (even in his own value-accents and reform tendencies) the essential timeless *structure* of personality with its value center ... I am convinced that these distinguished critical remarks will have a cleansing effect.[104]

Krueger did not criticize Jaensch so sharply in his publications. Rather it appeared possible for once to make his standpoint clear in an internal faculty *Habilitation* matter. This interpretation of this conflict also holds for explaining the conduct of another supporter of the *Habilitationsschrift*, Theodor Litt, as well as the opponent of Krueger and Litt, Arnold Gehlen. After Gehlen had vehemently opposed the *Habilitationsschrift* in a referee's report, Krueger commented once again in a second report. Within this report, Krueger takes up direct criticism of Jaensch. The lack of clarity criticized by Gehlen was not the fault of Rudert, rather of Jaensch's theory. Subsequent examinations made at the Leipzig institute to verify Jaensch's experiments had led to negative results. As far as theory was concerned, Krueger argued that Jaensch's typology did not penetrate to the heart of psychological existence and lacked a theory of feelings. Jaensch had recently connected 'in an undetermined manner ... valuations with grades and types of integration'. Finally he accused Jaensch of vague concepts, biologism and superficial comparisons of culture.[105]

This conflict in university politics, which finally ended with the *Habilitation* of Rudert against the sole resistance in the faculty on the part of Gehlen, had a significance that went beyond the assessment of the *Habilitation*. It was a matter of taking a stance on a theory which claimed to represent *the* National Socialist psychology. Perhaps the decisive point of difference between Jaensch and Krueger had been set up in a methodological respect even before the National Socialist period. Krueger was no biological reductionist. In contrast to Jaensch's later typology[106] and the race anthropology of Günther, physical determinations were not decisive for Krueger. In his lecture on the psychology of community life, he said indeed that 'the practical race care is on the right path', if the hereditary determinants of form 'outlined as "Nordic"' were especially strengthened; but at the same time he said that race could not be fixed by 'external physique'.[107] What is 'actually human' should be sought on the 'immaterial side'.[108] In the same article, however, Krueger also spoke of the 'blood-determined' communities of mother–child, family, clan, tribe and *Volk*. In the theoretical respect, this corresponds more to the spiritual concept of race found in Oswald Spengler and a metaphysical understanding of the connective function of blood than to the 'crass biological naturalism' and the 'crude blood science' of the *völkisch* and National Socialist ideology, even if in the political respect both came to similar conclusions.[109] But on the point of anti-Semitism, Krueger also distinguished himself from Jaensch at the level of political conclusions.

Krueger's pro-Semitic remarks and his retirement

In contrast to his other political statements, pro-Semitic remarks like the one Krueger obviously made in a lecture in the winter semester of

1935/36 are not documented in his writings – which given the political situation after 1933 is not surprising. Yet this remark, which led to the loss of his position as rector, will be examined more closely, for two reasons. Firstly, Krueger's political history at the University of Leipzig from 1935 to 1938, from his appointment as rector to his dispensation as professor, makes clear his ambivalent political stance towards National Socialism; secondly, this aspect of Krueger's biography has been used in order to portray Krueger as a conservative opponent of the regime and thereby to obscure the other side, his support of the National Socialist system.[110]

Krueger was known in Leipzig as a decisively German nationalist professor. In his 1939 retrospective survey of the history of the Leipzig institute,[111] he still presented exhaustively the struggle of his institute against Leipzig Social Democracy, boasted of the broad engagement of the Leipzig holistic psychologists even before 1933 in Hitler's 'Combat Union for German Culture', his own appearance at the 1932 demonstration of the right-wing-dominated Leipzig Student Organization, which had been banned by the university, and the activities of himself and Hans Volkelt as speakers before the National Socialist Teachers and Students Leagues. At the political rally of 1 May 1933 Krueger was the main speaker from the university. Subsequently, he was appointed rector of the University of Leipzig by the Reich Education Ministry (*Reichsministerium für Wissenschaft, Erziehung und Volksbildung*) for the summer semester of 1935. When he took up office, he was greeted by the head of the local National Socialist University Instructors League with the following words:

> We know that for years you were the leader of the reservoir against the [political] reaction and democracy, both in the national as well as *völkisch* respects. We know that before the seizure of power you marched together with the National Socialists of the university and, despite the prohibition by the bourgeois croakers of the time, gave a fiery speech against the shameful Treaty of Versailles, whose chains our leader Adolf Hitler has now finally broken.[112]

Despite this triumphal introduction, Krueger did not remain rector for long. On 3 January 1936 he was ordered to the Reich Education Ministry and there required to transfer his office for health reasons to the prorector Arthur Golf. This was caused by pro-Semitic remarks made by Krueger in his winter semester 1935/1936 lectures. The exact wording and the exact circumstances can today no longer be determined. However, some things can be ascertained from Krueger's personnel file and other documents.

In a newspaper article from the *Leipziger Tageszeitung* of 9 February 1936, a polemic was mounted against Krueger, without naming him directly, under the heading 'Abstract Intellectuality':

> It hardly seems possible that a German university professor sang the praises of the Jews in his course the other day! It concerned praise of the Portuguese-Jewish philosopher Baruch, who called himself Spinoza ...

Some German intellectuals practically die of sentimentality if they learn that some Jew falls under the [National Socialist anti-]Jewish laws, who according to their standards was the archetype of the famous 'decent Jew'!

According to Wellek,[113] Krueger spoke in a lecture of the 'noble Jew Heinrich Hertz' and in a subsequent lecture of 'noble Jews' like Spinoza, Mendelssohn and P. Heyse. The remark on Hertz is confirmed by a letter from Johannes Rudert to a colleague, in which on 21 June 1944 he passed on a petition to the faculty for awarding the Goethe Medal to Krueger: 'in particular he has been one of the few professors who before 1933 embraced anti-Semitism in a decisive manner. In contrast, the one clumsy remark (which included praise of Heinrich Hertz) is insignificant.'[114]

On 8 January 1936 the dean of the philosophical faculty wrote the following memo:

> Prorector Golf, who has been charged [by the Reich Education Ministry] with the operation of the rectorate, telephoned me this noon with the following message: Prof. Krueger had called him and told him that he would not continue the lectures until Thursday of the next week, since ovations for him had been announced, at which important men of science would also participate. The prorector pointed out the dangers of such ovations to Krueger and informed Mr Studentkowsky [Saxon Ministry of Education (*Sächsisches Ministerium für Volksbildung*)].[115]

Although in the meantime prorector Golf had been entrusted with the responsibility for the operation of the rectorate, at first Krueger insisted on continued recognition as legal rector and on being addressed in a corresponding manner. But after his remarks the political waves grew higher and higher. According to a complaint from Krueger to the Education Ministry, in January of 1936 a Hitler Youth Leader decreed a 'weekly order' against him, the contents of which, however, were rescinded in a new weekly order on 17 April after a reprimand from the Reich Governor (*Reichsstatthalter*) of Saxony.[116] Wellek[117] also reports weekly orders. There were obviously ovations in Krueger's lecture on 13 February; the next day the provisional director of the Saxon Ministry of Education, Studentkowsky, wrote to Krueger and forbade any further lecture or class by him for the rest of the semester, since in the previous lecture his instruction had been handled in a repugnant manner. The Reich Ministry of Education also removed Krueger as head of a planned delegation to the International Psychological Congress.[118] Jaensch took this opportunity to intervene for him with the Minister with the argument that Krueger was actually a fighter for anti-Semitism; the remarks about noble Jews should be taken as a somewhat unfortunate mistake.[119]

Unfortunately the personnel files do not show whether there was a direct, perhaps disciplinary connection between these events and Krueger's subsequent retirement. Krueger repeatedly had to cancel his lectures during the summer semester of 1937 because of heart trouble, as he wrote to the Dean. In September he therefore requested, that the Ministry release him from his official responsibilities and retire him. The personnel files do not give the impression that these reasons were merely excuses; for example, a doctor reported a heart attack on 18 May 1937. On 21 April 1939 Krueger's wife also cancelled her husband's participation in a *Habilitation* colloquium for Albert Wellek, whom *Krueger* had supported, because of angina pectoris-like heart attacks.[120] Of course a psychosomatic connection between the political events of the winter and the heart problems that followed shortly thereafter cannot be excluded.

Krueger was released from his official responsibilities as of 31 March 1938. A few months earlier a shameful examination of his 'descent' (*Abstammung*) had begun that dragged on until 1940. On 28 December 1937 the Saxon Ministry of Education informed Krueger that, according to the investigation of the Reich Office for Hereditary Research (*Reichsstelle für Sippenforschung*), he was not purely Aryan, rather had a full Jewish grandparent. On 4 January 1938 Krueger reacted to this remonstrance with a long response, in which he attempted on the one hand extensively to prove his Aryan descent, and on the other hand to insist on his political and scientific merits. Since the matter was not decided in his favour, a year later Krueger felt compelled to take the humiliating step of petitioning the Reich Office to reopen the investigation and to conduct a racial-biological and racial-psychological examination. In the second trimester of the year 1940, which began on 15 April, the university course prospectus no longer included his name. However, in June 1940 the Reich Office finally verified his Aryan descent. Thus nothing any longer stood in the way of the return of his name to the prospectus. Unfortunately the personnel files also do not show whether there was a connection between the opening of this procedure and Krueger's retirement, although only a few months lay in between. However, this matter would not have been decisive for Krueger's activity, since he had already been placed on leave as of October 1937 pending the outcome of his earlier request for early retirement.

Political ideology and psychology

Contemporaries have portrayed Krueger as a passionate German nationalist.[121] In fact he was the embodiment of the type of professor who opposed the new democracy during the Weimar period, who desired the right-wing conservative internal renewal of Germany and its external expansion, and who conceived of his own science as a contribution to the internal and external strengthening of the fatherland.[122] He was one of those securely established full professors (*Ordinarien*) who – just like Erich Rothacker or Martin Heidegger – initially turned to the National Socialist system of domination out of political conviction.[123] The idea that he did this out of opportunism must be rejected for a man like Krueger, who held Wundt's former chair, since 1910 was a full professor in Germany, since 1927 Chairman of the German Philosophical Society, and since 1933 Chairman of the German Society for Psychology. Krueger belonged to that conservative elite which had not reckoned with the possibility that the movement they had so gladly watched clear away the Weimar Republic, after its seizure of power would be immune to their efforts to impose their intellectual and political stamp upon it. Thus what was once said of the writer Hans Grimm might also hold for Krueger: 'as much as Grimm approved of the *ideas* of the new state, as little was he satisfied with the *masters* of power, who wanted to regiment everything'.[124] Krueger stood ideologically close to National Socialism, yet he shared the reserve of the rather aristocratic upper-middle-class conservatives towards the way the National Socialists exercised their power. He was not close to the movement as a propagandist, rather as a theoretician, who openly chose his own conservative *Weltanschauung* as a source of his theoretical efforts.

Krueger tried with his holistic psychology to achieve a solution to open problems of scientific psychology and especially to fill the need felt at the time for a theory of feeling, a theory of development and a social psychology. Yet he connected the development of his concepts with a political discourse in such a way that the development of the scientific discourse was completely determined by the political. The further development of Krueger's system of categories during the twenties and thirties was hardly more than an attempt to integrate general categories of right-wing conservative thought into psychology. However, Krueger was too independent with respect to his position to accommodate it completely to National Socialist ideology. Krueger's psychology thus also cannot be designated as the school of psychology which performed the greatest kowtow to the system.

Krueger attempted, in particular by means of his programmatic lectures as Chairman of the German Society for Psychology at the society's congresses, to raise the interpretation of Leipzig holistic psychology to an obligatory research programme for German psychology. However, this attempt failed. On the one hand, the state did not raise any particular direction in psychology to a politically obligatory paradigm. On the other hand, the competition between the schools and professors continued. Perhaps the dominance of representatives of holistic psychology in the psychological university chairs after the war in the Federal Republic of Germany has led to the false impression that psychology under National Socialism was more or less identical to Leipzig holistic psychology. However, it is correct that holistic psychology was able to gain in influence during National Socialism. Krueger could, for example, mold the image of two psychological congresses through extended lectures. He strove to carry his programme to the public, also beyond the walls of the university. He thereby presented as science a worldview which inevitably fed National Socialist policies. In contrast, the subsequent opposition on a few points hardly matters; it also cannot be an excuse for the fact that Krueger created this intellectual nourishment.

Appendix: A Brief Biography of Felix Krueger[125]

10 August 1874: born the son of a factory owner in Posen; attended the humanistic Friedrich-Wilhelm-Gymnasium.

1893–1897: studied philosophy, history, economics and physics in Strasbourg, Berlin and Munich.

22 July 1897: PhD with Theodor Lipps and Hans Cornelius in Munich with the work 'The concept of absolute values as a fundamental concept of moral philosophy' (fields of examination: philosophy, economics, physics).

1897–1899: study of philosophy, physiology and history, University of Leipzig; work at the Institute for Experimental Psychology with Wilhelm Wundt.

October 1899–April 1901: Assistant at the Psychological Seminar of the University of Kiel.

April 1901–October 1902: Assistant at the Physiological Institute of the University of Kiel.

October 1902–April 1906: Assistant to Wilhelm Wundt at the Institute for Experimental Psychology of the University of Leipzig.

28 April 1903: *Habilitation* at the University of Leipzig.

April 1906–April 1908: Professor of Philosophy and Psychology and Director of the Psychological Laboratory of the Instituto Nacional del Profesorado, Buenos Aires.

8 January 1907: appointed Professor and Director of the Laboratory for Applied Psychology in the Philosophical Faculty of the University of Buenos Aires.

March 1908: resigns his professorship; travels to Argentina, Chile, Uruguay and Brazil.

12 December 1909: appointed Associate Professor (*a.o. Professor*) at the University of Leipzig.

8 June 1910: inaugural lecture at the University of Leipzig.

2 August 1910: appointed Full Professor (*Ordinarius*) of Philosophy and Director of the Psychological Laboratory at the University of Halle (successor to Meumann).

Winter 1912–1913: Kaiser-Wilhelm Professor at Columbia University, New York.

August 1914: volunteered for military service; in the army until April 1917.

Summer 1917: held lectures at the University of Halle.

October 1917: called as successor to Wilhelm Wundt at the University of Leipzig; Professor of Philosophy and Director of the Psychological Institute.

1927–1934: Chairman of the German Philosophical Society.
1933–1936: Chairman of the German Society for Psychology.
1935: appointed Rector of the University of Leipzig.
October 1937: placed on leave.
31 March 1938: retirement.
End of 1944/beginning of 1945: moved to Switzerland.
1945: made his home in Basle.
25 February 1948: death in Basle.

Krueger was a member of, among others, the Saxon Academy of Sciences, the Imperial Leopold Academy in Halle, Corresponding member of the Society for Comparative Cultural Research in Oslo, and Honorary Member of the British Psychological Association; he edited the 'New Psychological Studies' and the 'Works on Developmental Psychology' and received an honorary doctorate from Columbia University in New York, Wittenberg College in Springfield, Ohio, and the Dresden Technical University.

11 | Pascual Jordan: quantum mechanics, psychology, National Socialism

M. NORTON WISE[1]

In Wahrheit ist das Licht weder Welle noch Korpuskel, sondern ein 'Drittes'.[2]

Pascual Jordan (1902–80) remains an enigma of *das Dritte Reich*. Precocious mathematician plagued by a stammer, co-author with Heisenberg and Born of the '*Drei-männer Arbeit*' of 1925–6 which formalized Heisenberg's quantum mechanics, and staunch opponent of '*Die deutsche Physik*' of Lenard and Stark, he was also an enthusiast for Freudian psychology, a proud *SA-Mann* and member of the NSDAP, and a religiously committed advocate of the view that the elusive spiritual side of life is manifested in '*ein Drittes*', the dualist physics of the material world. The interrelation of these activities constitutes my story. Consider first their political framework.[3]

In 1935 Jordan published a little propaganda piece designed to legitimate the theoretical physics of the twentieth century by identifying it with National Socialist ideology in the 'new epoch'. His cleverly titled *Physikalisches Denken in der neuen Zeit*[4] appeared under the imprint of the *Hanseatische Verlagsanstalt* in Hamburg, publishers of such Nazi visions as *Der Kampf um das geistige Reich: Bau und Schicksal der Universität*, by Julius Schmidhauser and *Die Massenwelt im Kampf um ihre Form*, by the Frankfurt sociologist Heinz Marr, as well as several of Ernst Jünger's calls to the romance of war and domination, such as *Der Arbeiter: Herrschaft und Gestalt*. Jordan's view of modern physics fit right in. Its technical application to airplanes, radio technology and weapons of all kinds provided 'the strongest and sharpest means of exercising power (*Machtmittel*) for the mighty battles of our century'. Moreover, the recent upheaval in theoretical physics and its explosive tempo of development presented 'a mirror image of the revolutionary transformation of the world'.[5] This mirror image will frame my analysis.

Under 'revolutionary' Jordan understood – to judge from frequency of usage – 'radical', 'brutal' and the 'liquidation' of enemies. Modern physics contributed not simply an analogue to the new world order but weapons for eliminating enemies, both material and intellectual. Intellectual enemy number one was the Enlightenment, with what Jordan saw as its mechanist-materialist reduction of the physical world, its elimination of life as a special category for organisms, its anti-religious stance, and of course the individualist social-political doctrines that it projected as natural law. Revolutionary quantum mechanics, coupled with revolutionary positivism, attacked this set of dogmas at the base of their legitimation, the mechanist-materialist physics of Newton–Laplace and the supposed capacity of scientific method to reveal the objective truth of nature itelf.

Jordan based his rejection of 'the idea of objective science' on what he regarded as the moral bankruptcy of Enlightenment ideology.

> The deepest tendency of this ideology is avoidance of the necessity of genuine decisions. Instead of the boldness and daring of faith-advancing religion, which assumes hostility between true believers and heretics, science understood in this way promises an objective certainty, in which, after overcoming prejudice and error, all human disharmonies must smooth out and come together. One believes in an 'objective truth', cognition of which is of an essentially *progressive* kind. It does not require, like religious perception, the risk of personal decision but rather its opposite, elimination of all '*prejudices*'. This cognition is in principle accessible to everyone who possesses the necessary receptiveness to impartiality ... Thereby scientific cognition attains *universality*: for it there are no differences of classes or peoples, races or cultures.[6]

Thus the very neutrality of the ideal of scientific objectivity is morally incapacitating. It also supports egalitarian notions, which deny obvious class, racial and cultural distinctions. In short, enlightenment ideology suppresses diversity and contest in order to maintain a simplistic ideology of universality. Jordan located a potent source for this critique in the human sciences.

> The present skepticism toward this conception finds allies in certain sciences themselves: in cultural history and in cultural anthropology. In that these sciences investigate the spiritual life of past epochs or of foreign peoples and cultures and in their comparative reflections also include our culture – and our science as a component of this culture – cultural history of necessity gives up the pretended *universality* of precisely our scientific knowledge.[7]

But Jordan here makes a turn from denouncing Enlightenment ideals to defending contemporary natural science, whose objectifying virtues he wished to preserve in a redefined form. Emphasizing that not only cultural critics like Oswald Spengler, but physicists and positivist philosophers themselves had vitiated the idea of absolute objectivity, even in mathematics, Jordan warned against overestimating cultural relativity in a fadish

'*Scheinradikalismus*'. Only limits to objectivity had been shown, not total invalidity. A minimal criterion for these limits existed, suitable to the new epoch: '*The differences of German and French mathematics are not more essential than the differencès of German and French machine guns.*'[8]

I will call this the machine gun principle of objectivity. Jordan called it 'objective efficacy' (*objektive Wirksamkeit*), stressing that national and cultural specificity were something to be overcome, not nurtured. Limited universalization had always been accomplished as *Realpolitik*. The machine gun principle itself showed that scientific objectivity is 'a politically definable concept' because criteria of transnational validity exist for everything related to war. 'War is the chief means for the creation of *objective historical facts* – meaning such facts whose actuality must be recognized also by opposing nations. And war forms the *objective probe* for comparison of the forces and weapons on both sides.'[9] Despite differences of style, if weapons work for and against the enemy, they possess transnational validity. Thus western mathematics possessed '*universal* meaning', extending even to Japan, 'after the Japanese have adopted European technology and European conduct of war'.[10]

Under the machine gun theory, modern physics promised an entirely new order of objective truth, that of nuclear weapons (an unusual prediction for 1935): 'a not-too-distant future may have at its disposal technical *energy sources* which make a Niagara power station appear trifling and *explosive materials* in comparison to which all present explosives are harmless toys'.[11] This new order of scientific objectivity would validate – in Jordan's singular version of positivist empiricism – a new political order, since 'according to the proof of historical evidence, war is the normal mode for attaining new historical creations'. The principle seemed clear: 'the minimum extent of the geographical regions ordered and pacified in themselves must remain larger than the effective radius of the longest range weapons available'; and so did the consequences: 'in this sense the present danger of war in Europe may prove in the long run to have been a mighty impulse for striving toward a better order in the totality of European social life'.[12]

Concretely, the new political order would ultimately extend at least as far as the objectivity of nuclear physics, meaning as far as the effectiveness of nuclear weapons to regulate and pacify a region. This capacity of weapons to enforce simultaneously a natural order and a political order represented to Jordan the technical-material side of historical development. To it corresponded an intellectual-cultural side.

> The political transformation already accomplished in so many European states, in the shape of a replacement of the old parliamentary forms of government by authoritative and dictatorial methods, signifies in no way merely a technical modernization of the apparatus of government; rather, it is the eruption of a revolutionary reconstruction of our entire thought, values and action, gradually encompassing all areas of life and culture.[13]

So the correlated Enlightenment ideals of universal knowledge and parliamentary government give way in the new epoch to a correlation of machine gun universalization with dictatorial rule. The Third Reich 'liquidates' the Enlightenment.[14] Throughout the 1930s Jordan sought in popular articles and books to show that this transformation of the western tradition should be understood as the necessary (zwangsläufig) result of twentieth-century physics and philosophy, especially quantum mechanics and positivism, whose basic ideas would also ground new trends in vitalist biology and spiritualist psychology. He also published a major text on quantum mechanics to reveal in technical detail how the characteristic appearances of life (Lebenserscheinungen) expressed themselves at the roots of physical nature. In what follows I want to examine this reciprocal fertilization, showing how the principle of dictatorship infuses each area. At the same time I will draw out the shifts of emphasis through which Jordan transforms meanings, therefore coopting ideas typically located in a liberal socialist context, often also Jewish, for the National Socialist cause. Bohr, Mach and Freud all suffer such violent reversals. This will lead to some generalizing conclusions. In the first instance, however, I will treat the material as intellectual spectacle, so unsettling in itself that contextualization would rob it of meaning.

Intuitive quantum mechanics

Those familiar with Paul Forman's 'Weimar Culture, Causality, and Quantum Theory', will have recognized already that Pascual Jordan's views on the revolutionary era epitomize many of the markers that Forman assigned to physicists in the Weimar period after World War I: vitalist Lebensphilosophie, Spenglerian cultural relativism, crisis mentality, and the search for non-mechanist, acausal explanation. Thus, if we extend Forman's argument, Jordan's National Socialist physics emerges as a natural continuation of Weimar physics (he completed his doctorate with Max Born at Göttingen in 1924, habilitated at Göttingen in 1926, and was called as professor ordinarius to Rostock in 1929). This narrative has much to recommend it, and I will present a version of it here. But for Forman's thesis, that rather suddenly in the Weimar period 'extrinsic influences led physicists to ardently hope for, actively search for, and willingly embrace an acausal quantum mechanics', Jordan's case suggests at least two weaknesses. Far from capitulating to a hostile culture, Jordan led the way; and the resources on which he drew for acausality did not suddenly emerge after the war. I will substitute participation for capitulation and continuity for suddenness. There is a third problem: the large number of people whom Forman bundles together as vitalists were an extremely diverse collection, all of whom pursued holistic explanation, but in different directions and with different motives. If applied to people he does not discuss, his criteria would lump Jordan with Bohr, with Gestalt psychologists like Köhler, and with positivists like Neurath, all of whom were hostile to Jordan's vitalist views and their political correlates. This criticism applies even more directly to John Heilbron's discussion of the 'missionaries of the Copenhagen spirit', where Bohr's holism opens the door to Jordan's Nazism. Certainly Nazi culture drew on holistic currents in Weimar culture, and certainly Jordan drew for his vitalist physics on Bohr's holism, but we should avoid colouring holism with a monochromatic Nazi tint.[15]

Elsewhere I have begun a longitudinal study from about 1870 of the concept of statistical causality in Central Europe, tracing its origins, development and ultimate refinement in physics.[16] That study should conclude with Jordan's quantum mechanics text of 1936, *Die anschauliche Quantentheorie*, where he presented the elegant statistical transformation theory for which he was known among physicists. But why does this book contain material on such subjects as parapsychology? The long-term perspective yields a relevant result. 'Statistical causality' originated as a coherent concept in the late nineteenth century in a specifically Central-European tradition of criticism and interpretation of social statistics. This tradition highlighted a distinction between *physical* causality and *psychical* causality, or *quantitative* causality versus *qualitative* causality. Applied to social statistics, *psychical* causality became statistical causality. From the beginning, therefore, psychology provided the structure of concepts within which statistical causality obtained its meaning.

Supplementing this historical development is the fact that many of the main actors in the actual formation of quantum mechanics looked to psychology for an understanding of the concepts they were struggling to develop. Best known in this regard are Bohr, Pauli and Jordan, but Richard von Mises and Hermann Weyl were others.[17] Thus Jordan's psychological perspective on statistical laws appears within a long and complex history which contains numerous points of intersection between physics and psychology and which includes a number of Jordan's associates among Central-European physicists. Most prominent of course was Niels Bohr.

Bohr's role

Jordan always advertised himself as a member of the Bohr 'school', along with Heisenberg and Pauli. Both in his own 'intuitive' formalization of the matrix-statistical viewpoint and in his attempts to extend that viewpoint into psychology and biology, he claimed to be merely elaborating Bohr's ideas of correspondence and complementarity. Citing the correspondence principle as 'without doubt the most important thought of the entire quantum theory', Jordan treated the new matrix formulation as 'nothing other than the fulfilment and elaboration of the tendencies expressed in Bohr's correspondence principle.'[18] Thus he devoted much of his quantum mechanics text to developing the correspondence viewpoint, or 'korrespondenzmässige quantelung'.

At the same time he intended the development to show that the 'dogmatic materialistic conception' of classical physics was completely inadequate even for the physical world and therefore doubly untenable as a basis for research in biology and psychology. Quantum mechanics would point the way toward an 'organic conception', a rigorous conceptual foundation for previously fuzzy ideas like 'finality' and 'wholeness'.[19] It would ground in physics itself, in its strictest mathematical form, a holistic, teleological viewpoint on all aspects of nature. At the outset, then, it is important to see how ideas like these entered the correspondence principle when Bohr established it in his classic *Quantum Theory of Line Spectra* of 1918.

Bohr's psychological understanding of complementarity is well known.[20] But the correspondence principle too requires interpretation in terms of the tradition in psychology to which I have pointed above. Once again, the central issue concerned the distinction of psychical causality from physical causality, which distinction supplied the conceptual ground for statistical causality.[21]

In its pre-1918 form, the correspondence principle had referred to simply-periodic states and to the fact that, at high quantum numbers, the quantum description of an electron transition gave the same results as one would expect classically from an electron in an orbit about a nucleus. That is, the classical electron should radiate light waves at a frequency ν given by the orbital frequency of the electron ω. Quantum mechanically, however, these two frequencies are very different. The radiation frequency is given by the energy change in the transition from one stationary state to another; while the orbital frequency, or periodicity, is involved only in fixing, or identifying, the stationary states. Only at high quantum numbers do the two frequencies correspond to each other and to the classical case, but still only numerically, not conceptually.

In 1918 Bohr considered more complex stationary states which depended for their identification on multiple periodicities. This multiple periodicity he represented by a Fourier series of simply-periodic components, exactly as one would decompose the motions of a vibrating string (Figure 11.1).

The correspondence principle now said that at high quantum numbers these various periodicities ω in the stationary states agreed with the radiation frequencies ν, just as they would for a classical electron orbit or a vibrating string. Furthermore, the radiation intensity at any one of the frequencies depended on the amplitude of the associated periodic component, again in correspondence with the classical case.

Looked at in terms of *classical causality*, electrons must emit all those frequencies which are present in their motion, and with intensities determined by amplitudes. Looked at in terms of *quantum causality*, pairs of stationary states are involved in a radiative transition. Electrons emit those

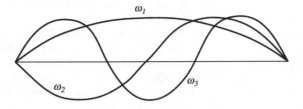

| Fig. 11.1   Vibrating String.

frequencies which are shared by both states in the various pairs of stationary states, with intensities depending on the amplitudes of the shared component.

But there is a problem with the analogy between quantum and classical cases. A single classical electron emits *all* of its frequencies simultaneously, while a single quantum electron emits only the one frequency which corresponds to the particular transition it undergoes. Each electron can emit only one frequency at a time because it can undergo only one transition at a time. Therefore, the correspondence analogy is a one–many analogy between one classical electron and a whole set of quantum electrons undergoing different transitions. This set must actually be a statistical ensemble, with weights determined by the amplitudes of the periodic components, if it is to correspond to the radiation from a single classical electron.

The statistical nature of the analogy between electron orbits and stationary states leads to the following conception. Each electron in a given stationary state is capable of all those transitions associated with the periodicities which identify it. The amplitudes of these periodic components determine propensities, or probabilities, for the various possible transitions. The causality involved in quantum transitions, therefore, is *statistical causality*.

Bohr's understanding of this result in psychological terms represents a fairly straightforward analogy with a version of psychical causality available to him locally, especially through his philosophical mentor Harald Høffding. Psychical causality thereby refers to the categories of *individuality* which Bohr stressed throughout his life: *identity* and *spontaneity*. They correlate closely with the two postulates of the Bohr atom, one for stationary states and the other for transitions (Figure 11.2).

Identity

Bohr's first postulate, applied to the hydrogen atom, asserts that discrete stationary states of the atom exist in which its electron continues to behave *as if* it obeyed the laws of classical mechanics, like a planet moving around the sun, without radiating energy. These 'quantized' states are defined by

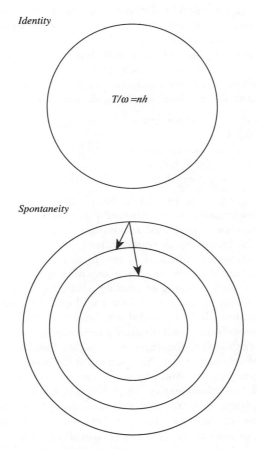

Identity

$T/\omega = nh$

Spontaneity

| **Fig. 11.2**   Identity and Spontaneity.

periodicity properties. In the simplest case of a circular orbit the defining relation is, $T/\omega = nh$, where T is kinetic energy, ω is the orbital frequency or periodicity, h is Planck's quantum of action, and n is any integer. To define periodicity requires many complete orbits. That is, as Bohr put it, the electron must 'get to know' the entire field of its action in order to establish its identity. The atom is then an *individual*, in the sense that its entire identity must be understood as a whole.[22]

Spontaneity
At the same time as the atom establishes its identity it establishes its possibilities for development via transitions between its possible stationary

states. That is, it can develop in all those ways that resonate with its identi-fying periodicities. But which way it will develop is indeterminate, or subject to spontaneous 'choice'. The choice cannot be submitted to a classical causal analysis, but only to a probabilistic analysis.

This account is subject to easy elaboration to include a set of related antinomies which had long been linked together in the tradition. Høffding in particular had subjected them to systematic analysis:

causality vs. development
whole vs. part
continuity vs. discontinuity
rationality vs. irrationality
definition vs. observation.

All of these antinomies are present in Bohr's 1918 paper. The last one, definition vs. observation, is the basis of the complementarity principle, which has so often been recognized as having a psychological foundation.

For Bohr, as for Høffding, the antinomies represented the categories of all knowledge, whether of physical or psychical states. Because they were general epistemological categories, their meaning in any one area could help to illuminate their meaning in another area by heuristic analogy. But analogy did not justify identification. One could usefully speak of the 'indi-viduality' of the atom, but atoms did not have personalities. Concerning definition vs. observation, psychological experience showed that attempts at observing one's thoughts disturbed the thoughts. Similarly, the condition of observation of an atom, a transition, changed the state of the atom. This similarity between psychical and physical states revealed a general relation of exclusion, of 'complementarity' in Bohr's 1929 formulation, between definition and observation. In another guise, complementarity appeared already in the correspondence principle, between the statistically defined Fourier analysis of the stationary states (classical) and the individual tran-sitions (quantum), then later between Schroedinger's wave functions for the stationary states and Heisenberg's matrices for the transitions, and again in wave–particle duality.

Jordan's text

In his *Anschauliche Quantentheorie* Jordan responded to the widespread charge that quantum mechanics, because it denied the possi-bility of unique causal description in space and time, was *unanschaulich* – unvisualizable and nonintuitive – therefore degenerate (*entartet* very much as in *entartete Kunst*) and ultimately false. He intended to build up a new image of *Anschaulichkeit* more suitable to the intuitions of a complex psychological inner world than to the outer world of spatio-temporal visu-alization. '*Doppelseitigkeit*' (double-sidedness) is the fundamental notion that Jordan wished to make *anschaulich* (now intuitive but not visualizable). Starting from the *doppelseitigkeit* of the correspondence principle, he would move gradually to the principle of complementarity in its most precise form. The goal is profoundly Idealist. It assumes that there are fundamental ideas which underlie *all* phenomena. The business of science is to extract those ideas from the phenomena and to put them in their most simple and most general mathematical form. This is the meaning of *Anschaulichkeit* in Jordan's sense. It is a view he shared with Heisenberg and Wolfgang Pauli, particularly on the significance of the matrix formulation of quantum mechanics.[23]

Speculative positivism

The new *Anschaulichkeit* rested on Jordan's interpretation of Machian positivism. Mach had insisted that physics and psychology, representing outer and inner worlds, both have the same foundation in our experience, or more specifically in our sense perceptions, from which we abstract a part called physics and a part called psychology. Agreeing in this, Jordan went further to emphasize not simply experiential fact as the basis of knowledge but the heuristic content of lived experience (*Erlebnis* even more than *Erfahrung*). The creative research seeks out more or less vaguely defined but nevertheless 'leading' (*führende*) principles which apply to concrete phenomena and then attempts to give them a precise and simple form.[24] The emphasis is on deep secrets and on revealing secrets. Typical is the title of his 1941 book, *Die Physik und das Geheimnis des organischen Lebens* and later *Schöpfung und Geheimnis* (1970). But in aiming to reveal deep secrets the new conception is also 'revolutionary', a term Jordan employed ubiquitously. Such revolutionary activity requires not only '*führende*' ideas but '*führende*' people. Through the insistent presence of this second key term in Jordan's suggestive vocabulary, Niels Bohr and his correspondence principle play their central role. They are the '*Leiter*' or '*Führer*' of the revolutionary new age in physical theory.[25] At least one of Jordan's critics, Hugo Dingler, took exception to this attempt to transplant the symbol of the *Führer* onto Bohr and his elite school (as well as Einstein), denouncing their views as '*the irrational personal opinion* of those members of this esoteric confederation, whom he [Jordan] regards as its leaders [*seine Führenden*]'. A Party member and positivist himself, but a defender of the experimentalists' craft and Lenard's *deutsche Physik*, Dingler portrayed theoretical speculation as a Jewish conspiracy to sabotage 'logical purity' and 'the great Aryan tradition of rigorous science' with 'unproven pseudoreligious fantasies'.[26] Dingler challenged Jordan's right to the symbols of the Reich as vehemently as his right to 'positivism'.

Nevertheless, in Jordan's unrepentant version, the positivist pursuit of radically new knowledge moves from the '*Primitivität*' of the concrete and the heuristic to the '*Einfachheit*' of the formal and the general. Primitivity supplies the driving force of revolution and simplicity its accomplishment. This methodology of the *Führer* structures Jordan's entire book. *Die an- schauliche Quantentheorie* moves from the vitalizing primitivity of the correspondence principle, through the principle of complementarity, to reach the elegant simplicity of Jordan's (and Dirac's) statistical trans- formation theory. Primitivity and simplicity, or vitality and beauty, are the two faces of *Anschaulichkeit*.[27]

In a slightly different form these two faces also characterize the physicist as a model participant in the new Reich. Physicists exhibit two prominent characteristics: love of beauty and will to power. For them, the beauty of things (*Schönheit der Dinge*) is captured in their theoretical representations, which resemble the artistic expressions of architecture and music; while their will to power (*Wille zur macht*) is 'one of the most sublime, most refined forms of the will to power, and yet filled with an almost brutal vitality'.[28] This juxtaposition of beauty with brutality was of course common in romantic ideology. Here, physicists' brutal vitality correlates with the primitivity of their *anschaulich* ideas, while their love of beauty is expressed in the search for mathematical simplicity.

In such characteristics of physicists Jordan saw 'a deep affinity with the spirit and desire of our epoch', which ever more clearly took the imprint of 'the resolute will to power'.[29] Politically, the significance of the physicists' will to power lay in weapons technology, as discussed above. Quantum mechanics would show how to release the energy of the atom, thereby extending the power of the state over ever larger boundaries. Such power should not be regarded negatively, according to Jordan, but as the positive precondition for building an ever-larger political unity, which required a central power strong enough to enforce its rule:

> only the force of the strongest powers will force the multiplicity of com- peting individual interests into a higher unity and protect against attempts at disruption. Therefore, in the wide spaces of the future, physics will also supply ... the positive, constructive means for great developments.

Thus the order and pacification ('*Ordnung und Befriedung*') attained under political unity presupposes the will to power, so that 'the destructive and the creative functions in a way fuse into one another'.[30]

These are the cultural terms in which Jordan understood the ideational dynamics of quantum mechanics, in which the primitivity of *anschaulich* ideas is the dialectical pole of their unified mathematical formulation. Of course the mass of normal people could never fully grasp these ideas, which were 'the intellectual work of the rare, surpassing researcher', nor could they appreciate that 'the brain of a *führenden* natural-scientific thinker is such a precious and irreplaceable entity'.[31] But with his *Anschauliche Quantentheorie* Jordan hoped to reach a somewhat more elevated audience.

Non-objectifiability

To characterize the revolutionary conceptual structure of quantum theory, Jordan employed not only 'primitivity' and 'simplicity' but also 'harmony', 'necessity' and 'wholeness'. So, for example, the 'inner necessity of the whole' is represented in the 'logical interrelation' of its constituent principles, leading to a harmonious totality which is fully unified, even though it stands in sharp contrast to the unity of classical physics.[32] More concretely and polemically, a positivist critique of classical physics, or 'the dogmatic materialistic conception of nature', shows that it makes a set of assumptions which are inconsistent with experience in the microphysical world of the atom. That is, in order fully to objectify the entities of its 'hypothetical-metaphysical reality' – whether planet, machine gun bullet or atom – the materialist view assumes a deterministic causality, which further assumes the continuity and lawlikeness of all physical processes. These assumptions allow one consistently to ascribe objective properties like position, momentum and energy to an entity. But quantum mechanics shows these assumptions to be untenable for individual atoms and to be valid only for the macroscopic world of inorganic objects. It replaces them in the microscopic realm with a new set of interrelated principles: discontinuity, acausality and non-objectifiability.[33]

Of these principles, non-objectifiability was most important to Jordan. It found expression in various forms of '*doppelseitigkeit*'. The correspondence principle, for example, expressed such double-sidedness because it related incommensurable quantum and classical descriptions through statistical causality. Similarly wave–particle duality expressed the fact that properties of atoms described by Schroedinger's probability waves, such as interference, follow classical spatio-temporal causality, while in their particle-like properties the atoms jump about without reason. From the statistical viewpoint the two sides are '*aufgehoben*' – in Jordan's implicit citation of Hegel – to form a new unity.[34]

The most directly telling *doppelseitigkeit* for Jordan, perhaps, was Pauli's concept of '*Zweideutigkeit*', according to which a state that would be single classically has a two-sidedness quantum mechanically. Thus a single orbital frequency for a classical electron would produce only one radiation frequency, but quantum mechanically it *corresponds* to two transition frequencies, upwards and downwards from a given stationary state. In a loosely similar fashion, the single valence electron in a silver atom is in a superposition state of two opposite states of spin. Any measurement of the spin will force the electron into either one or the other of the two distinct states, but prior to the measurement it is in some sense in both of them, in a superposition state of mutually incompatible states. Therefore the state is not objectifiable, not as a whole, *eine Ganzheit*.[35]

Complementarity and transformation theory

This brings us to the essence of the correspondence viewpoint in Jordan's eyes, namely to Bohr's principle of complementarity and his own transformation theory. Prior to a measurement, according to the so-called 'Copenhagen interpretation', a quantum mechanical system must be regarded as being in a very general condition which contains the potential for all those possible states which it might be forced into by a measurement, including incompatible states. This complex condition, however, can be represented by a matrix of probability amplitudes, definable statistically for a large number of identical systems. Here is the point of the statistical interpretation. It relates the non-objectifiable totality of all possible characteristics of a system to the result of a measurement made to fix the value of any one of them. Mutually incompatible characteristics are called *complementary*. Jordan intended his statistical transformation theory to express this primitive idea in its full, *anschaulich*, simplicity and generality.

The basic idea is that to make a measurement is to *transform* a system, in the following sense. The act of measuring, or observing, interferes with the statistically defined state of an individual system and forces it to take on, or better, *to express itself in terms of*, one of the characteristics possible to it. Actually, two measurements are involved, one to prepare the system as being of a particular kind, say in a state of determinate energy, and another to transform it so as to make it express another characteristic. Both the preparation and the transformation are represented by matrices. If two measurements are made successively two transformation matrices are involved, so that the system first expresses one characteristic and then another. Jordan (and Dirac) put this in an elegant form.

Assume for example a system represented by an energy matrix H which is a function of a position matrix q and a momentum matrix p, or $H = H(p, q)$. Assume further that the system has already been prepared by an energy measurement. Then the energy would be definite, meaning that H would be a diagonal matrix H_0, with zeroes in the off-diagonal or mixed positions and the possible measured energy values along the diagonal,

$$H = H_0 (p, q).$$

A subsequent measurement of q, the position, would be represented by a *transformation matrix* U, which diagonalizes q,

$$UqU^{-1} = q_0,$$

where U^{-1} is the inverse of U. Crucially, the elements of the transformation matrix U turn out to be probability amplitudes for transitions between the definite energy values of H_0 and the definite position values of q_0. This is the essense of the statistical transformation theory.[36]

In its utter simplicity Jordan's abstract representation contained the entire physics of quantum mechanical measurements. Within the same formalism, the complementarity principle, or the 'fundamental thought of the quantum theory', took on what he regarded as a particularly *anschaulich* form, subsuming '*every conceivable question altogether*', meaning, in his positivist vision, every question expressible in terms of measurement.[37] If two characteristics are complementary, so that they cannot be observed and measured simultaneously, the matrices representing them do not commute,

$$FG - GF \neq 0.$$

Position and momentum are such complementary, non-commuting, characteristics,

$$pq - qp = (h/2\pi i)I,$$

from which Heisenberg's principle of indeterminacy follows directly. So in its representation through transformation theory, quantum mechanics attains 'simplicity' in a few symbolic lines.[38]

Biology, psychology and parapschololgy

Following an esoteric treatment of current research in many-body theory and quantum electrodynamics, *Die anschauliche Quantentheorie* concludes in an unusual manner, with a chapter on the characteristic phenomena of life, including telepathy and clairvoyance. Herein lay the revolutionary potential of quantum ideas and the mission of Jordan's life. He first began publishing this material in 1931-2, but at least part of it, according to his own account, went back to 1919-22 when as a young student in Hannover and Göttingen he decided to go into physics to pursue Ernst Mach's positivist vision. Apparently he sought to unite Mach's (and Hume's) view of causality as a mere description of the observed order of phenomena – albeit uniquely determined – with the seemingly acausal, non-unique order of quantum phenomena.[39] No doubt he also found attractive Mach's view of the rather arbitrary demarcation of external physical from internal psychical phenomena, for in a positivist quantum mechanics he located the justification for rejecting any strict demarcation of observing subject from observed object. With strict causality and the correlated subject–object distinction 'liquidated', a scientific teleology of life could replace mechanist determinism: 'a deterministic conception of life processes cannot be brought into agreement with the results of natural science'. Jordan had expressed similar views already in his inaugural lecture at Göttingen in 1927 and by 1928 was prepared to elaborate them in a letter to Einstein.[40] In these expressions we see once again motives that Forman found to be common among Weimar scientists.

Verstärkertheorie *and phenomenological teleology*

Jordan began to publicize his message following his participation

in one of Bohr's Copenhagen conferences in March 1931, where he discussed with Bohr the relation of biology to physics. In May he sent for
Bohr's comments a draft manuscript which he subsequently published in
the widely read journal *Die Naturwissenschaften* as 'Die Quantenmechanik
und die Grundprobleme der Biologie und Psychologie'. Despite fundamental objections from Bohr, Jordan presented his conclusions as direct
elaborations of Bohr's views, a strategy that he continued in various other
forums from the propagandist *Physikalisches Denken* of 1935 to the esoteric *Anschauliche Quantentheorie* of 1936.[41] Constantly invoking the
image of Bohr as *Führer*, Jordan nevertheless did what seems unimaginable
for Bohr; he planted the *Führer* concept not only in political and scientific
life but in organisms themselves as the very principle of life. He developed
that idea in a highly controversial speculation called the *Verstärkertheorie*
(amplification theory).

Jordan's *Verstärkertheorie* rests on the premise that the acausal
behaviour of individual atoms in the micro-world can be amplified through
the 'structure' of organic molecules and larger systems to 'direct' or 'steer'
(not merely trigger or stimulate) their behaviour in the macro-world, thus
transferring acausality to entire organisms. As he put it to Einstein in 1928,
'*quite primitively* one can interpret [organic nature] to mean that the atoms
or electrons belonging to a living individual in a certain way coordinate
their otherwise statistically independent decisions'. This coordinated
activity would soon become Jordan's *amplified* acausality of organized
beings, responsible ultimately for freedom of the will: 'It is characteristic of
organic nature that the acausality of certain atomic reactions amplifies itself
(*sich verstärkt*) into macroscopically effective acausality'.[42] The free action
of a very few directing agents could thereby 'dictate' the unified behaviour
of organisms. In 1938 the political analogy became explicit:

> We know that in the body of the bacterium, there are among the enor-
> mously many molecules constituting this ... creature, a very small group
> of special molecules which are endowed with dictatorial authority over
> the total organism; they form a *Steuerungszentrum* [steering centre] of the
> living cell. Absorption of a light quantum anywhere *outside* this *Steuer-
> ungszentrum* can kill the cell just as little as a great nation can be annihi-
> lated by the killing of an individual soldier. But absorption of a light
> quantum in the *Steuerungszentrum* of the call can bring the entire
> organism to death and dissolution – similar to the way a successfully exe-
> cuted assault against a leading [*führenden*] statesman can set an entire
> nation into profound processes of dissolution.[43]

Jordan developed this idea as an exception to a common distinction
between microscopic and macroscopic objects in quantum theory. Individual atoms and electrons in the micro-world, as a consequence of their
non-objectifiability, have a certain '*Spielraum*' within which their
behaviour cannot be predicted. This *Spielraum* (again a key term in the

National Socialist legitimation of power) is given by Heisenberg's indeterminacy principle, which sets limits on the precision with which any observation can simultaneously establish position and momentum. A precise measurement, made to fix an electron's position, will force it to take on a definite position, but the experiment cannot influence which particular position it takes. The electron itself 'decides', as Jordan continually stressed.[44] With its position fixed, furthermore, the electron's *Spielraum* in momentum is correspondingly increased, so that its future course is just as indeterminate as ever.

In contrast, a macroscopic physical object behaves in a thoroughly determinate manner, because it contains so many atoms that the probability for their joint behaviour to follow classical causal laws becomes overwhelming. As an aggregate they are thereby objectified and have vanishingly small *Spielraum* for free choice. The only way they can avoid this fate is to follow the dictates of a quantum mechanical micro-entity, a directing molecule, making its decisions their own. Although Jordan had in hand no definite biological theory of how such life-giving structural organization of the whole might develop, post-quantum positivism justified assuming that it did, because it provided an efficient scheme for describing a universal 'primitive' experience, namely 'the subjective feeling of freedom of the will'.[45] Through the *Verstärkertheorie* organisms became non-objectifiable subjects, with all of the *Doppelseitigkeit* and complementarity of the atom.

Borrowing from Bohr, Jordan advanced the idea of 'biological complementarity', according to which the 'vitality' (*Lebendigkeit*) and the 'definiteness' (*Definiertheit*) of an organism are related as the observability of atoms (transitions; choice) to their definition (stationary states; identity) and as position to momentum. To demand the one is to lose the other. So to attempt to define precisely the acausal structure of an organism would be to kill it. It would then behave like a causally determined macroscopic object, an aggregate of atoms with no unity. 'The wholeness of the organism dissolves.'[46] Jordan everywhere referred to such one-sided operations as *Eingriffe*, calling up images of invasion and violation, even when referring to electron measurements.

On the surface much of this language sounds like Bohr, but from the beginning of his exchanges with Jordan, Bohr regularly insisted that biological complementarity was an analogy drawn for its epistemological value from the conceptual structure of quantum mechanics and employed to suggest how knowledge of organisms might be reformulated. He specifically rejected the idea that the quantum mechanical behaviour of atoms could explain the character of biological processes.[47] Jordan instead attempted with his *Verstärkertheorie* to make the new physics into the spiritual-material basis of life. More drastically, he did so in a way which made the dictator principle its essence, in complete violation of Bohr's liberal socialist values. I shall return to these reversals below.

Obviously Jordan was attempting to legitimate quantum mechanics by drawing on the legitimacy of National Socialist culture, and vice versa. More interesting are the concrete ways in which his mathematical physics entered this enterprise. With respect to biology, he focused on recent genetics and on how quantum mechanics might account for the directing role of genes. Three aspects are prominent.

The organism is a microscopic entity

From the fact that genes underwent mutations as a consequence of absorbing a single X-ray photon, Jordan concluded that genes provided the most convincing empirical evidence for the *Verstärkertheorie*. They seemed to be large protein molecules, containing large numbers of atoms, which were nevertheless controlled by individual atomic events. The structure of the gene, therefore, ought to be susceptible to quantum mechanical description as a whole, a *Ganzheit*. But this would require some relaxation of the principle of local causation (*Nahewirkungsprincip*), embodied in the equation Schroedinger had developed for wave functions underlying quantum probabilities. As a partial differential equation, it most naturally described propagating effects, not action at a distance. But Schroedinger himself had emphasized that the quantities which correlated with *observable* events, such as the matrix elements representing transition probabilities, were in fact *integrals* over the entire space of the wave functions. Jordan had originally (from 1926) heaped scorn on Schroedinger's differential formulation for continuous waves – calling it even here '*eine falsche Veranschaulichung*' – while promoting the integral matrix formulation for discontinuous jumps. Soon he learned to appreciate Bohr's correspondence view of wave–particle duality as a classical–quantum dialectic united by statistics. Still, the only observable phenomena for individual atoms were holistic jumps. And now genetics joined positivism in support of the '*Ganzheits-character*' of quantum events. Reciprocally the matrix theory seemed to offer a mathematical route to understanding the unity of genes through its integral formulation.[48]

Formation of integral structures

The unified wholeness of organisms, as opposed to inorganic bodies, Jordan believed, derived from their structures, 'wonderfully fine and most highly developed *structures*', which certainly descended to the level of genes and other macro-molecular proteins. These multi-atomic integral structures obtained plausibility from such systems as mercury vapour at high densities, which as a result of constructive interference between the atoms in its surface, acted *as a whole* to reflect individual photons.[49] More impressive to Jordan, however, was the theory of 'second quantization', the original quantum field theory of elementary particles, which he had helped to pioneer.

Second quantization attempted to explain not the states of individual particles, but the *existence* of many particles in an energy field, their creation, annihilation and total number. The quantization arose from treating field strength as ˆa matrix. This suggested to Jordan that the integral structures of organic molecules might have their origin in such quantized fields. He had in mind also that in this theory the Coulomb force acting between electrically charged particles (a retarded action at a distance in his understanding) results from photons passing between them through the quantized (and integral) electromagnetic field. As yet the theory had many problems, but it promised to make sense of the relation between action at a distance and integral structure.[50]

Purposiveness
Ever since Maupertuis and Euler introduced the 'action' integral and the Principle of Least Action into rational mechanics in the eighteenth century, integral formulations of the laws of physics had attracted those who sought purposiveness in nature. Such formulations promised to bring rigour to teleology through the variational calculus. They typically grounded nature's order on the requirement that some appropriate quantity integrated between initial and final states of a system, or over its entire space, be a maximum or a minimum. A final cause, or a principle of economy, could thus reveal itself as the foundation of the efficient causes (for example, forces) with which physics usually dealt. By the time Jordan entered the field, the principle of least action and other extremum principles dominated theoretical physics, classical and quantum (though not usually with the teleological metaphysics included). He naturally supposed that a principle of economy would also govern the integral structures of organic bodies.[51] Their purposive organization and development would find its proper mathematical expression in an equation derived from an extremum condition. With that expectation he labelled his program '*phänomenologische Teleologie*'. It seemed to hold the essential elements of a mathematical *Ganzheitsphilosophie*. But the ultimate stakes lay in psychology.

Psychoanalysis and parapsychology

Just as Jordan regarded the statistical transformation theory as the most *anschaulich* formulation of the principle of complementarity for physics, he regarded the psychological manifestations of complementarity as its most profound expression for life processes. Psychology, he remarked, is the most encompassing (*umfassendste*) of the sciences.[52] And he saw in Freud's theory of the unconscious, expressed as a theory of complementarity, the primitive ideas that would ultimately lead to an even more general theory than physics had produced.

The conscious and the unconscious were to Jordan like *observed* and *unobserved* states in quantum mechanics. To try to make the unconscious conscious necessarily involved a disruptive *Eingriff*, which forced the unconscious to take on one of the conscious expressions possible for it. So a kind of complementarity existed between, for example, conscious thought and sleeping. As in the case of biological complementarity, this 'psychological complementarity' was Bohr's (and Høffding's and James') before it was Jordan's, but again, where Bohr drew an analogy between the descriptions of physical and psychical states, Jordan sought more nearly to identify them, such that the 'primitive' experiences of self-observation would have their seat in the indeterminate behaviour of atoms united in organic structures. He regularly cited brain cells and the central nervous system as an example of the *Verstärkertheorie*. Since he lacked even the rudiments of a definite physical theory, however, his psychology remained analogical.[53]

Drawing on the associations with Heisenberg's indeterminacy principle of '*unbestimmt*', '*unbeobachtbar*' and '*undefiniert*', Jordan identified the unconscious (*Unbewusst*) as a non-objectifiable complex, a kind of potential consciousness containing the totality of our experience. Out of this totality we form our conscious images and make our conscious decisions, while being only vaguely aware of its existence. A too brutal *Eingriff* of consciousness will destroy the indeterminate totality by projecting it into linear reason. Normally this is unhealthy. But for pathogenic complexes in the unconscious, psychoanalytic therapy gains its effectiveness through the power of '*Bewusstmachung*' to destroy the complex. Freud, it seemed, had made therapy out of complementarity, in such remarks as, 'there exists also a relation of representation between this unconsciousness and the possibility of existence of the symptoms'.[54]

As Jordan developed his psychoanalytic perspective (partly in correspondence with Pauli and C. G. Jung in Zürich) he located the most direct expression of psychological complementarity in Freud's theory of repression (*Verdrängung*). Here parts of our unconscious, which would normally find conscious expression, are repressed by other parts of our personality which represent characteristics or values that are incompatible with the repressed ones. A shocking wish, such as oedipal love or hate, would provide a characteristic example.[55] This was the ground of Jordan's complementarity theory of psychical states, which he ultimately published as *Verdrängung und Komplementarität* in 1947. The idea found its most direct expression in the phenomena of split personality, in that two or more personalities, if they were incompatible, could never appear together. If the one were present, or objectified, and thus took on a particular expression, the other became completely undetermined. The two personalities repressed each other in the same way as complementary quantum characteristics did.[56]

More important to Jordan than psychoanalysis itself, however, was its heuristic value for parapsychology. The existence of a non-objectifiable realm of the unconscious, coupled with the *Verstärkertheorie*, made it plausible that individuals might communicate over space and time as though by some second-quantized field. On this basis he sought to make *anschaulich* the transmissions of telepathy (involving an active sender and an active receiver) and clairvoyance (with no consciously active sender). Stressing always their status as factual phenomena confirmed by rigorous empirical research, he used positivist methodology once again to legitimate forms of experience which mechanist dogma had excluded from the world.[57]

Of particular significance for Jordan was the 'fact' that these transmissions occurred without any consciousness on the part of either sender or receiver of the mechanism of transmission, whether through normal physical means like touch and whisper or through some seemingly 'supernormal' means over distances of 800 kilometers. Normal and supernormal, physical and psychical, passed over into one another in a continuous transition, without affecting the experience of the participants, which indicated that the essential process occurred in the unconscious. So it seemed reasonable to Jordan to speak of two or more people sharing an unconscious experience of the same things, whether objects or feelings. In fact, the equivalence of their experience made it impossible to ascribe the contents of the 'space of the unconscious' to one person at all. They possessed a reality or objectivity similar to that of things experienced intrasubjectively in the physical world. Thus one could justifiably speak of a 'real world of the unconscious', a highly 'social' world in which any two people observed the same objects. This social world of the unconscious would extend just as far as the sect of communicating participants.[58]

It will now be apparent why hints of telepathy and clairvoyance conclude *Die anschauliche quantentheorie*, whose most esoteric part is the mathematical theory of second quantization. People in the space of the unconscious would interact at a distance like charged particles exchanging photons in a quantum field version of Coulomb forces. It will also be apparent that through the world of the quantum unconscious Jordan reentered the National Socialist world with a potentially powerful model. Here psychological 'suggestion' occurred by telepathy, which was outside the conscious control of the participants. Here 'an astonishing degree of *amplification and intensification* can occur'. And here the '*Führer*' could exercise 'directing' power on the experience of others, and thereby on the construction of the real world of the unconscious.[59] Not surprisingly, Jordan found phenomena of mass hallucination and of the collective unconscious of special interest.[60]

Conclusions and morals

Jordan's story raises issues of considerable significance in the history of science and in German history generally. I will treat them as a series of warning flags: about the relation of science and ideology, about the relation of Nazi holism to holism in general, about the diversity of Nazi holism, about cooptation, and about the celebration of power.

Can Nazi ideology make good quantum mechanics?

I have attempted to display the degree to which Jordan's views on quantum mechanics were expressed in his biology, psychology and politics and how these subjects contributed to the formulation of quantum mechanics that he developed. His complex of commitments formed a consistent world view, however fantastic and however odious. This interpretation shows, as in many other cases, how political, religious and metaphysical commitments have provided crucial resources in the pursuit of scientific knowledge. We could as well be looking at Newton, Lavoisier, Kelvin or Helmholtz. But they all stood for liberal values. It costs us nothing to say that those values were essential ingredients in the science they produced. Jordan's Nazi values, on the other hand, stick in the craw. Can they have been important to his fundamental work in mathematical physics? Yes, according to the preceding analysis, Jordan's elegant transformation theory and his work on second quantization expressed directly his views on the hierarchical, organistic structure of the natural and the social order. It is necessary to make this point explicitly because we live with the tenacious myth that the acquisition of fundamental knowledge had to cease when scientists embraced Hitler. No real seekers after truth could also be pursuing Nazi political interests nor using those interests in the pursuit of knowledge. But of course they could, and did.

Reversals

More interesting is a broader question. Do the psychologistic and positivistic interpretations of quantum mechanics espoused by Bohr, Pauli, Heisenberg, Jordan and others express in *general* some tendency within Central European culture that opened the door to Nazism? Here I would raise within the history of mathematical physics issues which intellectual, social and political historians have intensely debated. The suspicion is still widespread that organistic, holist, teleological views of the natural and social order, coupled with positivist relativism, were major causes of the Nazi disaster. They opened the way to vitalism and mysticism and undermined the capacity of academics to stand up either for rationality or for the rights of the individual. This position is closely coupled with the so-called *Sonderweg* thesis, which argues that the failure of German liberalism in the formation of the Second Reich and afterwards left Germany with an unstable mix between a modern industrial economy and a basically feudal, or at least hierarchical and corporatist, social-political organization. The *Sonderweg*, or special path into the twentieth century, posits a continuous cultural progression from the 1870s to the crisis of Weimar in the 1920s and the collapse into Nazi dictatorship.

My own study confirms such continuity in the development of ideas like statistical causality, which was related at every point to holistic psychological and social theory. It does not, however, show that the continuity leads to national socialist perversions. It shows rather that subtle shifts in interpretation could take one across the political spectrum from Bohr's liberal individualist socialism to Jordan's conservative nationalist socialism. The mathematics of quantum mechanics could be read in widely different ways depending on which aspects one chose to emphasize. And not only holistic ideas were subject to such reversal. Positivist methodology and psychoanalysis, for all their analytic rationality, displayed similar plasticity.

We have seen that Jordan converted Bohr's egalitarian conception of the statistics of holism into the dictator principle through his theory of amplification, whereby the decisions of a central molecule became directives for a whole organism. He performed a similar trick with Freud by transferring the *individual* unconscious, read as quantum indeterminacy, to parapsychology and the *social* unconscious. And in perhaps his most stunning feat he coopted Mach and his heritage in modern positivism. A brief discussion of the latter episode will clarify why these reversals need to be recognized as such, and not as the natural consequences of Bohr's, Freud's and Mach's confused ideas or of holism.

Mach's weapon, like that of all positivists, was anti-metaphysics. Experiential fact alone would count as the basis of knowledge, a principle which Jordan belaboured in every publication. But for Mach, as for the Vienna Circle, the principle meant that experience would be analysed into its elements, ideally primitive elements, and then these elements would provide the basis for constructing the most economical representation possible. Any problem which could not be posed within this scheme was a 'Scheinproblem'. Realism, of course, was out of the question. Rudolph Carnap's *Der logische Aufbau der Welt* of 1928 became the standard reference. But what Mach took for granted, like Carnap and most other positivists of the Vienna Circle, was the analysability of experience into elements, and that the *Aufbau*, the building up of the world from the elements, would preserve this analysability in its reconstructions. Recognizing a gross assumption, Jordan simply treated it as the classical mechanical limit of a more general holistic *Aufbau* based on quantum mechanical epistemology and the acausal phenomena of life.[61] With remarkable audacity, he invoked not only Carnap's name but Moritz Schlick and Hans Reichenbach, co-editors of *Erkenntnis*, the official organ of Vienna and Berlin positivism, where he published his views on biology and psychology in 1934.[62] The entire force of positivist methodology was now supposed to support holism and National Socialism. Writing to Heisenberg, Jordan announced the pending publication of a closely related article for *Die Naturwissenschaften*, entitled 'The Positivistic Concept of Reality', with which he hoped to 'cause a few philosophers to explode with indignation: *somehow* I must finally work off my frustration'.[63] The response did not disappoint, whether from positivist or anti-positivist quarters.

Recognizing a cynical encroachment not only on their intellectual possessions but on their most cherished values and goals for humanity, official positivism flew to the defense in reviews and comments. But in truth, positivist philosophy offered little firm ground to stand on. Schlick attempted to undermine the conjuring force of *Ganzheit* in general (even while supporting Gestalt psychology) by attacking its vagueness and by dogmatically asserting that a holistic description could always in principle be reduced to a sum of elementry processes. Edgar Zilsel should have left off his own assault with evidence that the *Verstärkertheorie* was a piece of metaphysical speculation which seemed to violate all of those biological processes that depended on deterministic behaviour. Instead, he stumbled into Jordan's strongest territory with the doubtful claim that Heisenberg's indeterminacy principle introduced nothing fundamentally new into the problem of observer-disturbing-the-observed except a quantitative relation, and with the politically unfortunate suggestion that no reason existed to assume that a living organism, killed by a too-invasive investigation of its parts, differed from a disassembled electrical generator which could be reassembled and set to work again.[64]

The ever-liberal Reichenbach, pleased at having had his doubts about causality validated, objected to Zilsel branding Jordan with metaphysics. After all, Jordan had said nothing that overstepped the possibility of empirical proof and had explicitly identified his programme with theirs, even using Carnap's own formulation of the problem of objective existence. It came down to an empirical question about the *Aufbau* of the protein molecule; so philosophers, to avoid dogmatism, had to treat his views with respect. Reichenbach had no sense of reversals. Otto Neurath did. Perhaps because he had himself struggled to make holistic good sense out of socialism and scientific explanation simultaneously, he attacked Jordan's duplicitous intentions. The 'metaphysical mystifications' (*Verschwommenheiten*) were aimed not at furthering the positivist cause of clarification, said Neurath, but at connecting good new physics with obsolete scholastic metaphysics through 'vague analogies and conjectures'.[65]

Phillip Frank understood the stakes even more clearly. Bemoaning the fact that one could hardly open a book or journal without reading: 'bankruptcy of mechanistic physics', 'the end of animosity towards Spirit in natural science' or 'reconciliation between religion and natural science', he rejected out of hand the notion that the spiritualistic turn had been forced by the revolution in physics. Just as the mechanical world view had peaked with the ideals of the French Revolution, so opposition to mechanism had arisen along with the new revolution of the organic state: 'in a series of countries, especially in Italy and the German Reich, a completely antithetical conception of the world asserted itself'.[66] At least

Frank recognized that the argument against Jordan had to be cast in political terms.

But in this courageously open condemnation of Nazism and Fascism, Frank cast his net too widely, catching not only everyone who pursued holistic explanations, but all those mathematical idealists like Jeans and Eddington who believed that the world had been built according to the theorems of pure mathematics. This attempt to implant Jordan's National Socialism on anyone whose anti-mechanist ideas he might have employed had the same validity as would an attempt to implant him on the positivists or on psychoanalysts, whom he did freely employ, or on Gestalt psychologists, whom he did not. All of these people, of course, had to seek refuge during the Third Reich, having been tarred as Marxists and Jews.

By examining the ways in which Jordan turned Bohr, Freud and the self-proclaimed inheritors of Mach into supporters of dictatorship, I mean to have shown why these moves must be seen as reversals. At the same time, however, both Jordan and the heroes he inverted were the legitimate progeny of the *Sonderweg*. They all participated in the struggle to possess and define the past, to depict themselves as the true representatives of the present because the true inheritors of cultural tradition. Jordan's case shows just how precarious the contest was and how changeable the contestants. No one completely owned their own ideas, let alone the heritage of those ideas, or their future owners. Certainly not all cultures enter such unstable times as this one did, but its fragility should remind us that the *Sonderweg* must explain a wide diversity of movements at the same time as it explains the political-economic collapse. Quantum mechanics, psychoanalysis, positivism and National Socialism are neither historically isolable nor unifiable developments. Jordan impresses upon us that their adequate narration requires an unusual tolerance for ambiguity and contradiction.

Internationalism and anti-Semitism
One of the curious aspects of Jordan's career as a National Socialist is that so many of the people whose ideas he supported, borrowed and displaced were Jewish theorists, including his honoured mentor and mathematical collaborator Max Born and the 'notorious' Einstein. This brought down the wrath of *die deutsche Physik*, as noted previously for the positivist philosopher Hugo Dingler. So charges of *Schwärmerei* hit Jordan from left and right. In a tight spot, his strategy for survival becomes intriguing, particularly in relation to the reversals.

In 1935 in the lead article of the first volume of the NSDAP journal *Zeitschrift für die gesamte Naturwissenschaft*, one of its editors, the physician, eugenicist and Idealist philosopher Kurt Hildebrandt, set the tone for science in the interest of 'German nationhood' with an attack on positivism. The opening sentence brought Jordan under fire, and from there on he appeared as the intellectual supporter of positivist Jewish theoreticians whose abstract, relativist doctrines were weakening the Reich, producing 'an *Entartung* of thought' by denying the validity of 'human space–time *Anschauung*'. Jordan responded to this dangerous threat by directing against Hildebrandt the machine guns of objectivity deployed in his *Physikalisches Denken in der neuen Zeit*. He accused Hildebrandt of having defamed all of mathematical and physical research, the very foundation of Reich-defending and Reich-extending technology, which depended for its effectiveness on its international validity.[67] Now threatened himself, Hildebrandt played the honest critic, maligned and misunderstood in his contributions to 'spiritual *Aufbau*'. He had not meant to attack Jordan's contribution to rearmament, nor his *Verstärkertheorie*, only the positivism that corrupted his philosophy and associated him with enemies of the people like the mathematicians Hermann Weyl and Richard von Mises. Even Jordan would have to admit that his views actually contradicted those of the positivist group around Carnap, 'who in Prague and Paris will hardly have labored for the security of German armament'. But Hildebrandt still suspected Jordan's universalist *Weltanschauung*. After all, if machine guns worked for Germany they would work equally well for the enemy. The difference would come from 'the spirit of the *Volk*', not from international science. Others too maintained some scepticism about Jordan's commitment to National Socialism. Reporting to the Rector of the University of Rostock on Jordan's suitability for a conference in Paris, the Dozentenschaft judged that 'his works, especially his *weltanschauliche* attitude concerning the foundation and meaning of physics, are not without very significant objection'. Nevertheless they recommended support on a one-time, exceptional basis.[68]

Jordan was suspect because his physics depended on the contributions of Jews, but to defend his own identity he had to protect relativity and quantum mechanics. The obvious solution was to purify its content by rendering it culturally neutral, independent of the Jewishness of some of the people who had produced it, a product with no owner, available to be used as one wished. His concern, however, was not with the neutrality of science; it was with developing physics in its most powerful form, both ideationally and technically. From the technical side, the state that possessed the most effective machine guns, or nuclear weapons, would possess physics. Ideationally, the state that turned the new physics into a holistic biology of life and a powerful mass psychology would have made it its own by extending it over the culture. Therein lay the Germanness of German theoretical physics, not in the exclusion of non-Aryan contributors.

A still more insidious picture of Jordan's internationalism in defending science emerges from the Dingler affair. Dingler's review of his *Physik des 20. Jahrhunderts* appeared in the *Zeitschrift für die gesamte Naturwissenschaft* in December 1937. Dingler had tried to demonstrate, according to Jordan, that his presentation of modern physics expressed a 'pro-Jewish

attitude'. When Jordan learned of this charge in early February he
launched his counterattack, not in print but through the Party hierarachy.
Writing to the Directors of the local associations of professors and of
students (*Dozentenbund* and *Studentenbund*), to the Dean of the Philosophical Faculty at Rostock and to the Rector of the University, he strenuously protested this '*weltanschauliche* defamation' of a loyal party
member in a Party journal and requested that they report it to the central
administration of the national socialist *Dozentenbund*.[69] He had taken the
trouble to read Dingler's own major work of 1926, *Der Zusammenbruch
der Wissenschaft*, to discover that Dingler had undergone 'a certain *weltan-
schaulichen* metamorphosis'. Quoting directly, he showed that Dingler had
at that time identified his philosophy with classical Jewish learning and the
Talmud, even advertising that the head Rabbi of Vienna had praised his
earlier book, *Die Kultur der Juden: Eine Versöhnung zwischen Religion
und Wissenschaft*. In other philosophical writings, '*before* the *Machtergreifung*, Dingler expressly praised the "accustomed energy", the "industry
and acumen" of the Jewish race'. Jordan wanted simply to make the Rector
aware of the 'grotesque paradox' that such a 'pro-Jewish propagandist
should undertake to deliver a *weltanschauliche* correction and censure to a
Party member and *SA-Mann*, and that he should thereby obtain the
support of a Party official', the editor *Reichsfachgruppenleiter* Dr Kubach
who had made him a collaborator on the journal. And speaking as Party
comrade to Party comrade, this 'pseudo-scientist' had never received an
academic call between habilitation and retirement. 'It cannot serve the
positive work of *Aufbau*, in the sense of National Socialist *Kulturpolitik*,
when a man who is simultaneously a scientific zero and a fanatic *philosophical propagandist of Jewishness*, is named as a collaborator on the
Reichsfachgruppenleiter's Naturwissenschaft.'[70]

The confidence with which Jordan executed this turnabout of charges is
striking, but its basis becomes clear in the specifics. To Dingler's charge
that on page 120 he had written 'Kant has been revised by Einstein',
Jordan vehemently objected that 'Einstein' did not even appear on that
page. Of course 'relativity and quantum mechanics' do appear and 'Einstein' appears in many of his other writings. Implicit is the critical difference that Jordan, unlike Dingler, had never praised a person as a Jew, let
alone the Jewish race; he only approved theories. These were international.

It seems clear that Jordan adhered to some such attitude as this even in
his personal interactions with Jewish physicists. The interactions were
about ideas, not about the identity of their authors nor about the authors'
intentions for their ideas. Thus he never felt the need even to point out the
ways in which his *Führer*-physics violated Bohr's and Born's intentions, let
alone those of the more distant positivists and psychoanalysts. Jordan's
internationalist defense of theoretical physics left him free to employ the

ideas of Jews as he saw fit while simultaneously using anti-Semitism as a weapon against his enemies.

Machtpolitik – from NSDAP to CDU

Jordan's rhetoric grew ever more aggressive as German power expanded. In 1941 they both peaked. Jordan published *Die Physik und das Geheimnis des organischen Lebens* (*Physics and the Secret of Organic Life*), celebrating the supposed confirmation of his prescient speculations of the thirties, especially the *Verstärkertheorie* and the machine gun theory of objectivity, which had earlier appeared 'to the representatives of perishing liberalism as cynical brutality'. The modern revolution in science could now be recognized as the equivalent of the Scientific Revolution of the Renaissance, which 'transformed all areas of our lives and made possible the technical unfolding of power of our epoch and the supremacy of the white race'.[71] With his racism gone public, Jordan now disowned Einstein as having played any essential role in the development of relativity theory. If Einstein had not discovered it, someone else certainly would have; indeed, very recent historical research, not yet published, proved that the most essential content of the special theory was already known to Henri Poincaré before Einstein's publication.[72]

Jordan dated the introduction to this masterpiece from an unnamed airbase in the winter of 1940–41, adding the aura of real machine guns to the drama.[73] Democratic liberalism was dead, along with its deceptive insistence that the true value of science lay in the world of ideas, not material technology, while all along the only value it actually recognized was 'plutocratic plundering'. But since technology no longer served 'to enrich individual capitalists but rather the totality of life of the national community', raw power had been purified. 'We are not willing to see any abuse in the coupling of science to military might after military might has proven its compelling *aufbauende* force in the creation of a new Europe.'[74]

That was 1941. By 1943 Jordan apparently saw a different reality. Cleverly excising the introductory celebration of power from his *Geheimnis* he began the numbering on the title page (so that all pages after the introduction remained the same) and published a new edition under the old date from the airbase.[75] Having begun the cleansing process, and although he was called from Rostock to a professorship in Berlin in 1944, he largely disappeared from public controversy. That is, until the 1950s. Then a new cycle of power and polemics began, but in support of democracy and of a new party, the Christian Democratic Union (CDU) of Konrad Adenauer.

Throughout his career Jordan exhibited a remarkable capacity for rejuvenation (*Verjüngung*). The continuity of his position through these colour changes is nevertheless of interest. In June of 1934 he reported to Heisenberg, whom he had reason to believe shared his strategy, that he had been seeking since the previous autumn 'to rejuvenate myself through SA-

Dienst'.[76] He was hoping to gain Heisenberg's help in justifying to Born, Bohr, James Franck and others an obscure article that he had published earlier in the spring and that apparently enlisted science in the service of the new regime, especially for weapons technology. This 'literary slip', as Born called it in a letter to Franck, had aroused considerable distaste among his 'friends'. But he seems to have completely missed the point of their displeasure, in ways which illuminate both his capacity for the reversals discussed above and his later involvement in the armaments policy of Adenauer's government.

The great evil, if we can believe the thrust of Jordan's many *Führer* arguments, was not dictatorship, which seemed inevitable in light of modern science, but Marxist dictatorship. And only the strongest would win. So, he told Heisenberg, if Soviet scientists could convince their government of the importance of theoretical physics, it ought to be possible to do the same in Germany, despite Lenard–Stark.

> Naturally, as things stand, that is only possible if those aspects of physics and its significance are emphasized that offer positive possibilities for connection with the presently existing general conception of the life of the culture, state, etc. Not the intellectual-theoretical merits of our science, therefore, are to be propagated with some expectation of positive appreciation, but the practical consequences, above all with respect to war technology ... And the fact that today only a nation which also marches at the head of nuclear physics can be in a position in the long run to make use of the armament possibilities available to it in a manner equivalent to that of the scientifically 'higher-armed' states may be the single decisive argument if one wants to obtain attentive treatment and a positive evaluation of physics.[77]

Since Jordan made these remarks in order that Heisenberg could clear up the 'misunderstanding' of his article, it seems apparent that he simply could not grasp that to Born, Franck and Bohr his support for physics as a power-base for Nazi war aims presented a much greater threat than any Nazi degradation of physics or even the potential military strength of the Soviet Union.

After the Nazi cause failed, Jordan set about rejuvenating himself once again, through the denazification programme. He justified his actions, consistently, as defense of modern physics, while claiming, not so consistently, never to have been a supporter of Hitlerism. This standard ploy among physicists in the denazification programme succeeded '90% but not 100%', as Jordan put it to Born when seeking a testimonial in 1948. He enclosed a brief account of his activities during the Nazi period, minimizing his involvement with the Party, maximizing his heroic decision to stay in Germany actively to defend physics and the Jewish contribution to it against attacks from the 'radical-Nazi side' of Lenard–Stark, and concluding with a courageous decision not to contribute to rocketry or atomic energy.

Born politely declined to support this reincarnation, sending instead a list of his relatives and friends who had died under the Nazis. Heisenberg had accepted early on and provided at least two 'whitewash documents', stating that he had 'never reckoned with the possibility that [Jordan] could be a [true] National Socialist', while omitting any mention of his propaganda for weapons technology in the service of national power or for the principle of dictatorship.[78]

That Jordan emerged largely unblemished, and with a new professorship in Hamburg in 1947, may have depended less on testimonials than on the fact that he would have been a prime target at the Humboldt University in East Berlin for incorporation into the Soviet atomic bomb project, as he warned the President of the Göttingen Academy of Sciences in 1945.[79] By 1957, in any case, he was clean enough to be chosen by Adenauer to defend the nuclear armaments policy of the CDU against an anti-nuclear petition signed by eighteen prestigious German physicists at a meeting of the German Physical Society near Göttingen.

The 'Göttingen Eighteen', organized by C. F. von Weizsäcker but with strong support from Born and Heisenberg, were protesting the policy formulated by Adenauer's new Minister for Defense, Franz Joseph Strauss, to support massive nuclear armament of NATO forces in Europe and joint nuclear research with France. An unsatisfactory meeting with Strauss in January had preceded this public action. Professing their belief in the need of the Western world to protect freedom against Communism, the 'Eighteen' nevertheless stressed the 'unlimited potential of strategic atomic weapons for exterminating life' and the unreliability of mutual deterrence as a long-term policy for peace and freedom.[80]

No doubt the signers of the petition were motivated in part by their need to condemn or to divorce themselves from the *Machtpolitik* of the Nazi era and for some, like Heisenberg and von Weizsäcker, to confirm their self-representation as passive resisters. That route was hardly open to Jordan, having identified his own defense from 1934 with the necessity of *Machtpolitik* in a world of nuclear physics and in the face of the Soviet threat. But the new situation offered to him too an opportunity for self-justification. He would simply reassert his machine gun principle in the nuclear form it had always contained, converting it from an offensive to a defensive posture and deploying it in the interests of democratic rather than dictatorial government. This may seem a radical conversion, but apparently it did not seem so to Jordan, as he now defended freedom with the same imagination and intensity that he had formerly lavished on authority.

Jordan published his attack on his fellow scientists in *Wir müssen den Frieden retten* of 1957. His latest rejuvenation had already emerged, however, in *Der gescheiterte Aufstand* of 1956, his assessment of present and future prospects in the nuclear age. It is a document fit for present-day 'survivalists' and religious cults of doom and redemption, predicting the tyranny of nuclear gangs over peaceful countries, a mass of paid Soviet agents spreading Marxist propaganda, colonies on Mars and an ultimate overpopulation of the galaxy. More immediately and infamously, to survive the coming nuclear holocaust, Jordan proposed building underground cities over the next fifty years where 'humanity can remain for five years at a time without difficulty and discomfort until the atomic stink dies out'.[81] Full of such paranoid dreams of potency, Jordan condemned the 'Göttingen Eighteen' under the title 'We must save freedom'. In essence, he charged them with extreme naivety: 'the Göttingen manifesto of the 18 atomic researchers is an expression by extremely unpolitical and unworldly people who are certainly less capable of making judgments about fundamental political questions than the average democratic citizen'.[82]

One set of responses to these remarks, by Born and his wife Hedwig Born, will draw out the continuity of the story and its ultimate lesson. The Borns objected not so much to Jordan's political position as to his duplicity, to the fact that he continued to try to ingratiate himself in private while launching a personal attack in public and that this attack came from someone whose own political past reeked of compromise and fantasy. As he had in 1934 Jordan tried again to explain away the 'misunderstanding' of his intentions, protesting his 'deep human respect' for Born, his 'hurried writing in a deeply moved and alarmed state', his lack of knowledge that Weizsäcker had intended to campaign for a CDU seat, and that he had no idea how deeply Born was involved in the issue.[83]

But this time the Borns had exhausted their sympathy. Hedwig took the trouble 'to dig out your books, indeed, the uncleansed first editions', and to send excerpts to the Berlin newspaper *Die Deutsche Volkszeitung* (published under the title, 'Pascual Jordan, Propagandist in the Pay of the CDU').[84] Born himself let Jordan know that they finally understood the full consistency of his long-term commitments:

> You believe that dominance and power are the only valid arguments in the life of man. Even science, even our physics, is to you primarily a means to power ... Correspondingly you now support Adenauer's 'politics of strength' ... No one can reproach you for sticking by your viewpoint and similar opinions (such as, 'that the democratic idea is definitively dead'), so far as you honestly continue to profess it. However, since it seems to come down to power in itself for you, whoever may have it in hand, so you are yet again to be found with the presently ruling powers, church and democracy ... it appears to me that even after all your pronouncements you still would fit better in a totalitarian system on the Soviet model, while you indirectly suggest ... that we (the 'Eighteen') have played into the hands of the Soviets.[85]

Born's interpretation confirms the analysis of this paper. Jordan's picture of the world, from beginning to end, from physics to philosophy to politics, centred on the necessity for leadership through power in the organization of complex systems and on a willingness to manipulate other people and their ideas in the greater interest of justifying power. That in itself, I have tried to show, is the lesson we ought to draw from Jordan's history. We ought not to conclude that the pursuit of holistic interpretation of nature leads to either bad science or bad politics, but merely that the celebration of power for its own sake, and the violations of people that attend such celebration, has the same effects whether pursued in the cause of dictatorship or democracy, whether based on holism or mechanism, realism or relativism.

12 | The ideology of early particle accelerators: an association between knowledge and power

MARIA OSIETZKI

A lay person visiting one of the largest high energy laboratories probably finds the experience just as difficult to understand as the magic rituals of a native tribe. If one wants to gain acceptance by either of the 'communities', then a certain kind of 'initiation' is required.[1] In the case of high energy physics, this ideology would be shared not only by the elementary particle physicists, but also by those who are responsible for granting the tremendous sums necessary for building the accelerators. Thus by looking at the ideology of accelerator development, we can determine in an exemplary fashion the kind of mediation that takes place between highly specialized subdisciplines and the mental, social and economic motives of those social groups who accept and support them.

In order to investigate this subject, a few preliminary conceptual remarks are necessary. It makes sense to investigate ideologies in connection with science only if one abandons the traditional dichotomy between basis and superstructure, the (methodically problematic) concept of right or wrong, as well as the scheme of true or false. The 'critical concept of ideology' has helped overcome the theoretical dead ends whose roots lie in this dichotomy; it looks for meanings that are mobilized to secure and maintain power and dominance;[2] it deals with explicit statements and the consciousness conveyed within, as well as with social mechanisms, which allow certain meanings to achieve a status of 'truth' and this 'truth' to have a special kind of power.[3] This constellation of ideologies, which belongs to a social unconscious, allows us to see the alliance between knowledge and power, which was the general foundation for the expansion of modern science, especially for nuclear physics as the pioneer of accelerator development and for the subsequent high energy physics.

The ideologies that constitute power and dominance are certainly not limited to their linguistic meanings; artifacts also have a semiotic

255

dimension which can be ideological, in so far as they contribute to the establishment and maintenance of social stratification. In this manner the 'powerful' material effect of the ideology of technologies can also be seen in the reshaping of nature and the changing of social relationships. With regard to the development of accelerators in this conceptual context, several questions come to mind. Which meaning did accelerators receive in the field of nuclear and elementary particle physics because of their anticipated function for the production of scientific knowledge? Which symbolic meaning have they obtained because of changes in the social hierarchy of the scientific community? How did they contribute to the transformation of nature and society in the interest of small groups, but with severe effects for the whole society? How were all these functions connected with mechanisms of power, both inside science and within the greater society? Certainly not all of these questions can be treated exhaustively in this essay, instead they simply mark out the horizon of relevant questions and open up perspectives for the aspects addressed here.

The ideology that has accompanied the building of accelerators since its beginning in the thirties may be divided analytically into two main aspects. In the first place, it gave the accelerators legitimacy in the eyes of prospective investors. It is necessary to distinguish the early phase, in which the development of accelerators was justified within nuclear physics by their potential for applications, from the period after 1945, when high energy physics became a showpiece of 'pure science' within the scope of a politically accented research programme. Secondly, the ideology of accelerator development helps illuminate the mechanisms inside science for the distribution of power and social stratification. Both nuclear and high energy physics took up prestigious leadership positions in the hierarchy of disciplines and subdisciplines.

These two directions of effective internal and external scientific ideologies comprise consciously formulated reasoning strategies as well as ideological formations that refer to multiple unconscious structures and culturally sanctioned discourses. In particular, the obvious 'irrationality' of the tremendous expansion of accelerator development requires an interpretation from this 'third level'.[4] The genesis of accelerator construction for nuclear physics, as for high energy physics, was based on a scientific motivation and a social and political acceptance that cannot be reduced to the social, the economic, and certainly not to the purely functional dimension of an instrument.[5]

' ... Make the whole world one smiling Garden of Eden'[6]

Even today, the ideology is still propagated that the accelerator is simply a technical aid for the study of the subatomic structure of material and that the 'reason' for its development lies exclusively in this research problem. 'Thus, as a general rule, ideology has to obscure itself to achieve its prime effect.'[7] Accordingly the meaning of accelerators is narrowed to a scientific problem, and its ideological value for nuclear and elementary particle physics, which is decisive for the symbolic demonstration of power and prestige, is obscured.[8] At the same time, the connection between the symbolic function of accelerators and the ideological content of this sub-discipline is suppressed. This content may best be seen at its origin, when the ideological dependency of scientists' remarks was formed during the establishment of a specific relationship to society and to nature.

In spite of the changes that the creation of a new research direction can call forth in the identity of a discipline, it is still fundamentally based on the original programme. In the case of nuclear physics, it is based on modern science and especially on physics, which can be conceived of as a means methodically to control and conquer nature and as a deliberate trans-formation of human living conditions.[9] The discovery of radioactivity at the turn of the century brought this preset goal into a new phase, char-acterized by an 'intensified' grasp on nature, by the fantasy of an alchemi-cal transmutation of material and the exploitation of inexhaustible energy sources.[10] 'Atomic energy was coming to stand for things more important than atomic energy itself. First of all it was coming to stand for all the powers of science, powers for the better – or perhaps for the worse.'[11]

Given the fertile soil provided by the fantasies bound up in early atomic and nuclear physics, from which specific disciplinary and cultural context did the intensified grasp on nature originate?[12] In the first place, it is neces-sary to examine the transition from classical to modern physics, which was accompanied by the loss of the classical worldview to the discipline and thus provoked a crisis. While the programme of classical physics seemed close to fulfillment by the end of the nineteenth century – for older physi-cists a satisfactory, for younger ones a disturbing perspective – the dis-covery of X-rays and radioactivity opened new fields of research. During the twenties these research topics were embedded in a paradigmatic change of some of the fundamental principles of physics: quantum mechanics brought with it indeterminism and a partial forsaking of the principle of causality.[13] By making the 'truth' – which had been a pillar of the ideology of classical physics – relative, its function of creating a unifying worldview was lost. Since the physical formulae were no longer able to represent nature but only the 'knowledge' of nature, and this representation was no picture of nature, rather nothing more than a 'replica' of the relationship between scientist and nature,[14] the ideology accepted up until this time, that the explanation of the world by classical physics was 'true', had been abandoned. The dialectics inherent in physics between alienation and the delusion of grandeur, on the one hand its abstract mathematical–experimental practice and on the other its demand for truth, were as a consequence of its crisis reinforced in the following epoch of modern physics: the 'visibly alienated' research methods and the relativity of the 'truth' in the results of physics showed that nature could not be reached by knowledge in the traditional sense nor by uncovering or making visible the natural laws. From this point on, nature was submitted to systematic transformation, whereby 'knowledge' has been judged more and more by the effect of its power.[15]

These symptoms of an isolation of phenomena-orientated research practice and its progressive alienation from nature fitted quite well with the belief that science was value neutral, Physicists believed themselves to be responsible for progress, while society was blamed for the resulting crises. This ambivalence can also be seen in the interpretations of the future perspectives for scientific work with radioactivity. Ernest Rutherford, who in 1919 used a radioactive preparation to become the first to split an atom artificially, together with his co-worker, Frederic Soddy, saw the potential for destruction as well as for progress in their findings. Parallel to the awareness of the possibility of an atomic destruction of the earth, there existed hope for the salvation of civilization from its crisis by means of atomic energy.[16] According to Soddy, before the shrinking resources of an almost completely colonized world caused a regression to a primitive existence, mankind would be preserved by the 'transmutation' of elements as well as by the limitless energy gained from the atom.[17]

While the responsibility for the fulfillment of these fantasies was laid in the hands of physics, society had to deal with the inherent risks – a useful division for physics, since nuclear physicists felt responsible for creating a paradise but not for the possible risk of an apocalyptic downfall.[18] This 'liberation' of nuclear physics was completely entangled in the dialectics of alienation and the delusion of grandeur. It facilitated the further exemption of science from social responsibilities, but at the same time supported the delusion of grandeur of the unstoppable dynamics of 'progress'.

In the course of this development physics created radiation sources for the production of radioactive isotopes and thereby transcended a traditional instrumental relationship with nature. It facilitated an irreversibility of vegetable, animal and human hereditary matter by means of artificial radioactivity, thereby overshadowing all previous encroachments on nature. By pushing forward the boundaries of its command over nature to the subatomic regions, physics opened up unimagined possibilities for expansion, even including the kingdom of the living.[19] In this regard it should be mentioned that 'nucleus' and 'fission' were taken from the terms for cell nucleus and cell division. The possibilities for a calculated change in nature had thus taken on a new quality during the first decades of this century, a quality which displaced the preset goals of physics into the domain of the infinite – a perspective which, given the previous assumption that the edifice of classical physics was almost finished, obviously was compatible with 'saving' the discipline.

The interpretation of the year 1932 as the 'annus mirabilis' of nuclear physics must be seen in this context.[20] In this year not only had an artificial nucleus transformation been achieved with a high energy generator, but it had also been discovered that, due to its lack of charge, a projectile neutron could penetrate the atomic nucleus uninhibited. Both discoveries together promised to make possible the production of a given effect in the atomic nucleus by means of a neutron radiation technically variable in its intensity.

This specific function of accelerators certainly does not cover their entire meaning for nuclear physics. Just as the origins of accelerators cannot be reduced to scientific impulses, but must rather be interpreted as a product created in a certain phase of western culture, so the meaning of the technical equipment of a discipline cannot be limited to a scientific or technical spectrum of performance. On the contrary, accelerators have a share in the power effect of nuclear physics, since they have opened a power reservoir which manifests itself in the phantasm of inexhaustible energies slumbering in the atomic nucleus, as well as in the fascination caused by the 'transmutation' of material.

' ... interested in all kinds of extremes'[21]

The ideology of nuclear physics was not only the result of its ability to change nature and society. It was also concerned with mechanisms inside science, which were enriched by the trend towards an increasingly technical research practice using accelerators and other nuclear physics apparatus, resulting in new criteria for scientific competitiveness. Beginning in the 1930s, the relevance of the accelerators for the 'production' of scientific results challenged traditional criteria for scientific efficiency. The productivity of a research institute in the domain of nuclear physics was no longer dependent solely on the qualifications of its staff, but instead on its technical equipment.

The first years of particle acceleration opened up an instructive view into this change: first a competition was undertaken to construct a suitable high energy generator for the first artificial nucleus transformation. From now on scientific priority could be 'made'. If the technical preconditions for extreme, novel experimental conditions were available, then it was possible to make new fields of research accessible, to produce new results and to guarantee oneself the resulting merits.[22] Characteristic in this regard was the research strategy of Merle Tuve, one of the first to use a high energy construction as a source of radiation: he had always been interested in all kinds of extremes, high pressures and high temperatures, low pressures and low temperatures, as he said during an explanation of his experimental work during the early years of nuclear physics.[23] By investigating the subatomic domain at increasing levels of energy, thereby technically pushing back even further the limits of what was possible, there was a chance to be innovative and to produce top performances.

The ideology of this superlative lies in its meaning for the modification of criteria for scientific productivity, and so has consequences for the international structures of scientific competitiveness. This can be seen exemplarily in the development of the Radiation Laboratory at Berkeley, which was run by Ernest Orlando Lawrence, the inventor of a suitable neutron source, the cyclotron.[24] During this period he was obsessed with outperforming the Cavendish Laboratory in England in the field of artificial nucleus transformation. 'The system was something like this ... ', as one of the students described Lawrence's management of the institute, 'while we were doing research with the 27-inch and the 39-inch was being designed, he was dreaming up the 60. While we were using the 39-inch and the 60-inch cyclotron was being designed, the 184 was being dreamed of by Ernest Lawrence.'[25] This 'Berkeleyitis' was urged on by Lawrence's talent for management, demonstrated by his success in acquiring support for his research as well as leading an interdisciplinary team. He dedicated a great deal of the work at the Radiation Laboratory to the systematic search for unknown isotopes with the characteristics that would fulfill the needs of biological and medical research, and the foundations that were interested in these isotopes made the financing of larger and larger cyclotrons possible. The result was a dynamic of accelerator development emanating from the Radiation Laboratory, thus installing a new ideology of scientific research with the criteria 'bigger is better'. Lawrence thereby presented a fundamental challenge to the theoretically accented European leading role in physics, which had been founded on the quantum mechanics that had been developed there.

This change had an especially great effect on the physics community in Germany, which during the twenties had had high international ranking because of its contributions to theoretical quantum physics, but which only a decade later had to give up this position on the 'research front' – nuclear physics – to the USA. Although in the past American physicists had made pilgrimages to the leading quantum theorists in Europe, during the thirties the train of those eager to learn moved in the opposite direction. From this point on German physicists sought out the newest developments of nuclear physics in American laboratories. In particular, the revaluation of technical apparatus in scientific research, caused by the development of the accelerator, represented a fundamental challenge to the German understanding of science: the centre of attraction was no longer a famous physicist; his importance was reduced, and the increasing technical demands of nuclear physics now required extraordinary technical equipment for an institute. In the following decades and all over the world, unique accelerators developed into popular research centres for visitors.

Together with experimental nuclear physics and the modernization of scientific research by means of expensive equipment, team work and unconventional methods for collecting research funds, structural changes in physics were created which were contrary to the financial capacity as well as the mentality of the Gèrman community. Their idealistic concepts of physics concentrated on the personality of a scholar, in contrast to the costly equipment and interdisciplinary teamwork that was necessary for the development and usage of accelerators. The model for German scientific communities was much more the 'study room' and laboratory, in which first-rate research results were to be achieved using the 'simplest physics'. It was characteristic of the German research style that, in the beginnings of the race for the construction for efficient radiation sources in 1927, the Germans who engaged in this and cooperated with industry were engineers like Rolf Wideröe or young, unknown physicists like Fritz Lange.[26] For this group, just like the American community of physicists, accelerator technology was a vehicle for turning a second-rate scientific reputation into recognition as a world-class physicist.

During the mid-thirties at the latest, and under the influence of the international rivalry, German scientists' views of themselves became dysfunctional. Considering the mobilization of technology for physics in the USA, the hypostatization of the intellectual worker and of the individual personality of the researcher appeared to reverse the goal of placing themselves at the top of the social hierarchy. When after the second world war physicists analyzed their backwardness in comparison with the USA, they pointed out their inferior technological equipment, but at the same time justified their less technically-oriented research with the remark that 'German science grew up in the mentality of the poor man'.[27] In fact, early nuclear physics in Germany had suffered under low budgets, due to the world depression and the assumption of power by the National Socialists. But one must consider that renowned physicists like Peter Debye did not push for a special promotion of radiation research through cooperative efforts until two years after the 'annus mirabilis' of nuclear physics – a focal point which these physicists, because of their 'Gleichschaltung' (coordination) by the National Socialists, were unable to institutionalize.[28]

'Create ... something new for Germany'[29]

A noteworthy entry in accelerator construction began in Germany during the mid-thirties, when astonished reports of physicists and industrialists who had visited American accelerator centres became more frequent. To avoid falling too far behind, even the physicists – seeing the superiority of the American developments and especially of Lawrence and his team in the Radiation Laboratory – took up the initiative to try and secure the financing of accelerators.

In contrast to using a scientific legitimation for funding from the

Notgemeinschaft (literally translated as 'Emergency Society') for the costly development of radiation sources, arguments for building accelerators now had to be tailored to National Socialist ideologies. The sponsors of the programme were Bernhard Rust, *Reichsminister für Wissenschaft, Erziehung und Volksbildung* (Minister of Education), who had founded the *Reichsforschungsrat* (Reich Research Council) in 1937, which was to support the goals of the Four Year Plan; the *Heereswaffenamt* (Army Ordnance); the *Reichsministerium für Rüstungs- und Kriegsproduktion* (Ministry for Armaments); the *Reichsluftfahrtminister* (Minister of Aviation); and the *Reichspostministerium* (Postal Ministry). This list of 'willing' sponsors illustrates the economic and military motives of their support, complemented by private industry's interest in medical technology. Physicians were very interested in radiation sources that would enable better dosages and more accuracy and deeper penetration into the tissue, all of which were supposed to avoid visible damages to the skin surface.

The manner in which accelerators became ideologically significant under the National Socialist influence can be understood by examining the opinions of scientists during the early years of cyclotron development in Germany, when financing seemed possible through the founding of the *Reichsforschungsrat*. Wolfgang Gentner, the assistant of Walter Bothe, director of the Physics Department of the Kaiser Wilhelm Institute for Medical Research, wrote in a 1937 article that the 'tremendous expenditure for such an apparatus ... ' is justified 'by the grand success that this method has achieved for nuclear physics', but did not forget to point out the biological and medical uses of neutron radiation.[30]

The first to accomplish the financing of a cyclotron in 1937 through the support of the *Reichsforschungsrat*, the Saxon Ministry of Culture and the chairman of the *Helmholtz Gesellschaft* (an industrial foundation for the support of physical research), the powerful Ruhr-industrialist Albert Vögler, was Gerhard Hoffmann, Debye's successor in Leipzig. Hoffmann went to the firm Siemens & Halske AG with the suggestion of a joint cyclotron development in order to, as he put it, 'create something new for Germany'.[31] His suggestion seemed especially appealing to the engineer Desiderius Flir and the physicist Gustav Hertz, both employees at Siemens.

Flir, who had kept Heinrich von Boul, the chairman of the board, informed about the new developments in atom-smashing, artificial radiation and radiation therapy, mobilized arguments for a cooperation with Hoffmann from the discourse of national and private economical rivalry. He emphasized the Swiss Company Oerlikon, which had built a cyclotron for the physicist Joliot-Curie in Paris, and said that: 'The research institutes in Germany will not be able to delay work with cyclotrons any longer, and I believe that it would be a good idea if we, and not the AEG, would be the first to market this type of apparatus ... '[32] The Nobel laureate Gustav Hertz, who left his professorship at the Technical University of Berlin in

1935 and began working in Siemens' Research Laboratory II, which had been founded especially for physical research, was in favour of building a cyclotron as industrial research. With such a research and development programme, he would be able to secure a position of outstanding importance in nuclear technology for his research laboratory. During the preliminary discussions, he was able to legitimate this project as medical technology. 'Since the use of new radiation has become somewhat stylish', he argued, 'Siemens cannot afford to fall behind'.[33]

Despite the arguments for the practical use of the cyclotron, its meaning was not limited to its anticipated utility. The discourse on utility was always carefully tended, but it never covered the actual motives for the development. On the contrary, through its popularity at the Radiation Laboratory the cyclotron had attained such status by 1937 that it apparently no longer needed practical legitimation. Having a cyclotron was a desirable goal for a research institute because of its symbolic meaning, which allowed the institute to be distinguished from others and, *a priori*, to take a leading position in the domain of nuclear physics.

Therefore this ideology of powerful accelerators and its role in the race for power and prestige were already in place when the specific conditions in Germany molded it into the peculiarly German frame or scientific, capitalistic and national or National Socialist integration. In short, those who were involved in shaping scientific and public opinion wanted to build a cyclotron, and this desire was shaped by the existing symbolic ideological meaning of accelerators, which included arguments of national, economic and scientific competitiveness.

'Once our machine works, it will always work'[34]

The discourse on the medical applications of the cyclotron represented a mediation between scientific and industrial ambitions. During the times of financial hardship, this mediation made possible the unalterable alliance between scientific and industrial actors under the conditions of National Socialism for the realization of a cyclotron. When it came to the explicit execution of this realization, the different interests became divided over which construction type should be chosen. The conflict was touched off by the question of whether one should use a design made by Siemens itself, or a cyclotron model based on the American example.

The disputes became grave when Walter Bothe succeeded in securing the financing of a cyclotron and also turned to Siemens with his construction plans. His goal was to become engaged in the on-going developmental work in order to obtain a functioning cyclotron as soon as possible. He had sent his assistant Gentner to Lawrence's Radiation Laboratory, from which he returned with blueprints of the cyclotron there. They were supposed to be used as a pattern for the development at Siemens, or at least Bothe hoped so. He believed that his contacts with the Radiation Laboratory would be to his advantage in his competition in cyclotron construction with Hoffmann.

In general Bothe claimed that the first cyclotron built in Germany should be his. As the director of a Kaiser Wilhelm Institute he brought its high reputation into play, indeed when dealing with sponsors as well as with industry. He emphasized several times that his 'institute [was] the best place' for a cyclotron 'since he has the absolutely necessary good scientific and technical assistants and because any hindrance [of the work] through teaching responsibilities' (as with Hoffmann), which Bothe 'considered dangerous for the difficult and costly operation of the cyclotron' would be avoided.[35]

For Siemens this was no convincing reason to favour Bothe. On the contrary, since Bothe, unlike Hoffmann, with a certain arrogance had not agreed to a consulting contract with Siemens for research in the physics of medicine and insisted that the firm build him a model according to the American pattern, Siemens favoured a cooperation with Hoffmann. For him, Siemens devised a model that should already be fit for the market. Against Hoffmann's objection not to strive for a 'luxury model', but rather for an appropriate, versatile machine that could be taken apart and reconfigured, Siemens stuck to the goal it had had from the very beginning, to construct the perfect machine.[36] In this way the Siemens management believed that they could gain a monopoly over cyclotrons equally useful for medical and nuclear physics research. The self-confident goal was: 'Once our machine works, it will always work'.[37]

Completely new considerations entered the debate over the type and construction of the cyclotron after the discovery of nuclear fission, when the cyclotron took on military meaning with research into the neutrons released by a chain reaction.[38] For this purpose Kurt Diebner, since 1934 military advisor at the *Heereswaffenamt* for nuclear physics, favoured the construction of a 'giant cyclotron'. However, Siemens was able to persuade him that first of all experience should be gathered with the model intended for Hoffmann, which would then be used to build the larger machine. Even though Bothe demanded that his order be taken care of first, emphasizing that 'we have been given important war research', Siemens held to its strategy of using funds already granted by the state to develop a Siemens model which could be sold in large numbers.

But the cyclotron monopoly that Siemens hoped to gain in Germany appeared to be endangered by the plans for other projects. Vögler confirmed that there were parallel initiatives when he wrote to von Boul: 'I do not know whether you are aware that the Postal Minister Ohnesorge wants to construct a cyclotron. The *Führer* is supposedly interested in this plan. Thus the confusion is getting worse and worse.'[39] Siemens feared that a cyclotron would soon go into operation in Berlin and represent unwanted competition for the firm. For this reason the company administration decided to install in Berlin the machine that was meant for Leipzig.[40] An internal memorandum at Siemens argued that in order to improve future cyclotron models it would be to the firm's advantage 'that all of the physicists, chemists and physicians in Berlin should have some opportunity [to use the cyclotron] for their most important research at least once'.[41] When the Armaments Minister Albert Speer required Vögler to provide a survey of all the plans for cyclotrons in Germany as part of Speer's decision concerning the support to be given to nuclear physics, von Boul also saw a parallel chance to exclude the competing projects. Vögler and von Boul therefore decided to turn down Ohnesorge's request for new cyclotron projects as unnecessary, emphasizing the difficulties created by the war and portraying the delivery date for the magnets requested by the Postal Minister as unrealistic.[42] At the same time, Vögler was to inform Speer that the apparatus planned for Hoffmann would be set up in Berlin.[43] By placing a cyclotron in the metropolis, Berlin, Siemens hoped to attain a special status for its project and simultaneously to oppose the threat to the meaning of their own cyclotron development posed by rival projects. In Germany, competence for the construction of a cyclotron was to be associated with the name Siemens. The means used by Siemens to achieve this goal on the one hand were a strategic enhancement of their own project and on the other the exclusion and suppression rival projects. This was the only way Siemens felt it could ascribe its name to the meaning attributed to cyclotrons in Germany.

' ... a question of reputation for Germany ... '[44]

Siemens was able to assert the primacy of economic concerns over military needs in the construction of a cyclotron only because it did not appear to be crucial for the outcome of the war. Despite the fact that cyclotrons had been declared 'important for the war' (kriegswichtig) as part of the research project investigating the military applications of nuclear energy, a fundamental decision was made that nuclear energy research should be supported, but not forced.[45] In any case, in 1942 Speer decided that the further development of cyclotrons should be continued in the interest of international competitiveness. The construction of this apparatus had become a matter of prestige for Germany.[46] For this reason state support was given not only to Siemens' construction in Berlin, but also to Bothe's cyclotron project in Heidelberg, which had developed further once the magnets had been delivered. Both machines were about to go into operation shortly before the end of the war. This development was kept within the rational and ideological boundaries of national, economic and scientific rivalry. These had priority over any militaristic or National Socialist ideology of accelerator development, which had of course also existed.

Aggressive military or National Socialist terminology was usually used to enhance the meaning of a project or research organization. For example, when Carl Ramsauer, chairman of the German Physical Society and director of the AEG research laboratories, advocated stronger support for physics in Germany by emphasizing the exemplary Anglo–American lead in accelerator development, he portrayed physics as a 'weapon of the greatest, and sometimes decisive meaning for the economic and military competition between nations'.[47] Of course this kind of argument transcends the boundaries between economic, national and National Socialist motives.

The development of an efficient electron accelerator, named the betatron by Rolf Wideröe, is an example of how a project could be incorporated into the National Socialist-militaristic discourse. His work was supported by the German air force, which hoped to obtain radiation weapons useful against enemy airplanes. This episode, which belongs in the context of the myth of a 'wonder weapon', illustrates the integration of an accelerator project in a typical raster of National Socialist ideology.[48] Other usages illustrate another Fascist dimension of accelerator development, like the National Socialist dimension used to describe the effects of radiation in medicine. Especially significant in this regard are the definitions from Konrad Gund, who shortly before the end of the war was working at Siemens to develop a betatron for medical purposes. In 1952, when he published a survey of the origins of this apparatus, intended primarily for cancer therapy, he lapsed back into National Socialist terminology. He described this apparatus as a new weapon (*Kampfmittel*) for doctors, biologists and chemists against cancer, which was interpreted as a growth of 'degenerate' cells. Gund then compared the human organism with a cultural and economic community. Within such a nation, he argued, the danger exits that groups will come together that do not fit into the whole, rather such groups will lead an egoistical individual existence. According to Gund, such groups, like cancer, must be eradicated.[49]

In spite of the repeated use of Fascist terminology in accelerator development during the Third Reich, it remained primarily under the control of scientific and economic interest groups. Accelerators were vehicles for scientific and economic competitiveness and thus had become sources of power and prestige. Their symbolic meaning lay in the function of allowing individuals, institutes and industrial firms to distinguish themselves with the help of cyclotrons from their competitors. This was the primary motive for investing in their development. The ideological meaning of accelerators was derived from competition. It symbolized scientific superiority and control of the economic market. However, it must be emphasized that fascist-militaristic ideology could also be expressed by means of accelerators, since diverse motives could be ascribed to these machines, ranging from an instrument for killing degenerate cells to a wonder weapon. Thus fascist, economic and scientific interests met in a particular type of apparatus and led in spite of all their differences to a fundamental consensus on the necessity of its development.

'Basic research must come before all else'[50]

During the last years of the war the physicist Walter Gerlach, at that time Reich Plenipotentiary for nuclear physics in the *Reichsforschungsrat*, ordered the construction of several betatrons from Siemens as part of his efforts to use an improvement in equipment to strengthen basic physical research for the post-war era. The argument that support for basic research should be enhanced had been the subject of several appeals which began in 1942–3 and continued after World War II.[51] Physicists used the economic utility of their work as a justification, since given the desolate economic situation in Germany, this argument was the only way they could legitimate the increase in their budget. Indeed they tried to leave no room for doubt that Germany's economic competitiveness could only be founded on generously promoted basic research in physics. In this context 'pure' physics was often represented as the 'fertile soil' (*Nährboden*) for all technology used by the civilized world.

In order to enhance basic research, the ideology of 'pure' research was reinvigorated after 1945. After having been extremely oriented towards applications during the war, the researchers now tried to ensure the primacy of 'pure' basic research within the scientific community in order to liberate themselves from close ties to politics and the economy and the pressure for political and economical legitimacy that these ties entailed. This unreasonable demand had important consequences for the construction of accelerators, not only in Germany, but world-wide.

The extreme expansion in the development of accelerators after 1945 may thus be interpreted in this sense as an 'act of liberation' undertaken by the nuclear physicists. Their efforts in the USA to transfer the means of Mars to those of Minerva served the purpose of purifying the discipline of the stigma of an 'ambivalent' nuclear physics; the promotion of a 'pure' high energy physics would once again allow the public to associate physics exclusively with the struggle for truth.[52] In the USA, the ideology of the (extremely expensive) accelerator development immediately after World War II served the efforts to assert a positive 'meaning' for physics, which had been fundamentally shaken by the atomic bombs dropped on Hiroshima and Nagasaki. The promotion of enormous accelerator laboratories thus complemented the solution of the crisis of a physics that was no longer associated exclusively with progress. The huge post-war accelerators, symbols of a research completely free from applications and dedicated only to the search for the 'first principles' of matter, thus served the purpose of maintaining the traditional scientific ideology of the value-neutral quality of physics.

Given the great sums that had been given out for applications-oriented nuclear physics, the physics community found it desirable to direct the lion's share of these sums into plain basic research and thereby support the value-neutral ideology of science.[53] By means of such initiatives the American nuclear physicists were able to attach themselves to the American claim of superpower status and argue that their hegemony within nuclear physics depended on the generous support of their fundamental research questions. Thus the scientific ideologies fitted their political counterparts. Lawrence argued thus:

> one outstanding problem in physics has to do with the stability of nuclei and the forces which make them stable. The atomic bomb derives its energy from the splitting of the atomic nucleus, yet we do not understand the forces which hold the protons and neutrons in the nucleus together ... It is clear that any nucleonics program which did not attack this fundamental problem would have practically no foundation at all.[54]

With these words, some themes were transferred from nuclear physics – which at the end of the forties still included the entire complex of questions into the fundamental structure of matter and its conformity to natural laws, including the interpretation of nuclear forces as well as mesons and field theory – to elementary particle physics. This domain had previously been examined with the help of cosmic radiation research; however, physicists now strived for the artificial production of high particle energies in favour of controllable experimental conditions. Of course this functional aspect cannot sufficiently explain the construction of the 6 BeV bevatron at the Radiation Laboratory or the 3 BeV cosmotron at the Brookhaven National Laboratory. These giant accelerators, with which American physicists placed themselves in the forefront of elementary particle research and defended this position for more than two decades,[55] had only been made possible because of an alliance between superpower ideology and an ideology of physicists that asserted its superiority by way of the meaning of their 'pure' research.

With regard to scientific-technical competitiveness for the individual European states and Europe as a whole – England had a special status because of its own nuclear and accelerator programme – the large national research centres in the USA represented both a threat, because of the expected migration of physicists, as well as a model to be followed.[56] Pointing to the Brookhaven National Laboratory, a novel example of a cooperative research organization supported by nine American Universities, European physicists urged before the security council of the United Nations the creation of equivalent research centres, in which several European countries could work together on projects which would have overwhelmed a single country.[57] Their initiative eventually led to the establishment of the Centre Européen Recherche Nucléaire, the accelerator laboratory CERN in Geneva.

The emphasis placed on basic research for the examination of the smallest material particles in the USA and Europe correspondingly enhanced the initiative of the West German physicists. Their spokesman was Werner Heisenberg, director of the Max Planck Institute for Physics (at that time in Göttingen), who played a key role not only in the West German efforts in nuclear physics, but also in early accelerator development.[58] In order to satisfy the preconditions for success in these areas, he urged the modernization of research organization in West Germany, so that the institutional changes that had accompanied the Anglo-American development of nuclear and high energy physics would be introduced in West Germany.

However, the expansion of the research laboratories and the increases in financial support led to an increased dependence on governmental agencies, which ran counter to the general tendency towards the strengthening of research free from politics and applications. In an effort to deal with these two lines of development, both of which lay in the interest of physics, in 1949 Heisenberg created the *Deutscher Forschungsrat* (German Research Council), an elite scientific advisory committee consisting mainly of scientists, to safeguard the interests of science within the alliance between research and politics. His guiding principle during initiative in scientific organization and science policy was: 'And basic research must come before all else'.[59]

Of course the ideological emphasis on basic research was different in West Germany than in the USA. Common to the communities of physicists in both Germany and the United States were initiatives to maintain a social stratification, which was spearheaded by 'pure physics'. However, in Germany this ideology was tailored to the specific situation of a country that had been defeated and was fighting for scientific competitiveness. The arguments used to justify West German participation in the cooperative European efforts to establish a common laboratory for high energy research and the construction of a large accelerator emphasized the value of the political integration of West Germany into Europe. Indeed physicists at times spoke of physics as being the 'only form of foreign politics'.[60] The nuclear physicists also justified West German participation on the grounds that in this way they could gain access to research of the highest international standards. This argument was especially emphasized with respect to the meaning that a European laboratory would have for the training of West German physicists, both practically and psychologically. On the one hand these trained physicists were needed for the subsequent economic exploitation of atomic energy; on the other hand, it would be advantageous if young scientists had the feeling they were capable of doing 'good' physics in their own country.[61]

The physicists understood how to portray the power potential of their discipline during their effort to strengthen basic research. They simultaneously built political and economic rationales into their arguments, but also thereby defended the ideology that the value of research can only be fully realized when, spearheaded by basic research, it can develop freely. The success of this ideology within the rebuilding of scientific organizations in West Germany can hardly be explained merely by the primacy of science over politics. Instead one must assume, much rather proceed, on the assumption that state support of science was a result of efforts to enhance national scientific prestige. The enhancement of national power in turn was secured by science and its function for the production of knowledge. This symbiosis, which served to secure the reciprocal power of both the nation and science, was extremely ideological.

In sum, the meaning of accelerators since the thirties has lain in what they symbolized, especially when the international uniqueness or rarity of certain types attracted the attention of the scientific community. The prestige of scientific institutes increased because of these machines; R&D departments in industrial companies could demonstrate their ability by successfully constructing an accelerator or by producing the technically demanding accessories they required; the resulting enhanced scientific and industrial meaning increased the power of the state. However, the symbolic function of accelerators did not have a material effect until scientists began to use them in such processes as radiation sources for atom-smashing, the production of radioactive isotopes, the destruction of cells and gene manipulation. The ideological kernel of accelerators lay in the marriage of their symbolic character and their actual utility, whereby the effectiveness was manifested by intervening in nature.

13 | The 'Minerva' project. The accelerator laboratory at the Kaiser Wilhelm Institute/Max Planck Institute of Chemistry: continuity in fundamental research

BURGHARD WEISS

Introduction

From an equipment point of view, particle accelerators are generally regarded, along with nuclear reactors, as symbols of large-scale, state-subsidized or privately-financed scientific research involving large investments. A history of the development of accelerators in Germany has yet to be written. Of the publications devoted entirely to this subject,[1] or, as in the case of the numerous studies on the German uranium project, dealing with it marginally,[2] up to now all have concentrated on the development of the cyclotron.

This concentration on the cyclotron has distorted the historical picture by hiding the fact that from the middle of the 1930s onwards there already was a developed accelerator technology based on the principle of direct (linear) acceleration – a principle which today is still being applied successfully in low- and middle-energy nuclear physics. At this time in Germany there were numerous efforts to use this technology for research purposes, particularly in the production of artificially radioactive elements. Above all this work was done at the institutes of the *Kaiser Wilhelm Gesellschaft* (Kaiser Wilhelm Society; KWG), where accelerators of this type were either being constructed or were already in operation, namely at the Kaiser Wilhelm Institutes (KWI) of Brain Research, Chemistry, and Physics (all in Berlin); Biophysics (in Frankfurt); Medical Research, Physics Section (in Heidelberg) as well as at the Research Centre D (in Bisingen, Hohenzollern).[3]

Three possible reasons can be given for the fact that the history of the accelerator projects at the KWG has almost completely escaped the attention of historians: (1) all the accelerators, with the exception of the cyclotron, which was erected under the direction of Bothe at the KWI of Medical

271

Research (Physics Section) at Heidelberg, followed the principle of direct (linear) acceleration and were therefore based on a technology which, according to the view of some historians, was already 'outdated' around 1940; (2) up to the end of the war the accelerator projects of the KWG had not led to the sort of spectacular results which might find a place in the official history of science; they were unable to demonstrate their relevance from an equipment point of view before the end of the war and afterwards, with the exception of the case dealt with here, became victims of dismantling; and (3) the accelerator projects of the KWG (with the exception of the aforementioned cyclotron at Heidelberg) were not mentioned in the FIAT Review.[4] This source, regarded by historians as authoritative with respect to German research activity up to 1945, can be seen as a reason why up to now no comprehensive historical account of projects like 'Minerva' has been given.[5]

By concentrating on the history of the accelerator laboratory at the KWI/MPI of Chemistry, the present chapter attempts to extend by means of example the perspective ordinarily restricted to the cyclotron. Studying the 'Minerva' project enables us to support the thesis that Germany was backward in putting large-scale equipment into operation, even in the case of older technology (the linear accelerator), and at the same time to give the specific reasons for this backwardness. Over and above this, it allows us to raise the question of whether precisely this backwardness can be seen as a factor which allowed the continuity of research institutions through and beyond Germany's collapse.

Modest beginnings

The important successes achieved in the early 1930s in England and the USA with the help of accelerators did not go unnoticed at the KWI of Chemistry,[6] but neither did they lead to any spontaneous activity there. On the contrary, the entry into the new technology took place somewhat tentatively. The acquisition of a high-voltage apparatus was intended which, in combination with an evacuated acceleration tube, would allow the acceleration of protons and the production of neutrons. Room to set up the industrially-produced and modestly-dimensioned equipment was to be found in one of the normal laboratories on the ground floor of the Institute, thereby not necessitating structural alterations to the building. The suggestion from his assistants, that it might be better right from the beginning to erect a cyclotron, had been met by outright rejection from the director, Otto Hahn, who argued that the Institute lacked both the technical competence and the financial resources for this.[7] Lise Meitner, who as head of the Physical Department was responsible for such matters of equipment, also adopted a sceptical stance towards the innovative apparatus. In addition, she had scruples about asking the main financier of the Institute, the

Emil Fischer Society for the Furthering of Chemical Research, for a considerable amount of financial support for a research project, with no apparent benefit for the chemical industry.

Only in November 1934 did Hahn undertake the first attempt at obtaining the necessary funds from the Emil Fischer Society. To the treasurer,
Arthur von Weinberg, he directed the request that the Society provide the
first installment of 5,000 RM 'for the tackling of a special task', i.e. the
'building of equipment for smashing atoms with protons', the total cost of
which he estimated to be 10,000–12,000 RM. Such equipment represented,
as he pointed out, 'an urgent necessity on the basis of the present state of
atomic physics'.[8] Nevertheless the project did not move forward, because
the Emil Fischer Society, in spite of the treasurer's approval of the expenditure, did not find itself in the position to provide the money. It was finally
Carl Bosch who at the beginning of 1935 donated 20,000 RM out of his
own pocket.[9]

Subsequently, a high-voltage apparatus originally manufactured for
X-ray purposes by the company Koch and Sterzel (Dresden) and capable of
providing 220,000 volts was acquired. When connected to a canal ray tube
built in the workshop of the Institute it produced about 2×10^6 neutrons/
second, using deuterons as projectiles and heavy ice as target. The first
experimental work using this equipment was carried out by Hermann
Reddemann, who in May 1935 had joined the institute as Lise Meitner's
assistant.[10]

The motives for expansion

In July 1938 Lise Meitner had to leave Germany and her post of
head of the Physical Department became vacant. At precisely the same time
as Lise Meitner was awaiting her departure in a Berlin hotel room Hahn
undertook the first steps towards obtaining the financial means necessary
for erecting a larger high-voltage facility.[11] With just as little hesitation
Hahn also set about looking for Meitner's successor.[12] In October he wrote
to Josef Mattauch in Vienna, who accepted with enthusiasm Hahn's offer
of starting work in Berlin on 1 February 1939.[13]

Mattauch was one of the leading experts in the field of mass spectrome-
try.[14] Through his discovery with Richard Herzog of double focussing, he
had been able to increase considerably the sensitivity of the mass spectrograph. This instrument was of enormous importance for the further development of nuclear physics, since it enabled the spatial separation of isotopes not separable by chemical means. In November 1938 Mattauch
applied to the *Deutsche Forschungsgemeinschaft* (German Research Foundation; DFG) for funds of the order of 6,000 RM to construct a second
mass spectrograph.[15]

In the form of Mattauch's mass spectrographs, large-scale physical apparatus made their way into the KWI of Chemistry, with the result that older plans for structural extensions again became acute, and increasingly so. Hahn had wanted for a long time to extend the main building by means of 'the addition of a large or small wing'. There the 220 kV high-voltage equipment, already used by Lise Meitner and her assistants, was to be set up more satisfactorily than before in a larger room with a higher ceiling. Parts of Mattauch's department were also to be accommodated.[16] Back in October 1938 Hahn had approached the main financial contributor of his Institute, the Emil Fischer Society in Frankfurt, with the request for a further increase in the yearly contribution. Hahn was aware that the KWG would have to be prepared to make larger financial commitments if his plans were to be realised.[17] However, with this request he ran up against a brick wall with the managing director of the KWG, Ernst Telschow, who in the light of increasingly limited funding from the state pointed to the financial responsibility of those circles of industry that were interested in the work of the Institute.[18]

The laborious disentanglement of the products of nuclear fission, following its discovery in December 1938, made acutely clear to Hahn the necessity of having strong radiation sources,[19] particularly since Lise Meitner in exile reported by letter on the experimental possibilities of the cyclotrons in Copenhagen and Stockholm. The modest equipment she had left in Berlin was completely inadequate for this task.[20] Without its own high performance neutron source the KWI of Chemistry was therefore dependent on being allowed to use accelerators at other institutes in order to irradiate its preparations.[21] Considering the sometimes extremely short lifetime of the radioactive isotopes which were thereby produced, this was clearly a difficult and unsatisfactory state of affairs which demanded change.

Alongside this objective motive for acquiring the large-scale apparatus, i.e. its usage as determined by the needs of research, there was also a political-psychological one: a high-voltage apparatus of the type which had existed since 1938 in the neighbouring KWI of Physics headed by Peter Debye was an object of prestige emphasizing the importance of the Institute and ensuring its continued existence in difficult times. This link could not possibly remain hidden to Hahn: in the summer of 1939 discord was created between the two neighbouring KWIs when without his knowledge the *Deutsche Allgemeine Zeitung* illustrated an article by Siegfied Flügge, one of Mattauch's co-workers, on the use of atomic energy, with a picture of Peter Debye's high-voltage apparatus.[22] Flügge thereby 'found himself placed in a very embarrassing position vis-à-vis the men from the KWI of Physics' and demanded a written correction from the editorial department of the newspaper. Vis-à-vis Debye he expressed the hope that 'this wretched matter will thereby be eliminated without trace' and at the same time emphasized that nothing had been further from his aims 'than to swindle myself into higher circles using the equipment of your institute'.[23]

Because of its large-scale appearance, unusually spectacular for the time, as well as its being accommodated in its own tower construction (popularly called the 'tower of lightning') the high-voltage apparatus of the KWI of Physics had become a favourite photographic object of the press and was therefore regarded by the public as a sign of a new prestigious dimension of scientific research.[24]

The search for funds

Being an institute of the so-called 'A-Type' the KWI of Chemistry was almost entirely financed by private means. Before the war almost one hundred per cent of its resources came from the Emil Fischer Society for the Furthering of Chemical Research, based in Frankfurt. The society's resources in turn consisted mainly of donations from the chemical industry, the lion's share naturally coming from IG-Farben.[25]

In spring 1938 Hahn decided to undertake a new attempt at obtaining the extra financial support from the Emil Fischer Society. The latter had over the years steadily increased its contributions to the Institute, but did not, however, see itself in the position of being able to supplement its basic financial support with large investments such as the building of extensions.

Hahn therefore had to look around for new financial sources. In this respect first of all the *Heereswaffenamt* (Army Ordnance; HWA) came into question, which Hahn contacted immediately after the outbreak of war in the autumn of 1939.[26] This happened in agreement with Carl Friedrich von Weizsäcker, who recommended to Hahn, against his initial doubts, that he should allow his institute to be incorporated in the uranium club in order to emphasize the importance of the work on the chemistry of the products of fission for the war aims, and thereby to guarantee the future existence of Hahn's institute.[27] The sums of money which the Institute received from the HWA for the individual research projects remained, however, relatively modest and were certainly not sufficient to help finance the large laboratory planned.[28] The reserve on the part of the military could have been motivated equally by strategic and economic considerations: according to the wish of the HWA the uranium project was to be concentrated at the KWI of Physics, only a few hundred metres away from Hahn's institute, which had been specifically confiscated for this purpose in autumn 1939. As has already been mentioned the physics institute had a large high-voltage apparatus which had been planned by Peter Debye and delivered by the Siemens Company in 1938. In spring 1940 the KWI of Physics was commissioned by the HWA to convert Debye's equipment into a high performance neutron generator. This happened with the explicit instruction that the equipment should also be put at the disposal of Hahn and his assistants 'for experiments on the decay of uranium'.[29]

Since funds were obtainable neither from the chemical industry nor from the military for the realization of his plans, Hahn, along with two other institutes of the KWG, turned in 1940 to the *Deutsche Industriebank* (German Industrial Bank; DIB). In February 1941 the latter finally donated the considerable sum of 200,000 RM for 'the structural extension of the Kaiser Wilhelm Institute of Chemistry and the building·of high-voltage equipment for the continuation of experiments and work for the splitting or uranium'.[30] The total costs had been estimated by Hahn to be about 350,000 RM [31]

In spite of Hahn's eventual success in winning financial support, which was of course welcomed by the KWG, Telschow remained pessimistic about Hahn's and Mattauch's plans; their realization during wartime would be scarcely possible 'unless on the part of the army an urgent interest is expressed therein'.[32] This, however, was not in sight: although the HWA had been involved since 1939 in the financing of the Institute through individual projects, it showed no concrete sign of being interested in a large project on fundamental research in atomic physics, such as that represented by the accelerator laboratory conceived by Hahn and Mattauch.

Because of Telschow's sceptical remarks, the DIB could only assume that making funds available to the KWI of Chemistry would come into question 'after the end of the war at the earliest'.[33] Hahn's project was now in danger of losing the financial support which, after great efforts, was beginning to come in, since there were competitors within the KWG who were pursuing similar projects. This danger is reflected in the suggestion made by Schmidt-Ott to the DIB in July 1941 that it would be better to give the financial support awarded to Hahn instead to Boris Rajewsky, the director of the KWI of Biophysics in Frankfurt, since he 'desperately needs it for his high-voltage equipment'.[34] Indeed plans for large linear accelerators were here running parallel to each other.[35]

The persistent difficulties over financing, with which Hahn's project had up to this time been confronted, clearly show that it was not given any particular military value by government offices. Claiming military relevance for the transuranic research being carried out by Kurt Starke, Fritz Strassmann and himself at his institute and his prestige as the discoverer of fission were obviously not sufficient to ensure that the necessary financial means be allotted.

Towards the end of 1941 a fundamental change in the policy towards research began to emerge, from which also the 'Minerva' project was to profit. The end of the *Blitzkrieg* brought with it the necessity of re-evaluating research, which was carried out by Erich Schumann, head of the research section of the HWA. As a consequence, the HWA was preparing step by step to pull out of the uranium project, since nuclear research was no longer seen as being immediately decisive for the outcome of the war. The responsibility for the uranium project and nuclear research returned to the *Reichsforschungsrat* (Reich Research Council; RFR), which shortly afterwards was removed from the responsibility of the Ministry of Education and placed under the authority of the Aviation Ministry.[36]

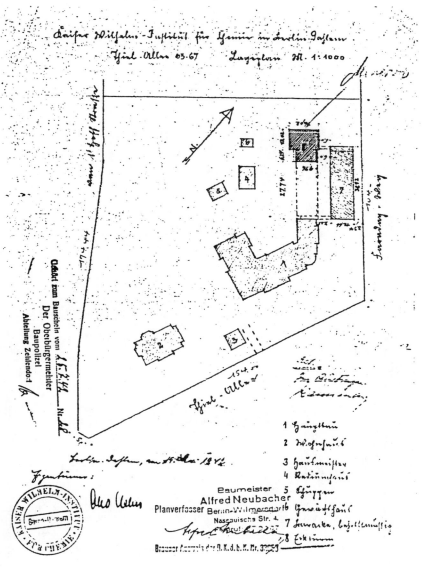

Fig. 13.1   Situation plan, KWI for Chemistry.

Hahn and Mattauch took advantage of the new, more favourable situation in order to translate into reality their plans which had taken on definite shape and size. They conceived a massive tower construction, not dissimilar to the 'tower of lightning' at the neighbouring KWI of Physics,

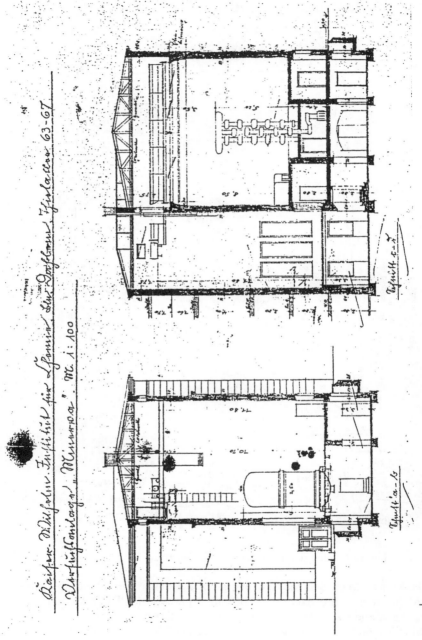

Fig. 13.2   Construction plan, KWI of Chemistry.

which was now to hold two accelerators: a cascade generator supplying 1.2 MV for the production of neutrons, as well as an electrostatic belt-generator on the model of Van de Graaff, supplying 3–5 MV for the production of energetic particle rays, which due to the high voltage had to be accommodated in a pressure tank filled with protective gas. Over and above this, a wooden barrack housing a part of Mattauch's Department of Mass Spectroscopy and connecting the tower with the main building was to be constructed (Figures 13.1, 13.2).[37]

In May 1942 the HWA finally gave its approval to the project, emphasizing the precondition 'that no additional workers are applied for from the employment exchange'.[38] At the same time Göring and Speer promised their support. Whereas the costs for the structural extensions were to be covered by the donation from the Industriebank, the two accelerators were to be financed through the Aviation Ministry's research assignment, for which 260,000 RM had now been made available.[39] In a letter to president Vögler, Hahn combined his pleasure that 'the building project planned for so long' was now finally getting under way, with the hope that in the case of further increases in costs the KWG alongside the Emil Fischer Society would also be prepared to make a contribution 'to this considerable increase in the value of our institute'.[40] In June 1942 director Hahn was able to draw the first payment of the funds provided by the DIB and to begin making orders to companies.[41]

At this time, when the Reich finally engaged itself in the financing of large-scale equipment, the nature of the tasks posed was no longer a military one: in the report that State Councillor Esau, the 'authorized representative on questions of nuclear physics' and 'head of the subject-branch physics at the *Reichsforschungsrat*', presented to the RFR in November 1942, only materials-testing and biological problems were named as potential fields of application for the neutron generators under construction.[42]

The realization

The shift in research policy to global financing came too late in order to take effect. Due to the wartime shortage of qualified personnel and special materials in 1942 German industry was no longer in a position to react quickly and flexibly enough to complicated development orders like those for neutron generators.

The Siemens Company, which in 1938 had supplied the cascade generator for the KWI of Physics, no longer came into consideration as a supplier, since it was completely overloaded with war orders. For this reason the Siemens Reiniger Werke (SRW) had in October already had to inform Rajewsky (KWI for Biophysics), in response to his inquiry, that the delivery time for high-voltage equipment for the production of neutrons would be

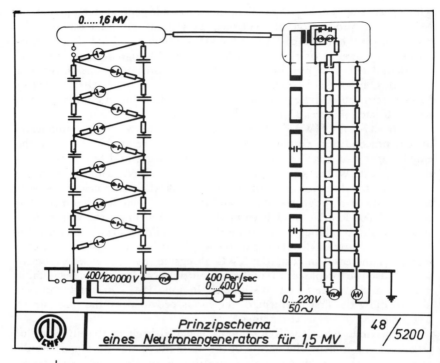

| Fig. 13.3.a   Neutron generator (cascade), part 1.

at least two years even when given the special status SS, and only if the shortage of qualified workers on account of the war did not increase further.[43] This was tantamount to a rejection of the order.

Since Siemens was ruled out as a supplier only the C.H.F. Müller Company in Hamburg now came into consideration. Nevertheless this choice was by no means completely obvious. In spite of its high reputation as one of the leading European manufacturers of X-ray tubes, the Hamburg company, which had a long tradition, had scarcely received any orders from government departments since 1933, because they were obliged to purchase exclusively 'German' products. Since 1927 the C.H.F. Müller Company had been owned by N.V. Philips Gloeilampenfabrieken in Eindhoven. The fact that most of the products manufactured in Hamburg had been developed in laboratories in Eindhoven was deemed by the Nazi government sufficient grounds for rejecting them as 'foreign'.[44] The German subsidiary of Philips was therefore forced to erect its own development laboratory in Hamburg, where work started in 1937. It was there under the direction of A. Kuntke, who had come over from Eindhoven,

| Fig. 13.3b   Neutron generator (cascade), part 2.

that the high-voltage cascade generator for 1.2 MV was now going to be constructed (Figure 13.3).[45]

The pressure tank required for the Van de Graaff generator was ordered from the Rheinmetall-Borsig Company in Berlin. The orders for the ion source as well as for the DC generator needed for the sparking device also went to Müller in Hamburg. The remaining components were to be developed in the Institute itself. The project was treated as a classified undertaking of the highest urgency. However, it was hindered by the bomb attacks on Hamburg which in summer 1943 had already forced the Müller Company to abandon its high-voltage workshop constructed for purposes of experimental tests and trials.

As surviving planning papers show, the short wing of Hahn's Institute was extended through the construction of a five-storey tower, whose visible height from the basement to the top of the roof measured just under 14 metres. The ground-plan of the building consisted in two long-sided rectangles next to each other, the larger of which, with an outside measurement of 12 × 16 metres, determined the main volume of the building. This part formed on the inside from the mezzanine upwards a large, hall-like room with space up to a height of 8.5 metres which served to accommodate the cascade generator along with auxiliary equipment. The cascade itself stood in a square-shaped depression about half a metre lower than the mezzanine itself and under which the engine room was situated. The smaller wing of the building, by not having a mezzanine, had an overall internal headroom of almost 12 metres and a floor area (outside measurement) of 6.2 × 9.8 meters. There the Van de Graaff generator (belt generator) was to be set up. The headroom in both the workshops was limited by two cranes set in a reinforced concrete ring and orthogonally orientated to each other, which with their crabs were able to reach the whole of the floor (Figure 13.2).[46]

In spring 1943 the construction work on the Minerva tower as well as on Mattauch's wooden barrack neared completion. The shell of the tower alone consumed the 200,000 RM donated by the DIB. The costly project required further funds. The Emil Fischer Society did not find itself in a position to increase the Institute's budget.[47] Thereupon Göring's Aviation Ministry undertook to pay the additional construction costs of 60,000 RM for Mattauch's barrack. The RFR also made its small contribution: in March 1943 Esau approved Mattauch's application for a grant of 37.900 RM for auxiliary apparatus using resources from the Subject-Branch Physics.[48] In order to cover the remaining costs expected for technical equipment, apparatus and measuring instruments, Hahn finally put in a request to the RFR in May 1943 for a further 200,000 RM and at the same time asked the Ministry of Education and Cultural Affairs as well as the KWG for an increase of 100,000 RM in the current budget of the Institute.[49]

The growing importance and complexity of the Nuclear Physics Department at the Institute, resulting from the increase in financial volume and the steady realization of large-scale research equipment, was taken into account by Hahn's recommendation of Mattauch as his deputy on the board of the Institute. After all, as Hahn emphasized in October 1943, it was thanks to Mattauch's planning and energy 'that now a high-voltage

| Fig. 13.4   KWI of Chemistry after the air raid of 15 February 1944.

generator and a pressure belt generator for artificial atomic transformation processes was being set up'.[50] The Senate of the KWG approved Hahn's application on 11 November: Joseph Mattauch was named Deputy Director of the KWI of Chemistry as of 1 November 1943.[51]

The relocation

The promotion of Mattauch and the completion of construction were followed by a setback: during an air raid on 15 February 1944 the KWI of Chemistry was hit by an aerial mine, which totally devastated the director's house and western wing of the Institute (Figure 13.4). Mattauch's valuable mass spectograph was destroyed, along with priceless papers.[52] The high-voltage room on the ground floor of the main building was also hit. As the roof threatened to collapse Meitner's old high-voltage equipment was dismantled and sent back for repairs to the company that had supplied it, where it was lost through bombing.[53]

About a month later, on 24 March 1944, during a further air raid the Minerva tower was hit by incendiary bombs. However, members of the Institute were able to extinguish the fire before large-scale damage was caused. The firebomb-safe roof construction with which the tower was subsequently provided proved itself, so that the building along with its contents survived the war undamaged,[54] whereas the newly-built barrack for Mattauch's department was completely burned down.[55]

The air raids forced the Institute to move to Tailfingen in South Württemberg-Hohenzollern, where it found accommodation in unused rooms of three textile factories which had been prepared for the transfer since summer 1943.[56] During this operation, carried out in March 1944, those parts of the accelerator which had been delivered but not yet assembled had for the time being to remain in Berlin.

On 30 September 1942 the foundations for the neutron generator had been built into the Berlin workshop while this was still in an early stage of construction. However, the assembly of the generator never happened. The deliveries sent to Berlin in the course of 1943, including parts for the Van de Graaff generator, were stored at first in the laboratory of the Reichspost at Miersdorf, from where in July 1944 they were sent on to the Institute which in the meantime had moved to Tailfingen. From then onwards the consignments went directly from Hamburg to Tailfingen, where by July 1944 about 80% of the equipment had been delivered. Due to the lack of a workshop in Tailfingen, however, they could not be assembled there either. The remaining components of the equipment were still waiting at the manufacturer's C.H.F. Müller in Hamburg, when the war ended. From the Van de Graaff generator, only the pressure tank supplied from the company Rheinmetall-Borsig remained in Berlin. This turned out to be a stroke of luck: whereas the prestigious accelerator belonging to the neighbouring KWI of Physics at the end of the war was dismantled by the Russians, there was at the KWI of Chemistry nothing to be dismantled; apart from the tank the Berlin workshop had remained empty.[57]

The policy of the French

After the end of the war the financing for the KWI of Chemistry was taken over by the Secretary of State for Education and Cultural Affairs in the French occupied zone of Württemberg. It was clear that the disadvantages of its location, created by the transfer, could best be overcome by moving it to a university town. The nearby town of Tübingen appeared to be just right for this purpose.[58] However, although the Secretary of State's office had agreed to the transfer of the Institute, it fell through in June 1946 when the old garrison hospital in Tübingen, envisaged for the accommodation of the Institute, was confiscated for French troops. Behind this confiscation stood the intention of the French to enhance the status of the University of Mainz, erected under their aegis, by settling the KWI there.

On 22 May 1946 the French reestablished the University of Mainz, which had been closed down in the Electoral Palatinate following the French revolution. This event, commonly described as the 'miracle of Mainz', could be seen superficially as the result of an initiative on the part of citizens there, who in August 1945 had distributed a memorandum demanding the reestablishment of the university. Under the circumstances prevailing at the time, however, the realization of such a project must have required massive support from the French occupation government, which in this respect pursued its own aims. In those circles of the military bureaucracy responsible for the administration of education and cultural affairs the predominating view was that the German universities were an 'anachronism'. Raymond Schmittlein, who was head of the Direction d'Education Publique and was resident in Baden-Baden, expressed the intention of 'making life difficult for these fossils by means of competing projects'. The reestablishment of the University of Mainz offered a welcome opportunity for laying down the principles of an alternative policy on education. If we follow the analysis of J. Kleindienst, there was also a strong psychological motive behind this view taken by the French education and cultural affairs bureaucracy: France, as a victorious power hopelessly inferior to the USA both economically and politically, saw in education and cultural affairs a field in which it could make its mark. Through reestablishing the University of Mainz, prestige could be won vis-à-vis not only the allies but also the German population, which in the face of a heavy burden of reparations under the French had had nothing to laugh about. All other considerations, such as denazification, were subjugated to the goal of establishing in Mainz a highly prestigious educational institution: the extremely lenient political investigation of applicants for the teaching staff of the new university led to the nasty rumour of 'a nest of nazis' (in the words of the Minister of the Interior of the Rhineland-Palatinate) being circulated.[59]

It was along the lines of this policy that the former KWIs still remaining in the French Zone of Occupation were to receive every conceivable help in order to regain opportunities for scientific work, while their future as institutions was to be closely tied in with the universities. In order to make the control from above palatable to the scientists at the KWI, they were assured by the occupying power that erection of the institute would take place at the same breath-taking pace as the rebuilding of the University of Mainz – a promise which, on account of the post-war shortage of materials, could not be kept.[60]

The construction work in Mainz took place under the direction of Mattauch but without the participation of Otto Hahn, who, having returned to Germany in January 1946 following British internment, had in April taken over the post of president of the KWG in Göttingen. After the decision on the new location in Mainz had been taken in July 1946, the task of realizing the accelerator laboratory originally planned for Berlin was able to begin.

Cooperation of the Allies

Apart from the slightly increased dimensions, the planning in Mainz was an exact copy of the Berlin 'Minerva'. The Van de Graaff accelerator was to be set up as well. However, this necessitated the transfer of the remains of the Institute still in Berlin, first and foremost the pressure tank. Although the equipment of the KWG in Berlin was formally under the control of the four victorious powers, the French and the Americans came to a separate agreement without the Allied Kommandantura (and therefore the Soviet Union) finding out about the planned removal.

In February 1946 the Education Committee of the Allied Control Authority had recommended the dissolution of the KWG. The operation of the individual institutes was, however, permitted in accordance with the laws of the zones of occupation and the Control Authority. Although this suggestion, an American initiative, was not placed in the statute book before the break-up of the Control Authority in the middle of 1948, the Americans forthwith adopted the position that the KWG was dissolved and that the individual institutes fell under the control of the occupying power in whose zone or sector they had found themselves at the end of the war. The US position created tension, since the institutes in Berlin, which lay in the American Sector, were financed out of the budget of the Berlin City Council. This budget required the approval of the Allied Kommandantura and therefore of all the four powers. The estimated provision for the KWIs in 1946/47 was vetoed by the Soviets. In order to get round the resulting obstructions, on 22 March 1948 the Americans took the remaining KWIs in Berlin out of the responsibility of the Allied Kommandantura by putting them under the direct control of their military governor in Germany.[61]

The legal position adopted by the Americans resulted in immediate permission for the dismantling of the equipment at Dahlem. As early as July 1946 Mattauch's assistants were able to apply for permission to travel to Berlin 'in order to be present at the dismantling of the Van de Graaff'.[62] With the technical assistance of the French, who provided a heavy-duty crane, in autumn 1946 the parts of the accelerator, including the twenty-one-ton pressure tank of the Van de Graaff, were dismantled and loaded onto four goods waggons. As part of a French troop train, and therefore removed from Soviet control, they arrived in Mainz on 9 November 1946.[63]

The British also showed themselves willing to cooperate. Already in autumn 1945, a few months after the end of the war, Mattauch had got in touch from Tailfingen with the manufacturers in Hamburg, in order to find out about the possibility of completing the equipment. The Müller company had not foreseen any technical problems, but had pointed out that before production in Hamburg could restart the permission of the British Military Government was necessary. This did not take a long time: in July 1946 the British representative responsible for research, Fraser, hinted that there were no longer reservations on the part of the British about the completion of the equipment now to be installed in Mainz. A few days later Colonel Cagniard from the Mission Scientifique came to Hamburg in order to regulate the details. As the head of the laboratory,

Kuntke, found out during his tour of inspection in Mainz in August 1946, a high-voltage workshop was to be erected there which essentially corresponded to the Dahlem plans. Only the measurements were going to be bigger, as Mattauch had expressed a wish to increase the maximum voltage of the equipment to 1.5 MV. This remained for the time being very much something for the future, since the permission given by the British Military Government was only for the completion of the original 1.2 MV equipment.[64] In February 1947, on the occasion of a meeting concerning the future of the KWI of Chemistry, Fraser gave the French assurances that the British would cooperate in the efforts to bring the accelerators existing in the French Zone of Occupation to completion. In return for this Joliot-Curie, as head of the Mission scientifique, declared himself willing to provide Heisenberg with one of the sets of equipment for his institute at Göttingen once they had all been completed.[65]

The restoration

Along with the relocation of the Institute from Tailfingen to Mainz went a change in the authority maintaining it. On 1 April 1949 the state of Rhineland-Palatinate took over the costs which up to then had been paid out of the budget for education and cultural affairs in South Württemberg-Hohenzollern. In taking on responsibility for financing the Institute, the state expected to be able to operate it as a state institution associated with the University of Mainz.

The reconstruction of the KWI of Chemistry took place on the extensive grounds of former anti-aircraft barracks, which the French had allocated to the University of Mainz as a campus.[66] In the expectation that the Institute would in the future be a research institution associated with the University, the construction was carried out technically and financially by the University of Mainz, which, in anticipation of the taking over of the financing through the state of Rhineland-Palatinate, had already made an advance payment of one million RM.

An alleviation of the costs incurred by the state as a result of the taking over of the Institute was hoped for by the government through the 'National agreement of the states of the three western zones on the financing of scientific research institutions with areas of activity covering more than one region' (The Königstein Agreement). Taking up the tradition of the old constitution of the German Empire, according to which the funding of scientific research was fundamentally a responsibility of the state, representatives of the latter had come together in Königstein (Taunus) in order to agree on guidelines for mutual financial help in respect of the financing of research institutions in advance of the reestablishment of central government departments. Article 6 of the agreement envisaged that the total amount of funds to be raised jointly would be spread over the individual states on the basis that 'two thirds corresponded to tax revenue and one third to size of population'. As one of the smaller and less well off states in the future Federal Republic of Germany, the Rhineland-Palatinate belonged, according to the National Agreement, to those states who were 'receivers'. At the conclusion of the National Agreement on 15 March 1949 the budget plan of the Institute at Mainz for 1949 (493,000 DM annually and a one-time payment of 500,000 DM) was therefore written into the text in full by the Minister of the Rhineland-Palatinate, Hoffmann.[67]

Completely undeterred by the financial commitments undertaken by the state government, the Finance Committee of the Landtag cut the budget plan for 1949 presented by the Institute from 993,000 DM to 774,000 DM just fourteen days later. The difference saved was to go to the state's own research institute for vine cultivation (already considered in the sum of 200,000 DM in the National Agreement), whose task was probably more obvious to members of parliament than that of the future state institute of chemistry.

The intervention of parliament led to a sharp protest from the President of the *Max Planck Gesellschaft*, (Max Planck Society; MPG), Otto Hahn, who, in anticipation of the intended restructuring of the Institute saw in the cuts a reduction of the approximately 12.5 million DM subsidy for the MPG, as set out in the National Agreement of the states. In addition, Hahn complained that the state government had insisted on having a say on the money allocated to the Institute. With reference to the instructions for the carrying out of the National Agreement, he pointed out that the funds going to the MPG were to be regarded as 'subsidies', 'which are granted to the individual research institutes without the necessity for items to be individually receipted'.[68]

Hahn's view, which saw in the institute of Mainz a potential member of the MPG, provoked the opposition of the state government. It was emphasized from the latter side that all the talks conducted by the Ministry of Finance were based on the assumption that it was dealing with a state institute.[69] The increasingly intense conflict between the MPG and the state over the future legal status of the Institute was finally settled by a third party on 13 October 1949 the military government of the Rhineland-Palatinate formally acknowledged the responsibility of the MPG for the former KWIs in the French Zone of Occupation. The institutes were now free to join the MPG if they wanted. Application for membership had however already been made of the Institute of Chemistry in Mainz to the MPG in Göttingen in September 1949.[70]

The state parliament of the Rhineland-Palatinate ratified the Königsstein Agreement on 10 November 1949. The protests of the MPG, as well as the changed legal status, had resulted in the original version being put to the vote: the budget of the Institute of Mainz was approved in full.

Because of the implementation of the National Agreement, money from now on flowed to Göttingen as part of a nationally allocated sum paid by the individual states. There it was centrally administered and alloted to the institutes according to their estimated budgets. Compared to the situation in the 'Third Reich', where Hahn had had to negotiate every year with the Emil Fischer Society over the budget of his institute, and where for larger investment projects like the 'Minerva' it had been necessary for him to gain sponsors from government and industry, things were now much simpler, guaranteeing a successful future existence. In place of a 'multiplicity of sponsorship' there was now national financing out of public funds.

The completion of the two accelerators nevertheless took more time than expected. First the cascade generator increased to 1.4 MV and delivered from Müller in September 1949 was put into operation. With its help a series of investigations was carried out, with participation from both the Chemistry and Physics Departments of the Institute, on nuclear isomerism, separation processes for radioactive isotopes, and the applications of radioactive isotopes in chemistry and medicine.[71] The completion of the Van de Graaff proved to be considerably more protracted, in spite of the 'saved' pressure tank. In view of the relocation of the Institute to Mainz and the reconstruction there of the pressure belt generator, a smaller belt generator providing 450,000 volts had been built and tested by Arnold Flammersfeld in 1947–8 whilst still in Tailfingen.[72] However, the director, Mattauch, did not show the necessary support for the project, because it took up a considerable amount of funds from the budget for mass spectroscopy. The work on the accelerators took place under the directorship of Flammersfeld until he accepted a chair at the Institute of Physics in Göttingen in 1954. His successor, Peter Jensen, suffered a fatal accident in August 1955. Finally, in 1956 Hermann Wäffler from Zürich was offered the post. Under his directorship the Van de Graaff was almost completely reconstructed and put into operation at the beginning of 1960.[73] It facilitated studies in the field of lower- and middle-energy nuclear reactions as well as the preparation of studies in the field of higher energies, for which a larger linear accelerator was conceived in cooperation with the University of Mainz.[74]

Conclusion

The history of the 'Minerva' project shows on a micro-sociological (institute) level the eventual successful efforts towards achieving continuity, which in general have marked the history of the KWG/MPG in the post-war period.[75] Transcending the total defeat of Germany, which for the Institute manifested itself physically in its transfer from Berlin to Tailfingen and later to Mainz, plans originating during the first years of the war could be realized. This success was due to three factors. Firstly, it was due to the identity of the individuals doing the research, who in the understandable desire to continue work and careers already begun, saw no reason to give up plans originally decided upon, although in the meantime requiring revision (continuity in personnel). Secondly, these individuals were able to fall back on the fact that the majority of the equipment already delivered had been saved and brought to the new location of the Institute, where it was supplemented and completed (continuity of apparatus). Thirdly, this goal in turn could only happen with the active support of the western allies, who, following the Control Authority initiative of the USA, after 1946 felt themselves individually responsible for the future of the institutes which belonged to their particular zone of occupation. In this respect it was, however, above all the French, who, moved by concern over their prestige as an occupying power, were interested in an early restoration of research capacity in their zone.

In order to realize these goals the allies were apparently prepared to disregard their own laws: not only the Control Authority Law No. 25 (on the regulation and monitoring of scientific research), with which the three powers in May 1946 had laid down the essential features of their joint policy on research, prohibiting applied research in the field of atomic physics; but also Law No. 22 from March 1950 (on the monitoring of materials, equipment and fittings in the field of atomic energy), which confirmed the ban on the operation of accelerators with energies exceeding 1 MeV. Under a strict interpretation of the law, 'Minerva' should have become a victim of allied legislation. However, the opposite was the case: ten years after planning had begun the 'Minerva' project became reality. The delay of a decade was probably taken as a sufficient guarantee for the harmlessness of the installation.

By bringing into service the first of the two accelerators, the continuity from the point of view of apparatus found its counterpart on the institutional level. Following the constitution of the MPG in the Bi-Zone the year before, in 1949 the French no longer placed any obstacles in the way of the Institute returning to it. Together with the other former KWIs in the French Zone of Occupation, it was able to join the MPG in October 1949. The 'release' to the successor of the KWG took place from the French point of view without anger or enthusiasm: as the French government confidentially informed its governor in Mainz, by 1949 she had already lost all her interest in the research work of the Institute. The reason given speaks volumes: 'The backwardness of German scholars is in effect such that one can scarcely say in advance if their work could be of any use to us'.[76]

In spite of his prestige, Hahn had needed about three years in order to procure support for 'Minerva' from the DIB and diverse Reich sources; the breakthrough came first with the change in research policy in the middle of 1942. The delay in the realization of the project, for which, alongside events in the war, above all the insufficient State funding of research in Nazi Germany was responsible, in the end turned out to be a favourable circumstance for the restoration of the Institute.

14 | The social system of mathematics and National Socialism: a survey

HERBERT MEHRTENS

Studies of the history of scientific disciplines in Nazi Germany have largely concentrated on the intrusion of Nazi ideology into scientific thinking.[1] Few works have addressed the process of the integration of a science into the society.[2] As a result, there has been no serious attempt to work out a comprehensive vision of the position of a science in German society and its development in the thirties and forties. Such a vision must include not only the core of scientific research and teaching, but also the position in the general system of education; the fields of application; the neighbouring scientific and technical disciplines; the political relations of the discipline; and the situation of individual scientists and their relation to the disciplinary sytems. In brief, it has to comprehend the complete system of the discipline and all its essential relations to its environment. For careful, fact-oriented historiography this would be an almost insurmountable problem. But it is also a problem of theory. What is the 'complete social system' of a science? How does it work? What are 'essential' environment relations? The basic understanding of a 'social system' used here follows from Luhmann.[3] It includes as essential an interest in the internal organization of the system, environment–system relations (where individuals are considered part of the environment), and the processes of identity formation and boundary maintenance.

The social system of mathematics

During the nineteenth century mathematics in Germany became an institutionalized, fully professional scientific discipline with a well-established and central position in the systems of knowledge production and education. 'Mathematics' means here the social system of the discipline with its central function of producing and disseminating novel knowledge

291

of a specific character. As two of the most important characteristics of mathematical knowledge, one might point out its pervasive role as a linguistic and theoretical tool in the production of scientific knowledge and the fact that it has no well-defined object in the material world and thus no clear boundaries to its applications. Further, the extremely compelling character of mathematical argument must be noted. Like other knowledge-producing social systems, mathematics defines its identity through the specificities of its knowledge. Because of the constitutive character of identity and difference (from other systems) the system has developed a core in which 'pure' mathematics is produced. 'Purity' thus serves an extremely important function by producing and reproducing the identity of the system and important elements of the identity of individuals taking part in the system.

Like other systems, mathematics has to care for productivity, social legitimacy, and professional autonomy if it is to survive. These functions have to be fulfilled in order to reproduce the internal coherence of the system but even more so to ensure stable environmental relations. Stable relations with the environment are important to intellectual endeavours such as mathematics, since they do not produce the material resources necessary for reproduction, but must depend upon others for them. The basic thesis presented here is that a scientific discipline exchanges its knowledge products plus political loyalty in return for material resources plus social legitimacy. Obviously such a trade is the result of continual bargaining and is subject to historical change. The systematic analysis would have to consider among other points the position of the discipline in the larger system of the sciences, the power of experts in politics or the economy, and the role of instrumental rationality in modern societies.

To ensure productivity the system has to care for recruitment of personnel; it has to allow room for some social and cognitive deviance in order to maintain creativity; and both internal and external communication has to be organized. Organized communication appears to be a most important characteristic of knowledge-producing social systems. Consequently the organization of journals, professional societies and conferences plays a central role. Furthermore a certain degree of social and cognitive coherence within the system is a precondition of sufficiently intense communication. The latter is produced by what has been called the paradigm or disciplinary matrix of the field.[4] The system itself is highly oriented towards knowledge that reinforces its productivity. Similarly the exchange of rewards, or the ways to gain scientific 'capital',[5] is also related to notions of productivity.

Social legitimacy for mathematics is basically attained in two ways: on one hand through the utility of mathematics; through its cultural value on the other. Cultural value can range from metaphors like 'honour of the human spirit' to 'expression of the German character', or from 'basic training of the mind' to 'core of modern rationality'. Since the utility of novelties in pure mathematics is usually not immediately visible (nor is its cultural value), mathematicians have frequently been defensive, complaining about the lack of understanding for their field. Social legitimacy has to be such that the basic and supporting institutions are preserved and possibly extended. Basic institutions are those where mathematical production takes place. In Germany this means almost exclusively universities and, since the end of the nineteenth century, institutes of technology. Supporting institutions would be places where mathematics is applied and taught. In the German system legitimacy of an academic subject that has no immediate field of application in society rests to a very large extent on the status of the subject in secondary education, since teacher education and scholarly production are combined in the universities. For this reason, school mathematics is a field of legitimation of extreme importance in Germany. There is the constant interest to maintain the identification of mathematics teachers with the academic subject. And in this field the cultural value of mathematics has been important, because in general the mathematics taught in schools appears to be of little use to the students. The utility of mathematics on the other hand is strongly expressed by its integration in the system of natural sciences and technology. Again a certain amount of identification with mathematics within other social systems has to be produced. The fact that mathematics has no defined field of application in the material world has the effect that strategies of legitimation are strongly mediated (that is, directed at other professions like teachers or natural scientists). Within this structure the role and development of 'applied mathematics' as a distinct subfield is of great interest.

The professional autonomy of mathematics is ensured mainly by monopolizing competence for the specific type of knowledge production. In the discussion of the modernization of mathematics below, I shall try to show how the development of knowledge in its basic characteristic interacts with its social function in ensuring autonomy. A dense and far-reaching (international) communication network within the system serves the goal of autonomy by monopolizing competence and means of communication but also via its productive function. A social system that depends on international communication for its central functions (production) gains autonomy in the face of national powers. On the other hand material resources come from national powers. Thus a dynamic equilibrium between autonomy and integration in the national society is necessary. A similar equilibrium is needed between utility and autonomy for legitimacy, since the competence to decide what mathematics is taught and where it is applied does not lie in the hands of the mathematicians. In times when the cultural value of the field is in doubt, the move towards a utility argument is a delicate problem.

This rough sketch of some basics of the social system of mathematics must suffice as a basis for the following discussions. It should have indicated that the system has necessary inner tensions and is of a highly dynamic stability.

Origins and power structures of the Third Reich

The following remarks are solely meant as a background to the specific theme of this paper. I can merely indicate a few basic problems which are still matters of intense discussion. But first of all two popular misconceptions have to be removed. First, the ideology of National Social-ism cannot be reduced to 'blood and soil'. The ideology is a large collection of pieces, some of which were decisive for political action while others were the object of cynical manipulation. This collection was hardly coherent as a cognitive system. Instead the parts could be combined and recombined as necessary into what may be called 'regional ideologies'. The concept of a 'Aryan' mathematics or physics was such a regional ideology that related to some core elements of general ideology but in a specific way, adapted to the social and cognitive situation of the discipline. Nazi ideology also embraced a cult of technics and naturalistic scientist modes of justi-fication. Thus regional ideologies in technology or in chemistry could be constructed along the lines of power, leadership, German imperialism and superiority, but excluding or at least playing down anti-Semitism, the cult of the soil and of rural life, and romantic irrationalism. The 'reactionary modernism' in Germany, as part of Nazi ideology, has recently been dis-cussed by Herf.[6]

Secondly the notion of a totalitarian, tightly structured and controlled state has to be revised. Power struggles were common at all levels below the *Führer*, and these conflicts included interests from outside the Party. Further, the system of Nazi-society was born mainly by four blocs of power: the party, state bureaucracy, industry and the army.[7] These powers cooperated and competed. Thus the environment for a social system like mathematics was much more diversified and dynamic than appears on first sight. Adaptive moves could relate to various sources of power. The immediate link to the state lay in university administration, and here the bureaucracy of the ministry of education was involved in constant conflicts with Party agencies. Systems like mathematics obviously preferred the bureaucratic rationality of ministerial administration. Similarly industry was a potential partner. The physicists' association, for example, elected an industrial physicist as president explicitly in order to use industrial power to counter party influence.

An important theory for the explanation of the rise of Fascism and especially National Socialism is to see it as a reaction to the problems of modernization. It is argued that rapid industrialization, urbanization, rationalization and bureaucratization in Germany did not find equivalent changes in politics, culture and mentality. National Socialism arose as an anti-modernist revolt mainly of those individuals who were in fear of, or actually subject to, social marginalization. In its effect, the argument goes, National Socialism modernized German society by destroying traditional institutions. The whole argument is subject to varied discussions. But it is, as an explanation of the rise of German Fascism and of its large support, at least partially valid. It is confirmed by the history of the sciences, but especially in this case needs a careful consideration of National Socialist modernism[8] and the role of technocracy in the power structures of the Third Reich.

Finally the Nazi system was changing during its twelve-year reign. For the history of mathematics and the natural sciences the years 1936–7 mark an important change. With the Four Year Plan and the intensification of war preparations several institutions strengthened the position of technocratic rationality to which social systems that produced technically applicable knowledge could relate. Another such change occurred in 1942–3, when the time of quick victories was over, and even party agencies that had stubbornly insisted on the value of a romanticist 'German' science dropped this notion in favour of technological and scientific rationality.

Modernism, anti-modernism and Nazi-ideology in mathematics

By 1930 it was quite clear what the term 'modern' meant when applied to mathematics: the conceptual study of abstract mathematical concepts characterized by axioms valid for sets of otherwise undefined elements and presented by proceeding from the elementary concepts to the more complicated structures; a hierarchical system of mathematical truths rigorously proved, the language applied having hardly any other function that to label the objects and to ensure the validity of statements. 'Modern' mathematics in this sense had no extra-mathematical meaning, did not indicate possible fields or objects of application, was devoid of hints to the historical or heuristical background of the theory, and at most was in a highly implicit manner structured along didactical guidelines.

The thesis presented here is that mathematical modernism emerged slowly through the nineteenth century, became fully visible around the turn of the century, and had gained its position as a dominant and productive research programme by the end of the 1920s. By then anti-modernist positions resided without influence in marginalized fields and groups. Attacks on the social and cognitive dominance of modernism occurred with the help of powers outside the discipline, as in Ludwig Bieberbach's attempt to establish a 'German mathematics' with the help of National Socialism. For the analysis of the latter development, a thorough analysis of the genesis and the structure of modernism and traditionalism in mathematics would be necessary.[9]

Sociologically it is crucial for such an analysis to understand the close interrelation of social and cognitive modernization of the discipline and the way this is embedded in the environment of mathematics. The key concepts are autonomy (both cognitive and social) and universality. Mathematics gained cognitive autonomy during the nineteenth century through de-ontologization, self-justification and productive self-reference. De-ontologization meant giving up the basic assumption that mathematics is concerned with real space and with magnitudes as applied in the real world. The legitimacy lost through giving up ontological ties to the real world was compensated through self-justification by method. Instead of the inquiry into the 'nature of the object' it was the methodologically and logically controlled conceptualization of relations and operations which became the object and justification of mathematical knowledge. With this mathematics became, in its 'pure' core of knowledge production, self-referential. Problems, objects and solution criteria were produced and controlled by mathematical thinking.

All this became visible most clearly in the rise of set theory, which on the one hand made it possible to talk and argue about objects which have no other characteristic than being capable of relations and operations. On the other hand, set theory gave access to the formal handling of infinity. A complementary event was the rise of mathematical logic and the axiomatic method which allowed for a rigid control of the syntax of mathematical expression and argument.

All this adds up to cognitive autonomy in so far as no other approach or field of knowledge can intervene in the basics of mathematics, neither philosophy nor physics, unless it becomes itself part of mathematics. No specific field of objects or relations or operations is presupposed. Anything can become the object of mathematical thought. At the same time mathematics is rigid and compelling. Accept the methods and the axioms and there is no way to evade the consequences. Thus mathematics is cognitively universal, both in its procedure and in its applicability.

As implied above, cognitive autonomy implies social autonomy to some extent. It means potentially complete monopoly of competence for a certain field of mental activities. Internally the rigid control of the syntax of mathematical expression and the tendency to push out various semantic dimensions from formalized mathematical discourse is oriented extremely toward the professional production of novel knowledge. The rigid discrimination of formal and informal discourse produces a highly esoteric core, inaccessible to outsiders. The specific structure of cognitive autonomy and universality is also productive in that it allows high interpenetrability of mathematical subfields, thus generating new problems and solutions. Given that mathematics is applicable and is used by others, the discipline is also socially universal. There are no intrinsic limitations to where mathematics may find its market. Any society, any social system, any other system of knowledge production can buy mathematical results and the competence to use it as needed.

Obviously modern mathematics has to complement its core autonomy with structural measures to ensure that there is demand for mathematics, either as a tool to be applied or as a paradigm for the prevalent type of rationality. Consequently, the social system of mathematics needs internal task-oriented subdivisions and institutionalized ties to its environment. Around the turn of the century, when modern mathematics became prominent, such task-oriented subsystems came into appearance. One was the institutionally emerging speciality of applied mathematics with a specific identity; the other, the field of a pedagogy of teacher education in mathematics and the relation between school and university mathematics. Both developed partly from outside-pressures from teachers, engineers, natural scientists and industrialists. The central cognitive definition of mathematics by its pure, modern core was related to those task-oriented fields. Lectures on 'elementary mathematics from a higher standpoint' served, for example, to relate the pedagogical branch to the development of scientific mathematics, and the attempt to axiomatize mathematical theories for physics aimed at an immediate relation between this field of application and pure mathematics. Applied mathematics, institutionalized with a wide range of very different tasks, had problems achieving coherence because there was no central governing theory or methodology which would cover most of the fields, from numerical analysis and graphical statics to mechanics and mathematical statistics.

This description is obviously idealized. The history is much more complicated. The relations indicated between various parts and functions of the system should not be taken as indicating historical causation. It should, on this level, be understood as the self-organization of a social system interacting with its environment. Further, it must be stressed that mathematics was embedded in the larger system of the sciences which fulfilled important functions for all subfields, for example the legitimation of scientific rationality.

Modernization in mathematics, as elsewhere, meant losses. The 'Loss of Certainty'[10] occurred cognitively as well as socially, because autonomy and universality imply that values and standards of action are no longer incorporated, but are rather a matter of implicit negotiation. Similarly, the sharper demarcations between, for example, formal and informal mathematical discourse, pure and applied mathematics, mathematics and physics imply a loss of connectedness of the whole system and its environment. Finally the modern mathematics, especially in formal discourse, no longer carried any meaning other than that for mathematical research work, and even there the heuristic context was obscured. As could be expected, modernization met with a sharp critique from traditionalist standpoints which sharpened when the paradoxes of set theory emerged around 1900. The critique centred on the loss of meaning. It was said that formalization and logic in mathematics had gone too far. Parts of mathematics became senseless and were uncontrollable because they could not be constructed out of elementary thought-action (like counting). Such mathematics no longer had any meaning in the real world. Further, 'intuition' (in various forms) was defended as a guideline, tool and justification of mathematics. This type of attack was frequently combined with the argument that modern mathematics would hinder the educational and applied tasks, while the establishment of a separate applied mathematics would destroy the unity of the discipline.

Ludwig Bieberbach, later the champion of 'Aryan' mathematics, used all these arguments during the twenties. In a lecture in 1926, for example, he sharply attacked Hilbert, the dean of mathematical modernity, and depicted the modern theories as 'skeletons in the sand of the desert of which nobody knows whence they come and what they have served for'.[11] Bieberbach was a mathematician of high reputation, well established and with a strong position in the German mathematical system. In his work, however, he considered himself as a 'geometrical thinker', relying on intuition and mental imagery. With this emphasis he had a tendency to be pushed to the margin of the official and progressive mathematics. He was a pure mathematician with strong interests in application, fearing a new field of applied mathematics as a 'wedge between mathematics and its users'. To him, the danger of modernity centred on both the loss of meaning, by extreme formalization, and the loss of unity, through differentiation.

To these combined motives for anti-modernism were added a series of conflicts, in which Bieberbach sided against the dominant position held by the mathematicians of the Göttingen Institute. Bieberbach sided with L. E. J. Brouwer's intuitionism and fought against David Hilbert's formalist programme. This struggle had strong elements of competition for social power in the discipline. Hilbert's victory was obvious when he succeeded in eliminating Brouwer, and Bieberbach with him, from the editorial board of the influential journal *Mathematische Annalen*. Bieberbach was involved in a series of further small conflicts which placed him in clear opposition to the dominant (modernist) Göttingen school. Most important for the present analysis was the combined effort of Bieberbach and Brouwer to organize a German boycott of the International Mathematics Congress of 1928. Previous congresses after World War I had excluded the Germans, and now nationalists called for a counter-boycott. These actions were strongly opposed by Hilbert who eventually led a large German group that attended the Congress. The obvious problem of interpretation is to understand the connection between political nationalism and the specific philosophical position in mathematics. Was there a systematic reason for this relation? Was intuitionism even pre-Fascist? I shall return to these questions after briefly sketching Bieberbach's Nazi activities.

To the surprise of his colleagues and students, Bieberbach, early in 1933, turned to the Nazis. Besides several Nazi-related activities at the university and the academy he made his reputation as *the* Nazi among mathematicians by his theories on the psychological (and thus racial) background of different mathematical styles, which he published in lectures and articles beginning in 1934. He was fairly careful not to express anti-Semitic or nationalist prejudices too bluntly, but gave an all too obvious basis to draw such conclusions about 'Jewish' and 'Aryan' mathematics. The core concepts reissued the anti-formalist position of earlier times. The 'positive, German type' would be intuitive, realistic, close to *Volk* and life; while the 'counter-type' would be a highly sophisticated juggler of formal concepts with no bonds to reality and no other motive than his own success. A key concept was *Anschauung*, indicating a variety of associations from Kantian philosophy via mental imagery down to the work with concrete geometrical figures. *Anschauung* had an imprecise but fairly well established meaning in mathematics, mainly as geometrical intuition in drawing conclusions from mental imagery in geometry or analysis. As a heuristic tool *Anschauung* had come into disrepute due to a series of spectacular findings during the second half of the nineteenth century which showed that such conclusions frequently were invalid. For example, the intuitive concept of dimension (i.e., a line has one dimension, a surface has two dimensions and a solid has three dimensions) was brought into question by the construction of a space-filling curve. *Anschauung* had since been pushed back into the role of a secret heuristics with no place in formal mathematical discourse. By praising *Anschauung*, Bieberbach attacked the esoteric, apparently meaningless character of formal mathematics and expressed the quest for the visibility of meaning and for bonding mathematics to reality. All this was framed in such a way that it had obvious relations to parts of Nazi ideology. Bieberbach attempted, so to speak, a scientific counter-revolution with the help of the new powers. His attempt to dominate mathematics in Germany failed, however. The Mathematicians' Association managed to exclude him in early 1935. He started a journal *Deutsche Mathematik* to create his own, competing organization, but did not find the support he needed from the Nazi ministry of education. By 1937 Bieberbach and his group were an ideological residue in the system of mathematics without substantial influence. The external reasons for the failure will be discussed in the second part of this paper.

In Bieberbach's counter-revolutionary enterprise there were three mistakes that led to his failure. First, he related mathematics via *Anschauung* to the Nazi world view as he understood it. That is, he opted for one of the two possible relations between science and politics. He almost explicitly rejected what may be called the instrumentality approach: scientific knowledge is a potential means of power; it can be turned into means of production, destruction or control. Bieberbach presented mathematics instead as part of the officially projected order of things. We may call this the metaphorical approach. *Anschauung* as a way to relate to the world is basically a metaphor. In mathematics it becomes the term for a certain method but is filled with a wealth of connotations. It can be and has been scientifically productive through the power of association. The same word could have been used in general Nazi ideology. The Nazi world view is largely based on *Anschauung*: the structure of the world is immediately visible; political power and hierarchy is made aesthetic in parades and architecture; friend and foe can be recognized by their noses, and so on. The metaphor is productive also in social and political thought. This double productivity of a metaphor frequently serves to relate scientific and political thinking. The ideological fallacy (frequently intended) occurs in the transfer of deductions or social legitimacy from one area to the other with the help of the metaphor. A more obvious example from biology is the concept of 'instinct' which was productive in Nazi Germany both politically and scientifically and served mutually to reinforce parts of Nazi ideology and biological ethology.[12]

Bieberbach's mistake was to put his stakes on this side. Nazi rule ultimately was much more interested in the instrumentality of the sciences and mathematics than in the correct world view. The background to this mistake is that Bieberbach did not simply fight for personal power but really wanted the Nazi revolution in mathematics to take place. Like other revolutionaries in the movement he was instrumental in establishing the power of the new rulers but was denied any substantial access to that power.

Bieberbach's second mistake was to attack the cognitive phenomenon of 'modern' mathematics not noticing that this was the definition of a well-established social system. Indeed the definition of this social system of mathematics by its cognitive product is a means to defend the system and to veil power structures and social relations within the system. To oppose this with an alternative concept like 'Aryan mathematics' in order to take over social power, when in fact the alternative system carries with it very little power, appears as a rather idealistic and helpless strategy. It is the strategy of the socially marginalized, of the losers in a basic social change, who believe that the glory they see in the old flag still bears some of the old power.

This type of critique may be applied to 'alternatives' in science today as well. Sciences need to give room on the margins to feed creativity into their system of mental production. But the basic 'paradigm' or self-definition of mainstream science rests on the safe basis of a well-established and flexible social structure which does not change flags easily.

The third mistake leads into the question of the relation of mathematical traditionalism (or intuitionism) and political nationalism (or Fascism). Colleagues held that Bieberbach's belief in a 'Aryan' mathematics was honest. If this is true – and it seems to be – he projected values and wishes of a general kind into a mathematical programme. But mathematics is just one of many trades in which an individual must deal with the constraints of the system. Just as a plumber cannot satisfy all his emotional needs in his trade; neither can a mathematician hope to satisfy his need for the connectedness of all life solely in his work. Secondly, the cognitive and social system of mathematics is structured such that these attempts are clearly rejected. Bieberbach implicitly attacked this structure and thus a central characteristic of the system. Unlike the student revolutionaries of the Nazi movement, calling indiscriminately for a 'politicized science', he could have known better.

But whence the possibility of such a projection, and why did he not know better? Bieberbach observed, historically and correctly, the existence of two 'styles' in mathematics, formalist and intuitionist (*anschaulich*), and the present dominance of the former. Bieberbach, along with most mathematicians, associated this intuitionist 'style' with the intuitionist programme for the foundation of mathematics developed by L. E. J. Brouwer mainly in the twenties, which attempted a reconstruction of what is meaningful in mathematics from the prime intuition of the one-after-the-other. Such a construction was highly restrictive for the existing mathematics and, therefore, never found a normative role (for which it was constructed). This programme wanted to construct roads that would carry 'meaning' into every remote branch of mathematics, the meaning which the relation to elementary mental action gave. The relation between technical intuitionism and the *anschaulich* style again was metaphorical. The metaphor normatively indicated that mathematics must not be cut off from the elements of human life. Brouwer's programme and the older intuitionist style indicated that this was possible. And what could be more convincing to a mathematician than a mathematics that has shown its possibilities, plus a technically developed programme for a mathematical foundation which would grant validity to the results? The problem was that the social system of mathematics was (and is) not interested in meaning and motive, but rather in production. The competing formalist style was obviously productive, and the corresponding foundational research programme, Hilbert's 'meta-mathematics', imposed no restrictions on existing mathematical theories except the demand for logical coherence. Hilbert attempted to build a wall against the intrusion of logical doubt by proving (with finite means) that no logical contradictions could occur. In this programme a mathematical concept 'existed' as soon as it was non-contradictory. This would grant a maximum of freedom in mathematical production. Although Hilbert's programme in the strict sense failed, it was strong enough to reject any traditionalist normative claims to be pushed into mathematics via the critique of foundations.

This struggle was intense both because of the technical problem of avoiding logical contradictions like the paradoxes of set theory and the competing styles, as well as the fact that it incorporated positions in disciplinary policy. Hilbert justified his programme with the 'pre-established harmony between mathematics and nature'. This can be translated into the harmony of the forces of the market. Formalist mathematics, it says, is productive and will sell. This accepts the social differentiation of mathematics and the social universality while demanding a maximum of autonomy for the 'pure' core. It is obviously compatible with disciplinary internationalism and nonpolitical specialism.

The intuitionists, on the other hand, saw fragmentation instead of differentiation, decadence instead of productive freedom, esotericism and discord instead of the harmony. The policy of the discipline should care for inner unity, for meaning that would shine into teaching and application, for showing the utility and cultural value of mathematics for humanity and for the nation. A mathematics that would be inherently tied to the essentials of human life would be the best means to support such a political programme.

Through this connection there is a clear potential to relate mathematical style and a foundational programme to political ends. Constructivism, and the metaphor of 'action' involved in it, gives an immediate relation to political or moral thought. The connecting hypothesis is that somebody who wants to relate his life and work as a mathematician to his political or moral views is looking for a highly connected and pervasive system of interpretation of facts, values and aims. He would rather opt for some sort of constructivism or intuitionism than for formalism, which defies the connectedness of a world view by walling off mathematics from the real world. Formalism seems to fit with liberal, pragmatic or politically uninterested positions. Intuitionism, on the other hand, seeks to connect mathematics and the real world of human action, allowing for an integration of professional and political views and values. Such a connection, formalism–liberalism and intuitionism – reactionary political romanticism, is obviously by no means necessary or inevitable. Counter-examples are easily found. But it is a potential that was to a significant extent realized at that time. In general, the social system and the cognitive structure of mathematics are opposed to such connections, defending the purely professional identity of the system (not of the individuals). Furthermore, the metaphorical connection of politics and mathematics, with its basis in 'action', does not prescribe specific details of either side, politics or science. Thus intuitionism need not be pre-fascist.

What is left to be explained historically is why this potential was realized at that point of history. Very briefly said, it is the experience of the losses through modernization which was complemented and reinforced by the experience of the German breakdown in World War I and the political, social, economic and cultural crisis of the following years. The feeling of 'crisis' was pervasive, and what was then called the 'foundational crisis' of mathematics was part of it. In the general situation a new understanding of the world had to be found, or the old one had to be reconstructed and defended against the powers of modernization. Nationalism, an emotional crutch in Germany in the face of the never completely realized national unity, was one of the means to preserve and re-erect a political identity after the experience of the war, the revolution and the Weimar crises. Many mathematicians were nationalistic, some let this show in their professional work, and a few made it explicitly part of their vision of mathematics and its social status. The longing for unity and identity was transported into the mathematical profession by pressing for unity there and for bonds to the real world and the political task of national resurrection. And this was leading to Fascism, to the violent attempt to construct a social world where it was easy to feel at home and safe, where there was unity and connectedness, a visible and simple structure of life and society, where it was easy to see who and what was responsible for the good and the bad.

But just this longing, this view of the world of mathematics, was marginalized by the force of its social and cognitive modernization. Mathematicians on this margin, not Bieberbach alone, took the chance for a revolt presented by the Nazi victory of 1933, and they were willing to use violence, more or less blindfolding themselves or being ruthlessly opportunistic.[13] This explanation is, I believe, in a very similar way applicable to 'Aryan' physics[14] which was more prominent because of the stronger cultural meaning of the mechanistic world view and its revolution through quantum and relativity theory.

Adaption and resistance of mathematics in Nazi Germany

The analysis of the process of integration of mathematics into the society of Nazi Germany will focus on the three professional societies. The story has been told in some detail elsewhere.[15] I shall concentrate now on the basic interpretations. The most important organization was the German Mathematicians' Association, the *Deutsche Mathematiker-Vereinigung* (DMV). Bieberbach was the permanent secretary of the DMV and one of the editors of its journal. The social status of the discipline was in danger because of the anti-intellectual thrust of Nazi ideology, and its autonomy was endangered by the quest for pervasive politicking. Thus one would expect a combination of adaptive and defensive moves. Adaptation was necessary for the social system since it depends wholly on the material resources granted by the society in which it exists. But professional autonomy and international relations also had to be preserved as essential constituents of the system. In Nazi Germany conflicts could not be evaded. The most interesting conflict is that with Bieberbach. He represented the danger of a loss of autonomy and, with his anti-modern aims, a loss of productivity. In some individual cases the fight against Bieberbach was or might have been motivated by morals and politics. The social system, however, knows nothing of morals and politics, and its representatives in general act accordingly.

In early 1934 Bieberbach had printed in the DMV journal an open letter that he had written as an answer to a sharp attack against his ideas of 'German' mathematics by a Danish mathematician. He did this without the consent of his co-editors and without the knowledge of the president of the DMV. Since Bieberbach could not be voted out of office, this event appeared to offer a way to force him to resign. When the matter was discussed at the 1934 business meeting, however, the DMV was not successful in separating this question of professional behaviour from matters of general politics. The resolution that was passed 'condemned sharply' the attack against Bieberbach 'in as far as one can find in it an attack on the new German state and on National Socialism' and it merely 'regretted' Bieberbach's behaviour.

In the atmosphere of fear created by the political and racial purges, the DMV adapted to the pressure of politicking from the 'new German state'. Internally, where cognitive autonomy was endangered, the defense was stronger. The move to make Bieberbach *Führer* of the society was voted down by a large majority. And an amendment of the statutes was passed, which looked somewhat like the National Socialist principle of hierarchical leadership (*Führerprinzip*), but which was meant to eliminate Bieberbach's influence by giving the president the right to dismiss officers of the association. The need to file the amendment at a special court, for which Bieberbach as secretary was responsible, led to a struggle, in which Bieberbach finally tried to use the power of the ministry and the help of some Nazi colleagues. But the result was that both the president of the DMV and Bieberbach were forced to resign. A politically reliable new president, Georg Hamel, came into office, and the DMV had to declare its loyalty to the state without being forced to amend the statutes.

Obviously, the ministry was not interested in making Bieberbach *Führer* of the German mathematicians. On the contrary, the political powers were willing to accept the professional autonomy of the specialists, as long as they were sufficiently loyal to the state. Thus the mathematics profession, by the threat coming from the Nazi revolutionary Bieberbach, was pushed into a compromise with the ministry, which was equally National Socialist but apparently less radical. This type of development can be found in many places. The social historian T. Mason expressed it thus: 'Conservative forces preserved social and state order for National Socialism by saving it initially from National Socialism'.[16] If Bieberbach had succeeded, the productivity of German mathematics would have been destroyed. Thus the DMV preserved a functioning mathematics for the Nazi state by protecting it from a Nazi revolution of mathematics. The immediate motive, which was most prominent in the fight against Bieberbach, was the fear that the DMV would lose its large foreign membership and thus its status in the international world of mathematics. This motive of internationalism embraced the preservation of productivity (as enforced by international communication), of autonomy (as enforced by recourse to structures out of reach of national powers), and of privileges as a resource of the disciplinary exchange system. We shall find such motives even clearer in the society of applied mathematicians.

A purely national organization was the *Reich* association of mathematical societies – in brief, *Reichsverband* (MR). The MR was closely connected with the DMV and acted as an autonomous department for mathematical interest policies. The object of its activities was teacher education and school curricula. Since its foundation in 1921, close relations were also kept with the association for the advancement of the teaching of mathematics and natural sciences, the so-called *Förderverein*. The MR was based in Berlin and its president was Georg Hamel, mathematics professor at the *Technische Hochschule*, Berlin.

Mathematics drew its social legitimacy mainly from its place in secondary education. For this reason the MR had been founded, and for this reason the MR followed the *Förderverein* in greeting National Socialism enthusiastically in 1933. Both organizations bowed to Nazi ideology and hastened to declare that mathematics and natural sciences were rooted in the German soul and thus were an indispensible part of National Socialist education. Even if Hamel was a nationalist, there is little reason to assume that he believed in what he said. He appears as the salesman of his discipline. The status of mathematics in the curricula of secondary schools appeared to be in danger. To defend that status while remaining allied with the teachers, the MR followed the submissive policy of the *Förderverein*. Furthermore, the members of the MR council were not likely to choose the way of political opposition. Indeed the activities of the MR and of Hamel met with no official opposition from the DMV, other than in the case of Bieberbach. This kind of salesmanship did not endanger professional autonomy or productivity. Furthermore it was institutionally dissociated from the DMV, so there appeared to be little need to feel responsible.

One of the first tasks the MR set for itself was the production of a handbook with exercises that would show the value of mathematics to the new powers. The book included military, economic and ideological topics of all kinds; for example: 'Building a lunatic asylum required 6 Million Reichsmark. How many new homes at 15,000 Reichsmark each could have been built for this sum?'

What was shown here and in numerous similar books was the instrumentality of mathematics. On one hand, mathematics in school could be an instrument of transport for Nazi ideology. On the other hand, mathematical, calculating rationality obviously could be used to gain power over the social and natural world in the fascist manner. The bureaucratic mentality of the administrators of slave labour and of death camps was prefigured in such exercises. The 'scientific' equivalent can be found in social statistics, for example, in the work and career of Siegfried Koller.[17]

The problem of analysis in this case, which needs further work, lies in the moral and political meaning of scientific instrumentality and in the social organization of social legitimation. The place of the MR on the margin between school and university mathematics was necessary for its political function. Being subject to pressures from the teachers, who out of their specific social and professional situation were tending strongly toward National Socialism, the MR forced the integration of mathematics into the Nazi system. Ideological salesmanship of the first years and the concentration on applied mathematics that followed were tolerable for the system of scientific production in mathematics. There was no systemic resistance against this movement of political adaptation. One could argue that, to the contrary, social universality and differentiation of modern mathematics was a precondition for such adaptation.[18]

The change around 1936–7 towards preference for the loyal and competent specialist, reinforced by the serious shortage of technical personnel, found complementary developments in the MR and the DMV. Both associations cooperated in creating the image of what was called the 'industrial mathematician' and developed a new university examination and curriculum which became effective in 1942 but had been discussed throughout the second half of the thirties. This move was adaptive to the chances offered by the need for technical specialists and by the fact that a few mathematicians were indeed working in industry, having been pushed into such careers by political pressures inhibiting academic careers. Basic autonomy was preserved, since the offer was to educate competent specialists. The mathematicians in universities and institutes of technology had to change their teaching programmes but hardly their fields of research. And what was taught and had to be put in textbooks was basic applied mathematics, thus not subject to the competence of engineers or physicists. In fact, the changes in the teaching were, at least in universities, slight. Even the thrust for the 'industrial mathematician' and applied mathematics appears to have been more propaganda than reality. Involved also were institutional conflicts between the representatives of various research specialities on one hand (that is, more or less applied) and between mathematicians at institutes of technology and at universities on the other. It has been noted that a change from the 'indoctrination function' to the 'qualification function' took place in school mathematics.[19]

For applied mathematicians the situation was in general different. Their society was the GAMM, the society for applied mathematics and mechanics. Here no problems like those Bieberbach created for the DMV occurred. But the GAMM had to face the racial purges. When in 1933 two of the three leading officers of the society decided to resign because of their Jewish descent, the president Ludwig Prandtl asked his colleague Erich

Trefftz whether he would take over the presidency. Trefftz however urged Prandtl to keep his position, adding: 'If we are forced to exclude Jewish members, I would hold the dissolution of the society to be the most honourable reaction.' Prandtl answered at length, arguing that the GAMM gave mechanics an adequate place besides mathematicians and physicists. This need, he wrote, 'persists today more than ever'. 'I feel that this has nothing to do with considerations of honour since it concerns simply a necessity of the discipline.'[20] After the war Prandtl called himself an 'unpolitical German'. In this case he acted as the 'unpolitical' representative of his discipline. The 'necessity of the discipline' was its survival in the face of competition from other fields and in the face of the growing demand for aircraft research. The moral position of Trefftz was brushed aside and did not reccur. Prandtl, his institute and his discipline had quite a career in the following years.

Prandtl actively defended the Jewish membership of the society. The main motive, however, lay not in human or moral values, but in the attempt to ensure and enlarge the international standing of the society and the discipline. The plan for an international congress for mechanics in Germany could be sold to the Aviation Ministry as a necessity for productive aircraft research. The exclusion of Jews would, Prandtl argued, jeopardize the congress. In the end, these plans failed, because the ministry of education was not willing to admit Jews unconditionally to the congress. Jewish members of the GAMM were excluded by 1938, formally on the basis of unpaid dues.

The GAMM was forced to give up much of its international relations. The combined disciplines of mechanics and applied mathematics, however, gained resources and status from the demand for their products and their competence. There were fairly few problems of integration into the Nazi system. Scientific internationalism appears as a professional value motivating resistance against political adaptation but it fell victim to the racist and imperialist politics of Nazi Germany.

The problem of analysis in this case has been merely touched upon. Viewed from the system of mathematics, the mechanics Prandtl represented is a different, and competing discipline. But applied mathematics had neither an autonomous social organization nor the cognitive core for a clear disciplinary identity. In the course of the foundation of the GAMM, Richard von Mises, the applied mathematician, formulated the identity of the field in terms of 'practical needs'.[21] Applied mathematics thus is much more dependent on the demand for its products. The lack of cognitive coherence has to be compensated for by stronger integration into its market environment. The combination with mechanics and thus with aircraft research turned out to be the best option during the thirties. Like the MR, the GAMM was an institution on the margin of the social system of mathematics, mediating influences and interests in both directions.

For a fairly complete survey of the social system of mathematics in Nazi Germany, the situation during the war should be analyzed. The empirical basis is, as yet, too small. It should just be noted here that matters of mathematics education lost prominence while application and applicability dominated disciplinary politics. Such politics were possible and promising after 1942, when the time of quick victories was over. Structures and functions of the disciplinary system remained basically unchanged but were obviously conditioned by the war. The new possibilities and the poor general organization of military research and development led to more and sharper conflicts within the discipline. Different groups and institutions cooperated and competed with wholly selfish interests, bound together mainly by a common fear of the end. The president of the DMV, who was re-elected in 1937 after a change in the statutes, became head of the newly founded mathematics branch of the Reich Research Council and managed to raise considerable funds for applied basic research. He was involved in calling mathematicians back into the institutes from military service, and finally even succeeded in creating a national research institute for mathematics which became a refuge for many mathematicians during the last months of the war and thereafter. This success was possible through close cooperation with many Nazi officials, including involvement in the creation of a mathematical institute in a concentration camp where scientific slave lavour was exploited.[22]

Conclusion

Mathematics was integrated into the social and political system of Nazi Germany. Specificity was the integrative mode for this society that was disintegrating and in which terror, violence and fear were the most important social bonds. I have hardly touched upon the problems of individual and social psychology involved in the understanding of this period. How, for example, were mathematicians able to blindfold themselves to the suffering of their Jewish friends and colleagues? This is an important question since the social system of mathematics was able to survive with the loss of some twenty to thirty per cent of its members as long as this remained tolerable to the remaining mathematicians. In fact, there are only very few cases of mathematicians who emigrated or isolated themselves because of this experience. From the point of view of the social system of mathematics, this is a question of environment relations. The mathematician as an individual (as a psychic system) is part of his environment. This dissociation of the individual scientist from the system of the discipline is certainly an unsolved theoretical problem in the sociology of science, but it appears as a very useful move for the (theoretically eclectic) historian to solve some of the historiographical problems involved in the present subject.

Rather, the social system in which individuals play their various roles is the perspective of this paper. Fear, opportunism and partial identification with Nazi politics have certainly been integrative forces on the mathematics system acting through the individuals. Further there was the move of the radical attack from revolutionary students and from Bieberbach pressing the system to seek cooperation with those blocks of power in which bureaucratic or technocratic rationality persisted (for example in ministerial bureaucracy or the Aviation Ministry). For such movements the social systems of the discipline preferred individuals who would manage the balance between adaptation and defense of the system's identity, as in the Prandtl–Trefftz case. There was also the offer of intensified technical development, to which mathematics reacted by enlarging its applied subsystem and by restructuring its educational functions.

Looking for the conditions of adaptability we find in the three professional associations a functional variance. The MR was largely in charge of the educational legitimation of the discipline. It fulfilled its task by deeply bowing to the new powers and following the main trends in the associated teaching profession. This submission to the political powers did not jeopardize any central necessities of survival of the discipline, since it had little to do with the system of knowledge production and was a purely national organization. The MR's declaration of loyalty, visibly coming from the closest vicinity of the DMV, relieved the latter from political pressure and gave the chance to defend the discipline against the radical Bieberbach. The fact that Hamel, the head of the MR, became the compromise president of the DMV after the resignation of Bieberbach and the former president is an expression of this relation.

The DMV represented all of mathematics, centred around its pure core. It declared its loyalty in a fairly strong way when it reached the compromise with the ministry. That meant some politicking since afterwards disciplinary identity and the borderlines of the system were less rigid. At the same time new possibilities of legitimation by utility opened up. The DMV, together with the MR, concentrated on the educational task, that is, on the production of mathematical competence to be applied in other social systems thus preserving the autonomy and legitimacy of pure mathematics as the indispensible basis for such competence. Since this went beyond the traditional task of the MR, the DMV took over much of the disciplinary policy involved, even more when the president was made re-electable in order to be politically efficient. And the then permanent president up to the end of the war worked in the interest of the survival of mathematics as a pure but applicable discipline.

The production of applied mathematics, that is of knowledge oriented towards specific tasks outside mathematics, was largely represented in the GAMM. This work could be easily identified with immediately visible development of technology in aircraft production, a technology which was an obvious means and expression of power. Thus there was a specific relation to Nazi ideology that made things easy for the GAMM. In its defense of international communication, the GAMM not only fought for its institutional status and its productivity but also presented visibly the necessities of scientific production for all of mathematics to the political powers.

Finally the Bieberbach group in Berlin has to be seen within this view of functional integration. Mathematicians, with the help of the ministry, managed to deprive Bieberbach of any substantial influence. But they were not interested in eliminating his influence completely; rather there were certain fields of cooperation. Large parts of traditional Nazi ideology became residual and had little to do with the social and economic realities of the country. They persisted however in providing an integrating function for the Nazi movement and its claim to complete power. The Bieberbach group related mathematics to that element of the Nazi system and kept for some time its role as an ideological showcase and stage. It lost that role only late in the war.

The variations of status and functions within the system of mathematics corresponded to variations in the definition of cognitive identity. To describe this in any detail again is an open problem. It is obvious, however, that the core function of this identity, namely to handle the difference to the environment and to preserve and, if necessary, adapt borderlines, remained with pure mathematics. The toleration of the Bieberbach group appears as such a temporary adaptation of the borderline. The existence of a stage for the Bieberbach type of deviance was necessary in this society. It remained, however, potentially dangerous to modern professional identity. This is part of the explanation for the fact that after the war Bieberbach was the only productive mathematician who never found a university position again. He became the symbol for Nazi deviance in mathematics while the disciplinary politicians of the field, despite their intense collaboration with the Nazi system, remained honoured representatives of German mathematics.

Finally I would like to address the question of the political meaning of this account. The Nazi experience has been used frequently to argue that natural science and mathematics are inherently democratic. I am afraid this is not the case. There is a tendency towards political liberalism inherent in the double function of international communication as being a condition of productivity as well as of autonomy in face of national powers. But the sciences are dependent on national societies for their material existence. They will adapt to political and social changes as long as there is the chance to preserve existence. The irrational, regressive side of German fascism was an existential danger to mathematics. Its technocratic, imperialist side, however, was compatible enough with the survival of the discipline. Mathematics offered a means of technological advancement, for instance by producing the aerodynamical theory and the calculational means for the V2 rocket, and it could offer means of social control (for example in the statistics of inheritance). And mathematicians did offer these services without becoming outcasts of the discipline. On the contrary, they also found a market with the victorious powers, immediately after the war.

Cognitive and social universality together with social differentiation of the system were the basis for survival of the discipline under extreme political and social changes. Universality makes the products saleable to any political power interested in new means of power. Social differentiation takes care of adaptive functions and at the same time ensures that individual moral or political aims will not jeopardize the existence of the system. As long as it is possible, the disciplinary system exchanges its products, loyalty and political neutrality, for material resources and legitimacy from its environment. I cannot find any reason why mathematics, and any other science, should not find a perfect partner in technocratic fascism. Except, perhaps, because of the need of such regimes to use means of social control that tend to destabilize social subsystems. It is this observation which makes the origins and power structures of the Third Reich more interesting and more important as a subject of further research in the history and sociology of science than the analysis of the obvious deviance in Bieberbach's 'Aryan' mathematics.

15 | The problem of anti-Fascist[1] resistance of 'apolitical' German scholars

REINHARD SIEGMUND-SCHULTZE

Several authors[2] have pointed out that concepts such as 'resistance', 'opposition' and 'nonconformity', applied to the political behavior of people in Nazi Germany, are themselves problematic and difficult to delimit from each other. This chapter does not pretend to solve this problem concerning the behaviour of scholars.[3] It uses these concepts in a rather vague sense, putting emphasis on examples mainly taken from mathematics and natural sciences. Before discussing these examples, the chapter outlines in its first two parts some historical roots of political behaviour of scholars under the special conditions found in Germany.

Scholarship (including natural and social sciences as well as the humanities) has become a political issue of paramount importance to the economy, military affairs and the production of ideology in the modern industrial society. However, the individual scholar is rarely politically active in a wider sense and, if involved at all, generally confines himself to politics pertaining to the interests of his profession. This is especially true of the natural and technical sciences, whose productivity and, therefore, the political function the ruling ideology requires it to fulfil, depends to a great extent on the 'unpolitical behaviour' of their representatives.[4]

A detailed discussion of the historical roots of this dominant pattern of behaviour of the 'unpolitical' scholar, impossible within the limited scope of this article, would have to consider the changes in the profession and the attitude of the scholars towards it, as well as the shifts between educational and research functions of the scientist, the ramifications for the internal and external structures of science, and the modifications of the criteria and values of research as well as of the public understanding of science which have taken place in the past 150 years.

312

(1)   Determinants of political behaviour for scholars

I should, however, like to point out *three determinants of the political behaviour of scholars*: the professional politics of the social subsystem of science; the obligations it has to the national culture and its devotion to political authorities; and the special interests of particular scientific disciplines.

The political behaviour of scholars in history has to be assessed primarily against the background of the fact that they were predominantly interested in the continuation of science and in the maintenance or the improvement of their working conditions. Social and political problems of a more general character (structure of political rule, international relations, military questions, treatment of religions and minorities, social problems) were and are being judged in general from a restricted horizon of social experience and, moreover, from the 'amoral' (*moralfrei*) point of view of their utility to science. Abstract principles and 'higher values' such as 'truth', 'impartiality', 'the internationality and universality of science', 'freedom' and 'equality', which in part are guiding principles within science and belong to the 'ethos of science' (though a critical and historically based sociology of science has shown the relativity of these criteria even in research) seldom determine political actions outside the sphere of science. Scholars often stress the general validity of these principles, but they seldom demand more than a selective realization of them, the selection being determined by the group interests of the scholars. A good example in this respect is the discussion of the notion of 'freedom of science' in Nazi Germany and the post-war years. Whilst in Nazi Germany the word 'freedom' was loaded with negative connotations such as 'liberalism' and 'democracy', scholars and even Nazi functionaries of science (for example Bernhard Rust) stressed the importance of the 'freedom of science' if complemented by 'national bonds and aims' ('*nationale Gebundenheit*').[5] After the war American scientists (for example Samuel Goudsmit) used the general condemnation of political suppression in Nazi Germany to trace the failure of the German atomic project back to the lack of a 'freedom of science'. This was an ahistorical simplification originating from the fact that American scientists wanted to loosen the regulations of secrecy which governed American military research.[6]

The demand for social equality – to mention another example of the interdependence of political behaviour and personal interests – met with resistance from scholars under the monarchy and the Weimar Republic insofar as the relative rise of the working classes was seen by them as a threat to their own social position.[7]

The internationality of science, which even on the cognitive level was not indisputable because of the existence of national scientific schools, was called into question even more by social and political loyalties (cf. below).

Where the traditional 'ethos of science' came into conflict with public life (superficiality and demagogy in the press, blaring publicity in politics and advertising campaigns), scholars felt repelled and 'alienated' rather than politivally motivated. They developed an often elitist and cynical relationship to 'the evils of the modern mass society', thus becoming 'unpolitical' – though not renouncing the politics immediately concerned with their discipline.[8]

These last remarks illustrate the fact that the political behaviour of scholars cannot be deduced merely from the criteria of research and the production of knowledge within their social subsystem. Being 'citizens' at the same time, the scholars and their interests are linked with other groups of society. A second problem arises as well: how does this dichotomy of scholar and citizen influence the political behaviour of scholars? The only kind of behaviour of immediate importance to the history of science is that, which is the result of one of those two determinants or of a mutual reinforcement or weakening of the scholars' scientific and social interests. Certainly there were individual cases of resistance by scholars against Nazi dictatorship which were caused by religious or 'purely humane' reasons (for example aid given to threatened fellow-citizens) and had nothing to do with the scholars' profession or with their social position as citizens. However, if the authority of the respective scholar and the effects of his behaviour on the public and the scientific community are taken into account, then such actions are of indirect importance for the history of science.

Wolfgang Abendroth, in his well-known article 'The unpolitical as a characteristic feature of the German university' (1966), pointed to the dual determination of the political behaviour of German scholars, both as citizens and as scientists, during the past hundred years.[9] Abendroth, who in this paper also had the reality of the then Federal Republic of Germany in mind, mentioned the unsuccessful bourgeois revolution of 1848–9 and the subsequent compromise between bourgeoisie and aristocracy as roots of the ideology of unpolitical behaviour. If we intend to specify the '*Weltanschauung*' (world view) of scholars, then we have to consider the congruities and the conflicts between the ideology of the scholar as a citizen and the ideology which is internal to science.[10]

The reception of the social and scientific aspects of the modern age, which was beginning to look increasingly contradictory around 1900, together with the discussion of the notion of 'progress', had far-reaching effects on the *Weltanschauung* of scholars.[11] Occasionally historians have oversimplified the situation by postulating a contradictory combination of social pessimism and scientific optimism among scholars of that time.[12] This interpretation certainly reflects the double determination of the scholars mentioned above, but it does not take into account the complexity of the mutual accommodation between scientific and social *Weltanschauung*.

The patterns of argumentation were developed at the beginning of this century, which supported the autonomy of science against political interference and determined the political behaviour of scholars under the conditions of the twenties and thirties, which were much more dangerous to science. Fritz K. Ringer has described this process with regard to social scientists in Germany, who reacted to the process of modernization by accentuating the academic traditions and rituals, centring *Weltanschauung* around the notion of '*Bildung*' (education), and emphasizing the role of scholars as 'civil servants'.[13]

In view of the substantial growth of natural and technical sciences in modern industrial society, a third question arises: how did different interests and social functions of different scientific disciplines influence the political behaviour and the *Weltanschauung* of their representatives? While it is not surprising that German social sciences and humanities experienced an adjustment of the scientific and general political convictions of their representatives, this is not so clear for the natural and technical sciences. Jeffrey Herf has shown, however, that the German technical scientists and engineers of the first third of this century aimed at glorifying technology, not only as their scientific work, but also as a cultural value in a conservative sense, while at the same time, they were often afraid of its social consequences.[14] Finally Paul Forman has established and made plausible the thesis that even some cognitive processes in the natural sciences of the twenties (for example, abandonment of strong deterministic causality in physics) were fostered by the scientists' conservative political convictions and by their willingness to accommodate themselves to any overriding interests they had in common with the humanities and social sciences.[15] However, one should not dispute the fact that different disciplines had different potentialities for resistance or collaboration according to their respective functions within the system. This is particularly true for Nazi Germany.

(2)   The strategy of the 'unpolitical scholar' under five German political systems

The works of Brigitte Schroeder-Gudehus and Paul Forman on the boycott of science in the twenties have made clear that, in cases of conflict between 'pure scientific interest' and national cultural, political and scientific traditions, the latter generally prevailed.[16] This is true of the following five quite different German political systems: the monarchy, the Weimar Republic, Nazi Germany, the Federal Republic of Germany, and the German Democratic Republic (GDR). It is therefore quite probable that the radical political changes in Germany in the past hundred years contributed to the development of the strategy of 'unpolitical behaviour' on the part of scholars, which seemed to be the most promising and safest strategy.

Under the Kaiser (but *before* the beginning of World War I), and in the Federal Republic of Germany, conflicts between pure scientific and social interests had been kept at a low level, not least because of the expansion of the social systems of science and the relatively favourable material conditions the sciences enjoyed. Nevertheless, even under these systems some scholars were ousted in spite of excellent scientific achievements if they dared to criticize society in too fundamental a manner (social democrats such as Leo Arons under the monarchy, communists in the Federal Republic) or did not satisfy certain social conventions (Jews under the monarchy).

Even the Weimar Republic cannot be considered a counter-example in this respect, though this 'republic without republicans' played a special role and represented a transitional system. The solidarity of professors against the 'system of Weimar' (cf. below) did not conform with the 'interest of science', but aimed at the restoration of the old privileges of the monarchy.

Under such extreme historical circumstances there were even attacks from some scientists on what Paul Forman has called the 'leading proposition in the ideology of scientific internationalism': the assertion of the universality of science.[17] Attacks came in 1914 predominantly from the French side ('*science allemande*').[18] In 1933 such attacks from the Nazi ideologues ('*Deutsche Physik*', '*Deutsche Mathematik*') were supported by some scientists of authority.[19] At the same time, and under extreme social conditions continuing until the fifties, there was interference by incompetent ideologues with the purely scientific discussion in the Soviet Union (Lysenkoism, 'idealism' debate in mathematics, cybernetics discussion),[20] whose after-effects even reached the German Democratic Republic.[21]

In Germany the Nazi and SED systems (SED, *Sozialistische Einheitspartei Deutschlands*, the Communist party in East Germany) defined the notion of the 'political' and of 'political activity' so strongly in the sense of 'ideological' that many scholars considered the traditional ideal of 'unpolitical science' to be a virtue, and adhering to it seemed an act of resistance. This is not to deny the fundamental differences in the political aims of both systems and in their attitudes towards science. Certainly the GDR leaders did not propagandize racial discrimination and war, and science was officially held in high esteem, contrary to its ambivalent status in Nazi Germany. But the mechanisms of the accommodation of GDR scholars were very similar to those in Nazi Germany.

In the course of the relative political stabilization in both systems, direct political interference into the scientific discussion ceased, at least in mathematics and the physical sciences. In Nazi Germany the 'revolution of science', which was propagandized by some Nazi ideologues (Alfred Rosenberg, Ernst Krieck), did not take place. In any case the propagation of this revolution had been predominantly a means of political coordination. In most sciences such propaganda would now be rather dangerous for the system itself – although ideological interference in some cases[22] proved 'fruitful' even for the disciplines.

In both the Nazi and GDR systems the decrease of political interference into the scientific discussion did not mean, however, that the demand for 'political activity' of scholars disappeared. But this demand was now rather a means to distract scholars and the public from the real situation of science and to give some scientists an excuse for perceived deficiencies. Moreover, if one was prepared to use officially sanctioned vocabulary, then one was considered a 'political scholar', although because of such self-delusion one understood the political importance of science less and less. There was undoubtedly a process of feedback in the course of time between activity (especially speaking) and thinking as described with reference to Nazi Germany by the mathematician Kurt Reidemeister:

> The general consequence of the infiltration of Nazi ideology was that one gradually abandoned the truth. The people in the National Socialist state in no way believed the officially sanctioned tenets taught in so many indoctrination courses and in so many papers. But they were willing to use the official vocabulary thoughtlessly.[23]

In the SED state politicization, in the sense of the ideology of the rulers, penetrated the scientific community to a much greater extent than in the Nazi state. Some of the many reasons for this are the much longer history of the GDR and the more homogeneous, in a certain sense even more 'totalitarian' (but certainly much less criminal!) structure of that system, but also the self-assessment of the GDR as the legitimate 'anti-Fascist' state, which ironically led to some similarities with Nazi Germany. That part of the motivation for politicization which stemmed from science itself was greatly dependent on the particular discipline and altogether contradictory.[24]

(3)   Patterns of political behaviour in Nazi Germany

After the National Socialists had seized power in 1933 they intended step by step to make all Germans accomplices in their crimes against minorities, in the brutal suppression of dissidents and in their preparations for war.

Active social engagement, or solidarity with other social groups for common aims, was not traditionally within the scope of German scholars. This is true of the majority of emigrants as well as of most scholars remaining in Germany. Conscious political resistance in an organized clandestine way, as was the case with the Berlin and Munich groups named 'Rote Kapelle' (Red Chapel) and 'Weisse Rose' (White Rose), was exceptional. Only a few scholars were involved, undergraduate students being in the majority.

Wolfgang Abendroth, in his article mentioned above, cited a passage from Thomas Mann's 'Reflections of an Unpolitical Man' (1918), in which he stated that 'the German people cannot love political democracy, simply because they cannot love politics itself'.

Certainly Thomas Mann's declaration was in accordance also with the vast majority of scholars. Although Thomas Mann himself, along with 'rational republicans' ('*Vernunftrepublikaner*') such as the historian Friedrich Meinecke, changed their views in what was for them a long and painful process, the overwhelming majority of German scholars, particularly the civil servants at the universities and technical colleges, remained, ideologically speaking, in the trenches of World War I. There was a fundamental consensus that the 'system of Weimar' had been forced on the German people by the 'November criminals' ('*Novemberverbrecher*') and by the 'shameful peace' ('*Schmachfrieden*') of Versailles.[25]

Considering themselves 'unpolitical', the German scholars rejected governmental interference in the fictitious autonomy of the universities as 'political'. They condemned leftist deviations from that 'fundamental consensus' by individual scholars such as Emil Julius Gumbel and Theodor Lessing. There was, however, a different attitude towards left-wing and right-wing deviations. Right-wing radicals, such as the mathematician Theodor Vahlen[26] and the physicists and Nobel prize-winners Philipp Lenard and Johannes Stark, were tolerated with regard to their general political convictions and condemned only because of political interference in the purely scientific discussion (e.g. the '*Anti-Einstein-Liga*').

It was that 'fundamental consensus' which contributed to the destruction of the Weimar Republic and promoted the rise of Fascism. Moreover it was that fundamental consensus and connected widespread militaristic thinking[27] which also were still alive in the years of the Nazi regime and were demagogically exploited in the preparations for war. The beginning of the war in 1939, for instance, saw a nationalist fraternization of politically moderate German mathematicians with exponents of the regime such as the mathematician Ludwig Bieberbach.[28] In 1941 Nazi officials integrated scientists into Fascist plans for the 'reconstruction' of European science, demagogically using the boycott of German science in the early twenties as an excuse.[29] In 1938 the statistician Gumbel wrote in exile:

> The nationalist-minded professors were disgusted with the limitations of their personal freedom. They disapprove of much that is being done in the Third Reich. But they do agree with the central imperialist goal of the present German rulers, and they therefore accept a lot into the bargain. The minority of liberal-minded lecturers is forced into silence.[30]

The brutal and anti-intellectual Fascist 'coordination' ('*Gleichschaltung*') of universities and technical colleges in 1933 certainly shocked the majority of German scholars. The 'idea of a political university', propagandized by Nazi philosophers such as Alfred Baeumler and Ernst Krieck, contradicted widespread convictions of the university's role as a 'refuge for pure science'. But soon it became evident that 'unpolitical' German scholars were unable to cope with the demagogy of the Nazis as well as with their tactics to play different academic groups off against each other (students and professors, assistants and professors). The homogeneity of the university, which had been a basis of resistance to the Weimar Republic, was broken. Resistance in the sense of academic group solidarity against the introduction of the Fascist 'leader principle' ('*Führerprinzip*') was partially successful only in those scientific associations which were of minor importance for the regime.[31]

The expulsion of leading scientists from the German universities and technical colleges generally met with a minimum of resistance. There were some petitions to the Fascist ministry of culture in favour of displaced colleagues (Wilhelm Blaschke for Kurt Reidemeister, Helmut Hasse for Emmy Noether). However, courageous public protest like that of the Göttingen physicist James Franck[32] was exceptional, also owing to the fact that the Nazi monopoly of the press greatly reduced any opportunities for public resistance.

The majority of scholars as well as other citizens were influenced by the diabolic anti-Semitic demagogy, which produced the egoistic feeling of being secure, of belonging to a privileged 'race'.[33] Moreover, the economic circumstances of German science around the time of 1933 (there was widespread academic unemployment) did not encourage solidarity with dismissed scholars.

Finally, there were only a few expulsions which were not based on racist 'arguments' but were otherwise politically motivated, since liberal and left-wing scholars had been kept away from the universities in the Weimar Republic. Political expulsions – insofar as they were not directed against so-called 'reactionaries' – therefore rather confirmed a certain identity of the interests of the regime with those of 'unpolitical' scholars.

Of course, many scholars were afraid of the international consequences of these expulsions, which damaged the prestige of German science abroad as well as international communication. The intensity of this fear corresponded to the degree of internationality of the respective discipline. As a matter of fact the problem of international relations bore in itself a latent potential for resistance, although in many respects modified by additional convictions the 'unpolitical' scholars may have held.

The problem of the losses caused by emigration was made a taboo subject in the years to come. Even in some critical memoirs concerning the situation in science (cf. below) there was no mention of this at all. The problem of emigration was so inseparably connected with officially sanctioned anti-semitism that criticism seemed useless from the very beginning. It was even considered an unheard-of event when the Dutch mathematician and professor at the university of Leipzig, B. L. Van Der Waerden, published a commemorative article[34] – though in the exclusiveness of a mathematical journal – for his teacher Emmy Noether, who had died in exile in 1935. Some sober-minded scholars may have regarded belated criticism of the expulsions as futile. Obviously there was also not enough political imagination around to foresee the further aggravation of anti-Semitism and campaigns leading to expulsion which actually were to come.

Certain strategies were used by the scientists to adapt the sciences to the regime and to eliminate moral considerations. The aerodynamicist Ludwig Prandtl spoke of the 'needs of the discipline', thus accepting the exclusion of Jewish scientists from the 'Society for Applied Mathematics and Mechanics'.[35] The geometer Wilhelm Blaschke considered 'service to the people and the state through a cultivation of science' as the main 'goal of the university'.[36] Moreover, he saw mathematics as a tool for the 'selection of our students', thus following the trend of using pseudo-biological phrases.

Mathematics, the applications of which are mainly transmitted via other disciplines, was under particular pressure to accommodate itself. It had to legitimate itself above all as an educational subject, while the educational system was dominated by the Fascist state. The *Mathematischer Reichsverband* (Reich Mathematical Union, henceforth MR), founded in 1921, was responsible for the school politics of the German mathematicians. Herbert Mehrtens[37] has shown how the functional ramifications of the system of mathematics enabled the majority of German mathematicians to continue their research unperturbed by any moral considerations in the shadow of submissiveness by the MR. In the anthology published by the MR 'Mathematics in the Service of National Political Education' (1935),[38] and in many mathematical school books of that time, exercises and problems were posed that amounted to the propagation of euthanasia and Fascist hegemony and thereby the dissemination of Nazi ideology. The leader (*Führer*) of the MR, Georg Hamel, even invented an 'intellectual congeniality of mathematics and the Third Reich'.[39]

Unlike the taboo in the case of the expulsion problem there were many other opportunities to discuss and criticize the effects of the National Socialist university reform on the quality of teaching and research. The regime was indeed interested in political indoctrination, but also in the rational control of science and technology for a future war. This duality of interests, as well as the well-known competence struggles within the Nazi system, made it possible for critical discussions to take place, like those that had been carried out in journals such as *'Der Biologe'* (*'The Biologist'*) and even in *'Militärisches Wochenblatt'* (*'Military Weekly'*) since the mid-thirties. There were discussions – veiled in National Socialist vocabulary – of the low standard of instruction in schools, as well as warnings against an impending shortage of qualified scientific manpower in industry, the military and universities.

Private memoirs such as those of the Dresden profesor of technology
W. Guertler (1940) addressed to Hitler,[40] and of the Berlin engineer
J. Rasch (1941) to the *Reichsforschungsrat* (Reich Research Council)[41]
deplored the gradual decline of German technology and engineering
mathematics compared with developments in America. Guertler demanded
a reduction in the political distractions for students, whereas Rasch asked
for editions of up-to-date mathematical function tables. Rasch's report
was to be a starting point for Wilhelm Süss, the chairman of the German
Mathematicians' Association, in his successful efforts to obtain a department of mathematics in the *Reichsforschungsrat* and a *Mathematisches
Reichsinstitut* (Imperial mathematical institute), which was founded in the
last months of the war. It was also Süss who, at a conference of university
rectors in Salzburg in 1943, drew a merciless picture of the state of German
science, especially in the field of pure research.[42] One cannot claim, therefore, that the rulers did not receive enough information from the scientists
about the waning strength of German science.

At a very early stage, in a paper read in November 1933, the Rostock
mathematician Gerhard Thomsen, who was a pupil of Blaschke, warned
against the 'danger of pushing back the exact sciences at schools and
universities'. Even Thomsen used National Socialist vocabulary, defending
fundamental science with the argument that also 'the whole theory of an
improvement of our race . . . presupposes a long-term process of at least one
hundred years'.[43] Thomsen did not call the Fascist rearmament policy into
question:

> We need the sports fields and drill grounds of brain training and con-
> centration schooling for the intellectual special soldiers of the Third
> Reich. We must realize, that in a future war an ingenious brain, which
> invents new weapons, can be more valuable than a thousand soldiers.[44]

Being a representative of the so-called exact sciences, Thomsen made an
even more fundamental criticism in his speech. Alluding to the National
Socialist university reform he remarked: 'This affects almost exclusively the
humanities, we as natural scientists are not concerned'.[45] And Thomsen
added as early as November 1933:

> The effectively revolutionary period of the National Socialist movement
> has ended. One of the most important tasks of the second period, which is
> now beginning, is to educate that part of the German people which can be
> used for special work to further the cause of the fatherland, for mental
> concentration on that work.[46]

This passage should be understood as a severe criticism from a conservative point of view of the Fascist methods of wielding power. Since political
activity in the Nazi sense was to be a prerequisite of a career for students of
science and young scientists as well in the years to come, it seems to be

exactly this passage in Thomsen's speech which crossed the borderline. There are strong indications[47] that Thomsen's suicide eight weeks later, on 4 January 1934, was connected with his speech of November 1933.

As a matter of fact the ideologically laden atmosphere, and with it the 'revolutionary period of the National Socialist movement' at the universities, was far from over in 1933. That atmosphere was one of several reasons for halving the student body between 1933 and 1939 and for the resulting problems with scientific manpower. Those losses often proved to be to the advantage of the army, which was wrongly considered by many as being 'ideologically clean'. However, the flight of many promising young scientists from the politically suppressive universities and technical colleges was often to the benefit of institutions for armaments research, which some scientists perceived as 'oases of freedom of opinion'.[48] Those losses should not be connected with political resistance. Rather one acquires a deeper understanding of the role and consequences of National Socialist ideology and politics with regard to the universities.

Even the refusal of the majority of scientists to accept the infiltration of '*Deutsche Physik*' (Aryan physics), '*Deutsche Mathematik*' (Aryan mathematics) and other abstruse derivatives of the National Socialist race doctrine into the scientific discussion cannot automatically be judged as political resistance. Insofar as scientists such as Werner Heisenberg and Oskar Perron turned to the public with their criticisms, this was certainly a mark of courage. Looking back today, however, one has to realize that pure 'professional resistance' of that kind was unable to trouble the regime, which gave those racist theories less support when science was needed for rearmament. Contrary to this conclusion, the discussion in the fifties and sixties in the Federal Republic of Germany contributed to the restoration of the ideal of the 'unpolitical scientist' by pointing to professional resistance in Nazi Germany. As we read in a history of Heidelberg Universities:[49]

> Ironically many German scientists after the defeat of Nazi Germany revived one of the central assertions of 'German physics': the thesis that a purely professional attitude was opposition against Fascism. This thesis is altogether wrong. The attacks of Lenard, Stark and others against professional physicists such as Heisenberg seemed to be dangerous to a certain extent, but they did not find support from the Fascist state in the long run.

It must certainly be added that '*Deutsche Physik*', '*Deutsche Mathematik*' and so on, had a function within the system at least until the mid-thirties, providing a pseudo-argument for expelling the Jewish lectures, preventing scientists from more serious kinds of protest and reconciling them with 'moderate' representatives of state bureaucracy.

Let me make some concluding remarks about the discussion of the resistance problem in both German states after 1945. In the Federal Republic of Germany the restoration of the ideal of 'unpolitical science' was connected with the rearmament discussion, with an uncritical reference to the traditions of Weimar, and with regard to living scientists. This restoration forsook a thorough examination of those problems at least until the end of the sixties. Since the eighties there has been a renaissance of these discussions in Western Germany, frequently inspired by burning problems such as the responsibility of scientists for the social and political consequences of modern science and technology.

In the German Democratic Republic the notion of 'anti-Fascism' was for a long time monopolized by the Communist party and the 'working class'. The political behaviour of the intelligentsia did not meet with much interest unless it was of a decidedly pro-Communist or pro-Fascist kind. Both the apparent yet misleading, as well as the obvious and real historical parallels between the structures of and the adaptation processes to the Nazi and SED systems also hindered the historiography of science. Furthermore, there was no critical examination of 'progressive science' itself, partly owing to the fact that GDR science and technology lagged behind its western rival to a great extent.

After the unification of Germany, there should certainly be a much broader discussion of the political function of science and its representatives, a discussion which is no longer disturbed by the mutual demarcation strategies of two German states.

16 Irresponsible purity: the political and moral structure of mathematical sciences in the National Socialist state[1]

HERBERT MEHRTENS

In April 1934 a brief correspondence was documented in the Parisian newspaper for German emigrants:[2]

> It concerns the response of the professor for mathematics in Berlin, Bieberbach, who earlier was a very respected scholar, but whose intellectual achievement today merely consists of work on the theme 'Mathematics and Race'. The correspondence began with a letter by Professor E. J. Gumbel, who previously taught in Heidelberg.
>
> From your letter I see that I am still a member of the *Deutschen-Mathematiker-Vereinigung* [German Mathematicians Association, henceforth DMV]. Since this organization, despite its statutes, has offered no resistance to the destruction of German science, I hasten to give up my membership and am only sorry that through ignorance I had not already done it earlier. E. J. Gumbel.
>
> As an answer to the pleasing letter to Herrn H. ...: Goetz von Berlichingen.[3] What do *you* know about *German* science? Bieberbach.
>
> I confirm the receipt of your displeasing letter and in the interest of the prestige of science, regret not being able to answer in the same neo-German swineherd tone. E. J. Gumbel.

Two extremes meet here, under the conditions of German Fascism in power, the exiled mathematical statistician and decisively pacifist Emil Julius Gumbel, and Ludwig Bieberbach, *Ordinarius* (full professor) for mathematics in Berlin, since 1933 adherent of National Socialism and propagandist of an '*arteigene*' (racially characteristic) German mathematics.[4] The great majority of German scientists took a position between these radical extremes in the attempt to accommodate themselves to the circumstances and keep their science 'pure'.[5]

Gumbel is especially known for his analysis of justice during the Weimar Republic. In 1931 he published a documentation of Fascist

324

murders since 1924 and drew the following conclusion:[6] 'Fascism shows its true face in these bloody crimes. It shows to the German people the methods it will use, if it comes to power.' Through such analyses, Gumbel incurred the hatred of the political Right. After he was named *Extra-ordinarius* (tenured, but not fully professor, and in this case poorly paid) in Heidelberg with great delay, his university withdrew his right to teach as early as 1932. Together with Albert Einstein and Julius Schaxel, he represented the sciences in the first expatriation list by the National Socialists. He wrote the first, and still valuable analysis of mathematics in the National Socialist state, which appeared in the book he edited in 1940.[7]

During the same years, Bieberbach became acting Vice-Chancellor of the University of Berlin and Dean of his faculty. His attempt to advance to '*Führer*' (leader) of the DMV failed in 1935. In order to create an institutional centre for 'nationalist-inclined' mathematics, in 1936 he began editing the journal *Deutsche Mathematik* ('German Mathematics'). He was amongst the few German professors who never regained a position after 1945.[8]

Symbols in collective memory

What these two extremes have in common is that the people concerned took public political positions and connected them with their science. But only Bieberbach is present in the memory of mathematics. Every mathematician knows of him and his 'Aryan Mathematics'. The name *Bieberbach* has become a symbol for the bad politicization of mathematics, similar to the names *Lenard* and *Stark* for physics and *Lysenko* for biology. Such symbols have their place in unofficial discussion, in what mathematicians call their folklore. In the official portion, where the discipline presents itself as science, they do not appear. Mathematics does not remember Gumbel, either officially or unofficially.

The journal of the DMV, the *Jahresbericht*, hardly poor when it comes to obituaries, has none for Gumbel, with the exception of the collective representation by Pinl, which only discusses Gumbel's mathematical activity.[9] Of course, Bieberbach is remembered:[10]

> He belongs to those personalities who have influenced the picture of mathematics in Germany throughout many decades of our century ... So it is proper that his work as a mathematician be remembered in the *Jahresbericht*. The clouding of the image of his personality through his unfortunate political aberrations during the National Socialist period changes nothing in this regard. This is not the place to discuss these matters ...

The official memory safeguards the person 'as mathematician', for other matters 'this is not the place', political or moral criteria play no role. 'As mathematician' Bieberbach is worth remembering, Gumbel is not. The collective memory of sciences – not only mathematics – produces the picture of the *pure* scientist.

Responsibility can be demanded only from individual people; for them moral judgments are meaningful. An institution or a social system has its ethics in the institutional arrangement and in the norms for language and conduct. Thus moral judgements of *science* or *mathematics* are meaningless. Instead, the question must be how science determines the self-image and conduct of the scientist. An ethics of science like that in vogue today, which considers norms, but thereby fails to scrutinize the enterprise of science itself and its connections to technology, politics and the economy in a historically educated manner, binds itself to the greatest possible impotence.

In 1979 Carl Friedrich von Weizsäcker called for 'reflections on the consequences of the second order for science'.[11] He mentioned drugs that 'heal illness and are therapeutic' as an example of the consequences of the first order. Effects of the second order would then be the undesired effects (side effects), including those that do not appear in the individual, rather in the '*Volksgesundheit*' (literally translated, 'public health'). As an aside, it should be noted that the primary goals of applied science are not always so clearly altruistic. One need only think of advertising psychology and military research. Moreover, here once again the showcase example of medicine is used, by which science identifies itself with one of the highest values of our society, the defense against sickness and death. It should also be noted that in this representative discussion by von Weizsäcker effects of null order, the science itself, is not a subject for debate.

'He who considers these effects of the second order, risks his career', says von Weizsäcker, this makes science into a 'calamity'. The scientists, on the other hand, strive towards 'knowledge', for which, and where, they are directly responsible. During a discussion at a large research institute, I have experienced how a scientist, who was partly responsible for a critical counter-Festschrift for the anniversary of the institute, was subtly but clearly threatened by the head of the institute. Anyone who uses his time in such a way, he was told, could hardly be a good scientist, because he is not concentrating sufficiently on his proper work. In a letter of recommendation such a statement can have a disastrous effect on a scientific career. In addition, up until that time the institute head had considered this individual to be a 'good scientist'. The reason for this threat was a controversy over the history and structure of the institute, in other words, over effects of the null order. The critical questioning of the enterprise of science and its portrayal in the official memory of the Festschrift is certainly dangerous for a career. Moreover, von Weizsäcker's observation need not lead only to the appeal to consider the consequences of the second order, rather also to the question of how such consideration can be hindered in the null order.

During a discussion of experts on a programme for the promotion of research in the history of science, a professor of biology, who had experience in this area, argued that it was irresponsible to encourage a young scientist to do work on the history of science under National Socialism. Such work would be 'scientific suicide'. In fact, political self-criticism on the activity and structure of scientific institutions is repulsed as strenuously as it can be, and not only when it concerns the most controversial historical themes. Instead of *pure* science, today the discussion is about *basic research*, and the arguments have become a shade more complex. However, the 'not-political' boundaries remain the same. As far as the history of science in the National Socialist state is concerned, during the last few decades some work has been done for the social and human sciences. For the natural sciences, however, there has been only one extensive, politically significant study, and that has come out of the USA.[12]

The collective memory of a discipline or a profession is part of its mythology, the framework of symbols and meanings, in which the common self-understanding, the social identity, is contained. Bieberbach is a negative symbol in the folklore of his discipline, whose justification is underscored through his recognition 'as mathematician'. The corresponding symbolic names for physics, Lenard and Stark, also have their place because, as it is routinely noted, both were Nobel laureates. These symbols contain the relationship between science and politics: the bogy-man, who causes fear and is defended against, is the one with scientific authority and bad politics. A counterpart, however, which would combine scientific authority and responsible politics, does not exist in this form. Gumbel would be suitable: an engaged and decisively political scientist who risked himself and his science, statistics. But he is forgotten. The explicit connection between science and politics is almost exclusively presented in stories which cause fear.

Thus a boundary is marked. He who goes beyond it, so the message goes, enters into danger, for which he cannot expect support from the institutions of his discipline. Only Albert Einstein appears suitable as a great symbol, as a scientific genius out of reach anyway, a mixture of the political and the symbolism of pure goals. Another scientist in the history of German physics who comes close to being a politically 'good' scientist is Max von Laue. There is no doubt that he deserves to be remembered for his upright stance, but his virtue was in fact caution. In 1933 he wrote to Einstein:[13] 'But why did you have to take a *political* stand? I am the last person to criticize you because of your opinions. The political struggle requires different methods and different natures than scientific research. As a rule, the scholar is crushed under the wheels.' Thus von Laue asserts the apolitical nature of the scholar. In the symbols the nature of science is fused with the nature of the scientist, and they are not allowed to have anything to do with politics. The danger is real, for in politics the true–false model, which is so easily combined with good–evil, does not hold.

Science as its own symbol

The concept of mathematics is itself a symbol through which the mathematician identifies himself. In the speech cited above, von Weizsäcker spoke of 'science' and 'knowledge' as if there could be no doubt what is meant. However, one of the most interesting books to appear during the past few years in science studies, a book in which the activities of scientists are observed very closely, replaces the concept *science* with *technoscience*.[14] The practice of the natural sciences is technoscience; *science* or *basic research* is imaginary, a standardized boundary and a symbol of identity. But the primary identification is the *discipline*, which does not bear this name for nothing.

In response to the question, what is mathematics?, there is no better answer than the usual: mathematics is what mathematicians do. Obviously one has to make this definition more precise, and a brief consideration leads to: mathematics is that which the mathematician does as mathematician. What mathematicians do, I can glean from the *Jahresbericht* of the DMV. However, I would thereby become afflicted with the partial amnesia of this caste. Mathematics defines itself in an extremely restrictive fashion. This is a core element of the problem: that to do mathematics, to be a mathematician, is identified exclusively by the process and result of reseach-oriented mental investigation of mathematical problems, thus turning mathematics – *mathematics proper* – into an apolitical and amoral matter.

This type of self-definition for scientific disciplines has a history, system and effect. Mathematics in this sense deals with abstract problems by means of abstract concepts and seeks solutions of general validity – a game played in an ivory tower, apparently without consequences and detached from the world. The research process for *pure* mathematics, which also plays a role in work oriented towards application, requires such an attitude: the mathematician must decidedly ignore non-mathematical consequences and possible concrete results in order to ensure the universal validity of his train of thought and conclusions. An epistemological excursion is needed here. Mathematics and mathematical theoretical science use specific methods of speech and thought, through which logical consistency, determinability, universality and translatability in principle can be ensured in technical thought and speech. Mathematical research is work on a symbolic language, whose symbols mean nothing other than the rules that have to be obeyed for their use. It is work on a language which can be mastered completely because it masters itself.[15]

Decisive in this regard is the separation of concepts from the world of things and actions. Theory consists (ideally) of a closed system of concepts which have nothing to do with the world outside of this structure. Thus the *proper* business of the mathematician occurs in an unreal world, which as such is without meaning or consequences for the real world. Here the researcher has responsibility only for the consistency of the world of concepts, the validity of the conclusions, the economy of linguistic construction. In a similar way, the experiment in physics is its own world. And even the scientist who aims at applications or technical products also knows these phases of work in the isolated world of linguistic or technical consistency and clarity. Indeed it is here that he experiences that he is a scientist. This separation is certainly comfortable, and for this reason the following question is discussed grudgingly or not at all: how nonetheless do mathematical theories not merely describe realities, but moreover alter and create them?

The self-definition and memory of mathematics force each mathematician to take his *proper* business more seriously than any other, thereby being optimally productive. The fact that science symbolizes itself with *knowledge*, which is its own world, has its function in its enterprise; in this way scientific productivity is ensured. At the same time, however, the other activities and connections are repressed – indeed also in a psychoanalytic sense. For example, the leading advocate of the political interests of mathematics (Wilhelm Süss) wrote the following in a report on pure mathematical research during the Second World War:[16]

> This report will demonstrate that, even in the period of this wretched war, the garden of the true scientific research could be tended in silence by its friends.

Atomic physicists, who had worked on the atomic bomb project, introduced their report with the following remark:[17]

> For the physicists of Germany, even during the war the will never slackened to do really good physics and not to allow the entanglements of personal fate to defile the purity of scientific knowledge (*Lauterkeit wissenschaftlichen Erkennens*).

Scientific knowledge is 'pure' and true research a 'silent garden:': apologetic protestations of purity. In opposition to this purity stand a 'wretched war' and the 'entanglements' of personal fate: formulations which deny responsibility. Such rhetorical figures can still be encountered today, identification with the *proper* profession of the scientist offers a symbol of purity that can be so effective for the researcher because it is based upon experience with the work in research. The *truth* furnished by a logical-mathematical train of thought or a laboratory experiment holds first of all only in the game of symbols and apparatus, mastered and brought to function according to rules. It is the truth of a game – innocent and 'pure'. The fact, however, that this experience of self- and world-oblivion is used apologetically as a symbol of purity, is another matter. If a Nazi bureaucrat involved in the extermination machine were to refer to the purity and neatness of his index-card system, we would be horrified at the banality of evil. Indeed, given the political environment, these physicists could well have allowed their will 'to do really good physics' to slacken. Research is no game; it is an occupation, well paid and interwoven in a network of norms, functions and meanings.

The self-definition of science is a pitfall, a door to 'pure' and methodical reason which makes it impossible simultaneously to be in another world which does not exclusively depend on rational methods. It is seductive to go through this door into the 'silent garden' and to leave the 'dirty' world behind. But one cannot overlook the fact that the methodical reality acquires its potential and its success from the separation from real meanings and consequences. The 'purity of knowledge' has its reality and is indispensable for successful scientific work. Too much realism might be a hindrance for the success of the researcher. This is one reason why an involvement with consequences of the second order or with the realities of the very scientific enterprise, can endanger the scientific career. Indeed, the leading norm is not simply knowledge, but discipline-specific productivity. *Great* discoveries have to fulfill three criteria: in a trivial sense they must be true and new, but they especially must be *fruitful* and *significant*. Fruitful means that they stimulate as much further technoscientific work as possible, significant, that they strengthen the significance of science as seen from the outside. The most productive results of science are those that (re)produce scientific production.

Thus there is a central dilemma for the question concerning political and moral responsibility. An examination of the connections into which scientific work is plugged, insight into the self-delusion induced by the symbols of science and the examination of the further consequences of knowledge are counterproductive. If possible the active scientist keeps his hands off and thus leaves it up to students, older scientists and the professionals of other disciplines such as philosophy and the social sciences. But the reflection is thus pushed over to where it remains inconsequential. With a few exceptions, the older scientists represent the norms and self-picture of science. Students and non-scientists have little influence in any case, they can easily be warded off by the charge of insufficient knowledge of the subject.

A way out of this dilemma is nowhere in sight. Whenever scientists themselves speak on the responsibility for science, there are good reasons to be mistrustful, for in such cases caste politicians are usually at work, who chiefly address themselves to those problems which can best be solved with science, problems which thus contribute to the consolidation of the public significance of science and its productivity. Benno Müller-Hill, who does not fall under this suspicion, has come to the conclusion that the scientist who has a 'conscience' must be 'schizophrenic', for he has to live in two irreconcilable worlds.[18] But also where Müller-Hill, discussing genetic engineering, has taken pains to provide a differentiated judgment, a schism between the worlds creeps in:[19] 'independent of all applications, a vast, hitherto dark world reveals itelf'.

Science as a social system: theses

At least analytically as a preliminary one can try to avoid the schizophrenia and scrutinize science under an aspect other than its self-definition. As the practice of the mathematician, as a social system,[20] mathematics is not only composed of methods of thought and theories, rather also of education, administration, interest politics, propaganda, ideology ... From such a perspective, these considerations can be summarized:

First thesis: the social system of a mathematical science defines itself through the process and product of work in pure research as an exclusively cognitive entity. This definition is functional for the productivity of the system. Thus mathematics separates itself clearly from non-mathematics and offers the persons involved a symbol of purity.

No matter what is used as methodology, philosophy or theory of science, it confirms this asocial structure. It is a matter of the true, scientific knowledge, of the laws that rule the world. It is no wonder that, especially in mathematics, one encounters a sort of theology of science. Even if such derived ethics have become brittle, they still function from the concepts and self-understanding of the discipline: science recognizes the order of the world; that is good, because this order is a divine law and the use of this law is good. The fact that mathematics first of all creates a language that can be mastered and then imposes it on reality wherever possible, and that physics and chemistry produce effects and thereby first of all manufacture the *nature* of the sciences, is not even considered by this theology of knowledge.[21]

The 'unfortunate involvement' and the 'clouded image of the personality' remain part of the folklore of the discipline kept private, far removed from cognition. Research into science, that is, a methodological reflection on scientific practice which examines the researchers (and reflexively, itself) in practice very closely, and with this ethnological perspective forgets neither the political nor the epistemological perspective, is very rare. Within the enterprise of the disciplines, where scientists learn to understand and to describe themselves as scientists, this perspective has no place. There are many reasons for the official unconsciousness with respect to the very worldly and impure existence of the 'silent garden', reasons that strengthen each other. In this way it becomes impossible to discuss caste politics or human weakness *as mathematician*, that is, in the language of mathematics. The sociological theoretician would put it thus: in this regard the system cannot thematize itself. However, one can assume that the system (and its representatives) also have no interest in this theme. By avoiding it, not only is repression made easy, it is also advantageous for caste politics.

For example, when in 1933 two of the three members of the board of the *Gesellschaft für angewandte Mathematik und Mechanik* (Society for Applied Mathematics and Mechanics, henceforth GAMM) felt forced to resign because of their Jewish origins, it was suggested to the non-Jewish member, Ludwig Prandtl, that 'if we *have to exclude* Jewish members, then I would consider the dissolution of the society to be the most honorable solution'. Prandtl's answer referred to the competition with the physicists and mathematicians and culminated in the statement that: 'even if the exclusion of Jewish members were demanded, we would still need the GAMM. In my opinion, this has nothing to do with considerations of what would be most honorable, since it is simply a matter of a necessity for the discipline.'

Prandtl was successful with his argument and his politics. His discipline, aerodynamics, expanded considerably. He himself played a leading role in the German aeronautic research up until the end of the war.[22] The argument for the 'necessity of the discipline' meant that work aimed at new knowledge should be carried out within the defined disciplinary boundaries, nothing else and nothing more. In fact, this has very little to do with morals, honour or dignity, and with politics only in so far as it justifies the politics of that discipline.

Second thesis: the restrictive self-definition of the discipline justifies a caste politics that obscures political or moral considerations, so long as they do not immediately concern the productivity of the discipline. The identification of the individual scientist with the discipline produces the type of scientist who can still consider himself apolitical even when acting in the political interests of his discipline.

The familiar lament, that the German educated class and especially professors are apolitical, is untenable as soon as one takes only a brief look at the universities during the 1920s. What passed for *apolitical* there, and what still passes today, is *science*, this higher sphere of thought and truth, which is established above all human weaknesses and the *'filth'* of politics. The schizophrenia described by Müller-Hill plays a role here. The scientist, mathematician or engineer is thereby 'apolitical' exactly because he defines himself and his work in this way. The fact that science is an occupation has been made sufficiently clear by Max Weber. When one is concerned with political responsibility, one must add, and analyze much more closely, the fact that in this occupation something special is produced, and that it is one occupation among and with others.

The caste politics of the mathematicians and scientists in the National Socialist state were not essentially different from the politics under other conditions, but they do make some things more visible. The separation of the sphere of politics also functions to defend this autonomy of the discipline. One fought against a 'characteristic' science which springs from the 'racial soul'; but there was no objection to the formulation that science had to serve for its country. Thus Ludwig Prandtl could defend international connections, for example, with the argument that only through such contacts could German aeronautic research be successful. The self-limitation through the definition of science had a double effect. It could serve to defend autonomy against political attacks on the core region of the profession, and it simultaneously contained the declaration that the scientists for their part would not intervene in politics. The best political strategy for the sciences appeared to be to define themselves as indifferent to the world of the political, in order to be able to accommodate themselves to changing conditions so long as the political world respected and supported the 'necessity of the discipline'. The National Socialist regime certainly had a technocratic rationality which made possible the cooperation between state bureaucracy, industries, the armed forces and science. The machinery of administration , conquest and extermination needed technical competence and thus in the last analysis also needed science and scientific rationality. Objectivity and functionality were certainly in demand.

Third thesis: by means of their self-definition and the resulting caste politics, the scientific discipline made themselves independent to a considerable degree from changes in their political surroundings. In this way the disciplines were able both to accommodate themselves to the National Socialist system and to contribute to its preservation. This is also why they were able to overcome the thresholds of 1933 and 1945 without great difficulty.

When one examines more closely the politics of accommodation and defense used by mathematicians or another scientific discipline in the National Socialist state, it quickly becomes clear that the division of labour of the sub-, hybrid- and boundary-areas of the discipline played an important role. The applied, technically oriented sciences pushed through to the foreground because they were the easiest to justify in an ideological and practical-political sense. Applied mathematics was institutionalized and became a theme for didacticians of mathematics, and the image of the industrial mathematician was created as a new goal of university education. But behind this unity were hidden very different structures and interests. Even the advocates of a race-specific mathematics, for example, once their attempt to seize power in the enterprise of mathematics had been stopped cold, had their place as a special decorative piece for those with eccentric tastes. The identification symbol of mathematics or science was used everywhere; it proved both to be sufficiently flexible and to have a continuing integrative value. It is striking that these systematically differentiated actions and reactions were almost never seen as a coordinated movement of the discipline. It is not only more difficult to see at once unity and diversity and to analyse the connections between them, it also leads to a concept of science with which it is not so easy for the individual scientist to identify.

Fourth thesis: the scientific disciplines, including mathematics, are systems with complex internal differentiations, in which applied or demand-oriented sciences in different forms has its place as well as caste politics and public work. The restrictive, cognitive self-definition of science is used everywhere, is flexible and integrative, and can serve to conceal the internal differentiation both internally and externally.

Science and power

A memo on the unreliability of scientific slave labour in the 'Mathematical Calculating Institute' in the concentration camp Oranien-burg closes with the suggestion to give the prisoners civilian dress and other privileges 'in order to give the impression that the individuals concerned are really working as scientists'.[23] According to the report, up until now this measure had been successful. To ask a mean question: are suitable privileges sufficient to allow the scientist to feel 'like a scientist' and to carry out his work satisfactorily? Is the concentration camp here like a microcosm of the world, in which the scientists are 'the race of useful dwarfs' of whom Brecht has spoken?

This story is at least characteristic in so far as the power relationships here are crassy asymmetric, but not completely one-sided. Scientists have the power to fight for privileges because they cannot be so easily replaced. No modern society can do without this work, not even Nazi Germany. But science as pure slave labour is inconceivable. The task and goals must be prescribed very precisely for slaves. Science, in contrast, must be organized publicly as 'generalized labour'. The regulative function is performed by the public significance of science or the individual disciplines and research organizations, by the command of financial means and the labour market for scientists. The sciences have a special kind of *market*.

Fifth thesis: the market for the sciences has constituted itself in particular as a labour market which is publicly organized and funded (in Germany, especially, full or partial state funding). Thus the power has lain funda-mentally on the side of the state. The sciences ensure themselves public legitimacy and limited access to social power through accommodation to specific power relationships and through their exploitation of antagonisms in the systems of social power. In addition, the natural sciences take advan-tage of the classical strategy of professions, to monopolize their competence as much as possible.

Mathematics and the natural sciences have their position and historical significance because they produce means of power. Whether or not one concedes to a researcher a playful instinct, an interest in 'pure' knowledge, altruism, or whatever other type of good will, he produces a kind of knowledge that most probably entails further the potential to exert control over oneself, someone else, or nature. Of course such researchers find themselves relatively seldom in positions of social power. The classical position of renouncing power, so to speak the non-interference clause in the social contract of the sciences, can be found in a 1663 draft of the statutes of the Royal Society:[24]

> The Business and Design of the Royal Society is: To improve the knowledge of natural things, and all useful Arts, Manufactures, Mechanick practices, Engynes and Inventions by Experiments – (not meddling with Divinity, Metaphysics, Moralls, Politicks, Grammar, Rhetorick, or Logick).

Sixth thesis: the natural sciences and mathematics produce potential means to power. They deliver technically and socially valuable knowledge. That is the decisive basis for their existence, also in the National Socialist state. The self-definition of sciences, with its restriction to the cognitive structure and the production of generally valid knowledge, ensured that the knowledge produced, as long as it lay in the hands of the scientists, remained only a potential means to power. The self-definition of the sciences includes the insurance of non-interference in questions of politics, economics and morality.

Von Laue's 'why did you have to take a *political* stand ...' alludes to the non-interference clause in the social contract of the natural sciences. The fact that the *völkisch*[25] ideologies of science in the National Socialist state (for example those of Bieberbach, Lenard, Stark, Dingler and Heidegger) failed almost without exception may have to do with their disregard of this clause. The caste politics of science stop at a very delicate boundary: even when they possess the means to power (i.e. influential positions), they renounce the use of these for goals that are defined as the goals of the political (or economic) system. The familiar demarcation, that politics is a 'dirty business' and that scientists because of their nature are unsuitable for it, reinforces the barriers and transforms the possible feeling of impotence into the self-portrait of 'purity', like the symbol of science suggests.

In one and the same interview with a psychiatrist, the daughter of Ernst Rüdin, who as director of the KWI for Psychiatry and member of the 'Hereditary Health Council' was responsible for the forced sterilization of psychiatric patients, the following sentences can be found:[26]

> ... so it was. What was he supposed to do? He would have sold himself to the devil in order to get money for his institute and his research ... He was a scientist, not a politician. Politics is dirty. Then like today.

The same mathematician who after the war spoke of a 'silent garden' from 1937 to 1945 was the most influential caste politician for his discipline. As late as 1944 he was able to establish a research institute for mathematics. For this goal he skilfully exploited the competition between the different research policymakers. The prerequisite for this success was the fact that the ministerial bureaucrats, SS leaders and politicians all recognized him as a specialist in mathematics and expected from him no political competition. Not only in this case was the respect for the boundary between science and politics the decisive prerequisite for successful caste politics.[27]

Some have liked to claim that Heisenberg and his collegues in the German atomic bomb project delayed and hushed up and therby hindered the bomb.[28] If that were true, then this modest power existed for the scientists only because the bomb project existed. But it was the scientists themselves who, after the discovery of nuclear fission, first made the possibility of a super-bomb clear to the state and military, who launched the project. No matter how pure the discovery of nuclear fission by Hahn, Strassmann and Meitner might have been, elsewhere in the enterprise of physics, in this case in Göttingen and Hamburg, there were institutes and colleagues who took advantage of business relationships with state power and immediately offered the unexpected potential of the new energy source to Army Ordnance and the Reich Ministry of Education. The power, resulting from the indispensability of competence, to make conditions for, or even to deny collaboration, presupposes that the competence has been made available and thus been made indispensable.

Responsible science

In the enterprise of science, to ponder the complicated game between knowledge and power is not only anything but opportune, it can endanger the career. But it is very necessary. In the meantime, it has become clear that science and technology have consequences that affect every aspect of human existence and which in the extreme case can come to the self-extermination of humanity. Science under the old institutional forms and the symbol 'science' is institutionalized irresponsibility. It plays unconsciously, but very well, its game with and for social power. Politically responsible conduct, however, requires considerable attention to the conditions and structures of one's own conduct, as well as the consciousness of the ambiguities and ambivalences. 'Science', however, is of another type, its conduct aims at clear, univalent results: the theorem has been proven, the theory has been confirmed so well that it can be considered true, the experiment or the machine functions. Pure science is irresponsible.

Science, however, as well as 'pure' mathematics, is a socially organized, productive practice, ambivalent through and through, political through and through. The pure type of conduct, 'science', plays an extremely important, indispensable role in this practice. But this conduct is not isolated and can be raised up to the central value only at the cost of other values and of the ability to think and act politically. The pure and innocent knowledge of an external nature is a phantasm, the 'purity' a childish denial of reality. The unavoidable conclusion is: science must be politicized. This conclusion means that the conditions and goals of research, social structure and interests must be discussed and criticized for the specific local work situation as well as globally for the relationship between the systems of science and politics. It also means that the discipline imposed by the discipline must be broken through. The discussion of 'responsibility' and 'ethics of science' that is heard today does not achieve this goal. The respect for the lines of demarcation and the great symbols is too strong. *Interdisciplinarity* is just as harmless and therefore inconsequential (and unsuccessful, except when it is directed towards results that are in obvious demand and thus well financed); *contra* is perhaps the single reasonable prefix to *disciplinary*.

It is extremely important to be concerned with the 'consequences of the second order', those that have already appeared and those that can be expected. But in order to be able to anticipate and correspondiingly handle such consequences, a type of science is necessary that recognizes its impurity and therefore can be responsible at all. I have used 'phantasm' and 'repression' above in order to make clear that it is not only a matter of social and political structures, rather also psychic. Together with *science*, *knowledge* and *purity*, the relationship of the scientist to himself and to other people is also open to debate. The collective memory of mathematics contains in particular the names of mathematicians. The symbols Gumbel and Bieberbach are threats – the one to be taken off the membership list and to be forgotten, the other to be branded. Separated from the great moral gesture and separated from the professional commandment of purity, both figures could be thought-provoking, for in life they were not symbols, rather people who took extreme paths in their occupation. The recognition of both as exemplars of different possibilities for conduct under the given political and professional conditions also means gaining the insight that innocence, purity, truth and security are not to be had in real life. But having these things is the declared dream and structural identity of 'science.' In the real life of science, however, in connection with politics and economics, this dream creates realities that are hardly dreamlike.

A science that wants to be politically responsible would have to be able to see itself, and to consider the consequences, realistically. The objection from a sociological systems-theorist, that this system is incapable of a realistic self-perception because it obligates itself to a code of true–false, is important. But this systems-theorist also represents 'sciences'. Political and scientific fantasy and reason are necessary and crucial. Science as science wears a cloak under which is hidden a completely normal participant in business life who commands several codes. One should observe him as such, not under his trademarks (truth, knowledge, nature ...). Finally:[29]

' . . . all professional ideologies are noble, and the hunters are hardly willing to call themselves the butchers of the forest'. Perhaps a certain schizophrenia is in fact necessary in order reasonably to distance oneself from scientific reason, for it is the professional ideology.

Notes

1 Scientists, engineers and National Socialism

1 We thank Mitchell Ash, Hans-Joachim Braun, Mikail Hård, Dieter Hoffmann, Herbert Mehrtens, Hartmut Petzold, Reinhard Siegmund-Schultze and Sheila Weiss for commenting on an earlier draft of this paper; also see two publications which appeared too late to be considered here: J. Olff-Nathan (ed.), *La science sous le Troisième Reich* (Paris, 1993); and C. Meinel and P. Voswinkel (eds.), *Medizin, Naturwissenschaft, Technik und National sozialismus* (forthcoming).

2 F. Neumann, *Behemoth. The Structure and Practice of National Socialism* (New York, 1942); P. Huttenberger, 'Nationalsozialistische Polykratie', *Geschichte und Gesellschaft*, 2 (1976), 417–42; M. Geyer, 'The State in National Socialist Germany', in C. Bright and S. Harding (eds.), *Statemaking and Social Movements: Essays in History and Theory* (Ann Arbor, 1984), pp. 193–232; I. Kershaw, *The Nazi Dictatorship: Problems and Perspectives of Interpretation*, 2nd edn (London, 1989), pp. 49–60.

3 M. Broszat, 'Soziale Motivation und Führer-Bindung des Nationalsozialismus', in *Nach Hitler. Der Schwierige Umgang mit unserer Geschichte*, 2nd edn (Munich, 1988), pp. 11–33.

4 I. Kershaw, *Hitler* (London, 1991), pp. 1–15, esp. 7–10.

5 For the controversy between the functionalists and intentionalists, see Kershaw, *Dictatorship*, pp. 1–17; and T. Mason, 'Intention and Explanation: A Current Controversy about the Interpretation of National Socialism', in G. Hirschfeld and L. Kettenacker (eds.), *Der 'Führerstaat': Mythos und Realität* (Stuttgart, 1981), pp. 23–40.

6 Quoted from Kershaw, *Hitler*, pp. 8 and 15, ' . . . die Pflicht eines jeden, zu versuchen, im Sinne des Führers ihm entgegen zu arbeiten'.

7 Kershaw, *Dictatorship*, pp. 61–81.

8 For the rocket research, see M. Neufeld's article in this collection as well as his forthcoming book, *The Rocket and the Reich: Peenemünde and the*

339

German Army Guided Missile Program (in press); for nuclear weapons, see M. Walker, *German National Socialism and the Quest for Nuclear Power, 1939–1949* (Cambridge, 1989); M. Walker, 'Legends surrounding the German Atomic Bomb', in T. Meade and M. Walker (eds.), *Science, Medicine, and Cultural Imperialism* (New York, 1991), pp. 178–204; M. Walker, 'Physics and Propaganda: Werner Heisenberg's Foreign Lectures under National Socialism', *Historical Studies in the Physical and Biological Sciences*, 22 (1992), 339–89; M. Walker, 'Myths of the German Atom Bomb', *Nature*, 359 (1992), 473–4; M. Walker, 'Legenden um die deutschen Atombombe (II): Farm Hall', *Vierteljahrshefte für Zeitgeschichte* (forthcoming).

9 Kershaw, *Hitler*, pp. 111–18.
10 O. Bartov, 'Soldiers, Nazis, and War in the Third Reich', *Journal of Modern History*, 63 (1991), 44–60.
11 For example, see P. Hayes, *Industry and Ideology: IG Farben in the Nazi Era* (Cambridge, 1987); G. Plumpe, *Die I. G. Farbenindustrie AG. Wirtschaft, Technik und Politik 1904–1945*; H. Pohl, 'Zur Zusammenarbeit von Wirtschaft und Wissenschaft im "Dritten Reich": Die "Fördergemeinschaft der Deutschen Industrie" von 1942', *Vierteljahrschrift für Sozial- und Wirtschaftsgeschichte*, 72 (1985), 508–36.
12 J. Caplan, *Government without Administration: State and Civil Service in Weimar and Nazi Germany* (Oxford, 1988).
13 Kershaw, *Hitler*, pp. 100–1, 116–17, 137–40.
14 H. Buchheim, M. Broszat, H-A. Jacobsen and H. Krausnick, *Anatomie des SS-Staates*, 2 vols., 3rd edn (Munich, 1982).
15 Geyer, 'The State', pp. 196–7.
16 For an example of Mentzel's and Schumann's activities, see Walker, *German*.
17 Hayes, *Industry*, pp. 155–60, 338–76; see also Plumpe, *Die I. G. Farbenindustrie*.
18 For technocracy also see J. Herf, *Reactionary Modernism: Technology, Culture, and Politics in Weimar and the Third Reich* (Cambridge, 1984) and K-H. Ludwig, *Technik und Ingenieure im Dritten Reich*, 2nd edn (Düsseldorf, 1979).
19 Kershaw, *Dictatorship*, pp. 79, 144–5; U. Herbert, *Fremdarbeiter. Politik und Praxis des "Ausländer-Einsatzes" in der Kriegswirtschaft des Dritten Reiches* (Berlin, 1985).
20 *Webster's Ninth New Collegiate Dictionary* (Springfield, 1983), p. 1211.
21 H. Elsner, *The Technocrats: Prophets of Automation* (Syracuse, 1967).
22 The German technocratic movement needs to be studied more closely.
23 H. Harden, 'Einleitung', *Technokratie*, No. 1 (1933), 1.
24 W. Kuntz, 'Deutsche Technokratie', *Technokratie*, No. 1 (1933), 2–5, here 3.
25 H. Triebel, 'Nationalsozialismus und Technokratie', *Technokratie*, No. 1 (1933), 6–8, the quotation is on 7; H. Triebel, 'Deutsche und amerikanische Technokratie', *Technokratie*, No. 1 (1935), 1–5.
26 J. Jeans, 'Das neue Weltbild der modernen Physik', *Technokratie*, No. 5 (1934), 85–92, here 88.

27 W. McDougall, *The Heavens and the Earth: A Political History of the Space Age* (New York, 1985), p. 5.

28 Thanks to Mikael Hård for this point.

29 McDougall, *Heavens*.

30 Thanks to both Mitchell Ash and Herbert Mehrtens for this point; see B. Latour, *Science in Action: How to Follow Scientists and Engineers through Society* (Milton Keynes, 1987).

31 Thanks to both Hans-Joachim Braun and Hartmut Petzold for this point; for example, see H-J. Braun, 'Fertigungsprozesse in deutschen Flugzeugbau 1926–1945', *Technikgeschichte*, 57 (1990), 111–35 and H-J. Braun, 'Aero-engine Production in the Third Reich', *History of Technology*, 14 (1992), 1–15; and H-J. Braun, 'Konstruktion, Destruktion und der Ausbau technischer Systeme Zwischen 1914 und 1945', in H-J. Braun and W. Kaiser (eds.), *Energiewirtschaft, Automatisierung, Information seit 1914* (Berlin, 1992), 11–282.

32 See Kershaw, *Dictatorship*, pp. 131–49; F. Bajohr, W. Johe and U. Lohalm (eds.), *Zivilisation und Barbarei. Die widersprüchlichen Potentiale der Moderne* (Hamburg, 1991); H. Mommsen, 'Nationalsozialismus als vorgetäuschte Modernisierung', in *Der Nationalsozialismus und die deutsche Gesellschaft* (Reinbek, 1991), pp. 405–27; D. Peukert, *The Weimar Republic. The Crisis of Classical Modernity* (New York, 1992); M. Prinz and R. Zitelmann (eds.), *Nationalsozialismus und Modernisierung* (Darmstadt, 1991).

33 Kershaw, *Dictatorship*, p. 418; also see Kershaw's criticism of interpretations of Hitler as a 'conscious modernizer' in I. Kershaw, 'Ideologe und Propagandist. Hitler im Lichte seiner Reden, Schriften und Anordungen', *Vierteljahrshefte für Zeitgeschichte*, 40 (1992), 263–71, here 270.

34 Mommsen, 'Nationalsozialismus', p. 423, 'Wenn man von Modernisierung im Dritten Reich sprechen will, so sind die perversen Anwendungen medizinischer Theorien wie die mit technischen Mitteln herbeigeführte Massenvernichtung deren spezifische Form'.

35 Peukert, *Weimar Republic*.

36 P. Forman, 'Weimar Culture, Causality, and Quantum Theory, 1918–1922: Adaptation by German Physicists and Mathematicians to a Hostile Environment', *Historical Studies in the Physical Sciences*, 3 (1971), 1–115.

37 Herf, *Reactionary Modernism*.

38 J. Noakes and G. Pridham (eds.), *Nazism 1919–1945: A Documentary Reader*, 2 vols. (New York, 1988), pp. 1086–208.

39 G. Bock, *Zwangssterilisation im Nationalsozialismus* (Opladen, 1986); also see G. Giles, 'The Most Unkind Cut of All: Castration, Homosexuality and Nazi Justice', *Journal of Contemporary History*, 27 (1992), 41–61.

40 Noakes and Pridham, *Nazism*, pp. 997–1048, 380–415, 496–520.

41 Noakes and Pridham, *Nazism*, pp. 167–87.

42 The classic studies of the *Gleichschaltung* of science and engineering are, respectively, A. Beyerchen, *Scientists under Hitler: Politics and the Physics Community in the Third Reich* (New Haven, 1977) as well as his retro-

spective discussion of his work, A. Beyerchen, 'What We Now Know about Nazism and Science', *Social Research*, 59 (1992), 615–41, here 620–8 and 638 for physics; and Ludwig, *Technik* for engineering; more recent studies include H. Mehrtens, 'The "Gleichschaltung" of Mathematical Societies in Nazi Germany', *The Mathematical Intelligencer*, 11 (1989), 48–60 on mathematics; U. Geuter, *The Professionalization of Psychology in Nazi Germany* (Cambridge, 1992) on psychology; and P. Lundgreen (ed.), *Wissenschaft im Dritten Reich* (Frankfurt a.M., 1983) for the social sciences and humanities.

43 J. L. Heilbron, *The Dilemmas of an Upright Man: Max Planck as Spokesman for German Science* (Berkeley, 1986), pp. 155–9; F. Stern, 'Einstein's Germany', in *Dreams and Delusions: The Drama of German History* (New York, 1987), pp. 25–50.

44 M. Bechstedt, '"Gestalthafte Atomlehre" – Zur "Deutschen Chemie" im NS-Staat', in H. Mehrtens and S. Richter (eds.), *Naturwissenschaft, Technik und NS-Ideologie. Beiträge zur Wissenschaftsgeschichte des Dritten Reiches* (Frankfurt a.M., 1980), p. 142–65.

45 H. Mehrtens, 'Bieberbach and "Deutsche Mathematik"' in E. Phillips (ed.), *Studies in the History of Mathematics* (Washington, D.C., 1987), pp. 195–241, and Mehrtens' first article in this volume; also see R. Siegmund-Schultze, 'Theodor Vahlen – zum Schuldanteil eines deutschen Mathematikers am faschistischen Missbrauch der Wissenschaft', *NTM – Schriftenreihe für Geschichte der Naturwissenschaften, Technik und Medizin*, 21 (1984), 17–32; R. Siegmund-Schultze, 'Faschistische Pläne zur "Neuordnung" der europäischen Wissenschaft', *NTM – Schriftenreihe für Geschichte der Naturwissenschaften, Technik und Medizin*, 23 (1986), 1–17; R. Siegmund-Schultze, 'Zur Sozialgeschichte der Mathematik an der Berliner Universität im Faschismus', *NTM – Schriftenreihe für Geschichte der Naturwissenschaften, Technik und Medizin*, 26 (1989), 49–68; R. Siegmund-Schultze, *Mathematische Berichterstattung in Hitlerdeutschland* (Göttingen, 1993); and the articles by Mehrtens, Siegmund-Schultze, and N. Schappacher in Olff-Nathan, *La science*, 33–102.

46 Beyerchen; *Scientists* and Beyerchen, 'What'; D. Cassidy, *Uncertainty: The Life and Science of Werner Heisenberg* (New York, 1991), pp. 297–500; Heilbron, *Dilemmas*, pp. 114–22, 1490–74; D. Hoffman, 'Die Physikdenkschriften von 1934/36 und zur Situation der Physik im faschistischen Deutschland', *Wissenschaft und Staat* (Berlin (East), 1989), pp. 185–211; A. Kleinert, 'Von der Science allemande zur Deutschen Physik: Nationalismus und moderne Naturwissenschaft in Frankreich und Deutschland zwischen 1914 und 1940', *Francia: Forschungen zur westeuropäischen Geschichte*, 6 (1978), 509–25; A. Kleinert's article in Olff-Nathan, *La science*, pp. 149–66; S. Richter, 'Die "Deutsche Physik"', in Mehrtens and Richter, *Naturwissenschaft*, pp. 116–41; Walker, *German*, pp. 60–80; Walker, 'Legends'; Walker, 'Propaganda'.

47 U. Geuter, 'Nationalsozialistische Ideologie und Psychologie', in M. Ash and U. Geuter (eds.), *Geschichte der deutschen Psychologie im 20. Jahr-*

hundert. Ein Überlick (Opladen, 1985), pp. 172–200; and U. Geuter, 'German Psychology in the Nazi Period', in M. Ash and W. Woodward (eds.), *Psychology in Twentieth-Century Thought and Society* (Cambridge, 1987), pp. 65–88.

48 See U. Deichmann, *Biologen unter Hitler. Vertreibung, Karrieren, Forschung* (Frankfurt a.M., 1992); K-H. Roth, 'Schöner neuer Mensch,' in H. Kaupen-Haas (ed.), *Der Griff nach der Bevölkerung* (Nördlingen, 1986), pp. 11–63.

49 Thanks to Herbert Mehrtens for this point.

50 Noakes and Pridham, *Nazism*, pp. 167–87.

51 For example, see Walker, 'Propaganda', 348–51.

52 Walker, *German*, pp. 60–80; Walker, 'Propaganda', 348–51.

53 For example, Walker, *German*, pp. 60–80.

54 For a survey of the debate over the Historicization, see Kershaw, *Dictatorship*, pp. 150–67; for the related *Historikerstreit*, see R. Evans, *In Hitler's Shadow: West German Historians and the Attempt to Escape from the Nazi Past* (New York, 1989); Kershaw, *Dictatorship*, pp. 150–67; C. Maier, *The Unmasterable Past* (Cambridge, MA, 1990); and H-U. Wehler, *Entsorgung der deutschen Vergangenheit? Ein polemischer Essay zum "Historikerstreit"* (Munich, 1988) also see H. Mehrten's article in Meinel and Voswinkel, *Medizin*.

55 Kershaw, *Dictatorship*, pp. 14–17.

56 Kershaw, *Dictatorship*, pp. 150–67.

57 It is no coincidence that the history of the University of Göttingen under National Socialism, which appeared in 1987, carried the subtitle 'The repressed chapter in her 250–year history'; H. N. Becker, H-J. Dahms and C. Wegeler (eds.), *Die Universität Göttingen unter dem Nationalsozialismus. Das verdrängte Kapitel ihrer 250jährigen Geschichte* (Munich, 1987); here we are concerned primarily with the majority of scientists and engineers, not only those few who were in the resistance to National Socialism.

58 Kershaw, *Dictatorship*, pp. 6–7.

59 The apologetic function is emphasized in Broszat, *Nach Hitler*, especially 'Eine Insel in der Geschichte? Der Historiker in der Spannung zwischen Bewerten und Verstehen', pp. 114–20.

60 M. Osietzki, *Wissenschaftsorganisation und Restauration. Der Aufbau ausseruniversitärer Forschungseinrichtungen und die Gründung des westdeutschen Staates 1945–1952* (Cologne, 1984).

61 Exceptions are the inventories taken by the Allies of the scientific and technological results in the Third Reich, and an abundance of memoirs written by scientists and engineers, which in particular serve the justification and distancing; see H. Mehrtens, 'Das "dritte Reich" in der Naturwissenschaftsgeschichte: Literaturbericht und Problemskizze' in Mehrtens and Richter, *Naturwissenschaft*, p. 15–87.

62 Literature in Mehrtens and Richter, *Naturwissenschaft*; for a rather negative assessment of this literature, see H. Heiber, *Universität unterm Haken-*

kreuz. Teil 1: Der Professor im Dritten Reich. Bilder aus der akademischen Provinz (Munich, 1991), pp. 12–13.

63 A complete list of the literature can be found in the register in Heiber, *Universität*.

64 For example, see the public controversy that Mark Walker's study of German nuclear power unleashed in a physics journal: M. Walker, 'Heisenberg, Goudsmit and the German atomic bomb', *Physics Today*, 43, No. 1 (1990), 52–60, and the subsequent letters to the editor in *Physics Today* 44, No. 5 (1991), 13–15, 90–6, as well as a comparable controversy touched off by G. Simonsohn, 'Physiker in Deutschland 1933–1945', *Physikalische Blätter*, 48 (1992), 23–8, especially the letters by S. Mengel and S. Wolff on pages 254 and 296 of the same volume.

65 The first such monograph was Beyerchen, *Scientists*; for the *völkisch* variants see also Mehrtens and Richter, *Naturwissenschaft*.

66 See Beyerchen, 'What'.

67 A discussion of this reconstruction can be found in Walker, *German*, pp. 179–221.

68 For one recent sensational example from biology, see B. Müller-Hill, *Murderous Science: Elimination by Scientific Selection of Jews, Gypsies and Others in Germany 1933–1945* (Oxford, 1988).

69 Mehrtens, 'Literaturbericht', in Mehrtens and Richter, *Naturwissenschaft*.

70 For example, H. Mehrtens, 'Angewandte Mathematik und Anwendungen der Mathematik im nationalsozialistischen Deutschland', *Geschichte und Gesellschaft*, 12 (1986), 317–47; Geuter, *Professionalization*; Walker, *German*.

71 This conclusion holds in particular for the field of population policy, in which ideologically-based goals were realized using technocratic means, see G. Aly and K-H. Roth, *Die restlose Erfassung* (Hamburg, 1984); G. Aly and S. Heim, *The Economics of the Final Solution: a Case Study from the General Government* (Los Angeles, 1988).

72 For *Ostforschung* in general, see M. Burleigh, *Germany Turns Eastwards: A Study of Ostforschung in the Third Reich* (Cambridge, 1988); for geography see M. Rössler, *"Wissenschaft und Lebensraum". Geographische Ostforschung im Nationalsozialismus* (Berlin, 1990).

73 Also see Deichmann, *Biologen*.

74 Race hygiene and eugenics have consciously been excluded from the scope of this book because of the wealth of existing literature on this topic: G. Baader and U. Schultz (eds.), *Medizin und Nationalsozialismus: Tabuisierte Vergangenheit – Ungebrochene Tradition* (Berlin, 1980); Bock, *Zwangssterilisation*; M. Kater, *Doctors under Hitler* (Chapel Hill, 1989); R. J. Lifton, *The Nazi Doctors: Medical Killing and the Psychology of Genocide* (New York, 1986); G. Lilienthal, *Der "Lebensborn e.V.": Ein Instrument nationalsozialistischer Rassenpolitik* (Stuttgart, 1985); B. Massin's article in Olff-Nathan, *La science*, pp. 197–262; Müller-Hill, *Murderous Science*; R. Proctor, *Racial Hygiene: Medicine under the Nazis* (Cambridge, MA, 1988); P. Weindling, *Health, Race, and German Politics between National Unification and Nazism, 1870–1945* (Cambridge, 1989);

P. Weingart, J. Kroll and K. Bayertz, *Rasse, Blut, Gene. Geschichte der Eugenik und Rassenhygiene in Deutschland* (Frankfurt a.M., 1988); S. Weiss, *Race Hygiene and National Efficiency: the Eugenics of Wilhelm Schallmayer* (Berkeley, 1987); 'The Race Hygiene Movement in Germany', *Osiris*, 3 (1987), 193–236; and 'Race and class in Fritz Lenz's Eugenics', *Medizinhistorisches Journal*, 27 (1992), 5–25.

75 Further examples include S. Richter, 'Die Kämpfe in der Physik in Deutschland nach dem Ersten Weltkrieg', *Studhoffs Archiv*, 57 (1973), 195–207; Mehrtens, 'Bieberbach'.

76 H. Trischler, *Luft- und Raumfahrtforschung in Deutschland, 1900–1970. Eine politische Wissenschaftsgeschichte* (Frankfurt a.M., 1992); H. Mehrtens, *Moderne – Sprache – Mathematik. Eine Geschichte des Streits um die Grundlagen der Disziplin und des Subjekts formaler Systeme* (Frankfurt a.M., 1990); H. Petzold, *Moderne Rechenkünstler. Die Industrialisierung der Rechentechnik in Deutschland* (Munich, 1992); J. Radkau, *Technik in Deutschland. Vom 18. Jahrhundert bis zur Gegenwart* (Frankfurt a.M., 1989); M. Ash, 'Psychology in twentieth-century Germany: science and profession', in K. Jarausch and G. Cocks (eds.), *German Professions, 1800–1950* (New York, 1990).

77 Also see the contributions by Wise and Geuter.

78 For example, see R. Vierhaus and B. vom Brocke (eds.), *Forschung im Spannungsfeld von Politik und Gesellschaft. Geschichte und Struktur der Kaiser-Wilhelm/Max-Planck-Gesellschaft* (Stuttgart, 1990); K. Macrakis, *Surviving the Swastika, Scientific Research in Nazi Germany*.

79 Becker *et al.*, *Die Universität*; F. Golczewski, *Kölner Universitätslehrer und der Nationalsozialismus. Personengeschichtliche Ansätze* (Cologne, 1988); E. Krause, L. Huber and H. Fischer (eds.), *Hochschulalltag im "Dritten Reich". Die Hamburger Universität 1933–1945*, 3 vols. (Berlin, 1991); K. Buselmeier, D. Harth and C. Jansen (eds.), *Auch eine Geschichte der Universität Heidelberg?* (Mannheim, 1985); also see H. Maier, *Erwin Marx (1893–1980), Ingenieurwissenschaftler in Braunschweig, und die Forschung und Entwicklung auf dem Gebiet der elektrischen Energieübertragung auf weiter Entfernung zwischen 1918 und 1950* (Stuttgart, 1993).

80 See the exceptional contribution from B. Vogel, 'Anpassung und Widerstand. Das Verhältnis Hamburger Hochschullehrer zum Staat 1919 bis 1945' in Krause *et al.*, *Hochschulalltag*, pp. 3–83, here p. 65.

81 Ludwig, *Technik*.

82 Vogel, 'Anpassung', p. 65.

83 On the 'normality' of adaptation in the social sciences, see O. Rammstedt, *Soziologie in Deutschland (oder: im Nationalsozialismus) 1933–1945. Die Normalität einer Anpassung* (Frankfurt a.M., 1986).

84 For example, see R. Giordano, *Die zweite Schuld oder von der Last Deutscher zu sein* (Hamburg, 1987).

85 Vierhaus and vom Brocke (eds.), *Forschung*; Müller-Hill, *Murderous Science*; university histories such as those in note 79; Walker, *German*.

86 See U. Albrecht, A. Heinemann-Grüder and A. Wellmann, *Die Spezialisten*.

Deutsche Naturwissenschaftler und Techniker in der Sowjetunion nach 1945 (Berlin, 1992); A. Heinemann-Grüder, *Die sowjetische Atombombe* (Münster, 1992); and J. Gimbel, *Science, Technology, and Reparations: Exploitation and Plunder in Postwar Germany* (Palo Alto, 1990).

87 The literature on the policies of the victorious powers is given in Heinemann-Grüder's chapter.

88 It is a matter of the change of the political system, not of the personal hardship entailed in such changes.

89 Once again, there are critical studies from the field of eugenics and genetics, for example, H. Kaupen-Haas (ed.), *Der Griff nach der Bevölkerung. Aktualität und Kontinuität nazistischer Bevölkerungspolitik* (Nördlingen, 1986); from other fields, M. Eckert and H. Schubert, *Crystals, Electrons, and Transistors* (New York, 1989); M. Eckert, *Die Atomphysiker* (Wiesbaden, 1993); Walker, *German*; also see M. Eckert and M. Osietzki, *Wissenschaft für Macht und Markt*. Kernforschung und Mikroelektronik in der Bundesrepublik Deutschland (Munich, 1989).

90 J. Radkau, *Aufstieg und Krise der deutschen Atomwirtschaft, 1945–1975. Verdrängte Alternativen in der Kerntechnik und der Ursprung der nuklearen Kontroverse* (Hamburg, 1983); H. Trischler, 'Historische Wurzeln der Grossforschung: Die Luftfahrtforschung vor 1945' in M. Szöllösi-Janze and H. Trischler (eds.), *Grossforschung in Deutschland* (Frankfurt a.M., 1990), pp. 23–37.

91 See M. Renneberg, 'Gründung und Aufbau des GKSS-Forschungszentrums Geesthacht. Ein Beitrag zur Geschichte der Grossforschungseinrichtungen in der Bundesrepublik Deutschland', (University of Hamburg PhD, 1989); G. Ritter, *Grossforschung und Staat in Deutschland. Ein historischer Überblick* (Munich, 1992); Szöllösi-Janze and Trischler; B. Weiss, *Grossforschung in Berlin. Geschichte des Hahn-Meiter-Instituts 1955–1980* (forthcoming); given the state of the literature, unfortunately it is not at present possible to include the German Democratic Republic in this analysis.

92 Kershaw, *Dictatorship*, p. 15, translates this term as 'morally neutral impenetrability or immunity rather than actively motivated opposition'.

93 Forman, 'Weimar Culture'.

94 Also see R. Proctor, *Value-Free Science. Purity and Power in Modern Knowledge* (Cambridge, MA., 1991); and C. Mukerji, *A Fragile Power. Scientists and the State* (Princeton, 1990).

2 *Keinerlei Untergang*: German armaments engineers during the Second World War and in the service of the victorious powers

1 *Keinerlei Untergang* (no downfall) is a play on words referring to A. Hillgruber, *Zweierlei Untergang. Die Zerschlagung des Deutschen Reiches und das Ende des europäischen Judentums* (Berlin, 1986) (English translation of title: 'Two Kinds of Downfall. The Destruction of the German Reich and the End of European Jewry'), which played a prominent role in the *Historikerstreit* (German Historians' Dispute).

2 G. Hortleder, *Das Gesellschaftsbild des Ingenieurs. Zum politischen Verhalten der technischen Intelligenz in Deutschland* (Frankfurt a.M., 1970); E. Kogon, *Die Stunde der Ingenieure* (Düsseldorf, 1976); and K-H. Ludwig, *Technik und Ingenieure im Dritten Reich* (Düsseldorf, 1974).

3 For example, the field of aeronautics has received a great deal of attention. See K. Kens and H. Nowarra, *Die deutschen Flugzeuge 1933–1945* (Munich, 1961); H. Nowarra, *Die deutsche Luftrüstung 1933–1945* (Koblenz, 1985); and R. Kosin, *Die Entwicklung der deutschen Jagdflugzeuge* (Koblenz, 1983).

4 See M. Geyer, *Deutsche Rüstungspolitik 1860–1980* (Frankfurt a.M., 1984); and J. Radkau, *Technik in Deutschland. Vom 18. Jahrhundert bis zur Gegenwart* (Frankfurt a.M., 1989).

5 A. Beyerchen, *Scientists under Hitler. Politics and the Physics Community in the Third Reich* (New Haven, 1977); M. Walker, *German National Socialist and the Quest for Nuclear Power, 1939–1949* (Cambridge, 1989); L. Graham, 'Science and values; the eugenics movement in Germany and Russia in the 1920s', *The American Historical Review*, 82 (1977), 1133–64; B. Müller-Hill, *From Daedalus to Mengele: The Dark Side of Human Genetics* (Genome, 1989).

6 Ludwig, *Technik*.

7 I have conducted interviews with Manfred von Ardenne (the owner of a private physics laboratory in Berlin during the war, afterwards part of the German atomic bomb team in the USSR); Fritz Bernhard (physicist, former colleague of von Ardenne in his so-called 'Secret Research Laboratory'; after the war Bernhard worked in the USSR); engineer Paul Blume (developer of cameras at the Zeiss company in Jena for the military; after the war he worked in the USSR); Helmuth Breuninger (developer of autopilots in wartime and later in the USSR); Irmgard Gröttrup (wife of the leading rocket (V–2) designer Helmuth Gröttrup); engineer Kurt Kracheel (specialist in rocket guidance technology); Gerhard Krüger (at the Technical University of Berlin in wartime, then a member of the German atomic bomb team in the USSR); engineer Hans Kuhl (specialist in rocket technology); engineer Georg Orlamünder (specialist in rocket guidance technology); Gustav Richter (physicist, in wartime he developed a torpedo detonator, afterwards he was part of the German atomic bomb team in the USSR); Werner Schütze (physicist at Siemens in wartime, afterwards part of the German atomic bomb team in the USSR); Klaus Thiessen (physicist, son of the chemist Peter-Adolf Thiessen, worked in the USSR after the war); Heinz Wadewitz (nuclear physicist, worked in the USSR after the war); Heinrich Wilhelmi (radar specialist, after the war also worked in the USSR); aircraft engineer Hans Wocke (former engineer at the Junkers company, then in the USSR).

8 See P. Weingart, 'Wissenschaftssoziologie und Technik. Die soziologische Analyse wissenschaftlicher und technischer Handlungsorientierung', in P. Lundgreen (ed.), *Zum Verhältnis von Wissenschaft und Technik. Erkenntnisziele und Erzeugungsregeln akademischen und technischen Wissens* (Bielefeld, 1981), pp. 6–31.

9 Regarding the philosophy of technology, see J. Herf, *Reactionary Modernism:*

Technology, Culture, and Politics in Weimar and Third Reich (Cambridge, 1984), pp. 152–88.

10 L. Brinkmann, *Der Ingenieur* (Frankfurt a.M., 1908), p. 11; see also W. Wendt, *Die Technik als Kulturmacht* (Berlin, 1906); and E. Meyer, *Technik und Kultur* (Berlin, 1906).

11 Brinkmann, *Der Ingenieur*, p. 16.

12 Brinkmann, *Der Ingenieur*, pp. 20ff.

13 B. Easlea, *Väter der Vernichtung. Männlichkeit, Naturwissenschaftler und der nukleare Rüstungswettlauf* (Reinbeck, 1986); of course Easlea is referring to Francis Bacon.

14 S. Wollgast, '"Technikphilosophie" während der Herrschaft des deutschen Faschismus', in G. Kovacs and S. Wollgast (eds.), *Technikphilosophie in Vergangenheit und Gegenwart* (Berlin, 1984), pp. 115ff.

15 See Hortleder, *Das Gesellschaftsbild*, p. 165; and Ludwig, *Technik*, p. 105.

16 Ludwig, *Technik*, p. 108.

17 K-H. Ludwig, 'Widersprüchlichkeiten der technischwissenschaftlichen Gemeinschaftsarbeit im Dritten Reich', *Technikgeschichte*, 8 (1979), 247.

18 A. Rosenberg, *Der Mythos des 20. Jahrhunderts. Eine Wertung der seelisch-geistigen Gestaltenkämpfe unserer Zeit* (Munich, 1941), p. 3; the first edition of this book appeared in 1925.

19 R. Heiss (ed.), *Die Sendung des Ingenieurs im neuen Staat* (Berlin, 1934), p. 10; see also G. Feder, 'Die Aufgaben der Technik beim Wiederaufbau der deutschen Wirtschaft', *Technik und Kultur*, 6 (1933), 93 and 96; A. Rosenberg, 'Weltanschauung und Technik', *Deutsche Technik*, No. 1 (1938), 1; and H. Dehnert, 'Vom Wesen der deutschen Technik', *Deutsche Technik*, No. 1 (1941), 17.

20 R. Heiss, 'Die Erziehung des Ingeniers zur Totalität', in Heiss, *Die Sendung*, p. 132.

21 See Feder, 'Die Aufgaben', p. 93; and Ludwig, 'Widersprüchlichkeiten', p. 245.

22 Ludwig, *Technik*, p. 159.

23 Ludwig, *Technik*, p. 245.

24 Hortleder, *Das Gesellschaftsbild*, p. 111.

25 W. Ostwald, 'NS-Technik', *Deutsche Technik*, No. 2 (1943), 48.

26 H. Ebert and H. Rupieper, 'Technische Wissenschaft und nationalsozialistische Rüstungspolitik: Die Wehrtechnische Fakultät der TH Berlin 1933–1945', in R. Rürup (ed.), *Wissenschaft und Gesellschaft. Beiträge zur Geschichte der TU Berlin 1879–1979* (Berlin, 1979), pp. 469–91.

27 The 'Faculty for General Technology' of the Technical University Berlin was renamed on 4 September 1935 the 'Faculty of Armaments Technology'.

28 Ebert and Rupieper, 'Technische Wissenschaft', p. 471.

29 Ebert and Rupieper, 'Technische Wissenschaft', p. 481.

30 See R. Sonnemann (ed.), *Geschichte der Technischen Universität Dresden 1828–1978* (Berlin, 1978), pp. 155–65.

31 Interview in Hamburg with Gerhard Krüger on 27 April 1989. Krüger reports that it was quite common in the Optical Institute of the Technical University Berlin to work on orders for the Air Force.

32 Ludwig, *Technik*, p. 239.

33 Ludwig, *Technik*, p. 222.
34 Ludwig, *Technik*, p. 264.
35 Ludwig, *Technik*, p. 264.
36 F. Brandner, *Ein Leben zwischen den Fronten* (Munich, 1976).
37 Brandner, *Ein Leben*, p. 42.
38 Brandner, *Ein Leben*, p. 68.
39 Brandner, *Ein Leben*, p. 70.
40 A similar 'fighting ethics' (*Kampfmoral*) can be found in the memoirs of air-craft designer and pilot G. Fieseler, *Meine Bahn am Himmel. Der Erbauer des Fieseler Storch und der V1 erzählt sein Leben* (Munich, 1979), p. 279.
41 Brandner, *Ein Leben*, p. 70.
42 Brandner, *Ein Leben*, pp. 74ff.
43 Brandner, *Ein Leben*, p. 79.
44 K. von Gersdorff, *Ludwig Bölkow und sein Werk – Ottobrunner Innovationen* (Koblenz, 1987), pp. 24ff.
45 An example for the reorientation of research during wartime is described by K. Lux, 'Technische Entwicklung und Forschung bei Telefunken während des Krieges', *Telefunkenzeitung*, 23 No. 87/88 (1950), 28–9.
46 K. von Gersdorff, 'Die Peenemünder Fernrakete A4 ("V–2")', in T. Benecke, K-H. Hedwig and J. Hermann (eds.), *Flugkörper und Lenkraketen* (Koblenz, 1987), pp. 77–85.
47 M. von Ardenne, *Sechzig Jahre für Forschung und Fortschritt. Autobiographie* (Berlin, 1987), p. 158.
48 von Ardenne, *Sechzig Jahre*, p. 159.
49 Interviews with Schütze (assistant to Nobel Prize-winner Gustav Hertz at the Siemens company) (16 November 1989); Gustav Richter (5 February 1990); Fritz Bernhard (8 February 1990); and Manfred von Ardenne (14 September 1989).
50 H. Barth, *Hermann Oberth. Leben – Werk – Wirkung* (Feucht, 1985), p. 195.
51 Interview with engineer Hans Wocke (28 April 1989), who worked as a development engineer at Junkers in Dessau until the end of the war, for example on the development of the aircraft Ju 287. Wocke was among the Junkers' engineers deported on 22 October 1946 to the USSR.
52 'Wir melden eine Leistungssteigerung', *Deutsche Technik*, No. 1 (1943), 19.
53 *Deutsche Technik*, No. 1 (1943), 1.
54 For example, a third of the 42,000 concentration-camp prisoners at 'Mittelbau' in Harz (Thuringia) worked in the underground facilities to build 'V-1' flying bombs and 'V-2' rockets; see Kommission zur 'Erforschung der Geschichte der örtlichen Arbeiterbewegung' der Kreisleitung der SED Nordhausen (ed.), *Antifaschistische Mahn- und Gedenkstätte Mittelbau-Dora* (Nordhausen, n.d.).
55 Brandner, *Ein Leben*, pp. 84ff.
56 Brandner, *Ein Leben*, p. 93.
57 Ludwig, *Technik*, p. 266.
58 H. D. Köhler, *Ernst Heinkel – Pionier der Schnellflugzeuge. Eine Biographie* (Koblenz, 1983), especially the chapter 'Der Volksjäger He 162 mit dem Huckepacktriebwerk', pp. 205ff.; also see U. Albrecht's chapter in this collection.

59 Brandner, *Ein Leben*, p. 80.
60 The reference to the Tank memorandum is in Ludwig, *Technik*, p. 267; Tank criticizes the lack of coordination between individual research and industrial production; see also Fieseler, *Meine Bahn*, p. 267; and W. Dornberger, *V2 – Der Schuss ins Weltall. Geschichte einer grossen Erfindung* (Esslingen, 1952), pp. 79, 122 and 124ff.
61 Brochure from the Messerschmidt-Bölkow-Blohm company, '75 Jahre Professor Dr. Ing. E. H. Willy Messerschmidt' (n.p., 1973).
62 For example NSDAP member Brandner writes: 'I preserved my humanity. More than once I defended colleagues, Jews, or forced laborers against the Party, Gestapo, or Labor Front, for the most part with success'; see Brandner, *Ein Leben*, p. 88.
63 Brandner, *Ein Leben*, p. 88.
64 W. Herzberg, *So war es. Lebensgeschichten zwischen 1900 und 1980* (Halle-Leipzig, 1985), p. 215, chapter 'Günter W'.
65 Herzberg, *So war es*, p. 215.
66 See the memoirs of a former electrical engineer at the Air Force Proving Grounds in Rechlin, K. Pflügel, *Schicksale deutscher Luftfahrtingenieure. Müritzsee – Dessau – Wolga 1945–1954. Rechliner Briefe* (Wessling/Oberbayern, n.d.); see also Dornberger, *V2*, p. 291; von Ardenne, *Sechzig Jahre*, p. 177 f.; and my interview with the nuclear physicist Walter Schutze (16 November 1989) also contains relevant confirmatory material.
67 Walker, *German*, p. 222.
68 Dornberger, *V2*, p. 135.
69 *Die Rakete*, 8 No. 2 (1987), 9.
70 *Die Rakete*, 8 No. 2 (1987), 2.
71 E. Klee and O. Merk, *Damals in Peenemünde. An der Geburtsstätte der Weltraumfahrt* (Oldenbourg, 1963), p. 21.
72 B. Ruland, *Wernher von Braun. Mein Leben für die Raumfahrt* (Offenburg, 1969), pp. 197ff.
73 Ruland, *Wernher von Braun*, p. 71.
74 E. Nolte used a similar typology in his study, 'Zur Typologie des Verhaltens der Hochschullehrer im Dritten Reich', *Aus Politik und Zeitgeschichte* (24 November 1965), pp. 3–14.
75 R. Italiaander, *Ein Deutscher namens Eckener. Luftfahrtpionier und Friedens politiker. Vom Kaiserreich bis in die Bundesrepublik* (Konstanz, 1981).
76 For example, a comparison of the cognitive process and the social system is characteristic of P. Lundgreen, 'Hochschulpolitik und Wissenschaft im Dritten Reich', in P. Lundgreen (ed.), *Wissenschaft im Dritten Reich* (Frankfurt a.M., 1985), pp. 9–30.
77 E. Senghaas-Knobloch and B. Vomerg, 'Integrierte Netze. Zur politischen Psychologie des Risikobewusstseins von Ingenieuren', *Bremer Beiträge zur Psychologie*, 63 (1987), pp. 1–21.
78 Senghaas-Knobloch and Vomerg, 'Integrierte Netze', pp. 13ff.
79 The term 'armaments specialists' includes both engineers and scientists who worked on practical armaments projects; also see U. Albrecht, A. Heinemann-Grüder and A. Wellmann, *Die Spezialisten. Deutsche*

Naturwissenschaftler und Techniker in der Sowjetunion nach 1945 (Berlin, 1992).

80 B. Meissner, *Russland, die Westmächte und Deutschland. Die sowjetische Deutschlandpolitik* (Hamburg, 1953), p. 51; Meissner refers to a version of the Molotov memorandum cited by E. R. Stettinius, *Roosevelt and the Russians: The Yalta Conference* (London, 1950), p. 154.

81 The official English version is published in *A Decade of American Foreign Policy: Basic Documents 1941–1949* (Washington, D.C., 1950), p. 33.

82 See K. von Gersdorff and K. Grasmann, *Flugmotoren und Strahltriebwerke* (Koblenz, 1985), pp. 226–44, chapter 'Deutsche Ingenieure im Ausland. Die Gruppen in Frankreich'; J. Gimbel, 'U.S. policy and German scientists: the early Cold War', *Political Science Quarterly*, 101 (1986), 433–51; T. Bower, *The Paperclip Controversy. The Hunt for the Nazi Scientists* (Boston, 1987); C. Lasby, *Project Paperclip. German Scientists and the Cold War* (New York, 1971); and J. Gimbel, *Science, Technology, and Reparations. Exploitation and Plunder in Postwar Germany* (Palo Alto, 1990).

83 P. Nettl, *The Eastern Zone and Soviet Policy in Germany, 1945–1950* (New York, 1977), pp. 200ff.

84 For more detail, see A. Heinemann-Grüder, *Die sowjetische Atombombe* (Münster, 1992).

85 von Ardenne, *Sechzig Jahre*, pp. 178ff.

86 Pose to Heisenberg (18 July 1946), Heisenberg Papers, Max-Planck-Institute for Physics in Munich, cited in Walker, *German*, pp. 184–5.

87 See 'Memorandum concerning the present situation of the German scientists and technical experts evacuated from the Thuringia area by the U.S. Army, Heidenheim, Jan. 1946', RG 260/OMGUS/ODI/17/11/1 Bundesarchiv Koblenz; in March 1946 American specialists camps still existed in Arnsdorf, Darmstadt, Heinenheim, Dillenburg, Rosenthal, Usingen and Weilburg, see 'Exploitation of German Scientific and Technical Personnel,' F.I.A.T. report (29 March 1946) in Bundesarchiv Koblenz RG 260/OMGUS/ODI/17/11/1 Bundesarchiv Koblenz; an exact figure for evacuated scientists and engineers cannot be given, Gimbel discusses several figures (1,294; 1,800; 4,000; 5,500) in 'U.S. policy', p. 443.

88 M. Bar-Zohar, *Die Jagd auf die deutschen Wissenschaftler (1944–1960)* (Frankfurt a.M., 1966), p. 147.

89 See 'Rote V2 in deutschen Werken', *Christ und Welt*, (15 June 1950), 3.

90 'Industrial and Scientific Enterprises under Control of USSR, which employ German scientists', in Bundesarchiv Koblenz RG 260/OMGUS/AGTS/37/1.

91 The Field Intelligence Agency Technical (F.I.A.T.) released special orders to try to prevent Soviet recruiting, see 'German Scientists and Technicians with Special Knowledge whom it may be desired to deny to Powers other than Great Britain and the U.S.A.', Enemy Personnel Exploitation Section F.I.A.T. (31 August 1946); 'Operations of Russian Mission in British and American Zones and Access of such Missions to F.I.A.T. (Br.) and Dustbin', (20 August 1946); 'Policy for Control of German Scientists and Engineers formerly engaged on Service Research and Development', Office of the Deputy Military Governor/Headquarters, Control Commission for

Germany (B.E.), Berlin B.A.O.R. (12 August 1946); all of the above-mentioned reports are in FO 1031/65 Public Record Office, London; cases of luring scientists and engineers are also reported by G. Klimow, *Berliner Kreml* (Cologne, 1951), pp. 276ff. and Lasby, *Project Paperclip*, pp. 140ff.

92 *Christ und Welt* (22 June 1950) and I. Gröttrup, *Die Besessenen und die Mächtigen. Im Schatten der Roten Rakete* (Stuttgart, 1958), p. 17.

93 'Return of Specified Specialists-Scientists to Russian zone', U.S. Group Control Council (Germany), F.I.A.T. (14 September 1945) RG 260/OMGUS/1945–46/41/16 Bundesarchiv Koblenz.

94 'The Employment of German Scientists and Technicians for Civil Industry in U.K.', British Intelligence Objectives Sub-Committee (B.I.O.S.) (18 December 1946) B.T. 211/60 Public Record Office, London.

95 Deputy chiefs of Staff Committee (D.C.O.S.), 27th meeting (11 September 1946) B.T. 211/60 Public Record Office, London.

96 Message from CONFOLK to BERCOMB (26 September 1946) B.T. 211/60 Public Record Office, London.

97 F.I.A.T. Forward Intelligence Group, Control Commission for Germany (24 May 1946) and F.I.A.T. Enemy Personnel Exploitation Section (31 May 1946), both in FO 1031/59 Public Record Office, London.

98 Lasby, *Project Paperclip*, pp. 151 and 180.

99 See H. Esche, *Die Ausplünderung des deutschen Ostens* (Munich, 1948), pp. 30ff.

100 H. and E. Barwich, *Das rote Atom* (Munich, 1967), pp. 19 and 21.

101 For example Gustav Hertz and Heinz Barwich.

102 See Gimbel, 'U.S. Policy', 434ff.

103 Gimbel, 'U.S. Policy', 437 and 445.

104 Gimbel, 'U.S. Policy', 446.

105 See Brandner, *Ein Leben*, p. 123.

106 See Lucius D. Clay to the Joint Chiefs of Staff, 'Removal of Scientific Equipment to U.S.', (6 December 1945) in J. E. Smith (ed.), *The Papers of General Lucius D. Clay: Germany 1945–1949*, vol. I (Bloomington, 1974), p. 129.

107 Gimbel, *Science*, p. 37.

108 This aspect is also underlined by Gimbel, 'U.S. Policy', 450.

109 Bower, *Paperclip Controversy*, pp. 3–8.

110 Bower, *Paperclip Controversy*, p. 254.

111 Esche, *Die Ausplünderung*, p. 31; see also 'Soviet sponsored Research Organizations currently active in Berlin', F.I.A.T. (1 March 1946) FO 1031/65 Public Record Office, London.

3   The guided missile and the Third Reich: Peenemünde and the forging of a technological revolution

*   The research for this article was made possible by a National Science Foundation Scholar's Award (DIR-8911103) and by fellowships from the National Air and Space Museum and the Smithsonian Institution. The

author would like to thank David DeVorkin, Robert Smith, Martin Collins, Peter Jakab, Dick Hallion, Ron Doel and the editors of this book for their comments, and Andy Dunar and Stephen Waring for providing draft chapters of their Marshall Space Flight Center history.

1 The only other achievement that comes close was the development of the turbojet engine and the first operational jet fighter, the Me 262. But the scale of the transformation of aircraft by the 'turbojet revolution', however impressive, does not equal the transformation of rocketry effected at Peenemünde from fireworks and amateur toys to the forerunner of the ICBM. See E. Constant II, *The Origins of the Turbojet Revolution* (Baltimore, 1980). Constant offers a model of technological revolution based on Thomas Kuhn, but he emphasizes conceptual revolutions in 'communities of technological practitioners' as a result of a 'normal technology' reaching its limitations. This seems less appropriate to my case than models of technological 'system-building'. The term 'technological revolution' is used here only informally to indicate the scale of the transformation.

2 *Die V-Waffen* (Stuttgart, 1984). For an earlier, unfootnoted version of the 'V' weapons struggle see D. Irving, *The Mare's Nest* (Boston, 1964), translated as *Die Geheimwaffen des Dritten Reiches* (Gutersloh, 1965). The most influential book in English, F. Ordway and M. Sharpe, *The Rocket Team* (New York, 1979), is riddled with errors, and it mythologizes the record of von Braun and his assistants.

3 On the military-industrial complex and its relationship to rocketry see W. McDougall, *The Heavens and the Earth. A Political History of the Space Age* (New York, 1985).

4 T. Hughes, *Networks of Power* (Baltimore, 1983), pp. 5–17; W. Bijker, T. Hughes and T. Pinch (eds.), *The Social Construction of Technological Systems* (Cambridge, Mass., 1987), pp. 51–82, 112–14.

5 For an introduction to the literature on the 'polycratic' character of the Third Reich see I. Kershaw, *The Nazi Dictatorship*, 2nd edn (London, 1989), pp. 65–81.

6 For details see F. Winter's *Prelude to the Space Age* (Washington, D.C., 1983), pp. 21–54.

7 For an elaboration of this argument see my 'Weimar Culture and Futuristic Technology: The Rocketry and Spaceflight Fad in Germany, 1923–1933', *Technology and Culture* 31 (1990), 725–52.

8 J. Winkler, 'Rückstoss–Arbeiten–Winkler', 8 May 1943, Deutsches Museum, Klee-Sammlung, Korrespondenzbd. 22 (1943), H. Kunze, 'Zur Zusammenarbeit von Hugo Junkers und Johannes Winkler', *NTM: Schriftenreihe für Geschichte der Naturwissenschaften, Technik und Medizin* 24 (1987), 62–82; Arthur Rudolph, oral history interview (hereafter abbreviated as OHI) with M. Neufeld, 4 August 1989, pp. 5–11, National Air and Space Museum (NASM).

9 Winter, *Prelude*, pp. 40–4; W. Ley, *Rockets, Missiles and Space Travel*, 2nd rev. edn (New York, 1962), chap. 6.

10 Lt. Gen. E. Schneider, 'Technik und Waffenentwicklung im Kriege', in

Bilanz des Zweiten Weltkrieges (Oldenbourg, 1953), pp. 225–47, here 236; R.-D. Müller, 'World Power Status Through the Use of Poison Gas? German Preparations for Chemical Warfare, 1919–1945', in W. Deist (ed.), *The German Military in the Age of Total War* (Leamington Spa, 1985), pp. 171–209.

11 On the relations between Army Ordnance and the rocketry pioneers see Bundesarchiv/Militärarchiv (hereafter BA/MA), RH 8/v. 1221–1226 (part of which is also available at the NASM archives on microfilm, NASM/FE 366) and with Heylandt, NASM/FE 724. Only summary descriptions of most archival sources are given here. Details will be given in my forthcoming book, *The Rocket and the Reich: Peenemünde and the German Army Guided Missile Program* (in press). See also W. Dornberger, *V-2* (New York, 1954), pp. 27–32.

12 W. von Braun, 'Konstruktive, theoretische und experimentelle Beiträge zu dem Problem der Flüssigkeitsrakete', (PhD Diss., University of Berlin, 1934), reprint, *Raketentechnik und Raumfahrtforschung*, Sonderheft 1, n.d. (c. 1960); Rudolph, OHI, NASM, 86–7.

13 Zanssen to Wimmer (Chief, Air Ministry Technical Office), 22 May 1935, NASM/FE 746c.

14 BA/MA RH 8/v. 1221–1226.

15 On contracts with industry see the correspondence on microfilm in NASM/FE 724, 744, 752. On Kreiselgeräte, NASM/FE 74b and Fritz Mueller, OHI by M. Neufeld, 6–8 Nov. 1989, NASM.

16 Correspondence with the Luftwaffe in NASM/FE 746; W. von Braun, 'Reminiscences of German Rocketry', *Journal of the British Interplanetary Society* 15 (1956), 133–4; Dornberger, *V-2*, pp. 38–9.

17 Rudolph, OHI, 75–7, NASM.

18 Hölsken, *Die V-Waffen*, pp. 19, 21; von Braun, 'Reminiscences', 137–8; Ordway and Sharpe, *The Rocket Team*, p. 35; H. Mehrtens, 'Angewandte Mathematik und Anwendeungen der Mathematik im nationalsozialistischen Deutschland', *Geschichte und Gesellschaft* 12 (1986), 334; 1939 meetings at Dresden and Kummersdorf in NASM technical file 'Peenemünde #2'. On Hase see the correspondence in NASM/FE 737.

19 von Braun, 'Reminscences', 138–9; Dornberger to Wa F (Schumann) 19 Sept. 1939, NASM file 'Peenemünde #2'; G. Reisig, 'Das kongeniale Vermächtnis Hermann Oberth's und Wernher von Braun's für die Raumfahrt-Entwicklung', *Astronautik* (1987), no. 4, 106. On the Reich Research Council see K.-H. Ludwig, *Technik und Ingenieure im Dritten Reich* (Düsseldorf, 1974), pp. 218–70 and M. Walker, *German National Socialism and the Quest for Nuclear Power 1939–1949* (Cambridge, 1989), p. 18.

20 G. Reisig, 'Von den Peenemünde "Aggregaten" zur amerikanischen "Mondrakete"', *Astronautik* (1986), 5–9, 44–7, 73–8, 111. My primary research confirms Reisig's main conclusions. On *Grossforschung*, see M. Szöllösi-Janze and H. Trischler (eds.), *Grossforschung in Deutschland* (Frankfurt a.M., 1990), especially pp. 13–20, 23–37.

21 For a preliminary synthesis of the Peenemünde guidance and control story

see D. MacKenzie, *Inventing Accuracy* (Cambridge, Mass., 1990), pp. 44–60. MacKenzie does not use the original sources, which are found in NASM/FE 23a, 23b, 74b, 119, 452, 746 and innumerable other files. For an older account which uses part of the original documents, but discusses only Siemens, see S. Karner, 'Die Steuerung der V2', *Technikgeschichte* 46 (1979), 45–66.

22 Gerhard Reisig, OHI by D. DeVorkin and M. Collins, 1985, NASM.
23 Hölsken, *Die V-Waffen*, pp. 20–1; A. Speer, *Inside the Third Reich* (New York, 1971), p. 469.
24 Dornberger Aktennotiz, 21 Aug. 1941, and *Oberkommando der Wehrmacht* [OKW] order of 15 Sept. 1941, in NASM/FE 341. For the best account of the priority battle to 1941 see Hölsken, *Die V-Waffen*, pp. 21–33, but this account contains errors. The original documents are found in the BA/MA Freiburg and on microfilm NASM/FE 341, 342 and 349. I have examined these questions in detail in 'Hitler, the V-2 and the Battle for Priority, 1939–1943', forthcoming in *The Journal of Military History* (July 1993).
25 Hölsken, *Die V-Waffen*, p. 19. The total cost of the programme, including 6,000 V-2s, was around RM 2,000 million.
26 'Milch Collection' documents of *Luftwaffe* development meetings in US National Archives microfilm publication T-321; Hölsken, *Die V-Waffen*, 25–38; E. Klee and O. Merk, *The Birth of the Missile* (New York, 1965), pp. 64–78.
27 Hölsken, *Die V-Waffen*, pp. 36–49; Reisig, OHI, 1985, NASM; and original documents in NASM/FE 342, 357, 358, 692f, 750.
28 Schubert chronicle entries for 23–6 Feb., 16–19 Mar. and 30 Apr. 1943 in BA/MA RH 8/v. 1210; Hölsken, *Die V-Waffen*, pp. 40–1; Dornberger, *V-2*, pp. 80–6.
29 Hölsken, *Die V-Waffen*, pp. 37, 50–1; M. Bornemann, *Geheimprojekt Mittelbau* (Munich, 1971).
30 HAP/VW chronicle entries and documents in BA/MA RH 8/v. 1210; F. Freund and B. Perz, *Das KZ in der Serbenhalle* (Vienna, 1987), pp. 55–91.
31 Hölsken, *Die V-Waffen*, pp. 67–9; von Braun, 'Reminiscences', 142–3; Dornberger *V-2*, pp. 200–7; Wernher von Braun file, Berlin Document Center.
32 Hölsken, *Die V-Waffen*, p. 72. The conversion to a corporation was in discussion no later than June as shown by Dir. Storch?, 'Die Aufgaben der Elektromechanische Werke G.m.b.H. (EMW)', 28 June 1944, NASM/FE 692f.
33 Hölsken, *Die V-Waffen*, p. 211.
34 C. Lasby, *Project Paperclip* (New York, 1971); T. Bower, *The Paperclip Conspiracy* (London, 1987); L. Hunt, *Secret Agenda* (New York, 1991); J. Gimbel, 'German Scientists, United States Denazification Policy, and the "Paperclip" Conspiracy"', *International History Review* 12 (Aug. 1990), 441–65. On the von Braun group under the US Army, the literature is poor. See Ordway and Sharpe, *Rocket Team*, pp. 344–404 and their bibliography.
35 R. Bilstein, *Stages to Saturn* (Washington, D.C., 1980), pp. 81–3, 262–92;

A. Dunar and S. Waring, draft chapters 1 and 2 of the NASA Marshall Space Flight Center history (ms., University of Alabama at Huntsville, 1989); G. Reisig, "Das kongeniale Vermächtnis', *Astronautik* (1988), no. 1, 10–11.

36 Hölsken, *Die V-Waffen*, pp. 203–8. Hölsken does not mention nuclear weapons.

4 Self-mobilization or resistance? Aeronautical research and National Socialism

1 I. Kershaw, *The Nazi Dictatorship: Problems and Perspectives of Interpretation*, 2nd edn (London, 1989), p. 151; cf. M. Broszat *et al.* (eds.), *Bayern in der NS-Zeit*, 6 Vols. (Munich, 1977–1983); M. Broszat and E. Fröhlich, *Alltag und Widerstand. Bayern im Nationalosozialismus* (Munich, 1987).

2 Broszat and Fröhlich, *Alltag*, pp. 49–52. For criticism see H. A. Winkler, 'Referat', in Institut für Zeitgeschichte (ed.), *Alltagsgeschichte der NS-Zeit: Neue Perspektive oder Trivialisierung?* (Munich, 1984), p. 31.

3 The term was coined by K-H. Ludwig, *Technik und Ingenieure im Dritten Reich* (Düsseldorf, 1974).

4 H. Möller, 'Nationalsozialistische Wissenschaftsideologie', in J. Tröger (ed.), *Hochschule und Wissenschaft im Dritten Reich* (Frankfurt a.M. 1986), pp. 65–76. This judgment has to be differentiated, if life sciences like eugenics are examined. For these sciences the historical research has detected within the last years an astonishingly powerful trend towards modernization; see, for example, P. Weindling, *Health, Race and German Politics between National Unification and Nazism, 1870–1945* (Cambridge, 1989); P. Weingart *et al.*, *Rasse, Blut und Gene: Geschichte der Eugenik und Rassenhygiene* (Frankfurt a.M., 1988).

5 A. Beyerchen, *Scientists under Hitler: Politics and the Physics Community in the Third Reich* (New Haven, 1977); M. Walker, 'National Socialism and German Physics', *Journal of Contemporary History* 24 (1989), 63–89; S. Richter, 'Die "Deutsche Physik"', in H. Mehrtens and S. Richter (eds.), *Naturwissenschaft, Technik und NS-Ideologie. Beiträge zur Wissenschaftsgeschichte des Dritten Reiches* (Frankfurt a.M., 1980), pp. 116–41.

6 H. Trischler, 'Historische Wurzeln der Grossforschung: Die Luftfahrtforschung vor 1945', in M. Szöllösi-Janze and H. Trischler (eds.), *Grossforschung in Deutschland* (Frankfurt a.M., 1990), pp. 23–37 and H. Trischler, *Luft- und Raumfahrtforschung in Deutschland 1900–1970* (Frankfurt a.M., 1992), especially pp. 34–88; J. C. Rotta, *Die Aerodynamische Versuchsanstalt in Göttingen, ein Werk Ludwig Prandtls. Ihre Geschichte von den Anfängen bis 1925* (Göttingen, 1990); also see H. Trischler (ed.), *Dokumente zur Geschichte der Luft- und Raumfahrtforschung in Deutschland 1900–1970* (Munich, 1993).

7 Prandtl to Telschow/KWG (11 Feb. 1933) (Archives of the Max-Planck-Gesellschaft [MPGA], I. Abt. Rep. 1 A/1508, pp. 17f.). Cf. H. Trischler, 'Die Luftfahrtforschung im Dritten Reich, Organisation, Steuerung und Effizienz im Zeichen von Aufrüstung und Krieg', in H. Boog (ed.), *Luftkrieg und Luftkriegsführung. Ein internationaler Vergleich* (Herford, 1993).

8 A. Baeumker, *Zur Geschichte der deutschen Luftfahrtforschung – Ein Beitrag* (Munich, 1944), pp. 31ff. See also W. Boje and K. Stuchtey (eds.), *Beiträge zur Geschichte der deutschen Luftfahrtforschung und -technik* (Berlin, 1941); L. Simon, *German Research in World War II* (New York, 1947).
9 Cf. H. Albrecht and A. Hermann, 'Die Kaiser-Wilhelm-Gesellschaft im Dritten Reich', in R. Vierhaus and B. vom Brocke (eds.), *Forschung im Spannungsfeld von Politik und Gesellschaft. Geschichte und Struktur der Kaiser-Wilhelm/Max-Planck-Gesellschaft* (Göttingen, 1990), pp. 356–406.
10 Cf. W. Abendroth, 'Die deutschen Professoren und die Weimarer Republik', in Tröger (ed.), *Hochschule*, pp. 11–25.
11 I. Kershaw, *The Hitler-Myth. Image and Reality in the Third Reich* (Oxford, 1987); I. Kershaw, *Popular Opinion and Political Dissent in the Third Reich, Bavaria 1933–1945* (Oxford, 1983).
12 Memo of Engelbrecht/AVA (1 Jan. 1938) (Historical Archives of the German Research Establishment for Aeronautics [HA/DLR], AVA).
13 Betz to Ackeret/Zurich (30 Oct. 1939), (HA/DLR, AVA).
14 A. Busemann, 'Ludwig Prandtl 1875–1953', *Biographical Memoirs of the Royal Society*, 5 (1959), pp. 193–205.
15 Cf. Trischler, 'Historische Wurzeln', pp. 28ff.
16 C. Tollmien, 'Das Kaiser-Wilhelm-Institut für Strömungsforschung verbunden mit der Aerodynamischen Versuchsanstalt', in Heinrich Becker *et al.* (eds.), *Die Universität Göttingen im Nationalsozialismus. Das verdrängte Kapitel ihrer 250 jährigen Geschichte* (Munich, 1988), pp. 464–88.
17 Göttingen Kreisleiter to Gauamtsleitung of the Amt für Technik der NSDAP (28 May 1937) (Berlin Document Centre henceforth BDC, Prandtl); see also the characterization of Betz from the Kreisleiter of Göttingen (28 May 1937) (BDC, Prandtl). I am very much indebted to Mark Walker for pointing these sources out to me.
18 See: Beyerchen, *Scientists*, passim; and U. Rosenow, 'Die Göttinger Physik unter dem Nationalsozialismus', in Becker *et al.*, *Die Universität Göttingen*, pp. 374–409.
19 Prandtl to Frick (27 Apr. 1933) (Archives of the Max-Planck-Institut für Strömungsforschung [MPIA]); Prandtl to Trefftz/Dresden (6 July 1933) (MPIA). Cf. H. Mehrtens, 'Angewandte Mathematik und Anwendungen der Mathematik im nationalsozialistischen Deutschland', in *Geschichte und Gesellschaft*, 12 (1986), 317–47; H. Mehrtens, 'Mathematics in the Third Reich: Resistance, Adaption and Collaboration of a Scientific Discipline', in R. P. Visser *et al.* (eds.), *New Trends in the History of Science* (Amsterdam 1989), pp. 151–66. As the second article by Mehrtens in this volume shows, Prandtl finally capitulated in the face of Nazi pressure.
20 Prandtl to Himmler (12 July 1938) (MPIA); cf. Beyerchen, *Scientists*; Walker, 'National Socialism', 66ff.
21 Prandtl to Milch (16 Oct. 1933) (MPIA); Milch to Preussischer Minister für Wissenschaft, Kunst und Volksbildung (9 Feb. 1934) (Zentrales Staatsarchiv Potsdam, RMI 26795/3, pp. 135ff.); Prandtl to Göring (28 Apr. 1941);

Prandtl to Raumsauer (8 June 1941); Prandtl to Milch (13 Nov. 1941); Prandtl to Rust (20 Jan. 1942); Prandtl to Joos (28 May 1941); Secretary of State/RLM to Prandtl (19 May 1941); Joos to Prandtl (9 June 1941); Raumsauer to Prandtl (19 June and 31 Oct. 1941); Lucht/RLM to Prandtl (3 Dec. 1941); Ramsauer to Rust (20 Jan. 1942) (MPIA). Citation from: Prandtl to Sommerfeld (10 Dec. 1941) (Deutsches Museum, Unpublished works of Sommerfeld). Cf. Walker, 'National Socialism', pp. 77–82.

22 Madelung to Prandtl (18 May 1942) (MPIA); Prandtl to Lucht (30 June 1942) (HA/DLR, AVA).

23 See Trischler, 'Luftfahrtforschung'.

24 Circular from Georgii (18 Apr. 1944), (MPIA).

25 Madelung to Prandtl (18 May 1942) (MPIA).

26 Prandtl to Telschow/KWG (23 Dec 1942) (MPGA, I. Abt. Rep. 1 A/1480); Prandtl to Baeumker (31 Jan. 1944) (MPIA).

27 For example, Betz to Glum/KWG (13 Oct. 1932) (MPGA, I. Abt. Rep. 1 A/1496, pp. 192–202).

28 Kamm to Baeumker (1 Mar. 1943), (MPIA).

29 Cf. M. Walker, *German National Socialism and the Quest for Nuclear Power, 1939–1949* (Cambridge, 1989), pp. 4–6; M. Walker, 'Legenden um die deutsche Atombombe', *Vierteljahrshefte für Zeitgeschichte* 38 (1990), 45–74, here 54–5.

30 L. Prandtl, 'Reflections of an unpolitical German on the denazification' (1947) (MPIA); cf. Tollmien, 'Das Kaiser-Wilhelm-Institut', pp. 481–3.

31 'Memo about the meeting of the Federal Ministry of Transportation with the "Amt Blank"', (15 June 1953) (Bundesarchiv Koblenz [BAK], B 108/42951); Seewald/DVL to Federal Minister for the Marshall Plan (7 May 1953) (BAK, B 108/42951).

32 See J. Weyer, *Soziale Innovation und Technikkonstruktion am Beispiel der Raumfahrt in der Bundesrepublik Deutschland (1945–1965)* (Bielefeld, 1990), pp. 53–123.

33 Seewald to von Heppe (6 Feb. 1953) (Hauptstaatsarchiv Düsseldorf, NW 178/1474, pp. 106–18).

34 'Minutes of the meeting of the commission of the Deutsche Forschungsgemeinschaft [DFG] for aeronautical research', (17 May 1952) (BA, B 108/42951); 'expert report of the commission of the Deutsche Forschungsgemeinschaft for aeronautical research', (17 Sep. 1952) (Hauptstaatsarchiv Stuttgart, EA 2/45 1348).

35 See H. Theissen, 'Der Geist weht, wo er will. Wissenschaftsgesellschaft ohne Wissenschaftspolitik', *Neue Politische Literatur*, 33 (1988), 383–92; Helmuth Trischler, 'Wissenschaft und Forschung aus der Perspektive des Historikers', *Neue Politische Literatur* 33 (1988), 393–416.

5   Military technology and National Socialist ideology

1 A first draft version of parts of this study was submitted to a symposium commemorating the fiftieth anniversary of World War II at the University

of Marburg (see the proceedings, N. Tschimer and H. W. Göbel (eds.), *Wissenschaft im Krieg – Krieg in der Wissenschaft* (Marburg, 1990), pp. 82–108); a preprint is to be found in *Informationsdienst Wissenschaft und Frieden* 7, No. 4 (1989), 21–8; for an engaged comment, see M. Grieger, 'Fakten der NS-Illusion. Produkte und Projekte der deutschen Rüstungswirtschaft am Ende des zweiten Weltkrieges', *Informationsdienst Wissenschaft und Frieden* 8, No. 1 (1990), 2–58.

2 H. Picker, *Hitlers Tischgespräche im Führerhauptquartier* (Stuttgart, 1977), p. 474 (28 July 1942); cf. also 'In war he who has and commands ... the most recent technological innovations emerges as the fittest, i.e. the most successful soldier' (9 February 1942), quoted from *Die Zeit* No. 43, (20 October 1990), p. 57.

3 This major research project, 'The German Empire and World War II', is published in a series of books; the volume meant here is the first publication, W. Deist, M. Messerschmidt, H-E. Volkmann and W. Wette, *Das Deutsche Reich und der Zweite Weltkrieg*, Vol. I *Ursachen und Voraussetzungen der deutschen Kriegspolitik* (Stuttgart, 1977).

4 I have given a brief account of the development of German chemical weapons until 1933 with the focus upon collaboration with the Soviet Union in U. Albrecht, *History of the Soviet Armaments Industry* (London, 1992).

5 Besides A. Speer's diaries, *Spandauer Tagebücher* (Frankfurt a.M., 1975), see H. Giesler, *Ein anderer Hitler* (Leoni, 1982) or P. Bonatz, *Leben und Bauen* (Stuttgart, 1950).

6 Cf. H. Trischler, 'Historische Wurzeln der Grossforschung: die Luftfahrtforschung vor 1945', in M. Szöllösi-Janze and H. Trischler (eds.), *Grossforschung in Deutschland* (Frankfurt a.M., 1990); C. Tollmien, 'Luftfahrtforschung: Die Aerodynamische Versuchsanstalt in Göttingen', in Tschimer and Göbel, *Wissenschaft im Krieg*, pp. 64–79.

7 For a recent detailed account, see O. Groehler, 'Aufbau- oder Zerstörungsinnovation: die Luftfahrtforschung Hugo Junkers im politischen und militärischen Spannungsfeld der zwanziger und dreissiger Jahre unseres Jahrhunderts', in Tschimer and Göbel, *Wissenschaft im Krieg*, pp. 374–84.

8 P. Gray and O. Thetford, *German Aircraft of the First World War* (London, 1962), p. 218.

9 Gray and Thetford, *German Aircraft*, p. 218.

10 Gray and Thetford, *German Aircraft*, pp. 473–4.

11 The description of Dornier's giant planes follows to some extent the sardonic description in chapter 12 of J. Gilbert, *The World's Worst Aircraft* (Dunton Green, 1978).

12 Gray and Thetford, *German Aircraft*, p. 582.

13 Gilbert, *World's Worst Aircraft*, p. 106, emphasis added.

14 Thus I accept the central argument by Greiger, 'Fakten', p. 25; Greiger provides additional details about SS involvements in the German armament effort.

15 K-H. Ludwig, *Technik und Ingenieure im Dritten Reich* (Düsseldorf, 1979),

p. 486: 'Nearly one month after the first discussion about the transfer of production to underground facilities the "Mittelwerke GmbH" was founded. As a subsidiary of the state "armaments office" (*Rüstungskontor*), it was administratively subordinate to the Central Branch for Economics and Finance (*Zentralabteilung für Wirtschaft und Finanzen*) in the Speer ministry ... In underground cages near Niedersachswerfen in the southern Harz mountains the new Mittelwerk was to prepare and start production of long-range missiles. Initial plans envisaged a "staff" [*Gefolgschaft*] of 16,000 "prisoners" and 2,000 "Germans".' There are good case studies about the use of concentration camps for the National Socialist armaments effort, but there is no comprehensive survey.

16 A good survey is provided by H. Mehrtens and S. Richter (eds.), *Naturwissenschaft, Technik und NS-Ideologie* (Frankfurt a.M., 1980).

17 M. Walker, *German National Socialism and the Quest for Nuclear Power, 1939–1949* (Cambridge, 1989).

18 Cf. Albrecht, *Soviet*, chapter 1.4.

19 R. Horten and P. Selinger, *Nurflügel. Die Geschichte der Horten-Flugzeuge 1933–1960*, 2nd edn (Graz, 1983), p. 75.

20 Cf. W. Spielberger, *Spezial-Panzer-Fahrzeuge des Deutschen Heeres* (Stuttgart, 1976), pp. 41–62 for the 'Maus', and pp. 71–91 for the E 100; R. M. Ogorkiewicz, *Design and Development of Fighting Vehicles* (London, 1967), p. 59; the proposal for a 1000 ton tank was submitted to Hitler on 23 June 1942 – Hitler listened with great interest to a presentation by the Krupp director Dipl.-Ing. Grote, otherwise special officer [*Sonderbeauftragter*] for submarine construction (!); see Spielberger, *Spezial-Panzer-Fahrzeuge*, p. 137.

21 The literature on these projects is abundant; the supergun is described in detail by K-H. Ludwig, 'Die "Hochdruckpumpe", ein Beispiel technischer Fehlentscheidung im 2.Weltkrieg', *Technikgeschichte* 2 (1971); for a recent semi-official account that places armour from the army of the Federal German Republic into this context, see T. Benecke *et al.*, *Flugkörper und Lenkraketen* (Koblenz, 1987); Benecke headed the West German procurement agency (*Bundesamt für Wehrtechnik und Beschaffung*) during the sixties.

22 H. Nowarra, *Die deutsche Luftrüstung 1933–1945*, 4 vols. (Koblenz, 1985–88), vol. I, p. 157; this voluminous edition represents a basically unchanged second edition of a twenty-year-old book (see the next note reference) which may not meet scholarly standards, but which nevertheless reflects the mainstream view in the German aerospace community of its ambivalent past and therefore must be taken into account; citations that are identical in both editions will be referred to both publications.

23 K. Kens and H. Nowarra, *Die deutschen Flugzeuge 1933–1945* (Munich, 1961), p. 323; Nowarra, *Luftrüstung*, vol. III, p. 33.

24 F. Hahn, *Deutsche Geheimwaffen 1939–1945* (Heidenheim, 1963), p. 409.

25 Kens and Norwarra, *Flugzeuge*, p. 283.

26 Saur's career is described in Ludwig, *Technik*.

27 A. Galland, *Die Ersten und die Letzten. Jagdflieger im zweiten Weltkrieg* (Munich, 1953), pp. 363–4.
28 A. Hiller, *Heinkel He 162 "Volksjäger"*. *Entwicklung – Produktion – Einsatz* (Vienna, 1984), p. 22.
29 Hiller, *Heinkel*, p. 22.
30 Hiller, *Heinkel*, p. 73.
31 Sammelbericht des Rüstungsstabs an Feldmarschall General Milch (21 October 1944), 1, reprinted in Hiller, *Heinkel*, p. 70.
32 Horten and Selinger, *Nurflügel*, p. 151.
33 G. Brütting, *Das Buch der deutschen Fluggeschichte* (Stuttgart, 1958), p. 292; cf. also H. D. Köhler, *Ernst Heinkel, Pioneer der Schnellflugzeuge* (Koblenz, 1983), pp. 205–12.
34 Hiller, *Heinkel*, p. 33.
35 R. Kosin, *Die Entwicklung der deutschen Jagdflugzeuge* (Koblenz, 1983), pp. 194ff.
36 Cf. Galland, *Die Ersten*, p. 363 and Hiller, *Heinkel*, p. 32.
37 E. Heinkel, *Stürmisches Leben*, 5th edn (Preetz, 1963), p. 511.
38 Quoted from Hiller, *Heinkel*, p. 30; Philipp Kessler was the chief executive of the Bergmann Electrical Society and chairman of the main industrial consultative committee for armaments production (*Rüstungsbeirat*); he directed 'forced action He 162' as a general commissioner, i.e. an industrialist chosen by the political leadership, not the management of the parent company.
39 Hiller, *Heinkel*, p. 35.
40 Hiller, *Heinkel*, p. 36.
41 Hiller, *Heinkel*, p. 58.
42 Saur quoted in Hiller, *Heinkel*, p. 30.
43 Industrierat des Reichsmarschalls für die Fertigung von Luftfahrtgerät, Umstellausschuss vom 21.11.1942, Bundesarchiv-Militärarchiv, RL 1/17, quoted from Helmut Maier, 'Vor den Karren der Kriegsforschung gespannt', *Informationsdienst Wissenschaft und Frieden* 9, No. 3 (1991), p. 39; Maier gives additional details about the conversion committee.
44 The use of wood in aircraft does not constitute a particular feature of National Socialist military technology *per se*; for constructions with limited stress loads such as high-flying reconnaissance aircraft, wood was occasionally used in other countries as well, for example in the famed DeHavilland DH 98 'Mosquito' plane; Russian aircraft also contained significant amounts of wood in the war years; resorting to wood and other 'surrogate materials' can be seen as specifically National Socialist if they were used for 'disposable equipment' and for jet aircraft designed to withstand stresses caused by high velocity; for opposition by designers to the use of wood in high-performance aircraft, see Hiller, *Heinkel*, p. 36.
45 Heinkel, *Stürmisches Leben*, p. 508; a report in *Der Spiegel* No. 32 (1989), p. 156 adds: 'joiners planed the wooden parts of the mini-fighter in Thuringia and Baden-Württemberg. Cyclists transported the finished parts through the bombed territory of the Reich in backpacks'.

46 Hiller, *Heinkel*, p. 68.
47 Hiller, *Heinkel*, p. 63.
48 Galland, *Die Ersten*, p. 363; also see Hiller, *Heinkel*, p. 33; according to Hiller, an experienced RAF test pilot, Eric Brown, evaluated the He 162 and confirmed this scepticism.
49 Hiller, *Heinkel*, p. 34.
50 Hiller, *Heinkel*, p. 34.
51 Galland, *Die Ersten*, p. 365.
52 Identical passages in Kens and Norwarra, *Flugzeuge*, p. 468 and Nowarra, *Luftrüstung*, vol. III, p. 239.
53 H. Reitsch, *Fliegen – mein Leben*, reprint edn (Munich, 1979), p. 295.
54 Reitsch, *Fliegen*, p. 297.
55 Kens and Norwarra, *Flugzeuge*, p. 469; Norwarra, *Luftrüstung*, vol. III, p. 239; for a more detailed account, see Reitsch, *Fliegen*, pp. 298–9.
56 Kens and Norwarra, *Flugzeuge*, p. 469.
57 Reitsch, *Fliegen*, p. 300.
58 Reitsch, *Fliegen*, p. 303.
59 Reitsch, *Fliegen*, p. 302.
60 W. Dornberger, *Peenemünde* (Esslingen, 1981), p. 158.
61 Dornberger, *Peenemünde*, p. 158.
62 W. von Braun and F. Ordway III, *Raketen* (Munich, 1949), p. 160.
63 O. Pabst, *Kurzstarter und Senkrechtstarter* (Koblenz, 1984), gives a different timetable: 'the invitation for tenders began in the spring of 1944 and lasted until August of 1944, when full-scale work began'.
64 NS 33/36, Fol. 10RS, quoted from Grieger, 'Fakten', p. 26; the most detailed account of the 'adder' project is given by Pabst, the head of development at Messerschmitt-Bölkow-Blohm, *Kurzstarter*, pp. 166–71.
65 Köhler, *Ernst Heinkel*, p. 220; Nowarra, *Luftrüstung*, vol. II, p. 252, evaluates 'Julia' as an 'intermediate solution between a manned air defense rocket . . . and a simplified fast mini-fighter'.
66 Details of the Soviet acquisition of Nazi military technology may be found in Albrecht, *Soviet*.
67 Nowarra, *Luftrüstung*, vol. II, p. 253.
68 Kens and Norwarra, *Flugzeuge*, p. 80; Nowarra, *Luftrüstung*, vol. I, p. 88.
69 Kens and Norwarra, *Flugzeuge*, p. 81; Nowarra, *Luftrüstung*, vol. I, p. 89.
70 Pabst, *Kurzstarter*, p. 170.
71 Kens and Norwarra, *Flugzeuge*, p. 81; Pabst, *Kurzstarter*, p. 170, gives a less dramatic account: 'despite a good start in the beginning, the flight ended unhappily with the death of the pilot, because the "adder" went off course at medium height and crashed into the ground'.
72 Pabst, *Kurzstarter*, p. 166.
73 Hiller, *Heinkel*, p. 22.
74 Nowarra, *Luftrüstung*, vol. I, p. 142.
75 Hiller, *Heinkel*, p. 22.
76 Brütting, *Das Buch*, p. 224.
77 The Institute for Aeronautical Engineering at the Braunschweig Technical

University received a development contract for such items, see for example Maier, 'Vor den Karren', p. 36.

78 Kens and Nowarra, *Flugzeuge*, p. 469.

79 Nowarra, *Luftrüstung*, vol. II, p. 253.

80 Nowarra, *Luftrüstung*, vol. IV, p. 48.

81 Cf. the polemics by Köhler, *Ernst Heinkel*, pp. 210ff, against a brief passage about the people's fighter Heinkel 162 in Ludwig, *Technik*; the author also came under attack from a senior broadcast aviation reporter when addressing the very same matter: 'It would be obscene to assume that the distinguished Ernst Heinkel would have considered putting the Nazi youth at the controls of the people's fighter' – but this was exactly the terms of the tender for this programme.

82 See R. Evans, *In Hitler's Shadow: West German Historians and the Attempt to Escape from the Nazi Past* (New York, 1989) and H-U. Wehler, *Entsorgung der deutschen Vergangenheit? Ein polemischer Essay zum "Historikerstreit"* (Munich, 1988).

83 Heinkel, *Stürmisches Leben*, p. 509; *Der Spiegel* No. 32 (1989), p. 156, defines the people's fighter concept as follows: 'Armaments minister Speer now wanted a mini-jet fighter, without many frills, inexpensive and unsophisticated in design. In addition, any Nazi youth should be able to master the equipment after short instruction'.

84 Nowarra, *Luftrüstung*, vol. III, p. 252.

85 Nowarra, *Luftrüstung*, vol. IV, p. 56.

86 Kens and Nowarra, *Flugzeuge*, p. 79; Nowarra, *Luftrüstung*, vol. I, p. 88.

87 Kosin, *Die Entwicklung*, p. 202.

88 Kosin, *Die Entwicklung*, p. 203.

89 Ludwig, *Technik*, p. 456.

90 G. Hortleder, *Das Gesellschaftsbild des Ingenieurs* (Frankfurt a.M., 1970); E. Korgon, *Die Stunde der Ingenieure* (Düsseldorf, 1976); A. Heinemann-Grüder's contribution to this volume; also see H. Trischler, *Luft- und Raumfahrtforschung in Deutschland, 1900–1970. Eine politische Wissenschaftsgeschichte* (Frankfurt a.M., 1992); H. Petzold, *Moderne Rechenkünstler. Die Industrialisierung der Rechentechnik in Deutschland* (Munich, 1992); and J. Radkau, *Technik in Deutschland. Vom 18. Jahrhundert bis zur Gegenwart* (Frankfurt a.M., 1989).

91 J. Herf, *Reactionary Modernism: Technology, Culture, and Politics in Weimar and the Third Reich* (Cambridge, 1984).

92 R. Hamann and J. Hermand, *Stilkunst um 1900* (Berlin, 1967).

6   'Area research' and 'spatial planning' from the Weimar Republic to the German Federal Republic

1 'Wie alle grossen Städte bestand sie aus Unregelmässigkeit, Wechsel, Vorgleiten, Nichtschritthalten, Zusammenstössen von Dingen und Angelengenheiten, bodenlosen Punkten der Stille dazwischen, Schlag und der ewigen Verstimmung und Verschiebung aller Rythem gegeneinander, und glich im

ganzen einer kochenden Blase, die in einem Gefäss ruht, das aus dem dauerhaften Stoff von Häusern, Gesetzen, Verordnungen und geschichtlichen Überlieferungen besteht.' R. Musil, *Der Mann ohne Eigenschaften* (Reinbek, 1978), p. 10.

2 The debate on modernity has been carried over to the National Socialist period since J. Herf's *Reactionary Modernism: Technology, Culture and Politics in the Weimar Republic and the Third Reich* (Cambridge, 1984).

3 J. Schulz zur Weisch, 'Regionalplanung', in H. Kerber and A. Schmieder (eds.), *Handbuch Soziologie* (Reinbek, 1984), p. 475.

4 E. Howard, *Garden Cities of Tomorrow* (London, 1902).

5 J. Reulecke, *Geschichte der Urbanisierung in Deutschland* (Frankfurt a.M., 1985), p. 85.

6 F. Schumacher, *Wesen und Organisation der Landesplanung im hamburgisch-preussischen Landesplanungsgebiet* (Hamburg, 1932); M. Rössler, 'Die Hochschularbeitsgemeinschaft für Raumforschung an der Hamburger Universität 1934 bis 1945', in E. Krause, L. Huber and H. Fischer (eds.), *Hochschulalltag im "Dritten Reich". Die Hamburger Universität 1933–1945* (Berlin, 1991), pp. 1035–78.

7 J. Short (ed.), *The Social Fabric of the Metropolis* (Chicago, 1971); M. Deegan, *Jane Addams and the Men of the Chicago School 1892–1918* (New Brunswick, 1990).

8 W. Christaller, *Die zentralen Orte in Süddeutschland. Eine Ökonomisch-geographische Untersuchung über die Gesetzmässigkeit der Verbreitung der Siedlungen mit städtischen Funktionen* (Jena, 1933); on Christaller's life and work see M. Rössler, 'Applied geography and area research in Nazi society: central place theory and planning, 1933 to 1945', *Environment and Planning D: Society and Space* 7 (1989), pp. 419–31; Christaller's concept became a model for the historical analyses of city-surroundings processes, see F. Irsigler, 'Stadt und Umland in der historischen Forschung. Theorien und Konzepte', in N. Bulst, J. Hooch and F. Irsigler (eds.), *Bevölkerung, Wirtschaft und Gesellschaft. Stadt-Landbeziehungen in Deutschland und Frankreich* (Trier, 1983), pp. 13–38.

9 See H. Weyl, 'Nachruf auf Josef Umlauf', *Nachrichten der Akademie für Raumforschung und Landesplanung* No. 49 (January 1990), pp. 1–3.

10 See J. Umlauf, *Zur Entwicklungsgeschichte der Landesplanung und Raumordnung* (Hannover, 1986), Veröffentlichungen der Akademie für Raumforschung und Landesplanung, Abhandlungen 90.

11 'Die Stadt ist das Instrument nichtpersonalen Lebens, die Gussform, in der Menschen, Interessen, Geschmackrichtungen in ihrer ganzen Komplexität und Vielfalt zusammenfliessen und gesellschaftlich erfahrbar werden.' R. Sennett, *Verfall und Ende des Öffentlichen Lebens. Die Tyrannei der Intimität* (Frankfurt a.M., 1985), p. 382.

12 K. Scherpe, 'Von der erzählten Stadt zur Stadterzählung', in J. Fohrmann and H. Müller (eds.), *Diskurstheorien und Literaturwissenschaft* (Frankfurt a.M., 1988), pp. 418–37, here p. 418.

13 R. Lindner, *Die Entdeckung der Stadtkultur. Soziologie aus der Erfahrung der Reportage* (Frankfurt a.M., 1990).

14 H. Mehrtens, *Moderne – Sprache – Mathematik. Eine Geschichte des Streits um die Grundlagen der Disziplin und des Subjekts formaler Systeme* (Frankfurt a.M., 1990).

15 D. Peukert, *Die Weimarer Republik* (Frankfurt a.M., 1987), p. 182.

16 Peukert, *Die Weimarer Republik*.

17 Peukert, *Die Weimarer Republik*, pp. 187–8.

18 See P. Nolte, *Staatsbildung als Gesellschaftsreform. Politische Reformen in Preussen und den süddeutschen Staaten 1800–1820* (Frankfurt a.M., 1990), pp. 54–75.

19 Hanns Kerrl became *Reichsminister ohne Geschäftsbereich* (Reichsminister without portfolio) in 1934, in 1935 leader of the *Reichsparteitag Nürnberg* (Reich Party Congress Nuremberg) committee and director of the '*Reichsstelle für Raumordnung*', and in 1936 Reichminister for Religious Affairs.

20 For example, the *Generalinspektor für das Strassenwesen*, the *Generalinspektor für die Reichshauptstadt*, the *Generalbaurat für die Hauptstadt der Bewegung* (Munich), the *Reichsbaurat für die Stadt Linz* and the *Reichsjugendführung*; with the exception of the latter, all of them were institutions of architecture and planning, which were directly under Hitler's authority.

21 *Meyers Lexikon* 4 (Leipzig, 1938), pp. 1182–3.

22 See M. Rössler, 'Die Institutionalisierung einer neuen Wissenschaft im Nationalsozialismus. Raumforschung und Raumordnung 1935–1945', *Geographische Zeitschrift* 75 (1987), pp. 176–94.

23 E. Pahl-Weber, 'Die Reichsstelle für Raumordnung und die Ostplanung', in M. Rössler and S. Schleiermacher (eds.), *Der Generalplan Ost. Aspekte der nationalsozialistischen Planungs-und Vernichtungspolitik* (Berlin, 1993).

24 *Meyers Lexikon* 4 (Leipzig, 1938), p. 1190.

25 I. Kershaw, *The Nazi Dictatorship: Problems and Perspectives of Interpretation*, 2nd edn (London, 1989).

26 The government president Minden to the Generalbevollmächtigten für die Reichsverwaltung, Minister of the Interior, (21 January 1942) Box No. 3 folder 256, Himmler Files, Hoover Institution Archives.

27 'Das kriegswichtige Forschungsprogramm', *Raumordnung und Raumforschung* (1939), p. 502.

28 Geisler to Jarmer (22 April 1940), R113/14.N Bundesarchiv Koblenz.

29 *Struktur und Gestalt der Zentralen Orte des Deutschen Ostens* (Leipzig, 1941).

30 *Struktur*, p. 129.

31 *Archiv für Wirtschaftsplanung* 1 (1941).

32 See the autobiography of K. Meyre, *Über Höhen und Tiefen. Ein Lebensbericht* (Salzderhelden, 1970); private property of Mrs Dina Meyre, Saizderhelden.

33 The *Bund Artam* was created in 1924 as a peasant movement and became a part of the Hitler Youth in 1933.

34 For example the East-Ministry of Rosenberg and the racial-political office.

35 C. Zentner and F. Bedürftig, *Das grosse Lexikon des Dritten Reiches* (Munich, 1985), p. 208). An overview on the new research is given by Rössler and Schleiermacher, *Der Generalplan*.

36 See for details M. Rössler, *Wissenschaft und Lebensraum. Geographische Ostforschung im Nationalsozialismus. Ein Beitrag zur Disziplingeschichte des Faches* (Berlin, 1990), pp. 168ff.

37 K. Meyer, 'Walter Christaller', in *Handwörterbuch der Raumforschung und Raumordnung* (Hannover, 1970), pp. 403–10, here p. 405.

38 Remarks by SS-Gruppenführer Greifelt to the Reichsführer-SS (10 August 1942) Box No. 3, folder 257, Himmler Files, Hoover Institution Archives.

39 As Bruno Wasser has pointed out in Rössler and Schleiermacher, *Der Generalplan.*

40 'Dass es kein totaler Neubeginn war, dass vielmehr über die weltpolitische Zäsur 1945 hinweg vielerlei politische und wirtschaftliche Kontinuitätslinien bald wieder wirksam wurden ... ist heute schon beinahe ein Gemeinplatz.' C. Klessmann, *Die doppelte Staatsgründung. Deutsche Geschichte 1945–1955* (Bonn, 1984), *Schriftenreihe der Bundeszentrale für politische Bildung* 37.

41 On the denazification of architects and architecture see K. von Beyme, *Der Wiederaufbau. Architektur und Städtebaupolitik in beiden deutschen Staaten* (Munich, 1987).

42 See remarks in R 113/2374, Bundesarchiv Koblenz.

43 'Arbeitsbericht der Akademie für Raumforschung und Landesplanung', in *Raumforschung und Raumordnung* 2 (1948), p. 68.

44 See the documentation of the dispute in the files of the Hochschulwesen II, Wh 59, Staatsarchiv Hamburg.

45 See 'Arbeitsbericht', p. 69.

46 *Das Deutsche Flüchtlingsproblem. Sonderheft der Zeitschrift für Raumforschung* (Bonn, 1950).

47 Klessmann, *Die doppelte Staatsgründung*, p. 37.

48 Klessmann, *Die doppelte Staatsgründung*, p. 243.

7   The ideological origins of institutes at the *Kaiser Wilhelm Gesellschaft* in National Socialist Germany

* I would like to thank Monika Renneberg and Mark Walker for their helpful comments on an earlier draft of this paper.

1 For two major works in English on race hygiene and *Deutsche Physik*, respectively, see R. Proctor, *Racial Hygiene: Medicine under the Nazis* (Cambridge, 1988), and A. Beyerchen, *Scientists under Hitler, Politics and the Physics Community in the Third Reich* (New Haven, 1977).

2 Recently the history of geography in National Socialist Germany and its relation to *Lebensraum* has received much attention. See M. Rössler, '*Wissenschaft und Lebensraum*': *Geographische Ostforschung im Nationalsozialismus* (Berlin, 1990).

3 For a detailed study of the Kaiser Wilhelm Gesellschaft during the Third Reich see K. Macrakis, *Surviving the Swastika: Scientific Research in Nazi Germany* (New York, 1993).

4 J. Johnson, *The Kaiser's Chemists: Science and Modernization in Imperial Germany* (Chapel Hill, 1990), pp. 48–67, 122–58.

5 See Macrakis, *Surviving the Swastika*, chs. 2 and 6 for more details on the founding of the institute for biology.

6 See Macrakis, *Surviving the Swastika*, ch. 2 for details about the individual industry-related institutes.

7 Paul Weindling, 'Weimar Eugenics, The Kaiser Wilhelm Institute for Anthropology, Human Heredity and Eugenics in Social Context', *Annals of Science* 42 (1985), 303–18.

8 Weindling, 'Eugenics'.

9 Weindling, 'Eugenics'.

10 I have found W. Smith. *The Ideological Origins of Nazi Imperialism*, (New York, 1986), invaluable in tracing the origins of the concept of *Lebensraum*. Much of this section is based on reading in Smith. For example Smith uses the terms 'migrationist colonialism' and 'romantic agrarianism'.

11 For the concept of 'reactionary modernism', see J. Herf, *Reactionary Modernism: Technology, Culture, and Politics in Weimar and the Third Reich* (Cambridge, 1984).

12 See W. Tornow, *Die Entwicklungslinien der landwirtschaftlichen Forschung in Deutschland* (Hiltrup bei Münster, 1955), pp. 144–7, for an overview of institutional developments in agricultural research in the Third Reich.

13 See V. Klemm. 'Agrarwissenschaften in der Zeit der faschistischen Diktatur – ihre Rolle als wissenschaftliches Erbe', *Tag.-Ber, Akad.Landwirtsch.-Wiss.DDR. Berlin* 254 (1987), 35–54, here 44. Klemm in turn has culled this information from H. Piegler's useful handbook: *Deutsche Forschungsstätten im Dienste der Nahrungsfreiheit* (Neudamm, 1940).

14 K. Düwell, *Deutschlands auswärtige Kulturpolitik, 1918–1932: Grundlinien und Dokumente* (Cologne, 1976) has made some useful typologies in his book, p. 36.

15 Zentrales Staatsachiv (ZStA, Potsdam), Reichserziehungsministerium (REM), Nr.3191, Minutes of Meeting on International Organizations on 12 November 1940, 11 December 1940, p. 9.

16 ZStA, Potsdam, Nr. 3191, p. 11.

17 ZStA, Potsdam, REM Nr.3190, a statement by Zschintzsch (from the Reich Ministry of the Interior) marked 'confidential', 10 October 1939.

18 ZStA, Potsdam, REM Nr.3190, Note on meeting of 17 January 1941.

19 ZStA, Potsdam, REM Nr.3190, Foreign Office to REM and Reich Ministry of the Interior, 17 September 1940. See R. Siegmund-Schultze, 'Faschistische Pläne zur "Neuordnung" der europaische Wissenschaft: Das Beispiel Mathematik', *NTM* 23 (1986), 1–17, for the example of mathematics in schemes for a new order of European science.

20 ZStA, Potsdam, REM Nr.3191, Minutes of 12 November 1940 Meeting, 11 December 1940, p. 40.

21 ZStA, Potsdam, REM Nr.3191, pp. 21–3.

22 ZStA, Potsdam, REM Nr.3191, p. 24.

368 | NOTES TO PAGES 146–149

23 Archiv der Akademie der Wissenschaften der Deutschen Demokratischen
   Republik (AAW), KWG, 7, Nationalsozialistische Deutsche Arbeiterspartei,
   Reichsleitung, signed Dr Bader, an den Direktor des Kaiser Wilhelm-
   Instituts für ausländisches Recht und Völkerrecht, 18 February 1942.
   Although referred to as 'Amt Rosenberg', the office is also known as the
   Rosenberg Ministry.
24 AAW, KWG Aktennotiz by Telschow, 9 March 1942.
25 AAW, KWG Aktennotiz by Telschow, 10 February 1942.
26 AAW, KWG Von Wettstein to Telschow, 9 March 1942.
27 Jahrbuch 1941 der Kaiser-Wilhelm-Gesellschaft zur Förderung der Wissenschaften, p. 83.
28 For the example of Werner Heisenberg as a goodwill ambassador see also
   M. Walker, *German National Socialism and the Quest for Nuclear Power,
   1939–1949*, (Cambridge, 1989), pp. 105–18, 222–8.
29 A very large Kaiser Wilhelm Institute for Animal Breeding was founded in
   Rostock in northeastern Germany in 1939, but will not be considered in
   detail here for reasons of conceptual unity, space, and because it related less
   to the ideology of *Lebensraum*.
30 Archives of the Max Planck Gesellschaft (MPGA), KWG, 138, Hauptver-
   sammlung.26, Der Oberbürgermeister der Hauptstadt Breslau to Planck, 24
   May 1937. The Mayor of Breslau had already written to Planck inviting the
   Society to hold its yearly meeting in Breslau, which it eventually did in 1939.
31 MPGA, KWG, 2912, 'Institut für landwirtschaftliche Arbeitswissenschaft in
   der KWG, 4 April 1940–6 December 1940'. Aktennotiz by Telschow, 4
   April 1940; Berlin Document Centre (BDC), 'Otto Fitzner'.
32 MPGA, KWG, 2912, 'Grundgedanken für ein Institut für landwirtschaftliche Arbeitswissenschaft'. Probably by Preuschen, the future director; 7
   April 1940.
33 MPGA, KWG, 2912, Aktennotiz by Telschow, 5 September 1940.
34 MPGA, KWG, 2912, Aktenvermerk, 20 September 1940.
35 MPGA, KWG, 2912, Aktenvermerk, 26 September 1940. Re: call of Preuschen about visit with Backe.
36 MPGA, KWG, 2912, Mentzel, from REM to the KWG, 11 October 1940.
37 MPGA, KWG, 2912, Telschow's speech at the founding meeting in Breslau,
   6 December 1940.
38 MPGA, KWG, 2912, Aktennotiz by Ernst Telschow, 4 April 1940.
39 BDC, NSDAP Party Card Gerhard Preuschen.
40 I would like to thank Monika Renneberg for helping me make this point
   more explicit.
41 MPGA, KWG, 2912, 'Institut für landwirtschaftliche Arbeitswissenschaft in
   der KWG, 4 April 1940–6 December 1940'. 'Tasks and work methods of the
   Institute for the science of agriculture.' Lecture by Dr G. Preuschen at the
   institute opening, 6 December 1940.
42 MPGA, KWG, 2912, 'Stichworte für die Rede von Prof. Dr Mentzel'.
43 MPGA, KWG, 2912, Stichworte für die Rede von Staatssekretär Backe'.
44 MPGA, KWG, 2912, See also newspaper clippings: 'Brücke zum europäischen Südosten', *Oberschlesischer Kurier*, 8 (December 1940).

45 MPGA, KWG, 2913, Institut für landwirtschaftliche Arbeitswissenschaft, 11.12.1940–23.1.1945. Note by Telschow, 22 February 1941.
46 N. Rich, *Hitler's War Aims: the Establishment of the New Order*, Vol. I (New York, 1974), p. 258.
47 H-J. Hoppe, *Bulgarien – Hitlers eigenwilliger Verbündeter* (Stuttgart, 1979).
48 MPGA, KWG, 2924, 'Deutsch–Bulgarisches Institut für landwirtschaftliche Forschung'. Telschow to the Reich Ministry for Nutrition and Agriculture, 1 April 1941.
49 MPGA, KWG, 2924, Telschow to the Reich Ministry for Nutrition and Agriculture, 1 April 1941.
50 MPGA, KWG, 2924, 'The tasks of the German–Bulgarian Institute for agricultural research'.
51 MPGA, KWG, 2924, 'Program für die Grundsteinlegung des Bulgarisch–Deutschen Instituts für Landwirtschaftliche Forschung in Sofia ... vom 11. bis zum 15. September 1942'.
52 MPGA, KWG, 2924, 12 September 1942, Pressenotiz.
53 MPGA, KWG, 2924, 'From a speech by a Bulgarian with no authorship.
54 MPGA, KWG, 2924, Aktennotiz by Telschow, 6 September 1942.
55 MPGA, KWG, 2924, Telschow to Mentzel, 14 January 1943.
56 BDC, file on Arnold Scheibe.
57 MPGA, KWG, 2927, 'Deutsch–Bulgarisches Institut für landwirtschaftliche Forschung'. Mentzel, President of the RFR, to Scheibe, 20 January 1944. See also the thirteen Deutsche Forschungsgemeinschaft (DFG) cards with a listing of contracts, BDC.
58 MPGA, KWG, 2931, Deutsch–Bulgarisches Institut für landwirtschaftliche Forschung, Kuratorium.
59 MPGA, KWG, 2931, Telschow to Mentzel, 14 January 1943.
60 MPGA, KWG, Deutsch–Griechisches Forschungsinstitut für Biologie, 2949. Three documents refer to 'Dr Tzonis' plan': 'Gutachten über Gründung eines Griechisch–Deutschen Forschungsinstitutes für Biologie', by Max Hartmann, 15 January 1938; Roth, Foreign Ministry, to the head of the KWG, c. 24 August 1940; Hartmann to Telschow, 26 August 1940.
61 MPGA, KWG, 2949, Gutachten über die Gründung eines Griechisch–Deutschen Forschungsinstitutes für Biologie' by Max Hartmann, 15 January 1938.
62 MPGA, KWG, 2949, 'Zweck und Richtungen des Deutschgriechischen Biologischen Instituts'.
63 MPGA, KWG, 2949, 'Gründungsstatut des Deutsch–Griechischen Instituts für Biologie'.
64 MPGA, Rep. 14, Deutsch–Griechisches Institut für Biologie, Fritz von Wettstein to Ernst Telschow, 4 January 1941.
65 MPGA, Rep. 14, Hartmann to Telschow, 26 August 1940.
66 MPGA, Rep. 14, Telschow to Roth at the Foreign Office, 30 August 1940.
67 MPGA, Rep. 14, 'Bericht über die Verhandlung von Prof. M. Hartmann über das deutsch–griechische Institut für Biologie in Athen vom 3. bis 17 Dezember 1941'.

68 MPGA, KWG, 2950, 'Bericht von Professor Dr M. Hartmann über seine Tätigkeit in Athen vom 9. Juni bis 10. Juli 1942 für das Deutsch–Griechische Institut für Biologie in Piräus'.

69 MPGA, KWG, 2946, 'Plan eines Deutsch–Ungarischen Instituts für landwirtschaftliche Forschung, 2.9.1941–15.6.1943'. Wilmowsky to Vögler, 2 September 1941.

70 MPGA, KWG, 2946, Note on a meeting at the Foreign Office on 13 October 1941 by Ernst Telschow.

71 MPGA, KWG, 2946, Rudolf Mentzel to the KWG, 21 October 1941; Albert Vögler to Mentzel, 6 November 1941; Mentzel to the President of the KWG, 26 February 1942.

72 R. Herzstein, *When Nazi Dreams Come True* (London, 1982), p. 110.

73 A. Fischer, 'Die Bedeutung der südosteuropäischen Länder für die Versorgung Deutschlands mit planzlichen Ölrohstoffen', *Leipziger Vierteljahrsschrift für Südosteuropa* 3(1939), 177–83. For the economic relationship between Greater Germany and southeastern Europe see R. Krugmann, *Südosteuropa und Grossdeutschland: Entwicklung und Zukunftsmöglichkeiten der Wirtschaftsbeziehungen* (Breslau, 1939).

74 ZStA, Potsdam, REM, Nr. 690, quoted by Rössler, *Wissenschaft*, p. 90. See also C. Klessmann, 'Osteuropaforschung und Lebensraumpolitik', in P. Lundgreen (ed.), *Wissenschaft im Dritten Reich* (Frankfurt a.M., 1985), pp. 364–7.

75 See R. Goguel, 'Über die Mitwirkung deutscher Wissenschaftler am Okkupationsregime in Polen im Zweiten Weltkrieg, untersucht an drei Institutionen der deutschen Ostforschung', (Dissertation Humboldt-Universität, Berlin (East), 1964), pp. 132–75, Klessmann, 'Osteuropaforschung', pp. 364–7, Rössler, *Wissenschaft*, pp. 84–102, for information on the German East Institute, and Goguel, 'Mitwirkung' pp. 90–131, Klessmann, 'Osteuropaforschung', p. 367–9, Rössler, *Wissenschaft*, pp. 103–11, for the Reich University in Poland. Rössler's discussion focuses primarily on geography at the two institutions. See also M. Burleigh, *German Turns Eastward: a Study of Ostforschung in the Third Reich* (Cambridge, 1988).

76 See Macrakis, *Surviving the Swastika*, Epilogue.

77 A. Scheibe, 'Plannung und Aufbau des "Deutsch–Bulgarischen Instituts für landwirtschaftliche Forschungen (Kaiser-Wilhelm-Institut)" in Sofia', in B. Rajewsky and G. Schreiber (eds.), *Aus der Deutschen Forschung der letzten Dezennien*, (Stuttgart, 1956).

78 G. Preuschen, 'Max-Planck-Institut für Landarbeit und Landtechnik in Bad Kreuznach', in *Jahrbuch der Max-Planck-Gesellschaft zur Förderung der Wissenschaften, Die Max-Planck-Gesellschaft und ihre Institute und Forschungsstellen* (Göttingen, 1961), p. 525.

79 Preuschen, 'Max-Planck-Institut', p. 527. The work of the institute is also covered in the reports published in *Die Naturwissenschaften* 38 (1951), 379.

80 See the minutes of the senate of the Max-Planck-Gesellschaft, MPGA, 29 October 1948, p. 13; 18 November 1949, pp. 11–13.

81 Preuschen, 'Max-Planck-Institut', p. 523.

82 Preuschen, 'Max-Planck-Institut', pp. 522–34.
83 By 1943 the Reich Nutrition Ministry had contributed 3,518,500 RM to the Society. This was even more than the REM contribution of 3,386,000 RM which had traditionally supported the Society and which supported research in many different areas, while the Reich Nutrition Ministry was primarily interested in research on agriculture and nutrition. For more details on financial support from the various ministries and for Backe's interest in becoming vice-president of the Society, see Macrakis, *Surviving the Swastika*, ch. 7.

8   Biological research at universities and Kaiser Wilhelm Institutes in Nazi Germany

Methods and sources

i. Biologists at universities: We collected the names of all *'habilitated'* biologists who worked between 1932 and 1944 at the botanical, zoological and the two contemporary genetic institutes at universities. The names were taken from prospectuses (*Vorlesungsverzeichnisse*) of the twenty-nine German and Austrian universities (including the contemporary German universities in Posen, Prague and Strassburg) and from five *Technische Hochschulen*.

ii. Biologists at Kaiser Wilhelm Institutes (KWIs): We collected: the names of all 'habilitated' biologists, including a few biochemists and biophysicists, who worked between 1932 and 1944 in the KWI for Biology in Berlin-Dahlem (founded in 1912), the Hydrobiological Station in Plön (taken over by the KWG in 1917), the KWI for Breeding Research in Müncheberg (founded in 1928) and its branch in East Prussia, the Research Department for Experimental Genetics of the KWI for Brain Research in Berlin-Buch (1925), and the KWI for Biophysics in Frankfurt (1937); the names of PhD 'non-habilitated' biologists at these KWIs were included if their names could be found in the *'Kürschners Deutsches Gelehrten Lexikon'* due to a later habilitation, and if they had received DFG grants or research stipends or if they had been dismissed during or after 1933. The list was compiled from the annual reports of the *Kaiser Wilhelm-Gesellschaft* between 1932 and 1943.

We located a total of 445 biologists who worked between 1933 and 1945 at universities (383) or at KWIs (62).

iii. Data on the dismissal and emigration of scientists was obtained from: the International Biographical Dictionary of Central European Emigrés, 1933–1945; lists of the *Notgemeinschaft Deutscher Wissenschaftler im Ausland*; records of the *Reichserziehungsministerium* in the *Bundesarchiv* in Koblenz (BAK); files of the Rockefeller Archive Center; files of the 'Society for the Protection of Science and Learning' (ms. SPSL) in the Bodleian Library in Oxford; files of the *Archiv der Max-Planck-Gesellschaft* (MPGA); files of Archives of German and Austrian Universities (UA); affiliations given in the scientific publications of biologists who presumably were emigrants.

iv. Information about the content of biological research and its funding was obtained from: the FIAT reviews of biological research in German science,

1939–1946: German scientists were required by the Allied occupation governments to write detailed reports about the progress in their particular fields of research during World War II. Four volumes deal with biology, four with biochemistry and two with biophysics; the DFG grants, which were consulted in the *Bundesarchiv* in Koblenz; of the 445 biologists mentioned above, 220 applied between 1933 and 1945 for grants from the DFG.

v. Information about the possible NSDAP membership of each of these biologists was obtained from the Berlin Document Center (BDC).

vi. The Science Citation Index 1945–1954 (SCI) was used to estimate the influence and quality of biological research. This SCI lists all citations of publications up to 1954. The number of citations of all of an individual researcher's articles may serve as an estimate of the influence of his or her research. This number divided by the number of articles cited should provide some indication of the quality of the research. We are aware of the fact that the number of citations does not only reflect the scientific importance of a person but also may depend on his or her prestige and the field of research.[79] In spite of this and other sources of error such as unequal accessibility of journals, a citation analysis of the research of groups of persons whose work covers a similar spectrum of subjects seems to be justified. We tried to avoid possible technical errors: we did not count recognizable autocitations; since some scientists cannot be differentiated by their names, citations were identified according to their contents. The same identification was made when names were misspelled in the SCI.

There is also the problem of multi-authorship, but that occurred much less often than it does today. The directors indeed are often first authors of multi-authored papers.

We thank Bob Jack and Diane Paul for their critical reading of this manuscript. This work was supported by grant Mu 575/4–1 of the Deutsche Forschungsgemeinschaft through *Schwerpunkt Wissenschaftsemigration*.

Notes

1 S. Goudsmit, *Alsos* (New York, 1947), p. 239.
2 Mentzel had been president of the *Deutsche Forschungsgemeinschaft* (DFG) since 1937; Schumann had been head of the department for scientific research and technology in the *Reichserziehungsministerium*.
3 See for example W. Heisenberg, *Notwendigkeit wissenschaftlicher Forschung*, in H. Eickemeyer (ed.), *Abschlussbericht des deutschen Forschungsrates* (Munich, 1953), p. 216; A. R. Michaelis and R. Schmidt, *Wissenschaft in Deutschland – Niedergang und neuer Aufstieg* (Stuttgart, 1983), p. 59; M. L. Zarnitz, *Molekulare und physikalische Biologie. Bericht zur Situation eines interdisziplinären Forschungsgebietes in der Bundesrepublik Deutschland* (Göttingen, 1968), p. 61.
4 See for example U. Geuter, *Die Professionalisierung der deutschen Psychologie im Nationalsozialismus* (Frankfurt a.M., 1984); M. Walker, *German National Socialism and the Quest for Nuclear Power, 1939–1949* (Cambridge, 1989), esp. pp. 60–80.

5 See for example E. Y. Hartshorne, *The German Universities and National Socialism* (London, 1937), esp. pp. 49–71; A. Beyerchen, *Scientists under Hitler* (New Haven, 1977), esp. pp. 9–14; Geuter, *Die Professionalisierung*, esp. pp. 99–115; for biology see Ute Deichmann, *Biologen unter Hitler. Vertreibung, Karrieren, Forschung* (Frankfurt a.M., 1992).

6 R. Vierhaus and B. von Brocke (eds.), *Forschung im Spannungsfeld von Politik und Gesellschaft – Geschichte und Struktur der Kaiser-Wilhelm-/Max-Planck-Gesellschaft* (Stuttgart, 1990), esp. pp. 356–75.

7 In a letter written on 27 April 1933 to all directors of KWIs, F. Glum referred to this law and gave the order to dismiss those persons from the institutes to whom the law was applicable (Arch. MPG, Abt. I, Rep. 1a). The KWI for Biology belonged to this category of institutes (Vierhaus and von Brocke, *Forschung im Spannungsfeld*, p. 619).

8 The *Habilitation* was an academic degree beyond the doctorate which allowed the holder to teach at a university and often was a necessary step in the scientific career.

9 There were several Jewish students at KWIs who emigrated after 1933. Among them was Charlotte Auerbach, who had not completed her PhD when she emigrated to Scotland where, in Edinburgh, she discovered the mutagenic effects of chemicals. These students are not included in these statistics. Also not included are the 'non-habilitated' Jewish assistants at biological institutes of universities, including E. Caspari and H. Grüneberg.

10 Max Delbrück, who left Germany in 1937 (he did not emigrate for political reasons, and he was not Jewish), is not included here, because he was then still a physicist. His influence on molecular genetics has been investigated in many publications, see for example the biography of him by P. Fischer, *Licht und Leben* (Konstanz, 1985).

11 M. Planck, *Die Naturwissenschaften* 22 (1934), 344. (Here as elsewhere all English translations from German publications and records are by the authors.) One may also interpret Planck's wording as implying that these scientists who had found other employment were of the highest quality.

12 M. Planck, *Die Naturwissenschaften* 25 (1937), 376.

13 She was dismissed as a 'non-Aryan' because of her Jewish ancestors, though, as in the case of M. Hertz, her parents and grandparents were baptized Protestants (Ministry of the Interiour to F. Glum, 3 March 1934, Arch, MPG, I.Abt. Rep. IA/543).

14 In 1934, Fanny de Bois-Reymond, granddaughter of the great physiologist Emil du Bois-Reymond, wrote to the Secretary General of the KWG, Glum, as follows: 'As I recently needed all my strength in order to show the required calmness in my appearance, I was not able to express what it means for me to have to leave the community of the K.W.G. In particular you, Professor, who have been concerned so much about the K.W.G., will understand how intensely (*innig*) I was connected to this community. Here I found the scientific atmosphere (*man atmet hier die Luft*), to which I was accustomed due to the highly scientific tradition of my family. This atmosphere was – even in my modest position – so familiar to me that I do not yet know how I shall be able to exist without it. I have always been

conscious of the honour of being part of it, an honour which I have been trying to justify for six and a half years by devoting myself to the work. May you be able to keep the tradition of the K.W.G. beautiful and pure in the future' (du Bois-Reymond to Glum, 30 March 1934, Arch. MPG, I.Abt. Rep.1A/543).

15 A quotation from a letter written by the zoologist Prof. E. Marcus to the Education Minister on 1 June 1936 may illustrate these feelings: 'Given that I was brought up as the son of a Prussian judge, permitted to do service as combatant (*Frontdienst*) in the Prussian guard, decorated with the Iron Cross (*Eis. Kreuz 1. Kl.*) as a non-commissioned officer (*Unteroffizier*), and have carried out all my work in the service of Prussia, it is not appropriate for me to beg for a place at charitable institutions. To have been ... expelled from my homeland (*Vaterland*) and made a homeless beggar, I regard as the greatest injustice and deepest offence that could have been done to me. This I did not deserve, in so far as decrees are taken according to the Prussian principle '*suum cuique*' (Zentrales Staatsarchiv Potsdam, Best. REM Nr. 1393 Bl. 26).

16 Beyerchen, *Scientists*, p. 44.

17 K. Fischer, 'Der quantitative Beitrag der nach 1933 emigrierten Naturwissenschaftler zur deutschsprachigen physikalischen Forschung', *Berichte zur Wissenschaftsgeschichte* 11 (1988), 83–104.

18 H. Becker, H. J. Dahms and C. Wegeler (eds.), *Die Universität Göttingen unter dem Nationalsozialismus* (Munich, 1987).

19 K. Zierold, *Forschungsförderung in 3 Epochen* (Wiesbaden, 1968), pp. 230 and 234. The political contributions of K. Meyer to the NS regime are discussed below in section 5.2

20 In 1972 all records of the NG/DFG from 1920–46 that had been saved during the war were transferred to the BAK. The files contain little information about grants given to biologists in the years 1920–32. Therefore the '*befürworteten*' grant applications from the '*Listen der von den Fachausschüssen (der Notgemeinschaft) begutachteten Einzelanträgen*' were evaluated for the years 1929 to 1933. BAK, R73/109–R73/118. The records contain almost all of these lists.

21 H. Albrecht and A. Hermann, 'Die Kaiser-Wilhelm-Gesellschaft im Dritten Reich', in Vierhaus and von Brocke, *Forschung im Spannungsfeld*, p. 377.

22 The KWIs for Biology, including the Division for Virology; for Breeding Research; for *Kulturpflanzenforschung*; the Genetic Department at the KWI for Brain Research; and the Hydrobiological Station.

23 For details of the research see the *FIAT reviews of German Science, 1939–1945* (Weinheim, 1948), in particular vols. 21, 22, 52 and 53, and Deichmann, *Biologen*. See also the PhD thesis of K. Macrakis, 'Scientific Research in National Socialist Germany: The Survival of the Kaiser Wilhelm-Gesellschaft', (unpublished PhD thesis, Harvard University, 1989). Macrakis gives some examples of research projects in virology and mutation research, and shows that basic biological research at KWIs was well funded even during World War II.

24 Foreword from the president of the KWG, M. Planck, to 25 *Jahre Kaiser Wilhelm-Gesellschaft* (Berlin, 1936).

25 F. Glum, 'Die Kaiser Wilhelm-Gesellschaft zur Förderung der Wissenschaften', in 25 *Jahre Kaiser Wilhelm-Gesellschaft*, p. 5.

26 Glum, 'Kaiser'.

27 Albrecht and Hermann, 'Die Kaiser-Wilhelm-Gesellschaft'.

28 Von Wettstein to the Minister of Education and Culture, München, 11 July 1934, UA München E–II–N Personalakt F. v. Wettstein.

29 Von Wettstein to the Minister of Education and Culture, München, 11 July 1934, UA München E–II–N Personalakt F. v. Wettstein.

30 In his letter to Prof. Glum, 29 August 1936, Prof. Spatz quoted from a letter of Prof. Vogt, 'The Americans had delivered an ultimatum to Timoféeff. Therefore he wanted to accept the offer from America. Understanding this, the Ministry of Culture promised to make him head of a Genetic Division of the present size in the institute, and promised to provide him with special funds', MPGA, Abt. 1, Rep. 1A/1582.

31 *Aktennotiz* by Telschow about a meeting with Backe, von Wettstein and Meyer in the *Reichserziehungsministerium*, 9 Feb. 1942, Arch. Akademie der Wissenschaften Berlin, KWG 7, also cited by Macrakis, 'Scientific Research', p. 229

32 *Aktennotiz* by Telschow, 10 Feb. 1942, *ibid.*

33 von Wettstein to Telschow, 9 March 1942, Arch. Akademie der Wissenschaften Berlin, KWG 7.

34 K. Meyer, 'Planung und Aufbau in den besetzten Ostgebieten', *Jahrbuch 1942 der KWG* pp. 250–75. K. Meyer was the person in the RFR who had to decide about most of the grant applications from biologists; see above, section 4.1.

35 Meyer, 'Planung', p. 255. Meyer also referred to the fact that the reorganization of the eastern territories was taking place under the leadership of Himmler, the *Reichsführer SS*.

36 'Der Generalplan Ost, vorgelegt von SS-Oberführer Professor Dr Konrad Meyer (Berlin, 1942), Inst. f. Zeitgeschichte, München, MA 1497.

37 'Generalplan', p. 2.

38 Meyer was indicted for creating the *Generalplan Ost* by the military court in Nuremberg after the war. He was, however, acquitted of all major charges (Becker, Dahms and Wegeler, *Universität*, p. 421). In 1956 he became full professor of '*Landesplannung*' at the university in Hannover. In 1957, he became a member of the Academy of '*Raumforschung und Landesplanung*'.

39 Inst. f. Zeitgeschichte, München, NO 2585, 'Bericht über die Sitzung vom 4.2.1942' in the *Ostministerium*.

40 H. Stubbe to RFR, 23 Jan. 1942, MPGA, Abt. 1, Rep. 1A/2564.

41 *Aktenvermerk* by Telschow, 31 Jan 1940, about a meeting with Backe on 25 Jan 1940, MPGA, Abt. 1, Rep. 1a/2963.

42 In 1947, before he could be indicted in the Nuremberg trial, Backe committed suicide in the Nuremberg prison of war criminals (R. Wistrich, *Wer war wer im Dritten Reich* (Frankfurt, a.M., 1987)). About the role of Backe in the genocide of the East, see also G. Aly and S. Heim, *Vordenker der*

Vernichtung. Auschwitz und die deutschen Pläne für eine neue europäische Ordnung (Hamburg, 1991).

43 *Jahrbuch 1942 der KWG*, p. 32.

44 Urgent war research projects of the RFR, BAK, R26III/271.

45 DFG File Hackbarth, BAK, R73/11415.

46 *Persönl. Stab Reichsführer-SS* to *SS-Gruppenführer* Lorenz, 6 June 1943, 'You will certainly know that the *Reichsführer-SS* has received the order of the *Führer* to promote the research, breeding, growing, and production of the rubber plant Kok-saghyz by all the means he has at his disposal. For this purpose all relevant agencies [...(3) the *Kaiser Wilhelm-Institut* ...] have placed themselves under the control of the *Reichsführer-SS*, 12 Feb. 1943, BDC, SS-record Vogel. 47 Waffen-SS to Reichsführer-SS, 12 Feb. 1943, BDC SS-HO 71396, p. 163.

48 Waffen-SS to Reichführer-SS, 12 Feb. 1943, BDC SS-HO 71396, p. 161.

49 Lorenz to Brandt, 27 July 1943, BDC, SS-record Vogel.

50 Report of the working meeting, BDC, SS-HO 7139a, pp. 28–31.

51 Report of the working meeting, BDC, SS-HO 7139a, pp. 28–31.

52 D. Czech, *Kalendarium der Ereignisse im Konzentrationslager Auschwitz-Birkenau 1939–1945* (Hamburg, 1989), p. 209.

53 BDC, SS-HO 71396, p. 161.

54 W. Rudorf remained Director of the KWI (MPI) for Breeding Research, which in 1945 was transferred to Voldagsen, and in 1955 to Köln-Vogelsang.

55 Inst. f. Zeitgeschichte, MA 441/1.

56 Gerlach to Prof. Beuthe, 3 March 1945, BAK, R 26 III/515. Zimmer thought that the negative effects of small doses, which were assumed harmless, could be attributed to the subnormal health of the subjects (Zimmer to Gerlach, 29 Dec. 1944, D. Irving microfilm DJ 31, p. 350).

57 Zimmer to the Army High Command, 23 Feb. 1943, D. Irving microfilm DJ 31, p. 306. Zimmer and Katsch also carried out biological research into radiation in cooperation with a research institute under the authority of the *Reichspostminister* Ohnesorge, D. Irving microfilm DJ 31, p. 342.

58 Gerlach to the *Kriegswirtschaftsstelle* in the RFR, 26 Feb. 1945, D. Irving microfilm 29, p. 1159.

59 Rajewsky to Gerlach, 9 Apr. 1944, D. Irving microfilm 31, p. 316.

60 Gerlach to *Oberst* Geist, 22 Feb. 1945, BAK, R 26 III/515.

61 Aktennotiz of Gerlach on the meeting of 26 Oct. 1944, D. Irving microfilm DJ 29, p. 1144. This high-tension apparatus became important for the physicists because other items of neutron-generating apparatus were lost or damaged by the war.

62 H. Stubbe, 'Erbkrankheiten bei Pflanzen', *Der Erbarzt* 8 (1935), 69.

63 N. V. Timoféeff-Ressovsky, 'Experimentelle Untersuchungen der erblichen Belastung von Populationen', *Der Erbarzt* 8 (1935), 117–18.

64 *Neues Volk*, Dec. 1938, 26–30. (The *Rassenpolitische Amt* was established by the NSDAP in order to coordinate indoctrination and propaganda in the fields of population and race policy.)

65 Research report from Timoféeff to the Education Minister for 1937/38, BAK, R21/11065.

66 H. Boehm, 'Das erbbiologische Forschungsinstitut in Alt-Rehse', *Ärzteblatt für Berlin* 42 (1937), 415–16, also cited by R. Proctor, *Racial Hygiene* (Cambridge, MA, 1988).

67 Secretary General Telschow wrote to the Education Minister on 8 Dec. 1938, that Boehm, who was a member of the 'Kuratorium' of the KWI for Brain Research, had accepted Timoféeff's decision not to change his citizenship and had explained it to the Ministry of Education. BAK, R 21/11065, p. 68.

68 For example, SS-*Hauptsturmführer* Greite decided in 1939 that Prof. Knoll should not yet become a member of the SS, because he had rejected the necessity of basic genetic research (Greite to Prof. Wüst, 7 June 1939, BDC, SS-file Prof. Knoll).

69 Gauleiter [name unreadable] to the Kreispersonalamt of the NSDAP, 10 May 1935, BDC, file A. Kühn.

70 H. Eickemeyer, *Abschlussbericht des deutschen Forschungsrates* (Munich, 1953), p. 62.

71 T. Nipperdey and L. Schmugge, *50 Jahre Forschungsförderung in Deutschland 1920–1970* (Berlin, 1970), p. 77.

72 F. Glum, 'Die Kaiser Wilhelm-Gesellschaft zur Förderung der Wissenschaften', p. 6.

73 The German physicists had not managed to produce an atomic reactor, not to mention the atomic bomb. O. Hahn wrote thus in his diary on 6 August 1945, after the German physicists who were interned in Farm Hall had received the news of the Hiroshima bomb: '[Gerlach] is desperate, apparently feels like a defeated general (*Feldherr*).' (O. Hahn, diary from 6 August, 1945, material for the report of Löhde, Zweites Deutsches Fernsehen (Second German TV) *'Der Kampf um die Atombombe'*, 1972, Deutsches Museum Munich.) In biology the decisive progress, in both physiological and molecular genetics, was made by Americans, in spite of the fact that a great deal of research in these fields had been carried out in Germany, in the former case even prior to the American work.

74 W. Heisenberg, Foreword to Eickemeyer, *Abschlussbericht*.

75 Eickemeyer, *Abschlussbericht*, p. 66.

76 Eickemeyer, *Abschlussbericht*, p. 64.

77 H. Haevecker, '40 Jahre Kaiser Wilhelm-Gesellschaft', *Jahrbuch 1951 der MPG*, pp. 7–59.

78 W. Heisenberg, 'Notwendigkeit wissenschaftlicher Forschung', in Eickemeyer, *Abschlussbericht*, p. 216.

79 P. Weingart und M. Winterhager, *Die Vermessung der Forschung -Theorie und Praxis der Wissenschaftsindikatoren* (Frankfurt, a.M, 1984).

9   Pedagogy, professionalism and politics: biology instruction during the Third Reich

An earlier version of this paper was presented at the American Historical Association Meetings on 29 December 1990 in New York. I would like to thank

Michael Neufeld, Sabine Schleiermacher and Tobias Eiselen for their comments and critique.

1 O. Rabes, 'Der biologische Lehrstoff der Oberstufe', *Aus der Natur* 16 (1919/20), 386–7.

2 *Volk* is literally translated as 'folk' and carries nationalist and racist connotations.

3 W. Schoenichen, *Der biologische Unterricht in der neuen Erziehung* (Leipzig, 1919), pp. 1–3.

4 Schoenichen, *Der biologische Unterricht*, pp. 8 and 17.

5 Schoenichen, *Der biologische Unterricht*, pp. 4–5.

6 Some of the other reform-minded biology pedagogues who stressed the *Arbeitsschulgedanke* in the biology classroom include H. Grupe, *Unsere erste Naturgeschichte. Aus der Arbeit der ersten Schuljahre* (Frankfurt a.M., 1923); C. Schmitt, *Naturliebe mein Unterrichtsziel*, (Freising, 1922) and *Heraus aus der Schulstube* (Langensalza, 1922); E. Schermer, 'Zur Reform des Biologieunterrichts in der Volksschule', *Die neue deutsche Schule* (DNDS) 1 (1927), 699–705; P. Brohmer, *Der naturkundliche Unterricht* (Leipzig, 1929).

7 For a discussion of the school garden in biology instruction see, for example, A. Senner, *Naturkunde auf der Grundlage der heimischen Scholle*, (Frankfurt a.M., 1927); K. Smalian, *Methodik des biologischen Unterrichts* (Berlin, 1927), esp. pp. 256–8; W. Schoenichen, *Methodik und Technik des naturgeschichtlichen Unterrichts*, (Leipzig, 1926), p. 168.

8 Schoenichen, *Der biologische Unterricht*, pp. 39–44.

9 Schoenichen, *Der biologische Unterricht*, p. 33.

10 Schoenichen, *Der biologische Unterricht*, pp. 33–6.

11 Brohmer, *Der naturkundliche Unterricht*, p. 7.

12 Schoenichen, *Der biologische Unterricht*, p. 69; *Volkskraft* may be translated as either 'national strength' or as the 'strength of the folk'.

13 For a discussion of the importance of 'Menschenkunde' see O. Rabes, 'Der biologische', 384–5; O. Krieger, 'Neuorientierung des biologischen und anthropologischen Unterrichts', *Hamburger Lehrerzeitung* 3 (1924), 214; Paul Brohmer, *Biologie* (Frankfurt a.M., 1932), p. 38; P. Depdolla, 'Der biologische Unterricht in dem neuen preussischen Lehrplane', *Unterrichtsblätter für Mathematik und Naturwissenschaften* 32 (1926), 87. On the problem of alcoholism see E. Dobers, 'Der Kampf gegen den Alkohol im Biologieunterricht', *Pädagogische Warte* 38 (1931), 101–8. The most important spokesman for the introduction of heredity and eugenics into the secondary-school biology curriculum was the Berlin *Schulrat* Philipp Depdolla. His position is clearly stated in the following articles: 'Eugenik und höhere Schulen', *Volksaufartung, Erblehre, Eheberatung* 1 (1928), 270–84; 'Die Eugenik im Unterricht der höheren Schulen', *Unterrichtsblätter* 35 (1929), 369–78; 'Vererbungslehre und naturwissenschaftlicher Unterricht', in G. Just (ed.), *Vererbung und Erziehung* (Berling, 1930), pp. 277–325.

14 'Richtlinien für die Lehrpläne der höheren Schulen Preussens Teil 1: Grundsätzliches und Methodisches', *Beilage zum Zentralblatt für die gesamte Unterrichtsverwaltung* No. 8 (1925), 36–7.

15 G. Beisinger, 'Die Biologie in den neuen hessischen Lehrplänen', *Naturwissenschaftliche Monatshefte für den biologischen, chemischen, geographischen und geologischen Unterricht* (NWM) 6 (1926), 132.

16 *Lehrpläne der höheren Schulen Hamburgs für Mathematik und Naturwissenschaften* (Hamburg, 1928), p. 25.

17 For a discussion of the fortunes of German biology education from the beginning of the nineteenth century until 1933 see I. Scheele's useful study, *Von Lüben bis Schmeil: Die Entwicklung von der Schulnaturgeschichte zum Biologieunterricht zwischen 1830 und 1933 Wissenschaftshistorische Studien*, Vol. I (Berlin, 1981).

18 R. Keckstein, 'Die Geschichte des biologischen Schulunterrichts in Deutschland', *biologica didactica* 3 (1980), 37–41; Scheele, *Von Lüben*, 99–101.

19 This goal was articulated at the *Versammlung deutscher Naturforscher und Aerzte* in Hamburg in 1901. See *Ueber die gegenwärtige Lage des biologischen Unterrichts an höheren Schulen. Verhandlungen der vereinigten Abteilungen für Zoologie, Botanik, Geologie, Anatomie und Physiologie der 73. Versammlung deutscher Naturforscher und Aerzte* (Jena, 1901), p. 43.

20 Scheele, *Von Lüben*, pp. 256–7.

21 See, for example, the comments of Ludwig Spilger on this point in his article 'Vererbungslehre und Rassenhygiene im biologischen Unterricht der höheren Schulen', *Archiv für Rassen- und Gesellschafts-Biologie* (ARGB) 19 (1927), p. 68.

22 Hamburg appears to have had a progressive tradition in biology education. As early as 1911, Darwin's theory of evolution and genetics were offered as part of the biology curriculum of one of Hamburg's most elite secondary schools, the Realgymnasium des Johanneums. In the 1928 curriculum reform, biology was accorded two hours in all Hamburg secondary-school classes. An important part of the biology curriculum of the *Oberstufe* was politically and ethically relevant eugenics instruction. Staatsarchiv Hamburg (STA-HH) Oberschulbehörde (OSB) II: A3 Nr. 27; A33 Nr. 27; A27 Nr. 27; Scheele, *Von Lüben*, pp. 266–7.

23 K. Oberkirsch, 'Die Stellung der Biologie in der Mittelschule', *Der Biologe* 1 (1931/32), 69–70; 'Mitteilungen', *Der Biologe* 1 (1931/32), 58.

24 For a discussion of the position of the natural sciences in the *Volksschule*, see Senner, *Naturkunde*, pp. 1–2.

25 For a discussion of the gap between the way school biology was taught and current trends in biological research see, Brohmer, 'Vorwort'.

26 Numerous biology didacticians and biology teachers emphasized the notion that their subject, far from being limited to a 'description of nature' (*Naturbeschreibung*), was nothing less than the 'science of life'. Biology education must stress the 'laws of biological phenomena', or, as Depdolla put it, the 'laws of life'. This preoccupation with biological laws was frequently coupled with the so-called organic perspective or *Ganzheitsgedanken*, the latter emphasizing the interdependence of all organs in an individual organism. Moreover, many biology pedagogues argued for an ecological perspective in biology education. They advocated studying *Lebensgemeinschaften* – ecological communities – as a way of understanding the inter-

relatedness of animate nature: Smalian, *Methodik*, p. v; Depdolla, 'Der bio-logische Unterricht', p. 82; Brohmer, *Der naturkundliche Unterricht*, pp. 15–16. For a more general discussion of the reasons for biology's stepchild-like position in the secondary schools see, E. Dobers, 'Die Bio-logie im Lehrplan der Pädagogischen Akademie', *DNDS* 5 (1931), pp. 15–21.

27 At least Depdolla believed that the Förderverein's lack of attention to biology was an important reason why many biologists formed the DBV. P. Depdolla, 'Biologie und Schule', *Der Biologe* 1 (1931/32), 12.

28 'Richtlinien für den biologischen Unterricht auf den höheren Schulen', *Der Biologe* 1 (1931/32), 145–6.

29 National Socialist Teacher League head Hans Schemm argued that 'Nation-alsozialismus ist politisch angewandte Biologie'. His words were frequently quoted by biology didacticians and schoolteachers during the Third Reich to promote their professional self-interest. See, for example, the use of the quote at the beginning of H. Feuerborn's article, 'Das Kernstück der deutschen Volksbildung: die Biologie', *Der Biologe* 4 (1935), 99; Interior Minister Frick's remarks that the scope of biology education must be broadened also gave biology teachers reason to believe that a new dawn had arrived for their discipline. See Frick's comments in *Erziehung zum lebendigen Volke* (Berlin, 1933), pp. 16–19.

30 An exact copy of the decree was reported in E. Dobers and K. Hielke, *Ras-senpolitische Unterrichtspraxis. Der Rassengedanke in der Unterrichtsges-taltung der Volksschulfächer*, 3rd edn (Leipzig, 1934), p. 354.

31 Rust's 1935 Reich decree was published in Dobers and Hielke, *Rassenpoliti-sche Unterrichtspraxis*, pp. 357–63. Between 1933 and 1934 Hamburg and Württemberg followed Prussia's lead in introducing racial science into their biology curricula. Zentralinstitut für Erziehung und Unterricht (ed.), *Deutsche Volkserziehung* (No. 2, Rassenkunde) (Berlin, 1934), pp. 82–3, 85–7.

32 H. Merkle, 'Rassen- und Bevölkerungskunde in UII und OI der höheren Lehranstalten', *Unterrichtsblätter* 39 (1933), 352.

33 For examples of biology teachers' optimism see, E. Giesbrecht, 'Ein neuer Kurs in der Schulbiologie', *Der Biologe* 2 (1932/33), 219; P. Linde, 'Zur Frage der Stoffverteilung im Biologieunterricht', *Der Biologe* 2 (1932/33), 335.

34 Scheele, *Von Lüben*, pp. 264–73; Dr med. H. C. von Behr-Pinnow, 'Verer-bungslehre und Eugenik in den Schulen', *ARGB* 20 (1927/28), 327–9; C. Vollmer, 'Die Stellung der Biologie im neuen sächsischen Landeslehr-plan', *Der Biologe* 1 (1932/33), 11–16; Beisinger, *Die Biologie*, 130–7; 'Lehr-plan für die höheren Schulen', *Amtsblatt des württembergischen Kultusmi-nisteriums* 21 (1928), 213.

35 On 8 June 1933, Günther Just, director of the Institute for Human Heredity and Eugenics at the University of Griefswald, delivered a lecture entitled 'Eugenik und Erziehung' at a meeting of the Deutscher Verein für das mit-tlere Schulwesen in Kiel. The paper was published in *Die Mittelschule*.

Zeitschrift für das gesamte mittlere Schulwesen 47 (1933), 431–4; Racial anthropologist and head of the Kaiser-Wilhelm-Institut für Anthropologie, menschliche Erblehre und Eugenik, Eugen Fischer, published an article designed for secondary-school teachers in which he openly praised the Nazis as being the first in history to take the racial future of their people into their own hands, 'Volkstum und Rasse als Frage der Nation', *Monatsschrift für die höhere Schule* 32 (1933), 263. And the prominent Hamburg anthropologist and race hygienist Walter Scheidt self-interestedly helped promote *Rassenbiologie* as *Wahlfach* for the training of future primary-school teachers. (STA-HH) OSB VI, F XI b1/1. Since there were relatively few employment options for biology and anthropology majors outside of teaching, it was in the interests of academic biologists, eugenicists and anthropologists to promote their subjects in the schools.

36 The only possible exception to my generalization is Hamburg. The 1928 Hamburg biology curriculum does mention that 'the scientifically proven conclusions of heredity and racial science' should be discussed in the *Oberstufe* of the secondary schools. No specifics, however, were given. *Lehrplane der höheren Schulen Hamburgs*, p. 25.

37 J. Graf, *Vererbungslehre und Erbgesundheitspflege: Einführung nach methodischen Grundsätzen* (Munchen, 1930). Graf's book was one of the first designed to acquaint teachers, students and mature schoolchildren with the basics of heredity and eugenics.

38 In fact, Nazi Party officials mandated that *Rassenkunde* not emphasize physical traits as a meaningful manifestation of the existence (or lack thereof) of Nordic blood. There was a general fear that an emphasis on the so-called physical traits of the Nordic – fair skin, blue eyes, long heads, etc. – would lead to divisions among Aryan Germans who did not look Nordic. In other words, it would serve to pit one 'national comrade' against the other, as class and occupational divisions had done in former times. Clearly Party and State wanted to avoid such potential problems, especially once war started. Teachers were instructed to stress that all Aryan Germans had a significant portion of Nordic blood running through their veins. See, for example, Rust's discussion of *Rassenkunde* in his 1935 decree extending the teaching of 'racial science' to the entire Reich. Dobers and Hielke, *Rassenpolitische Unterrichtspraxis*, p. 360; Instructive as well in this regard is the appraisal of August Hagemann, Hamburg Gausachbearbeiter for Biology in the National Socialist Teachers League, of a curriculum proposal for the teaching of biology in an Adolf Hitler school, (STA-HH) OSB VI, Abl 1977/1F VI d9/10 (319). Moreover, following the lead of Fritz Lenz, racial science textbooks stressed not the physical attributes of European races – which were seen as being of little intrinsic importance – but rather their alleged mental and character traits. Since, however, the character traits of the Nordic were the very meritocratic characteristics long praised by race hygienists, by concentrating on them one could effectively adopt a more traditional meritocratic/eugenic interpretation of 'race'. The 1938 curriculum reform for secondary-school

biology reflected this position. *Erziehung und Unterricht in der höheren Schule* (Berlin, 1938), p. 147.

39 E. Kruse and P. Wiedow, *Lebenskunde für Mittelschulen Klasse 6: Ausgabe für Mädchenschulen* (Leipzig, 1942), p. 119; A. Bauer, *Lebenskunde für die Abschlussklassen der höheren Lehranstalten* (Berlin/Leipzig, 1937), p. 179. Paul Brohmer, Ernst Dobers, Otto Rabes, Jakob Graf and Philipp Depdolla are just a few of the influential biology pedagogues active in both the Weimar and Nazi periods.

40 For use of these terms see, for example, M. Schwartz and H. Wolff, *Kurzgefasster Lehrgang de Biologie für die Abschlussklassen* (Frankfurt a.M., 1936), pp,. 66–7; E. Dobers, *Rassenkunde: Förderung und Dienst*, 2nd edn (Leipzig, 1939), pp. 68–9.

41 This experiment is reported in O. Ottweiler, *Die Volksschule im Nationalsozialismus* (Weinheim/Basel, 1979), pp. 180–1.

42 For a discussion of the need to show working-class children that they are genetically valuable, see Dobers, *Rassenkunde*, pp. 56–8; for examples of this watering down of elitist eugenic ideology during the Third Reich, see A. Hoffmann, *Rassenhygiene, Erblehre, Familienkunde. Ein Arbeitsheft mit neuen Hilfsmitteln* (Erfurt, 1935), pp. 22–3, and O. Steche, *Leitfaden der Rassenkunde und Vererbungslehre der Erbgesundheitspflege und Familienkunde für die Mittelstufe* (Leipzig, 1934), pp. 69–70.

43 For an in-depth discussion of the treatment of the 'Jewish question' in the classroom, see E. Dobers, *Die Judenfrage: Stoff und Behandlung in der Schule*, 4th edn (Leipzig, 1941). Virtually all racial textbooks published after 1935 depicted graphs and charts clarifying the Nuremberg Laws. See, for example, E. Meyer and K. Zimmerman, *Lebenskunde Lehrbuch der Biologie für höhere Schulen*, Vol. III, 2nd edn (Erfurt, n.d.), pp. 187–8.

44 In 1937 Rust published the *Richtlinien für den Unterricht in den vier unteren Jahrgängen der Volksschule* (Berlin, 1937).

45 While there is no special treatment of the Biology *Reichssachschaft* of the NSLB, there is a useful overview of the organization. See W. Feiten, *Der Nationalsozialistische Lehrerbund, Entwicklung und Organisation. Ein Beitrage zum Aufbau und zur Organisationsstruktur des nationalsozialistischen Herrschaftssystems* (Weinheim/Basel, 1981).

46 Work began on the construction of the NSLB *Biologielehrplan* at least as early as 1935; a draft of it appeared in the first 1936 issue of the NSLB journal, *Nationalsozialistisches Bildungswesen*. Apparently the original *Lehrplan* was modified after the collective experience of *Schulungslehrgänge* headed by the various *Gausachbearbeiter* for biology in the NSLB. The final draft as it appeared in *Der Biologe* was prepared by two secondary-school teachers, Dr H. Linder and Dr R. Lotze. Bundesarchiv (BA) NS 12, 845.

47 'Richtlinien für die Lehrpläne der höheren Schulen Preussens Teil II: Lehraufgaben', *Beilage zum Zentralblatt für die gesamte Unterrichtsverwaltung* No. 8 (1925), 74, 78, 87; 'Lehrplanentwurf für den biologischen Unterricht an den höheren Knabenschulen', *Der Biologe* 6 (1937), n.p.

48 Feiten, *Der Nationalsozialistische Lehrerbund*, p. 202.
49 'Lehrplanentwurf'.
50 It was expected that biology would receive three hours a week for the summer term and two hours a week for the winter term of every secondary-school class. (BA) NS 12, 845.
51 *Erziehung und Unterricht in der höheren Schule* (Berlin, 1938), pp. 140–64.
52 *Erziehung und Unterricht*, pp. 143–4.
53 *Erziehung und Unterricht*, p. 141.
54 Only in the natural science–mathematical section of the *Oberschule* for boys did physics and chemistry together receive seventeen hours to biology's sixteen. R. Fricke-Findkelburg (ed.), *Nationalsozialismus und Schule. Amtliche Erlasse und Richtlinien 1933–1945* (Opladen, 1989), p. 117.
55 Evidence for this is based on my examination of the *Reifeprüfungsprotokolle* of selected Prussian secondary schools housed in the *Archiv der Gutachterstelle für Deutsches Schul- und Studienwesen* located in the *Pädagogisches Zentrum Berlin*. Whether this was the case for other German states is unclear.
56 G. Scherf, 'Vom deutschen Wald zum deutschen Volk. Biologieunterricht in der Volksschule im Dienste nationalsozialistischer Weltanschauung', in R. Dithmar (ed.), *Schule und Unterricht im Dritten Reich* (Neuwied, 1989), pp. 219–20.
57 R. Benze and A. Pudelko (eds.), *Rassische Erziehung als Unterrichtsgrundsatz der Fachgebiete* (Frankfurt a.M., 1937), p. 10.
58 The four sets of textbooks for the higher secondary schools include Graf, *Lehrbuch der Biologie für höhere Schulen*; Steche-Stengel-Wagner, *Lehrbuch der Biologie für höhere Schulen*; Meyer-Zimmermann, *Lehrbuch der Biologie für höhere Schulen: Lebenskunde*; and Kraepelin-Schaffer-Franke, *Biologisches Unterrichtswerk für höhere Schulen*.
59 H. Mehrtens, 'Mathematik als Wissenschaft und Schulfach im NS-Staat', in Dithmar, *Schule*, p. 209.
60 I have presented evidence for this position in an article entitled, 'Biologie scolaire et enseignement de l'eugénisme sous le IIIème Reich', in J. Olff-Nathan (ed.), *La Science sous le Troisième Reich* (Paris, 1992), pp. 263–85.
61 For the comments of biology teachers on the subject of biology and Göring's Four-Year Plan see, for example, K. Reitz, 'Die Heilpflanzen im Vierjahresplan', DNDS 12 (1938), 376–9; O. Mehlan, 'Der Schulgarten im Dienste der Kriegserzeugungsschlacht 1940', *Der Deutsche Erzieher* (1940), 103–6; A. Erner, 'Der Vierjahresplan im Naturkunde-Unterricht der Mittelschule', *Die Mittelschule* 51 (1937), 363–5. For a discussion of the topic by the Biology Section of the NSLB, see its programmatic statement, 'Biologie und Vierjahresplan'; there are also NSLB 'Activity Reports' that mention the importance of the four-year plan as a topic discussed in the NSLB's *Arbeitsgemeinschaften* (BA) NS 12, 845; The DBV also worked together with the NSV and the NS Reichsnahrstand in the context of *Schädlingsbekämpfung*. (BA) NS 12, 845.

62 Following the 1936 Ministerial *Erlass* regarding the 'Förderung des Seiden-baues', all schools were encouraged to make their contribution to the pro-duction of raw silk. There are many important documents regarding the attempt to begin this project in the Hamburg area schools – with some measure of success. (STA-HH) OSB VI, F VI d 11/1 and 2.

63 Evidence for the continued use of biology textbooks written during the Empire and the Weimar Republic was obtained through an examination of a critical but little-known source, the *Jahresberichte der höheren Schulen Preussens*, housed in the *Archiv der Gutachterstelle für Deutsches Schul- und Studienwesen* located in the *Pädagogisches Zentrum Berlin*. These annual reports, which exist for all the Prussian secondary schools for the years 1920–40, contain much valuable information regarding the *Schulall-tag* both during the Weimar Republic and the Third Reich. Since it proved impossible to examine all the *Jahresberichte* for all the Prussian secondary schools throughout this entire twenty-year period, I selected a sample of boys' and girls' secondary schools from Berlin, from the rural Protestant areas of East Prussia and Pommerania, and from the Catholic areas of the Rhineland. I analyzed these documents for the years 1928–9, 1931–2, 1934–5 and 1937–40. The volumes examined are as follows: Pädagogisches Zentrum (PZ) Berlin 146, 221, 301, 353, 379, 404, 429, 160, 235, 315, 367, 392, 417, 441; PZ Ostpreussen 144, 219, 299, 351, 377, 402, 427, 158, 233, 313, 365, 390, 415, 439; PZ Pommern 147, 222, 302, 354, 380, 405, 430, 161, 244, 323, 375, 400, 425, 449; PZ Rheinland 156, 231, 311, 363, 388, 413, 437, 166, 244, 322, 375, 400, 425, 449.

64 PZ Reifeprüfungsprotokolle der Cecilienschule Berlin-Wilmersdorf; Reife-prüfungsprotokolle der Viktoria-Luise Schule Berlin-Wilmersdorf.

65 PZ Reifeprüfungsprotokolle der Cecilienschule Berlin-Wilmersforf; Reife-prüfungsprotokolle der Viktoria-Luise Schule Berlin-Wilmersdorf.

66 The increased emphasis on the war-relevant subjects of physics and chem-istry in the school curriculum parallels the growing influence of physics as a discipline during the Second World War. M. Walker, *German National Socialism and the Quest for Nuclear Power, 1939–1949* (Cambridge, 1989), pp. 73–80.

67 PZ Reifeprüfungsprotokolle.

68 These books are listed in the *Amtliche Richtlinien über die Ausmerzung des nationalsozialistischen, des militaristischen und imperialistischen Schrift-tums* published in 1945 by the *Landesamt für Volksbildung Thüringen*.

69 I was informed of the East German practice of placing Nazi literature and textbooks in special closets or rooms during my visit to the *Haus des Lehrers* in the former East Berlin. The library of the *Haus des Lehrers* holds a very large number of such 'brown' schoolbooks (still stored in a special room) that have only been accessible to the public since the *Wende*.

70 *Lehrpläne für die Grund- und Oberschulen in der Sowjetischen Besatzungs-zone Deutschlands*. Biologie (Deutsche Zentralverwaltung für Volksbildung in der Sowjetschen Besatzungszone Deutschlands, 1946), p. 3.

71 *Lehrpläne*, p. 21.

72 The elimination of Mendelian genetics and the resulting emphasis on the theories of Lysenko can be gleaned through an examination of the biology textbook employed in all secondary schools in the GDR, *Lehrbuch der Biologie für das 12. Schuljahr* (Berlin, 1953), pp. 91–112.

73 For example, during the Third Reich, biology didactician Ernst Kruse co-authored the standard biology textbook for the middle schools, *Lebenskunde für Mittelschulen* (Leipzig, 1942). Shortly after the war he came out with a revised version of the text entitled *Biologie: Ein Arbeits- und Lehrbuch für Mittelschulen, Realschulen und ähnliche Anstalten* (Stuttgart, 1951). And Ernst Stengel, co-author of one of the four state-sanctioned biology textbooks for the higher secondary schools during the Third Reich, *Lehrbuch der Biologie für höhere Schulen* (Leipzig, 1940), was also able to continue writing biology textbooks in the post-war period. Indeed, as late as the 1970s his co-authored book *Das Leben* (Stuttgart, 1974) was used in West German biology classrooms.

74 Keckstein, *Die Geschichte*, p. 71. During the 1950s, eugenics was part of the biology curriculum of the secondary schools in Lower Saxony. At present, I am uncertain as to whether it was taught in the biology classrooms of other West German *Länder*. *Richtlinien für den Unterricht an den Schulen des Landes Niedersachsen. Mathematik und Naturwissenschaften an höheren Schulen* (Braunschweig, n.d.), p. 47.

75 For a discussion of this point see E. Busche, B. Marquardt and M. Mauer (eds.), *Natur in der Schule. Kritik und Alternativen zum Biologieunterricht* (Hamburg, 1978).

10   **The whole and the community: scientific and political reasoning in the holistic psychology of Felix Krueger**

1 This essay originally appeared as U. Geuter, 'Das Ganze und die Gemeinschaft – Wissenschaftliches und politisches Denken in der Ganzheitspsychologie Felix Kruegers', in C-F. Graumann (ed.), *Psychologie im Nationalsozialismus* (Berlin, 1985), pp. 55–87.

2 R. Maikowski, P. Mattes and G. Rott, *Psychologie und ihre Praxis. Materialien zur Geschichte und Funktion einer Einzelwissenschaft in der Bundesrepublik* (Frankfurt a.M., 1976).

3 U. Geuter, 'Institutionelle und professionelle Schranken der Nachkriegsauseinandersetzungen über die Psychologie im Nationalsozialismus', *Psychologie- und Gesellschaftskritik* 4 (1980), 5–39; W. A. Russel and E. Roth, 'Psychologie in Deutschland und Amerika: Eine Studie in Gegensätzen', *Psychologie und Praxis* 2 (1958), 223–31.

4 F. Merz, 'Amerikanische und deutsche Psychologie', *Psychologie und Praxis* 4 (1960), 78–91.

5 Since the approach of the Red Army had caused Krueger to move his retirement home from Potsdam to Switzerland, Wellek even went so far as to claim that Krueger had '*emigrated* in the last weeks of the war ...'

(emphasis by the author), see A. Wellek, 'Deutsche Psychologie und Nationalsozialismus', *Psychologie und Praxis* 4 (1960), 177–82; here 179; as late as 1974 an article appeared in the magazine *Die Polizei* containing the historical perversion that Felix Krueger had left Germany 'indignant', see F. Stiebitz, '50 Jahre Psychologie im Dienste der Polizei', *Die Polizei* 65 (1974), 298–301, here 298.

6 F. Wyatt and H. L. Teuber, 'German psychology under the Nazi system 1933–1940', *Psychological Review* 51 (1944), 229–47, here 232.

7 W. Fischel, 'Rechenschaftsbericht über die Arbeit des Instituts für Psychologie der Karl-Marx-Universität', *Wissenschaftliche Zeitschrift der Karl-Marx-Universität Leipzig* 9 (1959), 257–60.

8 T. Herrmann, *Dichotomie und Duplizität. Festschrift für Ernst August Dölle* (Bern, 1974), pp. 16ff.

9 See U. Geuter, 'Die Zerstörung wissenschaftlicher Vernunft. Felix Krueger und die Leipziger Schule der Ganzheitspsychologie', *Psychologie heute* 7, No. 4 (1980), 35–43; W. Prinz, 'Ganzheits- und Gestaltpsychologie im Nationalsozialismus', in P. Lundgreen (ed.), *Wissenschaft im Dritten Reich* (Frankfurt a.M., 1985), pp. 55–81; for an earlier investigation, see 'Zur Situation in der westdeutschen Psychologie', *Forum* (1960), Wissenschaftliche Beilage, 1–4; also see Geuter, 'Institutionelle', 23ff.

10 G. Lukács, *Die Zerstörung der Vernunft*, Vols. I–III (Darmstadt, 1973).

11 D. Gasman, *The scientific origins of National Socialism* (London, 1971).

12 K. Sontheimer, *Antidemokratisches Denken in der Weimarer Republik* (Munich, 1978).

13 Wellek, 'Deutsche'.

14 U. Geuter, '"Gleichschaltung" von oben? Universitätspolitische Strategien und Verhaltensweisen in der Psychologie im Nationalsozialismus', *Psychologische Rundschau* 35 (1984), 198–213; U. Geuter, *Die Professionalisierung der deutschen Psychologie im Nationalsozialismus* (Frankfurt a.M., 1984); English edition: *The Professionalization of Psychology in Nazi Germany* (New York, 1992).

15 F. Krueger, 'Über Entwicklungspsychologie. Ihre sachliche und geschichtliche Notwendigkeit', *Arbeiten zur Entwicklungspsychologie* 1 (1915), for example, pp. 125 and 216.

16 For the sake of simplicity, citations from Krueger's work are taken where possible from the 1953 collection edited by E. Heuss and F. Krueger, *Zur Philosophie und Psychologie der Ganzheit. Schriften aus den Jahren 1918–1940* (Berlin, 1953), here p. 462.

17 F. Krueger, 'Wissenschaften und der Zusammenhang des Wirklichen', *Neue psychologische Studien* 3 (1928), IX–XXVII, here XIV.

18 F. Krueger, *Lehre von dem Ganzen. Seele, Gemeinschaft und das Göttliche* (Bern, 1948), p. 82.

19 F. Krueger, 'Der strukturelle Grund des Fühlens und Wollens', in O. Klemm (ed.), *Bericht über den 15. Kongress der Deutschen Gesellschaft für Psychologie 1936* (Jena, 1937), pp. 181–9, here p. 186.

20 Krueger, *Philosophie und Psychologie*, p. 148.

21 A. Wellek, 'Die genetische Ganzheitspsychologie der Leipziger Schule und ihre Verzweigungen. Rückblick und Ausblick', *Neue psychologische Studien* 15 (1954), 1–67, here 32.
22 Krueger, *Philosophie und Psychologie*, p. 146.
23 Krueger, *Philosophie und Psychologie*, p. 135.
24 F. Krueger, *Otto Klemm und das Psychologische Institut der Universität Leipzig* (Leipzig, 1939), p. 74.
25 F. Krueger, 'Vorrede (des Vorsitzenden der Deutschen Philosophischen Gesellschaft zur Tagung über 'Ganzheit und Form' in Breslau)', *Blätter für deutsche Philosophie* 6 (1932), 1–8, here 7.
26 M. Schlick, 'Über den Begriff der Ganzheit', *Actes du huitième Congrès international de philosophie à Prague 1934* (Prague, 1936), pp. 85–99.
27 F. Krueger, 'Das Problem der Ganzheit', *Blätter für deutsche Philosophie* 6 (1932), 111–39, here 111.
28 Krueger, *Philosophie und Psychologie*, p. 148.
29 Krueger, *Philosophie und Psychologie*, p. 171.
30 Krueger, *Philosophie und Psychologie*, p. 172.
31 Krueger, *Philosophie und Psychologie*, p. 174.
32 H. Driesch, *Das Ganze und die Summe* (Leipzig, 1921), p. 4; also see H. Driesch, *Die Maschine und der Organismus* (Leipzig, 1935).
33 Schlick, 'Über den Begriff'.
34 Sontheimer, *Antidemokratisches Denken*.
35 Sontheimer, *Antidemokratisches Denken*, p. 53.
36 P. Forman, 'Weimar culture, causality, and quantum theory, 1918–1927: Adaptation by German physicists and mathematicians to a hostile intellectual environment', *Historical Studies in the Physical Sciences* 3 (1971), 1–115.
37 See, Geuter, *Professionalisierung*, pp. 187ff.
38 F. Ringer, *The decline of the German mandarins. The German academic community, 1890–1933* (Cambridge, MA, 1969).
39 J. Habermas, 'Die deutschen Mandarine', in J. Habermas (ed.), 3rd edn *Philosophisch-politische Profile* (Frankfurt a.M., 1981), Vol. I, pp. 458–68.
40 J. Habermas, *Theorie des kommunikativen Handelns* (Frankfurt a.M., 1982), Vol. I, pp. 493ff.
41 E. Bloch, *Erbschaft dieser Zeit* (Frankfurt a.M., 1979), p. 304.
42 Krueger, *Philosophie und Psychologie*, p. 151 and F. Krueger, 'Über seelische Struktur', *Forschungen und Fortschritte* 6 (1930), 461–2, here 462.
43 F. Krueger, *Selbstbesinnung in deutscher Not* (Stuttgart, Enke Verlag, 1919), p. 8.
44 Krueger, *Selbstbesinnung*, p. 15.
45 F. Krueger, 'Wilhelm Wundt als deutscher Denker', *Beiträge zur Philosophie des Deutschen Idealismus* 2 (1922), 1–44.
46 Krueger, *Philosophie und Psychologie*, pp. 171ff.
47 Krueger, *Philosophie und Psychologie*, p. 140.
48 See von Dürckheim-Montmartin, 'Gemeinschaft', *Neue psychologische Studien* 12 (1935), 195–214.

49 F. Krueger, 'Psychologie des Gemeinschaftslebens', in O. Klemm (ed.), *Bericht über den 14. Kongress der Deutschen Gesellschaft für Psychologie in Tübingen 1934* (Jena, 1935), pp. 5–62, here 43.

50 Krueger, 'Gemeinschaftslebens', pp. 49ff.

51 Dürckheim-Montmartin, 'Gemeinschaft'.

52 W. Stern, *Studien zur Personwissenschaft, I. Teil: Personalistik als Wissenschaft* (Leipzig, 1930), p. 14.

53 Stern, *Studien*, p. 18.

54 Stern, *Studien*, p. 8.

55 See Sontheimer, *Antidemokratisches Denken*, for example pp. 115 and 172.

56 See F. W. Coker, *Organismic theories of the state. Ninteenth century interpretations of the state as organism or as person*, 2nd edn (New York, 1967), and E. Scheerer, 'Organische Weltanschauung und Ganzheitspsychologie', in Graumann, *Psychologie*, pp. 15–54.

57 This conception is implied in Prinz, 'Ganzheits- und Gestaltpsychologie'.

58 F. Krueger, 'Die Arbeit des Menschen als philosophisches Problem', *Blätter für deutsche Philosophie* 3 (1929/30), 159–92, here 167.

59 Krueger, 'Arbeit', 159.

60 P. Brückner, *Versuch, uns und anderen die Bundesrepublik zu erklären* (Berlin, 1978), pp. 72ff.

61 Lukács, *Die Zerstörung*, III, p. 60.

62 Krueger, *Philosophie und Psychologie*, p. 172.

63 F. Krueger, 'Sinn und Geist der deutschen Familie', *Deutsche Sängerschaft* 37 (1932), 4–18.

64 F. Krueger, 'Rückblick auf die 10. Tagung der Deutschen Philosophischen Gesellschaft', in F. Krueger (ed.), *Philosophie der Gemeinschaft* (Berlin, 1929), 143–68, here 144.

65 Krueger, 'Rückblick', 157.

66 Krueger, 'Rückblick', 166.

67 Krueger, 'Vorrede', 7.

68 Krueger, 'Das Problem der Ganzheit'.

69 Krueger, *Philosophie und Psychologie*, pp. 174ff.

70 Krueger, 'Familie', 6 and 9; a further example of Krueger's alarming, in part even embarrassing level in this article is his polemic against psychoanalysis: 'naked sex, entirely the intentional lust for sexual *pleasure*, such things might fulfill degenerate little men(!) ['Männchen'] such as those on the Vienna asphalt, for a time. Even among the animals it is usually different', Krueger, 'Families', 8.

71 Krueger, 'Familie', 18.

72 F. Krueger, *Bund, Volk und Reich* (Berlin, 1933), p. 14.

73 Krueger, *Bund*, p. 18.

74 Krueger, *Bund*, p. 23.

75 Krueger, *Bund*, p. 25.

76 Krueger, *Bund*, p. 24.

77 R. König, *Vom Wesen der deutschen Universität* (Berlin, 1935).

78 Krueger, 'Gemeinschaftslebens', 17.

79 H. Mommsen, 'Gesellschaftsbild und Verfassungspläne des deutschen
   Widerstandes', in W. Schmitthenner and H. Buchheim (ed.), *Widerstand
   gegen Hitler* (Köln, 1966), pp. 73–167, here 111.
80 Geuter, 'Zerstörung', 42.
81 F. Krueger, 'Die Lage der Seelenwissenschaft in der deutschen Gegenwart',
   in O. Klemm (ed.), *Bericht über den XIII. Kongress der Deutschen Gesellschaft für Psychologie in Leipzig vom 16.-19. Oktober 1933* (Jena, 1934),
   pp. 9–36, here 36.
82 Krueger, 'Gemeinschaftslebens', p. 21; Friedrich Sander, 'Deutsche Psychologie und nationalsozialistische Weltanschauung', *Nationalsozialistisches Bildungswesen* 2 (1937), 641–9, here 649.
83 A. Wellek, 'Psychologie der Gemeinschaft. Der 14. Kongress der
   Deutschen Gesellschaft für Psychologie in Tübingen', *Zeitschrift für angewandte Psychologie* 47 (1934), 125–50, here 126.
84 Krueger, 'Gemeinschaftslebens', 29.
85 See H. Marcuse, 'Der Kampf gegen den Liberalismus in der totalitären
   Staatsauffassung', in H. Marcuse (ed.), *Kultur und Gesellschaft I* (Frankfurt, 1968), pp. 17–54, here 20.
86 F. Krueger, 'Protest gegen Versailles. Ansprache zur Protest-Kundgebung
   der Leipziger Studentenschaft am 28. Juni 1932 im Kyffhäuserhaus', *Die
   Leipziger Studentenschaft* 16 (1932), 57–9, here 58.
87 *Rektorwechsel an der Universität Leipzig am 28. April 1935* (Leipzig,
   1935), p. 30.
88 Sander, 'Deutsche Psychologie', 642.
89 Sander, 'Deutsche Psychologie', 642.
90 Sander, 'Deutsche Psychologie', 643.
91 Krueger, 'Gemeinschaftslebens', 28.
92 Krueger, 'Gemeinschaftslebens', 42.
93 Krueger, 'Der strukturelle', 187.
94 Krueger, 'Der strukturelle', 188.
95 J. Rudert, *Charakter und Schicksal* (Potsdam, 1944), p. 6.
96 F. Krueger, 'Entwicklungspsychologie der Ganzheit', *Revista de Psihologie*
   2/3 (1939/1940), here pp. 73–4.
97 Krueger, *Philosophie und Psychologie*, pp. 161ff.
98 *Rektorwechsel*, p. 27.
99 Geuter, *Professionalisierung*, pp. 102ff.
100 See U. Geuter, 'Der Leipziger Kongress der Deutschen Gesellschaft für Psy-
    chologie 1933', *Psychologie- und Gesellschaftritik* 3 (1979), 6–25.
101 See Geuter, *Professionalisierung*, pp. 300–1.
102 Krueger, 'Seelenwissenschaft', 26ff.
103 A thorough description of the conflict is found in U. Geuter, 'Gleichschal-
    tung von oben? Universitätspolitische Strategien und Verhaltensweisen in
    der Psychologie während des Nationalsozialismus', *Bericht aus dem
    Archiv für Geschichte der Psychologie, Psychologisches Institut der Uni-
    versität Heidelberg, Historische Reihe* No. 11 (1983), 15–17.
104 PA 95, f. 14 f., University Archives Leipzig.
105 PA 95, f. 31, University Archives Leipzig.

106 See U. Geuter, 'Nationalsozialistische Ideologie und Psychologie', in M. Ash and U. Geuter (eds), *Geschichte der deutschen Psychologie im 20. Jahrhundert* (Opladen, 1985), pp. 172–200.
107 Krueger, 'Gemeinschaftslebens', pp. 15–16.
108 Krueger, 'Gemeinschaftslebens', p. 19.
109 Sontheimer, *Antidemokratisches Denken*, p. 250.
110 Wellek, 'Deutsche', 178–9.
111 Krueger, *Klemm*, pp. 30ff.
112 *Rektorwechsel*, p. 22.
113 Wellek, 'Deutsche'.
114 PA 664, f. 110d, University Archives Leipzig.
115 PA 664, f. 74, University Archives Leipzig.
116 49.01 REM 2945, f. 12, State Archives Potsdam; Krueger to Reichsministerium für Wissenschaft, Erziehung und Volksbildung (22 April 1936).
117 Wellek, 'Deutsche'.
118 See U. Geuter, 'The Eleventh and Twelfth International Congresses of Psychology – a note on politics and science between 1936 and 1948', in H. Carpintero & J. M. Peiró (eds), *Psychology in its Historical Context. Essays in Honor of Prof. Joseph Brožek* (Valencia, 1984), 127–40.
119 49.01 REM 2945, f. 129, State Archives Potsdam.
120 PA 1046, f. 47, University Archives Leipzig.
121 In conversations with the author, Hans Thomae, who was an assistant to Lersch in Leipzig, characterized Krueger as a German nationalist; Johannes Rudert, who was Krueger's assistant from 1929–36 and in 1941 became a Professor extraordinary in Leipzig, called him a 'passionate German nationalist romanticist'; see the conversations in U. Geuter, 'Gespräche zur Entwicklung der Psychologie in Deutschland von den 20er Jahren bis 1945. Eine Protokollsammlung', ZS/A 37, f. 90 and 191, Institut für Zeitgeschichte, Munich.
122 See H. P. Bleuel, *Deutschlands Bekenner. Professoren zwischen Kaiserreich und Diktatur* (Bern, 1968); Ringer, *Decline*; Schroeder-Gudehus, *Deutsche Wissenschaft und internationale Zusammenarbeit 1914–1928. Ein Beitrag zum Studium kultureller Beziehungen in politischen Krisenzeiten* (Geneva, 1966).
123 See M. Kater, 'Die nationalsozialistische Machtergreifung an den deutschen Hochschulen. Zum politischen Verhalten akademischer Lehrer bis 1939', in H. J. Vogel, H. Simon and A. Podleck (eds), *Die Freiheit des Anderen. Festschrift für Martin Hirsch* (Baden-Baden, 1981), pp. 49–75, here pp. 58ff.
124 H. Sarkowicz, 'Zwischen Sympathie und Apologie. Der Schriftsteller Hans Grimm und sein Verhältnis zum Nationalsozialismus', in K. Corino (ed.), *Intellektuelle im Bann des Nationalsozialismus* (Hamburg, 1980), pp. 120–35, here 123, italics by the author.
125 Sources: R21 Anh., f. 5567, Federal Archives Koblenz; PA 664 a, b, c, University Archives Leipzig.

11   Pascual Jordan: quantum mechanics, psychology, National
        Socialism

1 Department of History, Princeton University, Princeton, NJ 08544–1017,
  USA. I thank Elaine Wise and members of colloquia at Hamburg, Minne-
  sota, UC San Diego, UCLA and Cambridge universities for engaged discussions. I am most grateful to Mark Walker for locating and copying a variety
  of documents and to him and to Monika Renneberg for their critiques. The
  following abbreviations are used for works of Pascual Jordan: AQ = *Die
  anschauliche Quantentheorie: Eine Einführung in die moderne Auffassung
  der Quantenerscheinungen* (Berlin, 1936); PD = *Physikalisches Denken in
  der neuen Zeit* (Hamburg, 1935); 'Bemerkungen' = 'Quantenphysikalische
  Bemerkungen zur Biologie und Psychologie', *Erkenntnis* 4 (1934), 215–52;
  'Grundprobleme' = 'Die Quantenmechanik und die Grundprobleme der
  Biologie und Psychologie', *Die Naturwissenschaften* 20 (1932); *Geheimnis*
  = *Die Physik und das Geheimnis des organischen Lebens* (Braunschweig,
  1941); 'Parapsychischen' = 'Positivistische Bemerkungen über die parapsy-
  chischen Erscheinungen', *Zentralblatt für Psychotherapie* 9 (1936). Archives
  which I thank for permission to quote from their holdings are:
  HU = Universitätsarchiv der Humboldt-Universität zu Berlin; SB = Staatsbi-
  bliothek   Preussischer   Kulturbesitz,   Berlin,   Handschriftenabteilung;
  BSC = Bohr Scientific Correspondence, Archive for the History of Quantum
  Physics (American Institute of Physics, New York, and elsewhere);
  HN = Heisenberg Papers, Max Planck Institute for Physics, Munich',
  IG = 1st physikalishes Institut, Georg August Universität, Göttingen.
2 Pascual Jordan, 'Atom Vorgänge im biologischen Geschehen', *Bremer Beiträge zur Wissenschaft* 5 (1939), 61–72, here 65. 'In reality light is neither
  wave nor particle, rather a "third"'.
3 According to Jordan's official statement, he joined the NSDAP on 1 September 1933 and the SA in the autumn of 1933. Jordan an das Kuratorium
  der Universität Rostock, 25 May 1938, HU, UK. J69 I, 86. Jordan's personal
  life is difficult to reconstruct because his *Nachlass*, housed at the Staatsbi-
  bliothek Preussischer Kulturbesitz in Berlin, contains virtually nothing of
  personal-political relevance from the thirties and forties, even though it
  contains voluminous lecture notes from that period, often written on the
  back of used paper of all kinds, including letters.
4 Rembert Ramsauer objected to the deceptive '*Zweideutigkeit*' of this title in
  his review, *Zeitschrift für die gesamte naturwissenschaft* 1 (1935–6), 342–3.
5 PD, p. 7.
6 PD, p. 53.
7 PD, pp. 53–4.
8 PD, pp. 56–7.
9 PD, pp. 58–9.
10 PD, p. 57.
11 PD, p. 49.

12 PD, p. 51.

13 PD, p. 42.

14 PD, p. 8.

15 P. Forman, 'Weimar culture, causality, and quantum theory: adaptation by German physicists and mathematicians to a hostile intellectual environment', *Historical Studies in the Physical Sciences* 3 (1971), 1–115, here 3. The thesis is reaffirmed in his '*Kausalität, Anschaulichkeit*, and *Individualität*, or How Cultural Values Prescribed the Character and the Lessons Ascribed to Quantum Mechanics', in N. Stehr and V. Meja (eds.), *Society and Knowledge: Contemporary Perspectives in the Sociology of Knowledge* (New Brunswick 1984), pp. 333–47. Here Bohr does appear in much too close a relation with Jordan. John Heilbron, 'The earliest Missionaries of the Copenhagen Spirit', *Revue d'histoire des science* 38 (1985), 194–230.

16 M. Norton Wise, 'How do Sums Count? On the Cultural Origins of Statistical Causality', in *The Probabilistic Revolution*, 2 vols. (Cambridge, MA, 1987), Vol. I, *Ideas in History*, L. Krüger, L. J. Daston and M. Heidelberger (eds.), pp. 395–425.

17 M. Heidelberger, 'Fechner's Indeterminism: From Freedom to Laws of Chance', in Krüger *et al.*, *The Probabilistic Revolution* 1, pp. 117–56, esp. 145–7 for von Mises.

18 AQ, pp. 51, iii.

19 AQ, pp. 8–9.

20 J. Faye, *Niels Bohr: His Heritage and Legacy: An Anti-realist View of Quantum Mechanics* (Dordrecht, 1991), demonstrates how thoroughly Bohr employed concepts drawn from Harald Høffding, esp. pp. 127–46, for complementarity. K. M. Meyer-Abich, *Korrespondenz, Individualität und Komplementarität* (Wiesbaden, 1965). G. Holton, 'Roots of Complementarity', in *The Thematic Origins of Scientific Thought* (Cambridge, MA, 1973), pp. 115–61. L. Feuer, *Einstein and the Generations of Science* (New York, 1974). J. Faye, 'The Influence of Harald Høffding's philosophy on Niels Bohr's Interpretation of Quantum Mechanics', *Danish Yearbook of Philosophy* 16 (1979), 37–72.

21 The following description summarizes material from Wise, 'How do Sums Count?', containing full references.

22 Cf. Forman, '*Kausalität, Anschaualichkeit*, and *Individualität*', 340–3, where the issue of individuality is limited to whether an individual particle is fully and unambiguously knowable to an observer. Bohr was concerned instead with what the quantum-mechanical limitations on knowability implied about the nature of individuality. Forman's assertion that 'individuality does not exist in the atomic world' (p. 344) is highly problematic.

23 AQ, pp. 115, 131. On Heisenberg's earlier attempts to redefine *Anschaulichkeit* see Forman, '*Kausalität, Anschaulichkeit*, and *Individualität*', pp. 339ff, with reference to W. Heisenberg, 'Quantenmechanik', *Naturwissenschaften* 14 (1926), 989–94, and 'Ueber den anschaulichen Inhalt der quantentheoretischen Kinematik und Mechanik', *Zeitschrift für Physik* 43 (1927), 172–98. Also on *Anschaulichkeit* see R. McCormmach, *Night*

Thoughts of a Classical Physicist (Cambridge, MA, 1982), pp. 204–7; D. Serwer, 'Unmechanischer Zwang: Pauli, Heisenberg, and the Rejection of the Mechanical Atom, 1923–1925', *Historical Studies in the Physical Sciences* 8 (1977), 189–256; and J. Hendry, *The Creation of Quantum Mechanics and the Bohr–Pauli Dialogue* (Dordrecht, 1984), pp. 111–28.

24 AQ, p. v.

25 AQ, p. v, 51–2; PD, pp. 49–50.

26 H. Dingler, reviewing Jordan's *Physik des 20. Jahrhunderts*, in *Zeitschrift für die gesamte Naturwissenschaft* 3 (1937–8), 321–35, here 324, 335; (2nd edition) 4 (1938–39), 389–93, here 392.

27 AQ, pp. 37, 275–6, 301. P. Jordan, 'Ergänzende Bemerkungen über Biologie und Quantenmechanik', *Erkenntnis* 5 (1935), 348–52, here 348.

28 PD, pp. 39–40.

29 PD, p. 40.

30 PD, pp. 51–2.

31 PD, p. 50; also 40.

32 AQ, pp. v, 8–9, 37, 48, 52.

33 AQ, pp. 48, 52, 279–86, 306–9, 316.

34 AQ, pp. 65, 307.

35 AQ, pp. 41, 61, 83, 100. On *Zweideutigkeit* see Serwer, 'Unmechanischer Zwang', 232–3, 242–3; and Hendry, *Creation*, pp. 63–6.

36 AQ, pp. 167–75.

37 AQ, p. 171.

38 In a footnote Jordan claimed that Bohr and Heisenberg actually developed the complementarity viewpoint out of the Dirac–Jordan transformation theory. AQ, p. 171n.

39 P. Jordan, 'Quantenphysikalische Bemerkungen zur Biologie und Psychologie', *Erkenntnis* 4 (1934), 215–52, here 217; AQ, pp. vii–viii.

40 P. Jordan, 'Die Quantenmechanik und die Grundprobleme der Biologie und Psychologie', *Die Naturwissenschaften* 20 (1932), 815–21, here 820; 'Bemerkungen', 242; 'Philosophical Foundations of Quantum theory', *Nature* 119 (1927), 566–9 (trans. J. R. Oppenheimer).

41 Finn Aaserud describes Jordan's interaction with Bohr and perceptively analyses their differences in *Redirecting Science: Niels Bohr, Philanthropy, and the Rise of Nuclear Physics* (Cambridge, 1990), pp. 82–97. (I add Jordan's *Führer* concept to Aaserud's discussion.) The interaction had begun by 1926, when Bohr contributed money for treatment of Jordan's stammer, but effectively ended in 1934 when Jordan's distortions and Nazi associations had become manifest (pp. 82, 88). See also, D. Hoffman, 'Zur Teilnahme deutscher Physiker an den Kopenhagener Physikerkonferenzen nach 1933 sowie am 2. Kongress für Einheit der Wissenschaft, Kopenhagen 1936', *NTM – Schriftenreihe für Geschichte der Naturwissenschaften, Technik und Medizin* 25 (1988), 49–55.

42 Jordan to Einstein, 11 December 1928, Einstein Papers, Tel Aviv, Israel and Princeton, New Jersey; quoted in Aaserud, *Redirecting Science*, p. 83. 'Grundprobleme', p. 820.

43 P. Jordan, 'Die Naturwissenschaften und das Problem der Freiheit' (lecture, 1938), in *Geheimnis*, pp. 147–62, here 157.

44 'Grundprobleme', p. 817; 'Freiheit', in *Geheimnis*, p. 156.

45 'Grundprobleme', p. 820; AQ, pp. 300–1.

46 'Grundprobleme', p. 821.

47 See Aaserud's account of Bohr's initial response to Jordan in 1931 and his attempts to counter Jordan's misrepresentations during 1932–6, *Redirecting Science*, pp. 88–96. Bohr to Jordan, 23 June 1931, BSC (21,3). N. Bohr, 'Light and Life' (1932), in *Atomic Physics and Human Knowledge* (Cambridge, 1934), pp. 3–12, esp. p. 11; slightly revised from *Nature* 131 (1933), 421–3, 457–9.

48 AQ, pp. 154–7, 160–1, 241, 291, 297, 301. 'Ergänzende Bemerkungen', p. 351. See M. Beller, 'Are there Quantum Jumps', (forthcoming), on the Jordan–Schroedinger–Bohr relation.

49 AQ, pp. 42–3.

50 AQ, pp. 228–36, 241–2, 296.

51 AQ, pp. 290–2.

52 AQ, p. 315.

53 'Bemerkungen', pp. 247–8; AQ, pp. 313–14.

54 'Bemerkungen, pp. 243, 247–8; quoting S. Freud, *Vorlesungen über Psychoanalyse* (Vienna, 1920), p. 316.

55 P. Jordan, 'Positivistische Bemerkungen über die parapsychischen Erscheinungen', *Zentralblatt für Psychotherapie* 9 (1936), 3–17, here 10, 17.

56 P. Jordan, *Verdrängung und Komplementarität: Eine philosophische Untersuchung* (Hamburg, 1947), pp. 20–1. Jordan again acknowledged assistance from Pauli and Jung, pp. 8–9.

57 'Parapsychischen', pp. 6–7.

58 'Parapsychischen', pp. 15–16.

59 'Parapsychischen', pp. 8, 12–14.

60 'Parapsychischen', pp. 6, 11, 16; AQ, p. 318.

61 Literature and discussion in Helga Grebing, unter Mitarbeit von Doris von der Brelle-Lewien und Hans-Joachim Franzen, *Der "deutsche Sonderweg" in Europa, 1806–1945: Eine Kritik* (Stuttgart, 1986).

62 'Grundprobleme', 816n; 'Bemerkungen', 217–18.

63 Jordan to Heisenberg, 6 June 1934, HN. P. Jordan, 'Ueber den Positivistischen Begriff der Wirklichkeit', *Die Naturwissenschaften* 22 (1934), 485–90.

64 M. Schlick, 'Über den Begriff der Ganzheit', *Erkenntnis* 5 (1935), 52–5. E. Zilsel, 'P. Jordan's Versuch, den Vitalismus quantenmechanisch zu retten', *Erkenntnis* 5 (1935), 56–64.

65 H. Reichenbach, 'Zu Edgar Zilsel', *Erkenntnis* 5 (1935), 178–9. O. Neurath, 'Jordan, Quantentheorie und Willensfreiheit', *Erkenntnis* 5 (1935), 179–81. Additional remarks by Schlick and Frank follow.

66 P. Frank, *Erkenntnis* 5 (1935), 65–80, esp. 66–9.

67 K. Hildebrandt, 'Positivismus und Natur', *Zeitschrift für die gesamte naturwissenschaft* 1 (1935–6), 1–22, here 8. Jordan, PD, pp. 8–9.

68 K. Hildebrandt, 'In eigener Sache', *Zeitschrift für die gesamte Naturwissenschaft* 1 (1935–6), 340–2, here 340 and 341n; Hildebrandt, 'Positivismus und Natur', 11–18, for his critique of positivist *Weltanschauung* as 'the impoverishment of life, world-weariness'. Deflecting this critique, Jordan construed a proper *Weltanschauung* similarly: 'the sense of the word "*Weltanschauung*" has been essentially displaced: for our present sensibility it no longer refers in the first place to things which might be ascertained through thought and research, but to questions which are to be decided by the will and the political act'. *Geheimnis*, p. 166. Die Dozentenschaft der Universität Rostock an den Herrn Rektor der Universität Rostock, 23 August 1937, HU, UK. J69I.

69 Jordan an Herrn Gaudozentenbundführer Prof. Dr Gissel, 10 February 1938, HU, UK. J69II, 56; Jordan an den Dekan der philosophischen Fakultät der Universität Rostock, 11 February 1938, HU, UK. J69II, S7; Jordan an den Herrn Rektor der Universität Rostock, 23 February 1938, HU, UK, J69II, S4–5. All quotations below are from the latter.

70 Heisenberg attacked Dingler's review in a similar, if more subtle manner in 1940, but publication was delayed: W. Heisenberg, 'Die Bewertung der "modernen theoretischen Physik"' *Zeitschrift für die gesamte Naturwissenschaft* 9 (1943), 201–12, esp. 203–4.

71 *Geheimnis*, p. 8, P. Jordan, 'Gibt es eine "Krise" der modernen physikalischen Forschung?' (1936, previously unpublished), in *Geheimnis*, pp. 169–83, here 183.

72 Jordan, 'Krise', 173n. Again see Heisenberg's more subtle mode of de-emphasizing Einstein's contributiuon, Heisenberg' 'Bewertung', 205.

73 Jordan was a volunteer in the *Wehrmacht*. Jordan an Paul Rosbaud, 30 September 1941, SB, Nachlass Jordan, 765.

74 *Geheimnis*, p. 8–9.

75 P. Jordan, *Die Physik und das Geheimnis des organischen Lebens* (Braunschweig, 1943).

76 Jordan to Heisenberg, 6 June 1934, HN.

77 Jordan to Heisenberg, 6 June 1934, HN. See also, Born to Franck, 14 April 1934 and Franck to Born, 18 April 1934, SB, Born Nachlass, 954 and 229; Jordan to Bohr, June (?) 1934, and Bohr to Jordan, 30 June 1934, BSC (21,3); discussed in Aaserud, *Redirecting Science*, p. 88.

78 Jordan to Born, 23 July 1948 and 15 August 1948, SB, Nachlass, Born, 353. Born to Jordan, 30 October 1957, Born Nachlass, 1003. Heisenberg's testimonials are dated 21 October 1946 (quotation) and 18 January 1947, HN. For an excellent account of the use of *die deutsche Physik* as scapegoat in the denazification proceedings and for the form and function of Heisenberg's testimonials see M. Walker, *German National Socialism and the Quest for Nuclear Power, 1939–1949* (Cambridge, 1989), pp. 192–204. Heisenberg's testimonials follow the form of his own self-reconstruction.

79 Jordan to Prof. Dr. Correns, 29 December 1945, Pohl Papers, IG.

80 M. Cioc, *Pax Atomica: The Nuclear Defense Debate in West Germany*

during the Adenauer Era (New York, 1988), pp. 72–86, gives an account of the circumstances and a translation of the Göttingen petition, original reprinted in *Militärpolitik Dokumentation*, No. 25 (1982), 41–2; also C. F. von Weizsäcker, *Der bedrohte Frieden: Politische Aufsätze 1945–81* (Munich, 1981), 29–30.

81 P. Jordan, *Der gescheiterte Aufstand – Betrachtungen zur Gegenwart* (Frankfurt a.M., 1956). Cioc, *Pax Atomica*, pp. 80ff.
82 P. Jordan, *Wir müssen den Frieden retten*, (Cologne, 1957).
83 Jordan to Born, 21 October 1957, SB, Born Nachlass, 353.
84 Born to Jordan, 30 October 1957, SB, Born Nachlass, 1003. H. Born, 'Pasqual Jordan, Propagandist im Sold der CDU', *Deutsche Volkszeitung* 34 (1957); and, protesting the inflammatory title, 'An die Deutsche Volkszeitung' (2 September 1957), *Deutsche Volkszeitung* 36 (1957), 4.
85 Born to Jordan, 30 October 1957, SB, Born Nachlass, 1003.

12 The ideology of early particle accelerators; an association between knowledge and power

1 See S. Traweek, *Beamtimes and Lifetimes. The World of High Energy Physicists* (Cambridge, MA, 1988); this is an anthropological study that allows an insight into the initiation rituals of high energy physics.
2 Compare J. B. Thompson, *Studies in the Theory of Ideology* (Berkeley, 1984), especially chapter 1; Thompson distinguishes between the neutral concept of ideology, which searches for discursive meanings in the service of securing and ensuring power.
3 See Foucault's reflection on ideology, M. Foucault, *Dispositive der Macht. Über Sexualität, Wissenschaft und Wahrheit* (Berlin, 1978), p. 39 and *Archäologie des Wissens* (Frankfurt a.M., 1971).
4 In contrast to 'economy' and 'society', the 'third level' thematizes forms of consciousness, habits of thought and ideologies, however not in the sense of intellectual history, but rather as a 'structural history of the subjective', as a history of the complex and material forms of 'consciousness' or 'unconsciousness'; see P. Schöttler, 'Mentalitäten, Ideologien, Diskurse. Zur sozialgeschichtlichen Thematisierung der "dritten Ebene"', in A. Lüdtke (ed.), *Alltagsgeschichte, Zur Rekonstruktion historischer Erfahrungen und Lebensweisen* (Frankfurt a.M., 1989), pp. 85–136.
5 In my previous work on the early history of German particle accelerators, I restricted myself to a rather descriptive or socio-economic analysis, see M. Osietzki, 'Kernphysikalische Grossgeräte zwischen naturwissenschaftlicher Forschung, Industrie und Politik. Zur Entwicklung der ersten deutschen Teilchenbeschleuniger bei Siemens 1935–1945', *Technikgeschichte* 55 (1989), pp. 25–46; see also M. Eckert and M. Osietzki, *Wissenschaft für Macht und Markt. Kernforschung und Mikroelektronik in der Bundesrepublik Deutschland* (Munich, 1989), pp. 37–73.
6 F. Soddy, quoted according to S. Weart, *Nuclear Fear: A History of Images* (Cambridge, MA, 1988), p. 6.

7 J-M. Levy-Leblond, 'Ideology of/in Contemporary Physics', in H. Rose and S. Rose (eds), *The Radicalisation of Science. Ideology of/in Natural Sciences* (London, 1976), pp. 136–98, quote p. 136; to my knowledge this article is the best examination of the ideology of elementary particle physics.

8 Levy-Leblond, 'Ideology'.

9 My horizon of questions is based in part on the results of the scientific debate on gender and science, in which modern science is interpreted in the context of changing sexual relations as the result of a parallel process for the control of nature and of women; see the introductory essays and bibliographies in S. Rosser (ed.), *Women's Studies International Forum. In Memory of Ruth Bleier* 12, (1989).

10 B. Easlea, *Väter der Vernichtung. Männlichkeit, Naturwissenschaftler und der nukleare Rüstungswettlauf* (Reinbek, 1986); here Easlea interprets the motives of nuclear physicists as the wrestling away of the 'feminine' secrets of nature and liberating the energies enclosed in the atomic nucleus as compensation for the feminine ability to give birth, whereby the nuclear physicist is driven by ambition and lust for power.

11 Weart, *Nuclear Fear*, p. 16.

12 In the first chapter of his book *Nuclear Fear*, Spencer Weart has instructively worked out the images bound up with radioactivity and nuclear energy at the beginning of this century; even though this approach, inspired by the history of mentalities, allows new insight into the genesis of modern physics, in my opinion the fantasies upon which this genesis is based should be interpreted more from the perspective of social history; the images that stand behind the new dimensions for the control of nature by means of deliberate transformation of elements would then be derived historically from a specific form of society – an effort which in my opinion would be practicable by means of the critical concept of ideology.

13 P. Forman, 'Weimar Culture, Causality, and Quantum Theory, 1918–1927: Adaptation by German Physicists and Mathematicians to a Hostile Intellectual Environment', in *Historical Studies in the Physical Sciences* 3, (1971), pp. 1–115.

14 F. Wagner, *Die Wissenschaft und die gefährdete Welt. Eine Wissenschaftssoziologie der Atomphysik* (Munich, 1964), p. 76; also see Levy-Leblond, 'Ideology'.

15 Wagner, *Die Wissenschaft*, p. 98.

16 Weart examines these two motives associated with atomic energy: progress and doom.

17 T. Trenn, 'The Justification of Transmutation: Speculations of Ramsay and Experiments of Rutherford', *Ambix* 21 (1974), p. 53–77; see also 'The Central Role of Energy in Soddy's Holistic and Critical Approach to Nuclear Science, Economics, and Social Responsibility', *British Journal of the History of Science* 12 (1979), pp. 261–76.

18 For the social ideologies and fantasies of doom at the beginning of this century, compare K. D. Bracher, *Zeit der Ideologien. Eine Geschichte politischen Denkens im 20. Jahrhundert* (Munich, 1985).

19 E. Fox Keller, 'Fractured Images of Science, Language, and Power: A Postmodern Optic, or Just Bad Eyesight?' *Poetics Today* 12 (1991), pp. 227–43; Fox Keller thematizes the scientific attack on the sphere of life in molecular biology by means of its conceptual and social relations to physics.

20 C. Weiner, '1932 – Moving into a New Physics', *Physics Today* 25 (1972), pp. 40–9.

21 Quoted according to E. McMillan, 'Early History of Particle Accelerators', in R. Stuewer (ed.), *Nuclear Physics in Retrospect. Proceedings of a Symposium on the 1930s* (Minneapolis, 1979), pp. 113–29, here 117.

22 See Traweek, *Beamtimes*.

23 McMillan, 'Early History', p. 117; however, it must be noted that Tuve eventually took up the opposite position; see A. Baracca, '"Big Science" vs. "Little Science" in Post-War Physics', in M. De Maria, M. Grilli and F. Sebastiani (eds), *Proceedings of the International Conference on The Restructuring of Physical Sciences in Europe and the United States 1945– 1960* (Singapore, 1989), pp. 150–60; thanks to Monika Renneberg for this reference.

24 J. L. Heilbron and R. Seidel, *Lawrence and his Laboratory. A History of the Lawrence Berkeley Laboratory. Vol. 1* (Berkeley, 1989).

25 Quoted from H. Childs, *An American Genius: The Life of Ernest Orlando Lawrence* (New York, 1968), p. 297.

26 Akten des Hauptausschusses der Notgemeinschaft der deutschen Wissenschaft, Anträge von Lange aus den Jahren 1929/30 und 1930/31 BA R 73/110, 112, Bundesarchiv Koblenz.

27 Protokoll der 7. Sitzung des Ausschusses Angewandte Forschung am 29.4.1955, Teil I: Physikalische Apparate, p. 17, Archiv des Physikalischen Instituts der Universität Bonn.

28 See H. Konen, 'Strahlenforschung,' in 'Gesellschaft von Freunden und Förderern der Rheinischen Friedrich-Wilhelms-Universität zu Bonn' (ed.), *Bonner Mitteilungen* 2 (1929), 1–11, especially 9ff; for the cooperative research of the *Deutsche Forschungsgemeinschaft* see K. Zierold, *Forschungsförderung in drei Epochen. Deutsche Forschungsgemeinschaft. Geschichte, Arbeitsweise, Kommentare* (Wiesbaden, 1968); see also S. Richter, *Forschungsförderung in Deutschland 1920–1936. Dargestellt am Beispiel der Notgemeinschaft der deutschen Wissenschaft und ihrem Wirken für das Fach Physik* (Düsseldorf, 1972), especially pp. 49–52.

29 Hoffmann to Mehlhorn (12 January 1938), SAA 11/Lg 43, Siemens-Archives, Munich.

30 W. Gentner, 'Mitteilungen aus der Kernphysik', *Die Naturwissenschaften* 25 (1937), p. 479.

31 Hoffmann to Mehlhorn (12 January 1938), Siemens Archives.

32 Hoffmann to Mehlhorn (12 January 1938), Siemens Archives; Flir to von Boul (5 August 1937), Siemens Archives.

33 Flir to von Boul (5 August 1937), Siemens Archives; Aktennotiz: 'Betrifft Arbeitsteilung', (12 May 1936), Siemens Archives.

34 Aktennotiz: 'Betrifft Arbeitsteilung', (12 May 1936), Siemens Archives; Flir to von Boul (15 December 1940), Siemens Archives.

35 Bothe to Debye (18 May 1938), Bothe Papers 62, Archives of the Max-Planck-Gesellschaft, Berlin.

36 Hoffmann to von Boul (18 March 1940), Siemens Archives.

37 Hoffmann to von Boul (18 March 1940), Siemens Archives; Flir to von Boul (15 December 1940), Siemens Archives.

38 See M. Walker, *German National Socialism and the Quest for Nuclear Power, 1939–1949* (Cambridge, 1989), pp. 23–4.

39 The two cyclotron magnets ordered by Minister Ohnesorge were actually intended for Manfred Ardenne's private research institute in Berlin and the Post Office research institute in Zeuthen; see Vögler to von Boul (23 December 1941), Siemens Archives.

40 Fortunately for Siemens, a shortage of personnel had forced Hoffmann to transfer his claim on the first cyclotron to Bothe.

41 'Betrifft Zyklotronaufstellung bei S&H', (26 July 1942), Siemens Archives.

42 'Betrifft Zyklotronaufstellung bei S&H', (26 July 1942), Siemens Archives; Memo on the correspondence concerning the cyclotron between Speer, Ohnesorge and Vögler (19 March 1942), Siemens Archives.

43 Memo on the correspondence concerning the cyclotron between Speer, Ohnesorge and Vögler (19 March 1942), Siemens Archives; Von Boul to Hoffmann (20 December 1941), Siemens Archives.

44 Quotation from a memo by a Siemens employee concerning a relevant conference summoned by Speer: Dähne to Mehlhorn (13 June 1942), Siemens Archives.

45 See Walker, *German*, pp. 50–1.

46 Dähne to Mehlhorn (13 June 1942), Siemens Archives.

47 Quotation from Carl Ramsauer, chairman of the German Physical Society and director of the AEG research laboratories, who pointed out that Germany had fallen behind in nuclear technology by 1943; C. Ramsauer, 'Über Leistung und Organisation der angelsächsischen Physik mit Ausblicken auf die deutsche Physik. Vortrag gehalten auf der 2. Wissenschaftssitzung der Ordentlichen Mitglieder am 2. April 1943 der Akademie für Luftfahrtforschung', p. 10, Peenemünde Archives, Sondersammlungen des Deutschen Museums, Munich.

48 At times researchers and military authorities in Japan and England also hoped to be able to develop radiation weapons; see Weart, *Nuclear Fear*, p. 47.

49 K. Gund, 'Das jüngste Kampfmittel gegen den Krebs. Die Elektronen-Schleuder der Siemens-Reiniger-Werke', *Siemens Mitteilungen* 27, (1952), pp. 18ff.

50 Quotation from Werner Heisenberg in 1949 on the occasion of a speech about the 'Deutscher Forschungsrat', a science policy council of which he was the president and which he wanted to make into an instrument for the modernization of scientific organization in West Germany: 'Verlauf der Veranstaltung, Protokoll der auf Einladung des Koordinierungsbüros der Länder am 9. März 1949 stattgefundenen Vortragsveranstaltung', *Länderrat des amerikanischen Besatzungsgebietes – Koordinierungsbüro der Länder*, p. 2, Ordner Deutscher Forschungsrat, Heisenberg Papers, Munich.

51 Walker, *German*, pp. 76ff.
52 Levy-Leblond, 'Ideology', p. 164.
53 Levy-Leblond, 'Ideology', p. 139; elementary particle physics in the USA received 27% of the governmental and industrial support of basic research, while nuclear physics received only 13%; more data is found on p. 140 of the same reference.
54 R. Seidel, 'Accelerating Science: The Postwar Transformation of the Lawrence Radiation Laboratory', *Historical Studies in the Physical and Biological Sciences* 13 (1983), pp. 375–400, quotation from pp. 382ff.
55 Seidel, 'Accelerating Science'; see also J. L. Heilbron, R. Seidel and B. Wheaton, 'Lawrence and his Laboratory: Nuclear Science at Berkeley', *LBL Magazine* (Berkeley, 1981), pp. 76ff.
56 J. Krige, 'The Influence of Developments in American Nuclear Science of the Pioneers of CERN', in *Studies in CERN History* 1 (1983).
57 D. Pestre, 'The First Suggestions, 1949–June 1950', *History of CERN*, pp. 63–95, here pp. 69ff.
58 It was in this role that he came to be the chief ideologist of West German physics. At first, his early organisational and science policy activities took place in the 'Deutscher Forschungsrat'. This elite committee had been founded in March 1949 under Heisenberg's decisive influence. The physicist served as president of the *Deutscher Forschungsrat* from 1949 to 1951. This committee wanted to coordinate all scientific research and consultation in West Germany, as well as being the sole representative of German science in international affairs. See M. Osietzki, 'Forschungsorganisation zwischen Tradition und Modernisierung. Der Deutsche Forschungsrat 1949–51: eine Episode wissenschaftlichen Eliteanspruchs', (forthcoming).
59 Vortragsveranstaltung am 9. März 1949, p. 2, Heisenberg Papers.
60 Eckert and Osietzki, *Wissenschaft*, p. 72.
61 Eckert and Osietzki, *Wissenschaft*, p. 68.

13   The 'Minerva Project'

Archive abbreviations used: BAK: Bundesarchiv Koblenz; IFZ: Institut für Zeitgeschichte Munich; LAB: Landesarchiv Berlin; MPG: Archiv zur Geschichte der Max-Planck-Gesellschaft Berlin; MPI: Max-Planck-Institut für Chemie Mainz; PMS: Philips Medizin-Systeme (formerly C.H.F. Müller) Hamburg; SAM: Siemens-Archiv München; UAM: Universitätsarchiv Mainz.

Acknowledgement

I am gratefully indebted to J. Ahrens (MPI Chemistry Mainz), H. Bergmüller (Philips Medizin Systeme Hamburg) and E. Henning (Archiv für Geschichte der Max-Planck-Gesellschaft Berlin) for their continuous support of this study.

Notes

1 Compare M. Osietzki, 'Kernphysikalische Grossgeräte zwischen naturwiss-enschaftlicher Forschung, Industrie und Politik. Zur Entwicklung der ersten deutschen Teilchenbeschleuniger bei Siemens 1935–45', *Technikgeschichte* 55 (1988), 25–46; M. Osietzki, 'Physik, Industrie und Politik in der Frühge-schichte der deutschen Beschleunigerentwicklung' in M. Eckert and M. Osietzki (eds), *Wissenschaft für Macht und Markt. Kernforschung und Mikroelektronik in der Bundesrepublik Deutschland* (Munich, 1989), pp. 37–73.

2 The latest in this line is M. Walker, *German National Socialism and the Quest for Nuclear Power 1939–1949* (Cambridge, 1989).

3 A comparative study of these projects with respect to planning, funding and execution is currently under preparation by the author.

4 *Naturforschung und Medizin in Deutschland 1939–1949*, the German edition of the FIAT Review of German Science. The relevant volume is No. 14: W. Bothe and S. Flügge (eds), *Kernphysik und Kosmische Strahlen Teil II* (Weinheim, 1953). The article 'Hochspannungsanlagen' from F. Kirchner (Bothe and Flügge, *Kernphysik*, pp. 24–8) deals only with electrostatic generators, i.e. generators on the model of Van de Graaff. Cascade genera-tors are not considered. Since it was these generators that were preferred by the KWIs (see below), their high-voltage equipment was not taken into account by F. Kirchner. This at least led the editors to mention the cascade generators of the KWG in a footnote. The 'Minerva' project, however, was not mentioned at all.

5 References can be found in the publications of the MPG. See also F. Strass-mann, 'Das Max-Planck-Institut für Chemie', *Staats-Zeitung Rheinland-Pfalz* 2, No. 24 (17 June 1951), also reprinted in F. Frafft, *Im Schatten der Sensation. Leben und Wirken von Fritz Strassmann* (Weinheim, 1981), pp. 339–46. See also the references there in the footnotes from F. Krafft.

6 Lise Meitner had in June 1932 already found out about the first smashing of the atom, carried out by Cockcroft and Walton in Cambridge at the begin-ning of the year, from Max Delbrück in Bristol, with whom she correspon-ded at this time about his future work at the KWI. See the letters Delbrück to Meitner, 17 June 1932; Meitner to Delbrück, 27 June 1932 (MPI, file 'Mitarbeiter').

7 The chemist Otto Hahn was by no means alone in his doubts regarding the new technology. Similar doubts could be observed at all the nuclear physics laboratories in Europe, doubts which were fed by the complexity of the new equipment and the difficulties involved in its operation, which required a great deal of experience and experimental know-how. On these problems see J. L. Heilbron, 'The First European Cyclotrons', *Rivista di storia della scienza* 3 (1986), 1–44.

8 Hahn to A. von Weinberg, 9 November 1934 (MPI, file 'Verwaltungsaus-schuss').

9 Interview with A. Flammersfeld, Ebenhausen (15 November 1989).

10 See on this H. Reddemann, 'Untersuchungen mit schnellen Neutronen (I): Künstliche Neutronenquelle und Ausbeute an D + D − Neutronen', *Zeitschrift für Physik* 110 (1938), 373–88. See also the work reports of the KWG for the periods October 1935 to March 1937 and April 1937 to March 1938, *Naturwissenschaften* 25 (1937), 371; 26 (1938), 324.

11 Hahn to Bosch, 8 July 1938 (MPG, Abt. I. Rep. 1 A, Nr. 1154).

12 Compare on this Krafft, *Im Schatten*, p. 178.

13 Compare on this Mattauch to Hahn, 7 September 1955, published in Krafft, *Im Schatten*, pp. 200–3, and E. Henning and M. Kazemi, *Chronik der Kaiser-Wilhelm-Gesellschaft zur Förderung der Wissenschaften* (Berlin, 1988), p. 94.

14 On the contemporary evaluation of Mattauch's work compare H. Bomke, *Erzeugung von Atom- und Ionenstrahlen* (Braunschweig, 1939), pp. 103–8.

15 Mattauch to DFG, 6 November 1938 (BAK, R 73, Nr. 12980).

16 Hahn to Bosch, 8 July 1938 (MPG, Abt. I, Rep. 1A, Nr. 1154).

17 Hahn to Hörlein (Emil Fischer Society), copy, 26 October 1938 (MPG, Abt. I, Rep. 1 A, Nr. 1154, St. 34).

18 Telschow (KWG) to Hörlein (Emil Fischer Society), copy, 11 November 1938 (MPG, Abt. I, Rep. 1 A, Nr. 1154, St. 35).

19 Hahn complained repeatedly in his laboratory diaries as well as in his letters to Lise Meitner about the slowness of their work caused by the lack of sufficiently strong sources. See on this the documents reprinted in Krafft, *Im Schatten*: 'The trials are proceeding slowly ... In the English *Nature* journal five Japanese (Nishina etc.) report on the formation of UY out of thorium and neutrons. They have a cyclotron ... If we had stronger radiation sources we would get along faster'. (laboratory diary from 24.11.1938, p. 247); 'We are not having an easy time with the work. It is really incredible, how many trials we have to undertake using the small radioactivities. With the funds which other institutes have at their disposal we could carry out these trials very much more quickly and above all safely ... If we we preparations only five times stronger everything would go much quicker'. (O. H. to L. M., 5.6.1939, p. 118); 'It is a crying shame that we do not have stronger radiation sources. The McMillan preparations are 100,000 times stronger than ours. The UX resulting from the uranium slams the door in our face ...' (O. H., to L. M., 31.8.1940, p. 126).

20 Compare on this Hahn to the General Administration of the KWG, 26 May 1941 (MPG, Abt.I, Rep. 1 A, Nr. 1154) as well as Hahn, 'Die Transmutation der chemischen Elemente, ein Kapitel physikalischer und chemischer Zusammenarbeit', *Jahrbuch der Kaiser-Wilhelm-Gesellschaft* (1942), pp. 274–95, here p. 289).

21 In this respect only the laboratory of the Auer-Gesellschaft in Berlin-Buch (KWI of Brain Research) and Bohr's cyclotron in Copenhagen came into question. Compare on this the documents reprinted in Krafft, *Im Schatten*, concerning the Auer-Gesellschaft, p. 119 and p. 309; concerning the institute in Copenhagen, p. 307. The equipment in the neighbouring KWI of Physics did not become ready for operation until 1941 (see below).

22 S. Flügge, 'Die Ausnutzung der Atomenergie', *Deutsche Allgemeine Zeitung*, (DAZ), (15 August 1939), supplement.

23 Flügge to DAZ and Flügge to Debye, 8 September 1939 (MPG, Abt. III, Rep. 19, Nr. 218).

24 Picture subtitled 'Technology beyond the bounds of fantasy: the new atom-smashing equipment at the Kaiser Wilhelm Institute of Physics', *Sonderheft der Berliner Illustrierten Zeitung zur 700-Jahr Feier der Reichshauptstadt* (1939), p. 16. Compare also *Facts in Review* 2 (1940), No. 11, the front cover of which is adorned with a picture of the 'atom smasher'. This journal was distributed by the German Library of Information in the USA for propaganda purposes.

25 On the different modes of financing the KWI compare P.-C. Witt, 'Wissenschaftsfinanzierung zwischen Inflation und Deflation: Die Kaiser-Wilhelm-Gesellschaft 1918/19 bis 1934/35' in R. Vierhaus and B. vom Brocke (eds), *Forschung im Spannungsfeld von Politik und Gesellschaft. Geschichte und Struktur der Kaiser-Wilhelm-/Max-Planck-Gesellschaft* (Stuttgart, 1990), pp. 579–656.

26 Hahn to Hörlein, 14 September 1939 (MPI, file 'Verwaltungsausschuss').

27 Compare interview with C. F. von Weizsäcker, 'Ich gebe zu, ich war verrückt', *Der Spiegel* 17 (1991), 227–38.

28 The sums paid by the HWA to the KWI of Chemistry in 1939 came to 3,000 RM; in 1940, 25,573 RM; in 1941, 38,096 RM. In comparison the total funds provided by the Emil Fischer Society in 1939 were 216,000 RM; in 1940, 223,000 RM; in 1941, 245,600 RM. The subsidies from the Reich and from Prussia were only of a symbolic nature – in 1939, 6,249 RM; in 1940, 2,700 RM; in 1941, 4,650 RM. (Reports on the checking of receipts given from the MPG, Abt. I, Rep. 1 A, No. 13 (for 1939); No. 1153 (for 1940 and 1941)).

29 W. Maurer, W. Ramm and H. Geismann, 'Work report on the extension of the high-voltage equipment of the Kaiser-Wilhelm-Institute of Physics, Berlin-Dahlem, to become a neutron source, 19.2.1942', (MPG, Abt. I, Rep. 34). Considerable technical difficulties during the construction of the acceleration tube delayed the completion of the apparatus until March 1941.

30 DIB to Telschow (KWG), copy, 13 February 1941 (MPG, Abt. I, Rep. 1 A, Nr. 1153).

31 Hahn to the General Administration of the KWG, 26 May 1941 (MPG, Abt. I, Rep. 1 A, Nr. 1154).

32 Telschow (KWG) to W. Bötzkes (DIB), copy, 28 May 1941 (MPG, Abt. I, Rep. 1 A, Nr. 1153).

33 DIB board of directors, to Telschow (KWG), copy, 18 June 1941 (MPG, Abt. I, Rep. 1 A, Nr. 1154).

34 File note, Reinold and Forstmann (KWG), 26 July 1941 (MPG, Abt. I, Rep. 1 A, Nr. 1154).

35 Compare on the details BAK, R 73, Nr. 13774–13777.

36 On 9 July 1942 the long-prepared step was carried out by decree of Hitler.

37 Compare MPG, Abt. IV, Rep. 1 B, KWI of Chemistry.

38 Schumann (Research Department, Army High Command) to KWG, copy, 4 May 1942 (MPG, Abt. I, Rep. 1 A, Nr. 1154).

39 Hahn to Hörlein (IG Farben), 11 May 1942 (MPI, file 'Verwaltungsausschuss').

40 Hahn to Vögler (KWG), 12 May 1942 (MPG, Abt. I, Rep. 1 A, Nr. 1154).

41 Compare DIB General Secretary's office, to Telschow (KWG), copy, 6 June 1942 (MPG, Abt. I, Rep. 1 A, Nr. 1154).

42 Esau to Mentzel, 24 November 1942 (IFZ, ED 100 – Irving Papers – pp. 29.1036–29.1043).

43 SRW to Rajewsky, 9 October 1941 (SAM, Flir Papers).

44 For exactly this reason Peter Debye should also have ordered the high-voltage apparatus for his KWI of Physics from Siemens, even though this involved clear disadvantages in respect to delivery time. See on this Debye to Telschow, 11 March 1938, copy, (BAK, R 73, Nr. 10672).

45 Werner Fehr, C. H. F. Müller. *Mit Röntgen begann die Zukunft* (Hamburg, 1981), pp. 27–29.

46 Documents in MPG, Abt. IV, Rep. 1 B.

47 File note Forstmann, 18 March 1943 (MPG, Abt. I, Rep. 1 A, Nr. 1153).

48 Esau to DFG, March 1943 (BAK, R 73, Nr. 12980).

49 Hahn to Vögler (KWG), 4 May 1943. Identically worded, Telschow (KWG) to RFR, copy, 4 May 1943 (MPG, Abt. I, Rep. 1 A, Nr. 1153).

50 Hahn to Vögler (KWG), copy, 16 October 1943 (MPG, Abt. I, Rep. 1 A, Nr. 1145). The day before Mattauch and Flammersfeld had spoken at a secret conference on nuclear physics on the 'Pressure belt generator currently under construction and its possible applications'. See the conference programme (IFZ, ED 100, 29.1078-29.1080).

51 Chronicle of the KWG, p. 109.

52 Report on the bombing raid of 15.2.1944 (MPG, Abt. I, Rep. 1 A, Nr. 1145).

53 Interview with A. Flammersfeld, Ebenhausen (15 November 1989).

54 Layout plan of KWI of Chemistry, November 1947 (MPG, Abt. IV. Rep. 1 B, KWI of Chemistry).

55 Report on the bombing raid in the night of 24 March 1944 (MPG, Abt. I, Rep. 1 A, Nr. 1145).

56 O. Hahn 'Das Kaiser-Wilhelm-Institut für Chemie. Wandlungen einer Forschungsstätte', *Jahrbuch der Max-Planck-Gesellschaft* (1951), pp. 175–98, here 196.

57 PMS, internal note Kt/Lts/412, 3.4.1945; Report Nr. 1550, 23.8.1945. Compare 'Work report of the KWG, 1.1.1946 to 31.3.1951', *Naturwissenschaften*, 38 (1951), pp. 361–80, here 367.

58 H. Götte 'Report of the Kaiser Wilhelm Institute of Chemistry, Tailfingen/ Württ., 29 June 1945' (MPI, file 'MPG').

59 J. Kleindienst, 'Zur Hochschulpolitik Frankreichs in seiner Besatzungszone (1945–1949)' (unpublished thesis, University of Frankfurt, 1987), pp. 98–130.

60 'Bericht über die Lage des Kaiser-Wilhelm-Instituts für Chemie', Tailfingen

18.9.1946 (MPG, Abt. I, Rep. 11, Nr. 20, Bl. 39). In addition, interview with A. Flammersfeld, Ebenhausen (15 November 1989).

61 LAB, Rep. 36 (Office of Military Government Berlin Sector OMGBS), shipment 4, box 11–2, folder 37.

62 Unsigned 'Bericht über Reise vom 8.7. bis 15.7. 1946 (nach) Offenburg, Baden-Weiler, Baden-Baden' (MPG, Abt. I, Rep. 11, Nr. 20, Bll. 34–37).

63 Unsigned 'Bericht des Kaiser-Wilhelm-Instituts für Chemie über seine Tätigkeit seit dem Zusammenbruch', ca. December 1948 (MPI, file 'MPG'). In addition, interview with A. Flammersfeld, Ebenhausen (15 November 1989).

64 PMS, Tagesarchiv Labor I (Kuntke).

65 Procès-Verbal de la réunion du 3 Fèvrier 1947 à Baden-Baden au sujet des Kaiser Wilhelm Institute, copy (UAM, Bestd. 1/ 160). A second high-voltage apparatus originally manufactured by Müller had been confiscated by the French at the Forschungsstelle D in Bisingen and was dismantled.

66 The quarrels over the unsolved questions of ownership in respect of land and buildings which arose between the Institute and the University, represented by its curator, Eichholz, cannot be dealt with here. See on this MPI, file 'Eichholz', as well as Krafft, *Im Schatten*, passim.

67 MPI, file 'Kultusministerium'.

68 Hahn to the state Government of the Rhineland-Palatinate, 2 July 1949 (MPI, file 'Kultusministerium').

69 File note on the meeting between Frau Gantenberg, Secretary of state, Herr Becker, Head of Ministry Department, Schmitt and Jeuck, Senior civil servants from the Ministry of Education and Cultural Affairs, Seeliger, Director of the MPG, Arndt and Dr Götte, MPI of Chemistry, on 6 August 1949 (MPI, file 'Kultusministerium').

70 MPI, file 'Kultusministerium'.

71 Work report of the KWG, 1 January 1946 to 31 March 1951, *Naturwissenschaften*, 38 (1951), pp. 361–80 (p. 367). Compare O. Hahn 'Das Kaiser-Wilhelm-Institut', p. 197. The sources disagree over the neutron intensity of the cascade: Work report 5 kg RBE; according to Hahn: 7–8 kg RBE (RBE stands for 'Radium-Beryllium-Equivalent').

72 'Bericht über die Tätigkeit des Kaiser Wilhelm Instituts für Chemie im Jahre 1948' (MPG, Abt. I, Rep. 11, Nr. 22, Bll. 7–8).

73 J. Mattauch and F. A. Paneth, 'Über die Tätigkeit des Max-Planck-Instituts für Chemie seit 1951', *Mitteilungen der Max-Planck-Gesellschaft* (1956), pp. 131–49.

74 J. Mattauch , 'Max-Planck-Institut für Chemie in Mainz', *Jahrbuch der Max-Planck-Gesellschaft*, (1961), part 2, pp. 215–24 (p. 223).

75 Compare on this M. Heinemann, 'Der Wiederaufbau der Kaiser-Wilhelm-Gesellschaft und die Neugründung der Max-Planck-Gesellschaft (1945–1949)' in Vierhaus and vom Brocke, *Forschung*, pp. 407–70.

76 Haut Commissaire de la republique en Allemagne, i. V. R. Schmittlein, Directeur Général des Affaires Culturelles to Commissaire pour le Land Rhéno-Palatin, 4 October 1950, copy (UAM, Bstd. 1/ 160).

14   The social system of mathematics and National Socialism: a survey

1 This essay originally appeared as H. Mehrtens, 'The social system of mathematics and National Socialism: a survey', *Sociological Inquiry*, 57 (1987), 159–87; for example, A. Beyerchen, *Scientists under Hitler: Politics and the Physics Community in the Third Reich* (New Haven, 1977); H. Mehrtens and S. Richter (eds), *Naturwissenschaft, Technik und Ideologie: Beiträge zur Wissenschaftsgeschichte des Dritten Reiches* (Frankfurt a.M., 1980).

2 Cf. the excellent book, U. Geuter, *The Professionalization of German Psychology in Nazi Germany* (Cambridge, 1992).

3 N. Luhmann, *Soziale Systeme: Grundriss einer allgemeinen Theorie*, 2nd edn, enlarged (Frankfurt a.M., 1984).

4 T. Kuhn, *The Structure of Scientific Revolutions*, 2nd edn, enlarged (Chicago, 1971).

5 P. Bourdieu, 'The specificity of the scientific field and the social conditions of the progress of reason', *Social Science Information* 6 (1975), 19–47.

6 J. Herf, *Reactionary Modernism: Technology, Culture, and Politics in Weimar and the Third Reich* (Cambridge, 1984).

7 The notion of the four blocs of power is from F. Neumann, *Behemoth: The Structure and Practice of National Socialism* (New York, 1944). It certainly has to be revised in detail, but is valid in the general characterization of the system. For the discussion of the power struggles and the 'anarchy of competence' in Nazi Germany, cf. G. Hirschfeld and L. Kettenacker (eds), *Der 'Führerstaat', Mythos und Realität* (Stuttgart, 1981). A general discussion of the problems of interpretation of the history of science in relation to National Socialism is, together with a survey of the literature, given by H. Mehrtens, 'Die Naturwissenschaften im Nationalsozialismus', in R. Rürup (ed.), *Wissenschaft und Gesellschaft. Beiträge zur Geschichte der Technischen Universität Berlin 1879–1979* (Berlin, 1979) and 'Das "Dritte Reich" in der Naturwissenschaftsgeschichte: Literaturbericht und Problemskizze', in Mehrtens and Richter, *Naturwissenschaft*, pp. 15–87.

8 Cf. Herf, *Modernism*; cf. also M. Prinz and R. Zitelmann (eds), *Nationalsozialismus und Modernisierung* (Darmstadt, 1991), a collection in which science and technology are not treated.

9 For a more detailed (and less sociological) analysis of the genesis and structure of modernism in mathematics, see H. Mehrtens, *Moderne-Sprache-Mathematik. Eine Geschichte des Streits um die Grundlagen der Disziplin und des Subjekts formaler Systeme* (Frankfurt a.M., 1990).

10 M. Kline, *Mathematics: The Loss of Certainty* (New York, 1980).

11 The quote is from an unpublished manuscript which is described in more detail in H. Mehrtens, 'Ludwig Bieberbach and "Deutsche Mathematik"' in E. Phillips (ed.), *Studies in the History of Mathematics* (Washington, DC, 1987), pp. 195–241. For a contemporary reaction to Bieberbach's writings cf. G. Hardy, 'The J-type and the S-type among mathematicians', *Nature* 134 (1934), 250, reprinted in *Mathematical Intelligencer* 6, No. 3 (1984), 7.

For an analysis of his ideology see H. Linder, '"Deutsche" und "gegentypische" Mathematik. Zur Begründung einer "arteigenen" Mathematik im Dritten Reich durch Ludwig Bieberbach', in Mehrtens and Richter, *Naturwissenschaft*, pp. 88–115 and E. Quaisser, 'Zur "Deutschen" Mathematik', *Wissenschaftliche Zeitschrift der Ernst-Moritz-Arndt-Universität Greifswald, Mathematisch-Naturwissenschaftliche Reihe* 33 (1984), pp. 35–9.

12 T. Kalikow, 'Konrad Lorenz's ethological theory: Explanation and ideology, 1938–1943', *Journal of the History of Biology* 16 (1983), 39–73.

13 Bieberbach is historically the most important and in this paper the somewhat stylized ideal type of the mathematician introducing Nazism into his science out of largely professional motives. Support of Nazism in mathematics obviously also had other motives and different forms. Especially with younger mathematicians we find a strong dominance of purely political motives. To them it appears to have been much more important that their professors would support Nazism in general than that they found the correct 'German' mathematics. Oswald Teichmüller, famous for his mathematical achievements, is an example. He sided with Bieberbach, but appears to have regarded the discussion of a 'German' mathematics rather as a tactical means that could be used in the Nazification of the discipline. cf. N. Schappacher and E. Scholz (eds), 'Oswald Teichmüller – Leben und Werk', *Jahresbericht der Deutschen Mathematiker-Vereinigung* 94 (1992), pp. 1–39.

14 Beyerchen, *Scientists*; S. Richter, 'Die "Deutsche Physik"', in Mehrtens and Richter, *Naturwissenschaft*, pp. 116–41.

15 For the story of the three societies, cf. H. Mehrtens, 'The "Gleichschaltung" of Mathematical Societies in Nazi Germany', *The Mathematical Intelligencer* 11, No. 3 (1989), 48–60, as well as N. Schappacher and M. Kneser, 'Fachverband – Institut – Staat', in G. Fischer *et al.* (eds), *Ein Jahrhundert Mathematik 1890–1990: Festschrift zum Jubiläum der DMV* (Braunschweig, 1990), pp. 1–82. Cf. also R. Tobies, 'Zur Einflussnahme des Reichsverbandes deutscher mathematischen Gesellschaften und Vereine auf die Verstärkung der angewandten Mathematik in der Ausbildung', *Philosophie und Naturwissenschaften in Vergangenheit und Gegenwart* 19 (1980), 66–71 and 'Die "Gesellschaft für angewandte Mathematik und Mechanik" im Gefüge imperialistischer Wissenschaftsorganisation', *NTM Schriftenreihe zur Geschichte der Naturwissenschaft, Technik und Medizin* 19 (1982), 16–26; and for the Förderverein cf. A. Kremer, *Naturwissenschaftlicher Unterricht und Standesinteresse. Zur Professionalisierungsgeschichte der Naturwissenschaftslehrer an höheren Schulen* (Marburg, 1985).

16 T. Mason, *Sozialpolitik im Dritten Reich: Arbeiterklasse und Volksgemeinschaft*, 2nd edn (Opladen, 1978), p. 106.

17 Cf. G. Aly and K-H. Roth, *Die restlose Erfassung: Volkszählen, Identifizieren, Aussondern im Nationalsozialismus* (Berlin, 1984); R. Lorenz, 'Die Arbeiten Siegfried Kollers zur Rassenhygiene in der Zeit von 1933 bis 1945', *Biometrie und Informatik* 21 (1990), 196–240. On school mathematics see

H. Mehrtens, 'Nationalsozialistisch eingekleidetes Rechnen: Mathematik als Wissenschaft und Schulfach im NS-Staat', in R. Dithmar (ed.), *Schule und Unterricht im Dritten Reich* (Neuwied, 1989), pp. 205–16.
18 Cf. the argument at the end of this chapter.
19 E. Nyssen, *Schule im Nationalsozialismus* (Heidelberg, 1979).
20 Cf. Mehrtens, 'Gleichschaltung'.
21 R. von Mises, 'Über die Aufgaben und Ziele der angewandten Mathematik', *Zeitschrift für angewandte Mathematik und Mechanik* 1 (1921), 1–15.
22 For a more detailed analysis of mathematics in Germany during World War II see H. Mehrtens, 'Mathematics and war: aspects of the relationship, Germany 1900–1945', in J. Sánchez-Rón and P. Forman (eds), *National Military Establishments and the Advancement of Science and Technology: Studies in Twentieth Century History* (Dordrecht, forthcoming).

15   The problem of anti-Fascist Resistance of 'apolitical' German Scholars

1 I use the word 'Fascist' only with regard to the system, which was not only determined by the National Socialist party (NSDAP), while I use 'National Socialist' with regard to ideology as well as occasionally relating to the system.
2 Cf. I. Kershaw, 'The Führer Image and Political Integration: The Popular Conception of Hitler in Bavaria during the Third Reich', in G. Hirschfeld and L. Kettenacker (eds.), *The "Führer State": Myth and Reality* (Stuttgart, 1981), pp. 133–63.
3 'Scholars' in this article means representatives of the natural, technical and social sciences as well as of the humanities. The examples discussed below are mainly taken from mathematics and natural sciences.
4 The most prominent examples which show the pressure exerted on scientists in order to refrain from political judgments were certainly the political controversies surrounding the use of atomic bombs (cf. the 'Franck report' of 1945) and the development of hydrogen bombs (the 'case' of J. Robert Oppenheimer in 1949).
5 R. Siegmund-Schultze, 'Trois phases d'incorporation et de legitimation des mathématiques en allemagne fasciste', in J. Olff-Nathan (ed.), *La science sous le Troisième Reich* (Paris, 1993), pp. 91–102.
6 M. Walker, *German National Socialism and the Quest for Nuclear Power, 1939–1949* (Cambridge, 1989).
7 Cf. for example W. Kähler, 'Lage und Aufgaben der Universitäten in der Gegenwart', *Greifswalder Universitätsreden* 6 (1921), 1–16.
8 Cf. for example M. Walker, 'Legenden um die deutsche Atombombe', *Vierteljahrshefte für Zeitgeschichte* 38 (1990), 45–74, here 54–5.
9 W. Abendroth, 'Das Unpolitische als Wesensmerkmal der deutschen Universität', in *Nationalsozialismus und die deutsche Universität* Universitätstage 1966 (Berlin, 1966), pp. 189–208.
10 R. Siegmund-Schultze, 'Mathematics and Ideology in Fascist Germany', in

W. R. Woodward and R. S. Cohen (eds), *World Views and Scientific Discipline Formation: Science Studies in the German Democratic Republic* (Dordrecht, 1991), pp. 89–95.

11 H. Mehrtens, *Moderne, Sprache, Mathematik* (Frankfurt, a.M., 1990).

12 E. G. Lejkin, 'Die Idee vom wissenschaftlichen Fortschritt im bürgerlichen philosophischen und gesellschaftlichen Denken der Gegenwart', in G. Domin (ed.), *Wissenschaftskonzeptionen* (Berlin, 1978), pp. 11–76.

13 F. K. Ringer, *The Decline of the German Mandarins. The German Academic Community, 1890–1933* (Cambridge, MA, 1969).

14 J. Herf, *Reactionary Modernism. Technology, Culture and Politics in Weimar and the Third Reich* (Cambridge, 1984).

15 P. Forman, 'Weimar Culture, Causality, and Quantum Theory, 1918–1927: Adaptation of German Physicists and Mathematicians to a Hostile Intellectual Environment', *Historical Studies in the Physical Sciences* 3 (1971) 1–115.

16 In a recent article Schröder-Gudehus suggests, however, that those 'pure scientific interests' on both the western and the German sides were not jeopardized by the boycott as much as originally assumed. Cf. B. Schröder-Gudehus, 'Die Jahre der Entspannung: Deutsch-französische Wissenschaftsbeziehungen am Ende der Weimarer Republik', in Y. Cohen and K. Manfrass (eds), *Frankreich und Deutschland: Forschung, Technologie und industrielle Entwicklung im 19. und 20.Jahrhundert* (Munich, 1990), pp. 105–15.

17 P. Forman, 'Scientific Internationalism and the Weimar Physicists: The Ideology and its Manipulation in Germany after World War I', *Isis* 64 (1973), 151–80.

18 A. Kleinert, 'Von der Science allemande zur Deutschen Physik. Nationalismus und moderne Naturwissenschaft in Frankreich und Deutschland zwischen 1914 and 1940', *Francia* 6 (1978), 509–25.

19 H. Mehrtens, 'Ludwig Bieberbach and "Deutsche Mathematik"', in E. Phillips (ed.), *Studies in the History of Mathematics*, Studies in Mathematics, vol. 26 (Washington DC, 1987), pp. 195–241.

20 Cf. for example A. Shields, 'Klein and Bieberbach. Mathematics, Race, and Biology,' *The Mathematical Intelligencer* 10 (1988), No.3, 7–11 .

21 A. D. Alexandrow, 'Über den Idealismus in der Mathematik,' *Forum, Wissenschaftliche Beilage* (Berlin, 1952), No. 27, 3–16, No. 28, 3–7.

22 T. J. Kalikow, 'Die ethologische Theorie von Konrad Lorenz: Erklärung und Ideologie, 1938–1945' in H. Mehrtens and S. Richter (eds), *Naturwissenschaft, Technik und NS-Ideologie. Beiträge zur Wissenschaftgeschichte des Dritten Reiches* (Frankfurt, a.M., 1980), pp. 189–214.

23 K. Reidemeister, *Über Freiheit und Wahrheit* (Berlin 1947), pp. 35–6.

24 For example, mathematicians of the Berlin Academy of Sciences had a great deal of time for research, however there was a fundamental lack of funds, restrictions of foreign travel, and so on. Some sciences, such as economics, were totally politicized in their contents.

25 In spite of the existence of a strong latent anti-semitism, this was certainly not a part of the 'fundamental consensus'. Some influential conservative

scientists criticized anti-semitism, e.g. the Berlin mathematician Erhard Schmidt. Cf.: R. Siegmund-Schultze, 'Berliner Mathematik zur Zeit des Faschismus', *Mitteilungen der Mathematischen Gesellschaft der DDR* (1987) No. 4, 61–84, here 81. On the other hand some scholars of Jewish descent had strong German-nationalist feelings.

26 R. Siegmund-Schultze, 'Theodor Vahlen – zum Schuldanteil eines deutschen Mathematikers am faschistischen Missbrauch der Wissenschaft', *NTM – Schriftenreihe für Geschichte der Naturwissenschaften, Technik und Medizin* 21 (1984), No. 1, 17–32.

27 R. Siegmund-Schultze, 'Über die Haltung deutscher Mathematiker zur faschistischen Expansions- und Okkupationspolitik in Europa', in M. Tschirner and H-W. Göbel (eds), *Wissenschaft im Krieg – Krieg in der Wissenschaft* (Marburg, 1990), pp. 189–95.

28 R. Siegmund-Schultze, 'Das Ende des Jahrbuchs über die Fortschritte der Mathematik und die Brechung des deutschen Referatemonopols', *Mitteilungen der Mathematischen Gesellschaft der DDR* (1984), No. 1, 91–101, here 99; also see R. Siegmund-Schultze, *Mathematische Berichterstattung in Hitlerdeutschland* (Göttingen, 1993).

29 R. Siegmund-Schultze, 'Faschistische Pläne zur "Neuordnung" der europäischen Wissenschaft. Das Beispiel Mathematik', *NTM – Schriftenreihe für Geschichte der Naturwissenschaften, Technik und Medizin* 23 (1986), No. 2, 1–17.

30 E. J. Gumbel, 'Die Gleichschaltung der deutschen Hochschulen', in E. J. Gumbel (ed.), *Freie Wissenschaft. Ein Sammelbuch aus der deutschen Emigration* (Strasbourg, 1938), pp. 9–28, here 27.

31 For example Max von Laue's opposition against the election of Johannes Stark to the Berlin Academy, resistance to Bieberbach's attempts to take control of the German Mathematicians' Association. With regard to Bieberbach's attempts cf. H. Mehrtens, 'The *Gleichschaltung* of Mathematical Societies in Nazi Germany', *The Mathematical Intelligencer* 11 (1989), No. 3, 48–60.

32 Cf. *Exodus Professorum*, Göttinger Universitätsreden 86 (Göttingen, 1989), p. 16.

33 K. Pätzold, *Faschismus, Rassenwahn, Judenverfolgung* (Berlin, 1975).

34 B. L. van der Waerden, 'Nachruf auf Emmy Noether', *Mathematische Annalen* 111 (1935), 469–76.

35 Mehrtens, 'The Gleichschaltung', p. 57.

36 W. Blaschke, *Über das Studium der Mathematik und Naturwissenschaften* (Leipzig, 1935), p. 1.

37 Mehrtens, 'The Gleichschaltung', pp. 50–6.

38 A. Dorner, *Mathematik im Dienste der nationalpolitischen Erziehung* (Frankfurt, 1935).

39 G. Hamel, 'Die Mathematik im Dritten Reich', *Unterrichtsblätter für Mathematik und Naturwissenschaften*, 39 (1933), 306–9, here 309.

40 H. Seier, 'Niveaukritik und partielle Opposition. Zur Lage an den

deutschen Hochschulen 1939/40', *Archiv für Kulturgeschichte* 58 (1976), 227–46, here 231.

41 H. Mehrtens, 'Angewandte Mathematik und Anwendungen der Mathematik im nationalsozialistischen Deutschland', *Geschichte und Gesellschaft* 12 (1986), 317–47, here 339.

42 Mehrtens, 'Angewandte Mathematik', 338.

43 G. Thomsen, 'Über die Gefahr der Zurückdrängung der exakten Naturwissenschaften an den Schulen und Hochschulen', *Neue Jahrbücher für Wissenschaft und Jugendbildung* 10 (1934), 164–75, p. 165.

44 Thomsen, 'Über die Gefahr', p. 168.

45 Thomsen, 'Über die Gefahr', p. 166.

46 Thomsen, 'Über die Gefahr', p. 167.

47 Some evidence for this assumption is given in Thomsen's personal file in the Archives of Rostock University.

48 J. Weissinger, 'Erinnerungen an meine Zeit in der DVL 1937–1945', *Jahrbuch Überblicke Mathematik* (Mannheim) (1985), 105–29, here 129.

49 H. Breger, 'Streifzug durch die Geschichte der Mathematik und Physik an der Universität Heidelberg', in K. Buselmeier, D. Harth and C. Jansen (eds), *Auch eine Geschichte der Universität Heidelberg* (Mannheim, 1985), pp. 27–50, here 45.

16   Irresponsible purity: the political and moral structure of mathematical sciences in the National Socialist state

1 This essay originally appeared as H. Mehrtens, 'Verantwortungslose Reinheit: Thesen zur politischen und moralischen Struktur der mathematischen Wissenschaften am Beispiel des NS-States', in G. Fülgraff and A. Falter (eds), *Wissenschaft in der Verantwortung: Möglichkeiten der instutionellen Steuerung* (Frankfurt a.M., 1990), pp. 37–54.

2 *Pariser Tage-Blatt* (19 April 1934).

3 (Translator's note) 'Götz von Berlichingen' is the educated substitute for a specific coarse German expression roughly equivalent to 'kiss my ass' (*Leck mich am Arsch*).

4 For the German Mathematics movement and the history of mathematics under National Socialism, see H. Mehrtens, 'Angewandte Mathematik und Anwendungen der Mathematik im nationalsozialistischen Deutschland', *Geschichte und Gesellschaft* 12 (1986), 317–47; H. Mehrtens, 'Ludwig Bieberbach and "Deutsche Mathematik"' in E. Phillips (ed.), *Studies in the History of Mathematics* (Washington, DC, 1987), pp. 195–241; H. Mehrtens, 'The social system of mathematics and National Socialism: a survey', *Sociological Inquiry* 57 (1987), 159–82, reprinted in this collection; also see the thoroughly revised German version, 'Das soziale System der Mathematik und seine politische Umwelt', *Zentralblatt für Didaktik der Mathematik* 20 (1988), 28–37; H. Mehrtens, 'The 'Gleichschaltung" of Mathematical Societies in Nazi Germany', *The Mathematical Intelligencer* 11 (1989), 48–60;

H. Mehrtens, 'Mathematics in the Third Reich: Resistance, Adaptation and Collaboration of a Scientific Discipline', in R. P. W. Visser *et al.* (eds), *New Trends in the History of Science: Proceedings of a Conference Held at the University of Utrecht* (Amsterdam, 1989), pp. 141–66; H. Mehrtens, 'Nationalsozialistisch eingekleidetes Rechnen: Mathematik als Wissenschaft und Schulfach im NS-Staat', in R. Dithmar (ed.), *Schule und Unterrichtsfächer im Dritten Reich* (Neuwied, 1989), pp. 205–26; H. Mehrtens, 'Der französische Stil und der deutsche Stil: Nationalismus, Nationalsozialismus und Mathematik, 1900–1940', in Y. Cohen and K. Manfrass (eds), *Frankreich und Deutschland: Forschung, Technologie und industrielle Entwicklung im 19. und 20. Jahrhundert* (Munich, 1990).

5 For a general analysis of science under National Socialism, see H. Mehrtens, 'Das "Dritte Reich" in der Naturwissenschaftsgeschichte: Literaturbericht und Problemskizze', in H. Mehrtens and S. Richter (eds), *Naturwissenschaft, Technik und Ideologie: Beiträge zur Wissenschaftsgeschichte des Dritten Reiches* (Frankfurt a.M., 1980), pp. 15–87; H. Mehrtens, 'Naturwissenschaft und Nationalsozialismus', in S. Harbordt (ed.), *Wissenschaft und Nationalsozialismus* (Berlin, 1983), pp. 101–14; H. Mehrtens, 'Entartete Wissenschaft? Naturwissenschaft und Nationalsozialismus', 'Zur Diskussion: Naturwissenschaften, Hochschule, Nationalsozialismus', both in L. Siegele-Wenschkewitz and G. Stuchlik (eds), *Hochschule und Nationalsozialismus: Wissenschaftsgeschichte und Wissenschaftsbetrieb als Thema der Zeitgeschichte* (Frankfurt a.M., 1990), pp. 113–28.

6 E. Gumbel, *Auf der Suche nach Wahrheit. Ausgewählte Schriften*, A. Vogt (ed.) (Berlin, 1991), p. 80; this edition of selected writings contains a biographical essay on Gumbel by A. Vogt, cf. also W. Benz, 'Emil J. Gumbel: Die Karriere eines deutschen Pazifisten', in U. Walberer (ed.), *10. Mai 1933: Bücherverbrennungen in Deutschland und die Folgen* (Frankfurt, 1983), pp. 160–98.

7 E. Gumbel, 'Arische Naturwissenchaft', in E. Gumbel (ed.), *Freie Wissenschaft: Ein Sammelbuch aus der deutschen Emigration* (Strasbourg, 1938).

8 On Bieberbach, see Mehrtens, 'Bierbach'.

9 M. Pinl, 'Kollegen in einer dunklen Zeit. Teil III', *Jahresbericht der Deutschen Mathematiker-Vereinigung* 73 (1972), pp. 153–208, on Gumbel, pp. 158–62.

10 H. Grumsky, 'Ludwig Bieberbach zum Gedächtnis', *Jahresbericht der Deutschen Mathematiker-Vereinigung* 88 (1986), pp. 190–205, the quote is on p. 190.

11 C. F. von Weizsäcker, 'Forderung der Wissenschaft an sich selbst', *VDW intern – Vereinigung Deutscher Wissenschaftler* No. 78 (Oct. 1988), pp. 1, 25.

12 M. Walker, *German National Socialism and the Quest for Nuclear Power, 1939–1949* (Cambridge, 1989); M. Walker, 'Legends surrounding the German Atomic Bomb', in T. Meade and M. Walker (eds), *Science, Medicine, and Cultural Imperialism* (New York, 1991), pp. 178–204.

13 Einstein Papers (Duplicate Archive), Mudd Library, Princeton University, Box 19, 16–088,089; cf. G. Freise, ' "Der Gelehrte kommt in der Regel unter

die Räder ... ": Das Selbstverständnis von Naturwissenschaftlern im Nationalsozialismus', *Forum Wissenschaft* No. 2 (1985), pp. 8–17.

14 B. Latour, *Science in Action: How to Follow Scientists and Engineers through Society* (Milton Keynes, 1986).

15 H. Mehrtens, *Moderne-Sprache-Mathematik. Eine Geschichte des Streits um die Grundlagen der Disziplin und des Subjekts formaler Systeme* (Frankfurt a.M., 1990).

16 The quote from W. Süss is found in the unpaginated preface to volume 1 of *Naturforschung und Medizin in Deutschland 1939–1946. Für Deutschland bestimmte Ausgabe des FIAT Review of German Science* (Weinheim 1947–1949, Wiesbaden 1953).

17 *Naturforschung* vol. 14, p. 194.

18 B. Müller-Hill, 'Genetics after Auschwitz', *Holocaust and Genocide Studies* 2 (1987), 3–20, the quote is found on p. 17.

19 B. Müller-Hill, 'Gentechnologie als Beruf', *Die Tageszeitung* (1 February 1989), 13ff.

20 Cf. Mehrtens, 'soziale System'; Mehrtens 'Social System'

21 On mathematics as imposed on reality and on the theology of mathematics see P. Davis and R. Hersch, *Descartes' Dream. The World According to Mathematics* (San Diego, 1986).

22 For the quotes and more details of the story, cf. Mehrtens, 'Gleichschaltung'; on Prandtl cf. C. Tollmien, 'Das Kaiser-Wilhelm Institut für Strömungsforschung verbunden mit der Aerodynamischen Versuchsanstalt', in H. Becker, H-J. Dahms and C. Wegeler (eds), *Die Universität Göttingen unter dem Nationalsozialismus: Das verdrängte Kapitel ihrer 250jährigen Geschichte* (Munich, 1987), pp. 464–88.

23 Memo by Wolfram Sievers (4 August 1944), Nuremberg Trial files, NO 640, Institut für Zeitgeschichte, Munich.

24 Quoted on p. 138 in W. Van den Daele, 'Die soziale Konstruktion der Wissenschaft: Institutionalisierung und Definition der positiven Wissenschaft in der zweiten Hälfte des 17. Jahrhunderts', in G. Böhme, W. Van Daele and W. Krohn, *Experimentelle Philosophie: Ursprünge autonomer Wissenschaftsentwicklung* (Frankfurt a.M., 1977), pp. 129–82.

25 *Volk* is literally translated as 'folk', here it carries nationalist and racist connotations.

26 B. Müller-Hill, *Murderous Science. Elimination by Scientific Selection of Jews, Gypsies, and Others, Germany 1933–1945* (Oxford, 1988), pp. 120–3.

27 Cf. Mehrtens, 'Angewandte'.

28 For example, R. Jungk, *Heller als Tausend Sonnen. Das Schicksal der deutschen Atomforscher* (Bern, 1956); Jungk's later change of heart is expressed in his 'Vorwort' (preface) to M. Walker, *Die Uranmaschine. Mythos und Wirklichkeit der deutschen Atombombe* (Berlin, 1990), pp. 7–10, German translation of Walker, *Power*; on the myth of passive resistance cf. also Walker, 'Legends'.

29 R. Musil, *Der Mann ohne Eigenschaften* (Hamburg, 1952), chapter 72: 'Das In den Bart Lächeln der Wissenschaft oder Erste ausführliche Begegnung mit dem Bösen', p. 301.

Index

415

Ardenne, Baron Manfred von, 37, 44
armaments researchers, 16, 30–50
  specialists in the Soviet Union, 42–3, 49, 50
army (German)], 1, 4, 35, 51–2, 56–67, 70–1,
  90, 112, 177, 214, 294, 322
  Army Commission on Weapons and
    Equipment, 34, 56
  Army Ordnance, 3, 34–6, 56–7, 59–61, 70,
    262, 264, 275–6, 279, 336
Aryan race, 38, 189, 191, 196, 209, 211–12, 215,
  217, 233, 250, 319
Aryan science movements, 9–10, 13–14, 33, 73,
  139, 166, 224, 233, 247, 294, 298–300, 303,
  310–11, 316, 322, 324–5, 333, 335
  Aryan chemistry, 9
  Aryan mathematics, 294, 298–300, 303,
    301–11, 316, 322, 324–5, 333
  Aryan physics, 10, 14, 73, 139, 166, 224, 233,
    247, 294, 303, 316, 322
  Aryan technology, 33

Bachem, Erich, 116
Bachem-Werke, 116–19
Backe, Herbert, 148–9, 155, 159, 176–7
Baeumker, Adolf, 75–6
Baeumler, Alfred, 319
Barwich, Heinz, 44, 46
Becker, Karl, 34, 56, 58–61, 70–1
Behemoth model of National Socialism, 1–4,
  6–8, 10–11, 294
Benze, Rudolf, 193
Betz, Albert, 77, 80, 86
Bieberbach, Ludwig, 295, 298–301, 303–4, 306,
  309–10, 318, 324–5, 327, 335, 337
Big Science, 11, 51, 60, 182–3
Der Biologe, 188–9, 320
biology, 9, 15, 140–3, 146, 153–4, 160–96,
  227–9, 237–41, 244, 248, 325
  botany, 176, 178
  breeding research, 141, 143, 152
  genetics, 142, 180–1, 183, 187–90, 193–6, 240
  German Association of Biologists, 188
Blaschke, Wilhelm, 319–20
Blenk, Hermann, 82, 86
Bloch, Ernst, 204
Blohm & Voss Schiffswerft, 107–9, 119–20
Blome, Kurt, 166
blood and soil ideology, 5, 8, 143, 158
BMW, 101, 103, 107
Boehm, Hermann, 181
Bohr, Niels, 227–33, 236, 238–9, 242, 244–5,
  247, 249, 251
Bölkow, Ludwig, 37
bombing
  Allied, 37, 41, 88, 92, 282–4
  German, 87

Born, Hedwig, 253
Born, Max, 224, 227, 247, 249, 251–3
Bosch, Carl, 76, 149, 273
Bothe, Walther, 262–5, 271
Boul, Heinrich von, 262, 264–5
Brandner, Ferdinand, 36, 38–40
Brauchitsch, von, 59, 61
Braun, Wernher von, 37–8, 41, 47, 54, 56–7,
  59–62, 64–7, 70–1, 97, 114–16
Brinkmann, Ludwig, 31–2
Brookhaven National Laboratory, 268
Brouwer, L. E. J., 298, 301
Bruns, Victor, 145–6
Bulgaria, 150–5, 156

Caesar, Joachim, 179
Carnap, Rudolph, 245–6, 248
causality, 203, 224–54
central place theory, 128, 132–4
CERN, 268
chemical warfare, 56, 89–90, 95
chemistry, 9, 35, 140–1, 145, 193, 195
  Imperial Chemical Institute, 140
C.H.F. Müller, 280–2, 284, 286, 289
Christaller, Walter, 128, 132–5
civil service, 1–4, 9–11, 74, 82, 294, 315, 318
Clay, Lucius D., 45
Cold War, 13, 48, 86
Communism, 44, 252
  anti-Communism, 4, 40, 46–7, 247, 251
  German Communist Party, 181
  Socialist Unity Party (German Democratic
    Republic), 316–17, 323
concentration camp prisoners, 38, 62, 65–7,
  70–1, 88, 96, 98, 109, 116, 124, 177, 179,
  305, 308, 334
  at the Harz underground production
    facilities, 45, 96, 111
  at Mittelwerk, 65–7, 96, 109
  at the plant-breeding station in Auschwitz,
    179
  at the Tartun salt mine, 109
concentration camps, 38, 62, 65, 67, 71, 80,
  96–8, 109, 116, 178–9, 308, 334
  Auschwitz, 178–9
  Buchenwald, 97
  death camps, 40, 305
  Oranienburg, 334
continuity and discontinuity of National
  Socialism, 11–17
cultural imperialism, 139, 143–7, 158–9

Daimler-Benz, 98, 100
Darré, Walter, 156, 177
Darwinism, 143, 187, 195
Debye, Peter, 261–2, 274–5